McGraw-Hill's
HOMEWORK
MANAGER PLUS™

THE COMPLETE SOLUTION

Brewer Garrison Noreen

Managerial Accounting

McGraw-Hill's Homework Manager Plus combines the power of Homework Manager with the latest interactive learning technology to create a comprehensive, fully integrated online study package. Students working on assignments in Homework Manager can click a simple hotlink and instantly review the appropriate material in the Interactive Online Textbook. NetTutor rounds out the package by offering live tutoring with a qualified expert in the course material.

By including Homework Manager Plus with your textbook adoption, you're giving your students a vital edge as they progress through the course and ensuring that the help they need is never more than a mouse click away. Contact your McGraw-Hill representative or visit the book's website to learn how to add Homework Manager Plus to your adoption.

Interactive Online Version
of the Textbook

In addition to the textbook, students can rely on this online version of the text for a convenient way to study. The interactive content is fully integrated with Homework Manager to give students quick access to relevant content as they work through problems, exercises, and practice quizzes.

Features:

- Online version of the text integrated with Homework Manager

- Students referred to appropriate sections of the online book as they complete an assignment or take a practice quiz

- Direct link to related material that corresponds with the learning objective within the text

McGraw-Hill's
HM PLUS™

HOMEWORK **MANAGER**
HELPS YOU EFFICIENTLY

McGraw-Hill's

HOMEWORK
MANAGER

™

Problems and exercises from the book, as well as questions from the test bank, have been integrated into Homework Manager to give you a variety of options as you deliver assignments and quizzes to students via the web. You can choose from static or algorithmic questions and have the graded results automatically stored in your grade book online.

Have you ever wished that you could assign a different set of problems to each of your students, individualizing their educational experience? The algorithmic question capabilities of Homework Manager give you the opportunity to do so. The problem-making function inserts new numbers and data from an endless supply into the set question structure. Each student will have a different answer while learning the same principles from the text. This also enables the students to master concepts by revisiting the same questions with different data.

Assign coursework online.

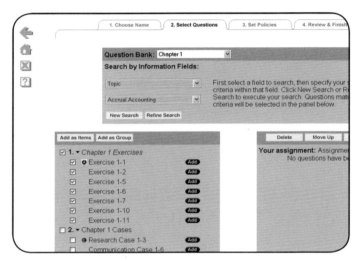

MANAGE YOUR CLASS.

Control how content is presented.

Homework Manager gives you a flexible and easy way to present course work to students. You determine which questions to ask and how much help students will receive as they work through assignments. You can determine the number of attempts a student can make with each problem or provide hints and feedback with each question. The questions can also be linked to an online version of the text for quick and simple reference while students complete an assignment.

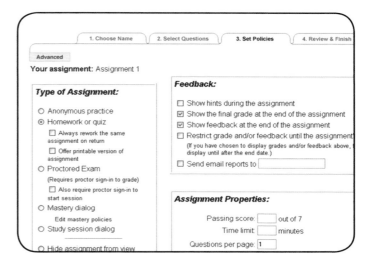

Track student progress.

Assignments are graded automatically, with the results stored in your private grade book. Detailed results let you see at a glance how each student does on an assignment or an individual problem. You can even see how many attempts it took them to solve it. You can monitor how the whole class does on each problem and even determine where individual students might need extra help.

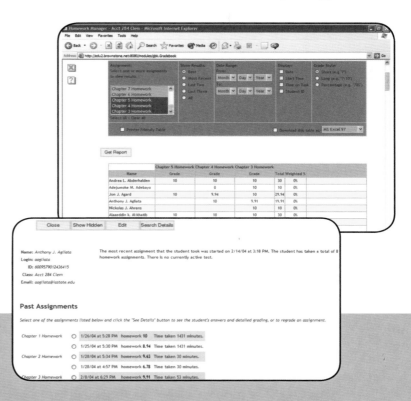

Introduction to
Managerial Accounting

3rd edition

PETER C. BREWER
Professor, Miami University

RAY H. GARRISON
Professor Emeritus, Brigham Young University

ERIC W. NOREEN
Professor Emeritus, University of Washington

McGraw-Hill Irwin

Boston   Burr Ridge, IL   Dubuque, IA   Madison, WI   New York   San Francisco   St. Louis
Bangkok   Bogotá   Caracas   Kuala Lumpur   Lisbon   London   Madrid   Mexico City
Milan   Montreal   New Delhi   Santiago   Seoul   Singapore   Sydney   Taipei   Toronto

McGraw-Hill
Irwin

INTRODUCTION TO MANAGERIAL ACCOUNTING

Published by McGraw-Hill/Irwin, a business unit of The McGraw-Hill Companies, Inc., 1221 Avenue of the Americas, New York, NY, 10020. Copyright © 2007 by The McGraw-Hill Companies, Inc. All rights reserved. No part of this publication may be reproduced or distributed in any form or by any means, or stored in a database or retrieval system, without the prior written consent of The McGraw-Hill Companies, Inc., including, but not limited to, in any network or other electronic storage or transmission, or broadcast for distance learning.

Some ancillaries, including electronic and print components, may not be available to customers outside the United States.

This book is printed on acid-free paper.

1 2 3 4 5 6 7 8 9 0 DOW/DOW 0 9 8 7 6

ISBN-13: 978-0-07-304883-3
ISBN-10: 0-07-304883-6

Editorial director: *Stewart Mattson*
Executive editor: *Tim Vertovec*
Developmental editor II: *Sarah Wood*
Marketing director: *Dan Silverburg*
Senior media producer: *Elizabeth Mavetz*
Lead project manager: *Pat Frederickson*
Production supervisor: *Gina Hangos*
Senior designer: *Kami Carter*
Senior photo research coordinator: *Jeremy Cheshareck*
Photo researcher: *Emily Tietz*
Media project manager: *Matthew Perry*
Senior supplement producer: *Carol Loreth*
Cover design: *Pam Verros, pvdesign*
Interior design: *Kami Carter*
Cover Image: *© Masterfile*
Typeface: *10.5/12 Times Roman*
Compositor: *TechBooks/GTS Companies, York, PA*
Printer: *R. R. Donnelley*

Library of Congress Cataloging-in-Publication Data

Brewer, Peter C.
    Introduction to managerial accounting / Peter C. Brewer, Ray H. Garrison, Eric W. Noreen.—3rd ed.
        p. cm.
    Includes index.
    ISBN-13: 978-0-07-304883-3 (alk. paper)
    ISBN-10: 0-07-304883-6 (alk. paper)
    1. Managerial accounting. I. Garrison. Ray H. II. Noreen, Eric W. III. Title.
HF5657.4.F65 2007
658.15'11—dc22

                                                            2005058386

www.mhhe.com

DEDICATION

To our families and to our many colleagues who use this book.
—Peter C. Brewer, Ray H. Garrison, and Eric W. Noreen

About the Authors

Peter C. Brewer is a professor in the Department of Accountancy at Miami University, Oxford, Ohio. He holds a BS degree in accounting from Penn State University, an MS degree in accounting from the University of Virginia, and a PhD from the University of Tennessee. He has published more than 25 articles in a variety of journals including: *Management Accounting Research*, *The Journal of Information Systems*, *Cost Management*, *Strategic Finance*, *The Journal of Accountancy*, *Issues in Accounting Education*, and *The Journal of Business Logistics*.

Professor Brewer is a member of the editorial board of *Issues in Accounting Education* and has served on the editorial board of *The Journal of the Academy of Business Education*. His article "Putting Strategy into the Balanced Scorecard" won the 2003 International Federation of Accountants' Articles of Merit competition and his article "Using Six Sigma to Improve the Finance Function" received the Institute of Management Accountants' Lybrand Gold Medal Award in 2005. He has received Miami University's Richard T. Farmer School of Business Teaching Excellence Award and has been recognized on two occasions by the Miami University Associated Student Government for "making a remarkable commitment to students and their educational development." He is a leading thinker in undergraduate management accounting curriculum innovation and is a frequent presenter at various professional and academic conferences.

Prior to joining the faculty at Miami University, Professor Brewer was employed as an auditor for Touche Ross in the firm's Philadelphia office. He also worked as an internal audit manager for the Board of Pensions of the Presbyterian Church (U.S.A.). He frequently collaborates with companies such as Harris Corporation, Cintas, Ethicon Endo-Surgery, Schneider Electric, Lenscrafters, and Fidelity Investments in a consulting or case writing capacity.

Ray H. Garrison

is emeritus professor of accounting at Brigham Young University, Provo, Utah. He received his BS and MS degrees from Brigham Young University and his DBA degree from Indiana University.

As a certified public accountant, Professor Garrison has been involved in management consulting work with both national and regional accounting firms. He has published articles in *The Accounting Review, Management Accounting*, and other professional journals. Innovation in the classroom has earned Professor Garrison the Karl G. Maeser Distinguished Teaching Award from Brigham Young University.

Eric W. Noreen is a globe-trotting academic who has held appointments at institutions in the United States, Europe, and Asia. He is emeritus professor of accounting at the University of Washington.

He received his BA degree from the University of Washington and MBA and PhD degrees from Stanford University. A Certified Management Accountant, he was awarded a Certificate of Distinguished Performance by the Institute of Certified Management Accountants.

Professor Noreen has served as associate editor of *The Accounting Review* and the *Journal of Accounting and Economics*. He has numerous articles in academic journals including: the *Journal of Accounting Research*; *The Accounting Review*; the *Journal of Accounting and Economics*; *Accounting Horizons*; *Accounting, Organizations and Society*; *Contemporary Accounting Research*; the *Journal of Management Accounting Research*; and the *Review of Accounting Studies*.

Professor Noreen has taught manage accounting at the undergraduate and m levels and has won a number of award students for his teaching.

Empowering Students to Rise to New Levels

"When will I ever use managerial accounting?"

y students ask this and similar
ns about the relevance
managerial accounting
oduction to Managerial
edition, by Brewer,
Noreen not only
managerial
also how
world.

nts will

skills

ss.

ment
aster's
s from

Here's how your colleagues have described *Introduction to Managerial Accounting*:

"A textbook that delivers **concise, yet relevant**, instruction on managerial accounting issues."

—DeWayne L. Searcy, Auburn University

"Excellent text that is **clearly written**, makes good use of graphics, and has **excellent problems** that map effectively back into the chapters."

—Howard Rockness,
University of North Carolina–Wilmington

"A good textbook, that **reads easy** and has a lot of illustrations, supplements and problems/exercises **for both the students and faculty** members to choose from."

—Jim Dougher, DeVry University

y written. It is a **concise and yet**
ctory managerial accounting text."

te University of New York College at Plattsburgh

Introduction to Managerial Accounting, *3rd edition*, by **BREWER/GARRISON/NOREEN** empowers your students by offering:

CONCISE COVERAGE

Your students want a text that is concise, and that presents material in a clear and readable manner. *Introduction to Managerial Accounting* presents everything your students should know, keeping the material accessible and avoiding advanced topics related to cost management. Similarly, their biggest concern is making sure they can solve the end-of-chapter problems after reading the chapter. Market research indicates that Brewer/Garrison/Noreen achieves—and helps students achieve—this better than any other concise managerial accounting text on the market. Additionally, the key supplements were written by Garrison, Noreen, and Brewer, ensuring that students and instructors will work with clear, well-written supplements that employ consistent terminology.

DECISION-MAKING FOCUS

Every student who passes through your class needs to know how accounting information is used to make business decisions, especially if they plan to be future managers. That's why Brewer, Garrison and Noreen make decision making a pivotal component of *Introduction to Managerial Accounting*. In every chapter, you'll find the following key features, each designed to teach your students how to use accounting information like a manager. **Decision Maker & You Decide** boxes challenge students to develop analytical and critical thinking skills in solving a managerial accounting problem, in both corporate and entrepreneurial settings. **Building Your Skills** cases give students' decision-making skills an added boost by presenting them with a more in-depth scenario to work through.

A CONTEMPORARY APPROACH TO LEARNING

Today's students rely on technology more than ever as a learning tool, and *Introduction to Managerial Accounting* offers the finest technology package of any text on the market. From interactive study aids to online grading and course management, our technology assets have one thing in common: they make your class time more productive, more stimulating, and more rewarding for you and your students. McGraw-Hill's *Homework Manager*™ uses text-based, algorithmically generated problems to develop problem-solving skills. For mastering the most difficult topics, *Topic Tackler* combines video, self-assessment, and PowerPoint lectures. Additionally, NetTutor and the Online Learning Center provide your students with a variety of multimedia aids to help them learn managerial accounting. *Homework Manager Plus*™ provides an online version of the text in addition to access to Homework Manager, NetTutor, and all of the assets offered on the Online Learning Center, giving students a convenient way to access everything they need to succeed in your course.

BREWER / GARRISON / NOREEN'S

Introduction to Managerial Accounting is full of pedagogy designed to make studying productive and hassle-free. On the following pages, you'll see the kind of engaging, helpful pedagogical features that have made Brewer one of the best-selling Managerial Accounting texts on the market.

OPENING VIGNETTE

Each chapter opens with a Business Focus feature that provides a real-world example for students, allowing them to see how the chapter's information and insights apply to the world outside the classroom. **Learning Objectives** alert students to what they should expect as they progress through the chapter.

SERVICE EXAMPLES

To reflect our service-based economy, the text is replete with examples from service-based businesses. A helpful icon distinguishes service-related examples in the text.

INFOGRAPHICS

Infographics help students visualize key accounting concepts, such as Planning and Control, the Activity-Based Costing Model, and Management by Exception.

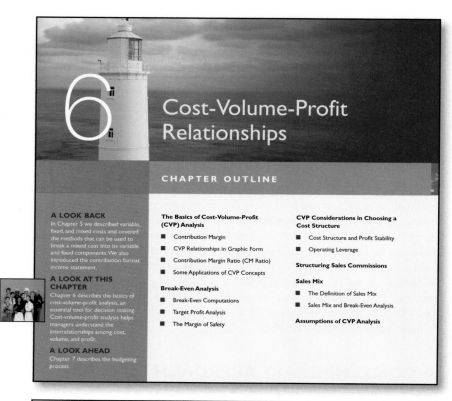

6 Cost-Volume-Profit Relationships

CHAPTER OUTLINE

A LOOK BACK
In Chapter 5 we described variable, fixed, and mixed costs and covered the methods that can be used to break a mixed cost into its variable and fixed components. We also introduced the contribution format income statement.

A LOOK AT THIS CHAPTER
Chapter 6 describes the basics of cost-volume-profit analysis, an essential tool for decision making. Cost-volume-profit analysis helps managers understand the interrelationships among cost, volume, and profit.

A LOOK AHEAD
Chapter 7 describes the budgeting process.

The Basics of Cost-Volume-Profit (CVP) Analysis
- Contribution Margin
- CVP Relationships in Graphic Form
- Contribution Margin Ratio (CM Ratio)
- Some Applications of CVP Concepts

Break-Even Analysis
- Break-Even Computations
- Target Profit Analysis
- The Margin of Safety

CVP Considerations in Choosing a Cost Structure
- Cost Structure and Profit Stability
- Operating Leverage

Structuring Sales Commissions

Sales Mix
- The Definition of Sales Mix
- Sales Mix and Break-Even Analysis

Assumptions of CVP Analysis

Planning   Control

*"Text uses companies that the **students can relate to** and understand their business process"*

—Monica M. Jeancola, Stetson University

POWERFUL PEDAGOGY

"BGN has done a nice job providing **numerical examples** and **real-world situations.**"
—Joon S. Yang, University of Minnesota—Duluth

Chapter Six

DECISION FEATURE

Forget the Theater—Make Money on Cable TV

"Several years ago, Hollywood experienced a phenomenon known as the 'straight-to-cable' era. What this phrase referred to was a well used (and abused!) movie-making principle that hinted that if anyone (and many times it really was just *anyone*) could produce a movie (quality was never an issue!) for under a million dollars, it'd automatically turn a profit from the sale of its cable TV rights. In essence, the 'movie' would bypass the theaters all together [sic] and still turn a profit. From a business standpoint, what this money-making scheme illustrates is [that] every product has a break-even point. Make more money than this and you turn a profit. Make less than this, and, well, you get the picture (pardon the pun)."

Source: Ben Chiu, "The Last Big-Budget Combat Sim," *Computer Games*, June 1999, p. 40.

LEARNING OBJECTIVES

After studying Chapter 6, you should be able to:

LO1 Explain how changes in activity affect contribution margin and net operating income.

LO2 Prepare and interpret a cost-volume-profit (CVP) graph.

LO3 Use the contribution margin ratio (CM ratio) to compute changes in contribution margin and net operating income resulting from changes in sales volume.

LO4 Show the effects on contribution margin of changes in variable costs, fixed costs, selling price, and volume.

LO5 Compute the break-even point in unit sales and dollar sales.

LO6 Determine the level of sales needed to achieve a desired target profit.

LO7 Compute the margin of safety and explain its significance.

LO8 Compute the degree of operating leverage at a particular level of sales and explain how it can be used to predict changes in net operating income.

"IN BUSINESS"

These helpful boxed features offer a glimpse into how real companies use the managerial accounting concepts discussed within the chapter. Every chapter contains these current examples.

Growing Sales at Amazon.com   IN BUSINESS

Amazon.com was deciding between two tactics for growing sales and profits. The first approach was to invest in television advertising. The second approach was to introduce free shipping on orders over a designated amount of sales. To evaluate the first option, Amazon.com invested in television ads in two markets—Minneapolis, Minnesota, and Portland, Oregon. The company quantified the profit impact of this choice by subtracting the increase in fixed advertising costs from the increase in contribution margin resulting from the advertising campaign. The advertising results paled in comparison to the free "super saver shipping" program, which the company introduced on orders over $99. In fact, the free shipping option proved to be so popular and profitable that within two years Amazon.com dropped its qualifying threshold to $49 and then again to a mere $25. At each stage of this progression, Amazon.com used cost-volume-profit analysis to determine whether the extra revenue from liberalizing the free shipping offer more than offset the associated increase in shipping costs.

Source: Rob Walker, "Because 'Optimism is Essential,'" *Inc.* April 2004, pp. 149–150.

---

1. The contribution margin ratio always increases when (you may select more than one answer):
   a. Sales increase.
   b. Fixed costs decrease.
   c. Total variable costs decrease.
   d. Variable costs as a percent of sales decrease.
2. Assume the selling price per unit is $30, the contribution margin ratio is 40%, and the break-even point is 5,000 units. What is the amount of total fixed costs?
   a. $20,000
   b. $30,000
   c. $50,000
   d. $60,000

CONCEPT CHECK ✔

CONCEPT CHECK

Concept Checks allow students to test their comprehension of topics and concepts covered at various stages throughout each chapter.

$$\text{Margin of safety percentage} = \frac{\text{Margin of safety in dollars}}{\text{Total budgeted (or actual) sales dollars}}$$

The calculation for the margin of safety for Acoustic Concepts is:

Sales (at the current volume of 400 speakers) (a)	$100,000
Break-even sales (at 350 speakers)	87,500
Margin of safety (in dollars) (b)	$ 12,500
Margin of safety as a percentage of sales, (b) ÷ (a)	12.5%

This margin of safety means that at the current level of sales and with the company's current prices and cost structure, a reduction in sales of $12,500, or 12.5%, would result in just breaking even.

In a single-product company like Acoustic Concepts, the margin of safety can also be expressed in terms of the number of units sold by dividing the margin of safety in dollars by the selling price per unit. In this case, the margin of safety is 50 speakers ($12,500 ÷ $250 per speaker = 50 speakers).

Loan Officer   DECISION MAKER

Sam Calagione owns Dogfish Head Craft Brewery, a microbrewery in Rehoboth Beach, Delaware. He charges his distributors $100 per case for premium beers such as World Wide Stout. The distributors tack on 25% when selling to retailers who in turn add a 30% markup before selling the beer to consumers. In the most recent year, Dogfish's revenue was $7 million and its net operating income was $800,000. Calagione reports that the costs of making one case of World Wide Stout are $30 for raw ingredients, $16 for labor, $6 for bottling and packaging, and $10 for utilities.

Assume that Calagione has approached your bank for a loan. As the loan officer you should consider a variety of factors, including the company's margin of safety. Assuming that the information related to World Wide Stout is representative of all Dogfish microbrews and that other information about the company is favorable, would you consider Dogfish's margin of safety to be comfortable enough to extend a loan?

Source: Patricia Huang, "Château Dogfish," Forbes, February 28, 2005, pp. 57–59.

The **DECISION MAKER** feature fosters critical thinking and decision-making skills by providing real world business scenarios that require the resolution of a business issue. The suggested solution is located at the end of the chapter.

Notice that use of ratios in the equation yields a break-even point in sales dollars rather than in units sold. The break-even point in units sold is the following:

$$\$87,500 \div \$250 \text{ per speaker} = 350 \text{ speakers}$$

Recruit   YOU DECIDE

Assume that you are being recruited by the ConneXus Corp. and have an interview scheduled later this week. You are interested in working for this company for a variety of reasons. In preparation for the interview, you did some research at your local library and gathered the following information about the company. ConneXus is a company set up by two young engineers, George Searle and Humphrey Chen, to allow consumers to order music CDs on their cell phones. Suppose you hear on the radio a cut from a CD that you would like to own. If you subscribe to their service, you would pick up your cell phone, punch "∗CD," and enter the radio station's frequency and the time you heard the song, and the CD would be on its way to you.

ConneXus charges about $17 for a CD, including shipping. The company pays its supplier about $13, leaving a contribution margin of $4 per CD. Because of the fixed costs of running the service (about $1,850,000 a year), Searle expects the company to lose about $1.5 million in its first year of operations on sales of 88,000 CDs.

What are your initial impressions of this company based on the information you gathered? What other information would you want to obtain during the job interview?

Source: Adapted from Peter Kafka, "Play It Again," Forbes, July 26, 1999, p. 94.

The **YOU DECIDE** feature challenges students to apply the tools of analysis and make decisions. The suggested solution is found at the end of the chapter.

The Contribution Margin Method The **contribution margin method** is a shortcut version of the equation method already described. The approach centers on the idea discussed earlier that each unit sold provides a certain amount of contribution margin that goes toward covering fixed costs. To find how many units must be sold to break even, divide the total fixed expenses by the unit contribution margin:

$$\text{Break-even point in units sold} = \frac{\text{Fixed expenses}}{\text{Unit contribution margin}}$$

Each speaker generates a contribution margin of $100 ($250 selling price, less $150 variable expenses). Since the total fixed expenses are $35,000, the break-even point in unit sales is computed as follows:

$$\frac{\text{Fixed expenses}}{\text{Unit contribution margin}} = \frac{\$35,000}{\$100 \text{ per speaker}} = 350 \text{ speakers}$$

A variation of this method uses the CM ratio instead of the unit contribution margin. The result is the break-even point in total sales dollars rather than in total units sold.

$$\text{Break-even point in total sales dollars} = \frac{\text{Fixed expenses}}{\text{CM ratio}}$$

In the Acoustic Concepts example, the calculation is as follows:

$$\frac{\text{Fixed expenses}}{\text{CM ratio}} = \frac{\$35,000}{0.40} = \$87,500$$

This approach, based on the CM ratio, is particularly useful when a company has multiple product lines and wishes to compute a single break-even point for the company as a whole. More is said on this point in a later section.

> *"It offers plenty of exercises/ problems as well as supplemental resources for students and instructors."*
>
> —Marilyn G. Ciolino,
> Delgado Community College

> *"Exercises, problems and building skills designed to meet my student's skill level."*
>
> —Lillian Grose,
> Delgado Community College

> *"Excellent quantity & quality of brief exercises, exercises and problems"*
>
> —Tamara Phelan,
> Northern Illinois University

END-OF-CHAPTER MATERIAL

Introduction to Managerial Acounting has earned a reputation for the best end-of-chapter review and discussion material of any text on the market. Our problem and case material continues to conform to AECC and AACSB recommendations and makes a great starting point for class discussions and group projects. Other helpful features include:

- *Spreadsheets have become an increasingly common budgeting tool for managerial accountants; therefore, to assist students in understanding how budgets look in a spreadsheet, all figures pertaining to budgeting will appear as Microsoft Excel® screen captures.*

- *Excel Spreadsheet Templates are available for use with select problems and cases.*

- *Ethics assignments serve as a reminder that good conduct is vital in business.*

- *Group projects can be assigned either as homework or as in-class discussion projects.*

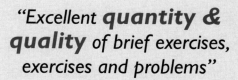

- *Internet assignments teach students how to find information online and apply it to managerial accounting situations.*

- *The Writing Icon denotes problems that require students to use critical thinking as well as writing skills to explain their decision.*

AUTHOR-WRITTEN SUPPLEMENTS

Unlike other managerial accounting texts, Brewer, Garrison and Noreen write all of the text's major supplements, ensuring a perfect fit between text and supplements. For more information on Introduction to Managerial Accounting's supplements package see page xviii.

Changes in the
3rd edition

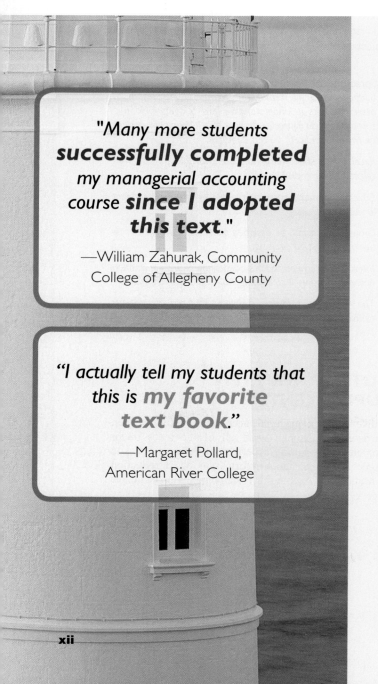

"Many more students ***successfully completed*** *my managerial accounting course* ***since I adopted this text.***"

—William Zahurak, Community College of Allegheny County

"I actually tell my students that this is ***my favorite text book.***"

—Margaret Pollard, American River College

Your feedback helps us continue to improve **Brewer, Garrison, and Noreen.** In response to faculty suggestions, we have added:

- Many new In Business boxes. Drawn from recent events, these boxes provide interesting examples of how managerial accounting concepts are used by real businesses.

- New end-of-chapter exercises. The authors have refreshed and updated all end-of-chapter problems and exercises.

Other improvements include:

- The Globalization section in the Prologue has been updated for currency.

- A section on Lean Production and a section on Six Sigma have been added to the Prologue.

- A discussion of Enterprise Systems, as well as new Corporate Governance and Enterprise Risk Management sections, have been added to the Prologue.

- A number of exhibits have been redrawn to enhance their clarity.

- Variable costing has been added in a new Appendix to Chapter 5.

- Chapter 10, particularly the section on ROI, has been extensively rewritten to improve the flow and simplify the presentation for students.

- The formulas in Chapter 12 dealing with the simple rate of return have been simplified.

- The Instructor's Resource Guide, prepared by Pete Brewer, features teaching notes, transparency masters, and numerous other enhancements that cut down your prep time and make your class a more lively and challenging place to learn for your students.

- In response to reviewer feedback, the test bank has been updated to include over 900 new questions, primarily easy and medium difficulty level. Additionally, an Algorithmic Diploma Test Bank allows instructors to create similarly structured problems with different values, allowing every student to be assigned a unique quiz or text.

- McGraw-Hill's Homework Manager™ is a web-based supplement that duplicates problem structures directly from the end-of-chapter material in the textbook, using algorithms to provide a limitless supply of online self-graded practice and assignment problems. The algorithmic test bank is also included in Homework Manager™. McGraw-Hill's Homework Manager Plus™ allows students to link directly to an online version of the text and web resources when working on the problem.

A Market-Leading Book Deserves
Market-Leading Technology

MCGRAW-HILL'S HOMEWORK MANAGER PLUS

McGraw-Hill's HOMEWORK MANAGER **HM** **PLUS**™ It can be a challenge remembering all the different access codes for the many online assets available with Managerial Accounting. To make life easier for your students, McGraw-Hill is pleased to introduce Homework Manager Plus. With McGraw-Hill's Homework Manager Plus, just one access code gets your students access to McGraw-Hill's Homework Manager, Topic Tackler Plus, NetTutor, and the online version of the textbook. Moreover, the Homework Manager Plus card fits in your student's wallets for safekeeping.

TOPIC TACKLER PLUS

This program is a complete tutorial focusing on those areas in the managerial accounting course that gives students the most trouble. Providing extensive help on two key topics for every chapter, this program delves into the material via the following:

- Video Clips
- PowerPoint slide shows
- Interactive exercises
- Self-grading quizzes
- Web site hotlinks

The highly engaging presentation will give your students command of the most fundamental aspects of managerial accounting. Students can access Topic Tackler Plus through the Online Learning Center.

> *"I really like the Topic Tackler and believe that they are **strategically placed** throughout the chapters **where they are most needed**."*
>
> —Dr. Benjamin L. Sadler, Miami Dade College

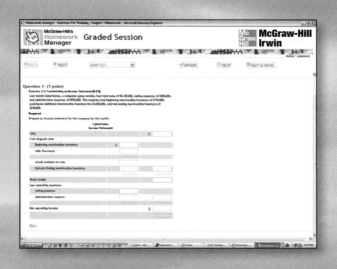

MCGRAW-HILL'S HOMEWORK MANAGER

Homework Manager is an exciting new web-based supplement that duplicates problems directly from the textbook end-of-chapter material, using algorithms to provide a limitless supply of online self-graded practice for students, or assignments and tests with unique versions of every problem. Say goodbye to cheating in your classroom; say hello to the power and flexibility you've been waiting for in creating assignments.

The enhanced version of McGraw-Hill's Homework Manager integrates all of Managerial Accounting's online and multimedia assets to allow your students to brush up on a topic before doing their homework. You now have the option to give your students pre-populated hints and feedback. The test bank has been added to Homework Manager so you can create online quizzes and exams and have them autograded and recorded in the same grade book as your homework assignments. Lastly, the enhanced version provides you with the option of incorporating the complete online version of the textbook, so your students can easily reference the chapter material as they do their homework assignment, even when their textbook is far away.

McGraw-Hill's Homework Manager is also a useful grading tool. All assignments can be delivered over the Web and are graded automatically, with the results stored in your private grade book. Detailed results let you see at a glance how each student does on an assignment or an individual problem—you can even see how many tries it took them to solve it.

Students receive full access to McGraw-Hill's Homework Manager when they purchase Homework Manager Plus or you can have Homework Manager pass codes shrinkwrapped with the textbook. Students can also purchase access to Homework Manager directly from your class home page.

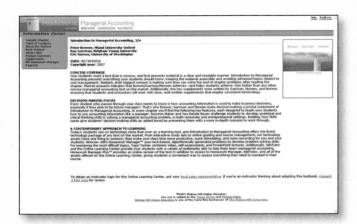

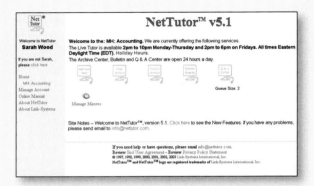

NetTutor

ONLINE LEARNING CENTER (OLC)
www.mhhe.com/brewer3e

More and more students are studying online. That's why we offer an Online Learning Center (OLC) that follows Introduction to Managerial Accounting chapter by chapter. It doesn't require any building or maintenance on your part. It's ready to go the moment you and your students type in the URL.

As your students study, they can refer to the OLC Web site for such benefits as:

- Internet-based activities
- Self-grading quizzes
- Alternate Problems
- Excel Spreadsheets
- Learning objectives
- Chapter overviews
- Internet factory tours
- PowerPoint slides

A secured Instructor Resource Center stores your essential course materials to save you prep time before class. The Instructor's Manual, Solutions, PowerPoint, and sample syllabi are now just a couple of clicks away. You will also find useful packaging information and transition notes.

OnePass gives students full use of all OLC features, including NetTutor and an online version of **Introduction to Managerial Accounting**.

The OLC Web site also serves as a doorway to other technology solutions like PageOut (see next page) which is free to Introduction to Managerial Accounting adopters.

Many students work or have other commitments outside of class, making it difficult for them to get help with their questions during regular hours. NetTutor is a breakthrough program that connects your student with qualified tutors online, so they can get help at their convenience. Students can communicate with tutors through the Live Tutor Center, where students can view tutor-created spreadsheets, T-accounts, and instant responses to their questions, or through the Q&A Center, which allows students to submit questions anytime and receive answers within 24 hours.

With Homework Manager Plus, students receive unlimited access to NetTutor for the length of the course.

Creating an Online Course Is Easy
WITH THE RIGHT GUIDE

For the instructor needing to educate students online, we offer *Introduction to Managerial Accounting* content for complete online courses. To make this possible, we have joined forces with the most popular delivery platforms currently available. These platforms are designed for instructors who want complete control over course content and how it is presented to students. You can customize the Managerial Accounting Online Learning Center content and author your own course materials. It's entirely up to you.

Products like WebCT, Blackboard, eCollege, and TopClass (a product of WBT) all expand the reach of your course. Online discussion and message boards will now complement your office hours. Thanks to a sophisticated tracking system, you will know which students need more attention–even if they don't ask for help. That's because online testing scores are recorded and automatically placed in your grade book, and if a student is struggling with coursework, a special alert message lets you know.

Remember, *Introduction to Managerial Accounting*'s content is flexible enough to use with any platform currently available. If your department or school is already using a platform, we can help. For information on McGraw-Hill/ Irwin's course management tool, visit **www.mhhe.com/solutions.**

PageOut—McGraw-Hill's Course Management System

PageOut is the easiest way to create a website for your accounting course.

There's no need for HTML coding, graphic design, or a thick how-to book. Just fill in a series of boxes with simple English and click on one of our professional designs. In no time, your course is online with a website that contains your syllabus!

Should you need assistance in preparing your website, we can help. Our team of product specialists is ready to take your course materials and build a custom website to your specifications; you simply need to call McGraw-Hill/Irwin PageOut specialist (1-800-634-3963) to start the process. Best of all, PageOut is free when you adopt *Introduction to Managerial Accounting*! To learn more, please visit www. pageout.net.

A Great Learning System

Introduction to Managerial Accounting authors Brewer, Garrison, and Noreen know from their own years of teaching experience what separates a great textbook from a merely adequate one. Every component of the learning package must be imbued with the same style and approach, and that's why the *Introduction to Managerial Accounting* authors write every major ancillary themselves, whether printed or online. It's one more thing that sets *Introduction to Managerial Accounting* far above the competition.

INSTRUCTOR SUPPLEMENTS

Instructor CD-ROM

ISBN: 0073264970
ISBN-13: 9780073264974

Allowing instructors to create a customized multimedia presentation, this all-in-one resource incorporates the Test Bank, PowerPoint® Slides, Instructor's Resource Guide, Solutions Manual, Teaching Transparency Masters, links to PageOut, and the Spreadsheet Application Template Software (SPATS).

Instructor's Resource Guide

ISBN: 0073264962
ISBN-13: 9780073264967

This supplement contains the teaching transparency masters and the video guide, extensive chapter-by-chapter lecture notes to help with classroom presentation, and useful suggestions for presenting key concepts and ideas.

Check Figures

These provide key answers for selected problems and cases. They are available on the text's website.

Solutions Transparencies

ISBN: 0073264997
ISBN-13: 9780073264998

These transparencies feature completely worked-out solutions to all assignment material. The font used in the solutions is large enough for the back row of any lecture hall. Masters of these transparencies are available in the Solutions Manual.

Solutions Manual

ISBN: 0073265004
ISBN-13: 9780073265001

This supplement contains completely worked-out solutions to all assignment material and a general discussion of the use of group exercises. In addition, the manual contains suggested course outlines and a listing of exercises, problems, and cases scaled according to difficulty.

Teaching Transparencies

ISBN: 0073265020
ISBN-13: 9780073265025

Contains a comprehensive set of over 260 teaching transparencies covering every chapter that can be used for classroom lectures and discussion.

PowerPoint® Slides

Prepared by Jon Booker, Charles Caldwell, and Richard Rand, all of Tennessee Technological University, and Susan Galbreath of Lipscomb University, these slides offer a great visual complement for your lectures. A complete set of slides covers each chapter. They are only available on the Instructor CD-ROM and the text's website.

Test Bank

ISBN: 0073265039
ISBN-13: 9780073265032

Over 2,000 questions are organized by chapter and include true/false, multiple-choice, and essay questions and computational problems.

Doesn't Stop with the Book.

Algorithmic-Diploma Test Bank (From Brownstone)

ISBN: 0073264946
ISBN-13: 9780073264943

New to the third edition this computerized test bank is an algorithmic problem generator enabling instructors to create similarly structured problems with different values, which allows every student to be assigned a unique quiz or test. The user-friendly interface gives faculty the ability to easily create different versions of the same test, change the answer order, edit or add questions, and even conduct online testing.

Excel Templates

Prepared by Jack Terry of ComSource Associates, Inc., these Excel templates offer solutions to the Student SPATS version. They are only available on the Instructor CD and the text's website.

Dallas County Community College Telecourse

These short, action-oriented videos, developed by Dallas County Community College, provide the impetus for lively classroom discussion. The focus is on the preparation, analysis, and use of accounting information for business decision making. (To acquire the complete telecourse, Accounting in Action, call Dallas TeleLearning at 972-669-6666, fax them at 972-669-6668, or visit their website at http://telelearning.dcccd.edu.)

STUDENT SUPPLEMENTS

Topic Tackler Plus

Free with the text, the Topic Tackler Plus helps students master difficult concepts in managerial accounting through a creative, interactive learning process. Designed for study outside the classroom, it delves into chapter concepts with graphical slides and diagrams, web links, video clips, and animations, all centered around engaging exercises designed to put students in control of their learning of managerial accounting topics. Topic Tackler Plus is available on the text's website.

Workbook/Study Guide

ISBN: 0073265012
ISBN-13: 9780073265018

This study aid provides suggestions for studying chapter material, summarizes essential points in each chapter, and tests students' knowledge using self-test questions and exercises.

Working Papers

ISBN: 0073265047
ISBN-13: 9780073265049

This study aid contains forms that help students organize their solutions to homework exercises and problems.

Excel Templates

Prepared by Jack Terry of ComSource Associates, Inc., this spreadsheet-based software uses Excel to solve selected problems and cases in the text. These selected problems and cases are identified in the margin of the text with an appropriate icon. The Excel Templates are only available on the text's website.

Reviewers

Suggestions have been received from many of our colleagues throughout the world who have used the prior edition of *Introduction to Managerial Accounting*. This is vital feedback that we rely on in each edition. Each of those who have offered comments and suggestions has our thanks.

The efforts of many people are needed to develop and improve a text. Among these people are the reviewers and consultants who point out areas of concern, cite areas of strength, and make recommendations for change. In this regard, the following professors provided feedback that was enormously helpful in preparing the third edition of *Introduction to Managerial Accounting*:

Omneya Abd-Elsalam – *Aston University*
L. M. Abney, *LaSalle University*
Dr. Nas Ahadiat, *California State Polytechnic University*
Sepeedeh Ahadiat, *California State Polytechnic University*
Sol. Ahiarah, *SUNY College at Buffalo*
Sol Ahiarah, *SUNY College at Buffalo*
Raquel Alexander, *University of North Carolina – Wilmington*
William Ambrose, *DeVry University*
Felix E. Amenkhienan, *Radford University*
Robert Appleton, *University of North Carolina – Wilmington*
Jeffrey J. Archambault, *Marshall University*
Sharad Asthana, *Fox School of Business and Management*
Leonard Bacon, *California State University, Bakersfield*
Roderick Barclay, *Texas A&M University*
Benjamin W. Bean, *Utah Valley State College*
Larry Bitner, *Hood College*
Jay Blazer, *Milwaukee Area Technical College*
Nancy Bledsoe, *Millsaps College*
William Blouch, *Loyola College*
Eugene Blue, *Governor State University*
Linda Bolduc, *Mount Wachusett Community College*
Marvin Bouillon, *Iowa State University*
Casey Bradley, *Troy State University*
Marley Brown, *Mt. Hood Community College*
Betty Jo Browning, *Bradley University*
Myra Bruegger, *Southeastern Community College*
Robert Burdette, *Salt Lake Community College*
Francis Bush, *Virginia Military Institute*
Rebecca Butler, *Gateway Community college*
June Calahan, *Redlands Community College*
John Callister, *Cornell University*
Annhenrie Campbell, *California State University, Stanislaus*
Elizabeth Cannata, *Stonehill College*
Dennis Caplan, *Iowa State University*
Kay Carnes, *Gonzaga University*
Siew Chan, *University of Massachusetts, Boston*
Chiaho Chang, *Montclair State University*
John Chandler, *University of Illinois – Champaign*
Lawrence Chin, *Golden Gate University*
Marilyn G. Ciolino, *Delgado Community College*
Carolyn Clark, *St. Joseph's University*
Joanne Collins, *California State University – Los Angeles*
Judith Cook, *Grossmont College*
Constance J. Crawford, *Rampo Colege of New Jersey*
Charles Croxford, *Merced College*
Richard Cummings, *Benedictine College*
Jill Cunningham, *Santa Fe Community College*
Alan Czyzewski, *Indiana State University*
Betty David, *Francis Marion University*
Alan E. Davis, *Community College of Philadelphia*
Deborah Davis, *Hampton University*
G. DiLorenzo, *Gloucester County College*
Jim Dougher, *DeVry University*
Keith Dusenbery, *Johnson State College*
Fara Elikai, *University of North Carolina – Wilmington*

James Emig, *Villanova University*
Martin L. Epstein, *Albuquerque TVI Community College*
Michael Farina, *Cerritos College*
John Farlin, *Ohio Dominican University*
Harriet Farney, *University of Hartford*
M.A. Fekrat, *Georgetown University*
Janice H. Fergusson, *University of South Carolina*
W. L. Ferrara, *Stetson University*
Jerry Ferry, *University of North Alabama*
Joan Foster, *Collge Misericordia*
James Franklin, *Troy State University Montgomery*
Mohamed Gaber, *State University of New York College at Plattsburgh*
Joseph Galante, *Millersville University of Pennsylvania*
David Gibson, *Hampden-Sydney College*
John Gill, *Jackson State University*
Jackson Gillespie, *University of Delaware*
Lisa Gillespie, *Loyola University*
Joe Goetz, *Louisiana State University*
Art Goldman, *University of Kentucky*
James Gravel, *Husson College*
Lillian Grose, *Delgado Community College*
Linda Hadley, *University of Dayton*
Rosalie C. Hallbauer, *Florida International University*
Anita Hape, *Farrant County Jr. College*
Dan Hary, *Southwestern Oklahoma State University*
Susan Hass, *Simmons College*
Robert Hayes, *Tennessee State University*
James Hendricks, *Northern Illinois University*
Aleecia Hibbets, *University of Louisiana Monroe*
Nancy Thorley Hill, *DePaul University*
Kathy Ho, *Niagra University*
Mary Hollars, *Vincennes University*
Norma Holter, *Towson University*
Kathy Horton, *College of DuPage*
Ronald Huntsman, *Texas Lutheran University*
Frank Ilett, *Boise State*
Wayne Ingalls, *University of Maine College*
David Jacobson, *Salem State College*
Martha Janis, *University of Wisconsin – Waukesha*
Monica M. Jeancola, *Stetson University*
Holly Johnston, *Boston University*
Sanford Kahn, *University of Cincinnati*
Mark Kaiser, *Plattsburgh State University*
John Karayan, *Cal Poly Pomona*
Marsha Kertz, *San Jose State University*
Michael Klimesh, *Gustav Adolphus University*
Greg Kordecki, *Clayton College and State University*
Michael Kulper, *Santa Barbara City College*
Christoper Kwak, *Ohlone College*
Steven LaFave, *Augsburg College*
Thomas Largay, *Thomas College*
Robert Larson, *Penn State University*
Chor Lau, *California State University, Los Angeles*
Minwoo Lee, *Western Kentucky University*
Angela Letourneau, *Winthrop University*
Barry Lewis, *Southwest Missouri State University*
Joan Litton, *Ferrum College*
G. D. Lorenzo, *Gloucester Community College*
Jordan Lowe, *Arizona State University*
Suzanne Lowensohn, *Colorado State University*
Jayne Maas, *Towson University*

Bob Mahan, *Milligan College*
Suneel Maheshwari, *Marshall University*
Leland Mansuetti, *Sierra College*
Lisa Martin, *Western Michigan University*
Jayne Mass, *Towson University*
Noel McKeon, *Florida Community College*
James E. Miller, *Gannon University*
Susan Minke, *Indiana-Purdue University at Fort Wayne*
Laura Morgan, *University of New Hampshire*
Andrew J. Morgret, *University of Memphis*
Anthony Moses, *Saint Anselm College*
Daniel Mugavero, *Lake Superior State University*
Muroki Mwaura, *William Patterson University*
Presha Neidermeyer, *Union College*
Trisha Newbanks, *Iowa State University*
Eizabeth Nolan, *Southwestern Oklahoma State University*
Michael O'Neill, *Seattle Central Community College*
George Otto, *Truman College*
Chei Paik, *George Washington University*
William D. Parrish, *Delgado Community College*
Wendy W. Peffley, *North Carolina Wesleyan College*
Tamara Phelan, *Northern Illinois University*
Eustace Phillip, *Emmanuel College*
Anthony Piltz, *Rocky Mountain College*
Margaret P. Pollard, *American River College*
H. M. Pomroy, *Elizabethtown College*
Alan Porter, *Eastern New Mexico University*
Barbara Prince, *Cambridge Community College*
Ahmad Rahman, *La Roche College*
Joan Reicosky, *University of Minnesota – Morris*
Roger Reynolds, *University of Dayton*
Howard Rockness, *University of North Carolina – Wilmington*
Leonardo Rodriguez, *Florida International University*
Gary Ross, *College of the Southwest*
Luther L. Ross, Sr., *Central Piedmont Community College*
Dr. Benjamin L. Sadler, *Miami Dade College*
Martha Sampsell, *Elmhurst College*
John Savash – *Elmira College*
Roger Scherser, *Edison Community College*
Henry Schwarzbach, *University of Colorado*
Eldon Schafer, *University of Arizona*
DeWayne L. Searcy, *Auburn University*
Deborah Shafer, *Temple College*
Marie Smith, *Central Texas College*
Ola Smith, *Michigan State University*
John Snyder, *Florida Technical*
Soliman Soliman, *Tulane University*
Alice Steljes, *Illinois Valley Community College*
Karen Grossman Tabak, *John E. Simon School of Business*
Diane Tanner, *University of North Florida*
Joseph Ugras, *LaSalle University*
Edward Walker, *University of Texas – Pan American*
Frank Walker, *Lee College*
Patricia Doran Walters, *Baruch College*
Robert Weprin, *Lourdes College*
Brent Wickham, *Owens Community College*
Geri Wink, *University of Texas at Tyler*
James Wolfson, *Wilson College*
Joon S. Yang, *University of Minnesota – Duluth*
William Zahurak, *Community College of Allegheny County*
Kristina Zvinakis, *California State University, Northridge*

We are grateful for the outstanding support from McGraw-Hill/Irwin. In particular, we would like to thank Stewart Mattson, Editorial Director; Tim Vertovec, Executive Editor; Sarah Wood, Developmental Editor; Pat Frederickson, Lead Project Manager; Gina Hangos, Production Supervisor; Kami Carter, Senior Designer; Carol Loreth, Senior Supplement Producer; Matthew Perry, Media Project Manager; Elizabeth Mavetz, Senior Media Tech Producer; and Jeremy Cheshareck, Senior Photo Research Coordinator.

Finally, we would like to thank Beth Woods and Barbara Schnathorst, for working so hard to ensure an error-free second edition.

We are grateful to the Institute of Certified Management Accountants for permission to use questions and/or unofficial answers from past Certificate in Management Accounting (CMA) examinations. Likewise, we thank the American Institute of Certified Public Accountants, the Society of Management Accountants of Canada, and the Chartered Institute of Management Accountants (United Kingdom) for permission to use (or to adapt) selected problems from their examinations. These problems bear the notations CMA, CPA, SMA, and CIMA, respectively.

Peter C. Brewer

Ray H. Garrison

Eric W. Noreen

BRIEF CONTENTS

CONTENTS

CHAPTER THREE
Systems Design: Activity-Based Costing   122

CHAPTER FOUR
Systems Design: Process Costing   164

CHAPTER EIGHT
Standard Costs 342

CHAPTER NINE
Flexible Budgets and Overhead Analysis 386

CHAPTER TEN
Decentralization 428

CHAPTER ELEVEN
Relevant Costs for Decision Making   458

CHAPTER TWELVE
Capital Budgeting Decisions   502

CHAPTER THIRTEEN
"How Well Am I Doing?" Statement of Cash Flows   548

CHAPTER FOURTEEN
"How Well Am I Doing?" Financial Statement Analysis   590

Managerial Accounting and the Business Environment

A LOOK AT THE PROLOGUE

Today's managers know that their world is constantly changing and becoming even more complex. Before we get down to the basics, this Prologue will introduce you to a few of the revolutionary changes that today's managers face.

A LOOK AHEAD

Chapter 1 describes the work performed by managers, stresses the need for managerial accounting information, contrasts managerial and financial accounting, and defines many of the cost terms that will be used throughout the textbook. You will begin to build your base there.

T hroughout this book you will study how management accounting functions within organizations. However, before embarking on the study of management accounting, you need to develop an appreciation for the larger business environment within which it operates. The Prologue is divided into nine sections: (1) globalization, (2) strategy, (3) organizational structure, (4) process management, (5) technology in business, (6) the importance of ethics in business, (7) corporate governance, (8) enterprise risk management, and (9) the Certified Management Accountant (CMA). Other business classes provide greater detail on many of these topics. Nonetheless, a broad discussion of these topics is useful for placing management accounting in its proper context.

GLOBALIZATION

The world has become more intertwined over the last 20 years. Reductions in tariffs, quotas, and other barriers to free trade; improvements in global transportation systems; an expansion in Internet usage; and increasing sophistication in international markets have created a truly global marketplace. Exhibit P-1 illustrates this fact from the standpoint of the United States. The top part of the exhibit shows the dollar value of imports (stated in millions of dollars) into the United States from six countries; the bottom half shows the dollar value of exports from the United States to those same six countries. As you can see, the increase in import and export activity from 1990 to 2004 was huge. Chinese trade expanded enormously while trade with Japan continued to be very significant. Members of the European Union (EU), such as the United Kingdom and Germany, increased their trade with the United States, as did Canada and Mexico, which are part of the North American Free Trade Association (NAFTA).

In a global marketplace, a company that has been very successful in its local market may suddenly find itself facing competition from halfway around the globe. For example, in the 1980s American automobile manufacturers began losing market share to Japanese competitors who offered American consumers higher quality cars at lower prices. For consumers, this type of heightened international competition promises a greater variety of goods and services, at higher quality and lower prices. However, heightened international competition threatens companies that may have been quite profitable in their own local markets.

Although globalization leads to greater competition, it also means greater access to new markets, customers, and workers. For example, the emerging markets of China, India, Russia, and Brazil contain more than 2.5 billion potential customers and workers.[1] Many

EXHIBIT P-1

United States Global Trade Activity (in millions of U.S. dollars)

U.S. Imports from:	1990	1995	2000	2004
Canada	$91,380	$144,370	$230,838	$255,928
China	$15,237	$45,543	$100,018	$196,699
Germany	$28,162	$36,844	$58,513	$77,236
Japan	$89,684	$123,479	$146,479	$129,595
Mexico	$30,157	$62,100	$135,926	$155,843
United Kingdom	$20,188	$26,930	$43,345	$46,402
U.S. Exports to:	**1990**	**1995**	**2000**	**2004**
Canada	$83,674	$127,226	$178,941	$190,164
China	$4,806	$11,754	$16,185	$34,721
Germany	$18,760	$22,394	$29,448	$31,381
Japan	$48,579	$64,343	$64,924	$54,400
Mexico	$28,279	$46,292	$111,349	$110,775
United Kingdom	$23,491	$28,857	$41,571	$35,960

Source: U.S. Census Bureau, Foreign Trade Division, Data Dissemination Branch, Washington, D.C. 20233. *www.census.gov/foreign-trade/balance.*

---

[1] *The Economist: Pocket World in Figures 2004*, Profile Books Ltd., London, U.K.

World Regions:	Internet Usage in 2000	(a) Internet Usage in 2004	(b) Population in 2004	(a ÷ b) Penetration Percentage in 2004
Africa	5	13	893	1.5%
Asia	114	258	3,607	7.2%
Europe	103	231	731	31.6%
Middle East	5	17	259	6.6%
North America	108	222	325	68.3%
South America	18	56	542	10.3%
Oceania/Australia	8	16	33	48.5%
Total	361	813	6,391	12.7%

Source: *internetworldstats.com*

U.S. companies such as FedEx, McDonald's, and Nike are actively seeking to grow their sales by investing in emerging markets. In addition, the movement of jobs from the United States and Western Europe to other parts of the world has been notable in recent years. For example, one research study estimates that by the end of the decade more than 825,000 financial services and high-tech jobs will transfer from Western Europe to less expensive labor markets such as India, China, Africa, Eastern Europe, and Latin America.[2]

As alluded to earlier, the Internet continues to fuel the globalization phenomenon by providing companies with greater access to geographically dispersed customers, employees, and suppliers. Exhibit P-2 summarizes global Internet usage through 2004. Notice that the number of Internet users worldwide more than doubled during the first four years of the new millennium. Nonetheless, only 12.7% of the world population uses the Internet and less than two percent of Africa's nearly 900 million people are connected. These facts indicate that the Internet's impact on global business has yet to fully develop.

The Implications of Globalization

IN BUSINESS

International competition goes hand-in-hand with globalization. China's entrance into the global marketplace has highlighted this stark reality for many U.S. companies. For example, from 2000 to 2003, China's wooden bedroom furniture exports to the United States climbed from $360 million to $1.2 billion. During this same time, the number of workers employed by U.S. furniture manufacturers dropped by 35,000, which is one of every three U.S. workers employed within that industry.

However, globalization means more than international competition. It brings opportunities for companies to enter new markets. FedEx has pushed hard to be an important player in the emerging Asian cargo market. FedEx makes 622 weekly flights to and from Asian markets, including service to 224 Chinese cities. FedEx currently has 39% of the U.S.–China express market and it plans to pursue continual growth in that region of the world.

Sources: Ted Fishman, "How China Will Change Your Business," *Inc.*, March 2005, pp. 70–84; Matthew Boyle, "Why FedEx Is Flying High," *Fortune*, November 1, 2004, pp. 145–150.

STRATEGY

In today's globally competitive environment, companies must have a viable *strategy* for succeeding in the marketplace. A **strategy** is a "game plan" that enables a company to attract customers by distinguishing itself from competitors. The focal point of a company's strategy should be its target customers. In other words, companies can only succeed if they create a reason for customers to choose them over a competitor. These reasons, or what are more formally called *customer value propositions*, are the essence of strategy.

[2]Job Exports: Europe's Turn, *BusinessWeek*, April 19, 2004, p. 50.

Customer value propositions tend to fall into three broad categories—*customer intimacy*, *operational excellence*, and *product leadership*. Companies that adopt a customer intimacy strategy are in essence saying to their target customers, "The reason that you should choose us is because we understand and respond to your individual needs better than our competitors." Ritz-Carlton, Nordstrom, and Starbucks rely primarily on a customer intimacy value proposition for their success. Companies that pursue operational excellence are saying to their target customers, "The reason that you should choose us is because we can deliver products and services faster, more conveniently, and at a lower price than our competitors." Southwest Airlines, Wal-Mart, and The Vanguard Group are examples of companies that succeed first and foremost because of their operational excellence. Companies pursuing the third customer value proposition, product leadership, are saying to their target customers, "The reason that you should choose us is because we offer higher-quality products than our competitors." BMW, Cisco Systems, and W.L. Gore (the creator of Gore-Tex fabrics) are examples of companies that succeed because of their product leadership. Although one company may offer its customers a combination of these three customer value propositions, one usually outweighs the others in terms of importance.[3]

Next, we turn our attention to how businesses create organizational structures to help accomplish their strategic goals.

IN BUSINESS

Operational Excellence Comes to the Diamond Business

An average engagement ring purchased from Blue Nile, an Internet diamond retailer, costs $5,200 compared to $9,500 if purchased from Tiffany & Co., a bricks-and-mortar retailer. Why is there such a difference? There are three reasons. First, Blue Nile allows wholesalers to sell directly to customers using its website. In the brick-and-mortar scenario, diamonds change hands as many as seven times before being sold to a customer—passing through various cutters, wholesalers, brokers, and retailers, each of whom demands a profit. Second, Blue Nile carries very little inventory and incurs negligible overhead. Diamonds are shipped directly from wholesalers after they have been purchased by a customer—no retail outlets are necessary. Bricks-and-mortar retailers tie up large amounts of money paying for the inventory and employees on their showroom floors. Third, Blue Nile generates a high volume of transactions by selling to customers anywhere in the world; therefore, it can accept a lower profit margin per transaction than local retailers, who complete fewer transactions to customers within a limited geographic radius.

Perhaps you are wondering why customers are willing to trust an Internet retailer when buying an expensive item such as a diamond? The answer is that all of the diamonds sold through Blue Nile's website are independently certified by the Gemological Institute of America in four categories—carat count, type of cut, color, and clarity. In essence, Blue Nile has turned diamonds into a commodity and is using an operational excellence customer value proposition to generate annual sales of $154 million.

Source: Victoria Murphy, "Romance Killer," *Forbes*, November 29, 2004, pp. 97–101.

ORGANIZATIONAL STRUCTURE

Our discussion of organizational structure is divided into two parts. First, we highlight the fact that presidents of all but the smallest companies cannot execute their strategies alone. They must seek the help of their employees by empowering them to make decisions—they

---

[3]These three customer value propositions were defined by Michael Treacy and Fred Wiersema in "Customer Intimacy and Other Value Disciplines," *Harvard Business Review*, January/February 1993, 84–93.

must *decentralize*. Next, we describe the most common formal decentralized organizational structure in use today—the functional structure.

Decentralization

Decentralization is the delegation of decision-making authority throughout an organization by giving managers the authority to make decisions relating to their area of responsibility. Some organizations are more decentralized than others. For example, consider Good Vibrations, an international retailer of music CDs with shops in major cities scattered across the Pacific Rim. Because of Good Vibrations' geographic dispersion and the peculiarities of local markets, the company is highly decentralized.

Good Vibrations' president (also often synonymous with the term *chief executive officer,* or *CEO*) sets the broad strategy for the company and makes major strategic decisions such as opening stores in new markets. However, much of the remaining decision-making authority is delegated to managers at various levels throughout the organization. Each of the company's numerous retail stores has a store manager as well as a separate manager for each music category such as international rock and classical/jazz. In addition, the company has support departments such as a central Purchasing Department and a Personnel Department.

The Functional View of Organizations

Exhibit P-3 shows Good Vibrations' organizational structure in the form of an **organization chart.** The purpose of an organization chart is to show how responsibility is divided among managers and to show formal lines of reporting and communication, or *chain of command.* Each box depicts an area of management responsibility, and the lines between the boxes

EXHIBIT P–3   Organization Chart, Good Vibrations.

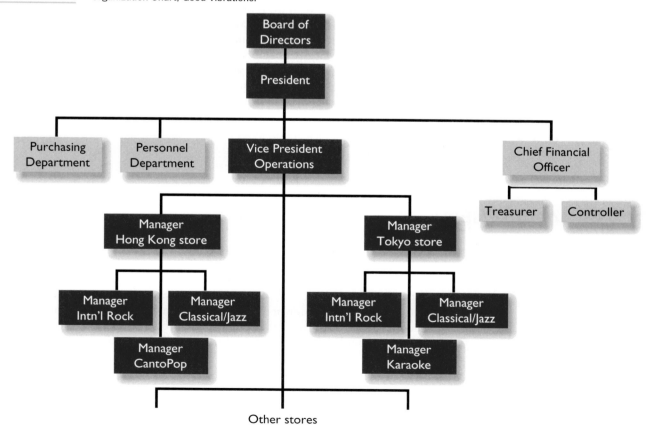

show the lines of formal authority between managers. The chart tells us, for example, that the store managers are responsible to the operations vice president. In turn, the operations vice president is responsible to the company president, who in turn is responsible to the board of directors. Following the lines of authority and communication on the organization chart, we can see that the manager of the Hong Kong store would ordinarily report to the operations vice president rather than directly to the president of the company.

An organization chart also depicts *line* and *staff* positions in an organization. A person in a **line** position is *directly* involved in achieving the basic objectives of the organization. A person in a **staff** position, by contrast, is only *indirectly* involved in achieving those basic objectives. Staff positions *support,* or provide assistance, to line positions or other parts of the organization, but they do not have direct authority over line positions. Refer again to the organization chart in Exhibit P-3. Because the basic objective of Good Vibrations is to sell recorded music at a profit, those managers whose areas of responsibility are directly related to selling music occupy line positions. These positions, which are shown in a darker color in the exhibit, include the managers of the various music departments in each store, the store managers, the operations vice president, the president, and the board of directors.

By contrast, the managers of the central Purchasing Department and the Personnel Department occupy staff positions, because their departments support other departments rather than carry out the company's basic missions. The chief financial officer is a member of the top management team who also occupies a staff position. The **chief financial officer (CFO)** is responsible for providing timely and relevant data to support planning and control activities and for preparing financial statements for external users. In the United States, a manager known as the **controller** often runs the accounting department and reports directly to the CFO. More than ever, the accountants who work under the CFO are focusing their efforts on supporting the needs of co-workers in line positions as one report concluded:

> Growing numbers of management accountants spend the bulk of their time as internal consultants or business analysts within their companies. Technological advances have liberated them from the mechanical aspects of accounting. They spend less time preparing standardized reports and more time analyzing and interpreting information. Many have moved from the isolation of accounting departments to be physically positioned in the [line] departments with which they work. Management accountants work on cross-functional teams, have extensive face-to-face communications with people throughout their organizations, and are actively involved in decision making . . . They are trusted advisors.[4]

The evolving role of management accountants as described in the quote above speaks to the importance of working cross-functionally to solve problems. This is the essence of the discussion in the next section.

PROCESS MANAGEMENT

A **business process** is a series of steps that are followed in order to carry out some task in a business. It is quite common for the linked set of steps constituting a business process to span departmental boundaries. The term *value chain* is often used when we look at how the functional departments of an organization interact with one another to form business processes. A **value chain,** as shown in Exhibit P-4, consists of the major business functions that add value to a company's products and services. The customer's needs are most effectively met by coordinating the business processes that span these functions.

---

[4]Gary Siegel Organization, *Counting More, Counting Less: Transformations in the Management Accounting Profession, The 1999 Practice Analysis of Management Accounting,* Institute of Management Accountants, Montvale, NJ, August 1999, p.3.

EXHIBIT P–4　Business Functions Making Up the Value Chain

Research and Development	Product Design	Manufacturing	Marketing	Distribution	Customer Service

This section discusses three different approaches to managing and improving business processes—lean production, the Theory of Constraints (TOC), and Six Sigma. Although each is unique in certain respects, they all share the common theme of focusing on managing and improving business processes.

Lean Production

Traditionally, managers in manufacturing companies have sought to minimize the unit costs of products on the theory that in the long run only the lowest-cost producer will survive and prosper. This strategy led managers to maximize output to spread the fixed costs of investments in equipment and other assets over as many units as possible. In addition, managers have traditionally felt that an important part of their job was to keep everyone busy—idleness wastes money. These traditional views, often aided and abetted by traditional management accounting practices, resulted in a number of practices that have come under criticism in recent years.

For example, in a traditional manufacturing company, work is *pushed* through the system in order to produce as much as possible and to keep everyone busy—even if products cannot be immediately sold and pile up in warehouses. The push process starts by accumulating large amounts of raw material inventories from suppliers so that operations can proceed smoothly even if unanticipated disruptions occur. Next, enough materials are released to workstations to keep everyone busy. When a workstation completes its tasks, the partially completed goods are "pushed" forward to the next workstation regardless of whether that workstation is ready to receive them. The result is that partially completed goods stack up, waiting for the next workstation to become available. They may not be completed for days, weeks, or even months. Additionally, when the units are finally completed, customers may or may not want them. If finished goods are produced faster than the market will absorb, the result is bloated finished goods inventories.

Although some may argue that maintaining large amounts of inventory has its benefits, it clearly has its costs. According to experts, in addition to tying up money, maintaining inventories encourages inefficient and sloppy work, results in too many defects, and dramatically increases the amount of time required to complete a product. For example, when partially completed goods are stored for long periods of time before being processed by the next workstation, defects introduced by the preceding workstation go unnoticed. If a machine is out of calibration or incorrect procedures are being followed, many defective units will be produced before the problem is discovered. And when the defects are finally discovered, it may be very difficult to track down the source of the problem. In addition, units may be obsolete or out of fashion by the time they are finally completed.

Large inventories of partially completed goods create many other problems that are best discussed in more advanced courses. These problems are not obvious—if they were, companies would have long ago reduced their inventories. Managers at Toyota are credited with the insight that large inventories often create many more problems than they solve. Toyota pioneered what is known today as *lean production*.

The Lean Thinking Model　The **lean thinking model** is a five-step management approach that organizes resources such as people and machines around the flow of business processes and that pulls units through these processes in response to customer

EXHIBIT P–5   The Lean Thinking Model

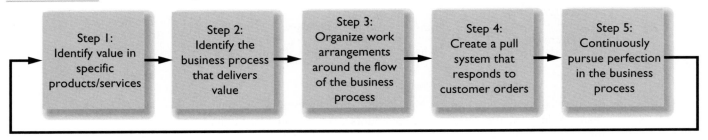

orders. The result is lower inventories, fewer defects, less wasted effort, and quicker customer response times. Exhibit P-5 depicts the five stages of the lean thinking model.[5]

The first step is to identify the value to customers in specific products and services. The second step is to identify the business process that delivers this value to customers.[6] As discussed earlier, the linked set of steps constituting a business process typically spans the departmental boundaries that are specified in an organization chart. The third step is to organize work arrangements around the flow of the business process. This is often accomplished by creating what is known as a *manufacturing cell*. The cellular approach takes employees and equipment from departments that were previously separated from one another and places them side-by-side in a work space called a *cell*. The equipment within the cell is aligned in a sequential manner that follows the steps of the business process. Each employee is trained to perform all the steps within his or her cell.

The fourth step in the lean thinking model is to create a pull system where production is not initiated until a customer has ordered a product. Inventories are reduced to a minimum by purchasing raw materials and producing units only as needed to meet customer demand. Under ideal conditions, a company operating a pull system would purchase only enough materials each day to meet that day's needs. Moreover, the company would have no goods still in process at the end of the day, and all goods completed during the day would be shipped immediately to customers. As this sequence suggests, work takes place just-in-time, in the sense that raw materials are received by each manufacturing cell just in time to go into production, manufactured parts are completed just in time to be assembled into products, and products are completed just in time to be shipped to customers. Not surprisingly, this facet of the lean thinking model is often called **Just-In-Time** production, or **JIT** for short.

The change from *push* to *pull* production is more profound than it may appear. Among other things, producing only in response to a customer order means that workers will be idle whenever demand falls below the company's production capacity. This can be an extremely difficult cultural change for an organization. It challenges the core beliefs of many managers and raises anxieties in workers who have become accustomed to being kept busy all of the time.

The fifth step of the lean thinking model is to continuously pursue perfection. In a traditional company, parts and materials are inspected for defects when they are received from suppliers, and quality inspectors inspect units as they progress along the production line. In a lean production system, the company's suppliers are responsible for the quality of incoming parts and materials. And instead of using quality inspectors, the company's production workers are directly responsible for spotting defective units. A worker who

---

[5]This exhibit is adapted from James P. Womack and Daniel T. Jones, *Lean Thinking: Banish Waste and Create Wealth in Your Corporation, Revised and Updated*, 2003, Simon & Schuster, New York, NY.
[6]The lean production literature uses the term *value stream* rather than business process.

discovers a defect immediately stops the flow of production. Supervisors and other workers go to the cell to determine the cause of the problem and correct it before any further defective units are produced. This procedure ensures that problems are quickly identified and corrected.

The lean thinking model can also be used to improve the business processes that link companies together. The term **supply chain management** is commonly used to refer to the coordination of business processes across companies to better serve end consumers. For example, Procter & Gamble and Costco coordinate their business processes to ensure that Procter & Gamble's products, such as Bounty, Tide, and Crest, are on Costco's shelves when customers want them. Both Procter & Gamble and Costco realize that their mutual success depends on working together to ensure Procter & Gamble's products are available to Costco's customers.

The Power of Lean   IN BUSINESS

Lean thinking can benefit all types of businesses. For example, Dell Inc.'s lean production system can produce a customized personal computer within 36 hours. Even more impressive, Dell doesn't start ordering components and assembling computers until orders are booked. By ordering right before assembly, Dell's parts are on average 60 days newer than those of its competitors, which translates into a 6% profit advantage in components alone. No wonder Dell continues to be the envy of the computer industry!

In the service arena, Jefferson Pilot Financial (JPF) realized that "[l]ike an automobile on the assembly line, an insurance policy goes through a series of processes, from initial application to underwriting, or risk assessment, to policy issuance. With each step, value is added to the work in progress—just as a car gets doors or a coat of paint." Given this realization, JPF organized its work arrangements into a cellular layout and synchronized the rate of output to the pace of customer demand. JPF's lean thinking enabled it to reduce attending physician statement turnaround times by 70%, decrease labor costs by 26%, and reduce reissue errors by 40%.

Sources: Gary McWilliams, "Whirlwind on the Web," *BusinessWeek*, April 7, 1997, p. 134; Stephen Pritchard, "Inside Dell's Lean Machine," *Works Management*, December 2002, pp. 14–16; and Cynthia Karen Swank, "The Lean Service Machine," *Harvard Business Review*, October 2003, pp. 123–129.

The Theory of Constraints (TOC)

A **constraint** is anything that prevents you from getting more of what you want. Every individual and every organization faces at least one constraint. You may not have enough time to study thoroughly for every subject and to go out with your friends on the weekend, so time is your constraint. United Airlines has only a limited number of loading gates available at its busy Chicago O'Hare hub, so its constraint is loading gates. Vail Resorts has only a limited amount of land to develop as home sites and commercial lots at its ski areas, so its constraint is land.

The **Theory of Constraints (TOC)** is based on the insight that effectively managing the constraint is the key to success. For example, long waiting periods for surgery are a chronic problem in the National Health Service (NHS), the government-funded provider of health care in the United Kingdom. The diagram in Exhibit P-6 illustrates a simplified version of the steps followed by a surgery patient. The number of patients who can be processed through each step in a day is indicated in the exhibit. For example, appointments for outpatient visits can be made for as many as 100 referrals from general practitioners in a day.

The constraint, or *bottleneck,* in a system is determined by the step that has the smallest capacity—in this case surgery. The total number of patients processed through the entire system cannot exceed 15 per day—the maximum number of patients who can be treated in surgery. No matter how hard managers, doctors, and nurses try

EXHIBIT P–6   Processing Surgery Patients at an NHS Facility (simplified)*

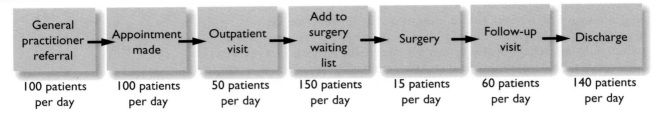

General practitioner referral	Appointment made	Outpatient visit	Add to surgery waiting list	Surgery	Follow-up visit	Discharge
100 patients per day	100 patients per day	50 patients per day	150 patients per day	15 patients per day	60 patients per day	140 patients per day

*This diagram originally appeared in the February 1999 issue of the U.K. magazine *Health Management.*

to improve the processing rate elsewhere in the system, they will never succeed in driving down wait lists until the capacity of surgery is increased. In fact, improvements elsewhere in the system—particularly before the constraint—are likely to result in even longer waiting times and more frustrated patients and health care providers. Thus, to be effective, improvement efforts must be focused on the constraint. A business process, such as the process for serving surgery patients, is like a chain. If you want to increase the strength of a chain, what is the most effective way to do this? Should you concentrate your efforts strengthening the strongest link, all the links, or the weakest link? Clearly, focusing your efforts on the weakest link will bring the biggest benefit.

The procedure to follow to strengthen the chain is clear. First, identify the weakest link, which is the constraint. In the case of the NHS, the constraint is surgery. Second, do not place a greater strain on the system than the weakest link can handle—if you do, the chain will break. In the case of the NHS, more referrals than surgery can accommodate leads to unacceptably long waiting lists. Third, concentrate improvement efforts on strengthening the weakest link. In the case of the NHS, this means finding ways to increase the number of surgeries that can be performed in a day. Fourth, if the improvement efforts are successful, eventually the weakest link will improve to the point where it is no longer the weakest link. At that point, the new weakest link (i.e., the new constraint) must be identified, and improvement efforts must be shifted over to that link. This simple sequential process provides a powerful strategy for optimizing business processes.

IN BUSINESS   **Watch Where You Cut Costs**

At one hospital, the emergency room became so backlogged that its doors were closed to the public and patients were turned away for over 36 hours in the course of a single month. It turned out, after investigation, that the constraint was not the emergency room itself; it was the housekeeping staff. To cut costs, managers at the hospital had laid off housekeeping workers. This created a bottleneck in the emergency room because rooms were not being cleaned as quickly as the emergency room staff could process new patients. Thus, laying off some of the lowest paid workers at the hospital had the effect of forcing the hospital to idle some of its most highly paid staff and most expensive equipment!

Source: Tracey Burton-Houle, "AGI Continues to Steadily Make Advances with the Adaptation of TOC into Healthcare," www.goldratt.com/toctquarterly/august2002.htm.

Six Sigma

Six Sigma is a process improvement method that relies on customer feedback and fact-based data gathering and analysis techniques to drive process improvement. Motorola and

General Electric are closely identified with the emergence of the Six Sigma movement. Technically, the term Six Sigma refers to a process that generates no more than 3.4 defects per million opportunities. Because this rate of defects is so low, Six Sigma is sometimes associated with the slogan *zero defects*.

3M Doubles its Efforts with Six Sigma

IN BUSINESS

In January 2001, Jim McNerney left General Electric to become the CEO at 3M. Given that General Electric was a Six Sigma pioneer, it is not surprising that McNerney introduced Six Sigma at 3M where it is used to do "everything from sharpening sales pitches to developing new kinds of duct tape. McNerney says Six Sigma also turns out to be a low-risk way to spot up-and-coming managers because it provides straightforward measurements of their performance. So far, a quarter of the 1,000 3M employees who have completed Six Sigma [training] have been promoted two steps or more."

Source: Michael Arndt, "3M's Rising Star," *BusinessWeek*, April 12, 2004, pp. 63–74.

The most common framework used to guide Six Sigma process improvement efforts is known as DMAIC (pronounced: du-may-ik), which stands for *D*efine, *M*easure, *A*nalyze, *I*mprove, and *C*ontrol. As summarized in Exhibit P-7, the Define stage of the process focuses on defining three things, namely the scope and purpose of the project, the flow of the current process, and the customer's requirements for the process. The Measure stage is used to gather baseline performance data concerning the existing process and to narrow the scope of the project to the most important problems. The Analyze stage focuses on identifying the root causes of the problems that were identified during the Measure stage. The Analyze stage often reveals that the process includes many *activities that do not add value to the product or service*. Activities that customers are not willing to pay for because they add no value are known as **non-value-added activities** and such activities should be eliminated wherever possible. The Improve stage is where potential solutions are developed, evaluated, and implemented to eliminate non-value-added activities and any other problems uncovered in the Analyze stage. Finally, the objective in the Control stage is to ensure that the problems remain fixed and that the new methods are improved over time.[7]

Stage	Goals
Define	• Establish the scope and purpose of the project. • Diagram the flow of the current process. • Establish the customer's requirements for the process.
Measure	• Gather baseline performance data related to the existing process. • Narrow the scope of the project to the most important problems.
Analyze	• Identify the root cause(s) of the problems identified in the Measure stage.
Improve	• Develop, evaluate, and implement solutions to the problems.
Control	• Ensure that problems remain fixed. • Seek to improve the new methods over time.

Source: Peter C. Brewer and Nancy A. Bagranoff, "Near Zero-Defect Accounting with Six Sigma," *Journal of Corporate Accounting and Finance*, January-February 2004, pp. 67–72.

EXHIBIT P–7

The Six Sigma DMAIC Framework

---

[7]Peter C. Brewer, "Six Sigma Helps a Company Create a Culture of Accountability," *Journal of Organizational Excellence*, Summer 2004, pp. 45–59.

Managers must be very careful when attempting to translate Six Sigma improvements into financial benefits. There are only two ways to increase profits—decrease costs or increase sales. Cutting costs may seem easy—lay off workers who are no longer needed because of improvements such as eliminating non-value-added activities. However, if this approach is taken, employees quickly get the message that process improvements lead to job losses and they will understandably resist further improvement efforts. If improvement is to continue, employees must be convinced that the end result of improvement will be more secure rather than less secure jobs. This can only happen if management uses tools such as Six Sigma to generate more business rather than to cut the workforce.

TECHNOLOGY IN BUSINESS

Technology is being harnessed in many ways by businesses. In this section we will discuss two of these ways—e-commerce and enterprise systems.

E-Commerce

E-commerce refers to business that is conducted using the Internet. At the start of the new millennium, e-commerce was riding high. The stock prices of dot.com companies (companies that focus on generating revenue exclusively through the Internet) were climbing by leaps and bounds. On January 30, 2000, more than 20 dot.com companies, such as Pets.com and Epidemic.com, paid as much as $3 million for 30-second commercials during the Super Bowl. However, by November of that same year, prospects for dot.com companies began to worsen as companies such as Pets.com, Garden.com and Furniture.com all failed. By the spring of 2001, EToys had folded and monthly statistics for dot.com layoffs and closures had peaked at 17,554 and 64, respectively. In short, the dot.com collapse was under way.[8]

Since the collapse of the dot.com bubble in 2001, e-commerce has slowly been rebuilding momentum. Internet advertising is projected to exceed $12 billion per year before the end of the decade.[9] And while e-commerce has already had a major impact on the sale of books, music, and airline tickets, it appears that companies such as Blue Nile, eBay, Amazon.com, Lending Tree, and Expedia will continue to disrupt and redefine other markets such as the jewelry, real estate, and hotel industries.[10] In addition to dot.com companies, established brick-and-mortar companies such as General Electric, Wells Fargo, and Target will undoubtedly continue to expand into cyberspace—both for business-to-business transactions and for retailing.

The growth in e-commerce is occurring because the Internet has important advantages over more conventional marketplaces for many kinds of transactions. For example, the Internet is an ideal technology for streamlining the mortgage lending process. Customers can complete loan applications over the Internet rather than tying up the time of a staffperson in an office. And data and funds can be sent back and forth electronically—no UPS or FedEx delivery truck needs to drop by the consumer's home to deliver a check.

In conclusion, building a successful dot.com business remains a tenuous and high-risk proposition. Nevertheless, e-commerce is here to stay. The stock prices of dot.com companies will rise and fall, but the benefits that the Internet provides to businesses and their customers will ensure that e-commerce grows over time.

---

[8]See the timeline published by BBC News in the United Kingdom. The web address for BBC news is http://news.bbc.co.uk.
[9]Stephen Baker, "Where the Real Internet Money is Made," *BusinessWeek*, December 27, 2004, p. 99.
[10]Timothy J. Mullaney, "E-Biz Strikes Again!" *BusinessWeek*, May 10, 2004, pp. 80–90.

Internet Innovations

Companies continue to develop new ways of using the Internet to improve their performance. Below is a summary of intriguing Internet applications categorized into four descriptive groups.

1. Collaboration
   - Eli Lilly has a website where scientific problems are posed to its global workforce. The best solutions earn cash rewards.
   - Lockheed Martin used the Internet to help 80 of its suppliers from around the world to collaborate in designing and building a new stealth fighter plane.
2. Customer Service
   - General Motors uses the Internet to auction off vehicles with expired leases.
   - IndyMac Bancorp uses the Internet to link its nationwide network of loan brokers to its central computers. Using these links, the brokers can electronically submit and then monitor their clients' loan applications.
3. Management
   - CareGroup's approximately 2,500 doctors are rated on 20 criteria related to the care they provide for insured patients. The results are summarized on digital report cards that have helped spot inefficiencies, saving the company $4 million annually.
   - Bristol-Myers Squibb uses the Internet to speed up drug research and development. The Web-based system has reduced by one third the time needed to develop new medications.
4. Cutting Edge
   - Fresh Direct is an on-line grocer in New York City. Using the Internet to streamline order processing, the company is able to charge prices as much as 35% below its competitors.
   - eArmyU is a virtual Internet-based university that provides educational opportunities to 40,000 geographically dispersed U.S. soldiers.

Source: Heather Green, "The Web Smart 50," *BusinessWeek*, November 24, 2003, pp. 82–106.

Enterprise Systems[11]

Historically, most companies implemented specific software programs to support specific business functions. For example, the accounting department would select its own software applications to meet its needs, while the manufacturing department would select different software programs to support its needs. The separate systems were not integrated and could not easily pass data back and forth. The end result was data duplication and data inconsistencies coupled with lengthy customer response times and high costs.

An **enterprise system** is designed to overcome these problems by integrating data across an organization into a single software system that enables all employees to have simultaneous access to a common set of data. There are two keys to the data integration inherent in an enterprise system. First, all data are recorded only once in the company's centralized digital data repository known as a database. When data are added to the database or are changed, the new information is simultaneously available to everyone across the organization on a real-time basis. Second, the unique data elements contained within the database can be linked together. For example, one data element, such as a customer identification number, can be related to other data elements, such as that customer's address, billing history, shipping history, merchandise returns history, and so on. The ability to forge such relationships among data elements explains why this type of database is called a *relational database*.

Data integration helps employees communicate with one another and it also helps them communicate with their suppliers and customers. For example, consider how the

---

[11]"Enterprise systems" is a broad term that encompasses many enterprise-wide computer applications such as customer relationship management and supply chain management systems. Perhaps the most frequently mentioned type of enterprise system is an Enterprise Resource Planning (ERP) system.

customer relationship management process is improved when enterprise-wide information resides in one location. Whether meeting the customer's needs requires accessing information related to billing (an accounting function), delivery status (a distribution function), price quotes (a marketing function), or merchandise returns (a customer service function) the required information is readily available to the employee interacting with the customer. Though expensive and risky to install, the benefits of data integration have led many companies to invest in enterprise systems.

IN BUSINESS

The Benefits of Data Integration

Nike's old supply-chain system was tenuously connected by 27 different computer systems, most of which could not talk to one another. The results for Nike were predictable—retailers ran out of hot-selling sneakers and were saddled with duds that didn't sell. Nike spent $500 million to fix the problem and the results have been impressive—the lead time for getting new sneaker styles to retail shelves has been cut from nine to six months. The percentage of shoes that Nike makes without a firm order from a retailer has dropped from 30% to 3%.

Agri Beef Company's enterprise system enables its accounts payable process to accomplish in two check runs what used to require 22 check runs. As Treasurer Kim Stuart commented: "Now we can post transactions straight through to another division's general ledger account . . . That change alone saves us 200 [labor] hours a month."

Sources: Stanley Holmes, "The New Nike," *BusinessWeek*, September 20, 2004, pp. 78–86; Doug Bartholomew, "The ABC's of ERP," *CFO-IT*, Fall 2004, pp. 19–21.

THE IMPORTANCE OF ETHICS IN BUSINESS

A series of major financial scandals involving Enron, Tyco International, HealthSouth, Adelphia Communications, WorldCom, Global Crossing, Rite Aid, and other companies have raised deep concerns about ethics in business. The managers and companies involved in these scandals have suffered mightily—from huge fines to jail terms and financial collapse. And the recognition that ethical behavior is absolutely essential for the functioning of our economy has led to numerous regulatory changes, some of which we will discuss in a later section on corporate governance. But why is ethical behavior so important? This is not a matter of just being "nice." Ethical behavior is the lubricant that keeps the economy running. Without that lubricant, the economy would operate much less efficiently—less would be available to consumers, quality would be lower, and prices would be higher.

Take a very simple example. Suppose that dishonest farmers, distributors, and grocers knowingly tried to sell wormy apples as good apples and that grocers refused to take back wormy apples. What would you do as a consumer of apples? Go to another grocer? But what if all grocers acted this way? What would you do then? You would probably either stop buying apples or you would spend a lot of time inspecting apples before buying them. So would everyone else. Now notice what has happened. Because farmers, distributors, and grocers could not be trusted, sales of apples would plummet and those who did buy apples would waste a lot of time inspecting them minutely. Everyone loses. Farmers, distributors, and grocers make less money, consumers enjoy fewer apples, and consumers waste time looking for worms. In other words, without fundamental trust in the integrity of businesses, the economy would operate much less efficiently. James Surowiecki summed up this point as follows:

> [F]lourishing economies require a healthy level of trust in the reliability and fairness of everyday transactions. If you assumed every potential deal was a rip-off or that the products you were buying were probably going to be lemons, then very little business would get done. More important, the costs of the transactions that did take place would be exorbitant, since you'd have to do enormous work to investigate each deal and you'd have to rely on the threat of legal action to enforce every contract. For an economy to prosper, what's needed is not a Pollyannaish faith that everyone else has your best interests at heart—"caveat emptor" [buyer

beware] remains an important truth—but a basic confidence in the promises and commitments that people make about their products and services.[12]

Thus, for the good of everyone—including profit-making companies—it is vitally important that business be conducted within an ethical framework that builds and sustains trust.

No Trust—No Enron

IN BUSINESS

Jonathan Karpoff reports on a particularly important, but often overlooked, aspect of the Enron debacle:

> As we know, some of Enron's reported profits in the late 1990s were pure accounting fiction. But the firm also had legitimate businesses and actual assets. Enron's most important businesses involved buying and selling electricity and other forms of energy. [Using Enron as an intermediary, utilities that needed power bought energy from producers with surplus generating capacity.] Now when an electric utility contracts to buy electricity, the managers of the utility want to make darned sure that the seller will deliver the electrons exactly as agreed, at the contracted price. There is no room for fudging on this because the consequences of not having the electricity when consumers switch on their lights are dire. . . .
>
> This means that the firms with whom Enron was trading electricity . . . had to trust Enron. And trust Enron they did, to the tune of billions of dollars of trades every year. But in October 2001, when Enron announced that its previous financial statements overstated the firm's profits, it undermined such trust. As everyone recognizes, the announcement caused investors to lower their valuations of the firm. Less understood, however, was the more important impact of the announcement; by revealing some of its reported earnings to be a house of cards, Enron sabotaged its reputation. The effect was to undermine even its legitimate and (previously) profitable operations that relied on its trustworthiness.
>
> This is why Enron melted down so fast. Its core businesses relied on the firm's reputation. When that reputation was wounded, energy traders took their business elsewhere. . . .

Energy traders lost their faith in Enron, but what if no other company could be trusted to deliver on its commitments to provide electricity as contracted? In that case, energy traders would have nowhere to turn. As a direct result, energy producers with surplus generating capacity would be unable to sell their surplus power. As a consequence, their existing customers would have to pay higher prices. And utilities that did not have sufficient capacity to meet demand on their own would have to build more capacity, which would also mean higher prices for their consumers. So a general lack of trust in companies such as Enron would ultimately result in overinvestment in energy-generating capacity and higher energy prices for consumers.

Source: Jonathan M. Karpoff, "Regulation vs. Reputation in Preventing Corporate Fraud," *UW Business, Spring 2002*, pp. 28–30.

The Institute of Management Accountants (IMA) of the United States has adopted an ethical code called the Standards of Ethical Conduct that describes in some detail the ethical responsibilities of management accountants. Even though the standards were specifically developed for management accountants, they have much broader application.

Code of Conduct for Management Accountants

The IMA's Standards of Ethical Conduct is presented in full in Exhibit P-8. The standards have two parts. The first part provides general guidelines for ethical behavior. In a nutshell, a management accountant has ethical responsibilities in four broad areas: First, to maintain a high level of professional competence; second, to treat sensitive matters with confidentiality; third, to maintain personal integrity; and fourth, to be objective in all disclosures. The second part of the standards specifies what should be done if an individual finds evidence of ethical misconduct. We recommend that you stop at this point and read the standards in Exhibit P-8.

---

[12]James Surowiecki, "A Virtuous Cycle," *Forbes*, December 23, 2002, pp. 248–256.

EXHIBIT P–8   Standards of Ethical Conduct Established by the Institute of Management Accountants (IMA)

Members of IMA have an obligation to the public, their profession, the organizations they serve, and themselves, to maintain the highest standards of ethical conduct. In recognition of this obligation, the IMA has promulgated the following standards of ethical conduct for its members. Members shall not commit acts contrary to these standards nor shall they condone the commission of such acts by others within their organizations.

Members shall abide by the more stringent code of ethical conduct, whether that is the standards widely practiced in their country or IMA's Standards of Ethical Conduct. In no case will a member conduct herself or himself by any standard that is not at least equivalent to the standards identified for members in IMA's Standards of Ethical Conduct.

COMPETENCE

Members have a responsibility to:

- Maintain an appropriate level of professional competence by ongoing development of their knowledge and skills.
- Perform their professional duties in accordance with relevant laws, regulations, and technical standards.
- Prepare complete and clear reports and recommendations after appropriate analyses of relevant and reliable information.

CONFIDENTIALITY

Members have a responsibility to:

- Refrain from disclosing confidential information acquired in the course of their work except when authorized, unless legally obligated to do so.
- Inform subordinates as appropriate regarding the confidentiality of information acquired in the course of their work and monitor their activities to assure the maintenance of that confidentiality.
- Refrain from using or appearing to use confidential information acquired in the course of their work for unethical or illegal advantage either personally or through third parties.

INTEGRITY

Members have a responsibility to:

- Avoid actual or apparent conflicts of interest and advise all appropriate parties of any potential conflict.
- Refrain from engaging in any activity that would prejudice their ability to carry out their duties ethically.
- Refuse any gift, favor, or hospitality that would influence or would appear to influence their actions.
- Refrain from either actively or passively subverting the attainment of the organization's legitimate and ethical objectives.
- Recognize and communicate professional limitations or other constraints that would preclude responsible judgment or successful performance of an activity.
- Communicate unfavorable as well as favorable information and professional judgments or opinions.
- Refrain from engaging in or supporting any activity that would discredit the profession.

OBJECTIVITY

Members have a responsibility to:

- Communicate information fairly and objectively.
- Disclose fully all relevant information that could reasonably be expected to influence an intended user's understanding of the reports, comments, and recommendations presented.

RESOLUTION OF ETHICAL CONFLICT

In applying the standards of ethical conduct, members may encounter problems in identifying unethical behavior or in resolving an ethical conflict. When faced with significant ethical issues, members should follow the established policies of the organization bearing on the resolution of such conflict. If these policies do not resolve the ethical conflict, such members should consider the following courses of action.

- Discuss such problems with the immediate superior except when it appears that the superior is involved, in which case the problem should be presented initially to the next higher managerial level. If a satisfactory resolution cannot be achieved when the problem is initially presented, submit the issues to the next higher managerial level. If the immediate superior is the chief executive officer, or equivalent, the acceptable reviewing authority may be a group such as the audit committee, executive committee, board of directors, board of trustees, or owners. Contact with levels above the immediate superior should be initiated only with the superior's knowledge, assuming the superior is not involved. Except where legally prescribed, communication of such problems to authorities or individuals not employed or engaged by the organization is not considered appropriate.
- Clarify relevant ethical issues by confidential discussion with an objective advisor (e.g., IMA Ethics Counseling service) to obtain a better understanding of possible courses of action. - Consult your own attorney as to legal obligations and rights concerning the ethical conflict.

If the ethical conflict still exists after exhausting all levels of internal review, there may be no other recourse on significant matters than to resign from the organization and to submit an informative memorandum to an appropriate representative of the organization. After resignation, depending on the nature of the ethical conflict, it may also be appropriate to notify other parties.

The ethical standards provide sound, practical advice for management accountants and managers. Most of the rules in the ethical standards are motivated by a very practical consideration—if these rules were not generally followed in business, then the economy and all of us would suffer. Consider the following specific examples of the consequences of not abiding by the standards:

- Suppose employees could not be trusted with confidential information. Then top managers would be reluctant to distribute such information within the company, and as a result, decisions would be based on incomplete information and operations would deteriorate.

- Suppose employees accepted bribes from suppliers. Then contracts would tend to go to suppliers who pay the highest bribes rather than to the most competent suppliers. Would you like to fly in aircraft whose wings were made by the subcontractor who paid the highest bribe? Would you fly as often? What would happen to the airline industry if its safety record deteriorated due to shoddy workmanship on contracted parts and assemblies?

- Suppose the presidents of companies routinely lied in their annual reports and financial statements. If investors could not rely on the basic integrity of a company's financial statements, they would have little basis for making informed decisions. Suspecting the worst, rational investors would pay less for securities issued by companies and may not be willing to invest at all. As a consequence, companies would have less money for productive investments—leading to slower economic growth, fewer goods and services, and higher prices.

As these examples suggest, if ethical standards were not generally adhered to, everyone would suffer—businesses as well as consumers. Essentially, abandoning ethical standards would lead to a lower standard of living with lower-quality goods and services, less to choose from, and higher prices. In short, following ethical rules such as those in the Standards of Ethical Conduct is absolutely essential for the smooth functioning of an advanced market economy.

Who Is to Blame?

IN BUSINESS

Don Keough, a retired Coca-Cola executive, recalls that, "In my time, CFOs [chief financial officers] were basically tough, smart, and mean. Bringing good news wasn't their function. They were the truth-tellers." But that had changed by the late 1990s in some companies. Instead of being truth-tellers, CFOs became corporate spokesmen, guiding stock analysts in their quarterly earnings estimates—and then making sure those earnings estimates were beaten using whatever means necessary, including accounting tricks and in some cases outright fraud. But does the buck stop there?

A survey of 179 CFOs published in May 2004 showed that only 38% of those surveyed believed that pressure to use aggressive accounting techniques to improve results had lessened relative to three years earlier. And 20% of those surveyed said the pressure had increased over the past three years. Where did the respondents say the pressure was coming from? Personal greed, weak boards of directors, and overbearing chief executive officers (CEOs) topped the list. Who is to blame? Perhaps that question is less important than focusing on what is needed—greater personal integrity and less emphasis on meeting quarterly earnings estimates.

Sources: Jeremy Kahn, "The Chief Freaked Out Officer," *Fortune*, December 9, 2002, pp. 197–202, and Don Durfee, "After the Scandals: It's Better (and Worse) Than You Think," *CFO*, May 2004, p. 29.

Company Codes of Conduct

Many companies have adopted formal ethical codes of conduct. These codes are generally broad-based statements of a company's responsibilities to its employees, its customers, its suppliers, and the communities in which the company operates. Codes rarely

EXHIBIT P–9

The Johnson & Johnson Credo

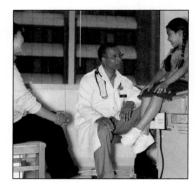

We believe our first responsibility is to the doctors, nurses and patients, to mothers and fathers and all others who use our products and services. In meeting their needs everything we do must be of high quality. We must constantly strive to reduce our costs in order to maintain reasonable prices. Customers' orders must be serviced promptly and accurately. Our suppliers and distributors must have an opportunity to make a fair profit.

We are responsible to our employees, the men and women who work with us throughout the world. Everyone must be considered as an individual. We must respect their dignity and recognize their merit. They must have a sense of security in their jobs. Compensation must be fair and adequate, and working conditions clean, orderly and safe. We must be mindful of ways to help our employees fulfill their family responsibilities. Employees must feel free to make suggestions and complaints. There must be equal opportunity for employment, development and advancement for those qualified. We must provide competent management, and their actions must be just and ethical.

We are responsible to the communities in which we live and work and to the world community as well. We must be good citizens—support good works and charities and bear our fair share of taxes. We must encourage civic improvements and better health and education. We must maintain in good order the property we are privileged to use, protecting the environment and natural resources.

Our final responsibility is to our stockholders. Business must make a sound profit. We must experiment with new ideas. Research must be carried on, innovative programs developed and mistakes paid for. New equipment must be purchased, new facilities provided and new products launched. Reserves must be created to provide for adverse times. When we operate according to these principles, the stockholders should realize a fair return.

spell out specific do's and don'ts or suggest proper behavior in a specific situation. Instead, they give broad guidelines. For example, Exhibit P-9 shows Johnson & Johnson's code of ethical conduct, which it refers to as a Credo. Johnson & Johnson created its Credo in 1943 and today it is translated into 36 languages. Johnson & Johnson surveys its employees every two to three years to obtain their impressions of how well the company adheres to its ethical principles. If the survey reveals shortcomings, corrective actions are taken.[13]

It bears emphasizing that establishing a code of ethical conduct, such as Johnson & Johnson's Credo, is meaningless if employees, and in particular top managers, do not adhere to it when making decisions. If top managers continue to say, in effect, that they will only be satisfied with bottom-line results and will accept no excuses, they are building a culture that implicitly coerces employees to engage in unethical behavior to get ahead. This type of unethical culture is contagious. In fact, one survey showed that "[t]hose who engage in unethical behavior often justify their actions with one or more of the following reasons: (1) the organization expects unethical behavior, (2) everyone else is unethical, and/or (3) behaving unethically is the only way to get ahead."[14]

Codes of Conduct on the International Level

The Code of Ethics for Professional Accountants, issued by the International Federation of Accountants (IFAC), governs the activities of all professional accountants throughout

---

[13]www.jnj.com/our_company/our_credo

[14]Michael K. McCuddy, Karl E. Reichardt, and David Schroeder, "Ethical Pressures: Fact or Fiction?" *Management Accounting* 74, no. 10, pp. 57–61.

Where Would You Like to Work?

Nearly all executives claim that their companies maintain high ethical standards; however, not all executives walk the talk. Employees usually know when top executives are saying one thing and doing another and they also know that these attitudes spill over into other areas. Working in companies where top managers pay little attention to their own ethical rules can be extremely unpleasant. Several thousand employees in many different organizations were asked if they would recommend their company to prospective employees. Overall, 66% said that they would. Among those employees who believed that their top management strives to live by the company's stated ethical standards, the number of recommenders jumped to 81%. But among those who believed top management did not follow the company's stated ethical standards, the number was just 21%.

Source: Jeffrey L. Seglin, "Good for Goodness' Sake," *CFO*, October 2002, pp. 75–78.

the world, regardless of whether they are practicing as independent CPAs, employed in government service, or employed as internal accountants.[15]

In addition to outlining ethical requirements in matters dealing with integrity and objectivity, resolution of ethical conflicts, competence, and confidentiality, the IFAC's code also outlines the accountant's ethical responsibilities in other matters such as those relating to taxes, independence, fees and commissions, advertising and solicitation, the handling of monies, and cross-border activities. Where cross-border activities are involved, the IFAC ethical requirements must be followed if they are stricter than the ethical requirements of the country in which the work is being performed.

CORPORATE GOVERNANCE

Effective corporate governance enhances stockholders' confidence that a company is being run in their best interests rather than solely in the interests of top managers. **Corporate governance** is the system by which a company is directed and controlled. If properly implemented it should provide incentives for the board of directors and top management to pursue objectives that are in the interests of the company's owners and it should provide for effective monitoring of performance.[16] Many would argue that, in addition, to protecting the interests of stockholders, an effective corporate governance system also should protect the interests of the company's many other *stakeholders*—its customers, creditors, employees, suppliers, and the communities within which it operates. These parties are referred to as stakeholders because their welfare is tied to the company's performance.

Unfortunately, history has repeatedly shown that unscrupulous top managers, if unchecked, can exploit their power to defraud stakeholders. This unpleasant reality became all too clear in 2001 when the fall of Enron kicked off an unprecedented wave of corporate scandals. These scandals were characterized by financial reporting fraud and misuse of corporate funds at the very highest levels—including CEOs and CFOs. While this was disturbing in itself, it also indicated that the institutions intended to prevent such abuses weren't working, thus raising fundamental questions about the adequacy of the existing corporate governance system. In an attempt to respond to these concerns, the U.S. Congress passed the most important reform of corporate governance in many decades— the Sarbanes-Oxley Act of 2002.

---

[15]A copy of this code can be obtained on the International Federation of Accountants' website www.ifac.org.

[16]This definition of corporate governance was adapted from the 2004 report titled OECD Principles of Corporate Governance published by the Organization for Economic Co-Operation and Development.

Spilled Milk at Parmalat

Corporate scandals have not been limited to the United States. In 2003, Parmalat, a publicly traded dairy company in Italy, went bankrupt. The CEO, Calisto Tanzi, admitted to manipulating the books for more than a decade so that he could skim off $640 million to cover losses at various of his family businesses. But the story doesn't stop there. Parmalat's balance sheet contained $13 billion in nonexistent assets, including a $5 billion Bank of America account that didn't exist. All in all, Parmalat was the biggest financial fraud in European history.

Source: Gail Edmondson, David Fairlamb, and Nanette Byrnes, "The Milk Just Keeps on Spilling," *BusinessWeek*, January 26, 2004, pp. 54–58.

The Sarbanes-Oxley Act of 2002

The **Sarbanes-Oxley Act of 2002** is intended to protect the interests of those who invest in publicly traded companies by improving the reliability and accuracy of corporate financial reports and disclosures. We would like to highlight six key aspects of the legislation.[17]

First, the act requires that both the CEO and CFO certify in writing that their company's financial statements and accompanying disclosures fairly represent the results of operations—with possible jail time if a CEO or CFO certifies results that they know are false. This creates very powerful incentives for the CEO and CFO to ensure that the financial statements contain no misrepresentations.

Second, the act established the Public Company Accounting Oversight Board to provide additional oversight over the audit profession. The act authorizes the board to conduct investigations, to take disciplinary actions against audit firms, and to enact various standards and rules concerning the preparation of audit reports.

Third, the act places the power to hire, compensate, and terminate the public accounting firm that audits a company's financial reports in the hands of the audit committee of the board of directors. Previously, management often had the power to hire and fire its auditors. Furthermore, the act specifies that all members of the audit committee must be independent, meaning that they do not have an affiliation with the company they are overseeing, nor do they receive any consulting or advisory compensation from the company.

Fourth, the act places important restrictions on audit firms. Historically, public accounting firms earned a large part of their profits by providing consulting services to the companies that they audited. This provided the appearance of a lack of independence since a client that was dissatisfied with an auditor's stance on an accounting issue might threaten to stop using the auditor as a consultant. To avoid this possible conflict of interests, the act prohibits a public accounting firm from providing a wide variety of non-auditing services to an audit client.

Fifth, the act requires that a company's annual report contain an *internal control report*. Internal controls are put in place by management to provide assurance to investors that financial disclosures are reliable. The report must state that it is management's responsibility to establish and maintain adequate internal controls and it must contain an assessment by management of the effectiveness of its internal control structure. The internal control report is accompanied by an opinion from the company's audit firm as to whether management's assessment of its internal control over financial reporting is fairly stated.[18]

---

[17]A summary of the Sarbanes-Oxley Act of 2002 can be obtained from the American Institute of Certified Public Accountants (AICPA) website www.aicpa.org/info/sarbanes_oxley_summary.

[18]The Public Company Accounting Oversight Board's Auditing Standard No. 2 requires the audit firm to issue a second opinion on whether its client maintained effective internal control over the financial reporting process. This opinion is in addition to the opinion regarding the fairness of management's assessment of the effectiveness of its own internal controls.

Sarbanes-Oxley: An Expensive Piece of Legislation

You wouldn't think 169 words could be so expensive! But that is the case with what is known as Section 404 of the Sarbanes-Oxley Act of 2002, which requires that a publicly traded company's annual report contains an internal control report certified by its auditors. Although this may sound simple enough, estimates indicate that Sarbanes-Oxley compliance will cost the Fortune 1000 companies alone about $6 billion annually—much of which will go to public accounting firms in fees. With the increased demand for audit services, public accounting firms such as KPMG, PricewaterhouseCoopers, Ernst & Young, and Deloitte are returning to campuses to hire new auditors in large numbers and students are flocking to accounting classes.

Source: Holman W. Jenkins Jr., "Thinking Outside the Sarbox," *The Wall Street Journal*, November 24, 2004, p. A13.

Finally, the act establishes severe penalties of as many as 20 years in prison for altering or destroying any documents that may eventually be used in an official proceeding and as many as 10 years in prison for managers who retaliate against a so-called whistle blower who goes outside the chain of command to report misconduct. Collectively, these six aspects of the Sarbanes-Oxley Act of 2002 should help reduce the incidence of fraudulent financial reporting.

ENTERPRISE RISK MANAGEMENT

Businesses face risks every day. Most risks are foreseeable. For example, a company could reasonably be expected to foresee the possibility of a natural disaster or a fire destroying its centralized data storage facility. Companies respond to this type of risk by having off-site backup data storage facilities. On the other hand, some risks are unforeseeable. For example, in 1982 Johnson & Johnson never could have imagined that a deranged killer would insert poison into bottles of Tylenol and then place these tainted bottles on retail shelves, ultimately killing seven people.[19] Johnson & Johnson—guided by the first line of its Credo (see page 18)—responded to this crisis by acting to reduce the risks faced by its customers and itself. First, it immediately recalled and destroyed 31 million bottles of Tylenol with a retail value of $100 million to reduce the risk of additional fatalities. Second, it developed the tamper-resistant packaging that we take for granted today to reduce the risk that the same type of crime could be repeated in the future.

Every business strategy or decision has risks associated with it. **Enterprise risk management** is a process used by a company to proactively identify the business risks that it faces and to develop responses to those risks that enable the company to be reasonably assured of satisfying stakeholder expectations.

Identifying and Controlling Business Risks

Companies should identify foreseeable risks before they occur rather than react to unfortunate events that have already happened. The left-hand column of Exhibit P-10 provides 12 examples of business risks. This list is not meant to be exhaustive, rather its purpose is to introduce you to the diverse nature of business risks that companies face. Whether the risks relate to the weather, computer hackers, complying with the law, employee theft, financial reporting, or strategic decision making, they all have one thing in common. If they are not managed effectively, they can infringe on a company's ability to meet its goals.

---

[19]Tamara Kaplan, "The Tylenol Crisis: How Effective Public Relations Saved Johnson & Johnson," in Glen Broom, Allen Center, and Scott Cutlip, *Effective Public Relations*, 1994, Prentice Hall, Upper Saddle River, NJ.

EXHIBIT P–10

Identifying and Controlling Business
Risks

Examples of Business Risks	Examples of Controls to Reduce Business Risks
• Intellectual assets being stolen from computer files	• Create firewalls that prohibit computer hackers from corrupting or stealing intellectual property
• Products harming customers	• Develop a formal and rigorous new product-testing program
• Losing market share due to the unforeseen actions of competitors	• Formalize an approach for legally gathering information about competitors' plans and practices
• Poor weather conditions shutting down operations	• Develop contingency plans for overcoming any disruptions due to weather
• A website malfunctioning	• Develop a pilot testing program before going "live" on the Internet
• A supplier strike halting the flow of raw materials	• Establish a relationship with two companies capable of providing needed raw materials
• An incentive compensation system causing employees to make poor decisions	• Create a balanced set of performance measures that motivates the desired behavior
• Financial statements unfairly reporting the value of inventory	• Count the physical inventory on hand to make sure that it agrees with the accounting records
• An employee stealing assets	• Segregate duties so that the same employee does not have physical custody of an asset and the ability to account for it
• An employee accessing unauthorized information	• Create password-protected barriers that prohibit employees from obtaining information not needed to do their jobs
• Inaccurate budget estimates causing excessive or insufficient production	• Implement a rigorous budget review process
• Failing to comply with equal employment opportunity laws	• Create a report that tracks key metrics related to compliance with the laws

Once a company identifies its risks, it can respond to them in various ways such as accepting, avoiding, sharing, or reducing the risk. Perhaps the most common risk management tactic is to reduce risks by implementing specific controls. The right-hand column of Exhibit P-10 provides an example of a control that could be implemented to help reduce each of the risks mentioned in the left-hand column of the exhibit. Again, the list of controls is far from exhaustive, rather it is meant to be illustrative.

In conclusion, a sophisticated enterprise risk management system cannot guarantee that a company will be able to satisfy the needs of its stakeholders. Nonetheless, many companies understand that managing risks is a superior alternative to reacting, perhaps too late, to unfortunate events.

IN BUSINESS

Managing Weather Risk

The National Oceanic and Atmospheric Administration claims that the weather influences one third of the U.S. gross domestic product. In 2004, the word "unseasonable" was used by more than 120 publicly traded companies to explain unfavorable financial performance. Indeed, it would be easy to conclude that the weather poses an uncontrollable risk to businesses, right? Wrong! Weather risk management is a growing industry with roughly 80 companies offering weather risk management services to clients.

For example, Planalytics is a weather consulting firm that helps Wise Metal Group, an aluminum can sheeting manufacturer, manage its natural gas purchases. Wise's $3 million monthly gas bill fluctuates sharply depending on the weather. Planalytics' software helps Wise plan its gas purchases in advance of changing temperatures. Beyond influencing natural gas purchases, the weather can also delay the boats that deliver Wise's raw materials and it can affect Wise's sales to the extent that cooler weather conditions lead to a decline in canned beverage sales.

Source: Abraham Lustgarten, "Getting Ahead of the Weather," *Fortune*, February 7, 2005, pp. 87–94.

THE CERTIFIED MANAGEMENT ACCOUNTANT (CMA)

An individual who possesses the necessary qualifications and who passes a rigorous professional exam earns the right to be known as a *Certified Management Accountant (CMA)*. In addition to the prestige that accompanies a professional designation, CMAs are often given greater responsibilities and higher compensation than those who do not have such a designation. Information about becoming a CMA and the CMA program can be accessed on the Institute of Management Accountants' (IMA) website at www.imanet.org or by calling 1-800-638-4427.

To become a Certified Management Accountant, the following four steps must be completed:

1. File an Application for Admission and register for the CMA examination.
2. Pass all four parts of the CMA examination within a three-year period.
3. Satisfy the experience requirement of two continuous years of professional experience in management and/or financial accounting prior to or within seven years of passing the CMA examination.
4. Comply with the IMA Standards of Ethical Conduct.

How's the Pay?

The Institute of Management Accountants has created the following table that allows an individual to estimate what her salary would be as a management accountant. (The table below applies specifically to women. A similar table exists for men.)

			Your Calculation
Start with this base amount		$62,234	$62,234
If you are top-level management	ADD	$6,249	
OR, if you are senior-level management	ADD	$15,642	
If you are entry-level management	SUBTRACT	$17,339	
Number of years in the field _____	TIMES	$314	
If you have an advanced degree	ADD	$5,941	
If you hold the CMA	ADD	$8,399	
OR, if you hold the CPA	ADD	$6,372	
OR, if you hold both the CMA and CPA	ADD	$11,779	_____
Your estimated salary level			_____

For example, if you make it to top-level management in 10 years and have an advanced degree and a CMA, your estimated salary would be $85,963 ($62,234 + $6,249 + 10 × $314 + $5,941 + $8,399).

Source: Karl E. Reichardt and David L. Schroeder, "Members' Salaries Still Increase," *Strategic Finance*, June 2004, pp. 29–42.

SUMMARY

Successful companies follow strategies that differentiate themselves from competitors. Strategies often focus on three customer value propositions—customer intimacy, operational excellence, and product leadership.

Most organizations rely on decentralization to some degree. Decentralization is formally depicted in an organization chart that shows who works for whom and which units perform line and staff functions.

Lean production, the Theory of Constraints, and Six Sigma are three management approaches that focus on business processes. Lean production organizes resources around business processes and pulls units through those processes in response to customer orders. The result is lower inventories, fewer defects, less wasted effort, and quicker customer response times. The Theory of Constraints emphasizes the importance of managing an organization's constraints. Since the constraint is whatever is holding back the organization, improvement efforts usually must be focused on the constraint to be effective. Six Sigma uses the DMAIC (Define, Measure, Analyze, Improve, and Control) framework to eliminate non-value-added activities and to improve processes.

E-commerce and enterprise systems are being used to reshape business practices. An enterprise system integrates data across the organization in a single software system that makes the same data available to all managers.

Ethical behavior is the foundation of a successful market economy. If we cannot trust others to act ethically in their business dealings with us, we will be inclined to invest less, scrutinize purchases more, and generally waste time and money trying to protect ourselves from the unscrupulous—resulting in fewer goods available to consumers at higher prices and lower quality.

Unfortunately, trust in our corporate governance system has been undermined in recent years by numerous high-profile financial reporting scandals. The Sarbanes-Oxley Act of 2002 was passed with the objective of improving the reliability of the financial disclosures provided by publicly traded companies.

GLOSSARY

At the end of each chapter, a list of key terms for review is given, along with the definition of each term. (These terms are printed in boldface where they are defined in the chapter.) Carefully study each term to be sure you understand its meaning. The list for the Prologue follows.

Business process   A series of steps that are followed to carry out some task in a business. (p. 6)

Chief financial officer (CFO)   The member of the top management team who is responsible for providing timely and relevant data to support planning and control activities and for preparing financial statements for external users. (p. 6)

Controller   The member of the top management team who is responsible for providing relevant and timely data to managers and for preparing financial statements for external users. The controller reports to the CFO. (p. 6)

Constraint   Anything that prevents an organization or individual from getting more of what it wants. (p. 9)

Corporate governance   The system by which a company is directed and controlled. If properly implemented it should provide incentives for top management to pursue objectives that are in the interests of the company and it should effectively monitor performance. (p. 19)

Decentralization   The delegation of decision-making authority throughout an organization by providing managers with the authority to make decisions relating to their area of responsibility. (p. 5)

Enterprise system   A software system that integrates data from across an organization into a single centralized database that enables all employees to access a common set of data. (p. 13)

Enterprise risk management   A process used by a company to help identify the risks that it faces and to develop responses to those risks that enable the company to be reasonably assured of meeting its goals. (p. 21)

Just-In-Time (JIT)   A production and inventory control system in which materials are purchased and units are produced only as needed to meet actual customer demand. (p. 8)

Lean thinking model   A five-step management approach that organizes resources around the flow of business processes and that pulls units through these processes in response to customer orders. (p. 7)

Line   A position in an organization that is directly related to the achievement of the organization's basic objectives. (p. 6)

Non-value-added activity   An activity that consumes resources but that does not add value for which customers are willing to pay. (p. 11)

Organization chart   A diagram of a company's organizational structure that depicts formal lines of reporting, communication, and responsibility between managers. (p. 5)

Sarbanes-Oxley Act of 2002   Legislation enacted to protect the interests of stockholders who invest in publicly traded companies by improving the reliability and accuracy of the disclosures provided to them. (p. 20)

Six Sigma   A method that relies on customer feedback and objective data gathering and analysis techniques to drive process improvement. (p. 10)

Staff   A position in an organization that is only indirectly related to the achievement of the organization's basic objectives. Such positions provide service or assistance to line positions or to other staff positions. (p. 6)

Strategy   A "game plan" that enables a company to attract customers by distinguishing itself from competitors. (p. 3)

Supply chain management   A management approach that coordinates business processes across companies to better serve end consumers. (p. 9)

Theory of Constraints (TOC)   A management approach that emphasizes the importance of managing constraints. (p. 9)

Value chain   The major business functions that add value to a company's products and services such as research and development, product design, manufacturing, marketing, distribution, and customer service. (p. 6)

1

An Introduction to Managerial Accounting and Cost Concepts

CHAPTER OUTLINE

DECISION FEATURE

Making Fact-Based Decisions in Real Time

Cisco Systems and Alcoa are on the leading edge of their industries and real-time management accounting is one of the keys to their success. Managers at these companies can drill down into the company's management accounting system to find the latest data on revenues, margins, order back-logs, expenses, and other data, by region, by business unit, by distribution channel, by salesperson, and so on. The Chief Financial Officer of Cisco, Larry Carter, says that with this kind of live information "you can empower all your management team to improve decision making." Richard Kelson, the Chief Financial Officer of Alcoa, says: "The earlier you get information, the easier it is to fix a problem." For example, with up-to-date data, managers at Alcoa saw softness in aerospace markets early enough to shift production from hard alloys that are used in aircraft to other products. John Chambers, the CEO of Cisco, says: "At any time in the quarter, first-line managers can look at margins and products and know exactly what the effect of their decisions will be."

Source: Thomas A. Stewart, "Making Decisions in Real Time," *Fortune,* June 26, 2000, pp. 332–333.

LEARNING OBJECTIVES

After studying Chapter 1, you should be able to:

LO1 Identify and give examples of each of the three basic manufacturing cost categories.

LO2 Distinguish between product costs and period costs and give examples of each.

LO3 Prepare an income statement including calculation of the cost of goods sold.

LO4 Prepare a schedule of cost of goods manufactured.

LO5 Define and give examples of variable costs and fixed costs.

LO6 Define and give examples of direct and indirect costs.

LO7 Define and give examples of cost classifications used in making decisions: differential costs, opportunity costs, and sunk costs.

M anagerial accounting is concerned with providing information to managers—that is, people *inside* an organization who direct and control its operations. In contrast, **financial accounting** is concerned with providing information to stockholders, creditors, and others who are *outside* an organization. Managerial accounting provides the essential data that are needed to run organizations. Financial accounting provides the essential data that are used by outsiders to judge a company's past financial performance.

Managerial accountants prepare a variety of reports. Some reports focus on how well managers or business units have performed—comparing actual results to plans and to benchmarks. Some reports provide timely, frequent updates on key indicators such as orders received, order backlog, capacity utilization, and sales. Other analytical reports are prepared as needed to investigate specific problems such as a decline in the profitability of a product line. And yet other reports analyze a developing business situation or opportunity. In contrast, financial accounting is oriented toward producing a limited set of specific prescribed annual and quarterly financial statements in accordance with generally accepted accounting principles (GAAP).

THE WORK OF MANAGEMENT AND THE NEED FOR MANAGERIAL ACCOUNTING INFORMATION

Every organization—large and small—has managers. Someone must be responsible for making plans, organizing resources, directing personnel, and controlling operations. This is true of the Bank of America, the Peace Corps, the University of Illinois, the Red Cross, and the Coca-Cola Corporation, as well as the local 7-Eleven convenience store. We will use a particular organization—Good Vibrations—to illustrate the work of management. What we have to say about the management of Good Vibrations, however, is very general and can be applied to virtually any organization.

Good Vibrations runs a chain of retail outlets that sell a full range of music CDs. The chain's stores are concentrated in Pacific Rim cities such as Sydney, Singapore, Hong Kong, Beijing, Tokyo, and Vancouver. The company has found that the best way to generate sales, and profits, is to create an exciting shopping environment. Consequently, the company puts a great deal of effort into planning the layout and decor of its stores—which are often quite large and extend over several floors in key downtown locations. Management knows that different types of clientele are attracted to different kinds of music. The international rock section is decorated with bold, brightly colored graphics, and the aisles are purposely narrow to create a crowded feeling much like one would experience at a popular nightclub on Friday night. In contrast, the classical music section is wood-paneled and fully sound insulated, with the rich, spacious feeling of a country club meeting room.

Managers at Good Vibrations, like managers everywhere, carry out three major activities—*planning, directing and motivating,* and *controlling.* **Planning** involves selecting a course of action and specifying how the action will be implemented. **Directing and motivating** involves mobilizing people to carry out plans and run routine operations. **Controlling** involves ensuring that the plan is actually carried out and is appropriately modified as circumstances change. Management accounting information plays a vital role in these basic management activities—but most particularly in the planning and control functions.

Planning

The first step in planning is to identify alternatives and then to select from among the alternatives the one that best furthers the organization's objectives. The basic objective of Good Vibrations is to earn profits for the owners of the company by providing superior service at competitive prices in as many markets as possible. To further this objective, every year top management carefully considers a number of alternatives for expanding into new geographic markets. This year management is considering opening new stores in Shanghai, Los Angeles, and Auckland.

When making this choice, management must balance the potential benefits of opening a new store against the costs. Management knows from bitter experience that opening a store in a major new market is a big step that cannot be taken lightly. It requires enormous amounts of time and energy from the company's most experienced, talented, and busy professionals. When the company attempted to open stores in both Beijing and Vancouver in the same year, resources were stretched too thinly. The result was that neither store opened on schedule, and operations in the rest of the company suffered. Therefore Good Vibrations plans very carefully before entering new markets.

Among other data, top management looks at the sales volumes, profit margins, and costs of the companys' established stores in similar markets. These data, supplied by the management accountant, are combined with projected sales volume data at the proposed new locations to estimate the profits that would be generated by the new stores. In general, virtually all important alternatives considered by management in the planning process impact revenues or costs, and management accounting data are essential in estimating those impacts.

After considering all of the alternatives, Good Vibrations' top management decided to open a store in the booming Shanghai market in the third quarter of the year, but to defer opening any other new stores to another year. As soon as this decision was made, detailed plans were drawn up for all parts of the company that would be involved in the Shanghai opening. For example, the Personnel Departments' travel budget was increased, since it would be providing extensive on-site training to the new personnel hired in Shanghai.

As in the case of the Personnel Department, the plans of management are often expressed formally in **budgets,** and the term *budgeting* is generally used to describe this part of the planning process. Budgets are usually prepared under the direction of the controller, who is the manager in charge of the Accounting Department. Typically, budgets are prepared annually and represent management's plans in specific, quantitative terms. In addition to a travel budget, the Personnel Department will be given goals in terms of new hires, courses taught, and detailed breakdowns of expected expenses. Similarly, the store managers will be given targets for sales volume, profit, expenses, pilferages losses, and employee training. Good Vibrations' management accountants will collect, analyze, and summarize this data in the form of budgets.

Directing and Motivating

In addition to planning for the future, managers oversee day-to-day activities and try to keep the organization functioning smoothly. This requires the ability to motivate and effectively direct people. Managers assign tasks to employees, arbitrate disputes, answer questions, solve on-the-spot problems, and make many small decisions that affect customers and employees. In effect, directing is that part of a manager's job that deals with the routine and the here and now. Managerial accounting data, such as daily sales reports, are often used in this type of day-to-day activity.

Controlling

In carrying out the **control** function, managers seek to ensure that the plan is being followed. **Feedback,** which signals whether operations are on track, is the key to effective control. In sophisticated organizations, this feedback is provided by various detailed reports. One of these reports, which compares budgeted to actual results, is called a **performance report.** Performance reports suggest where operations are not proceeding as planned and where some parts of the organization may require additional attention. For example, the manager of the new Shanghai store will be given sales volume, profit, and expense targets. As the year progresses, performance reports will be used to compare actual sales volume, profit, and expenses with those targets. If the actual results fall below the targets, top management will be alerted that the Shanghai store requires more

EXHIBIT 1-1   The Planning and Control Cycle

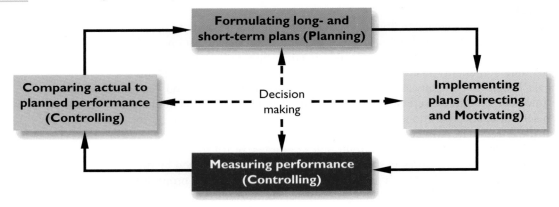

attention. Experienced personnel can be flown in to help the new manager, or top management may conclude that its plans need to be revised. As we shall see in following chapters, one of the central purposes of managerial accounting is to provide this kind of feedback to managers.

The End Results of Managers' Activities

When a customer enters a Good Vibrations store, the results of management's planning, directing and motivating, and controlling activities are evident in the many details that make the difference between a pleasant and an irritating shopping experience. The store is clean, fashionably decorated, and logically laid out. Featured artists' videos are displayed on TV monitors throughout the store, and the background rock music is loud enough to send older patrons scurrying for the classical music section. Popular CDs are in stock, and the latest hits are available for private listening on earphones. Specific titles are easy to find. Regional music, such as CantoPop in Hong Kong, is prominently featured. Checkout clerks are alert, friendly, and efficient. In short, what the customer experiences doesn't simply happen; it is the result of the efforts of managers who visualize and then fit together the processes that are needed to get the job done.

The Planning and Control Cycle

Exhibit 1–1 depicts the work of management in the form of the *planning and control cycle*. The **planning and control cycle** involves the smooth flow of management activities from planning through directing and motivating, controlling, and then back to planning again. All of these activities involve decision making, which is depicted as the hub around which the other activities revolve.

COMPARISON OF FINANCIAL AND MANAGERIAL ACCOUNTING

Financial accounting reports are prepared for external parties such as shareholders and creditors, whereas managerial accounting reports are prepared for managers inside the organization. This contrast in orientation results in a number of major differences between financial and managerial accounting, even though both disciplines often rely on the same underlying financial data. Exhibit 1–2 summarizes these differences.

As shown in Exhibit 1–2, financial and managerial accounting differ not only in their orientation but also in their emphasis on the past and the future, in the type of data provided to users, and in several other ways. These differences are discussed in the following paragraphs.

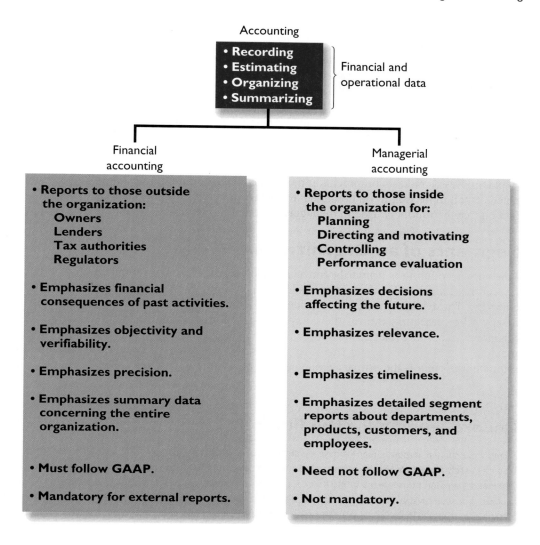

EXHIBIT 1–2

Comparison of Financial and Managerial Accounting

Emphasis on the Future

Since *planning* is such an important part of the manager's job, managerial accounting has a strong future orientation. In contrast, financial accounting primarily summarizes past financial transactions. These summaries may be useful in planning, but only to a point. The future is not simply a reflection of what has happened in the past. Changes constantly occur in economic conditions, customer needs and desires, competitive conditions, and so on. All of these changes demand that the manager's planning be based in large part on estimates of what will happen rather than on summaries of what has already happened.

Relevance of Data

Financial accounting data should be objective and verifiable. However, for internal uses, managers want information that is relevant even if it is not completely objective or verifiable. By relevant, we mean *appropriate for the problem at hand.* For example, it is difficult to verify estimated sales volumes for a proposed new store at Good Vibrations, but this is exactly the type of information that is most useful to managers. The managerial accounting information system should be flexible enough to provide whatever data are relevant for a particular decision.

Less Emphasis on Precision

Making sure that dollar amounts are accurate down to the last dollar or penny takes time and effort. While that kind of accuracy is required for external reports, most managers would rather have a good estimate immediately than wait for a more precise answer later. For this reason, managerial accountants often place less emphasis on precision than financial accountants do. In fact, one authoritative source recommends that, as a general rule, no one needs more than three significant digits in the data that are used in decision making.[1] For example, in a decision involving hundreds of millions of dollars, estimates that are rounded off to the nearest million dollars are probably good enough. In addition to placing less emphasis on precision than financial accounting, managerial accounting places much more weight on nonmonetary data. For example, data about customer satisfaction may be routinely used in managerial accounting reports.

Segments of an Organization

Financial accounting is primarily concerned with reporting for the company as a whole. By contrast, managerial accounting focuses much more on the parts, or **segments,** of a company. These segments may be product lines, sales territories, divisions, departments, or any other categorization of the company's activities that management finds useful. Financial accounting does require some breakdowns of revenues and costs by major segments in external reports, but this is a secondary emphasis. In managerial accounting, segment reporting is the primary emphasis.

IN BUSINESS

Recordkeeping for the Future

Properly maintained corporate records have significant future benefits and, as such, should be considered an essential asset. Reviews of recordkeeping policies should be performed periodically to ensure that important information, needed for reference in the future, is documented and can be retrieved. Most of the problems uncovered in such reviews tend to relate to how the records are organized rather than how much information is being documented. There is little value in information that cannot be retrieved when it is needed for decision making.

Source: J. Edwin Dietal, "Improving Corporate Performance," *Information Management Journal*, April 2000, pp. 18–26.

Generally Accepted Accounting Principles (GAAP)

Financial accounting statements prepared for external users must comply with generally accepted accounting principles (GAAP). External users must have some assurance that the reports have been prepared in accordance with a common set of ground rules. These common ground rules enhance comparability and help reduce fraud and misrepresentation, but they do not necessarily lead to the type of reports that would be most useful in internal decision making. For example, if management at Good Vibrations is considering selling land to finance a new store, they need to know the current market value of the land. However, GAAP requires that the land be stated at its original, historical cost on financial reports. The more relevant data for the decision—the current market value—is ignored under GAAP.

Managerial accounting is not bound by generally accepted accounting principles (GAAP). Managers set their own ground rules concerning the content and form of internal reports. The only constraint is that the expected benefits from using the information should outweigh the costs of collecting, analyzing, and summarizing the data. Nevertheless,

---

[1]*Statements on Management Accounting, Statement Number 5B, Fundamentals of Reporting Information to Managers,* Institute of Management Accountants, Montvale, NJ, p. 6.

as we shall see in subsequent chapters, it is undeniably true that financial reporting requirements have heavily influenced management accounting practice.

Managerial Accounting—Not Mandatory

Financial accounting is mandatory; that is, it must be done. Various outside parties such as the Securities and Exchange Commission (SEC) and the tax authorities require periodic financial statements. Managerial accounting, on the other hand, is not mandatory. A company is completely free to do as much or as little as it wishes. No regulatory bodies or other outside agencies specify what is to be done, or, for that matter, whether anything is to be done at all. Since managerial accounting is completely optional, the important question is always, "Is the information useful?" rather than, "Is the information required?"

As explained above, the work of management focuses on (1) planning, which includes setting objectives and outlining how to attain these objectives; and (2) control, which includes the steps taken to ensure that objectives are realized. To carry out these planning and control responsibilities, managers need *information* about the organization. From an accounting point of view, this information often relates to the *costs* of the organization.

In managerial accounting, the term *cost* is used in many different ways. The reason is that there are many types of costs, and these costs are classified differently according to the immediate needs of management. For example, managers may want cost data to prepare external financial reports, to prepare planning budgets, or to make decisions. Each different use of cost data demands a different classification and definition of costs. For example, the preparation of external financial reports requires the use of historical cost data, whereas decision making may require current cost data.

GENERAL COST CLASSIFICATIONS

All types of organizations incur costs—governmental, not-for-profit, manufacturing, retail, and service. Generally, the kinds of costs that are incurred and the way in which these costs are classified depend on the type of organization. For this reason, we will consider in our discussion the cost characteristics of a variety of organizations—manufacturing, merchandising, and service.

Our initial focus in this chapter is on manufacturing companies, since their basic activities include most of the activities found in other types of business organizations. Manufacturing companies such as Texas Instruments, Ford, and DuPont are involved in acquiring raw materials, producing finished goods, marketing, distributing, billing, and almost every other business activity. Therefore, an understanding of costs in a manufacturing company can be very helpful in understanding costs in other types of organizations.

Concept 1-1

In this chapter, we develop cost concepts that apply to diverse organizations. For example, these cost concepts apply to fast-food outlets such as KFC, Pizza Hut, and Taco Bell; movie studios such as Disney, Paramount, and United Artists; consulting firms such as Accenture and McKinsey; and your local hospital. The exact terms used in these industries may not be the same as those used in manufacturing, but the same basic concepts apply. With some slight modifications, these basic concepts also apply to merchandising companies such as Wal-Mart, The Gap, 7-Eleven, Nordstrom, and Tower Records. With that in mind, let's begin our discussion of manufacturing costs.

Manufacturing Costs

Most manufacturing companies divide their manufacturing costs into three broad categories: direct materials, direct labor, and manufacturing overhead. A discussion of each of these categories follows.

LEARNING OBJECTIVE 1

Identify and give examples of each of the three basic manufacturing cost categories.

Direct Materials   The materials that go into the final product are called **raw materials.** This term is somewhat misleading, since it seems to imply unprocessed natural resources like wood pulp or iron ore. Actually, raw materials refer to any materials that are used in the final product; and the finished product of one company can become the raw materials of another company. One study of 37 manufacturing industries found that materials costs averaged about 55% of sales revenues.[2]

Raw materials may include both direct and indirect materials. **Direct materials** are those materials that become an integral part of the finished product and that can be physically and conveniently traced to it. This would include, for example, the seats that Airbus purchases from subcontractors to install in its commercial aircraft. Another example is the tiny electric motor Panasonic uses in its DVD players to make the DVD spin.

Sometimes it isn't worth the effort to trace the costs of relatively insignificant materials to the end products. Such minor items would include the solder used to make electrical connections in a Sony TV or the glue used to assemble an Ethan Allen chair. Materials such as solder and glue are called **indirect materials** and are included as part of manufacturing overhead, which is discussed later in this section.

Direct Labor   **Direct labor** consists of labor costs that can be easily (i.e., physically and conveniently) traced to individual units of product. Direct labor is sometimes called *touch labor*, since direct-labor workers typically touch the product while it is being made. Examples of direct labor include assembly-line workers at Toyota, carpenters at the home builder Kaufman and Broad, and electricians who install equipment on aircraft at Bombardier Learjet.

Labor costs that cannot be physically traced to the creation of products, or that can be traced only at great cost and inconvenience, are termed **indirect labor.** Just like indirect materials, indirect labor is treated as part of manufacturing overhead. Indirect labor includes the labor costs of janitors, supervisors, materials handlers, and night security guards. Although the efforts of these workers are essential to production, it would be either impractical or impossible to accurately trace their costs to specific units of product. Hence, such labor costs are treated as indirect labor.

Major shifts have taken place and are taking place in the structure of labor costs in some industries. Sophisticated automated equipment, run and maintained by skilled indirect workers, is increasingly replacing direct labor. Indeed, direct labor averages only about 10% of sales revenues in manufacturing. In some companies, direct labor has become such a minor element of cost that it has disappeared altogether as a separate cost category. Nevertheless, the vast majority of manufacturing and service companies throughout the world continue to recognize direct labor as a separate cost category.

IN BUSINESS

Is Sending Jobs Overseas Always a Good Idea?

In recent years, many companies have sent jobs from high labor cost countries such as the United States to lower labor cost countries such as India and China. But is chasing labor cost savings always the right thing to do? In manufacturing, the answer is no. Typically, total direct labor costs are around 7% to 15% of cost of goods sold. Since direct labor is such a small part of overall costs, the labor savings realized by "offshoring" jobs can easily be overshadowed by a decline in supply chain efficiency that occurs simply because production facilities are located farther from the ultimate customers. The increase in inventory carrying costs and obsolescence costs coupled with slower response to customer orders, not to mention foreign currency exchange risks, can more than offset the benefits of employing geographically dispersed low-cost labor.

One manufacturer of casual wear in Los Angeles, California, understands the value of keeping jobs close to home in order to maintain a tightly knit supply chain. The company can fill orders for as many as 160,000 units in 24 hours. In fact, the company carries less than 30 days' inventory and is considering fabricating clothing only after orders are received from customers rather than attempting to forecast what items will sell and making them in advance. How would they do this? The company's entire supply chain—including weaving, dyeing, and sewing—is located in downtown Los Angeles, eliminating shipping delays.

Source: Robert Sternfels and Ronald Ritter, "When Offshoring Doesn't Make Sense," *The Wall Street Journal*, October 19, 2004, p. B8.

---

[2]Germain Boer and Debra Jeter, "What's New About Modern Manufacturing? Empirical Evidence on Manufacturing Cost Changes," *Journal of Management Accounting Research*, Volume 5, pp. 61–83.

Manufacturing Overhead   **Manufacturing overhead,** the third element of manufacturing cost, includes all costs of manufacturing except direct materials and direct labor. Manufacturing overhead includes items such as indirect materials; indirect labor; maintenance and repairs on production equipment; and heat and light, property taxes, depreciation, and insurance on manufacturing facilities. A company also incurs costs for heat and light, property taxes, insurance, depreciation, and so forth, associated with its selling and administrative functions, but these costs are not included as part of manufacturing overhead. Only those costs associated with *operating the factory* are included in manufacturing overhead. Manufacturing overhead averages about 16% of sales revenues.[3]

Various names are used for manufacturing overhead, such as *indirect manufacturing cost, factory overhead,* and *factory burden.* All of these terms mean the same thing as *manufacturing overhead.*

Manufacturing overhead combined with direct labor is called **conversion cost.** This term stems from the fact that direct labor costs and overhead costs are incurred to convert raw materials into finished products. Direct labor combined with direct materials is called **prime cost.**

Nonmanufacturing Costs

Nonmanufacturing costs are often divided into two categories: (1) selling costs and (2) administrative costs.

Selling costs include all costs necessary to secure customer orders and get the finished product into the customer's hands. These costs are often called *order-getting and order-filling costs.* Examples of selling costs include advertising, shipping, sales travel, sales commissions, sales salaries, and costs of finished goods warehouses.

Administrative costs include all executive, organizational, and clerical costs associated with the *general management* of an organization rather than with manufacturing, marketing, or selling. Examples of administrative costs include executive compensation, general accounting, secretarial, public relations, and similar costs involved in the overall, general administration of the organization *as a whole.*

Nonmanufacturing costs are often also called *selling and administrative costs.*

PRODUCT COSTS VERSUS PERIOD COSTS

In addition to classifying costs as manufacturing or nonmanufacturing costs, there are other ways to look at costs. For instance, they can also be classified as either *product costs* or *period costs.* To understand the difference between product costs and period costs, we must first refresh our understanding of the matching principle from financial accounting.

Generally, costs are recognized as expenses on the income statement in the period that benefits from the cost. For example, if a company pays for liability insurance in advance for two years, the entire amount is not considered an expense of the year in which the payment is made. Instead, one-half of the cost would be recognized as an expense each year. The reason is that both years—not just the first year—benefit from the insurance payment. The unexpensed portion of the insurance payment is carried on the balance sheet as an asset called *prepaid insurance.* You should be familiar with this type of *accrual* from your financial accounting coursework.

The *matching principle* is based on the accrual concept that *costs incurred to generate a particular revenue should be recognized as expenses in the same period that the revenue is recognized.* This means that if a cost is incurred to acquire or make something that will eventually be sold, then the cost should be recognized as an expense only when the sale takes place—that is, when the benefit occurs. Such costs are called *product costs.*

> **LEARNING OBJECTIVE 2**
> Distinguish between product costs and period costs and give examples of each.

---

[3]J. Miller, A. DeMeyer, and J. Nakane, *Benchmarking Global Manufacturing* (Homewood, IL: Richard D. Irwin), 1992, Chapter 2. The Boer and Jeter article previously cited contains a similar finding concerning the magnitude of manufacturing overhead.

Product Costs

For financial accounting purposes, **product costs** include all costs involved in acquiring or making a product. In the case of manufactured goods, these costs consist of direct materials, direct labor, and manufacturing overhead. Product costs "attach" to units of product as the goods are purchased or manufactured, and they remain attached as the goods go into inventory awaiting sale. Product costs are initially assigned to an inventory account on the balance sheet. When the goods are sold, the costs are released from inventory as expenses (typically called *cost of goods sold*) and matched against sales revenue. Since product costs are initially assigned to inventories, they are also known as **inventoriable costs.**

We want to emphasize that product costs are not necessarily treated as expenses in the period in which they are incurred. Rather, as explained above, they are treated as expenses in the period in which the related products *are sold*. This means that a product cost such as direct materials or direct labor might be incurred during one period but not recorded as an expense until a following period when the completed product is sold.

Period Costs

Period costs are all the costs that are not included in product costs. These costs are expensed on the income statement in the period in which they are incurred using the usual rules of accrual accounting. Period costs are not included as part of the cost of either purchased or manufactured goods. Sales commissions and office rent are examples of period costs. Neither commissions nor office rent are included as part of the cost of purchased or manufactured goods. Rather, both items are treated as expenses on the income statement in the period in which they are incurred. Thus, they are said to be period costs.

As suggested above, *all selling and administrative expenses are considered to be period costs.* Advertising, executive salaries, sales commissions, public relations, and other nonmanufacturing costs discussed earlier would all be period costs. They appear on the income statement as expenses in the period in which they are incurred.

Exhibit 1–3 contains a summary of the cost terms that we have introduced so far.

COST CLASSIFICATIONS ON FINANCIAL STATEMENTS

In your financial accounting training, you learned that companies prepare periodic financial reports for creditors, stockholders, and others to show the financial condition of the company and the company's earnings performance over some specified time interval. The reports you studied were probably those of merchandising companies, such as retail stores, which simply purchase goods from suppliers for resale to customers.

Bloated Selling and Administrative Expenses

Selling and administrative expenses tend to creep up during economic booms—creating problems when the economy falls into recession. Ron Nicol, a partner at the Boston Consulting Group, found that selling and administrative expenses at America's 1,000 largest companies grew at an average rate of 1.7% per year between 1985 and 1996 and then exploded to an average of 10% per year between 1997 and 2000. If companies had maintained their historical balance between sales revenues on the one hand and selling and administrative expenses on the other hand, Mr. Nicol calculates that selling and administrative expenses would have been about $500 million lower in the year 2000 for the average company on his list.

Source: Jon E. Hilsenrath, "The Outlook: Corporate Dieting Is Far from Over," *The Wall Street Journal*, July 9, 2001, p. A1.

EXHIBIT 1–3   Summary of Cost Terms

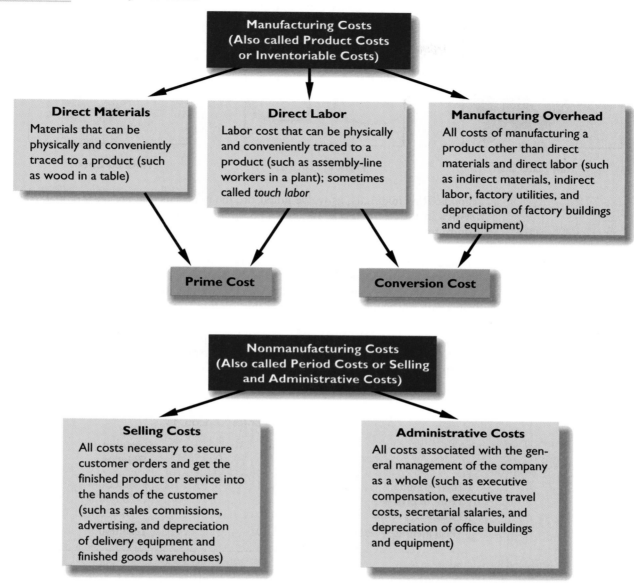

The financial statements prepared by a *manufacturing* company are more complex than the statements prepared by a merchandising company because a manufacturing company must produce its goods as well as market them. The production process involves many costs that do not exist in a merchandising company, and these costs must be properly accounted for on the manufacturing company's financial statements. In this section, we explain how these costs are recorded on the balance sheet and income statement.

The Balance Sheet

The balance sheet, or statement of financial position, of a manufacturing company is similar to that of a merchandising company. However, the inventory accounts differ between the two types of companies. A merchandising company has only one class of inventory—goods purchased from suppliers for resale to customers. In contrast, manufacturing companies have three classes of inventories—*raw materials*, *work in process*, and *finished*

Manufacturing Companies: Classifications of Inventory

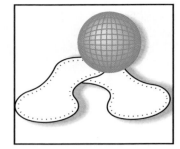

Raw Materials   Work in Process   Finished Goods

goods. Raw materials, as we've noted, are the materials that are used to make a product. **Work in process** consists of units of product that are only partially complete and will require further work before they are ready for sale to a customer. **Finished goods** consist of completed units of product that have not yet been sold to customers. The overall inventory figure shown on the balance sheet is usually broken down into these three classes of inventories in a footnote disclosure.

We will use two companies—Graham Manufacturing and Reston Bookstore—to illustrate the concepts discussed in this section. Graham Manufacturing is located in Portsmouth, New Hampshire, and makes precision brass fittings for yachts. Reston Bookstore is a small bookstore in Reston, Virginia, specializing in books about the Civil War.

The footnotes to Graham Manufacturing's Annual Report reveal the following information concerning its inventories:

Graham Manufacturing Corporation Inventory Accounts		
	Beginning Balance	**Ending Balance**
Raw materials	$ 60,000	$ 50,000
Work in process	90,000	60,000
Finished goods	125,000	175,000
Total inventory accounts	$275,000	$285,000

Graham Manufacturing's raw materials inventory consists largely of brass rods and brass blocks. The work in process inventory consists of partially completed brass fittings. The finished goods inventory consists of brass fittings that are ready to be sold to customers.

In contrast, the inventory account at Reston Bookstore consists entirely of the costs of books the company has purchased from publishers for resale to the public. In merchandising companies like Reston, these inventories may be called *merchandise inventory*. The beginning and ending balances in this account appear as follows:

Reston Bookstore Inventory Accounts		
	Beginning Balance	**Ending Balance**
Merchandise inventory	$100,000	$150,000

EXHIBIT 1–4 Comparative Income Statements: Merchandising and Manufacturing Companies

Merchandising Company
Reston Bookstore

The cost of merchandise inventory purchased from outside suppliers during the period.

Sales		$1,000,000
Cost of goods sold:		
Beginning merchandise inventory	$100,000	
Add: Purchases	650,000	
Goods available for sale	750,000	
Deduct: Ending merchandise inventory	150,000	600,000
Gross margin		400,000
Selling and administrative expenses:		
Selling expense	100,000	
Administrative expense	200,000	300,000
Net operating income		$ 100,000

Manufacturing Company
Graham Manufacturing

The manufacturing costs associated with the goods that were finished during the period. (See Exhibit 1–6 for details.)

Sales		$1,500,000
Cost of goods sold:		
Beginning finished goods inventory	$125,000	
Add: Cost of goods manufactured	850,000	
Goods available for sale	975,000	
Deduct: Ending finished goods inventory	175,000	800,000
Gross margin		700,000
Selling and administrative expenses:		
Selling expense	250,000	
Administrative expense	300,000	550,000
Net operating income		$ 150,000

The Income Statement

Exhibit 1–4 compares the income statements of Reston Bookstore and Graham Manufacturing. For purposes of illustration, these statements contain more detail about cost of goods sold than you will generally find in published financial statements.

At first glance, the income statements of merchandising and manufacturing companies like Reston Bookstore and Graham Manufacturing are very similar. The only apparent difference is in the labels of some of the entries in the computation of the cost of goods sold. In the exhibit, the computation of cost of goods sold relies on the following basic equation for inventory accounts:

> BASIC EQUATION FOR INVENTORY ACCOUNTS
>
> $$\underset{\text{balance}}{\text{Beginning}} + \underset{\text{to inventory}}{\text{Additions}} = \underset{\text{balance}}{\text{Ending}} + \underset{\text{from inventory}}{\text{Withdrawals}}$$

The logic underlying this equation, which applies to any inventory account, is illustrated in Exhibit 1–5. Any units that are in the inventory at the beginning of the period appear as the beginning balance. During the period, additions are made to the inventory through purchases or other means. The sum of the beginning balance and the additions to the account is the total amount of inventory available. During the period, withdrawals are made from inventory. The ending balance is whatever is left at the end of the period after the withdrawals.

LEARNING OBJECTIVE 3

Prepare an income statement including calculation of the cost of goods sold.

Concept 1-2

EXHIBIT 1–5   Inventory Flows

Beginning balance   + Additions   = Total available   − Withdrawals   = Ending balance

These concepts are used to determine the cost of goods sold for a merchandising company like Reston Bookstore as follows:

COST OF GOODS SOLD IN A MERCHANDISING COMPANY

$$\text{Beginning merchandise inventory} + \text{Purchases} = \text{Ending merchandise inventory} + \text{Cost of goods sold}$$

or

$$\text{Cost of goods sold} = \text{Beginning merchandise inventory} + \text{Purchases} - \text{Ending merchandise inventory}$$

To determine the cost of goods sold in a merchandising company like Reston Bookstore, we only need to know the beginning and ending balances in the Merchandise Inventory account and the purchases. Total purchases can be easily determined in a merchandising company by simply adding together all purchases from suppliers.

The cost of goods sold for a manufacturing company like Graham Manufacturing is determined as follows:

COST OF GOODS SOLD IN A MANUFACTURING COMPANY

$$\text{Beginning finished goods inventory} + \text{Cost of goods manufactured} = \text{Ending finished goods inventory} + \text{Cost of goods sold}$$

or

$$\text{Cost of goods sold} = \text{Beginning finished goods inventory} + \text{Cost of goods manufactured} - \text{Ending finished goods inventory}$$

To determine the cost of goods sold in a manufacturing company like Graham Manufacturing, we need to know the *cost of goods manufactured* and the beginning and ending balances in the Finished Goods inventory account. The **cost of goods manufactured** consists of the manufacturing costs associated with goods that were *finished* during the period. The cost of goods manufactured for Graham Manufacturing is derived in the *schedule of cost of goods manufactured* shown in Exhibit 1–6.

Schedule of Cost of Goods Manufactured

At first glance, the **schedule of cost of goods manufactured** in Exhibit 1–6 appears complex and perhaps even intimidating. However, it is all quite logical. The schedule of cost of goods manufactured contains the three elements of product costs that we discussed earlier—direct materials, direct labor, and manufacturing overhead.

EXHIBIT 1–6   Schedule of Cost of Goods Manufactured

Direct Materials →	Direct materials:		
	Beginning raw materials inventory*	$ 60,000	
	Add: Purchases of raw materials	400,000	
	Raw materials available for use	460,000	
	Deduct: Ending raw materials inventory	50,000	
	Raw materials used in production		$410,000
Direct Labor → {	Direct labor		60,000
	Manufacturing overhead:		
	Insurance, factory	6,000	
	Indirect labor	100,000	
Manufacturing	Machine rental	50,000	
Overhead →	Utilities, factory	75,000	
	Supplies	21,000	
	Depreciation, factory	90,000	
	Property taxes, factory	8,000	
	Total manufacturing overhead cost		350,000
Cost of Goods	Total manufacturing cost		820,000
Manufactured →	Add: Beginning work in process inventory		90,000
			910,000
	Deduct: Ending work in process inventory		60,000
	Cost of goods manufactured (taken to Exhibit 1–4)		$850,000

*We assume in this example that the Raw Materials inventory account contains only direct materials and that indirect materials are carried in a separate Supplies account. Using a Supplies account for indirect materials is a common practice. In Chapter 2, we discuss the procedure to be followed if *both* direct and indirect materials are carried in a single account.

The direct materials cost is not simply the cost of materials purchased during the period—rather it is the cost of materials used during the period. The purchases of raw materials are added to the beginning balance to determine the cost of materials available for use. The ending materials inventory is deducted from this amount to arrive at the cost of materials used in production. The sum of the three cost elements—materials, direct labor, and manufacturing overhead—is the total manufacturing cost. This is not the same thing, however, as the cost of goods manufactured for the period. The subtle distinction between the total manufacturing cost and the cost of goods manufactured is very easy to miss. Some of the materials, direct labor, and manufacturing overhead costs incurred during the period relate to goods that are not yet completed. As stated above, the cost of goods manufactured consists of the manufacturing costs associated with the goods that were finished during the period. Consequently, adjustments need to be made to the total manufacturing cost of the period for the partially completed goods that were in process at the beginning and at the end of the period. The costs that relate to goods that are not yet completed are shown in the work in process inventory figures at the bottom of the schedule. Note that the beginning work in process inventory must be added to the manufacturing costs of the period, and the ending work in process inventory must be deducted, to arrive at the cost of goods manufactured.

PRODUCT COST FLOWS

Earlier in the chapter, we defined product costs as those costs incurred to either purchase or manufacture goods. For manufactured goods, these costs consist of direct materials, direct labor, and manufacturing overhead. It will be helpful at this point to look briefly at the flow of costs in a manufacturing company. This will help us understand how product

EXHIBIT 1–7   Cost Flows and Classifications in a Manufacturing Company

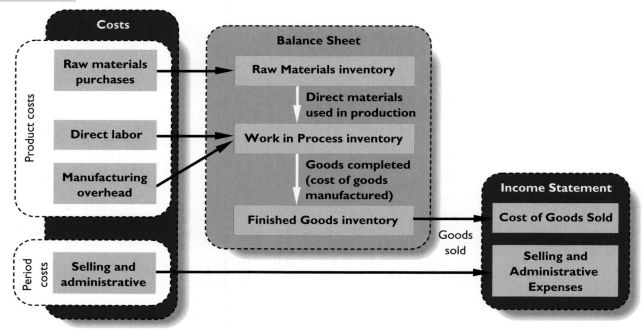

costs move through the various accounts and how they affect the balance sheet and the income statement.

Exhibit 1–7 illustrates the flow of costs in a manufacturing company. Raw materials purchases are recorded in the Raw Materials inventory account. When raw materials are used in production, their costs are transferred to the Work in Process inventory account as direct materials. Notice that direct labor cost and manufacturing overhead cost are added directly to Work in Process. Work in Process can be viewed most simply as products on an assembly line. The direct materials, direct labor, and manufacturing overhead costs added to Work in Process in Exhibit 1–7 are the costs needed to complete these products as they move along this assembly line.

Notice from the exhibit that as goods are completed, their costs are transferred from Work in Process to Finished Goods. Here the goods await sale to customers. As goods are sold, their costs are transferred from Finished Goods to Cost of Goods Sold. At this point the costs required to make the product are finally recorded as an expense. Until that point, these costs are in inventory accounts on the balance sheet.

Inventoriable Costs

As stated earlier, product costs are often called inventoriable costs. The reason is that these costs go directly into inventory accounts as they are incurred (first into Work in Process and then into Finished Goods), rather than going into expense accounts. Thus, they are termed *inventoriable costs. This is a key concept since such costs can end up on the balance sheet as assets if goods are only partially completed or are unsold at the end of a period.* To illustrate this point, refer again to Exhibit 1–7. At the end of the period, the materials, labor, and overhead costs that are associated with the units in the Work in Process and Finished Goods inventory accounts will appear on the balance sheet as assets. As explained earlier, these costs will not become expenses until the goods are completed and sold.

Selling and administrative expenses are not involved in making a product. For this reason, they are not treated as product costs but rather as period costs that are expensed as they are incurred as shown in Exhibit 1–7.

Benetton and the Value Chain

United Colors of Benetton, an Italian apparel company headquartered in Ponzano, is unusual in that it is involved in all activities in the "value chain" from clothing design through manufacturing, distribution, and ultimate sale to customers in Benetton retail outlets. Most companies are involved in only one or two of these activities. Looking at this company allows us to see how costs are distributed across the entire value chain. A recent income statement from the company contained the following data:

	Millions of Euros	Percent of Revenues
Revenues.	2,125	100.0%
Cost of sales	1,199	56.4
Selling and administrative expenses:		
Payroll and related cost	126	5.9
Distribution and transport.	45	2.1
Sales commissions	102	4.8
Advertising and promotion	125	5.9
Depreciation and amortization	62	2.9
Other expenses	141	6.6
Total selling and administrative expenses.	601	28.3%

Even though this company spends large sums on advertising and runs its own shops, the cost of sales is still quite high in relation to the net sales—56.4% of net sales. And despite the company's lavish advertising campaigns, advertising and promotion costs amounted to only 5.9% of net sales. (Note: One U.S. dollar was worth about 1.1218 euros at the time of this financial report.)

An Example of Cost Flows

To provide an example of cost flows in a manufacturing company, assume that a company's annual insurance cost is $2,000. Three-fourths of this amount ($1,500) applies to factory operations, and one-fourth ($500) applies to selling and administrative activities. Therefore, $1,500 of the $2,000 insurance cost would be a product (inventoriable) cost and would be added to the cost of the goods produced during the year. This concept is illustrated in Exhibit 1–8, where $1,500 of insurance cost is added into Work in Process. As shown in the exhibit, this portion of the year's insurance cost will not become an expense until the goods that are produced during the year are sold—which may not happen until the following year or even later. Until the goods are sold, the $1,500 will remain as part of inventory (either as part of Work in Process or as part of Finished Goods), along with the other costs of producing the goods.

By contrast, the $500 of insurance cost that applies to the company's selling and administrative activities will be expensed immediately.

Thus far, we have been mainly concerned with classifications of manufacturing costs for the purpose of determining inventory valuations on the balance sheet and cost of goods sold on the income statement in external financial reports. However, costs are used for many other purposes, and each purpose requires a different classification of costs. We will consider several different purposes for cost classifications in the remaining sections of this chapter. These purposes and the corresponding cost classifications are summarized in Exhibit 1–9. To help keep the big picture in mind, we suggest that you refer back to this exhibit frequently as you progress through the rest of this chapter.

EXHIBIT 1–8   An Example of Cost Flows in a Manufacturing Company

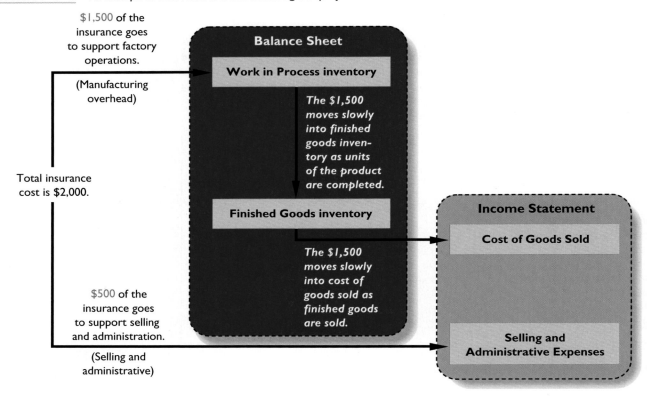

EXHIBIT 1–9

Summary of Cost Classifications

Purpose of Cost Classification	Cost Classifications
Preparing external financial statements	• Product costs (inventoriable) • Direct materials • Direct labor • Manufacturing overhead • Period costs (expensed) • Nonmanufacturing costs • Selling costs • Administrative costs
Predicting cost behavior in response to changes in activity	• Variable cost (proportional to activity) • Fixed cost (constant in total)
Assigning costs to cost objects such as departments or products	• Direct cost (can be easily traced) • Indirect cost (cannot be easily traced; must be allocated)
Making decisions	• Differential cost (differs between alternatives) • Sunk cost (past cost not affected by a decision) • Opportunity cost (forgone benefit)

Product or Period Cost?—Not Just an Academic Distinction

Whether a cost is considered a product or period cost can have an important impact on a company's financial statements and can create conflicts inside an organization. Consider the following excerpts from a conversation recorded on the Institute of Management Accountants' Ethics Hot Line:

Caller: My problem basically is that my boss, the division general manager, wants me to put costs into inventory that I know should be expensed.

Counselor: Have you expressed your doubts to your boss?

Caller: Yes, but he is basically a salesman and claims he knows nothing about GAAP. He just wants the "numbers" to back up the good news he keeps telling corporate [headquarters], which is what corporate demands. Also, he asks if I am ready to make the entries that I think are improper. It seems he wants to make it look like my idea all along. Our company had legal problems a few years ago with some government contracts, and it was the lower level people who were "hung out to dry" rather than the higher-ups who were really at fault.

Counselor: What does he say when you tell him these matters need resolution?

Caller: He just says we need a meeting, but the meetings never solve anything.

Counselor: Does your company have an ethics hot line?

Caller: Yes, but my boss would view use of the hot line as snitching or even whistle-blowing.

Counselor: If you might face reprisals for using the hot line, perhaps you should evaluate whether or not you really want to work for a company whose ethical climate is one you are uncomfortable in.

Source: Curtis C. Verschoor, "Using a Hot Line Isn't Whistle-Blowing," *Strategic Finance*, April 1999, pp. 27–28. Used with permission from *Strategic Finance* and the Institute of Management Accountants, Montvale, N.J., www.imanet.org.

---

1. Which of the following statements is false? (You may select more than one answer.)
   a. Conversion costs include direct material and direct labor.
   b. Indirect materials are included as part of manufacturing overhead.
   c. Prime costs are included as part of manufacturing overhead.
   d. Selling costs are considered period costs.
2. If the cost of goods sold is $100,000 and the ending finished goods inventory is $30,000 higher than the beginning finished goods inventory, what must be the amount of the cost of goods manufactured?
   a. $30,000
   b. $100,000
   c. $130,000
   d. $70,000

CONCEPT CHECK ✔

COST CLASSIFICATIONS FOR PREDICTING COST BEHAVIOR

Quite frequently, it is necessary to predict how a certain cost will behave in response to a change in activity. For example, a manager at AT&T may want to estimate the impact a 5% increase in long-distance calls would have on the company's total electric bill. **Cost behavior** is the way a cost will react to changes in the level of business activity. As the activity level rises and falls, a particular cost may rise and fall as well—or it may remain constant. For planning purposes, a manager must be able to anticipate which of these will happen; and if a cost can be expected to change, the manager must be able to estimate how much it will change. To help make such distinctions, costs are often categorized as variable or fixed.

LEARNING OBJECTIVE 5

Define and give examples of variable costs and fixed costs.

EXHIBIT 1–10   Variable and Fixed Cost Behavior

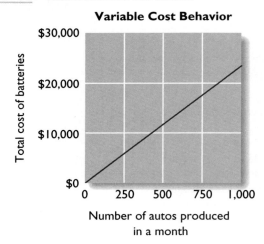

Variable Cost Behavior

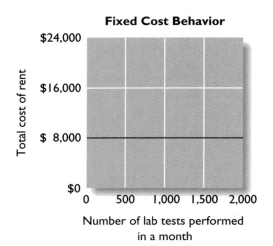

Fixed Cost Behavior

Variable Cost

A **variable cost** is a cost that varies, in total, in direct proportion to changes in the level of activity. The activity can be expressed in many ways, such as units produced, units sold, miles driven, beds occupied, lines of print, hours worked, and so forth. Direct materials is a good example of a variable cost. The cost of direct materials used during a period will vary, in total, in direct proportion to the number of units that are produced. As an example, consider the Saturn Division of General Motors. Each auto requires one battery. As the output of autos increases and decreases, the number of batteries used will increase and decrease proportionately. If auto production goes up 10%, then the number of batteries used will also go up 10%. The concept of a variable cost is shown graphically in Exhibit 1–10.

It is important to note that when we speak of a cost as being variable, we mean the *total* cost rises and falls as the activity level rises and falls. This idea is presented below, assuming that a Saturn's battery costs $24:

Number of Autos Produced	Cost per Battery	Total Variable Cost—Batteries
1	$24	$24
500	$24	$12,000
1,000	$24	$24,000

Note that a variable cost is constant if expressed on a *per unit* basis. Observe that the per unit cost of batteries remains constant at $24 even though the total cost of the batteries increases and decreases with activity.

There are many examples of costs that are variable with respect to the products and services provided by a company. In a manufacturing company, variable costs include items such as direct materials, shipping costs, sales commissions, and some elements of manufacturing overhead such as lubricants. We will usually assume that direct labor is a variable cost although direct labor may act more like a fixed cost in some situations, as we will see in a later chapter. In a merchandising company, the variable costs of carrying and selling products include items such as cost of goods sold, sales commissions, and billing costs. In a hospital, the variable costs of providing health care services to patients would include the costs of the supplies, drugs, meals, and perhaps nursing services.

When we say that a cost is variable, we ordinarily mean that it is variable with respect to the amount of goods or services the organization produces. However, costs can be variable with respect to other things. For example, the wages paid to employees at a Blockbuster Video outlet will depend on the number of hours the store is open and not strictly on the number of videos rented. In this case, we would say that wage costs are variable with respect to the hours of operation. Nevertheless, when we say that a cost is variable, we ordinarily mean it is variable with respect to the amount of goods and services produced. This could be how many Jeep Cherokees are produced, how many videos are rented, how many patients are treated, and so on.

Brown is Thinking Green

United Parcel Service (UPS) truck drivers travel more than 1.3 billion miles annually to deliver more than 4.5 billion packages. Therefore, it should come as no surprise that fuel is a huge variable cost for the company. Even if UPS can shave just a penny of cost from each mile driven, the savings can be enormous. This explains why UPS is so excited about swapping its old diesel powered trucks for diesel-electric hybrid vehicles, which have the potential to cut fuel costs by 50%. Beyond the savings for UPS, the environment would also benefit from the switch since hybrid vehicles cut emissions by 90%. As UPS television commercials ask, "What can Brown do for you?" Thanks to diesel-electric technology, the answer is that Brown can help make the air you breathe a little bit cleaner.

Source: Charles Haddad and Christine Tierney, "FedEx and Brown Are Going Green," *BusinessWeek*, August 4, 2003, pp. 60–62.

Fixed Cost

A **fixed cost** is a cost that remains constant, in total, regardless of changes in the level of activity. Unlike variable costs, fixed costs are not affected by changes in activity. Consequently, as the activity level rises and falls, total fixed costs remain constant unless influenced by some outside force, such as a price change. Rent is a good example of a fixed cost. Suppose the Mayo Clinic rents a machine for $8,000 per month that tests blood samples for the presence of leukemia cells. The $8,000 monthly rental cost will be sustained regardless of the number of tests that may be performed during the month. The concept of a fixed cost is shown graphically in Exhibit 1–10.

Food Costs at a Luxury Hotel

The Sporthotel Theresa (http://www.theresa.at/), owned and operated by the Egger family, is a four star hotel located in Zell im Zillertal, Austria. The hotel features access to hiking, skiing, biking, and other activities in the Ziller Alps as well as its own fitness facility and spa.

Three full meals a day are included in the hotel room charge. Breakfast and lunch are served buffet-style while dinner is a more formal affair with as many as six courses. A sample dinner menu appears below:

Tyrolean cottage cheese with homemade bread
***
Salad bar
***
Broccoli-terrine with saddle of venison and smoked goose-breast
Or
Chicken liver pâté with gorgonzola cheese ravioli and port wine sauce
***
Clear vegetable soup with fine vegetable strips
Or
Whey-yoghurt juice
***
Roulade of pork with zucchini, ham, and cheese on pesto ribbon noodles and saffron sauce
Or
Roasted fillet of Irish salmon and prawn with spring vegetables and sesame mash
Or
Fresh white asparagus with scrambled egg, fresh herbs, and parmesan

> **Or**
> **Steak of Tyrolean organic beef**
> ***
> **Strawberry terrine with homemade chocolate ice cream**
> **Or**
> **Iced Viennese coffee**

The chef, Stefan Egger, believes that food costs are roughly proportional to the number of guests staying at the hotel; that is, they are a variable cost. He must order food two or three days in advance from suppliers, but he adjusts his purchases to the number of guests who are currently staying at the hotel and their consumption patterns. In addition, guests make their selections from the dinner menu early in the day, which helps Stefan plan which foodstuffs will be required for dinner. Consequently, he is able to prepare just enough food so that all guests are satisfied and yet waste is held to a minimum.

Source: Conversation with Stefan Egger, chef at the Sport Hotel Theresa.

Very few costs are completely fixed. Most will change if activity changes enough. For example, suppose that the capacity of the leukemia diagnostic machine at the Mayo Clinic is 2,000 tests per month. If the clinic wishes to perform more than 2,000 tests in a month, it would be necessary to rent an additional machine, which would cause a jump in the fixed costs. When we say a cost is fixed, we mean it is fixed within some *relevant range*. The **relevant range** is the range of activity within which the assumptions about variable and fixed costs are valid. For example, the assumption that the rent for diagnostic machines is $8,000 per month is valid within the relevant range of 0 to 2,000 tests per month.

Fixed costs can create confusion if they are expressed on a per-unit basis. This is because the average fixed cost per unit increases and decreases *inversely* with changes in activity. In the Mayo Clinic, for example, the average cost per test will fall as the number of tests performed increases because the $8,000 rental cost will be spread over more tests. Conversely, as the number of tests performed in the clinic declines, the average cost per test will rise as the $8,000 rental cost is spread over fewer tests. This concept is illustrated in the table below:

Monthly Rental Cost	Number of Tets Performed	Average Cost per Test
$8,000	10	$800
$8,000	500	$16
$8,000	2,000	$4

Note that if the Mayo Clinic performs only 10 tests each month, the rental cost of the equipment will average $800 per test. But if 2,000 tests are performed each month, the average cost will drop to only $4 per test. More will be said later about the misunderstandings created by this variation in unit costs.

Examples of fixed costs include straight-line depreciation, insurance, property taxes, rent, supervisory salaries, administrative salaries, and advertising.

A summary of both variable and fixed cost behavior is presented in Exhibit 1–11.

Cost	Behavior of the Cost (within the relevant range)	
	In Total	**Per Unit**
Variable cost	Total variable cost increases and decreases in proportion to changes in the activity level.	Variable cost per unit remains constant.
Fixed cost	Total fixed cost is not affected by changes in the activity level within the relevant range.	Fixed cost per unit decreases as the activity level rises and increases as the activity level falls.

EXHIBIT 1–11

Summary of Variable and Fixed Cost Behavior

The Cost of a Call

On average, the variable cost of physically transporting a telephone call is about 7% of the price a customer pays for the call. It now costs more to bill for the call than to provide it. Then why aren't telephone companies fabulously profitable? In short, they have extremely high fixed costs for equipment, buildings, and personnel. The prices the telephone companies charge to consumers must cover these fixed costs as well as the relatively small variable costs of completing a particular call for a customer.

Source: Scott Woolley, "Meltdown," *Forbes,* July 3, 2000, pp. 70–71.

Financial Analyst

You are a financial analyst for several clients who are interested in making investments in stable companies. A privately owned airline that has been in business for 20 years needs to raise $75 million in new capital. When you call one of your clients about this possible investment, she replies that she avoids investing in airlines because of the high proportion of fixed costs in this industry. How would you reply to this statement?

COST CLASSIFICATIONS FOR ASSIGNING COSTS TO COST OBJECTS

Costs are assigned to cost objects for a variety of purposes including pricing, profitability studies, and control of spending. A **cost object** is anything for which cost data are desired—including products, product lines, customers, jobs, and organizational subunits. For purposes of assigning costs to cost objects, costs are classified as either *direct* or *indirect*.

LEARNING OBJECTIVE 6
Define and give examples of direct and indirect costs.

Direct Cost

A **direct cost** is a cost that can be easily and conveniently traced to the particular cost object under consideration. The concept of direct cost extends beyond just direct materials and direct labor. For example, if Reebok is assigning costs to its various regional and national sales offices, then the salary of the sales manager in its Tokyo office would be a direct cost of that office.

Indirect Cost

An **indirect cost** is a cost that cannot be easily and conveniently traced to the particular cost object under consideration. For example, a Campbell Soup factory may produce dozens of varieties of canned soups. The factory manager's salary would be an indirect cost of a particular variety such as chicken noodle soup. The reason is that the factory manager's salary is not caused by any one variety of soup but rather is incurred as a consequence of running the entire factory. *To be traced to a cost object such as a particular* *product, the cost must be caused by the cost object.* The factory manager's salary is called a *common cost* of producing the various products of the factory. A **common cost** is a cost that is incurred to support a number of cost objects but that cannot be traced to them individually. A common cost is a type of indirect cost.

A particular cost may be direct or indirect, depending on the cost object. While the Campbell Soup factory manager's salary is an *indirect* cost of manufacturing chicken noodle soup, it is a *direct* cost of the manufacturing division. In the first case, the cost object is the chicken noodle soup product. In the second case, the cost object is the entire manufacturing division.

COST CLASSIFICATIONS FOR DECISION MAKING

LEARNING OBJECTIVE 7

Define and give examples of cost classifications used in making decisions: differential costs, opportunity costs, and sunk costs.

Costs are an important feature of many business decisions. In making decisions, it is essential to have a firm grasp of the concepts *differential cost, opportunity cost,* and *sunk cost.*

Differential Cost and Revenue

Decisions involve choosing between alternatives. In business decisions, each alternative will have costs and benefits that must be compared to the costs and benefits of the other available alternatives. A difference in costs between any two alternatives is known as a **differential cost.** A difference in revenues between any two alternatives is known as **differential revenue.**

A differential cost is also known as an **incremental cost,** although technically an incremental cost should refer only to an increase in cost from one alternative to another; decreases in cost should be referred to as *decremental costs.* Differential cost is a broader term, encompassing both cost increases (incremental costs) and cost decreases (decremental costs) between alternatives.

The accountant's differential cost concept can be compared to the economist's marginal cost concept. When speaking of changes in cost and revenue, the economist uses the terms *marginal cost* and *marginal revenue.* The revenue that can be obtained from selling one more unit of product is called marginal revenue, and the cost involved in producing one more unit of product is called marginal cost. The economist's marginal concept is basically the same as the accountant's differential concept applied to a single unit of output.

IN BUSINESS

The Cost of a Healthier Alternative

In recent years, McDonald's has received growing pressure from critics to address the health implications of its menu. In response, McDonald's recently announced plans to switch from the partially hydrogenated vegetable oil that it had been using to fry foods to a new soybean oil that would cut trans-fat levels by 48%. After making the announcement, McDonald's came to the realization that the unhealthy oil is much cheaper than the soybean oil and it lasts twice as long. What were the cost implications of this change? A typical McDonald's restaurant uses 500 pounds of the relatively unhealthy oil per week at a cost of about $186. In contrast, the same restaurant would need to use 1,000 pounds of the new soybean oil per week at a cost of about $571. This is a differential cost of $385 per restaurant per week. This may seem like a small amount of money until the calculation is expanded to include 13,000 McDonald's restaurants operating 52 weeks a year. Now, the total tab rises to about $260 million per year.

Source: Matthew Boyle, "Can You Really Make Fast Food Healthy?" *Fortune*, August 9, 2004, pp. 134–139.

Differential costs can be either fixed or variable. To illustrate, assume that Nature Way Cosmetics, Inc., is thinking about changing its marketing method from distribution through retailers to distribution by a network of neighborhood sales representatives. Present costs and revenues are compared to projected costs and revenues in the following table:

	Retailer Distribution (present)	Sales Representatives (proposed)	Differential Costs and Revenues
Revenues (Variable)............	$700,000	$800,000	$100,000
Cost of goods sold (Variable).....	350,000	400,000	50,000
Advertising (Fixed).............	80,000	45,000	(35,000)
Commissions (Variable).........	0	40,000	40,000
Warehouse depreciation (Fixed)..	50,000	80,000	30,000
Other expenses (Fixed).........	60,000	60,000	0
Total expenses................	540,000	625,000	85,000
Net operating income	$160,000	$175,000	$ 15,000

According to the above analysis, the differential revenue is $100,000 and the differential costs total $85,000, leaving a positive differential net operating income of $15,000 under the proposed marketing plan.

The decision of whether Nature Way Cosmetics should stay with the present retail distribution or switch to sales representatives could be made on the basis of the net operating incomes of the two alternatives. As we see in the above analysis, the net operating income under the present distribution method is $160,000, whereas the net operating income with sales representatives is estimated to be $175,000. Therefore, using sales representatives is preferred, since it would result in $15,000 higher net operating income. Note that we would have arrived at exactly the same conclusion by simply focusing on the differential revenues, differential costs, and differential net operating income, which also show a $15,000 advantage for the sales representative method.

In general, only the differences between alternatives are relevant in decisions. Those items that are the same under all alternatives are not affected by the decision and can be ignored. For example, in the Nature Way Cosmetics example above, the "Other expenses" category, which is $60,000 under both alternatives, can be ignored, since it is not affected by the decision. If it were removed from the calculations, the sales representative method would still be preferred by $15,000. This is an extremely important principle in management accounting that we will revisit in later chapters.

Opportunity Cost

Opportunity cost is the potential benefit that is given up when one alternative is selected over another. To illustrate this important concept, consider the following examples:

Example 1   Vicki has a part-time job that pays $200 per week while she attends college. She would like to spend a week at the beach during spring break, and her employer has agreed to give her the time off, but without pay. The $200 in lost wages would be an opportunity cost of taking the week off to be at the beach.

Example 2   Suppose that Neiman Marcus is considering investing a large sum of money in land that may be a site for a future store. Rather than invest the funds in land, the company could invest the funds in high-grade securities. If the land is acquired, the opportunity cost is the investment income that could have been realized by purchasing the securities instead.

Example 3   Steve is employed by a company that pays him a salary of $38,000 per year. He is thinking about leaving the company and returning to school. Since returning to school would require that he give up his $38,000 salary, the forgone salary would be an opportunity cost of seeking further education.

Opportunity costs are not usually recorded in the accounts of an organization, but they are costs that must be explicitly considered in every decision a manager makes. Virtually every alternative involves an opportunity cost. In Example 3 above, for instance, if Steve decides to stay at his job, the higher income that could be realized in future years as a result of returning to school is an opportunity cost.

Using Those Empty Seats

Cancer patients who seek specialized or experimental treatments must often travel far from home. Flying on a commercial airline can be an expensive and grueling experience for these patients. Priscilla Blum noted that many corporate jets fly with empty seats and she wondered why these seats couldn't be used for cancer patients. Taking the initiative, she founded Corporate Angel Network (www.corpangelnetwork.org), an organization that arranges free flights on some 1,500 jets from over 500 companies. There are no tax breaks for putting cancer patients in empty corporate jet seats, but filling an empty seat with a cancer patient doesn't involve any significant incremental cost. Since its founding, Corporate Angel Network has provided over 16,000 free flights.

Sources: Scott McCormack, "Waste Not, Want Not," *Forbes,* July 26, 1999, p. 118; Roger McCaffrey, "A True Tale of Angels in the Sky," *The Wall Street Journal,* February 2002, p. A14; and Helen Gibbs, Communication Director, Corporate Angel Network, private communication.

YOU DECIDE

Your Decision to Attend Class

When you make the decision to attend class, what are the opportunity costs that are inherent in that decision?

Sunk Cost

A **sunk cost** is a cost *that has already been incurred* and that cannot be changed by any decision made now or in the future. Since sunk costs cannot be changed by any decision, they are not differential costs. Since only differential costs are relevant in a decision, sunk costs can and should be ignored.

To illustrate a sunk cost, assume that a company paid $50,000 several years ago for a special-purpose machine. The machine was used to make a product that is now obsolete and is no longer being sold. Even though in hindsight the purchase of the machine may have been unwise, the $50,000 cost has already been incurred and cannot be undone. And it would be folly to continue making the obsolete product in a misguided attempt to "recover" the original cost of the machine. In short, the $50,000 originally paid for the machine is a sunk cost that should be ignored in decisions.

CONCEPT CHECK

3. Which of the following cost behavior assumptions is false? (You may select more than one answer.)
   a. Variable costs are constant if expressed on a per unit basis.
   b. Total variable costs increase as the level of activity increases.
   c. The average fixed cost per unit increases as the level of activity increases.
   d. Total fixed costs decrease as the level of activity decreases.
4. Which of the following statements is false? (You may select more than one answer.)
   a. A common cost is one type of direct cost.
   b. A sunk cost is usually a differential cost.
   c. Opportunity costs are not usually recorded in the accounts of an organization.
   d. A particular cost may be direct or indirect depending on the cost object.

What Number Did You Have in Mind?

Caterpillar has long been at the forefront of management accounting practice. When asked by a manager for the cost of something, accountants at Caterpillar have been trained to ask "What are you going to use the cost for?" One management accountant at Caterpillar explains: "We want to make sure the information is formatted and the right elements are included. Do you need a variable cost, do you need a fully burdened cost, do you need overhead applied, are you just talking about discretionary cost? The cost that they really need depends on the decision they are making."

Source: Gary Siegel, "Practice Analysis: Adding Value," *Strategic Finance,* November 2000, pp. 89–90.

SUMMARY

LO1   Identify and give examples of each of the three basic manufacturing cost categories.
Manufacturing costs consist of two categories of costs that can be conveniently and directly traced to units of product—direct materials and direct labor—and one category that cannot be conveniently traced to units of product—manufacturing overhead.

LO2   Distinguish between product costs and period costs and give examples of each.
For purposes of valuing inventories and determining expenses for the balance sheet and income statement, costs are classified as either product costs or period costs. Product costs are assigned to inventories and are considered assets until the products are sold. A product cost becomes an expense—cost of goods sold— only when the product is sold. In contrast, period costs are taken directly to the income statement as expenses in the period in which they are incurred.

In a merchandising company, product cost is whatever the company paid for its merchandise. For external financial reports in a manufacturing company, product costs consist of all manufacturing costs. In both kinds of companies, selling and administrative costs are considered to be period costs and are expensed as incurred.

LO3   Prepare an income statement including calculation of the cost of goods sold.
See Exhibit 1–4 for examples of income statements for both a merchandising and a manufacturing company. In general, net operating income is computed by deducting the cost of goods sold and selling and administrative expenses from sales. Cost of goods sold is calculated by adding purchases to the beginning merchandise or finished goods inventory and then deducting the ending merchandise or finished goods inventory.

LO4   Prepare a schedule of cost of goods manufactured.
The cost of goods manufactured is the sum of direct materials, direct labor, and manufacturing overhead costs associated with the goods that were finished during the period. See Exhibit 1–6 for an example of a schedule of cost of goods manufactured.

LO5   Define and give examples of variable costs and fixed costs.
For purposes of predicting cost behavior—how costs will react to changes in activity—costs are commonly categorized as variable or fixed. Total variable costs, are strictly proportional to activity. Thus, the variable cost per unit is constant. Total fixed costs, remain the same when the level of activity fluctuates within the relevant range. Thus, the average fixed cost per unit decreases as the number of units increases.

LO6   Define and give examples of direct and indirect costs.
A direct cost is a cost that can be easily and conveniently traced to a cost object. Direct materials is a direct cost of making a product. An indirect cost is a cost that cannot be easily and conveniently traced to a cost object. For example, the salary of the administrator of a hospital is an indirect cost of serving a particular patient.

LO7   Define and give examples of cost classifications used in making decisions: differential costs, opportunity costs, and sunk costs.
The concepts of differential cost and revenue, opportunity cost, and sunk cost are vitally important for purposes of making decisions. Differential costs and revenues refer to the costs and revenues that differ between alternatives. Opportunity cost is the benefit that is forgone when one alternative is selected over another. Sunk cost is a cost that occurred in the past and cannot be altered. Differential costs and opportunity costs are relevant in decisions and should be carefully considered. Sunk costs are always irrelevant in decisions and should be ignored.

The various cost classifications discussed in this chapter are different ways of looking at costs. A particular cost, such as the cost of cheese in a taco served at Taco Bell, can be a manufacturing cost, a product cost, a variable cost, a direct cost, and a differential cost—all at the same time. Taco Bell essentially manufactures fast food. Therefore the cost of the cheese in a taco would be considered a manufacturing cost as well as a product cost. In addition, the cost of cheese would be considered variable with respect to the number of tacos served and would be a direct cost of serving tacos. Finally, the cost of the cheese in a taco would be considered a differential cost of the taco.

GUIDANCE ANSWERS TO *DECISION MAKER* AND *YOU DECIDE*

Financial Analyst (p. 49)

Fixed and *variable* are terms used to describe cost behavior or how a given cost will react or respond to changes in the level of business activity. A fixed cost is a cost that remains constant, in total, regardless of changes in the level of activity. However, on a per unit basis, a fixed cost varies inversely with changes in activity. The cost structures of a number of industries lean toward fixed costs because of the nature of their operations. Obviously, the cost of airplanes would be fixed, and within some relevant range, such costs would not change if the number of passengers flown changed. This would also be true in other industries, such as trucking and rail transportation. As a financial analyst you might suggest to your client that prior to making an investment decision it would be worthwhile to research the prospects for growth in this industry and for this company. If a downturn in business is not anticipated, a cost structure weighted toward fixed costs should *not* be used as the primary reason for turning down the investment opportunity. On the other hand, if a period of decline is anticipated, your client's initial impression might be on target. See Chapter 6 for further discussion of the impact of a company's cost structure on its profits.

Your Decision to Attend Class (p. 52)

Every alternative has some opportunity cost attached to it. If you brainstormed a bit, you probably came up with a few opportunity costs that accompany your choice to attend class. If you had trouble answering the question, think about what you could be doing instead of attending class.

- You could have been working at a part-time job; you could quantify that cost by multiplying your pay rate by the time you spend preparing for and attending class.
- You could have spent the time studying for another class; the opportunity cost could be measured by the improvement in the grade that would result from spending more time on the other class.
- You could have slept in or taken a nap; depending on your level of sleep deprivation, this opportunity cost might be priceless.

GUIDANCE ANSWERS TO CONCEPT CHECKS

1. **Choices a and c.** Conversion costs include direct labor and manufacturing overhead. Since prime costs include direct materials and direct labor, these costs are not part of manufacturing overhead.
2. **Choice c.** The cost of goods manufactured must be sufficient to cover the cost of goods sold of $100,000 plus the increase in the inventory account of $30,000.
3. **Choices c and d.** The average fixed cost per unit decreases, rather than increases, as the level of activity increases. Total fixed costs do not change as the level of activity decreases (within the relevant range).
4. **Choices a and b.** A common cost is one type of indirect cost, rather than direct cost. A sunk cost is not a differential cost. Sunk costs are irrelevant to decision making.

REVIEW PROBLEM 1: COST TERMS

Many new cost terms have been introduced in this chapter. It will take you some time to learn what each term means and how to properly classify costs in an organization. Consider the following example: Chippen Corporation manufactures furniture, including tables. Selected costs are given below:

1. The tables are made of wood that costs $100 per table.
2. The tables are made by workers, at a wage cost of $40 per table.

3. Workers making the tables are supervised by a factory supervisor who is paid $38,000 per year.
4. Electrical costs are $2 per machine-hour. Four machine-hours are required to produce a table.
5. The depreciation on the machines used to make the tables totals $10,000 per year. The machines have no resale value and do not wear out through use.
6. The salary of the president is $100,000 per year.
7. The company spends $250,000 per year to advertise its products.
8. Salespersons are paid a commission of $30 for each table sold.
9. Instead of producing the tables, the company could rent its factory space for $50,000 per year.

Required:

Classify these costs according to various cost terms used in the chapter. *Carefully study the classification of each cost.* If you don't understand why a particular cost is classified the way it is, reread the section of the chapter discussing the particular cost term. The terms *variable cost* and *fixed cost* refer to how costs behave with respect to the number of tables produced in a year.

Solution to Review Problem 1

	Variable Cost	Fixed Cost	Period (selling and adminis-trative) Cost	Product Cost — Direct Materials	Product Cost — Direct Labor	Product Cost — Manufacturing Overhead	Sunk Cost	Oppor-tunity Cost
1. Wood used in a table ($100 per table)	X			X				
2. Labor cost to assemble a table ($40 per table)	X				X			
3. Salary of the factory supervisor ($38,000 per year)		X				X		
4. Cost of electricity to produce tables ($2 per machine-hour)	X					X		
5. Depreciation of machines used to produce tables ($10,000 per year)		X				X	X*	
6. Salary of the company president ($100,000 per year)		X	X					
7. Advertising expense ($250,000 per year)		X	X					
8. Commissions paid to salespersons ($30 per table sold)	X		X					
9. Rental income forgone on factory space ($50,000 per year)								X†

*This is a sunk cost because the outlay for the equipment was made in a previous period.
†This is an opportunity cost because it represents the potential benefit that is lost or sacrificed as a result of using the factory space to produce tables. Opportunity cost is a special category of cost that is not ordinarily recorded in an organization's accounting books. To avoid possible confusion with other costs, we will not attempt to classify this cost in any other way except as an opportunity cost.

REVIEW PROBLEM 2: SCHEDULE OF COST OF GOODS MANUFACTURED AND INCOME STATEMENT

The following information has been taken from the accounting records of Klear-Seal Corporation for last year:

Selling expenses	$140,000
Raw materials inventory, January 1	$90,000
Raw materials inventory, December 31	$60,000
Utilities, factory	$36,000
Direct labor cost	$150,000
Depreciation, factory	$162,000
Purchases of raw materials	$750,000
Sales	$2,500,000
Insurance, factory	$40,000
Supplies, factory	$15,000
Administrative expenses	$270,000
Indirect labor	$300,000
Maintenance, factory	$87,000
Work in process inventory, January 1	$180,000
Work in process inventory, December 31	$100,000
Finished goods inventory, January 1	$260,000
Finished goods inventory, December 31	$210,000

Management wants these data organized in a better format so that financial statements can be prepared for the year.

Required:
1. Prepare a schedule of cost of goods manufactured as in Exhibit 1–6.
2. Compute the cost of goods sold.
3. Using data as needed from (1) and (2) above, prepare an income statement.

Solution to Review Problem 2

1.

Klear-Seal Corporation
Schedule of Cost of Goods Manufactured
For the Year Ended December 31

Direct materials:		
Raw materials inventory, January 1	$ 90,000	
Add: Purchases of raw materials	750,000	
Raw materials available for use	840,000	
Deduct: Raw materials inventory, December 31	60,000	
Raw materials used in production		$ 780,000
Direct labor		150,000
Manufacturing overhead:		
Utilities, factory	36,000	
Depreciation, factory	162,000	
Insurance, factory	40,000	
Supplies, factory	15,000	
Indirect labor	300,000	
Maintenance, factory	87,000	
Total manufacturing overhead costs		640,000
Total manufacturing costs		1,570,000
Add: Work in process inventory, January 1		180,000
		1,750,000
Deduct: Work in process inventory, December 31		100,000
Cost of goods manufactured		$1,650,000

2. The cost of goods sold would be computed as follows:

Finished goods inventory, January 1	$ 260,000
Add: Cost of goods manufactured	1,650,000
Goods available for sale	1,910,000
Deduct: Finished goods inventory, December 31	210,000
Cost of goods sold	$1,700,000

3.

Klear-Seal Corporation
Income Statement
For the Year Ended December 31

Sales		$2,500,000
Cost of goods sold (above)		1,700,000
Gross margin		800,000
Selling and administrative expenses:		
Selling expenses	$140,000	
Administrative expenses	270,000	
Total selling and administrative expenses		410,000
Net operating income		$ 390,000

GLOSSARY

Administrative costs All executive, organizational, and clerical costs associated with the general management of an organization rather than with manufacturing, marketing, or selling. (p. 35)

Budget A detailed plan for the future, usually expressed in formal quantitative terms. (p. 29)

Common cost A cost that is incurred to support a number of cost objects but cannot be traced to them individually. For example, the wage cost of the pilot of a 747 airliner is a common cost of all of the passengers on the aircraft. Without the pilot, there would be no flight and no passengers. But no part of the pilot's wage is caused by any one passenger taking the flight. (p. 50)

Control The process of instituting procedures and obtaining feedback to ensure that all parts of the organization are functioning effectively and moving toward overall company goals. (p. 29)

Controlling Ensuring that the plan is actually carried out and is appropriately modified as circumstances change. (p. 28)

Conversion cost Direct labor cost plus manufacturing overhead cost. (p. 35)

Cost behavior The way in which a cost reacts to changes in the level of activity. (p. 45)

Cost object Anything for which cost data are desired. Examples of possible cost objects are products, product lines, customers, jobs, and parts of the organization such as departments or divisions of a company. (p. 49)

Cost of goods manufactured The manufacturing costs associated with the goods that were finished during the period. (p. 40)

Differential cost A difference in cost between any two alternatives. Also see *Incremental cost.* (p. 50)

Differential revenue A difference in revenue between two alternatives. (p. 50)

Direct cost A cost that can be easily and conveniently traced to a specified cost object. (p. 49)

Direct labor Labor costs that can be easily traced to individual units of product. Also called *touch labor.* (p. 34)

Direct materials Materials that become an integral part of a finished product and whose costs can be conveniently traced to it. (p. 34)

Directing and motivating Mobilizing people to carry out plans and run routine operations. (p. 28)

Feedback Accounting and other reports that help managers monitor performance and focus on problems and/or opportunities. (p. 29)

Financial accounting The phase of accounting concerned with providing information to stockholders, creditors, and others outside the organization. (p. 28)

Finished goods   Units of product that have been completed but have not yet been sold to customers. (p. 38)

Fixed cost   A cost that remains constant, in total, regardless of changes in the level of activity within the relevant range. If a fixed cost is expressed on a per unit basis, it varies inversely with the level of activity. (p. 47)

Incremental cost   An increase in cost between two alternatives. Also see *Differential cost.* (p. 50)

Indirect cost   A cost that cannot be easily and conveniently traced to a specified cost object. (p. 49)

Indirect labor   The labor costs of janitors, supervisors, materials handlers, and other factory workers that cannot be conveniently traced directly to particular products. (p. 34)

Indirect materials   Small items of material such as glue and nails. These items may become an integral part of a finished product but their costs cannot be easily or conveniently traced to it. (p. 34)

Inventoriable costs   Synonym for *product costs.* (p. 36)

Managerial accounting   The phase of accounting concerned with providing information to managers for use in planning and controlling operations and in decision making. (p. 28)

Manufacturing overhead   All costs associated with manufacturing except direct materials and direct labor. (p. 35)

Opportunity cost   A potential benefit that is given up when one alternative is selected over another. (p. 51)

Performance report   A detailed report comparing budgeted data to actual data. (p. 29)

Period costs   Costs that are taken directly to the income statement as expenses in the period in which they are incurred or accrued. (p. 36)

Planning   Selecting a course of action and specifying how the action will be implemented. (p. 28)

Planning and control cycle   The flow of management activities through planning, directing and motivating, and controlling, and then back to planning again. (p. 30)

Prime cost   Direct materials cost plus direct labor cost. (p. 35)

Product costs   All costs that are involved in the purchase or manufacture of goods. In the case of manufactured goods, these costs consist of direct materials, direct labor, and manufacturing overhead. Also see *Inventoriable costs.* (p. 36)

Raw materials   Materials that are used to make a product. (p. 33)

Relevant range   The range of activity within which assumptions about variable and fixed cost behavior are valid. (p. 48)

Schedule of cost of goods manufactured   A schedule showing the direct materials, direct labor, and manufacturing overhead costs incurred during a period and the portion of those costs assigned to Work in Process and Finished Goods. (p. 40)

Segment   Any part of an organization that can be evaluated independently of other parts and about which the manager seeks financial data. Examples include a product line, a sales territory, a division, or a department. (p. 32)

Selling costs   All costs necessary to secure customer orders and get the finished product or service into the hands of the customer. (p. 35)

Sunk cost   A cost that has already been incurred and that cannot be changed by any decision made now or in the future. (p. 52)

Variable cost   A cost that varies, in total, in direct proportion to changes in the level of activity. (p. 46)

Work in process   Units of product that are only partially complete and will require further work before they are ready for sale to a customer. (p. 38)

QUESTIONS

1–1   What is the basic difference between the purposes of financial and managerial accounting?

1–2   What are the three major activities of a manager?

1–3   Describe the four steps in the planning and control cycle.

1–4   What are the major differences between financial and managerial accounting?

1–5   What are the three major elements of product costs in a manufacturing company?

1–6   Define the following: (a) direct materials, (b) indirect materials, (c) direct labor, (d) indirect labor, and (e) manufacturing overhead.

1–7   Explain the difference between a product cost and a period cost.

1–8   Describe how the income statement of a manufacturing company differs from the income statement of a merchandising company.

1–9   Describe the schedule of cost of goods manufactured. How does it tie into the income statement?

1–10   What inventory accounts are used by a manufacturing company? A merchandising company?

1–11 Why are product costs sometimes called inventoriable costs? Describe the flow of such costs in a manufacturing company from the point of incurrence until they finally become expenses on the income statement.

1–12 Is it possible for costs such as salaries or depreciation to end up as assets on the balance sheet? Explain.

1–13 What is meant by the term *cost behavior*?

1–14 "A variable cost is a cost that varies per unit of product, whereas a fixed cost is constant per unit of product." Do you agree? Explain.

1–15 How do fixed costs create difficulties in costing units of product?

1–16 Why is manufacturing overhead considered an indirect cost of a unit of product?

1–17 Define the following terms: differential cost, opportunity cost, and sunk cost.

1–18 Only variable costs can be differential costs. Do you agree? Explain.

BRIEF EXERCISES

BRIEF EXERCISE 1–1   Classifying Manufacturing Costs   (LO1)

The PC Works assembles custom computers from components supplied by various manufacturers. The company is very small and its assembly shop and retail sales store are housed in a single facility in a Redmond, Washington, industrial park. Listed below are some of the costs incurred by the company.

Required:

Classify each cost, as direct labor, direct materials, manufacturing overhead, selling, or an administrative cost.

1. The cost of a hard drive installed in a computer.
2. The cost of advertising in the *Puget Sound Computer User* newspaper.
3. The wages of employees who assemble computers from components.
4. Sales commissions paid to the company's salespeople.
5. The wages of the assembly shop's supervisor.
6. The wages of the company's accountant.
7. Depreciation on equipment used to test assembled computers before release to customers.
8. Rent on the facility in the industrial park.

BRIEF EXERCISE 1–2   Classification of Costs as Period or Product Cost   (LO2)

Classify the following costs as either product (inventoriable) costs or period (noninventoriable) costs in a manufacturing company:

1. Depreciation on salespersons' cars.
2. Rent on equipment used in the factory.
3. Lubricants used for maintenance of machines.
4. Salaries of finished goods warehouse personnel.
5. Soap and paper towels used by factory workers.
6. Factory supervisors' salaries.
7. Heat, water, and power consumed in the factory.
8. Materials used for boxing products for shipment overseas. (Units are not normally boxed.)
9. Advertising costs.
10. Workers' compensation insurance on factory employees.
11. Depreciation on chairs and tables in the factory lunchroom.
12. The wages of the receptionist in the administrative offices.
13. Lease cost of the corporate jet used by the company's executives.
14. Rent on rooms at a Florida resort for the annual sales conference.
15. Attractively designed box for packaging the company's product—breakfast cereal.

BRIEF EXERCISE 1–3   Constructing an Income Statement   (LO3)

Last month CyberGames, a computer game retailer, had total sales of $1,450,000, selling expenses of $210,000, and administrative expenses of $180,000. The company had beginning merchandise inventory of $240,000, purchased additional merchandise inventory for $950,000, and had ending merchandise inventory of $170,000.

Required:
Prepare an income statement for the company for the month.

BRIEF EXERCISE 1–4   Prepare a Schedule of Cost of Goods Manufactured   (LO4)
Lompac Products manufactures a variety of products in its factory. Data for the most recent month's operations appear below:

Beginning raw materials inventory	$60,000
Purchases of raw materials	$690,000
Ending raw materials inventory	$45,000
Direct labor	$135,000
Manufacturing overhead	$370,000
Beginning work in process inventory	$120,000
Ending work in process inventory	$130,000

Required:
Prepare a schedule of cost of goods manufactured for the company for the month.

BRIEF EXERCISE 1–5   Classification of Costs as Fixed or Variable   (LO5)
Below are a number of costs that are incurred in a variety of organizations.

Required:
Classify each cost as being variable or fixed with respect to the number of units of product or services sold by the organization by placing an X in the appropriate column.

	Cost Behavior	
Cost Item	**Variable**	**Fixed**
1. X-ray film used in the radiology lab at Virginia Mason Hospital in Seattle.		
2. The costs of advertising a Madonna rock concert in New York City.		
3. Rental cost of the space occupied by a McDonald's restaurant in Hong Kong.		
4. The electrical costs of running a roller coaster at Magic Mountain.		
5. Property taxes on your local cinema.		
6. Commissions paid to salespersons at Nordstrom.		
7. Property insurance on a Coca-Cola bottling plant.		
8. The costs of synthetic materials used to make Nike running shoes.		
9. The costs of shipping Panasonic televisions to retail stores.		
10. The cost of leasing an ultra-scan diagnostic machine at the American Hospital in Paris.		

BRIEF EXERCISE 1–6   Identifying Direct and Indirect Costs   (LO6)
Northwest Hospital is a full-service hospital that provides everything from major surgery and emergency room care to outpatient clinics.

Required:
For each cost incurred at Northwest Hospital, indicate whether it would most likely be a direct cost or an indirect cost of the specified cost object by placing an *X* in the appropriate column.

Cost	Cost object	Direct Cost	Indirect Cost
Ex. Catered food served to patients	A particular patient	X	
1. The wages of pediatric nurses	The pediatric department		
2. Prescription drugs	A particular patient		
3. Heating the hospital	The pediatric department		
4. The salary of the head of pediatrics	The pediatric department		
5. The salary of the head of pediatrics	A particular pediatric patient		
6. Hospital chaplain's salary	A particular patient		
7. Lab tests by outside contractor	A particular patient		
8. Lab tests by outside contractor	A particular department		

BRIEF EXERCISE 1–7   Differential, Opportunity, and Sunk Costs   (LO7)

Northwest Hospital's Radiology Department is considering replacing an old inefficient X-ray machine with a state-of-the-art digital X-ray machine. The new machine would provide higher quality X-rays in less time and at a lower cost per X-ray. It would also require less power and would use a color laser printer to produce easily readable X-ray images. Instead of investing the funds in the new X-ray machine, the Laboratory Department is lobbying the hospital's management to buy a new DNA analyzer.

Required:

For each of the items below, indicate by placing an X in the appropriate column whether it should be considered a differential cost, an opportunity cost, or a sunk cost in the decision to replace the old X-ray machine with a new machine. If none of the categories apply for a particular item, leave all columns blank.

Item	Differential Cost	Opportunity Cost	Sunk Cost
Ex. Cost of X-ray film used in the old machine	X		
1. Cost of the old X-ray machine			
2. The salary of the head of the Radiology Department			
3. The salary of the head of the Pediatrics Department			
4. Cost of the new color laser printer			
5. Rent on the space occupied by Radiology			
6. The cost of maintaining the old machine			
7. Benefits from a new DNA analyzer			
8. Cost of electricity to run the X-ray machines			

EXERCISES

EXERCISE 1–8   Product Cost Flows; Product versus Period Costs   (LO3)

The Devon Motor Company produces motorcycles. During April, the company purchased 8,000 batteries at a cost of $10 per battery. Devon withdrew 7,600 batteries from the storeroom during the month. Of these, 100 were used to replace batteries in motorcycles being used by the company's traveling sales staff. The remaining 7,500 batteries withdrawn from the storeroom were placed in motorcycles being produced by the company. Of the motorcycles in production during April, 90% were completed and transferred from work in process to finished goods. Of the motorcycles completed during the month, 30% were unsold at April 30.

There were no inventories of any type on April 1.

Required:

1. Determine the cost of batteries that would appear in each of the following accounts at April 30:
   a.   Raw Materials.
   b.   Work in Process.
   c.   Finished Goods.
   d.   Cost of Goods Sold.
   e.   Selling Expense.
2. Specify whether each of the above accounts would appear on the balance sheet or on the income statement at April 30.

EXERCISE 1–9 Classification of Costs as Variable or Fixed and as Selling and Administrative or Product   (LO2, LO5)

Below are listed various costs that are found in organizations.

1. Hamburger buns in a Wendy's outlet.
2. Advertising by a dental office.
3. Apples processed and canned by Del Monte.
4. Shipping canned apples from a Del Monte plant to customers.
5. Insurance on a Bausch & Lomb factory producing contact lenses.
6. Insurance on IBM's corporate headquarters.
7. Salary of a supervisor overseeing production of printers at Hewlett-Packard.
8. Commissions paid to pharmaceutical sales representatives.
9. Depreciation of factory lunchroom facilities at a General Electric plant.
10. Steering wheels installed in BMWs.

Required:

Classify each cost as being either variable or fixed with respect to the number of units produced and sold. Also classify each cost as either a selling and administrative cost or a product cost. Prepare your answer sheet as shown below, placing Xs in the appropriate columns.

	Cost Behavior		Selling and	
Cost Item	**Variable**	**Fixed**	**Administrative Cost**	**Product Cost**

EXERCISE 1–10   Definitions of Cost Terms   (LO2, LO5, LO7)

Following are a number of cost terms introduced in the chapter:

Variable cost	Product cost
Fixed cost	Sunk cost
Prime cost	Conversion cost
Opportunity cost	Period cost

Choose the term or terms above that most appropriately describe the cost identified in each of the following situations. A cost term can be used more than once.

1. Lake Company produces a tote bag that is very popular with college students. The cloth used to manufacture the tote bag would be called direct materials and classified as a _____. In terms of cost behavior, the cloth could also be described as a _____.
2. The direct labor cost required to produce the tote bags, combined with the manufacturing overhead cost involved, would be known as _____.
3. The company could have taken the funds that it has invested in production equipment and invested them in interest-bearing securities instead. The interest forgone on the securities would be called an _____.
4. Taken together, the direct materials cost and the direct labor cost required to produce tote bags would be called _____.
5. The company used to produce a smaller tote bag that was not very popular. Some three hundred of these smaller bags are stored in one of the company's warehouses. The amount invested in these bags would be called a _____.
6. The tote bags are sold through agents who are paid a commission on each bag sold. These commissions would be classified by Lake Company as a _____. In terms of cost behavior, commissions would be classified as a _____.
7. Depreciation on the equipment used to produce tote bags would be classified by Lake Company as a _____. However, depreciation on any equipment used by the company in selling and administrative activities would be classified as a _____. In terms of cost behavior, depreciation would probably be classified as a _____.
8. A _____ is also known as an inventoriable cost, since such costs go into the Work in Process inventory account and then into the Finished Goods inventory account before appearing on the income statement as part of cost of goods sold.
9. The salary of Lake Company's president would be classified as a _____, since the salary will appear on the income statement as an expense in the time period in which it is incurred.
10. Costs are often classified in several ways. For example, Lake Company pays $5,000 rent each month on its factory building. The rent would be part of manufacturing overhead. In terms of cost behavior, it would be classified as a _____. The rent can also be classified as a _____ and as part of _____.

EXERCISE 1-11 Preparing a Schedule of Cost of Goods Manufactured and Cost of Goods Sold (LO3, LO4)

The following cost and inventory data are taken from the accounting records of Mason Company for the year just completed:

Costs incurred:	
Direct labor cost	$70,000
Purchases of raw materials	$118,000
Indirect labor	$30,000
Maintenance, factory equipment	$6,000
Advertising expense	$90,000
Insurance, factory equipment	$800
Sales salaries	$50,000
Rent, factory facilities	$20,000
Supplies	$4,200
Depreciation, office equipment	$3,000
Depreciation, factory equipment	$19,000

	Beginning of the Year	End of the Year
Inventories:		
Raw materials	$7,000	$15,000
Work in process	$10,000	$5,000
Finished goods	$20,000	$35,000

Required:
1. Prepare a schedule of cost of goods manufactured.
2. Prepare the cost of goods sold section of Mason Company's income statement for the year.

EXERCISE 1-12 Cost Classification (LO5, LO6)

Various costs associated with the operation of factories are given below:

1. Electricity used in operating machines.
2. Rent on a factory building.
3. Cloth used in drapery production.
4. Production superintendent's salary.
5. Wages of laborers assembling a product.
6. Depreciation of air purification equipment used in furniture production.
7. Janitorial salaries.
8. Peaches used in canning fruit.
9. Lubricants needed for machines.
10. Sugar used in soft-drink production.
11. Property taxes on the factory.
12. Wages of workers painting a product.
13. Depreciation of cafeteria equipment.
14. Insurance on a building used in producing helicopters.
15. Cost of rotor blades used in producing helicopters.

Required:
Classify each cost as either variable or fixed with respect to the number of units produced and sold. Also indicate whether each cost would typically be treated as a direct cost or an indirect cost with respect to units of product. Prepare your answer sheet as shown below:

	Cost Behavior		To Units of Product	
Cost Item	Variable	Fixed	Direct	Indirect
Example: Factory insurance		X		X

EXERCISE 1–13   Classification of Costs   (LO1, LO2, LO5, LO7)
Wollogong Group Ltd. of New South Wales, Australia, acquired its factory building about 10 years ago. For several years the company has rented out a small annex attached to the rear of the building. The company has received a rental income of $30,000 per year on this space. The renter's lease will expire soon, and rather than renew the lease, the company has decided to use the space itself to manufacture a new product.

Direct materials cost for the new product will total $80 per unit. To have a place to store finished units of product, the company will rent a small warehouse at a cost of $500 per month. In addition, the company must rent equipment at a cost of $4,000 per month to make the new product. Workers will be hired to manufacture the new product, with direct labor cost amounting to $60 per unit. The space in the annex will continue to be depreciated on a straight-line basis in the amount of $8,000 per year.

Advertising costs for the new product will total $50,000 per year. A supervisor will be hired to oversee production; her salary will be $1,500 per month. Electricity for operating machines will be $1.20 per unit. Costs of shipping the new product to customers will be $9 per unit.

To provide funds to purchase materials, meet payrolls, and so forth, the company will have to liquidate some temporary investments. These investments are presently yielding a return of about $3,000 per year.

Required:
Prepare an answer sheet with the following column headings:

Name of the Cost	Variable Cost	Fixed Cost	Product Cost			Period (selling and administrative) Cost	Opportunity Cost	Sunk Cost
			Direct Materials	Direct Labor	Manufacturing Overhead			

List the different costs associated with the new product decision down the extreme left column (under Name of the Cost). Then place an *X* under each heading that helps to describe the type of cost involved. There may be *X's* under several column headings for a single cost. (For example, a cost may be a fixed cost, a period cost, and a sunk cost; you would place an *X* under each of these column headings opposite the cost.)

PROBLEMS

CHECK FIGURE
Boxes for packaging:
variable, direct

PROBLEM 1–14A   Cost Classification   (LO2, LO5, LO6)
Listed below are a number of costs typically found in organizations.

1. Property taxes, factory.
2. Boxes used for packaging detergent produced by the company.
3. Salespersons' commissions.
4. Supervisor's salary, factory.
5. Depreciation, executive autos.
6. Wages of workers assembling computers.
7. Insurance, finished goods warehouses.
8. Lubricants for machines.
9. Advertising costs.
10. Microchips used in producing calculators.
11. Shipping costs on merchandise sold.
12. Magazine subscriptions, factory lunchroom.
13. Thread in a garment factory.
14. Billing costs.
15. Executive life insurance.
16. Ink used in textbook production.
17. Fringe benefits, assembly-line workers.
18. Yarn used in sweater production.
19. Wages of receptionist, executive offices.

Required:
Prepare an answer sheet with column headings as shown below. For each cost item, indicate whether it would be variable or fixed with respect to the number of units produced and sold; and then whether it would be a selling cost, an administrative cost, or a manufacturing cost. If it is a manufacturing cost, indicate whether it would typically be treated as a direct cost or an indirect cost with respect to units of product. Three sample answers are provided for illustration.

Cost Item	Variable or Fixed	Selling Cost	Administrative Cost	Manufacturing (product) Cost	
				Direct	Indirect
Direct labor	V			X	
Executive salaries	F		X		
Factory rent	F				X

PROBLEM 1-15A Working with Incomplete Data from the Income Statement and Schedule of Cost of Goods Manufactured (LO3, LO4)

Supply the missing data in the following cases. Each case is independent of the others.

CHECK FIGURE
Case 1: Goods available for sale: $19,000

	Case			
	1	2	3	4
Schedule of Cost of Goods Manufactured				
Direct materials	$ 4,500	$ 6,000	$ 5,000	$ 3,000
Direct labor	?	3,000	7,000	4,000
Manufacturing overhead	5,000	4,000	?	9,000
Total manufacturing costs	18,500	?	20,000	?
Beginning work in process inventory	2,500	?	3,000	?
Ending work in process inventory	?	1,000	4,000	3,000
Cost of goods manufactured	$18,000	$14,000	$?	$?
Income Statement				
Sales	$30,000	$21,000	$36,000	$40,000
Beginning finished goods inventory	1,000	2,500	?	2,000
Cost of goods manufactured	?	?	?	17,500
Goods available for sale	?	?	?	?
Ending finished goods inventory	?	1,500	4,000	3,500
Cost of goods sold	17,000	?	18,500	?
Gross margin	13,000	?	17,500	?
Selling and administrative expenses	?	3,500	?	?
Net operating income	$ 4,000	$?	$ 5,000	$ 9,000

PROBLEM 1-16A Cost Classification and Cost Behavior (LO2, LO5, LO6)

The Dorilane Company specializes in producing a set of wood patio furniture consisting of a table and four chairs. The set enjoys great popularity, and the company has ample orders to keep production going at its full capacity of 2,000 patio sets per year. Annual cost data at full capacity follow:

CHECK FIGURE
(1) Total variable cost: $321,000

Factory labor, direct	$118,000
Advertising	$50,000
Factory supervision	$40,000
Property taxes, factory building	$3,500
Sales commissions	$80,000
Insurance, factory	$2,500
Depreciation, office equipment	$4,000
Lease cost, factory equipment	$12,000
Indirect materials, factory	$6,000
Depreciation, factory building	$10,000
General office supplies (billing)	$3,000
General office salaries	$60,000
Direct materials used (wood, bolts, etc.)	$94,000
Utilities, factory	$20,000

Required:

1. Prepare an answer sheet with the column headings shown below. Enter each cost item on your answer sheet, placing the dollar amount under the appropriate headings. As examples, this has been done already for the first two items in the list above. Note that each cost item is classified in two ways: first, as variable or fixed with respect to the number of units produced and sold; and second, as a selling and administrative cost or a product cost. (If the item is a product cost, it should also be classified as either direct or indirect with respect to units of product.)

Cost Item	Cost Behavior		Selling or Administrative Cost	Product Cost	
	Variable	Fixed		Direct	Indirect
Factory labor,.... direct	$118,000			$118,000	
Advertising		$50,000	$50,000		

2. Total the dollar amounts in each of the columns in (1) above. Compute the average product cost per patio set.
3. Assume that production drops to only 1,000 sets annually. Would you expect the average product cost per patio set to increase, decrease, or remain unchanged? Explain. No computations are necessary.
4. Refer to the original data. The president's brother-in-law has considered making himself a patio set and has priced the necessary materials at a building supply store. The brother-in-law has asked the president if he could purchase a patio set from the Dorilane Company "at cost," and the president agreed to let him do so.
   a. Would you expect any disagreement between the two men over the price the brother-in-law should pay? Explain. What price does the president probably have in mind? The brother-in-law?
   b. Since the company is operating at full capacity, what cost term used in the chapter might be justification for the president to charge the full, regular price to the brother-in-law and still be selling "at cost"?

PROBLEM 1–17A　Classification of Salary Cost as a Period or Product Cost　(LO2)
You have just been hired by Ogden Company to fill a new position that was created in response to rapid growth in sales. It is your responsibility to coordinate shipments of finished goods from the factory to distribution warehouses located in various parts of the United States so that goods will be available as orders are received from customers.

The company is unsure how to classify your annual salary in its cost records. The company's cost analyst says that your salary should be classified as a manufacturing (product) cost; the controller says that it should be classified as a selling expense; and the president says that it doesn't matter which way your salary cost is classified.

Required:

1. Which viewpoint is correct? Why?
2. From the point of view of the reported net operating income for the year, is the president correct in his statement that it doesn't matter which way your salary cost is classified? Explain.

CHECK FIGURE
Clay and glaze: variable,
direct materials

PROBLEM 1–18A　Classification of Various Costs　(LO1, LO2, LO5, LO7)
Staci Valek began dabbling in pottery several years ago as a hobby. Her work is quite creative, and it has been so popular with friends and others that she has decided to quit her job with an aerospace company and manufacture pottery full time. The salary from Staci's aerospace job is $3,800 per month.

Staci will rent a small building near her home for $500 per month to use as a place for manufacturing the pottery. She estimates that the cost of clay and glaze will be $2 for each finished piece of pottery. She will hire workers to produce the pottery at a labor rate of $8 per pot. To sell her pots, Staci feels that she must advertise heavily in the local area. An advertising agency states that it will handle all advertising for a fee of $600 per month. Staci's brother will sell the pots; he will be paid a commission of $4 for each pot sold. Equipment needed to manufacture the pots will be rented at a cost of $300 per month.

Staci has already paid the legal and filing fees associated with incorporating her business in the state. These fees amounted to $500. A small room has been located in a tourist area that Staci will use as a sales office. The rent will be $250 per month. A phone installed in the room for taking orders will cost $40 per month. In addition, a recording device will be attached to the phone for taking after-hours messages.

Staci has some money in savings that is earning interest of $1,200 per year. These savings will be withdrawn and used to get the business going. For the time being, Staci does not intend to draw any salary from the new company.

Required:

1. Prepare an answer sheet with the following column headings:

Name of the Cost	Variable Cost	Fixed Cost	Product Cost			Period (selling and administrative) Cost	Opportunity Cost	Sunk Cost
			Direct Materials	Direct Labor	Manufacturing Overhead			

List the different costs associated with the new company down the extreme left column (under Name of the Cost). Then place an *X* under each heading that helps to describe the type of cost involved. There may be *X*'s under several column headings for a single cost. (That is, a cost may be a fixed cost, a period cost, and a sunk cost; thus you would place an *X* under each of these column headings opposite the cost.)

Under the Variable Cost column, list only those costs that would be variable with respect to the number of units of pottery that are produced and sold.

2. All of the costs you have listed above, except one, would be differential costs between the alternatives of Staci producing pottery or staying with the aerospace company. Which cost is *not* differential? Explain.

PROBLEM 1–19A   Schedule of Cost of Goods Manufactured; Income Statement   (LO3, LO4)
Swift Company was organized on March 1 of the current year. After five months of start-up losses, management had expected to earn a profit during August. Management was disappointed, however, when the income statement for August also showed a loss. August's income statement follows:

CHECK FIGURE
(1) Cost of goods manufactured: $310,000

Swift Company Income Statement For the Month Ended August 31		
Sales		$450,000
Less operating expenses:		
Indirect labor cost	$ 12,000	
Utilities	15,000	
Direct labor cost	70,000	
Depreciation, factory equipment	21,000	
Raw materials purchased	165,000	
Depreciation, sales equipment	18,000	
Insurance	4,000	
Rent on facilities	50,000	
Selling and administrative salaries	32,000	
Advertising	75,000	462,000
Net operating loss		$ (12,000)

After seeing the $12,000 loss for August, Swift's president stated, "I was sure we'd be profitable within six months, but our six months are up and this loss for August is even worse than July's. I think it's time to start looking for someone to buy out the company's assets—if we don't, within a few months there won't be any assets to sell. By the way, I don't see any reason to look for a new controller. We'll just limp along with Sam for the time being."

The company's controller resigned a month ago. Sam, a new inexperienced assistant in the controller's office, prepared the income statement above. Additional information about the company follows:

a. Some 60% of the utilities cost and 75% of the insurance apply to factory operations. The remaining amounts apply to selling and administrative activities.

b. Inventory balances at the beginning and end of August were:

	August 1	August 31
Raw materials	$8,000	$13,000
Work in process	$16,000	$21,000
Finished goods	$40,000	$60,000

c.   Only 80% of the rent on facilities applies to factory operations; the remainder applies to selling and administrative activities.

The president has asked you to check over the income statement and make a recommendation as to whether the company should look for a buyer for its assets.

Required:
1. As one step in gathering data for a recommendation to the president, prepare a schedule of cost of goods manufactured for August.
2. As a second step, prepare a new income statement for August.
3. Based on your statements prepared in (1) and (2) above, would you recommend that the company look for a buyer?

CHECK FIGURE
(1) Cost of goods manufactured: $690,000

PROBLEM I–20A   Schedule of Cost of Goods Manufactured; Income Statement; Cost Behavior (LO1, LO2, LO3, LO4, LO5)

Selected account balances for the year ended December 31 are provided below for Superior Company:

Selling and administrative salaries	$110,000
Insurance, factory	$8,000
Utilities, factory	$45,000
Purchases of raw materials	$290,000
Indirect labor	$60,000
Direct labor	?
Advertising expense	$80,000
Cleaning supplies, factory	$7,000
Sales commissions	$50,000
Rent, factory building	$120,000
Maintenance, factory	$30,000

Inventory balances at the beginning and end of the year were as follows:

	Beginning of the Year	End of the Year
Raw materials	$40,000	$10,000
Work in process	?	$35,000
Finished goods	$50,000	?

The total manufacturing costs for the year were $683,000; the goods available for sale totaled $740,000; and the cost of goods sold totaled $660,000.

Required:
1. Prepare a schedule of cost of goods manufactured and the cost of goods sold section of the company's income statement for the year.
2. The company produced the equivalent of 40,000 units during the year. Compute the average cost per unit for direct materials used and the average cost per unit for rent on the factory building.
3. In the following year the company expects to produce 50,000 units. What average cost per unit and total cost would you expect to be incurred for direct materials? For rent on the factory building? (Assume that direct materials is a variable cost and that rent is a fixed cost.)
4. Explain to the president the reason for any difference in average cost per unit between (2) and (3) above.

PROBLEM 1–21A   Schedule of Cost of Goods Manufactured; Income Statement; Cost Behavior (LO3, LO4, LO5)

Various cost and sales data for Meriwell Company for the just completed year follow:

CHECK FIGURE
(1) Cost of goods manufactured: $290,000

File Edit View Insert Format Tools Data Window Help			
A	**B**	**C**	**D**
1 Finished goods inventory, beginning	$20,000		
2 Finished goods inventory, ending	$40,000		
3 Depreciation, factory	$27,000		
4 Administrative expenses	$110,000		
5 Utilities, factory	$8,000		
6 Maintenance, factory	$40,000		
7 Supplies, factory	$11,000		
8 Insurance, factory	$4,000		
9 Purchases of raw materials	$125,000		
10 Raw materials inventory, beginning	$9,000		
11 Raw materials inventory, ending	$6,000		
12 Direct labor	$70,000		
13 Indirect labor	$15,000		
14 Work in process inventory, beginning	$17,000		
15 Work in process inventory, ending	$30,000		
16 Sales	$500,000		
17 Selling expenses	$80,000		

Required:
1. Prepare a schedule of cost of goods manufactured.
2. Prepare an income statement.
3. The company produced the equivalent of 10,000 units of product during the year just completed. What was the average cost per unit for direct materials? What was the average cost per unit for factory depreciation?
4. The company expects to produce 15,000 units of product during the coming year. What average cost per unit and what total cost would you expect the company to incur for direct materials at this level of activity? For factory depreciation? (In preparing your answer, assume that direct materials is a variable cost and that depreciation is a fixed cost; also assume that depreciation is computed on a straight-line basis.)
5. Explain to the president any difference in the average cost per unit between (3) and (4) above.

BUILDING YOUR SKILLS

Case [LO3, LO4]
Hector P. Wastrel, a careless employee, left some combustible materials near an open flame in Salter Company's plant. The resulting explosion and fire destroyed the entire plant and administrative offices. Justin

Quick, the company's controller, and Constance Trueheart, the operations manager, were able to save only a few bits of information as they escaped from the roaring blaze.

"What a disaster," cried Justin. "And the worst part is that we have no records to use in filing an insurance claim."

"I know," replied Constance. "I was in the plant when the explosion occurred, and I managed to grab only this brief summary sheet that contains information on one or two of our costs. It says that our direct labor cost this year totaled $180,000 and that we have purchased $290,000 in raw materials. But I'm afraid that doesn't help much; the rest of our records are just ashes."

"Well, not completely," said Justin. "I was working on the year-to-date income statement when the explosion knocked me out of my chair. I instinctively held onto the page I was working on, and from what I can make out, our sales to date this year have totaled $1,200,000 and our gross margin rate has been 40% of sales. Also, I can see that our cost of goods available for sale to customers totals $810,000."

"Maybe we're not so bad off after all," exclaimed Constance. "My sheet says that prime cost has totaled $410,000 so far this year and that manufacturing overhead is 70% of conversion cost. Now if we just had some information on our beginning inventories."

"Hey, look at this," cried Justin. "It's a copy of last year's annual report, and it shows what our inventories were when this year started. Let's see, raw materials was $18,000, work in process was $65,000, and finished goods was $45,000.

"Super," yelled Constance. "Let's go to work."

To file an insurance claim, the company must determine the amount of cost in its inventories as of the date of the fire. You may assume that all materials used in production during the year were direct materials.

Required:
Determine the amount of cost in the Raw Materials, Work in Process, and Finished Goods inventory accounts as of the date of the fire. (Hint: One way to proceed would be to reconstruct the various schedules and statements that would have been affected by the company's inventory accounts during the period.)

Teamwork in Action (LO5)
Understanding the nature of fixed and variable costs is extremely important to managers. This knowledge is used in planning, making strategic and tactical decisions, evaluating performance, and controlling operations.

Required:
Form a team consisting of four persons. Each team member will be responsible for one of the following businesses:

a. Retail store that sells music CDs
b. Dental clinic
c. Fast-food restaurant
d. Auto repair shop

1. In each business decide what single measure best reflects the overall level of activity in the business and give examples of costs that are fixed and variable with respect to small changes in the measure of activity you have chosen.
2. Explain the relationship between the level of activity in each business and each of the following: total fixed costs, fixed cost per unit of activity, total variable costs, variable cost per unit of activity, total costs, and average total cost per unit of activity.
3. Discuss and refine your answers to each of the above questions with your group. Which of the above businesses seems to have the highest ratio of variable to fixed costs? The lowest? Which of the businesses' profits would be most sensitive to changes in demand for its services? The least sensitive? Why?

CHECK FIGURE
(1) Cost of goods manufactured: $870,000

Analytical Thinking (LO3, LO4)
Visic Corporation, a manufacturing company, produces a single product. The following information has been taken from the company's production, sales, and cost records for the just completed year.

Production in units	29,000
Sales in units	?
Ending finished goods inventory in units	?
Sales in dollars	$1,300,000
Costs:	
Advertising	$105,000
Entertainment and travel	$40,000

Direct labor	$90,000
Indirect labor	$85,000
Raw materials purchased	$480,000
Building rent (production uses 80% of the space; administrative and sales offices use the rest)	$40,000
Utilities, factory	$108,000
Royalty paid for use of production patent, $1.50 per unit produced	?
Maintenance, factory	$9,000
Rent for special production equipment, $7,000 per year plus $0.30 per unit produced	?
Selling and administrative salaries	$210,000
Other factory overhead costs	$6,800
Other selling and administrative expenses	$17,000

	Beginning of the Year	End of the Year
Inventories:		
Raw materials	$20,000	$30,000
Work in process	$50,000	$40,000
Finished goods	$0	?

The finished goods inventory is being carried at the average unit production cost for the year. The selling price of the product is $50 per unit.

Required:
1. Prepare a schedule of cost of goods manufactured for the year.
2. Compute the following:
   a. The number of units in the finished goods inventory at the end of the year.
   b. The cost of the units in the finished goods inventory at the end of the year.
3. Prepare an income statement for the year.

Ethics Challenge (LO2)

M. K. Gallant is president of Kranbrack Corporation, a company whose stock is traded on a national exchange. In a meeting with investment analysts at the beginning of the year, Gallant had predicted that the company's earnings would grow by 20% this year. Unfortunately, sales have been less than expected for the year, and Gallant concluded within two weeks of the end of the fiscal year that it would be impossible to ultimately report an increase in earnings as large as predicted unless some drastic action was taken. Accordingly, Gallant has ordered that wherever possible, expenditures should be postponed to the new year—including canceling or postponing orders with suppliers, delaying planned maintenance and training, and cutting back on end-of-year advertising and travel. Additionally, Gallant ordered the company's controller to carefully scrutinize all costs that are currently classified as period costs and reclassify as many as possible as product costs. The company is expected to have substantial inventories of work in process and finished goods at the end of the year.

Required:

1. Why would reclassifying period costs as product costs increase this period's reported earnings?
2. Do you believe Gallant's actions are ethical? Why or why not?

Taking it to the Net

As you know, the World Wide Web is a medium that is constantly evolving. Sites come and go and change without notice. To enable periodic updating of site addresses, these problems have been posted to the textbook website (www.mhhe.com/bgn3e). After accessing the site, enter the Student Center and select this chapter to find the Taking It to the Net problems.

2

Systems Design: Job-Order Costing

CHAPTER OUTLINE

DECISION FEATURE

Two College Students Succeeding as Entrepreneurs

When the University of Dayton athletic department needed 2,000 customized T-shirts to give away as part of a promotion for its first home basketball game of the year, it chose University Tees to provide the shirts. Numerous larger competitors could have been chosen, but University Tees won the order because of its fast customer response time, low price, and high quality.

University Tees is a small business that was started in February 2003 by two Miami University seniors—Joe Haddad and Nick Dadas (see the company's website at www.universitytees.com). The company creates the artwork for customized T-shirts and then relies on carefully chosen suppliers to manufacture the product. University Tees must provide a specific price quote for each potential customer order since each order is unique and the customer is always looking for the best deal.

Calculating the cost of a particular customer order is critically important to University Tees because the company needs to be sure that each price quote exceeds the cost associated with satisfying the order. The costs that University Tees factors into its bidding process include the cost of the T-shirts themselves, printing costs (which vary depending on the quantity of shirts produced and the number of colors printed per shirt), silk screen costs (which also vary depending on the number of colors included in a design), shipping costs, and the artwork needed to create a design. In addition to using cost information, the company also relies on knowledge of its competitors' pricing strategies when establishing price quotes.

Source: Conversation with Joe Haddad, cofounder of University Tees.

As discussed in the previous chapter, product costing is the process of assigning costs to the products and services provided by a company. An understanding of this costing process is vital to managers, since the way in which a product or service is costed can have a substantial impact on reported profits, as well as on key management decisions.

The essential purpose of any managerial costing system should be to provide cost data to help managers plan, control, direct, and make decisions. Nevertheless, external financial reporting and tax reporting requirements often heavily influence how costs are accumulated and summarized on managerial reports. This is true of product costing.

In this chapter, we use *absorption costing* to determine product costs. This method was also used in the previous chapter. In **absorption costing**, *all* manufacturing costs, fixed and variable, are assigned to units of product—units are said to *fully absorb manufacturing costs*. The absorption costing approach is also known as the **full cost** approach. In a later chapter, we look at an alternative to absorption costing known as *variable costing*.

In one form or another, most countries—including the United States—require absorption costing for both external financial reporting and for tax reporting. In addition, the vast majority of companies throughout the world also use absorption costing for managerial accounting purposes. Since absorption costing is the most common approach to product costing, we discuss it first and then deal with alternatives in subsequent chapters.

PROCESS AND JOB-ORDER COSTING

LEARNING OBJECTIVE 1

Distinguish between process costing and job-order costing and identify companies that would use each costing method.

Managers are faced with two complications when attempting to accurately compute the cost of a product or service. First, their companies often produce or provide a wide variety of products or services in a given period of time within the same factory or office. Second, many costs (such as rent) do not change from month to month despite fluctuations in the level of monthly output of products and services. Managers typically respond to these complications by averaging across time and outputs. The way in which this averaging is carried out depends heavily on the type of process involved. We will describe two different costing systems commonly used in manufacturing and service companies that rely on averaging in different ways—*process costing* and *job-order costing*. Our discussion of these costing systems focuses primarily on manufacturing applications; however, selected problems at the end of the chapter are used to help you understand how the concepts readily apply to service companies.

Process Costing

A **process costing system** is used in situations where the company produces many units of a single product for long periods. Examples include producing paper at Weyerhaeuser, refining aluminum ingots at Reynolds Aluminum, mixing and bottling beverages at Coca-Cola, and making wieners at Oscar Mayer. All of these industries are characterized by an essentially homogeneous product that flows through the production process on a continuous basis.

Process costing systems accumulate costs in a particular operation or department for an entire period (month, quarter, year) and then divide this total cost by the number of units produced during the period. The basic formula for process costing is:

$$\text{Unit product cost} = \frac{\text{Total manufacturing cost}}{\text{Total units produced}}$$

Since one unit of product is indistinguishable from any other unit of product, each unit produced during the period is assigned the same average cost. This costing technique results in a broad, average unit cost figure that applies to homogeneous units flowing in a continuous stream out of the production process.

Job-Order Costing

A **job-order costing system** is used in situations where many *different* products are produced each period. For example, a Levi Strauss clothing factory would typically make many different types of jeans for both men and women during a month. A particular order might consist of 1,000 stonewashed men's blue denim jeans, style number A312. This order of 1,000 jeans is called a *batch* or a *job*. In a job-order costing system, costs are traced and allocated to jobs and then the costs of the job are divided by the number of units in the job to arrive at an average cost per unit.

Other examples of situations where job-order costing would be used include large-scale construction projects managed by Bechtel International, commercial aircraft produced by Boeing, greeting cards designed and printed by Hallmark, and airline meals prepared by LSG Sky Chefs. All of these examples are characterized by diverse outputs. Each Bechtel project is unique and different from every other—the company may be simultaneously constructing a dam in Zaire and a bridge in Indonesia. Likewise, each airline orders a different type of meal from LSG Sky Chefs' catering service.

Job-order costing is also used extensively in service industries. Hospitals, law firms, movie studios, accounting firms, advertising agencies, and repair shops, for example, all use a variation of job-order costing to accumulate costs for accounting and billing purposes. Although the detailed example of job-order costing provided in the following section deals with a manufacturing company, the same basic concepts and procedures are used by many service organizations.

The record-keeping and cost assignment problems are more complex when a company sells many different products and services than when it has only a single product. Since the products are different, the costs are typically different. Consequently, cost records must be maintained for each distinct product or job. For example, an attorney in a large criminal law practice would ordinarily keep separate records of the costs of advising

Continuous Process Manufacturing vs. Job-Order Manufacturing

Continuous Process:

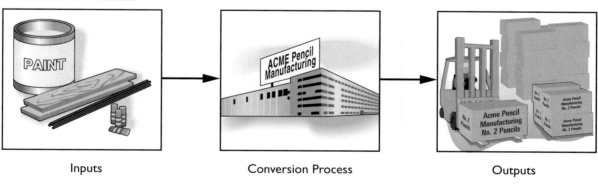

Inputs   Conversion Process   Outputs

Job-Order Process:

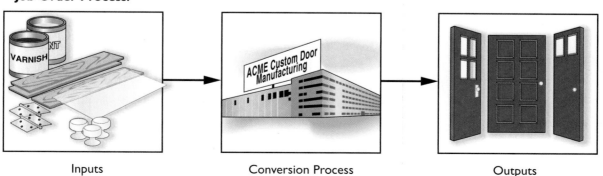

Inputs   Conversion Process   Outputs

and defending clients. And the Levi Strauss factory mentioned above would keep separate track of the costs of filling orders for particular styles of jeans. Thus, a job-order costing system requires more effort than a process-costing system. Nevertheless, job-order costing is used by over half of the manufacturers in the United States.

In this chapter, we focus on the design of a job-order costing system. In chapter 4, we focus on process costing and also look more closely at the similarities and differences between the two costing methods.

JOB-ORDER COSTING—AN OVERVIEW

LEARNING OBJECTIVE 2

Identify the documents used in a job-order costing system.

To introduce job-order costing, we will follow a specific job as it progresses through the manufacturing process at Yost Precision Machining, a small company that specializes in fabricating precision metal parts that are used in a variety of applications ranging from deep-sea exploration vehicles to the inertial triggers in automobile air bags. Loops Unlimited, a designer and builder of roller coaster rides, has ordered two experimental couplings from Yost Precision Machining. The couplings would connect the cars on a new high-speed roller coaster that is currently under development. Loops Unlimited has ordered just two couplings to evaluate their performance and safety.

Before we begin our discussion of the costing of these two experimental couplings, recall from the previous chapter that companies generally classify manufacturing costs into three broad categories: (1) direct materials, (2) direct labor, and (3) manufacturing overhead. As we study job-order costing, we will see how each of these three types of costs is recorded and accumulated.

Measuring Direct Materials Cost

Yost Precision Machining will require four G7 Connectors and two M46 Housings to make the two experimental couplings for Loops Unlimited. If this were a standard product, it would be accompanied by a *bill of materials*. A **bill of materials** is a document that lists the type and quantity of each raw material needed to complete a unit of product. In this case, there is no established bill of materials, so Yost's production staff determined the materials requirements from the blueprints submitted by the customer. Each coupling requires two connectors and one housing, so to make two couplings, four connectors and two housings are required.

A *production order* is issued when an agreement has been reached with the customer concerning the quantities, prices, and shipment date for the order. The Production Department then prepares a *materials requisition form* similar to the form in Exhibit 2–1.

EXHIBIT 2–1

Materials Requisition Form

Materials Requisition Number ___14873___   Date ___March 2___
Job Number to Be Charged ___2B47___
Department ___Milling___

Description	Quantity	Unit Cost	Total Cost
M46 Housing	2	$124	$248
G7 Connector	4	$103	412
			$660

Authorized Signature ___Bill White___

The **materials requisition form** is a detailed source document that (1) specifies the type and quantity of materials to be drawn from the storeroom, and (2) identifies the job that will be charged for the cost of the materials. The form is used to control the flow of materials into production and also for making entries in the accounting records.

The Yost Precision Machining materials requisition form in Exhibit 2–1 shows that the company's Milling Department has requisitioned two M46 Housings and four G7 Connectors for Job 2B47. This completed form is presented to the storeroom clerk who then issues these materials. The storeroom clerk is not allowed to release materials without a completed and properly authorized materials requisition form.

Job Cost Sheet

After being notified that the production order has been issued, the Accounting Department prepares a *job cost sheet* similar to the one presented in Exhibit 2–2. A **job cost sheet** is a form that records the materials, labor, and overhead costs charged to the job.

After direct materials are issued, the Accounting Department records their costs directly on the job cost sheet. Note from Exhibit 2–2, for example, that the $660 cost for direct materials shown earlier on the materials requisition form has been charged to Job 2B47 on its job cost sheet. The requisition number 14873 from the materials requisition form is also recorded on the job cost sheet to make it easier to identify the source document for the direct materials charge. In addition to serving as a means for charging costs to jobs, the job cost sheets also form a subsidiary ledger to the Work in Process account because the detailed records that they provide add up to the balance in Work in Process.

Concept 2-1

EXHIBIT 2–2

Job Cost Sheet

JOB COST SHEET

Job Number __2B47__ Date Initiated __March 2__

Date Completed _____

Department __Milling__ Units Completed _____

Item __Special order coupling__

For Stock _____

Direct Materials		Direct Labor			Manufacturing Overhead		
Req. No.	Amount	Ticket	Hours	Amount	Hours	Rate	Amount
14873	$660	843	5	$45			

Cost Summary		Units Shipped		
Direct Materials	$	Date	Number	Balance
Direct Labor	$			
Manufacturing Overhead	$			
Total Cost	$			
Unit Cost	$			

Measuring Direct Labor Cost

Direct labor cost is handled similarly to direct materials cost. Direct labor consists of labor charges that are easily traced to a particular job. Labor charges that cannot be easily traced directly to any job are treated as part of manufacturing overhead. As discussed in the previous chapter, this latter category of labor costs is called *indirect labor* and includes tasks such as maintenance, supervision, and cleanup.

IN BUSINESS

Relationship of Direct Labor to Product Cost

How much direct labor is in the products you buy? Sometimes not very much. During a visit to the Massachusetts Institute of Technology, Chinese Prime Minister Zhu Rongji claimed that, of the $120 retail cost of a pair of athletic shoes made in China, only $2 goes to the Chinese workers who assemble them. The National Labor Committee based in New York estimates that the labor cost to assemble a $90 pair of Nike sneakers is only $1.20.

Source: Robert A. Senser, letter to the editor, *Business Week,* May 24, 1999, pp. 11–12.

Workers use *time tickets* to record the time they spend on each job and task. A completed **time ticket** is an hour-by-hour summary of the employee's activities throughout the day. An example of an employee time ticket is shown in Exhibit 2–3. When working on a specific job, the employee enters the job number on the time ticket and notes the amount of time spent on that job. When not assigned to a particular job, the employee records the nature of the indirect labor task (such as cleanup and maintenance) and the amount of time spent on the task.

At the end of the day, the time tickets are gathered and the Accounting Department enters the direct labor-hours and costs on individual job cost sheets. (See Exhibit 2–2 for an example of how direct labor costs are entered on the job cost sheet.) The daily time tickets are source documents that are used as the basis for labor cost entries into the accounting records.

The system we have just described is a manual method for recording and posting labor costs. Many companies now rely on computerized systems and no longer record labor time by hand on sheets of paper. One computerized approach uses bar codes to capture the basic data. Each employee and each job has a unique bar code. When beginning work on a job, the employee scans three bar codes using a handheld device much like the bar code readers at grocery store check-out stands. The first bar code indicates that a job is being started; the second is the unique bar code on the employee's identity badge; and the third is the unique bar code of the job itself. This information is fed automatically via

EXHIBIT 2–3

Employee Time Ticket

Time Ticket No. 843 Date March 3
Employee Mary Holden Station 4

Started	Ended	Time Completed	Rate	Amount	Job Number
7:00	12:00	5.0	$9	$45	2B47
12:30	2:30	2.0	$9	18	2B50
2:30	3:30	1.0	$9	9	Maintenance
Totals		8.0		$72	

Supervisor *R.W. Pace*

an electronic network to a computer that notes the time and then records all of the data. When the task is completed, the employee scans a bar code indicating the task is complete, the bar code on his or her identity badge, and the bar code attached to the job. This information is relayed to the computer that again notes the time, and a time ticket is automatically prepared. Since all of the source data are already in computer files, the labor costs can be automatically posted to job cost sheets (or their electronic equivalents). Computers, coupled with technology such as bar codes, can eliminate much of the drudgery involved in routine bookkeeping activities while at the same time increasing timeliness and accuracy.

Concept 2-2

Application of Manufacturing Overhead

Manufacturing overhead must be included with direct materials and direct labor on the job cost sheet because manufacturing overhead is also a product cost. However, assigning manufacturing overhead to units of product can be difficult. There are three reasons for this.

1. Manufacturing overhead is an *indirect cost.* This means that it is either impossible or difficult to trace these costs to a particular product or job.
2. Manufacturing overhead consists of many different items ranging from the grease used in machines to the annual salary of the production manager.
3. Even though output may fluctuate due to seasonal or other factors, total manufacturing overhead costs tend to remain relatively constant due to the presence of fixed costs.

LEARNING OBJECTIVE 3

Compute predetermined overhead rates and explain why estimated overhead costs (rather than actual overhead costs) are used in the costing process.

Given these problems, about the only way to assign overhead costs to products is to use an allocation process. This allocation of overhead costs is accomplished by selecting an *allocation base* that is common to all of the company's products and services. An **allocation base** is a measure such as direct labor-hours (DLH) or machine-hours (MH) that is used to assign overhead costs to products and services.

The most widely used allocation bases are direct labor-hours and direct labor cost, with machine-hours and even units of product (where a company has only a single product) also used to some extent.

The allocation base is used to compute the **predetermined overhead rate** as follows:

$$\text{Predetermined overhead rate} = \frac{\text{Estimated total manufacturing overhead cost}}{\text{Estimated total amount of the allocation base}}$$

Note that the predetermined overhead rate is based on *estimates* rather than actual results.[1] This is because the *predetermined* overhead rate is computed *before* the period begins and is used to *apply* overhead cost to jobs throughout the period. The process of assigning overhead cost to jobs is called **overhead application.** The formula for determining the amount of overhead cost to apply to a particular job is:

$$\begin{matrix}\text{Overhead applied to} \\ \text{a particular job}\end{matrix} = \begin{matrix}\text{Predetermined} \\ \text{overhead rate}\end{matrix} \times \begin{matrix}\text{Amount of the allocation} \\ \text{base incurred by the job}\end{matrix}$$

For example, if the predetermined overhead rate is $8 per direct labor-hour, then $8 of overhead cost is *applied* to a job for each direct labor-hour incurred by the job. When the allocation base is direct labor-hours, the formula becomes:

$$\begin{matrix}\text{Overhead applied to} \\ \text{a particular job}\end{matrix} = \begin{matrix}\text{Predetermined} \\ \text{overhead rate}\end{matrix} \times \begin{matrix}\text{Actual direct labor-hours} \\ \text{incurred by the job}\end{matrix}$$

---

[1]Some experts argue that the predetermined overhead rate should be based on activity at capacity rather than on estimated activity. See Appendix 3A of Ray Garrison, Eric Noreen, and Peter Brewer *Managerial Accounting,* 11th edition, for details.

Using the Predetermined Overhead Rate

To illustrate the steps involved in computing and using a predetermined overhead rate, let's return to Yost Precision Machining. The company has estimated its total manufacturing overhead costs at $320,000 for the year and its total direct labor-hours at 40,000. Its predetermined overhead rate for the year would be $8 per direct labor-hour, as shown below:

$$\text{Predetermined overhead rate} = \frac{\text{Estimated total manufacturing overhead cost}}{\text{Estimated total amount of the allocation base}}$$

$$= \frac{\$320,000}{40,000 \text{ direct labor-hours}}$$

$$= \$8 \text{ per direct labour-hour}$$

The job cost sheet in Exhibit 2–4 indicates that 27 direct labor-hours (i.e., DLHs) were charged to Job 2B47. Therefore, a total of $216 of manufacturing overhead cost would be applied to the job:

$$\begin{array}{c}\text{Overhead applied to} \\ \text{Job 2B47}\end{array} = \begin{array}{c}\text{Predetermined} \\ \text{overhead rate}\end{array} \times \begin{array}{c}\text{Actual direct labor-hours} \\ \text{incurred by Job 2B47}\end{array}$$

$$= \$8 \text{ per direct labor-hour} \times 27 \text{ direct labor-hours}$$

$$= \$216 \text{ of overhead applied to Job 2B47}$$

This amount of overhead has been entered on the job cost sheet in Exhibit 2–4. Note that this is *not* the actual amount of overhead caused by the job. Actual overhead costs are *not*

EXHIBIT 2–4

A Completed Job Cost Sheet

JOB COST SHEET

Job Number __2B47__　　　　　　　　　　　　　Date Initiated __March 2__
　　　　　　　　　　　　　　　　　　　　　　　Date Completed __March 8__

Department __Milling__

Item __Special order coupling__　　　　　　　　Units Completed __2__

For Stock _____

Direct Materials		Direct Labor			Manufacturing Overhead		
Req. No.	Amount	Ticket	Hours	Amount	Hours	Rate	Amount
14873	$ 660	843	5	$ 45	27	$8/DLH	$216
14875	506	846	8	60			
14912	238	850	4	21			
	$1,404	851	10	54			
			27	$180			

Cost Summary		Units Shipped		
Direct Materials	$1,404	Date	Number	Balance
Direct Labor	$ 180	March 8	2	0
Manufacturing Overhead	$ 216			
Total Product Cost	$1,800			
Unit Product Cost	$ 900*			

*$1,800 ÷ 2 units = $900 per unit.

assigned to jobs—if that could be done, the costs would be direct costs, not overhead. The overhead assigned to the job is simply a share of the total overhead that was estimated at the beginning of the year. When a company applies overhead cost to jobs as we have done—that is, by multiplying the predetermined overhead rate by the actual activity—it is called a **normal cost system.**

The overhead may be applied as direct labor-hours are charged to jobs, or all of the overhead can be applied at once when the job is completed. The choice is up to the company. If a job is not completed at year-end, however, overhead should be applied to value the work in process inventory.

The Need for a Predetermined Rate

Instead of using a predetermined rate, a company could wait until the end of the accounting period to compute an actual overhead rate based on the *actual* total manufacturing costs and the *actual* total units in the allocation base for the period. However, managers cite several reasons for using predetermined overhead rates instead of actual overhead rates:

1. They would like to know the accounting system's valuation of completed jobs *before* the end of the accounting period. Suppose, for example, that Yost Precision Machining waits until the end of the year to compute its overhead rate. Then the cost of goods sold for Job 2B47 would not be known until the close of the year, even though the job was completed and shipped to the customer in March. The seriousness of this problem can be reduced to some extent by computing the actual overhead rate more frequently, but that immediately leads to another problem as discussed below.
2. If actual overhead rates are computed frequently, seasonal factors in overhead costs or in the allocation base can produce fluctuations in the overhead rates. For example, the costs of heating and cooling a production facility in Illinois will be highest in the winter and summer months and lowest in the spring and fall. If an overhead rate were computed each month or each quarter, the predetermined overhead rate would go up in the winter and summer and down in the spring and fall. Two identical jobs, one completed in the winter and one completed in the spring, would be assigned different costs if the overhead rate were computed on a monthly or quarterly basis. Managers generally feel that such fluctuations in overhead rates and costs serve no useful purpose and are misleading.
3. The use of a predetermined overhead rate simplifies record keeping. To determine the overhead cost to apply to a job, the accounting staff at Yost Precision Machining simply multiplies the direct labor-hours recorded for the job by the predetermined overhead rate of $8 per direct labor-hour.

For these reasons, most companies use predetermined overhead rates rather than actual overhead rates in their cost accounting systems.

Choice of an Allocation Base for Overhead Cost

Ideally, the allocation base used in the predetermined overhead rate should be the *cost driver* of the overhead cost. A **cost driver** is a factor, such as machine-hours, beds occupied, computer time, or flight-hours, that causes overhead costs. If a base is used to compute overhead rates that does not "drive" overhead costs, then the result will be inaccurate overhead rates and distorted product costs. For example, if direct labor-hours are used to allocate overhead, but in reality overhead has little to do with direct labor-hours, then products with high direct labor-hour requirements will be overcosted.

Most companies use direct labor-hours or direct labor cost as the allocation base for manufacturing overhead. However, as discussed in Chapter 1, major shifts are taking place in the structure of costs in many industries. In the past, direct labor accounted for up to 60% of the cost of many products, with overhead cost making up only a portion of the remainder. This situation has been changing for two reasons. First, sophisticated automated equipment has taken over functions that used to be performed by direct labor workers. Since the costs of acquiring and maintaining such equipment are classified as overhead, this increases overhead while decreasing direct labor. Second, products are themselves becoming more sophisticated and complex and are changed more frequently. This increases the need for highly skilled indirect workers such as engineers. As a result of these two trends, direct labor is decreasing relative to overhead as a component of product costs in many industries.

In companies where direct labor and overhead costs have been moving in opposite directions, it would be difficult to argue that direct labor "drives" overhead costs. Accordingly, managers in some companies use *activity-based costing* principles to redesign their cost accounting systems. Activity-based costing is a costing technique that is designed to more accurately reflect the demands that products, customers, and other cost objects make on overhead resources. The activity-based approach is discussed in more detail in Chapter 3.

We hasten to add that although direct labor may not be an appropriate allocation base in some industries, in others it continues to be a significant driver of manufacturing overhead. Indeed, most manufacturing companies in the United States continue to use direct labor as the primary or secondary allocation base for manufacturing overhead. The key point is that the allocation base used by the company should really drive, or cause, overhead costs, and direct labor is not always an appropriate allocation base.

IN BUSINESS

Waist Management

New research from the University of Michigan suggests that an important cost driver for a company's health care costs is the weight of its employees. In fact, the research indicates that workers who have added a few too many pounds can cost companies as much as $1,500 more annually to insure. So what is a company to do? Park Place Entertainment, a casino operator with more than 7,000 employees, decided to attack the problem by holding a weight-loss contest. Over two years, the company's workforce dropped 20 tons of weight. After the contest, 12 diabetics were able to stop using medications that cost $13,300 per year per employee. Additionally, the company believes that its contest has caused a decline in absenteeism and an increase in productivity.

Source: Jill Hecht Maxwell, "Worker Waist Management," *Inc.*, August 2004, p. 32; Jessi Hempel, "Dieting for Dollars," *BusinessWeek*, November 3, 2003, p. 10.

IN BUSINESS

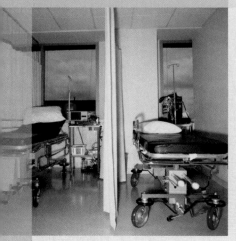

Understanding Cost Drivers Can Be Tricky Business

In recent years, hospitals have developed a keen interest in controlling their costs. Conventional wisdom in the health care industry was that costs could be reduced by reducing a patient's length of stay in a hospital. It seemed logical that reducing the number of days that a patient spends in the hospital should reduce the cost of treating that patient. However, researchers John Evans, Yuhchang Hwang, and Nandu Nagarajan provide evidence within one hospital that when doctors were motivated to reduce length of stay, it did not reduce costs. The researchers found that doctors compensated for a reduction in length of stay by increasing the number of procedures performed per patient per day. Thus, any potential savings from reducing one cost driver—length of stay—were offset by cost increases caused by increasing another cost driver—number of procedures performed per patient per day.

Source: John H. Evans, Yuhchang Hwang, and Nandu J. Nagarajan, "Management Control and Hospital Cost Reduction: Additional Evidence," *Journal of Accounting and Public Policy*, Spring 2001, pp. 73–88.

Computation of Unit Costs

With the application of Yost Precision Machining's $216 of manufacturing overhead to the job cost sheet in Exhibit 2–4, the job cost sheet is complete except for two final steps. First, the totals for direct materials, direct labor, and manufacturing overhead are transferred to the Cost Summary section of the job cost sheet and added together to obtain the total cost for the job. Then the total product cost ($1,800) is divided by the number of units (2) to obtain the unit product cost ($900). As indicated earlier, *this unit product cost is an average cost and should not be interpreted as the cost that would actually be incurred if another unit were produced.* Much of the actual overhead costs would not change if another unit were produced, so the incremental cost of an additional unit is less than the average unit cost of $900.

The completed job cost sheet is now ready to be transferred to the Finished Goods inventory account, where it will serve as the basis for valuing unsold units in ending inventory and for determining cost of goods sold.

Treasurer, Class Reunion Committee   DECISION MAKER

It is hard to believe that 10 years have passed so quickly since your graduation from high school. Take a minute to reflect on what has happened in that time frame. After high school, you attended the local community college, transferred to a state university, and graduated on time. You're juggling a successful career, classes in an evening MBA program, and a new family. And now, after reminiscing with one of your high school classmates, you've somehow agreed to handle the financial arrangements for your 10-year reunion. What were you thinking? Well, at least you can fall back on those accounting skills.

You call the restaurant where the reunion will be held and jot down the most important information. The meal cost (including beverages) will be $30 per person plus a 15% gratuity. An additional $200 will be charged for a banquet room with a dance floor. A band has been hired for $500. One of the members of the reunion committee informs you that there is just enough money left in the class bank account to cover the printing and mailing costs. He mentions that at least one-half of the class of 400 will attend the reunion and wonders if he should add the 15% gratuity to the $30 per person meal cost when he drafts the invitation, which will indicate that a check must be returned with the reply card.

How should you respond? How much will you need to charge to cover the various costs? After making your decision, label your answer with the managerial accounting terms covered in this chapter. Finally, identify any issues that should be investigated further.

Summary of Document Flows

The sequence of events discussed above is summarized in Exhibit 2–5. A careful study of the flow of documents in this exhibit will provide a good overview of the overall operation of a job-order costing system.

---

1. Which of the following statements is false? (You may select more than one answer.)   **CONCEPT CHECK**
   a. Absorption costing assigns fixed and variable manufacturing overhead costs to products.
   b. Job-order costing systems are used when companies produce many different types of products.
   c. A normal costing system assigns costs to products by multiplying the actual overhead rate by the actual amount of the allocation base.
   d. A company such as Coca-Cola is more likely to use a process costing system than a job-order costing system.

EXHIBIT 2–5 The Flow of Documents in a Job-Order Costing System

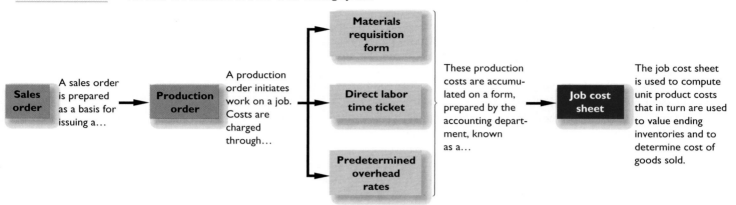

JOB-ORDER COSTING—THE FLOW OF COSTS

LEARNING OBJECTIVE 4

Prepare journal entries to record costs in a job-order costing system.

We are now ready to take a more detailed look at the flow of costs through a company's general ledger. To illustrate, we shall consider a single month's activity for Rand Company, a producer of gold and silver commemorative medallions. Rand Company has two jobs in process during April, the first month of its fiscal year. Job A, a special minting of 1,000 gold medallions commemorating the invention of motion pictures, was started during March. By the end of March, $30,000 in manufacturing costs had been recorded for the job. Job B, an order for 10,000 silver medallions commemorating the fall of the Berlin Wall, was started in April.

The Purchase and Issue of Materials

On April 1, Rand Company had $7,000 in raw materials on hand. During the month, the company purchased on account an additional $60,000 in raw materials. The purchase is recorded in journal entry (1) below:

(1)

Raw Materials	60,000	
Accounts Payable		60,000

As explained in the previous chapter, Raw Materials is an asset account. Thus, when raw materials are purchased, they are initially recorded as an asset—not as an expense.

Issue of Direct and Indirect Materials During April, $52,000 in raw materials were requisitioned from the storeroom for use in production. These raw materials include $50,000 of direct and $2,000 of indirect materials. Entry (2) records issuing the materials to the production departments.

(2)

Work in Process	50,000	
Manufacturing Overhead	2,000	
Raw Materials		52,000

The materials charged to Work in Process represent direct materials for specific jobs. These costs are also recorded on the appropriate job cost sheets. This point is illustrated in Exhibit 2–6, where $28,000 of the $50,000 in direct materials is charged to Job A's cost sheet and the remaining $22,000 is charged to Job B's cost sheet.

EXHIBIT 2–6   Raw Materials Cost Flows

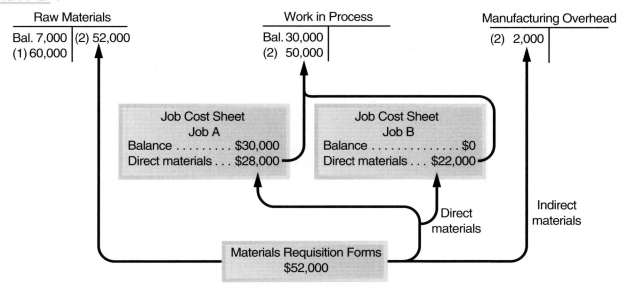

(In this example, all data are presented in summary form and the job cost sheet is abbreviated.)

The $2,000 charged to Manufacturing Overhead in entry (2) represents indirect materials used in production during April. Observe that the Manufacturing Overhead account is separate from the Work in Process account. The purpose of the Manufacturing Overhead account is to accumulate all manufacturing overhead costs as they are incurred during a period.

Before leaving Exhibit 2–6 we need to point out one additional thing. Notice from the exhibit that the job cost sheet for Job A contains a beginning balance of $30,000. We stated earlier that this balance represents the cost of work done during March that has been carried forward to April. Also note that the Work in Process account contains the same $30,000 balance. *The reason the $30,000 appears in both places is that the Work in Process account is a control account and the job cost sheets form a subsidiary ledger. Thus, the Work in Process account contains a summarized total of all costs appearing on the individual job cost sheets for all jobs in process at any given point in time.* (Since Rand Company had only Job A in process at the beginning of April, Job A's $30,000 balance on that date is equal to the balance in the Work in Process account.)

Issue of Direct Materials Only   Sometimes the materials drawn from the Raw Materials inventory account are all direct materials. In this case, the entry to record the issue of the materials into production would be as follows:

Work in Process	XXX	
Raw Materials		XXX

Labor Cost

As work is performed each day in various departments of Rand Company, employee time tickets are filled out by workers, collected, and forwarded to the Accounting Department. In the Accounting Department, wages are computed and the resulting costs are classified as either direct or indirect labor. In April, $60,000 was recorded for direct labor and $15,000 for indirect labor. This resulted in the following summary entry:

(3)

Work in Process	60,000	
Manufacturing Overhead	15,000	
Salaries and Wages Payable		75,000

EXHIBIT 2–7   Labor Cost Flows

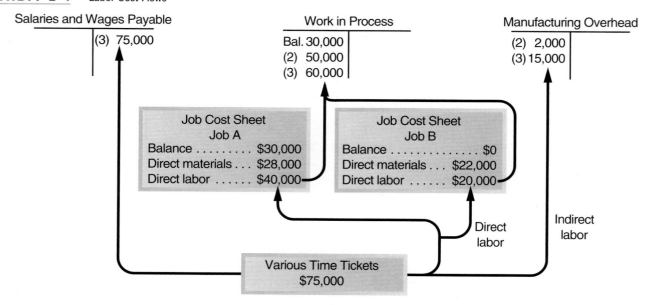

Only the direct labor cost of $60,000 is added to the Work in Process account. For Rand Company, this amounted to $60,000 for April.

At the same time that direct labor costs are added to Work in Process, they are also added to the individual job cost sheets, as shown in Exhibit 2–7. During April, $40,000 of direct labor cost was charged to Job A and the remaining $20,000 was charged to Job B.

The labor costs charged to Manufacturing Overhead represent the indirect labor costs of the period, such as supervision, janitorial work, and maintenance.

Manufacturing Overhead Costs

Recall that all costs of operating the factory other than direct materials and direct labor are classified as manufacturing overhead costs. These costs are entered directly into the Manufacturing Overhead account as they are incurred. To illustrate, assume that Rand Company incurred the following general factory costs during April:

Utilities (heat, water, and power)	$21,000
Rent on factory equipment	16,000
Miscellaneous factory overhead costs	3,000
Total	$40,000

The following entry records the incurrence of these costs:

(4)

Manufacturing Overhead	40,000	
Accounts Payable, Cash, etc.		40,000

In addition, let us assume that during April, Rand Company recognized $13,000 in accrued property taxes and that $7,000 in prepaid insurance expired on factory buildings and equipment. The following entry records these items:

(5)

Manufacturing Overhead	20,000	
Property Taxes Payable		13,000
Prepaid Insurance		7,000

Finally, let us assume that the company recognized $18,000 in depreciation on factory equipment during April. The following entry records the accrual of this depreciation:

(6)

Manufacturing Overhead........................	18,000	
Accumulated Depreciation..................		18,000

In short, *all* manufacturing overhead costs are recorded directly into the Manufacturing Overhead account as they are incurred. It is important to understand that Manufacturing Overhead is a control account for many—perhaps thousands—of subsidiary accounts such as Indirect Materials, Indirect Labor, Factory Utilities, and so forth. As the Manufacturing Overhead account is debited for costs during a period, the various subsidiary accounts are also debited. In the example above and also in the assignment material for this chapter, we omit the entries to the subsidiary accounts for the sake of brevity.

Applying Manufacturing Overhead

Since actual manufacturing costs are charged to the Manufacturing Overhead control account rather than to Work in Process, how are manufacturing overhead costs assigned to Work in Process? The answer is, by means of the predetermined overhead rate. Recall from our discussion earlier in the chapter that a predetermined overhead rate is established at the beginning of each year. The rate is calculated by dividing the estimated total manufacturing overhead cost for the year by the estimated total amount of the allocation base (measured in machine-hours, direct labor-hours, or some other base). The predetermined overhead rate is then used to apply overhead costs to jobs. For example, if direct labor-hours is the allocation base, overhead cost is applied to each job by multiplying the predetermined overhead rate by the number of direct labor-hours charged to the job.

> **LEARNING OBJECTIVE 5**
> Apply overhead cost to Work in Process using a predetermined overhead rate.

To illustrate, assume that Rand Company has used machine-hours to compute a predetermined overhead rate of $6 per machine-hour. Also assume that during April, 10,000 machine-hours were worked on Job A and 5,000 machine-hours were worked on Job B (a total of 15,000 machine-hours). Thus, $90,000 in overhead cost ($6 per machine-hour × 15,000 machine-hours = $90,000) would be applied to Work in Process. The following entry records the application of Manufacturing Overhead to Work in Process:

(7)

Work in Process..............................	90,000	
Manufacturing Overhead		90,000

The flow of costs through the Manufacturing Overhead account is shown in Exhibit 2–8.

The actual overhead costs in the Manufacturing Overhead account in Exhibit 2–8 are the costs that were added to the account in entries (2)–(6). Observe that the incurrence of these actual overhead costs [entries (2)–(6)] and the application of overhead to Work in Process [entry (7)] represent two separate and entirely distinct processes.

The Concept of a Clearing Account The Manufacturing Overhead account operates as a clearing account. As we have noted, actual factory overhead costs are debited to the account as they are incurred throughout the year. At certain intervals during the year, usually when a job is completed, overhead cost is applied to the job using the predetermined overhead rate, and Work in Process is debited and Manufacturing Overhead is credited. This sequence of events is illustrated below:

Manufacturing Overhead (A Clearing Account)	
Actual overhead costs are charged to this account as they are incurred throughout the period.	Overhead is removed from this account and is applied to Work in Process using the predetermined overhead rate.

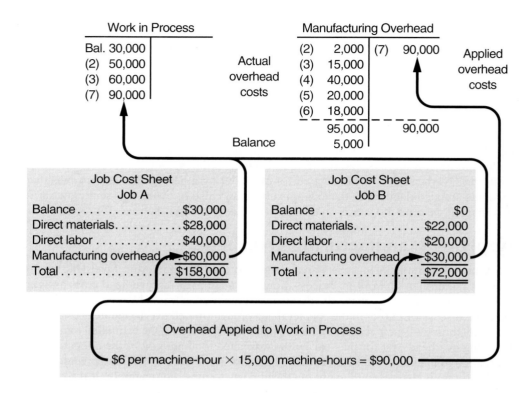

As we emphasized earlier, the predetermined overhead rate is based entirely on estimates of what overhead costs are *expected* to be, and it is established before the year begins. As a result, the overhead cost applied during a year will almost certainly turn out to be more or less than the overhead cost that is actually incurred. For example, notice from Exhibit 2–8 that Rand Company's actual overhead costs for the period are $5,000 greater than the overhead cost that has been applied to Work in Process, resulting in a $5,000 debit balance in the Manufacturing Overhead account. We will reserve discussion of what to do with this $5,000 balance until the next section, Problems of Overhead Application.

For the moment, we can conclude by noting from Exhibit 2–8 that the cost of a completed job consists of the actual direct materials cost of the job, the actual direct labor cost of the job, and the manufacturing overhead cost *applied* to the job. Pay particular attention to the following subtle but important point: *Actual overhead costs are not charged to jobs; actual overhead costs do not appear on the job cost sheet nor do they appear in the Work in Process account. Only the applied overhead cost, based on the predetermined overhead rate, appears on the job cost sheet and in the Work in Process account.*

Nonmanufacturing Costs

In addition to manufacturing costs, companies also incur selling and administrative costs. As explained in the previous chapter, these costs should be treated as period expenses and charged directly to the income statement. *Nonmanufacturing costs should not go into the Manufacturing Overhead account.* To illustrate the correct treatment of nonmanufacturing costs, assume that Rand Company incurred $30,000 in selling and administrative salary costs during April. The following entry records the accrual of salaries:

(8)		
Salaries Expense	30,000	
Salaries and Wages Payable*		30,000

Assume that depreciation on office equipment during April was $7,000. The entry would be:

(9)		
Depreciation Expense	7,000	
Accumulated Depreciation		7,000

Pay particular attention to the difference between this entry and entry (6) where we recorded depreciation on factory equipment. In journal entry (6), depreciation on factory equipment was debited to Manufacturing Overhead and is therefore a product cost. In journal entry (9) above, depreciation on office equipment is debited to Depreciation Expense. Depreciation on office equipment is considered to be a period expense rather than a product cost.

Finally, assume that advertising was $42,000 and that other selling and administrative expenses in April totaled $8,000. The following entry records these items:

(10)		
Advertising Expense	42,000	
Other Selling and Administrative Expense	8,000	
Accounts Payable*		50,000

Since the amounts in entries (8) through (10) all go directly into expense accounts, they will have no effect on product costs. The same will be true of any other selling and administrative expenses incurred during April, including sales commissions, depreciation on sales equipment, rent on office facilities, insurance on office facilities, and related costs.

Cost of Goods Manufactured

When a job has been completed, the finished output is transferred from the production departments to the finished goods warehouse. By this time, the accounting department will have charged the job with direct materials and direct labor cost, and manufacturing overhead will have been applied using the predetermined overhead rate. A transfer of these costs is made within the costing system that *parallels* the physical transfer of the goods to the finished goods warehouse. The costs of the completed job are transferred out of the Work in Process account and into the Finished Goods account. The sum of all amounts transferred between these two accounts represents the cost of goods manufactured for the period.

In the case of Rand Company, let us assume that Job A was completed during April. The following entry transfers the cost of Job A from Work in Process to Finished Goods:

LEARNING OBJECTIVE 6

Prepare schedules of cost of goods manufactured and cost of goods sold.

(11)		
Finished Goods	158,000	
Work in Process		158,000

The $158,000 represents the completed cost of Job A, as shown on the job cost sheet in Exhibit 2–8. Since Job A was the only job completed during April, the $158,000 also represents the cost of goods manufactured for the month.

---

*In addition to payables, other accounts such as cash may be credited.

Job B was not completed by month-end, so its cost will remain in the Work in Process account and carry over to the next month. If a balance sheet is prepared at the end of April, the cost accumulated thus far on Job B will appear as "Work in process inventory" in the assets section. The $158,000 cost of goods manufactured for the month is added to the $10,000 beginning balance in the Finished Goods account that is carried over from the previous month.

Cost of Goods Sold

As finished goods are shipped to customers, their costs are transferred from the Finished Goods account into the Cost of Goods Sold account. If a complete job is shipped, as in the case where a job has been done to a customer's specifications, then the entire cost appearing on the job cost sheet is transferred into the Cost of Goods Sold account. In most cases, however, only a portion of the units involved in a particular job will be immediately sold. In these situations, the unit product cost must be used to determine how much product cost should be removed from Finished Goods and charged to Cost of Goods Sold.

For Rand Company, we will assume 750 of the 1,000 gold medallions in Job A were shipped to customers by the end of the month for total sales revenue of $225,000. Since 1,000 units were produced and the total cost of the job from the job cost sheet was $158,000, the unit product cost was $158. The following journal entries would record the sale (all sales were on account):

(12)

| Accounts Receivable . . . . | 225,000 | |
| Sales . . . . | | 225,000 |

(13)

Cost of Goods Sold	118,500	
Finished Goods		118,500
(750 units × $158 per unit = $118,500)		

Entry (13) completes the flow of costs through our job-order costing system.

Summary of Cost Flows

LEARNING OBJECTIVE 7

Use T-accounts to show the flow of costs in a job-order costing system.

To pull the entire Rand Company example together, journal entries (1) through (13) are summarized in Exhibit 2–9. The flow of costs through the accounts is presented in T-account form in Exhibit 2–10.

Exhibit 2–11 presents a schedule of cost of goods manufactured and a schedule of cost of goods sold for Rand Company. Note particularly from Exhibit 2–11 that the manufacturing overhead cost on the schedule of cost of goods manufactured is the overhead applied to jobs during the month—not the actual manufacturing overhead costs incurred. The reason for this can be traced back to journal entry (7) and the T-account for Work in Process that appears in Exhibit 2–10. Under a normal costing system as illustrated in this chapter, applied—not actual—overhead costs are assigned to jobs and thus to Work in Process inventory. As a point of contrast, in Chapter 1 actual overhead costs were assigned to Work in Process and included in the schedule of cost of goods manufactured. This is because the concept of a normal costing system had not yet been introduced.

Note also, as shown in Exhibit 2-11, that the cost of goods manufactured for the month ($158,000) agrees with the amount transferred from Work in Process to Finished Goods for the month as recorded earlier in entry (11). Also note that this $158,000 is used in computing the cost of goods sold for the month.

An income statement for April is presented in Exhibit 2–12. Observe that the cost of goods sold on this statement ($123,500) is carried down from Exhibit 2–11.

EXHIBIT 2–9

Summary of Rand Company Journal Entries

(1)		
Raw Materials...................................	60,000	
Accounts Payable...........................		60,000
(2)		
Work in Process................................	50,000	
Manufacturing Overhead......................	2,000	
Raw Materials...............................		52,000
(3)		
Work in Process................................	60,000	
Manufacturing Overhead......................	15,000	
Salaries and Wages Payable		75,000
(4)		
Manufacturing Overhead......................	40,000	
Accounts Payable...........................		40,000
(5)		
Manufacturing Overhead......................	20,000	
Property Taxes Payable		13,000
Prepaid Insurance..........................		7,000
(6)		
Manufacturing Overhead......................	18,000	
Accumulated Depreciation...................		18,000
(7)		
Work in Process................................	90,000	
Manufacturing Overhead		90,000
(8)		
Salaries Expense	30,000	
Salaries and Wages Payable		30,000
(9)		
Depreciation Expense	7,000	
Accumulated Depreciation..................		7,000
(10)		
Advertising Expense	42,000	
Other Selling and Administrative Expense	8,000	
Accounts Payable...........................		50,000
(11)		
Finished Goods	158,000	
Work in Process		158,000
(12)		
Accounts Receivable..........................	225,000	
Sales		225,000
(13)		
Cost of Goods Sold	118,500	
Finished Goods.............................		118,500

EXHIBIT 2–10   Summary of Cost Flows—Rand Company

Accounts Receivable	
Bal. XX	
(12) 225,000	

Prepaid Insurance	
Bal. XX	
	(5) 7,000

Raw Materials	
Bal. 7,000	(2) 52,000
(1) 60,000	
Bal. 15,000	

Work in Process	
Bal. 30,000	(11) 158,000
(2) 50,000	
(3) 60,000	
(7) 90,000	
Bal. 72,000	

Finished Goods	
Bal. 10,000	(13) 118,500
(11) 158,000	
Bal. 49,500	

Accumulated Depreciation	
	Bal. XX
	(6) 18,000
	(9) 7,000

Manufacturing Overhead	
(2) 2,000	(7) 90,000
(3) 15,000	
(4) 40,000	
(5) 20,000	
(6) 18,000	
Bal. 5,000	

Accounts Payable	
	Bal. XX
	(1) 60,000
	(4) 40,000
	(10) 50,000

Salaries and Wages Payable	
	Bal. XX
	(3) 75,000
	(8) 30,000

Property Taxes Payable	
	Bal. XX
	(5) 13,000

Capital Stock	
	Bal. XX

Retained Earnings	
	Bal. XX

Sales	
	(12) 225,000

Cost of Goods Sold	
(13) 118,500	

Salaries Expense	
(8) 30,000	

Depreciation Expense	
(9) 7,000	

Advertising Expense	
(10) 42,000	

Other Selling and Administrative Expense	
(10) 8,000	

Explanation of entries:
(1)   Raw materials purchased.
(2)   Direct and indirect materials issued into production.
(3)   Direct and indirect factory labor cost incurred.
(4)   Utilities and other factory costs incurred.
(5)   Property taxes and insurance incurred on the factory.
(6)   Depreciation recorded on factory assets.
(7)   Overhead cost applied to Work in Process.
(8)   Administrative salaries expense incurred.
(9)   Depreciation recorded on office equipment.
(10) Advertising and other selling and administrative expense incurred.
(11) Cost of goods manufactured transferred into finished goods.
(12) Sale of Job A recorded.
(13) Cost of goods sold recorded for Job A.

EXHIBIT 2–11

Schedules of Cost of Goods
Manufactured and Cost of Goods Sold

Cost of Goods Manufactured

Direct materials:

Raw materials inventory, beginning	$ 7,000	
Add: Purchases of raw materials	60,000	
Total raw materials available	67,000	
Deduct: Raw materials inventory, ending	15,000	
Raw materials used in production	52,000	
Less indirect materials included in manufacturing overhead	2,000	$ 50,000
Direct labor		60,000
Manufacturing overhead applied to work in process		90,000
Total manufacturing costs		200,000
Add: Beginning work in process inventory		30,000
		230,000
Deduct: Ending work in process inventory		72,000
Cost of goods manufactured		$158,000

Cost of Goods Sold

Finished goods inventory, beginning	$ 10,000
Add: Cost of goods manufactured	158,000
Goods available for sale	168,000
Deduct: Finished goods inventory, ending	49,500
Unadjusted cost of goods sold	118,500
Add: Underapplied overhead	5,000
Adjusted cost of goods sold	$123,500

*Note that the underapplied overhead is added to cost of goods sold. If overhead were overapplied, it would be deducted from cost of goods sold.

EXHIBIT 2–12

Income Statement

Rand Company
Income Statement
For the Month Ending April 30

Sales		$225,000
Less cost of goods sold ($118,500 + $5,000)		123,500
Gross margin		101,500
Less selling and administrative expenses:		
Salaries expense	$30,000	
Depreciation expense	7,000	
Advertising expense	42,000	
Other expense	8,000	87,000
Net operating income		$ 14,500

PROBLEMS OF OVERHEAD APPLICATION

We need to consider two complications relating to overhead application: (1) the computation of underapplied and overapplied overhead and (2) the disposition of any balance remaining in the Manufacturing Overhead account at the end of a period.

Underapplied and Overapplied Overhead

LEARNING OBJECTIVE 8

Compute underapplied or overapplied overhead cost and prepare the journal entry to close the balance in Manufacturing Overhead to the appropriate accounts.

Since the predetermined overhead rate is established before a period begins and is based entirely on estimated data, the amount of overhead cost applied to Work in Process will generally differ from the amount of overhead cost actually incurred during a period. In the case of Rand Company, for example, the predetermined overhead rate of $6 per hour resulted in $90,000 of overhead cost being applied to Work in Process, whereas actual overhead costs for April proved to be $95,000 (see Exhibit 2–8). The difference between the overhead cost applied to Work in Process and the actual overhead costs of a period is called either **underapplied** or **overapplied overhead.** For Rand Company, overhead was underapplied because the applied cost ($90,000) was $5,000 less than the actual cost ($95,000). If the situation had been reversed and the company had applied $95,000 in overhead cost to Work in Process while incurring actual overhead costs of only $90,000, then the overhead would have been overapplied.

What is the cause of underapplied or overapplied overhead? The causes can be complex, and a full explanation will have to wait for later chapters. Nevertheless, the basic problem is that the method of applying overhead to jobs using a predetermined overhead rate assumes that actual overhead costs will be proportional to the actual amount of the allocation base incurred during the period. If, for example, the predetermined overhead rate is $6 per machine-hour, then it is assumed that actual overhead costs incurred will be $6 for every machine-hour that is actually worked. There are at least two reasons why this may not be true. First, much of the overhead often consists of fixed costs that do not change as the number of machine-hours incurred goes up or down. Second, spending on overhead items may or may not be under control. If individuals who are responsible for overhead costs do a good job, those costs should be less than were expected at the beginning of the period. If they do a poor job, those costs will be more than expected. As we indicated above, however, a fuller explanation of the causes of underapplied and overapplied overhead will have to wait for later chapters.

To illustrate what can happen, suppose that two companies—Turbo Crafters and Black & Howell—have prepared the following estimated data for the coming year:

	Turbo Crafters	Black & Howell
Allocation base	Machine-hours	Direct materials cost
Estimated manufacturing overhead cost (a)	$300,000	$120,000
Estimated total amount of the allocation base (b)	75,000 machine-hours	$80,000 direct materials cost
Predetermined overhead rate (a) ÷ (b)	$4 per machine-hour	150% of direct materials cost

Note that when the allocation base is dollars—such as direct materials cost in the case of Black & Howell—the predetermined overhead rate is expressed as a percentage of the allocation base. When dollars are divided by dollars, the result is a percentage.

Now assume that because of unexpected changes in overhead spending and changes in demand for the companies' products, the *actual* overhead cost and the actual activity recorded during the year in each company are as follows:

	Turbo Crafters	Black & Howell
Actual manufacturing overhead cost	$290,000	$130,000
Actual total amount of the allocation base	68,000 machine-hours	$90,000 direct materials cost

For each company, note that the actual data for both cost and the allocation base differ from the estimates used in computing the predetermined overhead rate. This results in underapplied and overapplied overhead as follows:

	Turbo Crafters		Black & Howell	
Actual manufacturing overhead cost	$290,000		$130,000	
Manufacturing overhead cost applied to Work in Process during the year:				
Predetermined overhead rate (a)	$4	per machine-hour	150%	of direct materials cost
Actual total amount of the allocation base (b) ...	68,000	machine-hours	$90,000	direct materials cost
Manufacturing overhead applied (a) × (b)	$272,000		$135,000	
Underapplied (overapplied) manufacturing overhead .	$18,000		$(5,000)	

For Turbo Crafters, notice that the amount of overhead cost that has been applied to Work in Process ($272,000) is less than the actual overhead cost for the year ($290,000). Therefore, overhead is underapplied. Also, notice that the original estimate of overhead for Turbo Crafters ($300,000) is not directly involved in this computation. Its impact is felt only through the $4 predetermined overhead rate.

For Black & Howell, the amount of overhead cost that has been applied to Work in Process ($135,000) is greater than the actual overhead cost for the year ($130,000), and so overhead is overapplied.

A summary of the concepts discussed above is presented in Exhibit 2–13.

Disposition of Underapplied or Overapplied Overhead Balances

What happens to any underapplied or overapplied balance remaining in the Manufacturing Overhead account at the end of a period? The simplest method is to close out the balance to Cost of Goods Sold. More complicated methods are sometimes used, but they are beyond the scope of this book. To illustrate the simplest method, recall that Rand

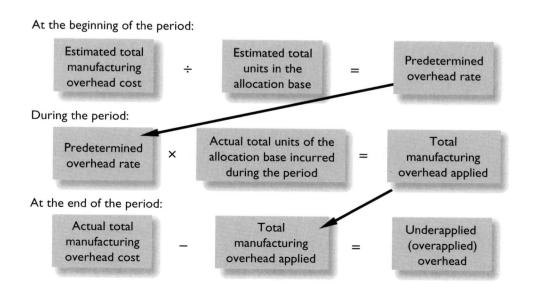

EXHIBIT 2–13

Summary of Overhead Concepts

At the beginning of the period:

Estimated total manufacturing overhead cost ÷ Estimated total units in the allocation base = Predetermined overhead rate

During the period:

Predetermined overhead rate × Actual total units of the allocation base incurred during the period = Total manufacturing overhead applied

At the end of the period:

Actual total manufacturing overhead cost − Total manufacturing overhead applied = Underapplied (overapplied) overhead

Company had underapplied overhead of $5,000. The entry to close this underapplied overhead to Cost of Goods Sold would be:

	(14)	
Cost of Goods Sold	5,000	
Manufacturing Overhead		5,000

Note that since the Manufacturing Overhead account has a debit balance, Manufacturing Overhead must be credited to close out the account. This has the effect of increasing Cost of Goods Sold for April by $5,000 to $123,500:

Unadjusted cost of goods sold [from entry (13)]	$118,500
Add underapplied overhead [entry (14) above]	5,000
Adjusted cost of goods sold	$123,500

After this adjustment has been made, Rand Company's income statement for April will appear as shown earlier in Exhibit 2–12.

YOU DECIDE | Remaining Balance in the Overhead Account

The simplest method for disposing of any balance remaining in the Overhead account is to close it out to Cost of Goods Sold. If there is a debit balance (that is, overhead has been underapplied), the entry to dispose of the balance would include a debit to Cost of Goods Sold. That debit would increase the balance in the Cost of Goods Sold account. On the other hand, if there is a credit balance, the entry to dispose of the balance would include a credit to Cost of Goods Sold. That credit would decrease the balance in the Cost of Goods Sold account. If you were the company's controller, would you want a debit balance, a credit balance, or no balance in the Overhead account at the end of the period?

A General Model of Product Cost Flows

Exhibit 2–14 presents a T-account model of the flow of costs in a product costing system. This model applies as much to a process costing system as it does to a job-order costing system. Examination of this model can be very helpful in understanding how costs enter a system, flow through it, and finally end up as Cost of Goods Sold on the income statement.

Multiple Predetermined Overhead Rates

Our discussion in this chapter has assumed that there is a single predetermined overhead rate for an entire factory called a **plantwide overhead rate.** This is a fairly common practice—particularly in smaller companies. But in larger companies, *multiple predetermined overhead rates* are often used. In a **multiple predetermined overhead rate** system, each production department may have its own predetermined overhead rate. Such a system, while more complex, is considered to be more accurate, since it can reflect differences across departments in how overhead costs are incurred. For example, overhead might be allocated based on direct labor-hours in departments that are relatively labor intensive and based on machine-hours in departments that are relatively machine intensive. When multiple predetermined overhead rates are used, overhead is applied in each department according to its own overhead rate as a job proceeds through the department.

EXHIBIT 2–14　A General Model of Cost Flows

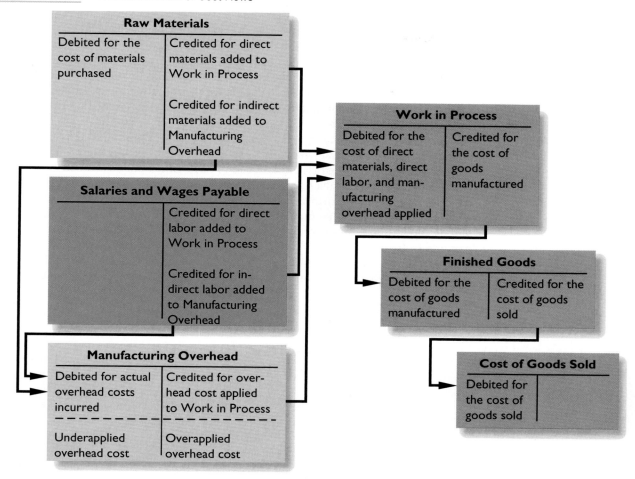

2. Which of the following statements is false? (You may select more than one answer.)
   a. The Manufacturing Overhead account is debited when manufacturing overhead is applied to Work in Process.
   b. Job cost sheets accumulate the actual overhead costs incurred to complete a job.
   c. When products are transferred from work in process to finished goods it results in a debit to Finished Goods and a credit to Work in Process.
   d. Selling expenses are applied to production using a predetermined overhead rate that is computed at the beginning of the period.

3. The predetermined overhead rate is $50 per machine hour, underapplied overhead is $5,000, and the actual amount of machine hours is 2,000. What is the actual amount of total manufacturing overhead incurred during the period?
   a. $105,000
   b. $95,000
   c. $150,000
   d. $110,000

CONCEPT CHECK ✓

JOB-ORDER COSTING IN SERVICE COMPANIES

Job-order costing is also used in service organizations such as law firms, movie studios, hospitals, and repair shops, as well as in manufacturing companies. In a law firm, for example, each client is considered to be a "job," and the costs of that job are accumulated day by day on a job cost sheet as the client's case is handled by the firm. Legal forms and similar inputs represent the direct materials for the job; the time expended by attorneys represents the direct labor; and the costs of secretaries, clerks, rent, depreciation, and so forth, represent the overhead.

In a movie studio such as Columbia Pictures, each film produced by the studio is a "job," and costs for direct materials (costumes, props, film, etc.) and direct labor (actors, directors, and extras) are charged to each film's job cost sheet. A share of the studio's overhead costs, such as utilities, depreciation of equipment, wages of maintenance workers, and so forth, is also charged to each film. However, there is considerable controversy about the methods used by some studios to distribute overhead costs among movies, and these controversies sometimes result in lawsuits. (See the accompanying In Business box.)

In sum, job-order costing is a versatile and widely used costing method that may be encountered in virtually any organization that provides diverse products or services.

IN BUSINESS

A Fair Share of Profits

"Net profit participation" contracts in which writers, actors, and directors share in the net profits of movies are common in Hollywood. For example, Winston Groom, the author of the novel *Forrest Gump,* has a contract with Paramount Pictures Corp. that calls for him to receive 3% of the net profits on the movie based on his novel. However, Paramount claims that *Forrest Gump* has yet to show any profits even though its gross receipts are among the highest of any film in history. How can this be?

Movie studios assess a variety of overhead charges including a charge of about 15% on production costs for production overhead, a charge of about 30% of gross rentals for distribution overhead, and a charge for marketing overhead that amounts to about 10% of advertising costs. After all of these overhead charges and other hotly contested accounting practices, it is a rare film that shows a profit. Fewer than 5% of released films show a profit for net profit participation purposes. Examples of "money-losing" films include *Rain Man, Batman,* and *Who Framed Roger Rabbit?* as well as *Forrest Gump.* Disgruntled writers and actors are increasingly suing studios, claiming unreasonable accounting practices that are designed to cheat them of their share of profits.

Source: Ross Engel and Bruce Ikawa, "Where's the Profit?" *Management Accounting,* January 1997, pp. 40–47.

SUMMARY

LO1 Distinguish between process costing and job-order costing and identify companies that would use each costing method.

Job-order costing and process costing are widely used to track costs. Job-order costing is used in situations where the organization offers many different products or services, such as in furniture manufacturing, hospitals, and law firms. Process costing is used where units of product are homogeneous, such as in flour milling or cement production.

LO2 Identify the documents used in a job-order costing system.

In a job-order costing system, each job has its own job cost sheet. Materials requisition forms and labor time tickets are used to record direct materials and direct labor costs. These costs, together with manufacturing overhead, are accumulated on the job cost sheet for a job.

LO3   Compute predetermined overhead rates and explain why estimated overhead costs (rather than actual overhead costs) are used in the costing process.

Manufacturing overhead costs are assigned to jobs using a predetermined overhead rate. The rate is determined at the beginning of the period so that jobs can be costed throughout the period rather than waiting until the end of the period. The predetermined overhead rate is determined by dividing the estimated total manufacturing cost for the period by the estimated total allocation base for the period.

LO4   Prepare journal entries to record costs in a job-order costing system.

Direct materials costs are debited to Work in Process when they are released for use in production. Direct labor costs are debited to Work in Process as incurred. Actual manufacturing overhead costs are debited to the Manufacturing Overhead control account as incurred. Manufacturing overhead costs are applied to Work in Process using the predetermined overhead rate. The journal entry that accomplishes this is a debit to Work in Process and a credit to the Manufacturing Overhead control account.

LO5   Apply overhead cost to work in process using a predetermined overhead rate.

Overhead is applied to jobs by multiplying the predetermined overhead rate by the actual amount of the allocation base used by the job.

LO6   Prepare schedules of cost of goods manufactured and cost of goods sold.

See Exhibit 2–11 for an example of these schedules.

LO7   Use T-accounts to show the flow of costs in a job-order costing system.

See Exhibit 2–14 for a summary of the cost flows through the T-accounts.

LO8   Compute underapplied or overapplied overhead cost and prepare the journal entry to close the balance in manufacturing overhead to the appropriate accounts.

The difference between the actual overhead cost incurred during a period and the amount of overhead cost applied to production is referred to as underapplied or overapplied overhead. Underapplied or overapplied overhead is closed out to Cost of Goods Sold. When overhead is underapplied, the balance in the Manufacturing Overhead control account is debited to Cost of Goods Sold. This has the effect of increasing the Cost of Goods Sold and occurs because costs assigned to products have been understated. When overhead is overapplied, the balance in the Manufacturing Overhead control account is credited to Cost of Goods Sold. This has the effect of decreasing the Cost of Goods Sold and occurs because costs assigned to products have been overstated.

GUIDANCE ANSWERS TO *DECISION MAKER* AND *YOU DECIDE*

Treasurer, Class Reunion Committee (p. 83)

You should charge $38.00 per person to cover the costs calculated as follows:

Meal cost	$30.00	Direct material cost
Gratuity ($30 × 0.15)	4.50	Direct labor cost
Room charge ($200 ÷ 200 expected attendees)	1.00	Overhead cost
Band cost ($500 ÷ 200 expected attendees)	2.50	Overhead cost
Total cost	$38.00	

The number of expected attendees (or estimated units in the allocation base) was used to allocate the band cost. Attendees who plan to leave immediately after dinner might object to this allocation. However, this personal choice probably should not override the decision to base the allocation on this very simple base.

   If exactly 200 classmates attend the reunion, the $7,600 of receipts (200 @ $38) will cover the expenditures of $7,600 [meal cost of $6,000 (or 200 @ $30) plus gratuity cost of $900 (or $6,000 × 0.15) plus the $200 room charge plus the $500 band cost]. Unfortunately, if less than 200 attend, the Reunion Committee will come up short in an amount equal to the difference between the 200 estimated attendees and the actual number of attendees times $3.50 (the total per person overhead charge). As such, you should talk to the members of the Reunion Committee to ensure that (1) the estimate is as reasonable as possible, and (2) there is a plan to deal with any shortage. On the other hand, if more than 200 attend, the Reunion Committee will collect more money than it needs to disburse. The amount would be equal to the difference between the actual number of attendees and the 200 estimated attendees times $3.50. Again, a plan should be in place to deal with this situation. (Perhaps the funds could be used to cover the mailing costs for the next reunion.)

Remaining Balance in the Overhead Account (p. 96)

A quick response on your part might have been that you would prefer a credit balance in the Overhead account. The entry to dispose of the balance would decrease the balance in the Cost of Goods Sold account and would cause the company's gross margin and net operating income to be higher than might have otherwise been expected. However, the impact on decision making during the period should be carefully considered.

Ideally, a controller would want the balance in the Overhead account to be zero. If there is no remaining balance in the Overhead account at the end of the period, that means that the actual overhead costs for the period (which are debited to the Overhead account) exactly equaled the overhead costs that were applied (or allocated to the products made by being added to the Work in Process account) during the period. As a result, the products made during the period would have had the "correct" amount of overhead assigned as they moved from the factory floor to the finished goods area to the customer. Typically, this would not be the case because the predetermined overhead rate (used to apply or allocate overhead to the products made) is developed using two estimates (the total amount of overhead expected and the total units in the allocation base expected during the period). It would be difficult, if not impossible, to accurately predict one or both estimates.

If there is a remaining balance in the Overhead account, then the products manufactured during the period either received too little overhead (if there is a debit or underapplied balance) or too much overhead (if there is a credit or overapplied balance).

GUIDANCE ANSWERS TO CONCEPT CHECKS

1. **Choice c.** A predetermined overhead rate rather than an actual overhead rate is used in a normal costing system.
2. **Choices a, b, and d.** The Manufacturing Overhead account is credited when manufacturing overhead is applied to Work in Process. Job cost sheets do not accumulate actual overhead costs. They accumulate the amount of the overhead that has been applied to the job using the predetermined overhead rate. Selling expenses are period costs. They are not applied to production.
3. **Choice a.** The amount of overhead applied to production is 2,000 hours multiplied by the $50 predetermined rate, or $100,000. If overhead is underapplied by $5,000, the actual amount of overhead is $100,000 + $5,000, or $105,000.

REVIEW PROBLEM: JOB-ORDER COSTING

Hogle Company is a manufacturer that uses job-order costing. On January 1, the beginning of its fiscal year, the company's inventory balances were as follows:

Raw Materials	$20,000
Work in Process	$15,000
Finished Goods	$30,000

The company applies overhead cost to jobs on the basis of machine-hours worked. For the current year, the company estimated that it would work 75,000 machine-hours and incur $450,000 in manufacturing overhead cost. The following transactions were recorded for the year:

a. Raw materials were purchased on account, $410,000.
b. Raw materials were requisitioned for use in production, $380,000 ($360,000 direct materials and $20,000 indirect materials).
c. The following costs were incurred for employee services: direct labor, $75,000; indirect labor, $110,000; sales commissions, $90,000; and administrative salaries, $200,000.
d. Sales travel costs were $17,000.
e. Utility costs in the factory were $43,000.
f. Advertising costs were $180,000.
g. Depreciation was recorded for the year, $350,000 (80% relates to factory operations, and 20% relates to selling and administrative activities).

h. Insurance expired during the year, $10,000 (70% relates to factory operations, and the remaining 30% relates to selling and administrative activities).

i. Manufacturing overhead was applied to production. Due to greater than expected demand for its products, the company worked 80,000 machine-hours during the year.

j. Goods costing $900,000 to manufacture according to their job cost sheets were completed during the year.

k. Goods were sold on account to customers during the year for a total of $1,500,000. The goods cost $870,000 to manufacture according to their job cost sheets.

Required:

1. Prepare journal entries to record the preceding transactions.
2. Post the entries in (1) above to T-accounts (don't forget to enter the beginning balances in the inventory accounts).
3. Is Manufacturing Overhead underapplied or overapplied for the year? Prepare a journal entry to close any balance in the Manufacturing Overhead account to Cost of Goods Sold.
4. Prepare an income statement for the year.

Solution to Review Problem

1. a. Raw Materials 410,000
         Accounts Payable   410,000
   b. Work in Process 360,000
         Manufacturing Overhead   20,000
         Raw Materials   380,000
   c. Work in Process   75,000
         Manufacturing Overhead 110,000
         Sales Commissions Expense   90,000
         Administrative Salaries Expense 200,000
         Salaries and Wages Payable   475,000
   d. Sales Travel Expense   17,000
         Accounts Payable   17,000
   e. Manufacturing Overhead   43,000
         Accounts Payable   43,000
   f. Advertising Expense 180,000
         Accounts Payable   180,000
   g. Manufacturing Overhead 280,000
         Depreciation Expense   70,000
         Accumulated Depreciation   350,000
   h. Manufacturing Overhead   7,000
         Insurance Expense   3,000
         Prepaid Insurance   10,000
   i. The predetermined overhead rate for the year would be computed as follows:

$$\text{Predetermined overhead rate} = \frac{\text{Estimated total manufacturing overhead cost}}{\text{Estimated total amount of the allocation base}}$$

$$= \frac{\$450,000}{75,000 \text{ machine-hours}}$$

$$= \$6 \text{ per machine-hour}$$

Based on the 80,000 machine-hours actually worked during the year, the company would have applied $480,000 in overhead cost to production: $6 per machine-hour × 80,000 machine-hours = $480,000. The following entry records this application of overhead cost:

          Work in Process 480,000
            Manufacturing Overhead   480,000
   j. Finished Goods 900,000
         Work in Process   900,000
   k. Accounts Receivable 1,500,000
         Sales   1,500,000
       Cost of Goods Sold 870,000
         Finished Goods   870,000

2.

Accounts Receivable				Manufacturing Overhead				Sales		
(k)	1,500,000			(b)	20,000	(i)	480,000			(k) 1,500,000

Accounts Receivable

(k) 1,500,000	

Prepaid Insurance

	(h) 10,000

Raw Materials

Bal. 20,000	(b) 380,000
(a) 410,000	
Bal. 50,000	

Work in Process

Bal. 15,000	(j) 900,000
(b) 360,000	
(c) 75,000	
(i) 480,000	
Bal. 30,000	

Finished Goods

Bal. 30,000	(k) 870,000
(j) 900,000	
Bal. 60,000	

Manufacturing Overhead

(b)	20,000	(i)	480,000
(c)	110,000		
(e)	43,000		
(g)	280,000		
(h)	7,000		
	460,000		480,000
		Bal. 20,000	

Accumulated Depreciation

	(g) 350,000

Accounts Payable

	(a)	410,000
	(d)	17,000
	(e)	43,000
	(f)	180,000

Salaries and Wages Payable

	(c) 475,000

Sales

	(k) 1,500,000

Cost of Goods Sold

(k) 870,000	

Commissions Expense

(c) 90,000	

Administrative Salaries Expense

(c) 200,000	

Sales Travel Expense

(d) 17,000	

Advertising Expense

(f) 180,000	

Depreciation Expense

(g) 70,000	

Insurance Expense

(h) 3,000	

3. Manufacturing overhead is overapplied for the year. The entry to close it out to Cost of Goods Sold is as follows:

Manufacturing Overhead	20,000	
Cost of Goods Sold		20,000

4.

Hogle Company
Income Statement
For the Year Ended December 31

Sales		$1,500,000
Cost of goods sold ($870,000 − $20,000)		850,000
Gross margin		650,000
Selling and administrative expenses:		
Commissions expense	$ 90,000	
Administrative salaries expense	200,000	
Sales travel expense	17,000	
Advertising expense	180,000	
Depreciation expense	70,000	
Insurance expense	3,000	560,000
Net operating income		$ 90,000

GLOSSARY

Absorption costing   A costing method that includes all manufacturing costs—direct materials, direct labor, and both variable and fixed manufacturing overhead—in the cost of a product. This term is synonymous with *full cost*. (p. 74)

Allocation base   A measure of activity such as direct labor-hours or machine-hours that is used to assign costs to cost objects. (p. 79)

Bill of materials   A document that shows the type and quantity of each major item of materials required to make a product. (p. 76)

Cost driver   A factor, such as machine-hours, beds occupied, computer time, or flight-hours, that causes overhead costs. (p. 81)

Full cost   See *Absorption costing*. (p. 74)

Job cost sheet   A form prepared for each job that records the materials, labor, and manufacturing overhead costs charged to the job. (p. 77)

Job-order costing system   A costing system used in situations where many different products, jobs, or services are produced each period. (p. 75)

Materials requisition form   A detailed source document that specifies the type and quantity of materials drawn from the storeroom and that identifies the job that is changed for the cost of those materials. (p. 77)

Multiple predetermined overhead rates   A costing system with multiple overhead cost pools with a different predetermined rate for each cost pool, rather than a single predetermined overhead rate for the entire company. Frequently, each production department is treated as a separate overhead cost pool. (p. 96)

Normal cost system   A costing system in which overhead costs are applied to jobs by multiplying a predetermined overhead rate by the actual amount of the allocation base incurred by the job. (p. 81)

Overapplied overhead   A credit balance in the Manufacturing Overhead account that occurs when the amount of overhead cost applied to Work in Process is greater than the amount of overhead cost actually incurred during a period. (p. 94)

Overhead application   The process of charging manufacturing overhead cost to job cost sheets and to the Work in Process account. (p. 79)

Plantwide overhead rate   A single predetermined overhead rate that is used throughout a plant. (p. 96)

Predetermined overhead rate   A rate used to charge overhead cost to jobs; the rate is established in advance for each period using estimates of total manufacturing overhead cost and of the total amount of the allocation base for the period. (p. 79)

Process costing system   A costing system used in situations where a single, homogeneous product (such as cement or flour) is produced for long periods of time. (p. 74)

Time ticket   A detailed source document that is used to record the amount of time an employee spends on various activities during a day. (p. 78)

Underapplied overhead   A debit balance in the Manufacturing Overhead account that arises when the amount of overhead cost actually incurred is greater than the amount of overhead cost applied to Work in Process during a period. (p. 94)

QUESTIONS

2–1   Why aren't actual overhead costs traced to jobs just as direct materials and direct labor costs are traced to jobs?

2–2   When would job-order costing be used in preference to process costing?

2–3   What is the purpose of the job cost sheet in a job-order costing system?

2–4   What is a predetermined overhead rate, and how is it computed?

2–5   Explain how a sales order, a production order, a materials requisition form, and a labor time ticket are involved in producing and costing products.

2–6   Explain why some production costs must be allocated rather than traced to products. Name several such costs. Would such costs be classified as *direct* or as *indirect* costs?

2–7   Why are predetermined overhead rates rather than actual manufacturing overhead costs used to apply manufacturing overhead to jobs?

2–8   What factors should be considered in selecting an allocation base?

2–9   If a company allocates all of its overhead costs to jobs, does this guarantee that the company will earn a profit?

2–10 What account is credited when overhead cost is applied to Work in Process? Would you expect the amount applied for a period to equal the actual overhead costs of the period? Why or why not?

2–11 What is underapplied overhead? Overapplied overhead? What disposition is made of these amounts at the end of the period?

2–12 Give two reasons why overhead might be underapplied in a given year.

2–13 What adjustment is made for underapplied overhead on the schedule of cost of goods sold? What adjustment is made for overapplied overhead?

2–14 What is a plantwide overhead rate? Why are multiple overhead rates, rather than a plantwide rate, used in some companies?

2–15 What happens to overhead rates based on direct labor when automated equipment replaces direct labor?

BRIEF EXERCISES

BRIEF EXERCISE 2–1   Process versus Job-Order Costing   (LO1)

Which method of determining product costs, job-order costing or process costing, would be more appropriate in each of the following situations?

a.   An Elmer's glue factory.
b.   A textbook publisher such as McGraw-Hill.
c.   An Exxon oil refinery.
d.   A facility that makes Minute Maid frozen orange juice.
e.   A Scott paper mill.
f.   A custom home builder.
g.   A shop that customizes vans.
h.   A manufacturer of specialty chemicals.
i.   An auto repair shop.
j.   A Firestone tire manufacturing plant.
k.   An advertising agency.
l.   A law office.

BRIEF EXERCISE 2–2   Job-Order Costing Documents   (LO2)

Cycle Gear Corporation has incurred the following costs on Job W456, an order for 20 special sprockets to be delivered at the end of next month.

> **Direct materials:**
> On April 10, requisition number 15673 was issued for 20 titanium blanks to be used in the special order. The blanks cost $15.00 each.
> On April 11, requisition number 15678 was issued for 480 hardened nibs also to be used in the special order. The nibs cost $1.25 each.
>
> **Direct labor:**
> On April 12, Jamie Unser worked from 11:00 AM until 2:45 PM on Job W456. He is paid $9.60 per hour.
> On April 18, Melissa Chan worked from 8:15 AM until 11:30 AM on Job W456. She is paid $12.20 per hour.

Required:
1. On what documents would these costs be recorded?
2. How much cost should have been recorded on each of the documents for Job W456?

BRIEF EXERCISE 2–3   Compute the Predetermined Overhead Rate   (LO3)

Harris Fabrics computes its predetermined overhead rate annually on the basis of direct labor hours. At the beginning of the year it estimated that its total manufacturing overhead would be $134,000 and the total direct labor would be 20,000 hours. Its actual total manufacturing overhead for the year was $123,900 and its actual total direct labor was 21,000 hours.

Required:
Compute the company's predetermined overhead rate for the year.

BRIEF EXERCISE 2–4   Prepare Journal Entries   (LO4)
Larned Corporation recorded the following transactions for the just completed month.

a. $80,000 in raw materials were purchased on account.
b. $71,000 in raw materials were requisitioned for use in production. Of this amount, $62,000 was for direct materials and the remainder was for indirect materials.
c.   Total labor wages of $112,000 were incurred. Of this amount, $101,000 was for direct labor and the remainder was for indirect labor.
d.   Additional manufacturing overhead costs of $175,000 were incurred.

Required:
Record the above transactions in journal entries.

BRIEF EXERCISE 2–5   Apply Overhead   (LO5)
Luthan Company uses a predetermined overhead rate of $23.40 per direct labor-hour. This predetermined rate was based on 11,000 estimated direct labor-hours and $257,400 of estimated total manufacturing overhead.
    The company incurred actual total manufacturing overhead costs of $249,000 and 10,800 total direct labor-hours during the period.

Required:
Determine the amount of manufacturing overhead that would have been applied to units of product during the period.

BRIEF EXERCISE 2-6   Prepare Schedules of Cost of Goods Manufactured and Cost of Goods Sold   (LO6)
Primare Corporation has provided the following data concerning last month's manufacturing operations.

Purchases of raw materials	$30,000
Indirect materials included in manufacturing overhead	$5,000
Direct labor	$58,000
Manufacturing overhead applied to work in process	$87,000
Underapplied overhead	$4,000

Inventories:	Beginning	Ending
Raw materials	$12,000	$18,000
Work in process	$56,000	$65,000
Finished goods	$35,000	$42,000

Required:
1. Prepare a schedule of cost of goods manufactured.
2. Prepare a schedule of cost of goods sold.

BRIEF EXERCISE 2–7   Prepare T-Accounts   (LO7)
Jurvin Enterprises recorded the following transactions for the just completed month. The company had no beginning inventories.

a. $94,000 in raw materials were purchased for cash.
b. $89,000 in raw materials were requisitioned for use in production. Of this amount, $78,000 was for direct materials and the remainder was for indirect materials.
c.   Total labor wages of $132,000 were incurred and paid. Of this amount, $112,000 was for direct labor and the remainder was for indirect labor.
d.   Additional manufacturing overhead costs of $143,000 were incurred and paid.
e.   Manufacturing overhead costs of $152,000 were applied to jobs using the company's predetermined overhead rate.
f.   All of the jobs in progress at the end of the month were completed and shipped to customers.
g.   The underapplied or overapplied overhead for the period was closed out to Cost of Goods Sold.

Required:
1. Post the above transactions to T-accounts.
2. Determine the cost of goods sold for the period.

BRIEF EXERCISE 2-8   **Underapplied and Overapplied Overhead**   (LO8)

Osborn Manufacturing uses a predetermined overhead rate of $18.20 per direct labor-hour. This predetermined rate was based on 12,000 estimated direct labor-hours and $218,400 of estimated total manufacturing overhead.

The company incurred actual total manufacturing overhead costs of $215,000 and 11,500 total direct labor-hours during the period.

Required:

1. Determine the amount of underapplied or overapplied manufacturing overhead for the period.
2. Assuming that the entire amount of the underapplied or overapplied overhead is closed out to Cost of Goods Sold, what would be the effect of the underapplied or overapplied overhead on the company's gross margin for the period?

EXERCISES

EXERCISE 2-9   **Varying Predetermined Overhead Rates**   (LO3, LO5)

Kingsport Containers, Ltd., of the Bahamas experiences wide variation in demand for the 200-liter steel drums it fabricates. The leakproof, rustproof steel drums have a variety of uses from storing liquids and bulk materials to serving as makeshift musical instruments. The drums are made to order and are painted according to the customer's specifications—often in bright patterns and designs. The company is well known for the artwork that appears on its drums. Unit product costs are computed on a quarterly basis by dividing each quarter's manufacturing costs (materials, labor, and overhead) by the quarter's production in units. The company's estimated costs, by quarter, for the coming year follow:

	Quarter			
	First	**Second**	**Third**	**Fourth**
Direct materials	$240,000	$120,000	$ 60,000	$180,000
Direct labor	128,000	64,000	32,000	96,000
Manufacturing overhead	300,000	220,000	180,000	260,000
Total manufacturing costs	$668,000	$404,000	$272,000	$536,000
Number of units to be produced	80,000	40,000	20,000	60,000
Estimated unit product cost	$8.35	$10.10	$13.60	$8.93

Management finds the variation in unit costs confusing and difficult to work with. It has been suggested that the problem lies with manufacturing overhead, since it is the largest element of cost. Accordingly, you have been asked to find a more appropriate way of assigning manufacturing overhead cost to units of product. After some analysis, you have determined that the company's overhead costs are mostly fixed and therefore show little sensitivity to changes in the level of production.

Required:

1. The company uses a job-order costing system. How would you recommend that manufacturing overhead cost be assigned to production? Be specific, and show computations.
2. Recompute the company's unit product costs in accordance with your recommendations in (1) above.

EXERCISE 2-10   **Journal Entries and T-Accounts**   (LO4, LO5, LO7)

The Polaris Company uses a job-order costing system. The following data relate to October, the first month of the company's fiscal year.

a.   Raw materials purchased on account, $210,000.
b.   Raw materials issued to production, $190,000 ($178,000 direct materials and $12,000 indirect materials).
c.   Direct labor cost incurred, $90,000; indirect labor cost incurred, $110,000.
d.   Depreciation recorded on factory equipment, $40,000.
e.   Other manufacturing overhead costs incurred during October, $70,000 (credit Accounts Payable).
f.   The company applies manufacturing overhead cost to production on the basis of $8 per machine-hour. A total of 30,000 machine-hours were recorded for October.
g.   Production orders costing $520,000 according to their job cost sheets were completed during October and transferred to Finished Goods.
h.   Production orders that had cost $480,000 to complete according to their job cost sheets were shipped to customers during the month. These goods were sold on account at 25% above cost.

Required:
1. Prepare journal entries to record the information given above.
2. Prepare T-accounts for Manufacturing Overhead and Work in Process. Post the relevant information above to each account. Compute the ending balance in each account, assuming that Work in Process has a beginning balance of $42,000.

EXERCISE 2–11 Applying Overhead; Cost of Goods Manufactured (LO5, LO6, LO8)

The following cost data relate to the manufacturing activities of Chang Company during the just completed year:

Manufacturing overhead costs incurred:	
Indirect materials	$15,000
Indirect labor	130,000
Property taxes, factory	8,000
Utilities, factory	70,000
Depreciation, factory	240,000
Insurance, factory	10,000
Total actual manufacturing overhead costs incurred	$473,000
Other costs incurred:	
Purchases of raw materials (both direct and indirect)	$400,000
Direct labor cost	$60,000
Inventories:	
Raw materials, beginning	$20,000
Raw materials, ending	$30,000
Work in process, beginning	$40,000
Work in process, ending	$70,000

The company uses a predetermined overhead rate to apply overhead cost to production. The rate for the year was $25 per machine-hour. A total of 19,400 machine-hours were recorded for the year.

Required:
1. Compute the amount of underapplied or overapplied overhead cost for the year.
2. Prepare a schedule of cost of goods manufactured for the year.

EXERCISE 2–12 Applying Overhead in a Service Company (LO2, LO3, LO5)

Leeds Architectural Consultants began operations on January 2. The following activity was recorded in the company's Work in Process account for the first month of operations:

Work in Process			
Costs of subcontracted work	230,000	To completed projects	390,000
Direct staff costs	75,000		
Studio overhead	120,000		

Leeds Architectural Consultants is a service firm, so the names of the accounts it uses are different from the names used in manufacturing companies. Costs of Subcontracted Work is comparable to Direct Materials; Direct Staff Costs is the same as Direct Labor; Studio Overhead is the same as Manufacturing Overhead; and Completed Projects is the same as Finished Goods. Apart from the difference in terms, the accounting methods used by the company are identical to the methods used by manufacturing companies.

Leeds Architectural Consultants uses a job-order costing system and applies studio overhead to Work in Process on the basis of direct staff costs. At the end of January, only one job was still in process. This job (Lexington Gardens Project) had been charged with $6,500 in direct staff costs.

Required:
1. Compute the predetermined overhead rate that was in use during January.
2. Complete the following job cost sheet for the partially completed Lexington Gardens Project.

```
┌─────────────────────────────────────────────────────────┐
│          Job Cost Sheet—Lexington Gardens Project        │
│                    As of January 31                      │
│                                                          │
│   Costs of subcontracted work  . . . . . . . . . . . . .   $ ?   │
│   Direct staff costs  . . . . . . . . . . . . . . . . . . . .      ?   │
│   Studio overhead  . . . . . . . . . . . . . . . . . . . . .      ?   │
│   Total cost to January 31  . . . . . . . . . . . . . . . .   $ ?   │
└─────────────────────────────────────────────────────────┘
```

EXERCISE 2–13   Applying Overhead; Journal Entries; T-Accounts   (LO3, LO4, LO5, LO7)
Dillon Products manufactures various machined parts to customer specifications. The company uses a job-order costing system and applies overhead cost to jobs on the basis of machine-hours. At the beginning of the year, it was estimated that the company would work 240,000 machine-hours and incur $4,800,000 in manufacturing overhead costs.

 The company spent the entire month of January working on a large order for 16,000 custom-made machined parts. The company had no work in process at the beginning of January. Cost data relating to January follow:

a. Raw materials purchased on account, $325,000.
b. Raw materials requisitioned for production, $290,000 (80% direct materials and 20% indirect materials).
c. Labor cost incurred in the factory, $180,000 (one-third direct labor and two-thirds indirect labor).
d. Depreciation recorded on factory equipment, $75,000.
e. Other manufacturing overhead costs incurred, $62,000 (credit Accounts Payable).
f. Manufacturing overhead cost was applied to production on the basis of 15,000 machine-hours actually worked during the month.
g. The completed job was moved into the finished goods warehouse on January 31 to await delivery to the customer. (In computing the dollar amount for this entry, remember that the cost of a completed job consists of direct materials, direct labor, and *applied* overhead.)

Required:
1. Prepare journal entries to record items (a) through (f) above [ignore item (g) for the moment].
2. Prepare T-accounts for Manufacturing Overhead and Work in Process. Post the relevant items from your journal entries to these T-accounts.
3. Prepare a journal entry for item (g) above.
4. Compute the unit product cost that will appear on the job cost sheet.

EXERCISE 2–14   Journal Entries; Applying Overhead   (LO4, LO7, LO8)
The following information is taken from the accounts of Latta Company. The entries in the T-accounts are summaries of the transactions that affected those accounts during the year.

```
┌──────────────────────────────────────────────────────────────────────────────────────┐
│        Manufacturing Overhead                          Work in Process                 │
│                                                                                        │
│  (a)    460,000  │ (b)   390,000          Bal.    15,000  │ (c)    710,000             │
│  Bal.    70,000  │                                260,000  │                           │
│                  │                                 85,000  │                           │
│        Finished Goods                          (b)   390,000  │                         │
│                                                Bal.    40,000  │                         │
│  Bal.    50,000  │ (d)   640,000                                                        │
│  (c)    710,000  │                                  Cost of Goods Sold                  │
│  Bal.   120,000  │                                                                      │
│                                                (d)    640,000  │                         │
└──────────────────────────────────────────────────────────────────────────────────────┘
```

Required:
1. Identify reasons for entries (a) through (d).
2. Assume that the company closes any balance in the Manufacturing Overhead account directly to Cost of Goods Sold. Prepare the necessary journal entry.

EXERCISE 2–15   Applying Overhead with Differing Bases   (LO3, LO5, LO8)

Estimated cost and operating data for three companies for the upcoming year follow:

	Company		
	X	Y	Z
Direct labor-hours	80,000	45,000	60,000
Machine-hours	30,000	70,000	21,000
Direct materials cost	$400,000	$290,000	$300,000
Manufacturing overhead cost	$536,000	$315,000	$480,000

Predetermined overhead rates are computed using the following bases in the three companies:

Company	Overhead Rate Based on—
X	Direct labor-hours
Y	Machine-hours
Z	Direct materials cost

Required:

1. Compute the predetermined overhead rate to be used in each company during the upcoming year.
2. Assume that Company X works on three jobs during the upcoming year. Direct labor-hours recorded by job are: Job 418, 12,000 hours; Job 419, 36,000 hours; Job 420, 30,000 hours. How much overhead cost will the company apply to Work in Process for the year? If actual overhead costs total $530,000 for the year, will overhead be underapplied or overapplied? By how much?

PROBLEMS

PROBLEM 2–16A   Departmental Overhead Rates   (LO2, LO3, LO5)

White Company has two departments, Cutting and Finishing. The company uses a job-order cost system and computes a predetermined overhead rate in each department. The Cutting Department bases its rate on machine-hours, and the Finishing Department bases its rate on direct labor cost. At the beginning of the year, the company made the following estimates:

CHECK FIGURE
(2) Overhead applied to Job 203: $870

	Department	
	Cutting	Finishing
Direct labor-hours	6,000	30,000
Machine-hours	48,000	5,000
Manufacturing overhead cost	$360,000	$486,000
Direct labor cost	$50,000	$270,000

Required:

1. Compute the predetermined overhead rate to be used in each department.
2. Assume that the overhead rates that you computed in (1) above are in effect. The job cost sheet for Job 203, which was started and completed during the year, showed the following:

	Department	
	Cutting	Finishing
Direct labor-hours	6	20
Machine-hours	80	4
Materials requisitioned	$500	$310
Direct labor cost	$70	$150

Compute the total overhead cost applied to Job 203.

3. Would you expect substantially different amounts of overhead cost to be assigned to some jobs if the company used a plantwide overhead rate based on direct labor cost, rather than using departmental rates? Explain. No computations are necessary.

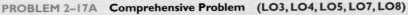

PROBLEM 2–17A   Comprehensive Problem   (LO3, LO4, LO5, LO7, LO8)

Gold Nest Company of Guandong, China, is a family-owned enterprise that makes birdcages for the South China market. A popular pastime among older Chinese men is to take their pet birds on daily excursions to teahouses and public parks where they meet with other bird owners to talk and play mahjong. A great deal of attention is lavished on these birds, and the birdcages are often elaborately constructed from exotic woods and contain porcelain feeding bowls and silver roosts. Gold Nest Company makes a broad range of birdcages that it sells through an extensive network of street vendors who receive commissions on their sales. The Chinese currency is the renminbi, which is denoted by Rmb. All of the company's transactions with customers, employees, and suppliers are conducted in cash; there is no credit.

The company uses a job-order costing system in which overhead is applied to jobs on the basis of direct labor cost. At the beginning of the year, it was estimated that the total direct labor cost for the year would be Rmb200,000 and the total manufacturing overhead cost would be Rmb330,000. At the beginning of the year, the inventory balances were as follows:

Raw materials	Rmb25,000
Work in process	Rmb10,000
Finished goods	Rmb40,000

During the year, the following transactions were completed:

a.   Raw materials purchased for cash, Rmb275,000.
b.   Raw materials requisitioned for use in production, Rmb280,000 (materials costing Rmb220,000 were charged directly to jobs; the remaining materials were indirect).
c.   Costs for employee services were incurred as follows:

Direct labor	Rmb180,000
Indirect labor	Rmb72,000
Sales commissions	Rmb63,000
Administrative salaries	Rmb90,000

d.   Rent for the year was Rmb18,000 (Rmb13,000 of this amount related to factory operations, and the remainder related to selling and administrative activities).
e.   Utility costs incurred in the factory, Rmb57,000.
f.   Advertising costs incurred, Rmb140,000.
g.   Depreciation recorded on equipment, Rmb100,000. (Rmb88,000 of this amount was on equipment used in factory operations; the remaining Rmb12,000 was on equipment used in selling and administrative activities.)
h.   Manufacturing overhead cost was applied to jobs, Rmb ___?___ .
i.   Goods that had cost Rmb675,000 to manufacture according to their job cost sheets were completed during the year.
j.   Sales for the year totaled Rmb1,250,000. The total cost to manufacture these goods according to their job cost sheets was Rmb700,000.

Required:
1. Prepare journal entries to record the transactions for the year.
2. Prepare T-accounts for inventories, Manufacturing Overhead, and Cost of Goods Sold. Post relevant data from your journal entries to these T-accounts (don't forget to enter the beginning balances in your inventory accounts). Compute an ending balance in each account.
3. Is Manufacturing Overhead underapplied or overapplied for the year? Prepare a journal entry to close any balance in the Manufacturing Overhead account to Cost of Goods Sold.
4. Prepare an income statement for the year. (Do not prepare a schedule of cost of goods manufactured; all of the information needed for the income statement is available in the journal entries and T-accounts you have prepared.)

PROBLEM 2–18A Applying Overhead in a Service Company; Journal Entries (LO4, LO5, LO8)
Vista Landscaping uses a job-order costing system to track the costs of its landscaping projects. The company provides garden design and installation services for its clients. The table below provides data concerning the three landscaping projects that were in progress during April. There was no work in process at the beginning of April.

	Project		
	Harris	Chan	James
Designer-hours	120	100	90
Direct materials cost	$4,500	$3,700	$1,400
Direct labor cost	$9,600	$8,000	$7,200

Actual overhead costs were $30,000 for April. Overhead costs are applied to projects on the basis of designer-hours since most of the overhead is related to the costs of the garden design studio. The predetermined overhead rate is $90 per designer-hour. The Harris and Chan projects were completed in April; the James project was not completed by the end of the month.

Required:
1. Compute the amount of overhead cost that would have been charged to each project during April.
2. Prepare a journal entry showing the completion of the Harris and Chan projects and the transfer of costs to the Completed Projects (i.e., Finished Goods) account.
3. What is the balance in the Work in Process account at the end of the month?
4. What is the balance in the Overhead account at the end of the month? What is this balance called?

PROBLEM 2–19A Applying Overhead: T-Accounts; Journal Entries (LO3, LO4, LO5, LO7, LO8)
Harwood Company is a manufacturer that operates a job-order costing system. Overhead costs are applied to jobs on the basis of machine-hours. At the beginning of the year, management estimated that the company would incur $192,000 in manufacturing overhead costs and work 80,000 machine-hours.

Required:
1. Compute the company's predetermined overhead rate.
2. Assume that during the year the company works only 75,000 machine-hours and incurs the following costs in the Manufacturing Overhead and Work in Process accounts:

Manufacturing Overhead		Work in Process	
(Maintenance) 21,000	?	(Direct materials) 710,000	
(Indirect materials) 8,000		(Direct labor) 90,000	
(Indirect labor) 60,000		(Overhead) ?	
(Utilities) 32,000			
(Insurance) 7,000			
(Depreciation) 56,000			

Copy the data in the T-accounts above onto your answer sheet. Compute the amount of overhead cost that would be applied to Work in Process for the year and make the entry in your T-accounts.
3. Compute the amount of underapplied or overapplied overhead for the year and show the balance in your Manufacturing Overhead T-account. Prepare a journal entry to close out the balance in this account to Cost of Goods Sold.
4. Explain why the manufacturing overhead was underapplied or overapplied for the year.

PROBLEM 2–20A Journal Entries; T-Accounts; Cost Flows (LO4, LO5, LO7, LO8)
Almeda Products, Inc., uses a job-order cost system. The company's inventory balances on April 1, the start of its fiscal year, were as follows:

Raw materials	$32,000
Work in process	$20,000
Finished goods	$48,000

During the year, the following transactions were completed:

a.   Raw materials were purchased on account, $170,000.
b.   Raw materials were issued from the storeroom for use in production, $180,000 (80% direct and 20% indirect).
c.   Employee salaries and wages were accrued as follows: direct labor, $200,000; indirect labor, $82,000; and selling and administrative salaries, $90,000.
d.   Utility costs were incurred in the factory, $65,000.
e.   Advertising costs were incurred, $100,000.
f.   Prepaid insurance expired during the year, $20,000 (90% related to factory operations, and 10% related to selling and administrative activities).
g.   Depreciation was recorded, $180,000 (85% related to factory assets, and 15% related to selling and administrative assets).
h.   Manufacturing overhead was applied to jobs at the rate of 175% of direct labor cost.
i.   Goods that cost $700,000 to manufacture according to their job cost sheets were transferred to the finished goods warehouse.
j.   Sales for the year totaled $1,000,000 and were all on account. The total cost to manufacture these goods according to their job cost sheets was $720,000.

Required:
1. Prepare journal entries to record the transactions for the year.
2. Prepare T-accounts for Raw Materials, Work in Process, Finished Goods, Manufacturing Overhead, and Cost of Goods Sold. Post the appropriate parts of your journal entries to these T-accounts. Compute the ending balance in each account. (Don't forget to enter the beginning balances in the inventory accounts.)
3. Is Manufacturing Overhead underapplied or overapplied for the year? Prepare a journal entry to close this balance to Cost of Goods Sold.
4. Prepare an income statement for the year. (Do not prepare a schedule of cost of goods manufactured; all of the information needed for the income statement is available in the journal entries and T-accounts you have prepared.)

CHECK FIGURE
(2) WIP balance: $17,300
(4) Net operating income: $18,700

PROBLEM 2–21A   T-Accounts; Applying Overhead   (LO5, LO7, LO8)
Hudson Company's trial balance as of January 1, the beginning of its fiscal year, is given below:

Cash	$ 7,000	
Accounts Receivable	18,000	
Raw Materials	9,000	
Work in Process	20,000	
Finished Goods	32,000	
Prepaid Insurance	4,000	
Plant and Equipment	210,000	
Accumulated Depreciation		$ 53,000
Accounts Payable		38,000
Capital Stock		160,000
Retained Earnings		49,000
Total	$300,000	$300,000

Hudson Company is a manufacturer that uses a job-order costing system. During the year, the following transactions took place:

a.   Raw materials purchased on account, $40,000.
b.   Raw materials were requisitioned for use in production, $38,000 (85% direct and 15% indirect).
c.   Factory utility costs incurred, $19,100.
d.   Depreciation was recorded on plant and equipment, $36,000. Three-fourths of the depreciation related to factory equipment, and the remainder related to selling and administrative equipment.
e.   Advertising expense incurred, $48,000.
f.   Costs for salaries and wages were incurred as follows:

Direct labor	$45,000
Indirect labor	$10,000
Administrative salaries	$30,000

g. Prepaid insurance expired during the year, $3,000 (80% related to factory operations, and 20% related to selling and administrative activities).

h. Miscellaneous selling and administrative expenses incurred, $9,500.

i. Manufacturing overhead was applied to production. The company applies overhead on the basis of $8 per machine-hour; 7,500 machine-hours were recorded for the year.

j. Goods that cost $140,000 to manufacture according to their job cost sheets were transferred to the finished goods warehouse.

k. Sales for the year totaled $250,000 and were all on account. The total cost to manufacture these goods according to their job cost sheets was $130,000.

l. Collections from customers during the year totaled $245,000.

m. Payments to suppliers on account during the year, $150,000; payments to employees for salaries and wages, $84,000.

Required:

1. Prepare a T-account for each account in the company's trial balance and enter the opening balances shown above.

2. Record the transactions above directly into the T-accounts. Prepare new T-accounts as needed. Key your entries to the letters (a) through (m) above. Find the ending balance in each account.

3. Is manufacturing overhead underapplied or overapplied for the year? Make an entry in the T-accounts to close any balance in the Manufacturing Overhead account to Cost of Goods Sold.

4. Prepare an income statement for the year. (Do not prepare a schedule of cost of goods manufactured; all of the information needed for the income statement is available in the T-accounts.)

PROBLEM 2–22A Multiple Departments; Applying Overhead (LO3, LO5, LO8)

High Desert Potteryworks makes a variety of pottery products that it sells to retailers such as Home Depot. The company uses a job-order costing system in which predetermined overhead rates are used to apply manufacturing overhead cost to jobs. The predetermined overhead rate in the Molding Department is based on machine-hours, and the rate in the Painting Department is based on direct labor cost. At the beginning of the year, the company's management made the following estimates:

CHECK FIGURE
(3) $78.16 per unit

	Department	
	Molding	**Painting**
Direct labor-hours	12,000	60,000
Machine-hours	70,000	8,000
Direct materials cost	$510,000	$650,000
Direct labor cost	$130,000	$420,000
Manufacturing overhead cost	$602,000	$735,000

Job 205 was started on August 1 and completed on August 10. The company's cost records show the following information concerning the job:

	Department	
	Molding	**Painting**
Direct labor-hours	30	85
Machine-hours	110	20
Materials placed into production	$470	$332
Direct labor cost	$290	$680

Required:

1. Compute the predetermined overhead rate used during the year in the Molding Department. Compute the rate used in the Painting Department.

2. Compute the total overhead cost applied to Job 205.

3. What would be the total cost recorded for Job 205? If the job contained 50 units, what would be the unit product cost?

4. At the end of the year, the records of High Desert Potteryworks revealed the following *actual* cost and operating data for all jobs worked on during the year:

	Department	
	Molding	Painting
Direct labor-hours	10,000	62,000
Machine-hours	65,000	9,000
Direct materials cost	$430,000	$680,000
Direct labor cost	$108,000	$436,000
Manufacturing overhead cost	$570,000	$750,000

What was the amount of underapplied or overapplied overhead in each department at the end of the year?

CHECK FIGURE
(2) Cost of Goods Manufactured: $1,340,000

PROBLEM 2–23A Schedule of Cost of Goods Manufactured; Overhead Analysis [LO3, LO5, LO6, LO8]

Gitano Products operates a job-order costing system and applies overhead cost to jobs on the basis of direct materials *used in production* (*not* on the basis of raw materials purchased). In computing a predetermined overhead rate at the beginning of the year, the company's estimates were: manufacturing overhead cost, $800,000; and direct materials to be used in production, $500,000. The company has provided the following data in the form of an Excel worksheet:

	A	B	C
1		Beginning	Ending
2	Raw Materials	$20,000	$80,000
3	Work in Process	$150,000	$70,000
4	Finished Goods	$260,000	$400,000
5			
6	The following actual costs were incurred during the year:		
7	Purchase of raw materials (all direct)		$510,000
8	Direct labor cost		$90,000
9	Manufacturing overhead costs:		
10	Indirect labor		$170,000
11	Property taxes		$48,000
12	Depreciation of equipment		$260,000
13	Maintenance		$95,000
14	Insurance		$7,000
15	Rent, building		$180,000

Required:
1. a. Compute the predetermined overhead rate for the year.
   b. Compute the amount of underapplied or overapplied overhead for the year.
2. Prepare a schedule of cost of goods manufactured for the year.
3. Compute the Cost of Goods Sold for the year. (Do not include any underapplied or overapplied overhead in your cost of goods sold figure.)
4. Job 215 was started and completed during the year. What price would have been charged to the customer if the job required $8,500 in direct materials and $2,700 in direct labor cost and the company priced its jobs at 25% above the job's cost according to the accounting system?
5. Direct materials made up $24,000 of the $70,000 ending Work in Process inventory balance. Supply the information missing below:

Direct materials	$24,000
Direct labor	?
Manufacturing overhead	?
Work in process inventory	$70,000

PROBLEM 2–24A **Cost Flows; T-Accounts; Income Statement (LO3, LO5, LO7, LO8)**
Supreme Videos, Inc., produces short musical videos for sale to retail outlets. The company's balance sheet accounts as of January 1, the beginning of its fiscal year, are given below.

CHECK FIGURE
(3) Overapplied by $9,400
(4) Net operating income: $78,400

Supreme Videos, Inc.
Balance Sheet
January 1
Assets

Current assets:		
Cash		$ 63,000
Accounts receivable		102,000
Inventories:		
Raw materials (film, costumes)	$ 30,000	
Videos in process	45,000	
Finished videos awaiting sale	81,000	156,000
Prepaid insurance		9,000
Total current assets		330,000
Studio and equipment	730,000	
Less accumulated depreciation	210,000	520,000
Total assets		$850,000

Liabilities and Stockholders' Equity

Accounts payable		$160,000
Capital stock	$420,000	
Retained earnings	270,000	690,000
Total liabilities and stockholders' equity		$850,000

Since the videos differ in length and in complexity of production, the company uses a job-order costing system to determine the cost of each video produced. Studio (manufacturing) overhead is charged to videos on the basis of camera-hours of activity. At the beginning of the year, the company estimated that it would work 7,000 camera-hours and incur $280,000 in studio overhead cost. The following transactions were recorded for the year:

a. Film, costumes, and similar raw materials purchased on account, $185,000.
b. Film, costumes, and other raw materials issued to production, $200,000 (85% of this material was considered direct to the videos in production, and the other 15% was considered indirect).
c. Utility costs incurred in the production studio, $72,000.
d. Depreciation recorded on the studio, cameras, and other equipment, $84,000. Three-fourths of this depreciation related to actual production of the videos, and the remainder related to equipment used in marketing and administration.
e. Advertising expense incurred, $130,000.
f. Costs for salaries and wages were incurred as follows:

Direct labor (actors and directors)	$82,000
Indirect labor (carpenters to build sets, costume designers, and so forth)	$110,000
Administrative salaries	$95,000

g. Prepaid insurance expired during the year, $7,000 (80% related to production of videos, and 20% related to marketing and administrative activities).
h. Miscellaneous marketing and administrative expenses incurred, $8,600.
i. Studio (manufacturing) overhead was applied to videos in production. The company recorded 7,250 camera-hours of activity during the year.

    j.   Videos that cost $550,000 to produce according to their job cost sheets were transferred to the finished videos warehouse to await sale and shipment.

    k.   Sales for the year totaled $925,000 and were all on account. The total cost to produce these videos according to their job cost sheets was $600,000.

    l.   Collections from customers during the year totaled $850,000.

    m. Payments to suppliers on account during the year, $500,000; payments to employees for salaries and wages, $285,000.

Required:

1. Prepare a T-account for each account on the company's balance sheet and enter the beginning balances.
2. Record the transactions directly into the T-accounts. Prepare new T-accounts as needed. Key your entries to the letters (a) through (m) above. Find the ending balance in each account.
3. Is the Studio (manufacturing) Overhead account underapplied or overapplied for the year? Make an entry in the T-accounts to close any balance in the Studio Overhead account to Cost of Goods Sold.
4. Prepare an income statement for the year. (Do not prepare a schedule of cost of goods manufactured; all of the information needed for the income statement is available in the T-accounts.)

CHECK FIGURE
(3) Indirect labor: $30,000
(7) Overapplied: $10,000

PROBLEM 2–25A   T-Account Analysis of Cost Flows   (LO3, LO6, LO8)

Selected ledger accounts of Moore Company are given below for the just completed year:

Raw Materials				Manufacturing Overhead			
Bal. 1/1	15,000	Credits	?	Debits	230,000	Credits	?
Debits	120,000						
Bal. 12/31	25,000						

Work in Process				Factory Wages Payable			
Bal. 1/1	20,000	Credits	470,000	Debits	185,000	Bal. 1/1	9,000
Direct						Credits	180,000
materials	90,000						
Direct labor	150,000					Bal. 12/31	4,000
Overhead	240,000						
Bal. 12/31	?						

Finished Goods				Cost of Goods Sold			
Bal. 1/1	40,000	Credits	?	Debits	?		
Debits	?						
Bal. 12/31	60,000						

Required:

1. What was the cost of raw materials put into production during the year?
2. How much of the materials in (1) above consisted of indirect materials?
3. How much of the factory labor cost for the year consisted of indirect labor?
4. What was the cost of goods manufactured for the year?
5. What was the cost of goods sold for the year (before considering underapplied or overapplied overhead)?
6. If overhead is applied to production on the basis of direct labor cost, what rate was in effect during the year?
7. Was manufacturing overhead underapplied or overapplied? By how much?

8. Compute the ending balance in the Work in Process inventory account. Assume that this balance consists entirely of goods started during the year. If $8,000 of this balance is direct labor cost, how much of it is direct materials cost? Manufacturing overhead cost?

BUILDING YOUR SKILLS

Communicating In Practice (LO1, LO3, LO5)

Look in the yellow pages or contact your local chamber of commerce or local chapter of the Institute of Certified Management Accountants to find the names of manufacturing companies in your area. Call or make an appointment to meet with the controller or chief financial officer of one of these companies.

Required:

Ask the following questions and write a brief memorandum to your instructor that addresses what you found out.

1. What are the company's main products?
2. Does the company use job-order costing, process costing, or some other method of determining product costs?
3. How is overhead assigned to products? What is the overhead rate? What is the basis of allocation? Is more than one overhead rate used?
4. Has the company recently changed its cost system or is it considering changing its cost system? If so, why? What changes were made or what changes are being considered?

Ethics Challenge (LO3, LO5, LO8)

Terri Ronsin had recently been transferred to the Home Security Systems Division of National Home Products. Shortly after taking over her new position as divisional controller, she was asked to develop the division's predetermined overhead rate for the upcoming year. The accuracy of the rate is of some importance, since it is used throughout the year and any overapplied or underapplied overhead is closed out to Cost of Goods Sold at the end of the year. National Home Products uses direct labor-hours in all of its divisions as the allocation base for manufacturing overhead.

To compute the predetermined overhead rate, Terri divided her estimate of the total manufacturing overhead for the coming year by the production manager's estimate of the total direct labor-hours for the coming year. She took her computations to the division's general manager for approval but was quite surprised when he suggested a modification in the base. Her conversation with the general manager of the Home Security Systems Division, Harry Irving, went like this:

Ronsin: Here are my calculations for next year's predetermined overhead rate. If you approve, we can enter the rate into the computer on January 1 and be up and running in the job-order costing system right away this year.

Irving: Thanks for coming up with the calculations so quickly, and they look just fine. There is, however, one slight modification I would like to see. Your estimate of the total direct labor-hours for the year is 440,000 hours. How about cutting that to about 420,000 hours?

Ronsin: I don't know if I can do that. The production manager says she will need about 440,000 direct labor-hours to meet the sales projections for the year. Besides, there are going to be over 430,000 direct labor-hours during the current year and sales are projected to be higher next year.

Irving: Teri, I know all of that. I would still like to reduce the direct labor-hours in the base to something like 420,000 hours. You probably don't know that I had an agreement with your predecessor as divisional controller to shave 5% or so off the estimated direct labor-hours every year. That way, we kept a reserve that usually resulted in a big boost to net operating income at the end of the fiscal year in December. We called it our Christmas bonus. Corporate headquarters always seemed as pleased as punch that we could pull off such a miracle at the end of the year. This system has worked well for many years, and I don't want to change it now.

Required:

1. Explain how shaving 5% off the estimated direct labor-hours in the base for the predetermined overhead rate usually results in a big boost in net operating income at the end of the fiscal year.
2. Should Terri Ronsin go along with the general manager's request to reduce the direct labor-hours in the predetermined overhead rate computation to 420,000 direct labor-hours?

Teamwork in Action   (LO3, LO4, LO5, LO7, LO8)

In an attempt to conceal a theft of funds, Snake N. Grass, controller of Bucolic Products, Inc., placed a bomb in the company's record vault. The ensuing explosion left only fragments of the company's factory ledger, as shown below:

Raw Materials		Manufacturing Overhead	
Bal. 6/1 8,000		Actual costs for June 79,000	
			Overapplied overhead 6,100
Work in Process		**Accounts Payable**	
Bal. 6/1 7,200			Bal. 6/30 16,000
Finished Goods		**Cost of Goods Sold**	
Bal. 6/30 21,000			

To bring Mr. Grass to justice, the company must reconstruct its activities for June. Your team has been assigned to perform the task of reconstruction. After interviewing selected employees and sifting through charred fragments, you have determined the following additional information:

a. According to the company's treasurer, the accounts payable are for purchases of raw materials only. The company's balance sheet, dated May 31, shows that Accounts Payable had a $20,000 balance at the beginning of June. The company's bank has provided photocopies of all checks that cleared the bank during June. These photocopies show that payments to suppliers during June totaled $119,000. (All materials used during the month were direct materials.)

b. The production superintendent states that manufacturing overhead cost is applied to jobs on the basis of direct labor-hours. However, he does not remember the rate currently being used by the company.

c. Cost sheets kept in the production superintendent's office show that only one job was in process on June 30, at the time of the explosion. The job had been charged with $6,600 in materials, and 500 direct labor-hours at $8 per hour had been worked on the job.

d. A log is kept in the finished goods warehouse showing all goods transferred in from the factory. This log shows that the cost of goods transferred into the finished goods warehouse from the factory during June totaled $280,000.

e. The company's May 31 balance sheet indicates that the finished goods inventory totaled $36,000 at the beginning of June.

f. A charred piece of the payroll ledger, found after sifting through piles of smoking debris, indicates that 11,500 direct labor-hours were recorded for June. The company's Personnel Department has verified that, as a result of a union contract, all factory employees earn the same $8 per hour rate.

g. The production superintendent states that there was no under- or overapplied overhead in the Manufacturing Overhead account at May 31.

Required:
1. Assign one of the following sets of accounts to each member of the team:
    a. Raw Materials and Accounts Payable.
    b. Work in Process and Manufacturing Overhead.
    c. Finished Goods and Cost of Goods Sold.

Determine the types of transactions that would be posted to each account and present a summary to the other team members. When agreement is reached, the team should work together to complete steps 2 through 4.

2. Determine the company's predetermined overhead rate and the total manufacturing overhead applied for the month.
3. Determine the June 30 balance in the company's Work in Process account.
4. Prepare the company's T-accounts for the month. (It is easiest to complete the T-accounts in the following order: Accounts Payable, Work in Process, Raw Materials, Manufacturing Overhead, Finished Goods, Cost of Goods Sold.)

Analytical Thinking   (LO3, LO5)

Kelvin Aerospace, Inc., manufactures parts such as rudder hinges for the aerospace industry. The company uses a job-order costing system with a plantwide predetermined overhead rate based on direct labor-hours. On December 16, 2005, the company's controller made a preliminary estimate of the predetermined overhead rate for the year 2006. The new rate was based on the estimated total manufacturing overhead cost of $3,402,000 and the estimated 63,000 total direct labor-hours for 2006:

$$\text{Predetermined overhead rate} = \frac{\$3,402,000}{63,000 \text{ direct labor-hours}}$$

$$= \$54 \text{ per direct labor-hour}$$

This new predetermined overhead rate was communicated to top managers in a meeting on December 19. The rate did not cause any comment because it was within a few pennies of the overhead rate that had been used during 2005. One of the subjects discussed at the meeting was a proposal by the production manager to purchase an automated milling machine built by Sunghi Industries. The president of Kelvin Aerospace, Harry Arcany, agreed to meet with the sales representative from Sunghi Industries to discuss the proposal.

On the day following the meeting, Mr. Arcany met with Jasmine Chang, Sunghi Industries' sales representative. The following discussion took place:

Arcany: Wally, our production manager, asked me to meet with you since he is interested in installing an automated milling machine. Frankly, I'm skeptical. You're going to have to show me this isn't just another expensive toy for Wally's people to play with.

Chang: This is a great machine with direct bottom-line benefits. The automated milling machine has three major advantages. First, it is much faster than the manual methods you are using. It can process about twice as many parts per hour as your present milling machines. Second, it is much more flexible. There are some up-front programming costs, but once those have been incurred, almost no setup is required to run a standard operation. You just punch in the code for the standard operation, load the machine's hopper with raw material, and the machine does the rest.

Arcany: What about cost? Having twice the capacity in the milling machine area won't do us much good. That center is idle much of the time anyway.

Chang: I was getting there. The third advantage of the automated milling machine is lower cost. Wally and I looked over your present operations, and we estimated that the automated equipment would eliminate the need for about 6,000 direct labor-hours a year. What is your direct labor cost per hour?

Arcany: The wage rate in the milling area averages about $32 per hour. Fringe benefits raise that figure to about $41 per hour.

Chang: Don't forget your overhead.

Arcany: Next year the overhead rate will be $54 per hour.

Chang: So including fringe benefits and overhead, the cost per direct labor-hour is about $95.

Arcany: That's right.

Chang: Since you can save 6,000 direct labor-hours per year, the cost savings would amount to about $570,000 a year. And our 60-month lease plan would require payments of only $348,000 per year.

Arcany: That sounds like a no-brainer. When can you install the equipment?

Shortly after this meeting, Mr. Arcany informed the company's controller of the decision to lease the new equipment, which would be installed over the Christmas vacation period. The controller realized that this decision would require a recomputation of the predetermined overhead rate for the year 2006 since the decision would affect both the manufacturing overhead and the direct labor-hours for the year. After talking with both the production manager and the sales representative from Sunghi Industries, the controller discovered that in addition to the annual lease cost of $348,000, the new machine would also require a skilled technician/programmer who would have to be hired at a cost of $50,000 per year to maintain and program the equipment. Both of these costs would be included in factory overhead. There would be no other changes in total manufacturing overhead cost, which is almost entirely fixed. The controller assumed that the new machine would result in a reduction of 6,000 direct labor-hours for the year from the levels that had initially been planned.

When the revised predetermined overhead rate for the year 2006 was circulated among the company's top managers, there was considerable dismay.

Required:
1. Recompute the predetermined rate assuming that the new machine will be installed. Explain why the new predetermined overhead rate is higher (or lower) than the rate that was originally estimated for the year 2006.
2. What effect (if any) would this new rate have on the cost of jobs that do not use the new automated milling machine?
3. Why would managers be concerned about the new overhead rate?
4. After seeing the new predetermined overhead rate, the production manager admitted that he probably wouldn't be able to eliminate all of the 6,000 direct labor-hours. He had been hoping to accomplish the reduction by not replacing workers who retire or quit, but that had not been possible. As a result, the real labor savings would be only about 2,000 hours—one worker. Given this additional information, evaluate the original decision to acquire the automated milling machine from Sunghi Industries.

Taking It To The Net
As you know, the World Wide Web is a medium that is constantly evolving. Sites come and go and change without notice. To enable periodic updating of site addresses, these problems have been posted to the textbook website (www.mhhe.com/bgn3e). After accessing the site, enter the Student Center and select this chapter to find the Taking It to the Net problems.

3

Systems Design: Activity-Based Costing

CHAPTER OUTLINE

A LOOK BACK

Chapter 2 provided an overview of job-order costing. Direct materials and direct labor costs are traced directly to jobs. Manufacturing overhead is applied to jobs using a predetermined overhead rate.

A LOOK AT THIS CHAPTER

In Chapter 3, we continue the discussion of allocation of overhead. Activity-based costing is a technique that uses a number of allocation bases to assign overhead costs to products.

A LOOK AHEAD

After comparing job-order and process costing systems, we provide an overview of a process costing system in Chapter 4.

Chapter Three

DECISION FEATURE

The Payoff from Activity-Based Costing

Implementing an activity-based costing system can be expensive. To be worthwhile, the data supplied by the system must actually be used to make decisions and improve profitability. Insteel Industries manufactures a range of products, such as concrete reinforcing steel, industrial wire, and bulk nails, for the construction, home furnishings, appliance, and tire manufacturing industries. The company implemented an activity-based costing system at its manufacturing plant in Andrews, South Carolina, and immediately began using activity-based data to make strategic and operating decisions.

In terms of strategic decisions, Insteel dropped some unprofitable products, raised prices on others, and in some cases even discontinued relationships with unprofitable customers. Of course, Insteel realized that simply discontinuing products and customers does not improve profits. The company needed to either deploy its freed-up capacity to increase sales, or it needed to eliminate its freed-up capacity to reduce costs. Insteel chose the former and used its activity-based costing system to identify which new business opportunities to pursue.

In terms of operational improvements, Insteel's activity-based costing system revealed that its 20 most expensive activities consumed 87% of the plant's $21.4 million in physical and human resource costs. Almost $4.9 million was being consumed by non-value-added activities. Teams were formed to reduce quality costs, material handling and freight costs, and maintenance costs. Within one year, quality costs had been cut by $1,800,000 and freight costs by $550,000. Overall, non-value-added activity costs dropped from 22% to 17% of total activity costs.

Source: V. G. Narayanan and R. Sarkar, "The Impact of Activity-Based Costing on Managerial Decisions at Insteel Industries—A Field Study," *Journal of Economics & Management Strategy,* Summer 2002, pp. 257–288.

As discussed in earlier chapters, direct materials and direct labor costs can be directly traced to products. Overhead costs, on the other hand, cannot be easily traced to products and some other means must be found for assigning them to products for financial reporting and other purposes. In the previous chapter, overhead costs were assigned to products using a plantwide predetermined overhead rate. This method is simpler than the methods of assigning overhead costs to products described in this chapter, but this simplicity has a cost. A plantwide predetermined overhead rate spreads overhead costs uniformly over products in proportion to whatever allocation base is used—most commonly, direct labor-hours. This procedure results in high overhead costs for products with a high direct labor-hour content and low overhead costs for products with a low direct labor-hour content. However, the real causes of overhead may have little to do with direct labor-hours and as a consequence, product costs may be distorted. Activity-based costing attempts to correct these distortions by more accurately assigning overhead costs to products.

ASSIGNING OVERHEAD COSTS TO PRODUCTS

Companies use three common approaches to assign overhead costs to products. The simplest method is to use a plantwide overhead rate. A slightly more refined approach is to use departmental overhead rates. The most complex method is activity-based costing, which is the most accurate of the three approaches to overhead cost assignment.

Plantwide Overhead Rate

The preceding chapter assumed that a single overhead rate, called a *plantwide overhead rate,* was used throughout an entire factory. This simple approach to overhead assignment can result in distorted unit product costs, as we shall see below.

When cost systems were developed in the 1800s, cost and activity data had to be collected by hand and all calculations were done with paper and pen. Consequently, the emphasis was on simplicity. Companies often established a single overhead cost pool for an entire facility or department as described in Chapter 2. Direct labor was the obvious choice as an allocation base for overhead costs. Direct labor-hours were already being recorded for purposes of determining wages and direct labor time spent on tasks was often closely monitored. In the labor-intensive production processes of that time, direct labor was a large component of product costs—larger than it is today. Moreover, managers believed direct labor and overhead costs were highly correlated. (Two variables, such as direct labor and overhead costs, are highly correlated if they tend to move together.) And finally, most companies produced a very limited variety of similar products, so in fact there was probably little difference in the overhead costs attributable to different products. Under these conditions, it was not cost-effective to use a more elaborate costing system.

Conditions have changed. Many companies now sell a large variety of products that consume significantly different amounts of overhead resources. Consequently, a costing system that assigns essentially the same overhead cost to every product may no longer be adequate. Additionally, factors other than direct labor often drive overhead costs.

On an economywide basis, direct labor and overhead costs have been moving in opposite directions for a long time. As a percentage of total cost, direct labor has been declining, whereas overhead has been increasing.[1] Many tasks previously done by hand are now done with largely automated equipment—a component of overhead. Furthermore, product diversity has increased. Companies are introducing new products and

---

[1]Germain Böer provides some data concerning these trends in "Five Modern Management Accounting Myths," *Management Accounting*, January 1994, pp. 22–27. Since 1849, on average, material cost has been fairly constant at 55% of sales. Labor cost has always been less important than direct materials and has declined steadily from 23% of sales in 1849 to about 10% in 1987. Overhead has grown from about 18% of sales to about 33% of sales over the last 50 years.

services at an ever-accelerating rate. Managing and sustaining this product diversity requires many more overhead resources such as production schedulers and product design engineers, and many of these overhead resources have no obvious connection with direct labor. Finally, computers, bar code readers, and other technology have dramatically reduced the costs of collecting and processing data—making more complex (and accurate) costing systems such as activity-based costing much less expensive to build and maintain.

Nevertheless, direct labor remains a viable base for applying overhead to products in some companies—particularly for external reports. Direct labor is an appropriate allocation base for overhead when overhead costs and direct labor are highly correlated. And indeed, most companies throughout the world continue to base overhead allocations on direct labor or machine-hours. However, if factorywide overhead costs do not move in tandem with factorywide direct labor or machine-hours, some other means of assigning overhead costs must be found or product costs will be distorted.

Departmental Overhead Rates

Rather than use a plantwide overhead rate, many companies use departmental overhead rates. The nature of the work performed in a department will determine the department's allocation base. For example, overhead costs in a machining department may be allocated on the basis of machine-hours. In contrast, the overhead costs in an assembly department may be allocated on the basis of direct labor-hours.

Unfortunately, even departmental overhead rates will not correctly assign overhead costs in situations where a company has a range of products and complex overhead costs. The reason is that the departmental approach usually relies on volume as the base for allocating overhead cost to products. For example, if the machining department's overhead is applied to products on the basis of machine-hours, it is assumed that the department's overhead costs are caused by, and are directly proportional to, machine-hours. However, the department's overhead costs are probably more complex than this and are caused by a variety of factors, including the range of products processed in the department, the number of batch setups that are required, the complexity of the products, and so on. A more sophisticated method like *activity-based costing* is required to adequately account for these diverse factors.

ABC Changes the Focus

Euclid Engineering makes parts and components for the big automobile manufacturers. As a result of an ABC study, Euclid's managers "discovered that the company was spending more in launching new products than on direct labor expenses to produce existing products. Product development and launch expenses were 10% of expenses, whereas direct labor costs were only 9%. Of course, in the previous direct labor cost system, all attention had been focused on reducing direct labor costs . . . Product development and launch costs were blended into the factory overhead rate applied to products based on direct labor cost. Now Euclid's managers realized that they had a major cost reduction opportunity by attacking the product launch cost directly."

The new information produced by the ABC study also helped Euclid in its relations with customers. The detailed breakdown of the costs of design and engineering activities helped customers to make trade-offs, with the result that they would often ask that certain activities whose costs exceeded their benefits be skipped.

Source: Robert S. Kaplan and Robin Cooper, *Cost & Effect: Using Integrated Cost Systems to Drive Profitability and Performance* (Boston: Harvard Business School Press, 1998), pp. 219–222.

Activity-Based Costing (ABC)

Activity-based costing (ABC) is a technique that attempts to assign overhead costs more accurately to products than the simpler methods discussed thus far. The basic idea underlying the activity-based costing approach is illustrated in Exhibit 3–1. A customer order

Concept 3-1

EXHIBIT 3–1 The Activity-Based Costing Model

Cost Objects

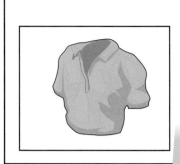  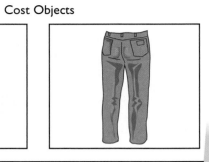 

Customer Orders Require:

Activities

| Scheduling | Sewing | Inspection | Shipping |

Activities Consume:

Resources

 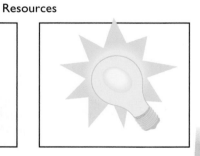 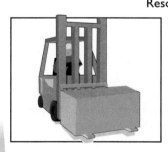 

| Labor | Equipment | Energy | Supplies |

Consumption of Resources Incur:

Costs

Account Title	Dr.	Cr.
Salary Expense	XX	
Depreciation	XX	

Account Title	Dr.	Cr.
Utilities Expense	XX	
Supplies Expense	XX	

triggers a number of activities. For example, if Nordstrom orders a line of women's skirts from Calvin Klein, a production order is generated, patterns are created, materials are ordered, textiles are cut to pattern and then sewn, and the finished products are packed for shipping. These activities consume resources. For example, ordering the appropriate materials consumes clerical time—a resource the company must pay for. In activity-based costing, an attempt is made to trace these costs directly to the products that cause them.

Rather than a single allocation base such as direct labor-hours or machine-hours, in activity-based costing a company uses a number of allocation bases for assigning costs to products. Each allocation base in an activity-based costing system represents a major *activity* that causes overhead costs. An **activity** in activity-based costing is an event that causes the consumption of overhead resources. Examples of activities in various organizations include the following:

- Setting up machines.
- Admitting patients to a hospital.
- Scheduling production.
- Performing blood tests at a clinic.
- Billing customers.
- Maintaining equipment.
- Ordering materials or supplies.
- Stocking shelves at a store.
- Meeting with clients at a law firm.
- Preparing shipments.
- Inspecting materials for defects.
- Opening an account at a bank.

Activity-based costing focuses on these activities. Each major activity has its own overhead cost pool (also known as an *activity cost pool*), its own *activity measure*, and its own predetermined overhead rate (also known as an *activity rate*). An **activity cost pool** is a "cost bucket" in which costs related to a particular activity measure are accumulated. The **activity measure** expresses how much of the activity is carried out and it is used as the allocation base for applying overhead costs to products and services. For example, *the number of patients admitted* is a natural choice of an activity measure for the activity *admitting patients to the hospital.* An **activity rate** is a predetermined overhead rate in an activity-based costing system. Each activity has its own activity rate that is used to apply overhead costs to cost objects.

Shedding Light on Product Profitability

Reichhold, Inc., one of the world's leading suppliers of synthetic materials, adopted activity-based costing to help shed light on the profitability of its various products. Reichhold's prior cost system used one allocation base, reactor hours, to assign overhead costs to products. The ABC system uses four additional activity measures—preprocess preparation hours, thin-tank hours, filtration hours, and waste disposal costs per batch—to assign costs to products. Reichhold has rolled out ABC to all 19 of its North American plants because the management team believes that ABC helps improve the company's "capacity management, cycle times, value-added pricing decisions, and analysis of product profitability."

Source: Edward Blocher, Betty Wong, and Christopher McKittrick, "Making Bottom-Up ABC Work at Reichhold, Inc.," *Strategic Finance*, April 2002, pp. 51–55.

For example, the activity *setting up machines to process a batch* would have its own activity cost pool. Products are ordinarily processed in batches. And since each product has its own machine settings, machines must be set up when changing over from a batch of one product to another. If the total cost in this activity cost pool is $150,000 and the total expected activity is 1,000 machine setups, the predetermined overhead rate (i.e., activity rate) for this activity would be $150 per machine setup ($150,000 ÷ 1,000 machine setups = $150 per machine setup). Each product that requires a machine setup would be charged $150. Note that this charge does not depend on how many units are produced after the machine is set up. A small batch requiring a machine setup would be charged $150—just the same as a large batch.

Taking each activity in isolation, this system works exactly like the job-order costing system described in the last chapter. A predetermined overhead rate is computed for each activity and then applied to jobs and products based on the amount of activity consumed by the job or product.

IN BUSINESS

Is E-Tailing Really Easier?

The company art.com™ sells prints and framed prints over the web. An ABC study identified the following 12 activities carried out in the company:

1. Service customers
2. Website optimization
3. Merchandise inventory selection and management
4. Purchasing and receiving
5. Customer acquisition and retention—paid-for marketing
6. Customer acquisition and retention—revenue share marketing (affiliate group)
7. Sustain information system
8. Sustain business—administration
9. Sustain business—production
10. Maintain facility—administrative
11. Maintain facility—production
12. Sustain business—executive

For example, the activity "merchandise inventory selection and management" involves scanning, describing, classifying, and linking each inventory item to search options. "Staff must carefully manage each change to the database, which is similar to adding and removing inventory items from the shelf of a store. They annotate added inventory items and upload them into the system, as well as remove obsolete and discontinued items . . . The number of inventory items for an e-tailer is typically much greater than for a brick-and-mortar [store], which is a competitive advantage, but experience shows managing a large inventory consumes substantial resources."

Source: Thomas L. Zeller, David R. Kublank, and Philip G. Makris, "How art.com™ Uses ABC to Succeed," *Strategic Finance*, March 2001, pp. 25–31. Reprinted with permission from the IMA, Montvale, NJ, USA, www.imanet.org.

DESIGNING AN ACTIVITY-BASED COSTING SYSTEM

The most important decisions in designing an activity-based costing system concern what activities will be included in the system and how the activities will be measured. In most companies, hundreds or even thousands of different activities cause overhead costs. These activities range from taking a telephone order to training new employees. Setting up and maintaining a complex costing system that includes all of these activities would be prohibitively expensive. The challenge in designing an activity-based costing system is to identify a reasonably small number of activities that explain the bulk of the variation in overhead costs. This is usually done by interviewing a broad range of managers in the organization to find out what activities they think are important and that consume most of the resources they manage. This often results in a long list of potential activities that could be included in the activity-based costing system. This list is refined and pruned in consultation with top managers. Related activities are frequently combined to reduce the amount of detail and record-keeping cost. For example, several actions may be involved in handling and moving raw materials, but these may be combined into a single activity titled *material handling*. The end result of this stage of the design process is an *activity dictionary* that defines each of the activities that will be included in the activity-based costing system and how the activities will be measured.

Some of the activities commonly found in activity-based costing systems in manufacturing companies are listed in Exhibit 3–2. In the exhibit, activities have been grouped into a four-level hierarchy: *unit-level activities, batch-level activities, product-level activities,* and *facility-level activities.* This cost hierarchy is useful in understanding the difference between activity-based costing and conventional approaches. It also serves as a guide when simplifying an activity-based costing system. In general, activities and costs should be combined in the activity-based costing system only if they fall within the same level in the cost hierarchy.

Hierarchy of Activities

Unit-level activities are performed each time a unit is produced. The costs of unit-level activities should be proportional to the number of units produced. For example, providing power to run processing equipment would be a unit-level activity since power tends to be consumed in proportion to the number of units produced.

Batch-level activities consist of tasks that are performed each time a batch is processed, such as processing purchase orders, setting up equipment, packing shipments to customers, and handling material. Costs at the batch level depend on *the number of batches processed* rather than on the number of units produced. For example, the cost of processing a purchase order is the same no matter how many units of an item are ordered. Furthermore, the total cost of processing purchase orders is a function of the *number* of orders placed rather than the total number of units ordered.

Product-level activities (sometimes called *product-sustaining activities*) relate to specific products and typically must be carried out regardless of how many batches or units of the product are manufactured. Product-level activities include maintaining inventories of parts for a product, issuing engineering change notices to modify a product to meet a customer's specifications, and developing special test routines when a product is first placed into production.

Facility-level activities (also called *organization-sustaining activities*) are activities that are carried out regardless of which products are produced, how many batches are run,

Level	Activities	Activity Measures
Unit-level	Processing units on machines	Machine-hours
	Processing units by hand	Direct labor-hours
	Consuming factory supplies	Units produced
Batch-level	Processing purchase orders	Purchase orders processed
	Processing production orders	Production orders processed
	Setting up equipment	Number of setups; setup hours
	Handling material	Pounds of material handled; number of times material moved
Product-level	Testing new products	Hours of testing time
	Administering parts inventories	Number of part types
	Designing products	Hours of design time
Facility-level	General factory administration	Direct labor-hours*
	Plant building and grounds	Direct labor-hours*

*Facility-level costs cannot be traced on a cause-and-effect basis to individual products. Nevertheless, these costs are usually allocated to products for external reports using some arbitrary allocation basis such as direct labor-hours.

EXHIBIT 3–2

Examples of Activities and Activity Measures in Manufacturing Companies

or how many units are made. Facility-level costs include items such as factory management salaries, insurance, property taxes, and building depreciation. The costs of facility-level activities must be allocated to products for external financial reports. This is usually accomplished by combining all facility-level costs into a single cost pool and allocating those costs to products using an arbitrary allocation base such as direct labor-hours. However, as we will see later in the book, allocating such costs to products results in misleading data that can lead to bad decisions.

IN BUSINESS

Dining in the Canyon

Western River Expeditions (www.westernriver.com) runs river rafting trips on the Colorado, Green, and Salmon rivers. One of its most popular trips is a six-day trip down the Grand Canyon, which features famous rapids such as Crystal and Lava Falls as well as the awesome scenery accessible only from the bottom of the Grand Canyon. The company runs trips of one or two rafts, each of which carries two guides and up to 18 guests. The company provides all meals on the trip, which are prepared by the guides.

In terms of the hierarchy of activities, a guest can be considered as a unit and a raft as a batch. In that context, the wages paid to the guides are a batch-level cost since each raft requires two guides regardless of the number of guests in the raft. Each guest is given a mug to use during the trip and to take home at the end of the trip as a souvenir. The cost of the mug is a unit-level cost since the number of mugs given away is strictly proportional to the number of guests on a trip.

What about the costs of food served to guests and guides—is this a unit-level cost, a batch-level cost, a product-level cost, or an organization-sustaining cost? At first glance, it might be thought that food costs are a unit-level cost—the greater the number of guests, the higher the food costs. However, that is not quite correct. Standard menus have been created for each day of the trip. For example, the appetizer on the first night's menu might specify shrimp cocktail, steak, cornbread, salad, and cheesecake. The day before a trip begins, all of the food needed for the trip is taken from the central warehouse and packed in modular containers. It isn't practical to finely adjust the amount of food for the actual number of guests planned to be on a trip—most of the food comes prepackaged in large lots. For example, the shrimp cocktail menu may call for two large bags of frozen shrimp per raft and that many bags will be packed regardless of how many guests are expected on the raft. Consequently, the costs of food are not a unit-level cost that varies with the number of guests actually on a trip. Instead, the costs of food are a batch-level cost.

Source: Conversations with Western River Expeditions personnel.

An Example of an Activity-Based Costing System Design

The complexity of an activity-based costing system will differ from company to company. For some companies, the structure of their activity-based costing system will be simple with only one or two activity cost pools at the unit, batch, and product levels. For other companies, the structure will be much more complex.

Under activity-based costing, the manufacturing overhead costs at the top of Exhibit 3–3 are allocated to products via a two-stage process. In the first stage, overhead costs are assigned to the activity cost pools. In the second stage, the costs in the activity cost pools are allocated to products using activity rates and activity measures. For example, in the first stage cost assignment, various manufacturing overhead costs are assigned to the production-order activity cost pool. These costs could include the salaries of engineers who modify products for individual orders, the costs of scheduling and monitoring orders, and other costs that are incurred as a consequence of the number of different orders received and processed by the company. We will not go into the details of how these first-stage cost assignments are made. In all of the examples and assignments in this book, the first-stage cost assignments have already been completed. Once the amount of cost in the production-order activity cost pool is known, procedures from Chapter 2 can be followed. The activity rate for the production-order cost pool is computed by dividing the total cost in

EXHIBIT 3–3   Graphic Example of Activity-Based Costing

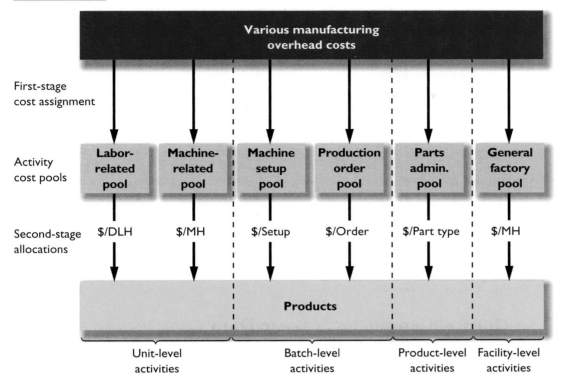

First-stage
cost assignment

Activity
cost pools

Second-stage
allocations

$/DLH $/MH $/Setup $/Order $/Part type $/MH

Products

Unit-level
activities

Batch-level
activities

Product-level
activities

Facility-level
activities

the production-order activity cost pool by the anticipated number of orders for the upcoming year. For example, the total cost in the production-order activity cost pool might be $450,000 and the company might expect to process a total of 1,200 orders. In that case, the activity rate would be $375 per order. Each order would be charged $375 for production-order costs. This is no different from the way overhead was applied to products in Chapter 2 except that the number of orders is the allocation base rather than direct labor-hours.

1. Which of the following statements is false? (You may select more than one answer.)
   a. In recent years, most companies have experienced increasing manufacturing overhead costs in relation to direct labor costs.
   b. Activity-based costing systems may use direct labor-hours and/or machine-hours to assign unit-level costs to products.
   c. Facility-level costs are not caused by particular products.
   d. Product-level costs are larger for high-volume products than for low-volume products.

CONCEPT
CHECK

USING ACTIVITY-BASED COSTING

Different products place different demands on resources. This difference in demand on resources is not recognized by conventional costing systems, which assume that overhead resources are consumed in direct proportion to direct labor-hours or machine-hours. The following example illustrates the distortions in product costs that can result from using a traditional costing system.

Comtek Sound, Inc., makes two products, a radio with a built-in CD player (called a CD unit) and a radio with a built-in DVD player (called a DVD unit). Both of these products are sold to automobile manufacturers for installation in new vehicles. Recently, the company has been losing bids to supply CD players, which management regards as its main product, because competitors have been bidding less than Comtek Sound has been willing to bid. At the same time, Comtek Sound has been winning every bid it has submitted for its DVD player, which management regards as a secondary product. The marketing manager has been complaining that at the prices Comtek Sound is willing to bid, competitors are taking the company's high-volume CD business and leaving Comtek Sound with just low-volume DVD business. However, the prices competitors quote on the CD players are below Comtek Sound's manufacturing cost for these units—at least according to Comtek Sound's conventional accounting system that applies manufacturing overhead based on direct labor-hours. Production managers suspected that the conventional costing system might be distorting the relative costs of the CD player and the DVD player—the DVD player takes more overhead resources to make than the CD player and yet their manufacturing overhead costs are identical under the conventional costing system. With the enthusiastic cooperation of the company's accounting department, a cross-functional team was formed to develop an activity-based costing system to more accurately assign overhead costs to the two products.

Comtek Sound, Inc.'s Basic Data

The ABC team immediately began gathering basic information relating to the company's two products. As a basis for its study, the team decided to use the cost and other data planned for the current year. A summary of some of this information follows. For the current year, the company's budget provides for selling 50,000 DVD units and 200,000 CD units. Both products require two direct labor-hours to complete. Therefore, the company plans to work 500,000 direct labor-hours (DLHs) during the current year, computed as follows:

	Hours
DVD units: 50,000 units × 2 DLHs per unit	100,000
CD units: 200,000 units × 2 DLHs per unit	400,000
Total direct labor-hours	500,000

Costs for materials and labor for one unit of each product are given below:

	DVD Units	CD Units
Direct materials	$90	$50
Direct labor (at $10 per DLH)	$20	$20

The company's estimated manufacturing overhead costs for the current year total $10,000,000. The ABC team discovered that although the same amount of direct labor time is required for each product, the more complex DVD units require more machine time, more machine setups, and more testing than the CD units. Also, the team found that it is necessary to manufacture the DVD units in smaller batches, so they require more production orders than the CD units.

The company has always used direct labor-hours as the base for assigning overhead costs to its products.

With this data in hand, the ABC team was prepared to begin the design of the new activity-based costing system. But first, they wanted to compute the cost of each product using the company's existing cost system.

Direct Labor-Hours as a Base

Under the company's existing costing system, the predetermined overhead rate would be $20 per direct labor-hour, computed as follows:

$$\text{Predetermined overhead rate} = \frac{\text{Estimated total manufacturing overhead}}{\text{Estimated total amount of the allocation base}}$$

$$= \frac{\$10,000,000}{500,000 \text{ DLHs}} = \$20 \text{ per DLH}$$

Using this rate, the ABC team computed the unit product costs as given below:

	DVD Units	CD Units
Direct materials (above)	$ 90	$ 50
Direct labor (above)	20	20
Manufacturing overhead (2 DLHs × $20 per DLH)	40	40
Unit product cost	$150	$110

The problem with this costing approach is that it relies entirely on direct labor-hours to assign overhead cost to products and does not consider the impact of other factors—such as setups and testing—on the overhead costs of the company. Since these other factors are being ignored and the two products require equal amounts of direct labor, they are assigned equal amounts of overhead cost.

While this method of computing costs is fast and simple, it is accurate only in those situations where other factors affecting overhead costs are not significant. These other factors *are* significant in the case of Comtek Sound, Inc.

Computing Activity Rates

The ABC team then analyzed Comtek Sound, Inc.'s operations and identified six major activities to be included in the new activity-based costing system. (These six activities are identical to those illustrated earlier in Exhibit 3–3.) Cost and other data relating to the activities are presented in Exhibit 3–4.

As shown in the Basic Data at the top of Exhibit 3–4, the ABC team estimated the amount of overhead cost for each activity cost pool, along with the expected amount of activity for the current year. The machine setups activity cost pool, for example, was assigned $1,600,000 in overhead cost. The company expects to complete 4,000 setups during the year, of which 3,000 will be for DVD units and 1,000 will be for CD units. Data for other activities are also shown in the exhibit.

The ABC team then computed an activity rate for each activity. (See the middle panel in Exhibit 3–4.) The activity rate of $400 per machine setup, for example, was computed by dividing the total estimated overhead cost in the activity cost pool, $1,600,000, by the expected amount of activity, 4,000 setups. This process was repeated for each of the other activities in the activity-based costing system.

Computing Product Costs

Once the activity rates were calculated, it was easy to compute the overhead cost that would be allocated to each product. (See the bottom panel of Exhibit 3–4.) For example, the amount of machine setup cost allocated to DVD units was determined by multiplying the activity rate of $400 per setup by the 3,000 expected setups for DVD units during the year. This yielded a total of $1,200,000 in machine setup costs to be assigned to the DVD units.

Note from the exhibit that the use of an activity approach has resulted in $97.80 in overhead cost being assigned to each DVD unit and $25.55 to each CD unit. The ABC team then used these amounts to determine unit product costs under activity-based costing, as presented in the table at the bottom of page134. For comparison, the table also shows the unit product costs derived earlier when direct labor-hours were used as the base for assigning overhead costs to the products.

Concept 3-2

EXHIBIT 3–4   Comtek Sound's Activity-Based Costing System

Basic Data

Activities and Activity Measures	Estimated Overhead Cost	Expected Activity DVD Units	CD Units	Total
Labor related (direct labor-hours)	$ 800,000	100,000	400,000	500,000
Machine related (machine-hours)	2,100,000	300,000	700,000	1,000,000
Machine setups (setups)	1,600,000	3,000	1,000	4,000
Production orders (orders)	3,150,000	800	400	1,200
Parts administration (part types)	350,000	400	300	700
General factory (machine-hours)	2,000,000	300,000	700,000	1,000,000
	$10,000,000			

Computation of Activity Rates

Activities	(a) Estimated Overhead Cost	(b) Total Expected Activity	(a) ÷ (b) Activity Rate
Labor related	$800,000	500,000 DLHs	$1.60 per DLH
Machine related	$2,100,000	1,000,000 MHs	$2.10 per MH
Machine setups	$1,600,000	4,000 setups	$400.00 per setup
Production orders	$3,150,000	1,200 orders	$2,625.00 per order
Parts administration	$350,000	700 part types	$500.00 per part type
General factory	$2,000,000	1,000,000 MHs	$2.00 per MH

Computation of the Overhead Cost per Unit of Product

Activities and Activity Rates	DVD Units Expected Activity	Amount	CD Units Expected Activity	Amount
Labor related, at $1.60 per DLH	100,000	$ 160,000	400,000	$ 640,000
Machine related, at $2.10 per MH	300,000	630,000	700,000	1,470,000
Machine setups, at $400 per setup	3,000	1,200,000	1,000	400,000
Production orders, at $2,625 per order	800	2,100,000	400	1,050,000
Parts administration, at $500 per part type	400	200,000	300	150,000
General factory, at $2.00 per MH	300,000	600,000	700,000	1,400,000
Total overhead costs assigned (a)		$4,890,000		$5,110,000
Number of units produced (b)		50,000		200,000
Overhead cost per unit (a) ÷ (b)		$ 97.80		$ 25.55

	Activity-Based Costing DVD Units	CD Units	Direct-Labor Based Costing DVD Units	CD Units
Direct materials	$ 90.00	$50.00	$ 90.00	$ 50.00
Direct labor	20.00	20.00	20.00	20.00
Manufacturing overhead	97.80	25.55	40.00	40.00
Unit product cost	$207.80	$95.55	$150.00	$110.00

The ABC team members were shocked by their findings, which they summarized as follows in the team's report:

> In the past, the company has been charging $40.00 in overhead cost to a unit of either product, whereas it should have been charging $97.80 in overhead cost to each DVD unit and only $25.55 to each CD unit. Thus, unit costs have been badly distorted as a result of using direct labor-hours as the allocation base. The company may even have been suffering a loss on the DVD units without knowing it because the cost of these units has been so vastly understated. Through activity-based costing, we have been able to more accurately assign overhead costs to each product.
>
> Although in the past we thought our competitors were pricing below their cost on the CD units, it turns out that we were overcharging for these units because our costs were overstated. Similarly, we always used to believe that our competitors were overpricing the DVD units, but now we realize that our prices have been way too low because the cost of our DVD units was being understated. It turns out that we, not our competitors, had everything backwards.

The pattern of cost distortion shown by the ABC team's findings is quite common. Such distortion can happen in any company that relies on direct labor-hours or machine-hours in assigning overhead cost to products and ignores other significant causes of overhead costs.

Shifting of Overhead Cost

When a company implements activity-based costing, overhead cost often shifts from high-volume products to low-volume products, with a higher unit product cost resulting for the low-volume products. We saw this happen in the example above, where overhead cost was shifted to the DVD units—the low-volume product—and their unit product cost increased from $150.00 to $207.80 per unit. This results from the existence of batch-level and product-level costs. When these costs are spread across lower volumes, it results in higher average costs. For example, consider the cost of issuing production orders, which is a batch-level activity. As shown in Exhibit 3–4, the average cost to Comtek Sound to issue a single production order is $2,625. This cost is assigned to a production order regardless of how many units are processed in that order. The key here is to realize that fewer DVD units (the low-volume product) are processed per production order than CD units:

LEARNING OBJECTIVE 4
Contrast the product costs computed under activity-based costing and conventional costing methods.

	DVD Units	CD Units
Number of units produced per year (a)	50,000	200,000
Number of production orders issued per year (b)	800	400
Number of units processed per production order (a) ÷ (b)	62.5	500

Spreading the $2,625 cost to issue a production order over the number of units processed per order results in the following average cost per unit:

	DVD Units	CD Units
Cost to issue a production order (a)	$2,625	$2,625
Average number of units processed per production order (above) (b)	62.5	500
Production order cost per unit (a) ÷ (b)	$42.00	$5.25

Thus, the production order cost for a DVD unit (the low-volume product) is $42, which is *eight times* the $5.25 cost for a CD unit.

Product-level costs—such as parts administration—have a similar impact. In a conventional costing system, these costs are spread more or less uniformly across all units that are produced. In an activity-based costing system, these costs are assigned more accurately to products. Since product-level costs are fixed with respect to the number of units processed, the average cost per unit of an activity such as parts administration will be higher for low-volume products than for high-volume products.

IN BUSINESS

Finding that Golden Top 20%

According to Meridien Research of Newton, Massachusetts, 20% of a bank's customers generate about 150% of its profits. At the other end of the spectrum, 30% of a bank's customers drain 50% of its profits. The question becomes how do banks identify which customers are in that golden top 20%? For many banks, the answer is revealed through customer relationship management software that provides activity-based costing capability.

"We had some customers that we thought, on the surface, would be very profitable, with an average of $300,000 in business accounts," said Jerry Williams, chairman and chief executive officer of First Bancorp. "What we didn't pull out was the fact that some write more than 275 checks a month. Once you apply the labor costs, it's not a profitable customer."

Meridien Research estimates that large commercial banks are increasing their spending on customer profitability systems by 14% a year with total annual expenditures exceeding $6 billion dollars.

Source: Joseph McKendrick, "Your Best Customers May Be Different Tomorrow," *Bank Technology News,* July 2001, pp. 1–4.

TARGETING PROCESS IMPROVEMENTS

Activity-based costing can also be used to identify activities that would benefit from process improvements. Indeed, this is the most widely cited benefit of activity-based costing by managers.[2] When used in this way, activity-based costing is often called *activity-based management*. Basically, **activity-based management** involves focusing on activities to eliminate waste, decrease processing time, and reduce defects. Activity-based management is used in organizations as diverse as manufacturing companies, hospitals, and the U.S. Marine Corps. When "40 percent of the cost of running a hospital involves storing, collecting and moving information," there is obviously a great deal of room for eliminating waste.[3]

The first step in any improvement program is to decide what to improve. The Theory of Constraints approach discussed in the Prologue is a powerful tool for targeting the area in an organization whose improvement will yield the greatest benefit. Activity-based management provides another approach. The activity rates computed in activity-based costing can provide valuable clues concerning where there is waste and opportunity for improvement. For example, looking at the activity rates in Exhibit 3–4, Comtek's managers may conclude that $2,625 to process a production order is far too expensive for an activity that adds no value to the product. As a consequence, they may target production-order processing for process improvement using Six Sigma as discussed in the Prologue.

Benchmarking is another way to leverage the information in activity rates. **Benchmarking** is a systematic approach to identifying the activities with the greatest room for improvement. It is based on comparing the performance in an organization with the performance of other, similar organizations known for their outstanding performance. If a particular part of the organization performs far below the world-class standard, managers will be likely to target that area for improvement.

---

[2]Dan Swenson, "The Benefits of Activity-Based Cost Management to the Manufacturing Industry," *Journal of Management Accounting Research* 7, pp. 167–180.
[3]Kambiz Foroohar, "Rx: Software," *Forbes,* April 7, 1997, p. 114.

Costs in Health Care

Owens & Minor, a $3 billion medical supplies distributor, offers an activity-based billing option to its customers. Instead of charging a fixed amount for items that are ordered by customers, the charges are based on activities required to fill the order as well as on the cost of the item ordered. For example, Owens & Minor charges extra for weekend deliveries. These charges encourage customers to reduce their weekend delivery requests. This results in decreased costs for Owens & Minor, which can then be passed on to customers in the form of lower charges for the specific items that are ordered. As many as 25% of Owens & Minor's 4,000 health care customers have used this billing option to identify and realize cost reduction opportunities. For example, Bill Wright of Sutter Health in Sacramento, California, said that Owens & Minor's activity-based billing has motivated his company to eliminate weekend deliveries, place more items per order, align purchase quantities with prepackaged specifications, and transmit orders electronically. The end result is that one Sutter affiliate decreased its purchasing costs from 4.25% of product costs to 3.75%. In all, Owens & Minor has identified about 250 activity-driven procurement costs that hospitals can manage more efficiently to reduce costs.

Source: Todd Shields, "Hospitals Turning to Activity-Based Costing to Save and Measure Distribution Costs," *Healthcare Purchasing News*, November 2001, pp. 14–15.

EVALUATION OF ACTIVITY-BASED COSTING

Activity-based costing improves the accuracy of product costs, helps managers to understand the nature of overhead costs, and helps target areas for improvement through benchmarking and other techniques. These benefits are discussed in this section.

The Benefits of Activity-Based Costing

Activity-based costing improves the accuracy of product costs in three ways. First, activity-based costing usually increases the number of cost pools used to accumulate overhead costs. Rather than accumulating all overhead costs in a single, plantwide pool, or accumulating them in departmental pools, the company accumulates costs for each major activity. Second, the activity cost pools are more homogeneous than departmental cost pools. In principle, all of the costs in an activity cost pool pertain to a single activity. In contrast, departmental cost pools contain the costs of many different activities carried out in the department. Third, activity-based costing uses a variety of activity measures to assign overhead costs to products, some of which are correlated with volume and some of which are not. This differs from conventional approaches that rely exclusively on direct labor-hours or other measures of volume such as machine-hours to assign overhead costs to products.

Because conventional costing systems typically apply overhead costs to products using direct labor-hours, it may appear to managers that overhead costs are caused by direct labor-hours. Activity-based costing makes it clear that batch setups, engineering change orders, and other activities cause overhead costs rather than just direct labor. Managers thus have a better understanding of the causes of overhead costs, which should lead to better decisions and better cost control.

Finally, activity-based costing highlights the activities that could benefit most from Six Sigma and other improvement initiatives. Thus, activity-based costing can be used as a part of programs to improve operations.

Limitations of Activity-Based Costing

Any discussion of activity-based costing is incomplete without some cautionary warnings. First, the cost of implementing and maintaining an activity-based costing system may outweigh the benefits. Second, it would be naïve to assume that product costs provided even by an activity-based costing are always relevant when making decisions. These limitations are discussed below.

The Cost of Implementing Activity-Based Costing   Implementing ABC is a major project that involves a great deal of effort. First, the cost system must be designed—preferably by a cross-functional team. This requires taking valued employees away from other tasks for a major project. In addition, the data used in the activity-based costing system must be collected and verified. In some cases, this requires collecting data that has never been collected before. In short, implementing and maintaining an activity-based costing system can present a formidable challenge, and management may decide that the costs are too great to justify the expected benefits. Nevertheless, it should be kept in mind that the costs of collecting and processing data have dropped dramatically over the last several decades due to bar coding and other technologies, and these costs can be expected to continue to fall.

When are the benefits of activity-based costing most likely to be worth the cost? Companies that have some of the following characteristics are most likely to benefit from activity-based costing:

1. Products differ substantially in volume, batch size, and in the activities they require.
2. Conditions have changed substantially since the existing cost system was established.
3. Overhead costs are high and increasing and no one seems to understand why.
4. Management does not trust the existing cost system and ignores cost data from the system when making decisions.

The Survey Says . . .

Professors John Innes, Falconer Mitchell, and Donald Sinclair have conducted two surveys designed to study ABC adoption trends within the United Kingdom across a five-year time span. The professors' initial survey results are based on responses from 352 of the U.K.'s largest companies, while the follow-up survey results obtained five years later are based on responses from 177 of the U.K.'s largest companies.

The initial survey results indicated that 21% of respondents were currently using ABC, 29.6% were considering ABC adoption, 13.3% had rejected ABC after considering its implementation, and 36.1% were not considering ABC. Five years later the follow-up survey showed that 17.5% of respondents were currently using ABC, 20.3% were considering ABC adoption, 15.3% had rejected ABC after considering implementation, and 46.9% were not considering ABC. The professors summarized their findings by saying "These results are indicative of no growth in the popularity of ABC, and are consistent with both a leveling off in interest in it and the adoption of it over this five-year period."

Source: John Innes, Falconer Mitchell, and Donald Sinclair, "Activity-Based Costing in the U.K.'s Largest Companies: A Comparison of 1994 and 1999 Survey Results," *Management Accounting Research,* September 2000, pp. 349–362.

Limitations of the ABC Model   The activity-based costing model relies on a number of critical assumptions.[4] Perhaps the most important of these assumptions is that the cost in each activity cost pool is strictly proportional to its activity measure. What little evidence we have on this issue suggests that overhead costs are less than proportional to activity.[5] Economists call this increasing returns to scale—as activity increases, the

---

[4]Eric Noreen, "Conditions under Which Activity-Based Cost Systems Provide Relevant Costs," *Journal of Management Accounting Research,* Fall 1991, pp. 159–168.

[5]Eric Noreen and Naomi Soderstrom, "The Accuracy of Proportional Cost Models: Evidence from Hospital Service Departments," *Review of Accounting Studies* 2, 1997; and Eric Noreen and Naomi Soderstrom, "Are Overhead Costs Proportional to Activity? Evidence from Hospital Service Departments," *Journal of Accounting and Economics,* January 1994, pp. 253–278.

average cost drops. As a practical matter, this means that product costs computed by a traditional or activity-based costing system will be overstated for the purposes of making decisions. The product costs generated by activity-based costing are almost certainly more accurate than those generated by a conventional costing system, but they should nevertheless be viewed with caution. Managers should be particularly alert to product costs that contain allocations of facility-level costs. As we shall see later in the book, product costs that include facility-level or organization-sustaining costs can easily lead managers astray.

Bakery Owner   YOU DECIDE

You are the owner of a bakery that makes a complete line of specialty breads, pastries, cakes, and pies for the retail and wholesale markets. A summer intern has just completed an activity-based costing study that concluded, among other things, that one of your largest recurring jobs is losing money. A local luxury hotel orders the same assortment of desserts every week for its Sunday brunch buffet for a fixed price of $975 per week. The hotel is quite happy with the quality of the desserts the bakery has been providing, but it would seek bids from other local bakeries if the price were increased.

The activity-based costing study conducted by the intern revealed that the cost to the bakery of providing these desserts is $1,034 per week, resulting in an apparent loss of $59 per week or over $3,000 per year. Scrutinizing the intern's report, you find that the weekly cost of $1,034 includes facility-level costs of $329. These facility-level costs include portions of the rent on the bakery's building, your salary, depreciation on the office personal computer, and so on. The facility-level costs were arbitrarily allocated to the Sunday brunch job on the basis of direct labor-hours.

Should you demand an increase in price from the luxury hotel for the Sunday brunch desserts to at least $1,034? If an increase is not forthcoming, should you withdraw from the agreement and discontinue providing the desserts?

Modifying the ABC Model   The discussion in this chapter has assumed that the primary purpose of an activity-based costing system is to provide more accurate product costs for external reports. If the product costs are to be used by managers for internal decisions, some modifications should be made. For example, for decision-making purposes, the distinction between manufacturing costs on the one hand and selling and administrative expenses on the other hand is unimportant. Managers need to know what costs a product causes, and it doesn't matter whether the costs are manufacturing costs or selling and administrative expenses. Consequently, for decision-making purposes, some selling and administrative expenses should be assigned to products as well as manufacturing costs. Moreover, as mentioned above, facility-level and organization-sustaining costs should be removed from product costs when making decisions. Nevertheless, the techniques covered in this chapter provide a good basis for understanding the mechanics of activity-based costing. For a more complete coverage of the use of activity-based costing in decisions, see more advanced texts.[6]

Activity-Based Costing and Service Industries

Although initially developed as a tool for manufacturing companies, activity-based costing is also being used in service industries. Successful implementation of an activity-based costing system depends on identifying the key activities that generate costs and tracking how many of those activities are performed for each service the organization provides. Activity-based costing has been implemented in a wide variety of service industries including railroads, hospitals, banks, and data services companies.

---

[6]See, for example, Chapter 8 and its appendix in Ray Garrison, Eric Noreen, and Peter Brewer, *Managerial Accounting,* 11th edition, Irwin/McGraw-Hill, © 2006.

IN BUSINESS

ABC in the Public Sector

Robin Cooper and Robert S. Kaplan report that: "The U.S. Veterans Affairs Department has identified the cost of the 10 activities performed to process death benefits and uses this information to monitor and improve the underlying cost structure for performing this function. The U.S. Immigration and Naturalization Service (INS) uses its ABC cost information to set fees for all of its outputs, including administering citizenship exams and issuing permanent work permits (green cards)." The City of Indianapolis made ABC a cornerstone of its privatization efforts and its drive to provide more services at lower cost to citizens. As the mayor of the city, Stephen Goldsmith, explained: "Introducing competition and privatization to government services requires real cost information. You can't compete if you are using fake money." When city workers became aware of the costs of carrying out activities such as filling potholes in streets and were faced with the possible transfer of such tasks to the private sector, they became highly motivated to reduce costs. Instead of going out to fill potholes with a five- or six-man repair crew, plus a supervisor, they started doing the same job with a three- or four-man crew without a supervisor. The number of politically appointed supervisors, which had stood at 36 for 75 employees, was slashed by half.

Source: Robert S. Kaplan and Robin Cooper, *Cost & Effect: Using Integrated Cost Systems to Drive Profitability and Performance,* Harvard Business School Press, Boston, 1998, pp. 245–250.

DECISION MAKER

Legal Firm Business Manager

You have been hired to manage the business aspects of a local legal firm with a staff of 6 attorneys, 10 paralegals, and 5 staffpersons. Clients of the firm are billed a fixed amount per hour of attorney time. The fixed hourly charge is determined each year by dividing the total cost of the legal office for the preceding year by the total billed hours of attorney time for that year. A markup of 25% is then added to this average cost per hour of billed attorney time to provide for a profit and for inflation.

The firm's partners are concerned because the firm has been unprofitable for several years. The firm has been losing its smaller clients to other local firms—largely because the firm's fees have become uncompetitive. And the firm has been attracting larger clients with more complex legal problems from its competitors. To serve these demanding larger clients, the firm must subscribe to expensive on-line legal reference services, hire additional paralegals and staffpersons, and lease additional office space.

What do you think might be the reason for the unprofitable operations in recent years? What might be done to improve the situation for the coming year?

CONCEPT CHECK ✓

2. Which of the following statements is false? (You may select more than one answer.)
   a. Activity-based costing systems usually shift costs from low-volume products to high-volume products.
   b. Benchmarking can be used to identify activities with the greatest potential for improvement.
   c. Activity-based costing is most valuable to companies that manufacture products that are similar in terms of their volume of production, batch size, and complexity.
   d. Activity-based costing systems are based on the assumption that the costs included in each activity cost pool are strictly proportional to the cost pool's activity measure.

3. A company manufactures and sells 10,000 units of A and 5,000 units of B. The average batch sizes for A and B are 1,000 and 250 units, respectively. Which of the following statements is false? (You may select more than one answer.)
   a. A costing system that relies solely on a unit-level activity measure to assign all manufacturing overhead to products will overcost product A.
   b. A costing system that relies solely on a unit-level activity measure to assign manufacturing overhead to products will overcost product B.
   c. An activity-based costing system would assign 67 percent of the batch-level overhead costs to product B.
   d. An activity-based costing system would assign 67 percent of the unit-level overhead costs to product A.

COST FLOWS IN AN ACTIVITY-BASED COSTING SYSTEM

In Chapter 2, we discussed the flow of costs in a job-order costing system. The flow of costs through Raw Materials, Work in Process, and other accounts is the same under activity-based costing. The only difference in activity-based costing is that more than one predetermined overhead rate is used to apply overhead costs to products. Our purpose in this section is to provide a detailed example of cost flows in an activity-based costing system.

> **LEARNING OBJECTIVE 5**
> Record the flow of costs in an activity-based costing system.

An Example of Cost Flows

The company in the following example has five activity cost pools and therefore must compute five predetermined overhead rates (i.e., activity rates). Except for that detail, the journal entries, T-accounts, and general cost flows are the same as described in Chapter 2.

Basic Data Sarvik Company uses activity-based costing for its external financial reports. The company has five activity cost pools, which are listed below along with relevant data for the coming year.

Activity Cost Pool	Activity Measure	Estimated Overhead Cost	Expected Activity
Machine related	Machine-hours	$175,000	5,000 MHs
Purchase orders	Number of orders	$63,000	700 orders
Machine setups	Number of setups	$92,000	460 setups
Product testing	Number of tests	$160,000	200 tests
General factory	Direct labor-hours	$300,000	25,000 DLHs

At the beginning of the year, the company had inventory balances as follows:

Raw materials	$3,000
Work in process	$4,000
Finished goods	$0

Selected transactions recorded by the company during the year are given below:

a. Raw materials were purchased on account, $915,000.
b. Raw materials were requisitioned for use in production, $900,000 ($810,000 direct and $90,000 indirect).

c. Labor costs were incurred in the factory, $370,000 ($95,000 direct labor and $275,000 indirect labor).

d. Depreciation was recorded on factory assets, $180,000.

e. Miscellaneous manufacturing overhead costs were incurred, $230,000.

f. Manufacturing overhead cost was applied to production. Actual activity during the year was as follows:

Activity Cost Pool	Actual Activity
Machine related	4,600 MHs
Purchase orders	800 orders
Machine setups	500 setups
Product testing	190 tests
General factory	23,000 DLHs

g. Goods costing $1,650,000 to manufacture according to the activity-based costing system were completed during the year.

Tracking the Flow of Costs   The predetermined overhead rates (i.e., activity rates) for the activity cost pools would be computed as follows:

Activity Cost Pools	(a) Estimated Overhead Cost	(b) Total Expected Activity	(a) ÷ (b) Activity Rate
Machine related	$175,000	5,000 machine-hours	$35 per machine-hour
Purchase orders	$63,000	700 orders	$90 per order
Machine setups	$92,000	460 setups	$200 per setup
Product testing	$160,000	200 tests	$800 per test
General factory	$300,000	25,000 direct labor-hours	$12 per direct labor-hour

The following journal entries would be used to record transactions (a) through (g) above:

a.	Raw Materials	915,000	
	Accounts Payable*.......................		915,000
b.	Work in Process............................	810,000	
	Manufacturing Overhead	90,000	
	Raw Materials............................		900,000
c.	Work in Process............................	95,000	
	Manufacturing Overhead	275,000	
	Salaries and Wages Payable*		370,000
d.	Manufacturing Overhead	180,000	
	Accumulated Depreciation		180,000
e.	Manufacturing Overhead	230,000	
	Accounts Payable*.......................		230,000

Recall from Chapter 2 the formula for computing applied overhead cost, which is:

Predetermined overhead rate × Actual activity = Applied overhead cost

*Other accounts, such as Cash, may be credited.

In activity-based costing, this formula is applied for each activity cost pool using its own predetermined overhead rate (i.e., activity rate). The computations are as follows:

Activities	(1) Activity Rate	(2) Actual Activity	(1) × (2) Applied Overhead Cost
Machine related	$35 per MH	4,600 MHs	$161,000
Purchase orders	$90 per order	800 orders	72,000
Machine setups	$200 per setup	500 setups	100,000
Product testing	$800 per test	190 tests	152,000
General factory	$12 per DLH	23,000 DLHs	276,000
Total			$761,000

By totaling these five applied overhead cost figures, we find that the company applied $761,000 in overhead cost to products during the year. The following entry would be used to record this application of overhead cost:

f. | Work in Process .... | 761,000 |
   | Manufacturing Overhead .... | | 761,000

Finally, the following journal entry would be used to record the completion of work in process as described in transaction (g) above:

g. | Finished Goods............................. | 1,650,000 |
   | Work in Process .... | | 1,650,000

The T-accounts corresponding to the above journal entries appear below:

Raw Materials			
Bal.	3,000	(b)	900,000
(a)	915,000		
Bal.	18,000		

Work in Process			
Bal.	4,000	(g)	1,650,000
(b)	810,000		
(c)	95,000		
(f)	761,000		
Bal.	20,000		

Finished Goods			
Bal.	0		
(g)	1,650,000		

Accumulated Depreciation			
		(d)	180,000

Accounts Payable			
		(a)	915,000
		(e)	230,000

Salaries and Wages Payable			
		(c)	370,000

Manufacturing Overhead			
(b)	90,000	(f)	761,000
(c)	275,000		
(d)	180,000		
(e)	230,000		
	775,000		761,000
Bal.	14,000		

The overhead is underapplied by $14,000. This can be determined directly, as shown below, or by reference to the balance in the Manufacturing Overhead T-account above.

Actual manufacturing overhead incurred	$775,000
Manufacturing overhead applied	761,000
Overhead underapplied	$ 14,000

SUMMARY

LO1   Understand the basic approach in activity-based costing and how it differs from conventional costing.

Activity-based costing was developed to more accurately assign overhead costs to products. Activity-based costing differs from conventional costing as described in Chapter 2 in two major ways. First, in activity-based costing, each major activity that consumes overhead resources has its own cost pool and its own activity rate, whereas in Chapter 2 there was only a single overhead cost pool and a single predetermined overhead rate. Second, the allocation bases (or activity measures) in activity-based costing are diverse. They may include machine setups, purchase orders, engineering change orders, and so on, in addition to direct labor-hours or machine-hours. Nevertheless, within each activity cost pool, the mechanics of computing overhead rates and of applying overhead to products are the same as described in Chapter 2. However, the increase in the number of cost pools and the use of better activity measures generally result in more accurate product costs.

LO2   Compute activity rates for an activity-based costing system.

Each activity in an activity-based costing system has its own cost pool and its own activity measure. The activity rate for a particular activity is computed by dividing the total cost in the activity's cost pool by the total amount of activity.

LO3   Compute product costs using activity-based costing.

Product costs in activity-based costing, as in conventional costing systems, consist of direct materials, direct labor, and overhead. In both systems, overhead is applied to products using predetermined overhead rates. In the case of an activity-based costing system, each activity has its own predetermined overhead rate (i.e., activity rate). The activities required by a product are multiplied by their respective activity rates to determine the amount of overhead that is applied to the product.

LO4   Contrast the product costs computed under activity-based costing and conventional costing methods.

Under conventional costing methods, overhead costs are applied to products using some measure of volume such as direct labor-hours or machine-hours. This results in most of the overhead cost being applied to high-volume products. In contrast, under activity-based costing, some overhead costs are applied on the basis of batch-level or product-level activities. This change in allocation bases results in shifting overhead costs from high-volume products to low-volume products. Accordingly, product costs for high-volume products are commonly lower under activity-based costing than under conventional costing methods, and product costs for low-volume products are higher.

LO5   Record the flow of costs in an activity-based costing system.

The journal entries and general flow of costs in an activity-based costing system are the same as they are in a conventional costing system. The only difference is the use of more than one predetermined overhead rate (i.e., activity rate) to apply overhead to products.

GUIDANCE ANSWERS TO *DECISION MAKER* AND *YOU DECIDE*

Bakery Owner (p. 139)

The bakery really isn't losing money on the weekly order of desserts from the luxury hotel. By definition, facility-level costs are not affected by individual products and jobs—these costs would continue unchanged even if the weekly order were dropped. Recalling the discussion in Chapter 1 concerning decision making, only those costs and benefits that differ between alternatives in a decision are relevant. Since the facility-level costs would be the same whether the dessert order is kept or dropped, they are not relevant in this decision and should be ignored. Hence, the real cost of the job is $705 ($1,034 − $329), which reveals that the job actually yields a weekly profit of $270 ($975 − $705) rather than a loss.

No, the bakery owner should not press for a price increase—particularly if that would result in the hotel seeking bids from competitors. And no, the bakery owner certainly should not withdraw from the agreement to provide the desserts.

Legal Firm Business Manager (p. 140)

The recent problems the firm has been facing can probably be traced to its simplified billing system. Rather than carefully tracing costs to clients, costs are arbitrarily allocated to clients on the basis of attorney hours. Large, demanding clients require much more overhead resources than smaller clients, but the costs of these overhead resources are arbitrarily allocated to all clients on the basis of attorney hours. This results in shifting overhead costs to the smaller, less demanding clients and increasing their charges. It also results in under-charging larger, more demanding clients. Consequently, the firm has been losing smaller clients to competitors and has been attracting larger, demanding clients. Unfortunately, this change in the mix of clients has led to much higher costs and reduced profits.

The situation can be improved by using activity-based costing to trace more costs directly to clients. This should result in shifting costs from the smaller, less demanding clients to the larger, more demanding clients that cause those costs. Smaller clients will face lower charges and hence will be more likely to stay with the firm. Larger, more demanding clients will face higher charges that will fully cover the costs they impose on the firm.

GUIDANCE ANSWERS TO CONCEPT CHECKS

1. **Choice d.** Product-level costs are unrelated to the amount of a product that is made.
2. **Choices a and c.** Activity-based costing systems usually shift costs from high-volume products to low-volume products. Activity-based costing is most valuable for companies with highly diverse products rather than with similar products.
3. **Choice b.** Relying solely on a unit-level activity measure will result in 33% of the total overhead costs being assigned to product B. While product B should be assigned 33% of the unit-level over-head costs, it should be assigned 67% of the batch-level overhead costs.

REVIEW PROBLEM: ACTIVITY-BASED COSTING

Aerodec, Inc., manufactures and sells two types of wooden deck chairs: Deluxe and Tourist. Annual sales in units, direct labor-hours (DLHs) per unit, and total direct labor-hours per year are provided below:

	Total Hours
Deluxe deck chair: 2,000 units × 5 DLHs per unit	10,000
Tourist deck chair: 10,000 units × 4 DLHs per unit	40,000
Total direct labor-hours	50,000

Costs for materials and labor for one unit of each product are given below:

	Deluxe	Tourist
Direct materials	$25	$17
Direct labor (at $12 per DLH)	$60	$48

Manufacturing overhead costs total $800,000 each year. The breakdown of these costs among the company's six activity cost pools is given below. The activity measures are shown in parentheses.

Activities and Activity Measures	Estimated Overhead Cost	Expected Activity		
		Deluxe	Tourist	Total
Labor related (direct labor-hours)	$ 80,000	10,000	40,000	50,000
Machine setups (number of setups)	150,000	3,000	2,000	5,000
Parts administration (number of parts)	160,000	50	30	80
Production orders (number of orders)	70,000	100	300	400
Material receipts (number of receipts)	90,000	150	600	750
General factory (machine-hours)	250,000	12,000	28,000	40,000
	$800,000			

Required:

1. Classify each of Aerodec's activities as either a unit-level, batch-level, product-level, or facility-level activity.
2. Assume that the company applies overhead cost to products on the basis of direct labor-hours.
   a. Compute the predetermined overhead rate.
   b. Determine the unit product cost of each product, using the predetermined overhead rate computed in (2)(a) above.
3. Assume that the company uses activity-based costing to compute overhead rates.
   a. Compute the activity rate (i.e., predetermined overhead rate) for each of the six activities listed above.
   b. Using the rates developed in (3)(a) above, determine the amount of overhead cost that would be assigned to a unit of each product.
   c. Determine the unit product cost of each product and compare this cost to the cost computed in (2) (b) above.

Solution to Review Problem

1.

Activity Cost Pool	Type of Activity
Labor related	Unit level
Machine setups	Batch level
Parts administration	Product level
Production orders	Batch level
Material receipts	Batch level
General factory	Facility level

2. a.

$$\text{Predetermined overhead rate} = \frac{\text{Estimated total manufacturing overhead}}{\text{Estimated total amount of the allocation base}} = \frac{\$800,000}{50,000 \text{ DLHs}} = \$16 \text{ per DLH}$$

b.

	Deluxe	Tourist
Direct materials	$ 25	$ 17
Direct labor	60	48
Manufacturing overhead applied:		
Deluxe: 5 DLHs × $16 per DLH	80	
Tourist: 4 DLHs × $16 per DLH		64
Unit product cost	$165	$129

3. a.

Activities	(a) Estimated Overhead Cost	(b) Total Expected Activity	(a) ÷ (b) Activity Rate
Labor related	$80,000	50,000 DLHs	$1.60 per DLH
Machine setups	$150,000	5,000 setups	$30.00 per setup
Parts administration	$160,000	80 parts	$2,000.00 per part
Production orders	$70,000	400 orders	$175.00 per order
Material receipts	$90,000	750 receipts	$120.00 per receipt
General factory	$250,000	40,000 MHs	$6.25 per MH

b.

Activities and Activity Rates	Deluxe		Tourist	
	Expected Activity	Amount	Expected Activity	Amount
Labor related, at $1.60 per DLH	10,000	$ 16,000	40,000	$ 64,000
Machine setups, at $30 per setup	3,000	90,000	2,000	60,000
Parts administration, at $2,000 per part	50	100,000	30	60,000
Production orders, at $175 per order	100	17,500	300	52,500
Material receipts, at $120 per receipt	150	18,000	600	72,000
General factory, at $6.25 per MH	12,000	75,000	28,000	175,000
Total overhead cost assigned (a)		$316,500		$483,500
Number of units produced (b)		2,000		10,000
Overhead cost per unit, (a) ÷ (b)		$ 158.25		$ 48.35

c.

	Deluxe	Tourist
Direct materials........................	$ 25.00	$ 17.00
Direct labor	60.00	48.00
Manufacturing overhead (see above)	158.25	48.35
Unit product cost	$243.25	$113.35

Under activity-based costing, the unit product cost of the Deluxe deck chair is much greater than the cost computed in (2)(b) above, and the unit product cost of the Tourist deck chair is much less. Using volume (direct labor-hours) in (2)(b) to apply overhead cost to products results in too little overhead cost being applied to the Deluxe deck chair (the low-volume product) and too much overhead cost being applied to the Tourist deck chair (the high-volume product).

GLOSSARY

Activity An event that causes the consumption of overhead resources. (p. 127)

Activity-based costing (ABC) A two-stage costing method in which overhead costs are applied to products on the basis of the activities they require. (p. 125)

Activity-based management A management approach that focuses on managing activities as a way of eliminating waste and reducing delays and defects. (p. 136)

Activity cost pool A "bucket" in which costs are accumulated that relate to a single activity measure in an activity-based costing system. (p. 127)

Activity measure An allocation base in an activity-based costing system; ideally, a measure of whatever causes the costs in an activity cost pool. (p. 127)

Activity rate A predetermined overhead rate in activity-based costing. Each activity cost pool has its own activity rate which is used to apply overhead to products and services. (p. 127)

Batch-level activities Activities that are performed each time a batch of goods is handled or processed, regardless of how many units are in a batch. The amount of resources consumed depends on the number of batches run rather than on the number of units in the batch. (p. 129)

Benchmarking A systematic approach to identifying the activities with the greatest room for improvement. It is based on comparing the performance in an organization with the performance of other, similar organizations known for their outstanding performance. (p. 136)

Facility-level activities Activities that relate to the overall costs of maintaining and managing productive capacity and that can't be traced to specific products. (p. 129)

Product-level activities Activities that relate to specific products that must be carried out regardless of how many units are produced and sold or batches run. (p. 129)

Unit-level activities Activities that arise as a result of the total volume of goods and services that are produced, and that are performed each time a unit is produced. (p. 129)

QUESTIONS

3–1   What are the three common approaches for assigning overhead costs to products?
3–2   Why is activity-based costing growing in popularity?
3–3   Why do departmental overhead rates sometimes result in inaccurate product costs?
3–4   What are the four hierarchical levels of activity discussed in the chapter?
3–5   Why is activity-based costing described as a "two-stage" costing method?
3–6   Why do overhead costs often shift from high-volume products to low-volume products when a company switches from a conventional costing method to activity-based costing?
3–7   What are the three major ways in which activity-based costing improves the accuracy of product costs?
3–8   What are the major limitations of activity-based costing?

BRIEF EXERCISES

BRIEF EXERCISE 3–1   ABC Cost Hierarchy   (LO1)
The following activities occur at Greenwich Corporation, a company that manufactures a variety of products.

a.   Receive raw materials from suppliers.
b.   Manage parts inventories.
c.   Do rough milling work on products.
d.   Interview and process new employees in the personnel department.
e.   Design new products.
f.   Perform periodic preventive maintenance on general-use equipment.
g.   Use the general factory building.
h.   Issue purchase orders for a job.

Required:
Classify each of the activities above as either a unit-level, batch-level, product-level, or facility-level activity.

BRIEF EXERCISE 3–2   Compute Activity Rates   (LO2)
Kramer Corporation is a diversified manufacturer of consumer goods. The company's activity-based costing system has the following seven activity cost pools:

Activity Cost Pool	Estimated Overhead Cost	Expected Activity
Labor related	$48,000	20,000 direct labor-hours
Machine related	$67,500	45,000 machine-hours
Machine setups	$84,000	600 setups
Production orders	$112,000	400 orders
Product testing	$58,500	900 tests
Packaging	$90,000	6,000 packages
General factory	$672,000	20,000 direct labor-hours

Required:
  1. Compute the activity rate for each activity cost pool.
  2. Compute the company's predetermined overhead rate, assuming that the company uses a single plantwide predetermined overhead rate based on direct labor-hours.

BRIEF EXERCISE 3–3   Compute ABC Product Costs   (LO3)
Klumper Corporation is a diversified manufacturer of industrial goods. The company's activity-based costing system contains the following six activity cost pools and activity rates:

Activity Cost Pool	Activity Rates
Labor related	$6.00 per direct labor-hour
Machine related	$4.00 per machine-hour
Machine setups	$50.00 per setup
Production orders	$90.00 per order
Shipments	$14.00 per shipment
General factory	$9.00 per direct labor-hour

Cost and activity data have been supplied for the following products:

	K425	M67
Direct materials cost per unit	$13.00	$56.00
Direct labor cost per unit	$5.60	$3.50
Number of units produced per year	200	2,000

	Total Expected Activity	
	K425	M67
Direct labor-hours	80	500
Machine-hours	100	1,500
Machine setups	1	4
Production orders	1	4
Shipments	1	10

Required:
Compute the unit product cost of each product listed above.

BRIEF EXERCISE 3–4   Contrast ABC and Conventional Product Costs   (LO4)
Midwest Industrial Products Corporation makes two products, Product H and Product L. Product H is expected to sell 50,000 units next year and Product L is expected to sell 10,000 units. A unit of either product requires 0.2 direct labor-hours.
    The company's total manufacturing overhead for the year is expected to be $1,920,000.

Required:
1. The company currently applies manufacturing overhead to products using direct labor-hours as the allocation base. If this method is followed, how much overhead cost would be applied to each product? Compute both the overhead cost per unit and the total amount of overhead cost that would be applied to each product. (In other words, how much overhead cost is applied to a unit of Product H? Product L? How much overhead cost is applied in total to all the units of Product H? Product L?)
2. Management is considering an activity-based costing system and would like to know what impact this change might have on product costs. For purposes of discussion, it has been suggested that all of the manufacturing overhead be treated as a product-level cost. The total manufacturing overhead would be divided in half between the two products, with $960,000 assigned to Product H and $960,000 assigned to Product L.
      If this suggestion is followed, how much overhead cost per unit would be applied to each product?
3. Explain the impact on unit product costs of the switch in costing systems.

BRIEF EXERCISE 3–5   Cost Flows in an ABC System   (LO5)
Larker Corporation implemented activity-based costing several years ago and uses it for its external financial reports. The company has four activity cost pools, which are listed below.

Activity Cost Pool	Activity Rate
Machine related	$24 per MH
Purchase orders	$85 per order
Machine setups	$175 per setup
General factory	$16 per DLH

At the beginning of the year, the company had inventory balances as follows:

Raw materials	$18,000
Work in process	$24,000
Finished goods	$46,000

Selected transactions recorded by the company during the year are given below:

a. Raw materials were purchased on account, $854,000.
b. Raw materials were requisitioned for use in production, $848,000 ($780,000 direct and $68,000 indirect).
c. Labor costs were incurred in the factory, $385,000 ($330,000 direct labor and $55,000 indirect labor).
d. Depreciation was recorded on factory assets, $225,000.
e. Miscellaneous manufacturing overhead costs were incurred, $194,000.
f. Manufacturing overhead cost was applied to production. Actual activity during the year was as follows:

Activity Cost Pool	Actual Activity
Machine related.........................	3,800 MHs
Purchase orders	700 orders
Machine setups...........................	400 setups
General factory	22,000 DLHs

g. Completed products were transferred to the company's finished goods warehouse. According to the company's costing system, these products cost $1,690,000.

Required:
1. Prepare journal entries to record transactions (a) through (g) above.
2. Post the entries in part (1) above to T-accounts.
3. Compute the underapplied or overapplied overhead cost in the Manufacturing Overhead account.

EXERCISES

EXERCISE 3–6   Cost Hierarchy and Activity Measures   (LO1)
The following activities are carried out in Greenberry Company, a manufacturer of consumer goods.

a. Direct labor workers assemble a product.
b. Engineers design a new product.
c. A machine is set up to process a batch.
d. Numerically controlled machines cut and shape materials.
e. The personnel department trains new employees concerning company policies.
f. Raw materials are moved from the receiving dock to the production line.
g. A random sample of 10 units in each batch is inspected for defects.

Required:
1. Classify each activity as a unit-level, batch-level, product-level, or facility-level cost.
2. Provide at least one example of an allocation base (i.e., activity measure) that could be used to allocate the cost of each activity listed above.

EXERCISE 3–7   Computing ABC Product Costs   (LO2, LO3)
Fogerty Company makes two products, titanium Hubs and Sprockets. Data regarding the two products follow:

	Direct Labor-Hours per Unit	Annual Production
Hubs	0.80	10,000 units
Sprockets	0.40	40,000 units

Additional information about the company follows:

a. Hubs require $32 in direct materials per unit, and Sprockets require $18.
b. The direct labor wage rate is $15 per hour.
c. Hubs are more complex to manufacture than Sprockets and they require special equipment.
d. The ABC system has the following activity cost pools:

Activity Cost Pool	Activity Measure	Estimated Overhead Cost	Activity		
			Hubs	Sprockets	Total
Machine setups	Number of setups	$72,000	100	300	400
Special processing	Machine-hours	$200,000	5,000	0	5,000
General factory	Direct labor-hours	$816,000	8,000	16,000	24,000

Required:

1. Compute the activity rate (i.e., predetermined overhead rate) for each activity cost pool.
2. Determine the unit product cost of each product according to the ABC system.

EXERCISE 3–8 Cost Flows in Activity-Based Costing (LO2, LO5)

Sylvan Company uses activity-based costing to determine product costs for external financial reports. The company's partially completed Manufacturing Overhead T-account for the current year is shown below:

Manufacturing Overhead

(a)   1,302,000 |

Required:

1. What does the entry (a) above represent?
2. At the beginning of the year, the company made the following estimates of cost and activity for its five activity cost pools:

Activity Cost Pool	Activity Measure	Estimated Overhead Cost	Expected Activity
Labor related	Direct labor-hours	$280,000	40,000 DLHs
Purchase orders	Number of orders	$90,000	1,500 orders
Parts management	Number of part types	$120,000	400 part types
Board etching	Number of boards	$360,000	2,000 boards
General factory	Machine-hours	$400,000	80,000 MHs

Compute the activity rate (i.e., predetermined overhead rate) for each of the activity cost pools.
3. During the year, actual activity was recorded as follows:

Activity Cost Pool	Actual Activity
Labor related	41,000 DLHs
Purchase orders	1,300 orders
Parts management	420 part types
Board etching	2,150 boards
General factory	82,000 MHs

Determine the amount of manufacturing overhead cost applied to production for the year.
4. Determine the amount of underapplied or overapplied overhead cost for the year.

EXERCISE 3–9 Assigning Overhead to Products in ABC (LO3)

Refer to the data in Exercise 3–8 for Sylvan Company. Activities during the year were distributed across the company's four products as follows:

Activity Cost Pool	Actual Activity			
	Product A	Product B	Product C	Product D
Labor related (DLHs)	8,000	12,000	15,000	6,000
Purchase orders (orders)	100	300	400	500
Parts management (part types)	20	90	200	110
Board etching (boards)	0	1,500	650	0
General factory (MHs)	16,000	24,000	30,000	12,000

Required:
Compute the amount of overhead cost applied to each product during the year.

EXERCISE 3–10   Contrast ABC and Conventional Product Costs   (LO2, LO3, LO4)
Harrison Company makes two products and uses a conventional costing system in which a single plantwide predetermined overhead rate is computed based on direct labor-hours. Data for the two products for the upcoming year follow:

	Rascon	Parcel
Direct materials cost per unit	$13.00	$22.00
Direct labor cost per unit	$6.00	$3.00
Direct labor-hours per unit	0.40	0.20
Number of units produced	20,000	80,000

These products are customized to some degree for specific customers.

Required:
1. The company's manufacturing overhead costs for the year are expected to be $576,000. Using the company's conventional costing system, compute the unit product costs for the two products.
2. Management is considering an activity-based costing system in which half of the overhead would continue to be allocated on the basis of direct labor-hours and half would be allocated on the basis of engineering design time. This time is expected to be distributed as follows during the upcoming year:

	Rascon	Parcel	Total
Engineering design time (in hours)	3,000	3,000	6,000

   Compute the unit product costs for the two products using the proposed ABC system.
3. Explain why the product costs differ between the two systems.

PROBLEMS

PROBLEM 3–11A   ABC Cost Hierarchy   (LO1)
Juneau Company manufactures a variety of products in a single facility. Consultants hired by the company to do an activity-based costing analysis have identified the following activities carried out in the company on a routine basis:

a.   Machines are set up between batches of different products.
b.   The company's grounds crew maintains planted areas surrounding the factory.
c.   A percentage of all completed goods are inspected on a random basis.
d.   Milling machines are used to make components for products.
e.   Employees are trained in general procedures.
f.   Purchase orders are issued for materials required in production.
g.   The maintenance crew does routine periodic maintenance on general-purpose equipment.
h.   The plant controller prepares periodic accounting reports.
i.   Material is received on the receiving dock and moved to the production area.
j.   The engineering department makes modifications in the designs of products.
k.   The human resources department screens and hires new employees.
l.   Production orders are issued for jobs.

Required:
1. Classify each of the above activities as a unit-level, batch-level, product-level, or facility-level activity.
2. For each of the above activities, suggest an activity measure that could be used to allocate its costs to products.

PROBLEM 3–12A Contrasting ABC and Conventional Product Costs (LO2, LO3, LO4)

Siegel Corporation manufactures a product that is available in both a deluxe and a regular model. The company has made the regular model for years; the deluxe model was introduced several years ago to tap a new segment of the market. Since introduction of the deluxe model, the company's profits have steadily declined. Sales of the deluxe model have been increasing rapidly.

Overhead is applied to products on the basis of direct labor-hours. At the beginning of the current year, management estimated that $2,000,000 in overhead costs would be incurred and the company would produce and sell 5,000 units of the deluxe model and 40,000 units of the regular model. The deluxe model requires 1.6 hours of direct labor time per unit, and the regular model requires 0.8 hours. Materials and labor costs per unit are given below:

	Deluxe	Regular
Direct materials cost per unit	$150	$112
Direct labor cost per unit	$16	$8

Required:

1. Compute the predetermined overhead rate using direct labor-hours as the basis for allocating overhead costs to products. Compute the unit product cost for one unit of each model.
2. An intern suggested that the company use activity-based costing to cost its products. A team was formed to investigate this idea. It came back with the recommendation that four activity cost pools be used. These cost pools and their associated activities are listed below:

Activity Cost Pool and Activity Measure	Estimated Overhead Cost	Activity Deluxe	Activity Regular	Activity Total
Purchase orders (number of orders)	$ 84,000	400	800	1,200
Rework requests (number of requests)	216,000	300	600	900
Product testing (number of tests)	450,000	4,000	11,000	15,000
Machine-related (machine-hours)	1,250,000	20,000	30,000	50,000
	$2,000,000			

Compute the activity rate (i.e., predetermined overhead rate) for each of the activity cost pools.
3. Assume that actual activity is as expected for the year. Using activity-based costing, do the following:
   a. Determine the total amount of overhead that would be applied to each model for the year.
   b. Compute the unit product cost for one unit of each model.
4. Can you identify a possible explanation for the company's declining profits? If so, what is it?

PROBLEM 3–13A Compute and Use Activity Rates to Determine the Costs of Serving Customers (LO2, LO3, LO4)

Jordan's Lakeside is a popular restaurant located on Lake Washington in Seattle. The owner of the restaurant has been trying to better understand costs at the restaurant and has hired a student intern to conduct an activity-based costing study. The intern, in consultation with the owner, identified the following major activities:

Activity Cost Pool	Activity Measure
Serving a party of diners	Number of parties served
Serving a diner	Number of diners served
Serving drinks	Number of drinks ordered

A group of diners who ask to sit at the same table are counted as a party. Some costs, such as the costs of cleaning linen, are the same whether one person is at a table or the table is full. Other costs, such as washing dishes, depend on the number of diners served.

Data concerning these activities are displayed below.

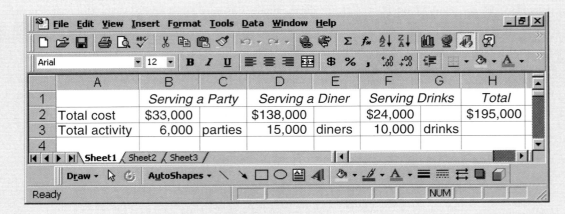

	Serving a Party		Serving a Diner		Serving Drinks		Total
1							
2 Total cost	$33,000		$138,000		$24,000		$195,000
3 Total activity	6,000	parties	15,000	diners	10,000	drinks	
4							

Prior to the activity-based costing study, the owner knew very little about the costs of the restaurant. She knew that the total cost for the month was $195,000 and that 15,000 diners had been served. Therefore, the average cost per diner was $13 ($195,000 ÷ 15,000 diners = $13 per diner).

Required:
1. Compute the activity rates for each of the three activities.
2. According to the activity-based costing system, what is the total cost of serving each of the following parties of diners?
   a. A party of four diners who order three drinks in total.
   b. A party of two diners who do not order any drinks.
   c. A lone diner who orders two drinks.
3. Convert the total costs you computed in part (1) above to costs per diner. In other words, what is the average cost per diner for serving each of the following parties?
   a. A party of four diners who order three drinks in total.
   b. A party of two diners who do not order any drinks.
   c. A lone diner who orders two drinks.
4. Why do the costs per diner for the three different parties differ from each other and from the overall average cost of $13 per diner?

CHECK FIGURE
(3a) Mono-relay overhead
cost: $10.80

PROBLEM 3–14A Contrasting ABC and Conventional Product Costs (LO2, LO3, LO4)
For many years, Zapro Company manufactured a single product called a mono-relay. Then three years ago, the company automated a portion of its plant and at the same time introduced a second product called a bi-relay that has become increasingly popular. The bi-relay is a more complex product, requiring one hour of direct labor time per unit to manufacture and extensive machining in the automated portion of the plant. The mono-relay requires only 0.75 hour of direct labor time per unit and only a small amount of machining. Manufacturing overhead costs are currently assigned to products on the basis of direct labor-hours.

Despite the growing popularity of the company's new bi-relay, profits have been declining steadily. Management is beginning to believe that there may be a problem with the company's costing system. Material and labor costs per unit are as follows:

	Mono-Relay	Bi-Relay
Direct materials	$35	$48
Direct labor (0.75 hour and 1.0 hour @ $12 per hour)	$9	$12

Management estimates that the company will incur $1,000,000 in manufacturing overhead costs during the current year and 40,000 units of the mono-relay and 10,000 units of the bi-relay will be produced and sold.

Required:
1. Compute the predetermined manufacturing overhead rate assuming that the company continues to apply manufacturing overhead cost on the basis of direct labor-hours. Using this rate and other data from the problem, determine the unit product cost of each product.

2. Management is considering using activity-based costing to apply manufacturing overhead cost to products for external financial reports. The activity-based costing system would have the following four activity cost pools:

Activity Cost Pool	Activity Measure	Estimated Overhead Cost
Maintaining parts inventory	Number of part types	$ 180,000
Processing purchase orders	Number of purchase orders	90,000
Quality control	Number of tests run	230,000
Machine related	Machine-hours	500,000
		$1,000,000

	Expected Activity		
Activity Measure	Mono-Relay	Bi-Relay	Total
Number of part types	75	150	225
Number of purchase orders	800	200	1,000
Number of tests run	2,500	3,250	5,750
Machine-hours	4,000	6,000	10,000

Determine the activity rate (i.e., predetermined overhead rate) for each of the four activity cost pools.

3. Using the activity rates you computed in part (2) above, do the following:

   a. Determine the total amount of manufacturing overhead cost that would be applied to each product using the activity-based costing system. After these totals have been computed, determine the amount of manufacturing overhead cost per unit of each product.

   b. Compute the unit product cost of each product.

4. From the data you have developed in parts (1) through (3) above, identify factors that may account for the company's declining profits.

PROBLEM 3–15A Activity-Based Costing Cost Flows and Income Statement (LO2, LO5)
Aucton Corporation is a manufacturing company that uses activity-based costing for its external financial reports. The company's activity cost pools and associated data for the coming year appear below:

CHECK FIGURE
(4) Total overhead
overapplied: $8,000

Activity Cost Pool	Activity Measure	Estimated Overhead Cost	Expected Activity
Machining	Machine-hours	$180,000	1,000 MHs
Purchase orders	Number of orders	$90,000	600 orders
Parts management	Number of part types	$60,000	300 part types
Testing	Number of tests	$150,000	250 tests
General factory	Direct labor-hours	$280,000	20,000 DLHs

At the beginning of the year, the company had inventory balances as follows:

Raw materials	$7,000
Work in process	$6,000
Finished goods	$10,000

The following transactions were recorded for the year:

a. Raw materials were purchased on account, $595,000.

b. Raw materials were withdrawn from the storeroom for use in production, $600,000 ($560,000 direct and $40,000 indirect).

c. The following costs were incurred for employee services: direct labor, $90,000; indirect labor, $300,000; sales commissions, $85,000; and administrative salaries, $245,000.

d. Sales travel costs were incurred, $38,000.
e. Various factory overhead costs were incurred, $237,000.
f. Advertising costs were incurred, $190,000.
g. Depreciation was recorded for the year, $270,000 ($210,000 related to factory operations and $60,000 related to selling and administrative activities).
h. Manufacturing overhead was applied to products. Actual activity for the year was as follows:

Activity Cost Pool	Actual Activity
Machining	1,050 MHs
Purchase orders	580 orders
Parts management	330 part types
Testing	265 tests
General factory	21,000 DLHs

i. Goods were completed and transferred to the finished goods warehouse. According to the company's activity-based costing system, these finished goods cost $1,450,000 to manufacture.
j. Goods were sold on account to customers during the year for a total of $2,100,000. According to the company's activity-based costing system, the goods cost $1,400,000 to manufacture.

Required:
1. Compute the predetermined overhead rate (i.e., activity rate) for each activity cost pool.
2. Prepare journal entries to record transactions (a) through (j) above.
3. Post the entries in part (2) above to T-accounts.
4. Compute the underapplied or overapplied manufacturing overhead cost. Prepare a journal entry to close any balance in the Manufacturing Overhead account to Cost of Goods Sold. Post the entry to the appropriate T-accounts.
5. Prepare an income statement for the year.

CHECK FIGURE
(2d) Total overhead
underapplied: $17,000

PROBLEM 3–16A Activity-Based Costing Cost Flows (LO2, LO3, LO5)
Munoz Corporation uses activity-based costing to determine product costs for external financial reports. At the beginning of the year, management made the following estimates of cost and activity in the company's five activity cost pools:

Activity Cost Pool	Activity Measure	Estimated Overhead Cost	Expected Activity
Labor related	Direct labor-hours	$210,000	35,000 DLHs
Purchase orders	Number of orders	$72,000	900 orders
Product testing	Number of tests	$168,000	1,400 tests
Template etching	Number of templates	$315,000	10,500 templates
General factory	Machine-hours	$840,000	70,000 MHs

Required:
1. Compute the activity rate (i.e., predetermined overhead rate) for each of the activity cost pools.
2. During the year, actual overhead cost and activity were recorded as follows:

Activity Cost Pool	Actual Overhead Cost	Actual Activity
Labor related	$ 205,000	32,000 DLHs
Purchase orders	74,000	950 orders
Product testing	160,000	1,300 tests
Template etching	338,000	11,500 relays
General factory	825,000	68,000 MHs
Total manufacturing overhead cost . .	$1,602,000	

a. Prepare a journal entry to record the incurrence of actual manufacturing overhead cost for the year (credit Accounts Payable). Post the entry to the company's Manufacturing Overhead T-account.
b. Determine the amount of overhead cost applied to production during the year.

c.   Prepare a journal entry to record the application of manufacturing overhead cost to work in process for the year. Post the entry to the company's Manufacturing Overhead T-account.

d.   Determine the amount of underapplied or overapplied manufacturing overhead for the year.

3.   The actual activity for the year was distributed among the company's four products as follows:

Activity Cost Pool	Actual Activity			
	Product A	Product B	Product C	Product D
Labor related (DLHs)	6,000	7,500	10,000	8,500
Purchase orders (orders)	150	300	100	400
Product testing (tests)	400	175	225	500
Template etching (templates)	0	4,500	0	7,000
General factory (MHs)	10,000	20,000	17,000	21,000

a.   Determine the total amount of overhead cost applied to each product.

b.   Does the total amount of overhead cost applied to the products above tie in to the T-accounts in any way? Explain.

PROBLEM 3–17A   Contrast Activity-Based Costing and Conventional Product Costs (LO2, LO3, LO4)

Ellix Company manufactures two models of ultra-high fidelity speakers, the X200 model and the X99 model. Data regarding the two products follow:

	Direct Labor-Hours per Unit	Annual Production (units)	Total Direct Labor-Hours
Model X200	1.8	5,000	9,000
Model X99	0.9	30,000	27,000
			36,000

Additional information about the company follows:

a.   Model X200 requires $72 in direct materials per unit, and model X99 requires $50.

b.   The direct labor wage rate is $10 per hour.

c.   The company has always used direct labor-hours as the base for applying manufacturing overhead cost to products.

d.   Model X200 is more complex to manufacture than model X99 and requires the use of special equipment. Consequently, the company is considering the use of activity-based costing to apply manufacturing overhead cost to products. Three activity cost pools have been identified as follows:

Activity Cost Pool	Activity Measure	Estimated Overhead Cost
Machine setups	Number of setups	$ 360,000
Special processing	Machine-hours	180,000
General factory	Direct labor-hours	1,260,000
		$1,800,000

Activity Measure	Expected Activity		
	Model X200	Model X99	Total
Number of setups	50	100	150
Machine-hours	12,000	0	12,000
Direct labor-hours	9,000	27,000	36,000

Required:

1. Assume that the company continues to use direct labor-hours as the base for applying overhead cost to products.
   a. Compute the predetermined overhead rate.
   b. Compute the unit product cost of each model.
2. Assume that the company decides to use activity-based costing to apply manufacturing overhead cost to products.
   a. Compute the predetermined overhead rate for each activity cost pool and determine the amount of overhead cost that would be applied to each model using the activity-based costing system.
   b. Compute the unit product cost of each model.
3. Explain why manufacturing overhead cost shifts from Model X99 to Model X200 under activity-based costing.

CHECK FIGURE
(2d) Total overhead
overapplied: $15,000

PROBLEM 3–18A   Cost Flows and Unit Product Costs in Activity-Based Costing
(LO2, LO3, LO5)

Hunter Corporation uses activity-based costing to determine product costs for external financial reports. At the beginning of the year, management made the following estimates of cost and activity in the company's five activity cost pools:

Activity Cost Pool	Activity Measure	Estimated Overhead Cost	Expected Activity
Labor related	Direct labor-hours	$270,000	30,000 DLHs
Production orders	Number of orders	$60,000	750 orders
Material receipts	Number of receipts	$180,000	1,200 receipts
Relay assembly	Number of relays	$320,000	8,000 relays
General factory	Machine-hours	$840,000	60,000 MHs

Required:

1. Compute the activity rate (i.e., predetermined overhead rate) for each of the activity cost pools.
2. During the year, actual overhead cost and activity were recorded as follows:

Activity Cost Pool	Actual Overhead Cost	Actual Activity
Labor related	$ 279,000	32,000 DLHs
Production orders	58,000	700 orders
Material receipts	190,000	1,300 receipts
Relay assembly	320,000	7,900 relays
General factory	847,000	61,000 MHs
Total overhead cost	$1,694,000	

   a. Prepare a journal entry to record the incurrence of actual manufacturing overhead cost for the year (credit Accounts Payable). Post the entry to the company's Manufacturing Overhead T-account.
   b. Determine the amount of overhead cost applied to production during the year.
   c. Prepare a journal entry to record the application of manufacturing overhead cost to Work in Process for the year. Post the entry to the company's Manufacturing Overhead T-account.
   d. Determine the amount of underapplied or overapplied manufacturing overhead for the year.
3. The actual activity for the year was distributed among the company's four products as follows:

	Actual Activity			
Activity Cost Pool	Product A	Product B	Product C	Product D
Labor related (DLHs)	8,000	11,000	4,000	9,000
Production orders (orders)	160	200	130	210
Materials receipts (receipts)	100	460	240	500
Relay assembly (relays)	2,700	0	5,200	0
General factory (MHs)	13,000	18,000	14,000	16,000

a. Determine the total amount of overhead cost applied to each product.
b. Does the total amount of overhead cost applied to the products above tie in to the T-accounts in any way? Explain.

BUILDING YOUR SKILLS

Communicating in Practice   (LOI)

You often provide advice to Maria Graham, a client who is interested in diversifying her company. Maria is considering the purchase of a small manufacturing company that assembles and packages its many products by hand. She plans to automate the factory and her projections indicate that the company will once again be profitable within two to three years. During her review of the company's records, she discovered that the company currently uses direct labor-hours to allocate overhead to its products. Because of its simplicity, Maria hopes that this approach can continue to be used.

Required:

Write a memorandum to Maria that addresses whether or not direct labor should continue to be used as an allocation base for overhead.

Ethics Challenge   (LOI)

You and your friends go to a restaurant as a group. At the end of the meal, the issue arises of how the bill for the group should be shared. One alternative is to figure out the cost of what each individual consumed and divide up the bill accordingly. Another alternative is to split the bill equally among the individuals.

Required:

Which system for dividing the bill is more equitable? Which system is easier to use? How does this issue relate to the material covered in this chapter?

Teamwork in Action   (LOI)

Your team should visit and closely observe the operations at a fast food restaurant.

Required:

Identify activities and costs at the restaurant that fall into each of the following categories:

a. Unit-level activities and costs.
b. Customer-level activities and costs. (This is like a batch-level activity at a manufacturing company.)
c. Product-level activities and costs.
d. Facility-level activities and costs.

Case   [LO2, LO3, LO4]

CHECK FIGURE
(2b) Overhead cost per pound of Viet Select: $1.90

Java Source, Inc. (JSI), is a processor and distributor of a variety of blends of coffee. The company buys coffee beans from around the world and roasts, blends, and packages them for resale. JSI offers a large variety of different coffees that it sells to gourmet shops in one-pound bags. The major cost of the coffee is raw materials. However, the company's predominantly automated roasting, blending, and packing processes require a substantial amount of manufacturing overhead. The company uses relatively little direct labor.

Some of JSI's coffees are very popular and sell in large volumes, while a few of the newer blends sell in very low volumes. JSI prices its coffees at manufacturing cost plus a markup of 25%, with some adjustments made to keep the company's prices competitive.

For the coming year, JSI's budget includes estimated manufacturing overhead cost of $2,200,000. JSI assigns manufacturing overhead to products on the basis of direct labor-hours. The expected direct labor cost totals $600,000, which represents 50,000 hours of direct labor time. Based on the sales budget and expected raw materials costs, the company will purchase and use $5,000,000 of raw materials (mostly coffee beans) during the year.

The expected costs for direct materials and direct labor for one-pound bags of two of the company's coffee products appear below.

	Kenya Dark	Viet Select
Direct materials	$4.50	$2.90
Direct labor (0.02 hours per bag)	$0.24	$0.24

JSI's controller believes that the company's traditional costing system may be providing misleading cost information. To determine whether or not this is correct, the controller has prepared an analysis of the year's expected manufacturing overhead costs, as shown in the following table:

Activity Cost Pool	Activity Measure	Expected Activity for the Year	Expected Cost for the Year
Purchasing	Purchase orders	2,000 orders	$ 560,000
Material handling	Number of setups	1,000 setups	193,000
Quality control	Number of batches	500 batches	90,000
Roasting	Roasting hours	95,000 roasting hours	1,045,000
Blending	Blending hours	32,000 blending hours	192,000
Packaging	Packaging hours	24,000 packaging hours	120,000
Total manufacturing overhead cost			$2,200,000

Data regarding the expected production of Kenya Dark and Viet Select coffee are presented below.

	Kenya Dark	Viet Select
Expected sales	80,000 pounds	4,000 pounds
Batch size	5,000 pounds	500 pounds
Setups	2 per batch	2 per batch
Purchase order size	20,000 pounds	500 pounds
Roasting time per 100 pounds	1.5 roasting hours	1.5 roasting hours
Blending time per 100 pounds	0.5 blending hours	0.5 blending hours
Packaging time per 100 pounds . . .	0.3 packaging hours	0.3 packaging hours

Required:
1. Using direct labor-hours as the base for assigning manufacturing overhead cost to products, do the following:
   a. Determine the predetermined overhead rate that will be used during the year.
   b. Determine the unit product cost of one pound of the Kenya Dark coffee and one pound of the Viet Select coffee.
2. Using activity-based costing as the basis for assigning manufacturing overhead cost to products, do the following:
   a. Determine the total amount of manufacturing overhead cost assigned to the Kenya Dark coffee and to the Viet Select coffee for the year.
   b. Using the data developed in part (2a) above, compute the amount of manufacturing overhead cost per pound of the Kenya Dark coffee and the Viet Select coffee. Round all computations to the nearest whole cent.
   c. Determine the unit product cost of one pound of the Kenya Dark coffee and one pound of the Viet Select coffee.
3. Write a brief memo to the president of JSI explaining what you have found in parts (1) and (2) above and discussing the implications to the company of using direct labor as the base for assigning manufacturing overhead cost to products.

(CMA, adapted)

CHECK FIGURE
(2) Standard model unit product cost: $29.98 per unit

Analytical Thinking   [LO2, LO3, LO4]
"A dollar of gross margin per briefcase? That's ridiculous!" roared Art Dejans, president of CarryAll, Inc. "Why do we go on producing those standard briefcases when we're able to make over $15 per unit on our specialty items? Maybe it's time to get out of the standard line and focus the whole plant on specialty work."

Mr. Dejans is referring to a summary of unit costs and revenues that he had just received from the company's Accounting Department:

	Standard Briefcases	Specialty Briefcases
Selling price per unit	$36	$40
Unit product cost	35	25
Gross margin per unit	$ 1	$15

CarryAll produces briefcases from leather, fabric, and synthetic materials in a single plant. The basic product is a standard briefcase that is made from leather lined with fabric. The standard briefcase is a high-quality item and has sold well for many years.

Last year, the company decided to expand its product line and produce specialty briefcases for special orders. These briefcases differ from the standard in that they vary in size, they contain the finest leather and synthetic materials, and they are imprinted with the buyer's name. To reduce labor costs on the specialty briefcases, automated machines do most of the cutting and stitching. These machines are used to a much lesser degree in the production of standard briefcases.

"I agree that the specialty business is looking better and better," replied Sally Henrie, the company's marketing manager. "And there seems to be plenty of specialty work out there, particularly since the competition hasn't been able to touch our price. Did you know that Armor Company, our biggest competitor, charges over $50 a unit for its specialty items? Now that's what I call gouging the customer!"

A breakdown of the manufacturing cost for each of CarryAll's product lines is given below:

	Standard Briefcases	Specialty Briefcases
Units produced each month	10,000	2,500
Direct materials:		
Leather	$15.00	$ 7.50
Fabric	5.00	5.00
Synthetic	0	5.00
Total direct materials	20.00	17.50
Direct labor (0.5 DLH and 0.25 DLH @ $12 per DLH)	6.00	3.00
Manufacturing overhead (0.5 DLH and 0.25 DLH @ $18 per DLH)	9.00	4.50
Total cost per unit	$35.00	$25.00

Manufacturing overhead is applied to products on the basis of direct labor-hours. The rate of $18 per direct labor-hour is determined by dividing the total manufacturing overhead cost for a month by the direct labor-hours:

$$\text{Predetermined overhead rate} = \frac{\text{Manufacturing overhead}}{\text{Direct labor-hours}} = \frac{\$101,250}{5,625 \text{ DLHs}} = \$18 \text{ per DLH}$$

The following additional information is available about the company and its products:

a. Standard briefcases are produced in batches of 200 units, and specialty briefcases are produced in batches of 25 units. Thus, the company does 50 setups for the standard items each month and 100 setups for the specialty items. A setup for the standard items requires one hour of time, whereas a setup for the specialty items requires two hours of time.

b. All briefcases are inspected to ensure that quality standards are met. A total of 300 hours of inspection time is spent on the standard briefcases and 500 hours of inspection time is spent on the specialty briefcases each month.

c. A standard briefcase requires 0.5 hour of machine time, and a specialty briefcase requires 2 hours of machine time.

d. The company is considering the use of activity-based costing as an alternative to its traditional costing system for computing unit product costs. Since these unit product costs will be used for external financial reporting, all manufacturing overhead costs are to be allocated to products and nonmanufacturing costs are to be excluded from product costs. The activity-based costing system has already been designed and costs allocated to the activity cost pools. The activity cost pools and activity measures are detailed below:

Activity Cost Pool	Activity Measure	Estimated Overhead Cost
Purchasing	Number of orders	$ 12,000
Material handling	Number of receipts	15,000
Production orders and setup	Setup hours	20,250
Inspection	Inspection-hours	16,000
Frame assembly	Assembly-hours	8,000
Machine related	Machine-hours	30,000
		$101,250

	Expected Activity		
Activity Measure	Standard Briefcase	Specialty Briefcase	Total
Number of orders:			
Leather	34	6	40
Fabric	48	12	60
Synthetic material	0	100	100
Number of receipts:			
Leather	52	8	60
Fabric	64	16	80
Synthetic material	0	160	160
Setup hours	?	?	?
Inspection-hours	?	?	?
Assembly-hours	800	800	1,600
Machine-hours	?	?	?

Required:

1. Using activity-based costing, determine the amount of manufacturing overhead cost that would be applied to each standard briefcase and each specialty briefcase.
2. Using the data computed in part (1) above and other data from the case as needed, determine the unit product cost of each product line from the perspective of the activity-based costing system.
3. Within the limitations of the data that have been provided, evaluate the president's concern about the profitability of the two product lines. Would you recommend that the company shift its resources entirely to production of specialty briefcases? Explain.
4. Sally Henrie stated that "the competition hasn't been able to touch our price" on specialty business. Why do you suppose the competition hasn't been able to touch CarryAll's price?

Adapted from a case written by Harold P. Roth and Imogene Posey, "Management Accounting Case Study: CarryAll Company," *Management Accounting Campus Report,* Institute of Management Accountants (Fall 1991), p. 9. Used by permission.

Taking It to the Net

As you know, the World Wide Web is a medium that is constantly evolving. Sites come and go and change without notice. To enable periodic updating of site addresses, these problems have been posted to the textbook website (www.mhhe.com/bgn3e). After accessing the site, enter the Student Center and select this chapter to find the Taking It to the Net problems.

4

Systems Design: Process Costing

LEARNING OBJECTIVES

After studying Chapter 4, you should be able to:

LO1 Record the flow of materials, labor, and overhead through a process costing system.

LO2 Compute the equivalent units of production using the weighted-average method.

LO3 Prepare a quantity schedule using the weighted-average method.

LO4 Compute the costs per equivalent unit using the weighted-average method.

LO5 Prepare a cost reconciliation using the weighted-average method.

DECISION FEATURE

Costing the "Quicker-Picker-Upper"

If you have ever spilled milk, there is a good chance that you used Bounty paper towels to clean up the mess. Procter & Gamble (P&G) manufactures Bounty in two main processing departments—Paper Making and Paper Converting. In the Paper Making Department, wood pulp is converted into paper and then spooled into 2,000 pound rolls that are inventoried and retrieved as needed to supply the paper converting process. In the Paper Converting Department, two 2,000 pound rolls of paper are simultaneously unwound into a machine that creates a two-ply paper towel that is decorated, perforated, and embossed to create texture. The large sheets of paper towels that emerge from this process are wrapped around a cylinder-shaped cardboard core measuring eight feet in length. Once enough sheets wrap around the core, the eight-foot roll is cut into individual rolls of Bounty that are sent down a conveyor to be wrapped, packed, and shipped.

In this type of manufacturing environment, costs cannot be readily traced to individual rolls of Bounty; however, given the homogeneous nature of the product, the total costs incurred in the Paper Making Department can be spread uniformly across its output of 2,000 pound rolls of paper. Similarly, the total costs incurred to produce a particular style of Bounty in the Paper Converting Department (including the cost of the 2,000 pound rolls that are transferred in from the Paper Making Department) can be spread uniformly across the number of cases produced of that style.

P&G uses a similar costing approach for many of its products such as Tide, Crest toothpaste, and Pringles.

Source: Conversation with Brad Bays, retired financial executive from Procter & Gamble.

As explained in Chapter 2, job-order costing and process costing are two common methods for determining unit product costs. A job-order costing system is used in situations where many different jobs or products are worked on each period. Examples of industries that would typically use job-order costing include furniture manufacturing, special-order printing, shipbuilding, and many types of service organizations.

By contrast, **process costing** is most commonly used in industries that produce essentially homogenous (i.e., uniform) products on a continuous basis, such as bricks, corn flakes, or paper. Process costing is particularly used in companies that convert basic raw materials into homogenous products, such as Reynolds Aluminum (aluminum ingots), Scott Paper (toilet paper), General Mills (flour), Exxon (gasoline and lubricating oils), Coppertone (sunscreens), and Kellogg (breakfast cereals). In addition, process costing is sometimes used in companies with assembly operations. A form of process costing may also be used in utilities that produce gas, water, and electricity.

Our purpose in this chapter is to explain how product costing works in a process costing system.

COMPARISON OF JOB-ORDER AND PROCESS COSTING

In some ways process costing is very similar to job-order costing, and in some ways it is very different. In this section, we focus on these similarities and differences to provide a foundation for the detailed discussion of process costing that follows.

Similarities between Job-Order and Process Costing

Much of what was learned in Chapter 2 about costing and cost flows applies equally well to process costing in this chapter. That is, we are not throwing out all that we have learned about costing and starting from "scratch" with a whole new system. The similarities between job-order and process costing can be summarized as follows:

1. Both systems have the same basic purposes—to assign material, labor, and manufacturing overhead costs to products and to provide a mechanism for computing unit product costs.
2. Both systems use the same basic manufacturing accounts, including Manufacturing Overhead, Raw Materials, Work in Process, and Finished Goods.
3. The flow of costs through the manufacturing accounts is basically the same in both systems.

As can be seen from this comparison, much of the knowledge that we have already acquired about costing is applicable to a process costing system. Our task now is to refine and extend this knowledge to process costing.

Differences between Job-Order and Process Costing

There are four differences between job-order and process costing. First, process costing is used when a company produces a continuous flow of units that are indistinguishable from one another. Job-order costing is used when a company produces many different jobs that have unique production requirements. Second, under process costing, it makes no sense to try to identify materials, labor, and overhead costs with a particular customer order (as we did with job-order costing), since each order is just one of many that are filled from a continuous flow of virtually identical units from the production line. Accordingly, process costing accumulates costs *by department* (rather than by order) and assigns these costs uniformly to all units that pass through the department during a period. Third, since process costing focuses on departments, job cost sheets (which we used for job-order costing) are *not* used to accumulate costs. Instead, process costing systems use a **production report** to accumulate costs departmentally and to summarize all activity in a department's Work in Process account during a period. Fourth, process costing systems use the

Job-Order Costing	Process Costing
1. Many different jobs are worked on during each period, with each job having different production requirements.	1. A single product is produced either on a continuous basis or for long periods of time. All units of product are identical.
2. Costs are accumulated by individual job.	2. Costs are accumulated by department.
3. The *job cost sheet* is the key document controlling the accumulation of costs by a job.	3. The *department production report* is the key document showing the accumulation of costs in a department.
4. Unit costs are computed *by job* on the job cost sheet.	4. Unit costs are computed *by department* on the department production report.

EXHIBIT 4–1

Differences between Job-Order and Process Costing

production report to compute unit costs by department. This differs from job-order costing where unit costs are computed by job on the job cost sheet. Exhibit 4–1 summarizes the differences just described.

A Hybrid Approach

Managers of successful pharmacies understand product costs. Some pharmacies use a hybrid approach to costing drugs. For example, a hospital pharmacy may use process costing to develop the cost of formulating the base solution for parenterals (that is, drugs delivered by injection or through the blood stream), and then use job-order costing to accumulate the additional costs incurred to create specific parenteral solutions. These additional costs include the ingredients added to the base solution and the time spent by the pharmacist to prepare the specific prescribed drug solution.

Source: "Pharmaceutical Care: Cost Estimation and Cost Management," *Drug Store News,* February 16, 1998, p. CP21 (5 pages).

COST FLOWS IN PROCESS COSTING

Before going through a detailed example of process costing, it will be helpful to see how manufacturing costs flow through a process costing system.

Processing Departments

A **processing department** is an organizational unit where work is performed on a product and where materials, labor, or overhead costs are added to the product. For example, a Nalley's potato chip factory might have three processing departments—one for preparing potatoes, one for cooking, and one for inspecting and packaging. A brick factory might have two processing departments—one for mixing and molding clay into brick form and one for firing the molded brick. Some products may go through a number of processing departments, while others may go through only one or two. Regardless of the number, the processing departments all have two essential features. First, the activity in the processing department must be performed uniformly on all of the units passing through it. Second, the output of the processing department must be homogeneous—that is, all units produced should be identical.

Products in a process costing environment such as bricks or potato chips typically flow in sequence from one department to another as in Exhibit 4–2.

EXHIBIT 4–2

Sequential Processing Departments

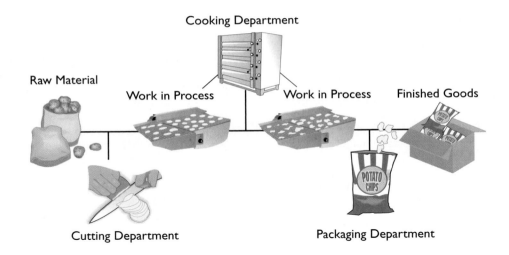

Cooking Department

Raw Material   Work in Process   Work in Process   Finished Goods

Cutting Department   Packaging Department

The Flow of Materials, Labor, and Overhead Costs

Cost accumulation is simpler in a process costing system than in a job-order costing system. In a process costing system, instead of having to trace costs to perhaps hundreds of different jobs, costs are traced to only a few processing departments.

A T-account model of materials, labor, and overhead cost flows in a process costing system is presented in Exhibit 4–3. Several key points should be noted from this exhibit. First, note that a separate Work in Process account is maintained for *each processing department*. In contrast, in a job-order costing system the entire company may have only one Work in Process account. Second, note that the completed production of the first processing department (Department A in the exhibit) is transferred to the Work in Process account of the second processing department (Department B). After further work in Department B, the

EXHIBIT 4–3   T-Account Model of Process Costing Flows

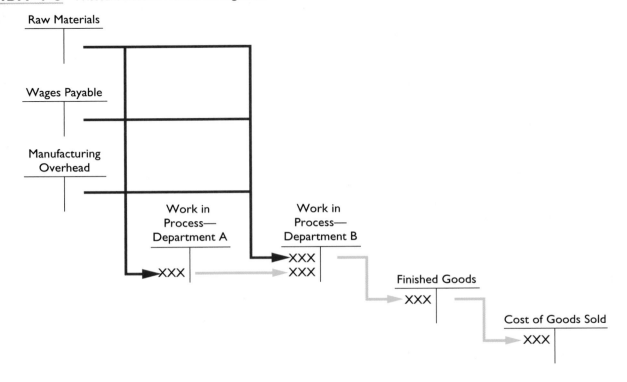

Raw Materials

Wages Payable

Manufacturing Overhead

Work in Process— Department A

Work in Process— Department B

XXX   XXX
       XXX

Finished Goods
XXX

Cost of Goods Sold
XXX

completed units are transferred to Finished Goods. (In Exhibit 4–3, we show only two processing departments, but a company can have many processing departments.)

Finally, note that materials, labor, and overhead costs can be added in *any* processing department—not just the first. Costs in Department B's Work in Process account would consist of the materials, labor, and overhead costs incurred in Department B plus the costs attached to partially completed units transferred in from Department A (called **transferred-in costs**).

Materials, Labor, and Overhead Cost Entries

To complete our discussion of cost flows in a process costing system, in this section we show journal entries relating to materials, labor, and overhead costs at Megan's Classic Cream Soda, a company that has two processing departments—Formulating and Bottling. In the Formulating Department, ingredients are checked for quality and then mixed and injected with carbon dioxide to create bulk cream soda. In the Bottling Department, bottles are checked for defects, filled with cream soda, capped, visually inspected again for defects, and then packed for shipping.

> **LEARNING OBJECTIVE 1**
> Record the flow of materials, labor, and overhead through a process costing system.

Materials Costs　　As in job-order costing, materials are drawn from the storeroom using a materials requisition form. Materials can be added in any processing department, although it is not unusual for materials to be added only in the first processing department, with subsequent departments adding only labor and overhead costs as the partially completed units move along toward completion.

At Megan's Classic Cream Soda, some materials (i.e., water, flavors, sugar, and carbon dioxide) are added in the Formulating Department and some materials (i.e., bottles, caps, and packing materials) are added in the Bottling Department. The journal entry to record the materials used in the first processing department, the Formulating Department, is as follows:

| Work in Process—Formulating .... | XXX | |
| Raw Materials .... | | XXX |

The journal entry to record the materials used in the second processing department, the Bottling Department, is the following:

| Work in Process—Bottling .... | XXX | |
| Raw Materials .... | | XXX |

Labor Costs　　In process costing, labor costs are traced to departments—not to individual jobs. The following journal entry records the labor costs in the Formulating Department at Megan's Classic Cream Soda:

| Work in Process—Formulating .... | XXX | |
| Salaries and Wages Payable .... | | XXX |

Overhead Costs　　In process costing, as in job-order costing, predetermined overhead rates are usually used. Manufacturing overhead cost is applied to units of product as they move through the department. The following journal entry records the cost for the Formulating Department:

| Work in Process—Formulating .... | XXX | |
| Manufacturing Overhead .... | | XXX |

Completing the Cost Flows　　Once processing has been completed in a department, the units are transferred to the next department for further processing, as illustrated in the T-accounts in Exhibit 4–3. The following journal entry is used to transfer the costs of partially completed units from the Formulating Department to the Bottling Department:

| Work in Process—Bottling .... | XXX | |
| Work in Process—Formulating .... | | XXX |

After processing has been completed in the final department, the costs of the completed units are transferred to the Finished Goods inventory account:

| Finished Goods .... | XXX | |
| Work in Process—Bottling .... | | XXX |

Finally, when a customer's order is filled and units are sold, the cost of the units is transferred to Cost of Goods Sold:

| Cost of Goods Sold .... | XXX | |
| Finished Goods .... | | XXX |

To summarize, the cost flows between accounts are basically the same in a process costing system as they are in a job-order costing system. The only difference at this point is that in a process costing system each department has a separate Work in Process account.

EQUIVALENT UNITS OF PRODUCTION

Double Diamond Skis, a company that manufactures a high-performance deep-powder ski, uses process costing to determine its unit product costs. The production process is illustrated in Exhibit 4–4. The basic idea in process costing is to add together all of the costs incurred in a department in a period and then spread those costs uniformly across the units processed in that department during that period. For example, if $80,000 in costs are incurred in a department to produce 2,000 units, the cost per unit in the department would be $40. However, units that have only been partially completed pose a problem. It does not seem reasonable to count partially completed units as equivalent to fully completed units when counting the department's output. Therefore, in process costing, partially completed units are mathematically translated into an equivalent number of fully completed units. This translation is accomplished using the following formula:

Equivalent units = Number of partially completed units × Percentage completion

As the formula states, **equivalent units** is defined as the product of the number of partially completed units and the percentage completion of those units. Roughly speaking, the equivalent units is the number of complete units that could have been obtained from the materials and effort that went into the partially complete units.

For example, suppose the Molding Department at Double Diamond has 500 units in its ending work in process inventory that are 60% complete. These 500 partially complete units are equivalent to 300 fully complete units (500 × 60% = 300). Therefore, the ending work in process inventory contains 300 equivalent units. These equivalent units would be added to any units completed during the period to determine the department's output for the period—called the *equivalent units of production.*

The equivalent units of production can be computed using either the *weighted-average method* or the *FIFO method.* The weighted-average method is a little simpler, and for that reason, it is the method used in this chapter. The details of the FIFO method are contained in a supplement to this chapter that can be downloaded at www.mhhe.com/bgn3e. In broad terms, in the **FIFO method** the equivalent units and unit costs relate only to work done during the current period. In contrast, the

EXHIBIT 4–4 The Production Process at Double Diamond Skis*

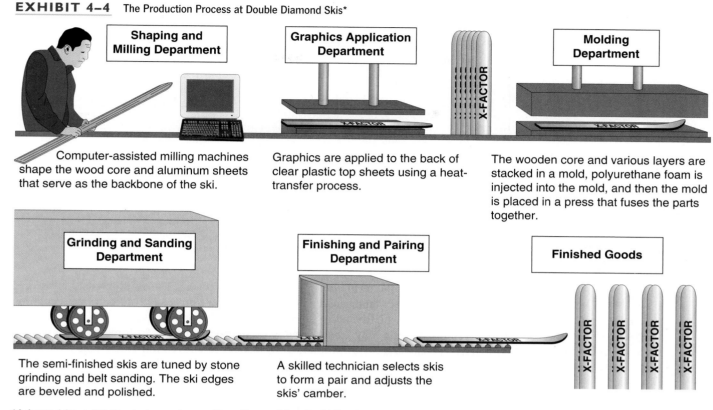

Computer-assisted milling machines shape the wood core and aluminum sheets that serve as the backbone of the ski.

Graphics are applied to the back of clear plastic top sheets using a heat-transfer process.

The wooden core and various layers are stacked in a mold, polyurethane foam is injected into the mold, and then the mold is placed in a press that fuses the parts together.

The semi-finished skis are tuned by stone grinding and belt sanding. The ski edges are beveled and polished.

A skilled technician selects skis to form a pair and adjusts the skis' camber.

*Adapted from Bill Gout, Jesse James Doquilo, and Studio M D, "Capped Crusaders," *Skiing*, October 1993, pp. 138–144.

weighted-average method blends together units and costs from the current period with units and costs from the prior period. In the weighted-average method, the **equivalent units of production** for a department are the number of units transferred to the next department (or to finished goods) plus the equivalent units in the department's ending work in process inventory.

Weighted-Average Method

Under the weighted-average method, a department's equivalent units are computed as follows:

> **Weighted-Average Method**
> **(a separate calculation is made for each cost category in each processing department)**
>
> Equivalent units = Units transferred to the next department or to finished goods
> of production + Equivalent units in ending work in process inventory

Note that the computation of the equivalent units of production involves adding the number of units transferred out of the department to the equivalent units in the department's ending inventory. There is no need to compute the equivalent units for the units transferred out of the department—they are 100% complete with respect to the work done in that department or they would not be transferred out. In other words, each unit transferred out of the department is counted as one equivalent unit.

Consider the Shaping and Milling Department at Double Diamond. This department uses computerized milling machines to precisely shape the wooden core and metal sheets

Concept 4-1

that will be used to form the backbone of the ski. (See Exhibit 4–4 for an overview of the production process at Double Diamond.) The following activity took place in the department in May:

Shaping and Milling Department			
		Percent Completed	
	Units	**Materials**	**Conversion**
Work in process, May 1	200	55%	30%
Units started into production during May	5,000		
Units completed during May and transferred to the next department	4,800	100%*	100%*
Work in process, May 31	400	40%	25%

*It is always assumed that units transferred out of a department are 100% complete with respect to the processing done in that department.

Note the use of the term *conversion* in the table above. **Conversion cost,** as defined in Chapter 1, is direct labor cost plus manufacturing overhead cost. In process costing, conversion cost may be treated as a single element of product cost.

Also note that the May 1 beginning work in process was 55% complete with respect to materials costs and 30% complete with respect to conversion costs. This means that 55% of the materials costs required to complete the units in the department had already been incurred. Likewise, 30% of the conversion costs required to complete the units had already been incurred.

Two equivalent unit figures must be computed—one for materials and one for conversion. The equivalent units computations are shown in Exhibit 4–5.

Note that the computations in Exhibit 4–5 ignore the fact that the units in the beginning work in process inventory were partially complete. For example, the 200 units in beginning inventory were already 30% complete with respect to conversion costs. Nevertheless, the weighted-average method is concerned only with the 4,900 equivalent units that are in ending inventories and in units transferred to the next department; it is not concerned with the fact that the beginning inventory was already partially complete. In other words, the 4,900 equivalent units computed using the weighted-average method include work that was accomplished in prior periods. This key point in the weighted-average method is easy to overlook.

Computation of equivalent units of production is illustrated in Exhibit 4–6. Study this exhibit carefully before going on.

Cutting Conversion Costs

CEMEX S.A., the world's third largest cement maker, owns 54 plants that each consumes 800 tons of fuel a day heating kilns to 2,700 degrees Fahrenheit. Not surprisingly, energy costs account for 40% of the company's overall conversion costs. Historically, Cemex relied exclusively on coal to heat its kilns; however, faced with soaring coal prices and shrinking profits, the company desperately needed a lower cost heat source. Cemex turned its attention to an oil industry waste product called petroleum coke that burns hotter than coal and costs half as much. The company spent about $150 million to convert its manufacturing processes to accommodate petroleum coke and set up an office in Houston, Texas, to negotiate bulk petroleum coke purchases from locally headquartered oil companies. Overall, Cemex has cut its energy bills by 17%, thus helping it earn higher profit margins than its biggest rivals.

Source: John Lyons, "Expensive Energy? Burn Other Stuff, One Firm Decides," *The Wall Street Journal*, September 1, 2004, pp. A1 and A8.

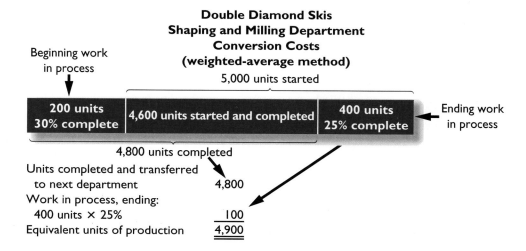

Shaping and Milling Department	Materials	Conversion
Units transferred to the next department	4,800	4,800
Work in process, May 31:		
400 units × 40% complete with respect to materials	160	
400 units × 25% complete with respect to conversion ...		100
Equivalent units of production	4,960	4,900

EXHIBIT 4–5

Equivalent Units of Production: Weighted-Average Method

**Double Diamond Skis
Shaping and Milling Department
Conversion Costs
(weighted-average method)**
5,000 units started

Beginning work in process

| 200 units 30% complete | 4,600 units started and completed | 400 units 25% complete |

Ending work in process

4,800 units completed

Units completed and transferred to next department   4,800
Work in process, ending:
  400 units × 25%   100
Equivalent units of production   4,900

EXHIBIT 4–6

Visual Perspective of Equivalent Units of Production

PRODUCTION REPORT—WEIGHTED-AVERAGE METHOD

The purpose of the production report developed in this section is to summarize for management all of the activity that takes place in a department's Work in Process account for a period. This activity includes the units and costs that flow through the Work in Process account. As illustrated in Exhibit 4–7, a separate production report is prepared for each department.

Home Runs Galore

IN BUSINESS

In 1999 Rawlings, the baseball manufacturer, was forced to open its Turrialba facility in Costa Rica to a delegation from Major League Baseball to dispel rumors that Rawlings balls were behind the record numbers of home runs.

The delegation found that the production process was unchanged from earlier years. The red pills (rubber-coated corks purchased from a company in Mississippi) are wound three times with wool yarn and then once with cotton string. The balls are weighed, measured, and inspected after each wind. The covers, cut from sheets of rawhide, are hand-stitched and then machine-rolled. After a trip through a drying room to remove the moisture that keeps the leather soft during the sewing process, the balls are stamped with logos. After they are weighed, measured, and inspected once again, the balls are wrapped in tissue and packed in boxes. Balls that don't meet Major League specifications (5–5¼ ounces and 9–9¼ inches in circumference) are sold elsewhere.

Source: "Behind-the-Seams Look: Rawlings Throws Open Baseball Plant Door," *USA Today,* May 24, 2000, pp. 1C–2C.

EXHIBIT 4–7   The Position of the Production Report in the Flow of Costs

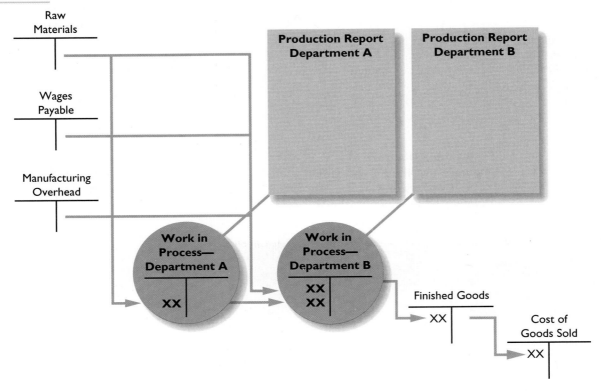

Cost Analyst

Assume that you are a cost analyst in the Rawlings plant in Costa Rica that supplies baseballs to Major League Baseball. Your assignment is to identify the production departments in that facility. How many production reports will be needed?

Earlier, when we outlined the differences between job-order costing and process costing, we stated that the production report takes the place of a job cost sheet in a process costing system. The production report is a key management document. It has three separate (though highly interrelated) parts:

1. A quantity schedule, which shows the flow of units through the department and a computation of equivalent units.
2. A computation of costs per equivalent unit.
3. A reconciliation of all cost flows into and out of the department during the period.

We will use the data that follows for the May operations of the Shaping and Milling Department of Double Diamond Skis to illustrate the production report. Keep in mind that this report is only one of the five reports that would be prepared for the company since the company has five processing departments.

Shaping and Milling Department Data for May Operations

Work in process, beginning:

Units in process	200
Stage of completion with respect to materials	55%
Stage of completion with respect to conversion	30%

Costs in the beginning inventory:

Materials cost	$ 9,600
Conversion cost	5,575
Total cost in the beginning inventory	$ 15,175

Units started into production during May	5,000
Units completed and transferred out	4,800

Costs added to production during May:

Materials cost	$368,600
Conversion cost	350,900
Total cost added in the department	$719,500

Work in process, ending:

Units in process	400
Stage of completion with respect to materials	40%
Stage of completion with respect to conversion	25%

In this section, we show how a production report is prepared when the weighted-average method is used to compute equivalent units and unit costs.

Step 1: Prepare a Quantity Schedule and Compute the Equivalent Units

The first part of a production report consists of a **quantity schedule,** which shows the flow of units through the department and the computation of equivalent units.

LEARNING OBJECTIVE 3

Prepare a quantity schedule using the weighted-average method.

Shaping and Milling Department
Quantity Schedule and Equivalent Units

	Quantity Schedule	Equivalent Units	
		Materials	Conversion
Units to be accounted for:			
Work in process, May 1 (materials 55% complete; conversion 30% complete)	200		
Started into production	5,000		
Total units to be accounted for	5,200		
Units accounted for as follows:			
Transferred to next department	4,800	4,800	4,800
Work in process, May 31 (materials 40% complete; conversion 25% complete)	400	160*	100†
Total units accounted for	5,200	4,960	4,900

*400 units × 40% = 160 equivalent units.
†400 units × 25% = 100 equivalent units.

The quantity schedule shows how many units moved through the department during the period as well as the stage of completion of any in-process units. The quantity schedule provides data for preparing the remaining parts of the production report.

YOU DECIDE

Term Paper Writer

Assume that all of your professors have assigned short papers this term. In fact, you have to turn in four separate five-page papers early next month. During the month, you began and finished two papers and wrote the first two and one-half pages of the other two papers. You turned in the papers that you had finished to your instructors on the last day of the month.

If instead you had focused all your efforts into starting *and* completing papers this month, how many complete papers would you have written this month? After answering that question, reconfigure your answer as a computation of equivalent units of production by (1) preparing a quantity schedule and (2) computing the number of equivalent units for labor.

Step 2: Compute the Costs per Equivalent Unit

LEARNING OBJECTIVE 4

Compute the costs per equivalent unit using the weighted-average method.

As stated earlier, the weighted-average method blends together the work that was accomplished in the prior period with the work that was accomplished in the current period. That is why it is called the weighted-average method; it averages together units and costs from both the prior and current periods. These computations are shown below for the Shaping and Milling Department for May:

Shaping and Milling Department Costs per Equivalent Unit				
	Total Cost	Materials	Conversion	Whole Unit
Cost to be accounted for:				
Work in process, May 1	$ 15,175	$ 9,600	$ 5,575	
Cost added during the month in the Shaping and Milling Department	719,500	368,600	350,900	
Total cost to be accounted for (a)	$734,675	$378,200	$356,475	
Equivalent units (Step 1 above) (b)		4,960	4,900	
Cost per equivalent unit, (a) ÷ (b)		$76.25 +	$72.75 =	$149.00

The cost per equivalent unit (EU) that we have computed for the Shaping and Milling Department will be used to apply costs to units that are transferred to the next department, Graphics Application, and will also be used to compute the cost in the ending work in process inventory. For example, each unit transferred out of the Shaping and Milling Department to the Graphics Application Department will carry with it a cost of $149. Since the costs are passed on from department to department, the unit cost of the last department, Finishing and Pairing, will represent the final cost of a completed unit of product.

LEARNING OBJECTIVE 5

Prepare a cost reconciliation using the weighted-average method.

Step 3: Prepare a Cost Reconciliation

The purpose of a **cost reconciliation** is to show how the costs that have been charged to a department during a period are accounted for. Typically, the costs charged to a department will consist of the following:

1. Cost in the beginning work in process inventory.
2. Materials, labor, and overhead costs added during the period.
3. Cost (if any) transferred in from the preceding department.

In a production report, these costs are titled "Cost to be accounted for." They are accounted for in the production report by computing the following amounts:

1. Cost transferred out to the next department (or to Finished Goods).
2. Cost remaining in the ending work in process inventory.

Concept 4-2

In short, when a cost reconciliation is prepared, the "Cost to be accounted for" from step 2 is reconciled with the sum of the cost transferred out during the period plus the cost in the ending work in process inventory. This concept is illustrated in Exhibit 4–8. Study this exhibit carefully before going on to the cost reconciliation for the Shaping and Milling Department.

Example of a Cost Reconciliation   To prepare a cost reconciliation, follow the quantity schedule line for line and show the cost associated with each group of units. This is done in Exhibit 4–9, where we present a completed production report for the Shaping and Milling Department.

The quantity schedule in the exhibit shows that 200 units were in process on May 1 and that an additional 5,000 units were started into production during the month. Looking at the "Cost to be accounted for" in the middle part of the exhibit, notice that the units in process on May 1 had $15,175 in cost attached to them and that the Shaping and Milling Department added another $719,500 in cost to production during the month. Thus, the department has $734,675 ($15,175 + $719,500) in cost to be accounted for.

This cost is accounted for in two ways. As shown on the quantity schedule, 4,800 units were transferred to the Graphics Application Department, the next department in the production process. Another 400 units were still in process in the Shaping and Milling Department at the end of the month. Thus, part of the $734,675 "Cost to be accounted for" goes with the 4,800 units to the Graphics Application Department, and part of it remains with the 400 units in the ending work in process inventory in the Shaping and Milling Department.

Each of the 4,800 units transferred to the Graphics Application Department is assigned $149.00 in cost, for a total of $715,200. The 400 units still in process at the end of the month are assigned costs according to their stage of completion. To determine the stage of completion, we refer to the equivalent units computation and bring the equivalent units figures down to the cost reconciliation part of the report. We then assign costs to these units, using the cost per equivalent unit figures already computed.

After cost has been assigned to the ending work in process inventory, the total cost that we have accounted for ($734,675) agrees with the amount that we had to account for ($734,675). Thus, the cost reconciliation is complete.

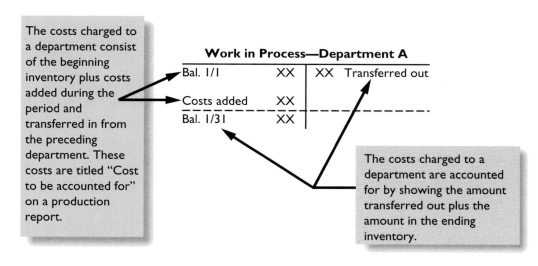

EXHIBIT 4–8

Graphic Illustration of the Cost Reconciliation Part of a Production Report

EXHIBIT 4–9 Production Report—Weighted-Average Method

Double Diamond Skis
Shaping and Milling Department Production Report
(Weighted-Average Method)

Quantity Schedule and Equivalent Units

	Quantity Schedule		
Units to be accounted for:			
Work in process, May 1 (materials 55% complete; conversion 30% complete) ...	200		
Started into production	5,000		
Total units to be accounted for	5,200		

		Equivalent Units (EU)	
		Materials	**Conversion**
Units accounted for as follows:			
Transferred to next department	4,800	4,800	4,800
Work in process, May 31 (materials 40% complete; conversion 25% complete) ...	400	160*	100†
Total units accounted for	5,200	4,960	4,900

Costs per Equivalent Unit

	Total Cost	Materials	Conversion	Whole Unit
Cost to be accounted for:				
Work in process, May 1	$ 15,175	$ 9,600	$ 5,575	
Cost added in the department	719,500	368,600	350,900	
Total cost to be accounted for (a)	$734,675	$378,200	$356,475	
Equivalent units (b)		4,960	4,900	
Cost per EU, (a) ÷ (b)		$76.25 +	$72.75 =	$149.00

Cost Reconciliation

	Total Cost	Equivalent Units (above)	
		Materials	**Conversion**
Cost accounted for as follows:			
Transferred to the next department:			
4,800 units × $149.00 per unit	$715,200	4,800	4,800
Work in process, May 31:			
Materials, at $76.25 per EU	12,200	160	
Conversion, at $72.75 per EU	7,275		100
Total work in process, May 31	19,475		
Total cost accounted for	$734,675		

*400 units × 40% = 160 equivalent units.
†400 units × 25% = 100 equivalent units.
EU = Equivalent unit.

1. Beginning work in process includes 400 units that are 20% complete with respect to conversion costs and 30% complete with respect to materials. Ending work in process includes 200 hundred units that are 40% complete with respect to conversion costs and 50% complete with respect materials. If 2,000 units were started during the period, what are the equivalent units of production for the period according to the weighted-average method?
   a. Conversion EU = 2,280 units; Material EU = 2,100 units
   b. Conversion EU = 1,980 units; Material EU = 2,080 units
   c. Conversion EU = 2,480 units; Material EU = 1,980 units
   d. Conversion EU = 2,280 units; Material EU = 2,300 units

2. Assume the same facts as above in Concept Check 1. Also, assume that $9,900 of material costs and $14,880 of conversion costs were in the beginning inventory and $180,080 of material and $409,200 of conversion costs were added to production during the period. What is the total cost per equivalent unit using the weighted-average method?
   a. $268.60
   b. $267.85
   c. $280.00
   d. $265.00

CONCEPT CHECK ✓

SUMMARY

LO1 Record the flow of materials, labor, and overhead through a process costing system.
The journal entries to record the flow of costs in process costing are basically the same as in job-order costing. Direct materials costs are debited to Work in Process when the materials are released for use in production. Direct labor costs are debited to Work in Process as incurred. Manufacturing overhead costs are applied to Work in Process by debiting Work in Process. Costs are accumulated by department in process costing and by job in job-order costing.

LO2 Compute the equivalent units of production using the weighted-average method.
To compute unit costs for a department, the department's output in terms of equivalent units must be determined. In the weighted-average method, the equivalent units for a period are the sum of the units transferred out of the department during the period and the equivalent units in ending work in process inventory at the end of the period.

LO3 Prepare a quantity schedule using the weighted-average method.
The activity in a department is summarized on a production report which has three separate (though highly interrelated) parts. The first part is a quantity schedule, which includes a computation of equivalent units and shows the flow of units through the department during the period. The quantity schedule shows the units to be accounted for—the units in beginning Work in Process inventory and the units started into production. These units are accounted for by detailing the units transferred to the next department and the units still in process in the department at the end of the period. This part of the report also shows the equivalent units of production for the units still in process.

LO4 Compute the costs per equivalent unit using the weighted-average method.
The cost per equivalent unit is computed by dividing the total cost for a particular cost category such as conversion costs by the equivalent units of production for that cost category.

LO5 Prepare a cost reconciliation using the weighted-average method.
In the cost reconciliation report, the costs of beginning Work in Process inventory and the costs added during the period are reconciled with the costs of the units transferred out of the department and the costs of ending Work in Process inventory.

GUIDANCE ANSWERS TO *DECISION MAKER* AND *YOU DECIDE*

Cost Analyst (p. 174)
The Rawlings baseball production facility in Costa Rica might include the following production departments: winding, cutting, stitching, rolling, drying, stamping, inspecting, and packaging. Each department would have its own production report.

Term Paper Writer (p. 176)
You wrote a total of 15 pages (5 + 5 + 2.5 + 2.5) this month. For the same effort, you could have written three complete five-page papers.

	Quantity Schedule
Units (papers) to be accounted for:	
Work in process, beginning of month	0
Started into production	4
Total units	4

	Quantity Schedule	Equivalent Units Labor
Units accounted for as follows:		
Transferred (handed in) to instructors	2	2
Work in process, end of month (50% of labor added this month)	2	1*
Total units and equivalent units of production	4	3

*2 units (papers) × 50% = 1

GUIDANCE ANSWERS TO CONCEPT CHECKS

1. **Choice d.** Material EU is 2,200 units completed and transferred to the next department + 100 EU in ending work in process (200 units × 50%). Conversion EU is 2,200 units completed and transferred to the next department plus 80 EU in ending work in process (200 units × 40%).
2. **Choice a.** ($189,980 ÷ 2,300 EU) + ($424,080 ÷ 2,280 EU) = $268.60.

REVIEW PROBLEM: PROCESS COST FLOWS AND REPORTS

Luxguard Home Paint Company produces exterior latex paint, which it sells in one-gallon containers. The company has two processing departments—Base Fab and Finishing. White paint, which is used as a base for all the company's paints, is mixed from raw ingredients in the Base Fab Department. Pigments are added to the basic white paint, the pigmented paint is squirted under pressure into one-gallon containers, and the containers are labeled and packed for shipping in the Finishing Department. Information relating to the company's operations for April follows:

a. Raw materials were issued for use in production: Base Fab Department, $851,000; and Finishing Department, $629,000.
b. Direct labor costs were incurred: Base Fab Department, $330,000; and Finishing Department, $270,000.

c. Manufacturing overhead cost was applied: Base Fab Department, $665,000; and Finishing Department $405,000.
d. The cost of basic white paint transferred from the Base Fab Department to the Finishing Department, was $1,850,000.
e. Paint that had been prepared for shipping was transferred from the Finishing Department to Finished Goods. Its cost according to the company's cost system was $3,200,000.

Required:
1. Prepare journal entries to record items (a) through (e) above.
2. Post the journal entries from (1) above to T-accounts. The balance in the Base Fab Department's Work in Process account on April 1 was $150,000; the balance in the Finishing Department's Work in Process account was $70,000. After posting entries to the T-accounts, find the ending balance in each department's Work in Process account.
3. Prepare a production report for the Base Fab Department for April. The following additional information is available regarding production in the Base Fab Department during April:

Production data:	
Units (gallons) in process, April 1: materials 100% complete, labor and overhead 60% complete	30,000
Units (gallons) started into production during April	420,000
Units (gallons) completed and transferred to the Finishing Department	370,000
Units (gallons) in process, April 30: materials 50% complete, labor and overhead 25% complete	80,000
Cost data:	
Work in process inventory, April 1:	
Materials	$ 92,000
Labor	21,000
Overhead	37,000
Total cost of work in process	$ 150,000
Cost added during April:	
Materials	$ 851,000
Labor	330,000
Overhead	665,000
Total cost added during April	$1,846,000

Solution to Review Problem

1. a.	Work in Process—Base Fab Department	851,000	
	Work in Process—Finishing Department	629,000	
	Raw Materials		1,480,000
b.	Work in Process—Base Fab Department	330,000	
	Work in Process—Finishing Department	270,000	
	Salaries and Wages Payable		600,000
c.	Work in Process—Base Fab Department	665,000	
	Work in Process—Finishing Department	405,000	
	Manufacturing Overhead		1,070,000
d.	Work in Process—Finishing Department	1,850,000	
	Work in Process—Base Fab Department		1,850,000
e.	Finished Goods	3,200,000	
	Work in Process—Finishing Department		3,200,000

2.

Raw Materials				Salaries and Wages Payable		
Bal.	XXX	(a)	1,480,000		(b)	600,000

Work in Process—Base Fab Department				Manufacturing Overhead		
Bal.	150,000	(d)	1,850,000	(Various actual	(c)	1,070,000
(a)	851,000			costs)		
(b)	330,000					
(c)	665,000					
Bal.	146,000					

Work in Process—Finishing Department				Finished Goods		
Bal.	70,000	(e)	3,200,000	Bal.	XXX	
(a)	629,000			(e)	3,200,000	
(b)	270,000					
(c)	405,000					
(d)	1,850,000					
Bal.	24,000					

3.

Luxguard Home Paint Company
Production Report—Base Fab Department
For the Month Ended April 30

Quantity Schedule and Equivalent Units

Quantity Schedule

Units (gallons) to be accounted for:	
Work in process, April 1 (materials 100% complete, labor and overhead 60% complete)	30,000
Started into production	420,000
Total units to be accounted for	450,000

		Equivalent Units (EU)		
		Materials	Labor	Overhead
Units (gallons) accounted for as follows:				
Transferred to Finishing Department	370,000	370,000	370,000	370,000
Work in process, April 30 (materials 50% complete, labor and overhead 25% complete)	80,000	40,000*	20,000*	20,000*
Total units accounted for	450,000	410,000	390,000	390,000

Costs per Equivalent Unit

	Total Cost	Materials	Labor	Overhead	Whole Unit
Cost to be accounted for:					
Work in process, April 1	$ 150,000	$ 92,000	$ 21,000	$ 37,000	
Cost added by the Base Fab Department	1,846,000	851,000	330,000	665,000	
Total cost to be accounted for (a)	$1,996,000	$943,000	$351,000	$702,000	
Equivalent units of production (b)		410,000	390,000	390,000	
Cost per EU, (a) ÷ (b)		$2.30 +	$0.90 +	$1.80 =	$5.00

(continued)

(concluded)

Cost Reconciliation

	Total Cost	Equivalent Units (above)		
		Materials	Labor	Overhead
Cost accounted for as follows:				
Transferred to Finishing Department:				
370,000 units ×				
$5.00 per unit	$1,850,000	370,000	370,000	370,000
Work in process, April 30:				
Materials, at $2.30 per EU .	92,000	40,000		
Labor, at $0.90 per EU	18,000		20,000	
Overhead, at $1.80				
per EU	36,000			20,000
Total work in process	146,000			
Total cost accounted for	$1,996,000			

*Materials: 80,000 units × 50% = 40,000 EUs; labor and overhead: 80,000 units × 25% = 20,000 EUs.
EU = Equivalent unit.

GLOSSARY

Conversion cost   Direct labor cost plus manufacturing overhead cost. (p. 172)

Cost reconciliation   The part of a department's production report that shows the cost to be accounted for during a period and how those costs are accounted for. (p. 176)

Equivalent units   The product of the number of partially completed units and their percentage of completion with respect to a particular cost. Equivalent units are the number of complete whole units one could obtain from the materials and effort contained in partially completed units. (p. 170)

Equivalent units of production (weighted-average method)   The units transferred to the next department (or to finished goods) during the period plus the equivalent units in the department's ending work in process inventory. (p. 171)

FIFO method   A method of accounting for cost flows in a process costing system in which equivalent units and unit costs relate only to work done during the current period. (p. 170)

Process costing   A costing method used when essentially homogeneous products are produced on a continuous basis. (p. 166)

Processing department   An organizational unit where work is performed on a product and where materials, labor, or overhead costs are added to the product. (p. 167)

Production report   A report that summarizes all activity in a department's Work in Process account during a period and that contains three parts: a quantity schedule and a computation of equivalent units, a computation of total and unit costs, and a cost reconciliation. (p. 166)

Quantity schedule   The part of a production report that shows the flow of units through a department during a period and a computation of equivalent units. (p. 175)

Transferred-in cost   The cost attached to products that have been received from a prior processing department. (p. 169)

Weighted-average method   A method of process costing that blends together units and costs from both the current and prior periods. (p. 171)

QUESTIONS

4–1   Under what conditions would it be appropriate to use a process costing system?

4–2   In what ways are job-order and process costing similar?

4–3   Costs are accumulated by job in a job-order costing system; how are costs accumulated in a process costing system?

4–4   Why is cost accumulation easier under a process costing system than it is under a job-order costing system?

4–5   How many Work in Process accounts are maintained in a company using process costing?

4–6 Assume that a company has two processing departments, Mixing and Firing. Prepare a journal entry to show a transfer of partially completed units from the Mixing Department to the Firing Department.

4–7 Assume again that a company has two processing departments, Mixing and Firing. Explain what costs might be added to the Firing Department's Work in Process account during a period.

4–8 What is meant by the term *equivalent units of production* when the weighted-average method is used?

4–9 What is a quantity schedule, and what purpose does it serve?

4–10 Under process costing, it is often suggested that a product is like a rolling snowball as it moves from department to department. Why is this an apt comparison?

BRIEF EXERCISES

BRIEF EXERCISE 4–1 Process Costing Journal Entries (LO1)

Quality Brick Company produces bricks in two processing departments—Molding and Firing. Information relating to the company's operations in March follows:

a. Raw materials were issued for use in production: Molding Department, $23,000; and Firing Department, $8,000.

b. Direct labor costs were incurred: Molding Department, $12,000; and Firing Department, $7,000.

c. Manufacturing overhead was applied: Molding Department, $25,000; and Firing Department, $37,000.

d. Unfired, molded bricks were transferred from the Molding Department to the Firing Department. According to the company's process costing system, the cost of the unfired, molded bricks was $57,000.

e. Finished bricks were transferred from the Firing Department to the finished goods warehouse. According to the company's process costing system, the cost of the finished bricks was $103,000.

f. Finished bricks were sold to customers. According to the company's process costing system, the cost of the finished bricks sold was $101,000.

Required:
Prepare journal entries to record items (a) through (f) above.

BRIEF EXERCISE 4–2 Computation of Equivalent Units—Weighted-Average Method (LO2)

Clonex Labs, Inc., uses a process costing system. The following data are available for one department for October:

		Percent Completed	
	Units	Materials	Conversion
Work in process, October 1	30,000	65%	30%
Work in process, October 31	15,000	80%	40%

The department started 175,000 units into production during the month and transferred 190,000 completed units to the next department.

Required:
Compute the equivalent units of production for October assuming that the company uses the weighted-average method of accounting for units and costs.

BRIEF EXERCISE 4–3 Preparation of Quantity Schedule—Weighted-Average Method (LO3)

Hielta Oy, a Finnish company, processes wood pulp for various manufacturers of paper products. Data relating to tons of pulp processed during June are provided below:

		Percent Completed	
	Tons of Pulp	Materials	Labor and Overhead
Work in process, June 1	20,000	90%	80%
Work in process, June 30	30,000	60%	40%
Started into production during June	190,000		

Required:

1. Compute the number of tons of pulp completed and transferred out during June.
2. Prepare a quantity schedule for June assuming that the company uses the weighted-average method.

BRIEF EXERCISE 4–4   Cost per Equivalent Unit—Weighted-Average Method   (LO4)

Superior Micro Products uses the weighted-average method in its process costing system. Data for the Assembly Department for May appear below:

	Materials	Labor	Overhead
Work in process, May 1	$18,000	$5,500	$27,500
Cost added during May	$238,900	$80,300	$401,500
Equivalent units of production	35,000	33,000	33,000

Required:

1. Compute the cost per equivalent unit for materials, for labor, and for overhead.
2. Compute the total cost per equivalent whole unit.

BRIEF EXERCISE 4–5   Cost Reconciliation—Weighted-Average Method   (LO5)

Superior Micro Products uses the weighted-average method in its process costing system. During January, the Delta Assembly Department completed its processing of 25,000 units and transferred them to the next department. The cost of beginning inventory and the costs added during January amounted to $599,780 in total. The ending inventory in January consisted of 3,000 units, which were 80% complete with respect to materials and 60% complete with respect to labor and overhead. The costs per equivalent unit for the month were as follows:

	Materials	Labor	Overhead
Cost per equivalent unit	$12.50	$3.20	$6.40

Required:

1. Compute the total cost per equivalent unit for the month.
2. Compute the equivalent units of material, of labor, and of overhead in the ending inventory for the month.
3. Prepare the cost reconciliation portion of the department's production report for January.

EXERCISES

EXERCISE 4–6   Process Costing Journal Entries   (LO1)

Chocolaterie de Geneve, SA, is located in a French-speaking canton in Switzerland. The company makes chocolate truffles that are sold in popular embossed tins. The company has two processing departments—Cooking and Molding. In the Cooking Department, the raw ingredients for the truffles are mixed and then cooked in special candy-making vats. In the Molding Department, the melted chocolate and other ingredients from the Cooking Department are carefully poured into molds and decorative flourishes are applied by hand. After cooling, the truffles are packed for sale. The company uses a process costing system. The T-accounts below show the flow of costs through the two departments in April (all amounts are in Swiss francs):

Work in Process—Cooking			
Balance 4/1	8,000	Transferred out	160,000
Direct materials	42,000		
Direct labor	50,000		
Overhead	75,000		

Work in Process—Molding			
Balance 4/1	4,000	Transferred out	240,000
Transferred in	160,000		
Direct labor	36,000		
Overhead	45,000		

Required:
Prepare journal entries showing the flow of costs through the two processing departments during April.

EXERCISE 4–7   Quantity Schedule, Equivalent Units, and Cost per Equivalent Unit—Weighted-Average Method   (LO2, LO3, LO4)
Pureform, Inc., manufactures a product that passes through two departments. Data for a recent month for the first department follow:

	Units	Materials	Labor	Overhead
Work in process, beginning	5,000	$4,320	$1,040	$1,790
Units started in process	45,000			
Units transferred out	42,000			
Work in process, ending	8,000			
Cost added during the month		$52,800	$21,500	$32,250

The beginning work in process inventory was 80% complete with respect to materials and 60% complete with respect to processing. The ending work in process inventory was 75% complete with respect to materials and 50% complete with respect to processing.

Required:
1. Assume that the company uses the weighted-average method of accounting for units and costs. Prepare a quantity schedule and a computation of equivalent units for the month for the first department.
2. Determine the costs per equivalent unit for the month.

EXERCISE 4–8   Equivalent Units and Cost per Equivalent Unit—Weighted-Average Method (LO2, LO4)
Helox, Inc., manufactures a product that passes through two production processes. A quantity schedule for the month of May for the first process follows:

	Quantity Schedule	Equivalent Units	
		Materials	Conversion
Units to be accounted for:			
Work in process, May 1 (materials 100% complete, conversion 40% complete)	5,000		
Started into production	180,000		
Total units to be accounted for	185,000		
Units accounted for as follows:			
Transferred to the next department ...	175,000	?	?
Work in process, May 31 (materials 100% complete, conversion 30% complete)	10,000	?	?
Total units accounted for	185,000	?	?

Costs in the beginning work in process inventory of the first processing department were: materials, $1,500; and conversion cost, $4,000. Costs added during the month were: materials, $54,000; and conversion cost, $352,000.

Required:

1. Assume that the company uses the weighted-average method of accounting for units and costs. Determine the equivalent units for the month for the first process.
2. Compute the costs per equivalent unit for the month for the first process.

EXERCISE 4–9   Cost Reconciliation—Weighted-Average Method   (LO5)

(This exercise should be assigned only if Exercise 4–8 is also assigned.) Refer to the data for Helox, Inc., in Exercise 4–8 and to the equivalent units and costs per equivalent unit you have computed there.

Required:

Complete the following cost reconciliation for the first process:

Cost Reconciliation			
	Total Cost	**Equivalent Units**	
		Materials	**Conversion**
Cost accounted for as follows:			
Transferred to the next department:			
(? units × $? per unit)	$?		
Work in process, May 31:			
Materials, at _____ per EU	?	?	
Conversion, at _____ per EU	?		?
Total work in process, May 31	?		
Total cost accounted for	$?		

EXERCISE 4–10   Quantity Schedule and Equivalent Units—Weighted-Average Method (LO2, LO3)

The Alaskan Fisheries, Inc., processes salmon for various distributors. Two departments are involved—Cleaning and Packing. Data relating to pounds of salmon processed in the Cleaning Department during July are presented below:

	Pounds of Salmon	**Percent Completed***
Work in process, July 1	20,000	30%
Started into processing during July	380,000	
Work in process, July 31	25,000	60%
*Labor and overhead only.		

All materials are added at the beginning of processing in the Cleaning Department.

Required:

Prepare a quantity schedule and a computation of equivalent units for July for the Cleaning Department assuming that the company uses the weighted-average method of accounting for units.

PROBLEMS

PROBLEM 4–11A   Equivalent Units; Cost Reconciliation—Weighted-Average Method   (LO2, LO5)   CHECK FIGURE
Martin Company manufactures a single product. The company uses the weighted-average method in its   (2) 6/30 WIP: $4,510
process costing system. Activity for June has just been completed. An incomplete production report for the first processing department follows:

Quantity Schedule and Equivalent Units

Quantity Schedule

Units to be accounted for:	
Work in process, June 1 (materials 100% complete; labor and overhead 75% complete)	8,000
Started into production	45,000
Total units	53,000

		Equivalent Units (EU)		
		Materials	Labor	Overhead
Units accounted for as follows:				
Transferred to the next department	48,000	?	?	?
Work in process, June 30 (materials 100% complete; labor and overhead 40% complete)	5,000	?	?	?
Total units	53,000	?	?	?

Costs per Equivalent Unit

	Total Cost	Materials	Labor	Overhead	Whole Unit
Cost to be accounted for:					
Work in process, June 1	$ 7,130	$ 5,150	$ 660	$ 1,320	
Cost added by the department	58,820	29,300	9,840	19,680	
Total cost (a)	$65,950	$34,450	$10,500	$21,000	
Equivalent units (b)		53,000	50,000	50,000	
Cost per EU, (a) ÷ (b)		$0.65 +	$0.21 +	$0.42 =	$1.28

Cost Reconciliation

	Total Cost
Cost accounted for as follows:	
?	?

Required:
1. Prepare a schedule showing how the equivalent units were computed for the first processing department.
2. Complete the "Cost Reconciliation" part of the production report for the first processing department.

CHECK FIGURE
(2) Materials: $1.50 per unit
(3) 5/31 WIP: $16,500

PROBLEM 4–12A Step-by-Step Production Report—Weighted-Average Method (LO2, LO3, LO4, LO5)
Builder Products, Inc., manufactures a caulking compound that goes through three processing stages prior to completion. Information on work in the first department, Cooking, is given below for May:

Production data:	
Units in process, May 1: materials 100% complete; labor and overhead 80% complete	10,000
Units started into production during May	100,000
Units completed and transferred out	95,000
Units in process, May 31: materials 60% complete; labor and overhead 20% complete	?

```
Cost data:
  Work in process inventory, May 1:
    Materials cost .................................................  $1,500
    Labor cost .....................................................  $1,800
    Overhead cost ..................................................  $5,400
  Cost added during May:
    Materials cost .................................................  $154,500
    Labor cost .....................................................  $22,700
    Overhead cost ..................................................  $68,100
```

Materials are added at several stages during the cooking process, whereas labor and overhead costs are incurred uniformly. The company uses the weighted-average method.

Required:

Prepare a production report for the Cooking Department for May. Use the following three steps in preparing your report:

1. Prepare a quantity schedule and a computation of equivalent units.
2. Compute the costs per equivalent unit for the month.
3. Using the data from (1) and (2) above, prepare a cost reconciliation.

PROBLEM 4–13A Production Report—Weighted-Average Method (LO2, LO3, LO4, LO5)
Sunspot Beverages, Ltd., of Fiji makes blended tropical fruit drinks in two stages. Fruit juices are extracted from fresh fruits and then blended in the Blending Department. The blended juices are then bottled and packed for shipping in the Bottling Department. The following information pertains to the operations of the Blending Department for June. (The currency in Fiji is the Fijian dollar.)

CHECK FIGURE
6/30 WIP: $87,500

	Units	Percent Complete	
		Materials	Conversion
Work in process, beginning	20,000	100%	75%
Started into production	180,000		
Completed and transferred out	160,000		
Work in process, ending	40,000	100%	25%
		Materials	Conversion
Work in process, beginning		$25,200	$24,800
Cost added during June		$334,800	$238,700

Required:

Prepare a production report for the Blending Department for June assuming that the company uses the weighted-average method.

PROBLEM 4–14A Interpreting a Production Report—Weighted-Average Method (LO2, LO3, LO4)
Cooperative San José of southern Sonora state in Mexico makes a unique syrup using cane sugar and local herbs. The syrup is sold in small bottles and is prized as a flavoring for drinks and for use in desserts.

The bottles are sold for $12 each. (The Mexican currency is the peso and is denoted by $.) The first stage in the production process is carried out in the Mixing Department, which removes foreign matter from the raw materials and mixes them in the proper proportions in large vats. The company uses the weighted-average method in its process costing system.

A hastily prepared report for the Mixing Department for April appears below:

Quantity Schedule

Units to be accounted for:	
Work in process, April 1 (materials 90% complete; conversion 80% complete)	30,000
Started into production	200,000
Total units to be accounted for	230,000
Units accounted for as follows:	
Transferred to the next department	190,000
Work in process, April 30 (materials 75% complete; conversion 60% complete)	40,000
Total units accounted for	230,000

Total Cost

Cost to be accounted for:	
Work in process, April 1	$ 98,000
Cost added during the month	827,000
Total cost to be accounted for	$925,000

Cost Reconciliation

Cost accounted for as follows:	
Transferred to the next department	$805,600
Work in process, April 30	119,400
Total cost accounted for	$925,000

Cooperative San José has just been acquired by another company, and the management of the acquiring company wants some additional information about Cooperative San José's operations.

Required:

1. What were the equivalent units for the month?
2. What were the costs per equivalent unit for the month? The beginning inventory consisted of the following costs: materials, $67,800; and conversion cost, $30,200. The costs added during the month consisted of: materials, $579,000; and conversion cost, $248,000.
3. How many of the units transferred to the next department were started and completed during the month?
4. The manager of the Mixing Department, anxious to make a good impression on the new owners, stated, "Materials prices jumped from about $2.50 per unit in March to $3 per unit in April, but due to good cost control I was able to hold our materials cost to less than $3 per unit for the month." Should this manager be rewarded for good cost control? Explain.

PROBLEM 4–15A   Comprehensive Process Costing Problem—Weighted-Average Method (LO1, LO2, LO3, LO4, LO5)

Lubricants, Inc., produces a special kind of grease that is widely used by race car drivers. The grease is produced in two processing departments: Refining and Blending.

Raw materials are introduced at various points in the Refining Department.

The following incomplete Work in Process account is available for the Refining Department for March:

Work in Process—Refining Department		
March 1 inventory (20,000 gallons; materials 100% complete; labor and overhead 90% complete) 38,000	Completed and transferred to Blending (? gallons) ?	
March costs added: Raw materials (390,000 gallons) 495,000		
Direct labor 72,000		
Overhead 181,000		
March 31 inventory (40,000 gallons; materials 75% complete; labor and overhead 25% complete) ?		

The March 1 work in process inventory in the Refining Department consists of the following cost elements: raw materials, $25,000; direct labor, $4,000; and overhead, $9,000.

Costs incurred during March in the Blending Department were: materials used, $115,000; direct labor, $18,000; and overhead cost applied to production, $42,000. The company uses the weighted-average method in its process costing.

Required:

1. Prepare journal entries to record the costs incurred in both the Refining Department and Blending Department during March. Key your entries to the items (a) through (g) below.
   a. Raw materials were issued for use in production.
   b. Direct labor costs were incurred.
   c. Manufacturing overhead costs for the entire factory were incurred, $225,000. (Credit Accounts Payable.)
   d. Manufacturing overhead cost was applied to production using a predetermined overhead rate.
   e. Units that were complete with respect to processing in the Refining Department were transferred to the Blending Department, $740,000.
   f. Units that were complete with respect to processing in the Blending Department were transferred to Finished Goods, $950,000.
   g. Completed units were sold on account, $1,500,000. The Cost of Goods Sold was $900,000.

2. Post the journal entries from (1) above to T-accounts. The following account balances existed at the beginning of March. (The beginning balance in the Refining Department's Work in Process account is given above.)

Raw Materials	$618,000
Work in Process—Blending Department	$65,000
Finished Goods	$20,000

After posting the entries to the T-accounts, find the ending balances in the inventory accounts and the manufacturing overhead account.

3. Prepare a production report for the Refining Department for March.

PROBLEM 4–16A   Preparation of Production Report from Analysis of Work in Process—Weighted-Average Method   (LO2, LO3, LO4, LO5)

Weston Products manufactures an industrial cleaning compound that goes through three processing departments—Grinding, Mixing, and Cooking. All raw materials are introduced at the start of work in the Grinding Department, with conversion costs being incurred evenly throughout the

CHECK FIGURE
(1) Materials: $0.80 per unit; 5/31 WIP: $25,000

eXcel

grinding process. The Work in Process T-account for the Grinding Department for a recent month is given below:

Work in Process—Grinding Department			
Inventory, May 1 (18,000 pounds; labor and overhead 1/3 complete)	21,800	Completed and transferred to mixing (? pounds)	?
May costs added:			
Raw materials (167,000 pounds)	133,400		
Labor and overhead	226,800		
Inventory, May 31 (15,000 pounds; labor and overhead 2/3 complete)	?		

The May 1 work in process inventory consists of $14,600 in materials cost and $7,200 in labor and overhead cost. The company uses the weighted-average method to account for units and costs.

Required:

1. Prepare a production report for the Grinding Department for the month.
2. What criticism can be made of the unit costs that you have computed on your production report if they are used to evaluate how well costs have been controlled?

CHECK FIGURE
(1) Labor: $2.20 per EU
(2) 12/31 WIP: $903.000
(4) COGS: $3,339,000

PROBLEM 4–17A   Equivalent Units; Costing Inventories; Journal Entries; Cost of Goods Sold—Weighted-Average Method   (LO1, LO2, LO4, LO5)

You are employed by Spirit Company, a manufacturer of digital watches. The company's chief financial officer is trying to verify the accuracy of the ending work in process and finished goods inventories prior to closing the books for the year. You have been asked to assist in this verification. The year-end balances shown on Spirit Company's books are as follows:

	Units	Costs
Work in process, December 31 (labor and overhead 50% complete)	300,000	$660,960
Finished goods, December 31	200,000	$1,009,800

Materials are added to production at the beginning of the manufacturing process, and overhead is applied to each product at the rate of 60% of direct labor cost. There was no finished goods inventory at the beginning of the year. A review of Spirit Company's inventory and cost records has disclosed the following data:

	Units	Costs	
		Materials	Labor
Work in process, January 1 (labor and overhead 80% complete)	200,000	$200,000	$315,000
Units started into production	1,000,000		
Cost added during the year:			
Materials cost		$1,300,000	
Labor cost			$1,995,000
Units completed during the year	900,000		

The company uses the weighted-average method.

Required:

1. Determine the equivalent units and costs per equivalent unit for materials, labor, and overhead for the year.
2. Determine the amount of cost that should be assigned to the ending work in process and finished goods inventories.

3. Prepare the necessary correcting journal entry to adjust the work in process and finished goods inventories to the correct balances as of December 31.

4. Determine the cost of goods sold for the year assuming there is no underapplied or overapplied overhead.

(CPA, adapted)

PROBLEM 4–18A Comprehensive Process Costing Problem—Weighted-Average Method (LO1, LO2, LO3, LO4, LO5)

Hilox, Inc., produces an antacid product that goes through two departments—Cooking and Bottling. The company has recently hired a new assistant accountant, who has prepared the following summary of production and costs for the Cooking Department for May using the weighted-average method.

Cooking Department costs:	
Work in process inventory, May 1: 70,000 quarts; materials 60% complete and labor and overhead 30% complete	$ 61,000*
Materials added during May	570,000
Labor added during May	100,000
Overhead applied during May	235,000
Total departmental costs	$966,000
Cooking Department costs assigned to:	
Quarts completed and transferred to the Bottling Department: 400,000 quarts at __?__ per quart	$?
Work in process inventory, May 31: 50,000 quarts; materials 70% complete and labor and overhead 40% complete	?
Total departmental costs assigned	$?

*Consists of materials, $39,000; labor, $5,000; and overhead, $17,000.

The new assistant accountant has determined the cost per quart transferred to be $2.415, as follows:

$$\frac{\text{Total departmental costs}}{\text{Quarts completed and transferred}} = \frac{\$966,000}{400,000 \text{ quarts}} = \$2.415 \text{ per quart}$$

However, the assistant accountant is unsure how to use this unit cost figure in assigning cost to the ending work in process inventory. In addition, the company's general ledger shows only $900,000 in cost transferred from the Cooking Department to the Bottling Department, which does not agree with the $966,000 figure above.

The general ledger also shows the following costs incurred in the Bottling Department during May: materials used, $130,000; direct labor cost incurred, $80,000; and overhead cost applied to products, $158,000.

Required:

1. Prepare journal entries as follows to record activity in the company during May. Key your entries to the letters (a) through (g) below.
   a. Raw materials were issued to the two departments for use in production.
   b. Direct labor costs were incurred in the two departments.
   c. Manufacturing overhead costs were incurred, $400,000. (Credit Accounts Payable.) The company maintains a single Manufacturing Overhead account for the entire plant.
   d. Manufacturing overhead cost was applied to production in each department using predetermined overhead rates.
   e. Units completed as to processing in the Cooking Department were transferred to the Bottling Department, $900,000.
   f. Units completed as to processing in the Bottling Department were transferred to Finished Goods, $1,300,000.
   g. Units were sold on account, $2,000,000. The Cost of Goods Sold was $1,250,000.

2. Post the journal entries from (1) above to T-accounts. Balances in selected accounts on May 1 are given below:

Raw Materials	$710,000
Work in Process—Bottling Department	$85,000
Finished Goods	$45,000

After posting the entries to the T-accounts, find the ending balance in the inventory accounts and the Manufacturing Overhead account.

3. Prepare a production report for the Cooking Department for May.

BUILDING YOUR SKILLS

Communicating in Practice   (LO5)

Assume that you are the cost analyst who prepared the Production Report that appears in Exhibit 4–9. You receive a call from Minesh Patel, a new hire in the company's accounting staff who is not sure what needs to be done with the cost reconciliation portion of the report. He wants to know what journal entries should be prepared and what balances need to be checked in the company's accounts.

Required:

Write a memorandum to Mr. Patel that explains the steps that should be taken. Refer to specific amounts on the Cost Reconciliation portion of the Production Report to ensure that he properly completes the steps.

Analytical Thinking   (LO2, LO3, LO4, LO5)

"I think we goofed when we hired that new assistant controller," said Ruth Scarpino, president of Provost Industries. "Just look at this production report that he prepared for last month for the Finishing Department. I can't make heads or tails out of it."

CHECK FIGURE:
(1) 4/30 WIP: $7,182

Finishing Department costs:	
Work in process inventory, April 1, 450 units; materials 100% complete; conversion costs 60% complete	$ 8,208*
Costs transferred in during the month from the preceding department, 1,950 units	17,940
Materials cost added during the month (materials are added when processing is 50% complete in the Finishing Department)	6,210
Conversion costs incurred during the month	13,920
Total departmental costs	$46,278
Finishing Department costs assigned to:	
Units completed and transferred to finished goods, 1,800 units at $25.71 per unit	$46,278
Work in process inventory, April 30, 600 units; materials 0% complete; processing 35% complete	0
Total departmental costs assigned	$46,278

*Consists of: cost transferred in, $4,068; materials cost, $1,980; and conversion cost, $2,160.

"He's struggling to learn our system," replied Frank Harrop, the operations manager. "The problem is that he's been away from process costing for a long time, and it's coming back slowly."

"It's not just the format of his report that I'm concerned about. Look at that $25.71 unit cost that he's come up with for April. Doesn't that seem high to you?" said Ms. Scarpino.

"Yes, it does seem high; but on the other hand, I know we had an increase in materials prices during April, and that may be the explanation," replied Mr. Harrop. "I'll get someone else to redo this report and then we may be able to see what's going on."

Provost Industries manufactures a ceramic product that goes through two processing departments—Molding and Finishing. The company uses the weighted-average method in its process costing.

Required:

1. Prepare a revised production report for the Finishing Department.
2. Explain to the president why the unit cost on the new assistant controller's report is so high.

Teamwork In Action   (LO2, LO3, LO4, LO5)

The Production Report includes a quantity schedule, the computation of equivalent costs and costs per equivalent units, and a cost reconciliation.

Required:

1. *Learning teams* of three (or more) members should be formed. Each team member must select one of the following sections of the Production Report (as illustrated in Exhibit 4–9) as an area of expertise (each team must have at least one expert in each section).
   a.   Quantity Schedule and Equivalent Units.
   b.   Costs per Equivalent Unit.
   c.   Cost Reconciliation.
2. *Expert teams* should be formed from the individuals who have selected the same area of expertise. Expert teams should discuss and write up a brief summary that each expert will present to his/her learning team that addresses the following:
   a.   The purpose of the section of the Production Report.
   b.   The manner in which the amounts appearing in this section of the report are determined.
3. Each expert should return to his/her learning team. In rotation, each member should present his/her expert team's report to the learning team.

Ethics Challenge   (LO2, LO4, LO5)

Gary Stevens and Mary James are production managers in the Consumer Electronics Division of General Electronics Company, which has several dozen plants scattered in locations throughout the world. Mary manages the plant located in Des Moines, Iowa, while Gary manages the plant in El Segundo, California. Production managers are paid a salary and get an additional bonus equal to 5% of their base salary if the entire division meets or exceeds its target profits for the year. The bonus is determined in March after the company's annual report has been prepared and issued to stockholders.

Shortly after the beginning of the new year, Mary received a phone call from Gary that went like this:

Gary: How's it going, Mary?

Mary: Fine, Gary. How's it going with you?

Gary: Great! I just got the preliminary profit figures for the division for last year and we are within $200,000 of making the year's target profits. All we have to do is pull a few strings, and we'll be over the top!

Mary: What do you mean?

Gary: Well, one thing that would be easy to change is your estimate of the percentage completion of your ending work in process inventories.

Mary: I don't know if I can do that, Gary. Those percentage completion figures are supplied by Tom Winthrop, my lead supervisor, who I have always trusted to provide us with good estimates. Besides, I have already sent the percentage completion figures to corporate headquarters.

Gary: You can always tell them there was a mistake. Think about it, Mary. All of us managers are doing as much as we can to pull this bonus out of the hat. You may not want the bonus check, but the rest of us sure could use it.

The final processing department in Mary's production facility began the year with no work in process inventories. During the year, 210,000 units were transferred in from the prior processing department and 200,000 units were completed and sold. Costs transferred in from the prior department totaled $39,375,000. No materials are added in the final processing department. A total of $20,807,500 of conversion cost was incurred in the final processing department during the year.

Required:

1. Tom Winthrop estimated that the units in ending inventory in the final processing department were 30% complete with respect to the conversion costs of the final processing department. If this estimate of the percentage completion is used, what would be the Cost of Goods Sold for the year?
2. Does Gary Stevens want the estimated percentage completion to be increased or decreased? Explain why.
3. What percentage completion would result in increasing reported net operating income by $200,000 over the net operating income that would be reported if the 30% figure were used?
4. Do you think Mary James should go along with the request to alter estimates of the percentage completion?

Taking It To The Net

As you know, the World Wide Web is a medium that is constantly evolving. Sites come and go and change without notice. To enable periodic updating of site addresses, these problems have been posted to the textbook website (www.mhhe.com/bgn3e). After accessing the site, enter the Student Center and select this chapter to find the Taking It to the Net problems.

5

Cost Behavior: Analysis and Use

CHAPTER OUTLINE

Chapter Five

DECISION FEATURE

A Costly Mistake

After spending countless hours tracking down the hardware and fixtures he needed to restore his Queen Anne–style Victorian house, Stephen Gordon recognized an opportunity. He opened Restoration Hardware, Inc., a specialty store carrying antique hardware and fixtures. The company's products are described by some as nostalgic, old-fashioned, and obscure. Customers can shop at one of the 90 Restoration Hardware stores, by catalog, or online at the company's website www.restorationhardware.com.

1998 was a year of phenomenal growth and change for Restoration Hardware. Twenty-four new stores were opened, increasing the total number in the chain to 65. The company's newly launched catalog business was an instant success. Net sales approached $200 million, an increase of almost 114% from the prior year. Gordon, chairman and CEO, took the company public.

The success enjoyed by the company in 1998 did not recur in 1999. Gordon's biggest mistake was a failure to consider cost behavior when making decisions to promote the company's products. The most popular furniture items in the store were discounted during the first quarter to encourage customer interest. The company spent $1 million to advertise this big sale, which was far more "successful" than Gordon had imagined. Sales for the first quarter increased by 84% to $60 million. However, much of the increase arose from sales of discounted goods. As a result, margins (that is, differences between sale prices and the cost of the goods that were sold) were lower than usual. Further, because the items placed on sale were larger and heavier than average, the costs to move them from the distribution centers to the stores were considerably higher. The company ended up reporting a loss of $2.7 million for the quarter.

Sources: Restoration Hardware website July 2000; Stephen Gordon, "My Biggest Mistake," *Inc.*, September 1999, p. 103; and Heather Chaplin, "Past? Perfect," *American Demographics*, May 1999, pp. 68–69.

LEARNING OBJECTIVES

After studying Chapter 5, you should be able to:

LO1 Understand how fixed and variable costs behave and how to use them to predict costs.

LO2 Use a scattergraph plot to diagnose cost behavior.

LO3 Analyze a mixed cost using the high-low method.

LO4 Prepare an income statement using the contribution format.

LO5 (Appendix) Use variable costing to prepare a contribution format income statement and contrast absorption costing and variable costing.

In Chapter 1, we stated that costs can be classified by behavior. Cost behavior refers to how a cost will change as the level of activity changes. Managers who understand how costs behave can predict how costs will change under various alternatives. Conversely, managers who attempt to make decisions without a thorough understanding of cost behavior patterns can create disastrous consequences. For example, cutting back production of a particular product line might result in far less cost savings than managers assume if they confuse fixed costs with variable costs—leading to a decline in profits. To avoid such problems, managers must be able to accurately predict what costs will be at various activity levels.

This chapter briefly reviews the definitions of variable and fixed costs and then discusses the behavior of these costs in greater depth than was done in Chapter 1. The chapter also introduces the concept of a mixed cost, which is a cost that has both variable and fixed cost elements. The chapter concludes by introducing a new income statement format—called the *contribution format*—in which costs are organized by behavior rather than by the traditional functions of production, sales, and administration.

TYPES OF COST BEHAVIOR PATTERNS

Concept 5-1

In Chapter 1 we mentioned only variable and fixed costs. In this chapter we will examine a third cost behavior pattern, known as a *mixed* or *semivariable* cost. All three cost behavior patterns—variable, fixed, and mixed—are found in most organizations. The relative proportion of each type of cost present in an organization is known as the organization's **cost structure.** For example, an organization might have many fixed costs but few variable or mixed costs. Alternatively, it might have many variable costs but few fixed or mixed costs. In this chapter we will concentrate on gaining a fuller understanding of the behavior of each type of cost. In the next chapter we explore how cost structure impacts decisions.

LEARNING OBJECTIVE 1

Understand how fixed and variable costs behave and how to use them to predict costs.

Variable Costs

We explained in Chapter 1 that a variable cost is a cost whose total dollar amount varies in direct proportion to changes in the activity level. If the activity level doubles, the total variable cost also doubles. If the activity level increases by only 10%, then the total variable cost increases by 10% as well.

Selling Online

By making investments in technology, cutting-edge companies have created cost structures radically different from those of traditional companies. John Labbett, the CFO of Onsale, an Internet auctioneer of discontinued computers, was previously employed at House of Fabrics, a traditional retailer. The two companies have roughly the same total revenues of about $250 million. However, House of Fabrics, with 5,500 employees, has a revenue per employee of about $45,455. At Onsale, with only 200 employees, the figure is $1.25 million per employee. Moreover, Internet companies are often able to grow at very little cost. If demand grows, an Internet company may not have to do much more than just add another computer server. If demand grows at a traditional retailer, the company may have to invest in new facilities and additional inventory and may have to hire additional employees.

Source: George Donnelly, "New@ttitude," *CFO*, June 1999, pp. 42–54.

We also found in Chapter 1 that a variable cost remains constant if expressed on a *per unit* basis. To provide an example, consider Nooksack Expeditions, a small company that provides daylong whitewater rafting excursions on rivers in the North Cascade Mountains. The company provides all of the necessary equipment and experienced guides, and it serves gourmet meals to its guests. The meals are purchased from an exclusive caterer for $30 a person for a daylong excursion. If we look at the cost of the meals on a *per person* basis, it remains constant at $30. This $30 cost per person will not change, regardless of how many people participate in a daylong excursion. The behavior of this variable cost, on both a per unit and a total basis, is tabulated below:

Number of Guests	Cost of Meals per Guest	Total Cost of Meals
250	$30	$7,500
500	$30	$15,000
750	$30	$22,500
1,000	$30	$30,000

The idea that a variable cost is constant per unit but varies in total with the activity level is crucial to understanding cost behavior patterns. We shall rely on this concept repeatedly in this chapter and in chapters ahead.

Exhibit 5–1 illustrates variable cost behavior. Note that the graph of the total cost of the meals slants upward to the right. This is because the total cost of the meals is directly proportional to the number of guests. In contrast, the graph of the per unit cost of meals is flat because the cost of the meal per guest is constant at $30.

The Activity Base   For a cost to be variable, it must be variable *with respect to something*. That "something" is its *activity base*. An **activity base** is a measure of whatever causes the incurrence of variable cost. An activity base is also sometimes referred to as a *cost driver*. Some of the most common activity bases are direct labor-hours, machine-hours, units produced, and units sold. Other examples of activity bases (cost drivers) include the number of miles driven by salespersons, the number of pounds of laundry cleaned by a hotel, the number of calls handled by technical support staff at a software company, and the number of beds occupied in a hospital.

People sometimes get the notion that if a cost doesn't vary with production or with sales, then it is not a variable cost. This is not correct. As suggested by the range of bases listed above, costs are caused by many different activities within an organization. Whether a cost is variable or fixed depends on whether it is caused by the activity under consideration. For example, when analyzing the cost of service calls under a product warranty, the

EXHIBIT 5–1   Variable Cost Behavior

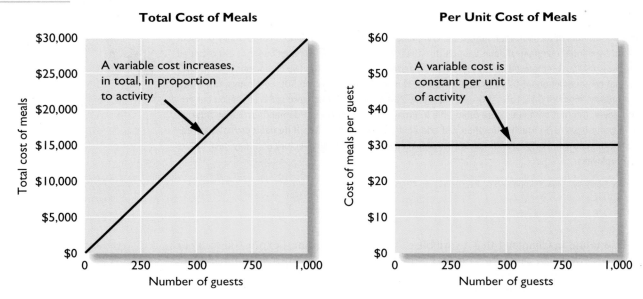

Total Cost of Meals

A variable cost increases, in total, in proportion to activity

(y-axis: Total cost of meals — $0, $5,000, $10,000, $15,000, $20,000, $25,000, $30,000)
(x-axis: Number of guests — 0, 250, 500, 750, 1,000)

Per Unit Cost of Meals

A variable cost is constant per unit of activity

(y-axis: Cost of meals per guest — $0, $10, $20, $30, $40, $50, $60)
(x-axis: Number of guests — 0, 250, 500, 750, 1,000)

relevant activity measure is the number of service calls made. Those costs that vary in total with the number of service calls made are the variable costs of making service calls.

Nevertheless, unless stated otherwise, you can assume that the activity base under consideration is the total volume of goods and services provided by the organization. So, for example, if we ask whether direct materials at Ford is a variable cost, the answer is yes, since the cost of direct materials is variable with respect to Ford's total volume of output. We will specify the activity base only when it is something other than total output.

Extent of Variable Costs   The number and type of variable costs in an organization will depend in large part on the organization's structure and purpose. A public utility like Florida Power and Light, with large investments in equipment, will tend to have few variable costs. Most of the costs are associated with its plant, and these costs tend to be insensitive to changes in levels of service provided. A manufacturing company like Black and Decker, by contrast, will often have many variable costs; these costs will be associated with both manufacturing and distributing its products to customers.

A merchandising company like Wal-Mart or J. K. Gill will usually have a high proportion of variable costs in its cost structure. In most merchandising companies, the cost of merchandise purchased for resale, a variable cost, constitutes a very large component of total cost. Service companies, by contrast, have diverse cost structures. Some service companies, such as the Skippers restaurant chain, have fairly large variable costs because of the costs of their raw materials. On the other hand, service companies involved in consulting, auditing, engineering, dental, medical, and architectural activities have very large fixed costs in the form of expensive facilities and highly trained salaried employees.

Some of the more frequently encountered variable costs are listed in Exhibit 5–2. This exhibit is not a complete listing of all costs that can be considered variable. Moreover, some of the costs listed in the exhibit may behave more like fixed than variable costs in some organizations and in some circumstances. We will see examples of this later in the chapter. Nevertheless, Exhibit 5–2 provides a useful listing of many of the costs that normally would be considered variable with respect to the volume of output.

True Variable versus Step-Variable Costs

Not all variable costs have exactly the same behavior pattern. Some variable costs behave in a *true variable* or *proportionately variable* pattern. Other variable costs behave in a *step-variable* pattern.

EXHIBIT 5–2

Examples of Variable Costs

Type of Organization	Costs that Are Normally Variable with Respect to Volume of Output
Merchandising company	Cost of goods (merchandise) sold
Manufacturing company	Manufacturing costs: 　　Direct materials 　　Direct labor* Variable portion of manufacturing overhead: 　　Indirect materials 　　Lubricants 　　Supplies
Both merchandising and manufacturing companies	Selling and administrative costs: 　　Commissions 　　Clerical costs, such as invoicing 　　Shipping costs
Service organizations	Supplies, travel, clerical

*Direct labor may or may not be variable in practice. See the discussion later in this chapter.

True Variable Costs　Direct materials is a true or proportionately variable cost because the amount used during a period will vary in direct proportion to the level of production activity. Moreover, any amounts purchased but not used can be stored and carried forward to the next period as inventory.

Step-Variable Costs　The wages of maintenance workers are often considered to be a variable cost, but this labor cost doesn't behave in the same way as the cost of direct materials. Unlike direct materials, a maintenance worker's time can only be obtained in large chunks. Moreover, any maintenance time not utilized cannot be stored as inventory and carried forward to the next period. Furthermore, a maintenance crew can work at a leisurely pace if pressures are light but intensify its efforts if pressures build up. For this reason, small changes in the level of production may have no effect on the number of maintenance people employed by the company.

The cost of a resource (such as the cost of maintenance workers) that is obtainable only in large chunks and increases or decreases only in response to fairly wide changes in activity is known as a **step-variable cost.** Exhibit 5–3 contrasts the behavior of a step-variable cost with the behavior of a true variable cost.

Notice that the need for maintenance help changes only with fairly wide changes in volume and that when additional maintenance time is obtained, it comes in large, indivisible chunks. Great care must be taken in working with these kinds of costs to prevent "fat" from building up in an organization. There may be a tendency to employ additional help more quickly than needed, and there is a natural reluctance to lay people off when volume declines.

Direct Materials (true variable)　**Maintenance Help (step variable)**

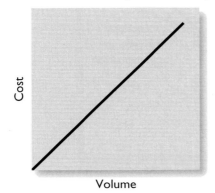

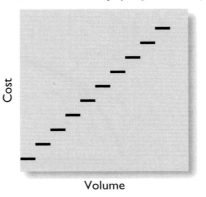

EXHIBIT 5–3

True Variable versus
Step-Variable Costs

Coping with the Fallout from September 11

Costs can change for reasons having nothing to do with changes in volume. Filterfresh company services office coffee machines, providing milk, sugar, cups, and coffee. The company's operations were profoundly affected by the security measures many companies initiated after the terrorist attacks on the World Trade Center and the Pentagon on September 11, 2001. Heightened security at customer locations means that Filterfresh's 250 deliverymen can no longer casually walk through a customer's lobby with a load of supplies. Now a guard typically checks the deliveryman's identification and paperwork at the loading dock and may search the van before permitting the deliveryman access to the customer's building. These delays have added an average of about an hour per day to each route, which means that Filterfresh needs 24 more delivery people to do the same work it did prior to September 11. That's a 10% increase in cost without any increase in the amount of coffee sold.

Source: Anna Bernasek, "The Friction Economy," *Fortune*, February 18, 2002, pp. 104–112.

The Linearity Assumption and the Relevant Range

In dealing with variable costs, we assume a strictly linear relationship between cost and volume, except in the case of step-variable costs. Economists correctly point out that many costs that the accountant classifies as variable actually behave in a *curvilinear* fashion. The behavior of a **curvilinear cost** is shown in Exhibit 5–4.

Although many costs are not strictly linear when plotted as a function of volume, a curvilinear cost can be satisfactorily approximated with a straight line within a narrow band of activity known as the *relevant range*. The **relevant range** is that range of activity within which the assumptions made about cost behavior are valid. For example, note that the dashed line in Exhibit 5–4 approximates the curvilinear cost with very little loss of accuracy within the shaded relevant range. However, outside of the relevant range this particular straight line is a poor approximation to the curvilinear cost. Managers should always keep in mind that assumptions made about cost behavior may be invalid if activity falls outside of the relevant range.

Fixed Costs

In our discussion of cost behavior patterns in Chapter 1, we stated that total fixed costs remain constant within the relevant range of activity. To continue the Nooksack Expeditions

EXHIBIT 5–4

Curvilinear Costs and the
Relevant Range

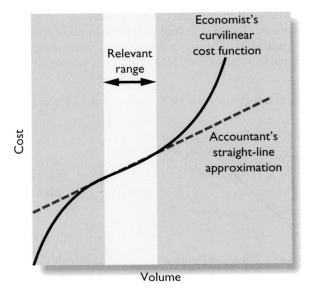

example, assume the company decides to rent a building for $500 per month to store its equipment. Within the relevant range, the *total* amount of rent paid is the same regardless of the number of guests the company takes on its expeditions during any given month. Exhibit 5–5 depicts this cost behavior pattern.

Since fixed costs remain constant in total, the amount of fixed cost computed on a *per-unit* basis becomes progressively smaller as the level of activity increases. If Nooksack Expeditions has only 250 guests in a month, the $500 fixed rental cost would amount to $2 per guest. If there are 1,000 guests, the fixed rental cost would amount to only 50 cents per guest. Exhibit 5–5 illustrates this aspect of the behavior of fixed costs. Note that as the number of guests increases, the average fixed cost per unit drops, but it drops at a decreasing rate. The first guests have the biggest impact on the average fixed cost per unit.

It is necessary in some contexts to express fixed costs on an average per-unit basis. For example, in Chapter 2 we showed how unit product costs computed for use in *external* financial statements contain both variable and fixed costs. As a general rule, however, we caution against expressing fixed costs on an average per-unit basis in *internal* reports because it creates the false impression that fixed costs are like variable costs and that total fixed costs actually change as the level of activity changes. To avoid confusion in internal reporting and decision-making situations, fixed costs should be expressed in total rather than on a per-unit basis.

Costing the Trek

Jackson Hole Llamas is owned and operated by Jill Aanonsen/Hodges and David Hodges. The company provides guided tours to remote areas of Yellowstone National Park and the Jedediah Smith Wilderness, with the llamas carrying the baggage for the multiday treks.

Jill and David operate out of their ranch in Jackson Hole, Wyoming, leading about 10 trips each summer season. All food is provided as well as tents and sleeping pads. Based on the number of guests on a trip, Jill and David will decide how many llamas will go on the trip and how many will remain on the ranch. Llamas are transported to the trailhead in a special trailer.

The company has a number of costs, some of which are listed below:

Cost	Cost Behavior
Food and beverage costs	Variable with respect to the number of guests and the length of the trip in days.
Truck and trailer operating costs	Variable with respect to the number of miles to the trailhead.
Guide wages	Step variable; Jill and David serve as the guides on most trips and hire guides only for larger groups.
Costs of providing tents	Variable with respect to the number of guests and length of the trip in days. Jackson Hole Llamas owns its tents, but they wear out through use and must be repaired or eventually replaced.
Cost of feeding llamas	Variable with respect to the number of guests, and hence the number of llamas, on a trip. [Actually, the cost of feeding llamas may *decrease* with the number of guests on a trip. When a llama is on a trek, it lives off the land—eating grasses and other vegetation found in meadows and along the trail. When a llama is left on the ranch, it may have to be fed purchased feed.]
Property taxes	Fixed.

Source: Jill Aanonsen/Hodges and David Hodges, owners and operators of Jackson Hole Llamas, www.jhllamas.com.

EXHIBIT 5–5 Fixed Cost Behavior

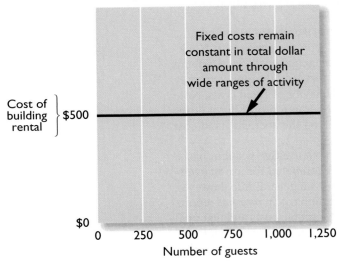

Total Fixed Cost of Renting the Building

Fixed costs remain constant in total dollar amount through wide ranges of activity

Cost of building rental } $500

$0

0   250   500   750   1,000   1,250
Number of guests

Per Unit Fixed Cost of Renting the Building

$5.00
$4.50
$4.00
$3.50
$3.00
$2.50
$2.00
$1.50
$1.00
$0.50
$0

Fixed costs decrease on a per unit basis as the activity level increases

0   250   500   750   1,000   1,250
Number of guests

Types of Fixed Costs

Fixed costs are sometimes referred to as capacity costs, since they result from outlays made for buildings, equipment, skilled professional employees, and other items needed to provide the basic capacity for sustained operations. For planning purposes, fixed costs can be viewed as being either *committed* or *discretionary*.

Committed Fixed Costs

Committed fixed costs relate to the investment in facilities, equipment, and the basic organizational structure of a company. Examples of such costs include depreciation of buildings and equipment, taxes on real estate, insurance, and salaries of top management and operating personnel.

Committed fixed costs are long term in nature and can't be reduced to zero even for short periods of time without seriously impairing the profitability or long-run goals of the organization. Even if operations are interrupted or cut back, the committed fixed costs will still continue largely unchanged. During a recession, for example, a company won't usually discharge key executives or sell off key facilities. The basic organizational structure and facilities ordinarily are kept intact. The costs of restoring them later are likely to be far greater than any short-run savings that might be realized.

Since it is difficult to change a committed fixed cost once the commitment has been made, management should approach these decisions with particular care. Decisions to acquire major equipment or to take on other committed fixed costs involve a long planning horizon. Management should make such commitments only after careful analysis of the available alternatives. Once a decision is made to build a certain size facility, a company becomes locked into that decision for many years to come. Decisions relating to committed fixed costs will be examined in Chapter 12.

Sharing Office Space

Even committed fixed costs may be more flexible than they would appear at first glance. Doctors in private practice have been under enormous pressure in recent years to cut costs. Dr. Edward Betz of Encino, California, reduced the committed fixed costs of maintaining his office by letting a urologist use the office on Wednesday afternoons and Friday mornings for $1,500 a month. Dr. Betz uses this time to work on paperwork at home and he makes up for the lost time in the office by treating some patients on Saturdays.

Source: Gloria Lau and Tim W. Ferguson, "Doc's Just an Employee Now," *Forbes*, May 18, 1998, pp. 162–172.

Committed vs. Discretionary Fixed Costs

Discretionary Fixed Costs   **Discretionary fixed costs** (often referred to as *managed fixed costs*) usually arise from *annual* decisions by management to spend on certain fixed cost items. Examples of discretionary fixed costs include advertising, research, public relations, management development programs, and internships for students.

Two key differences exist between discretionary fixed costs and committed fixed costs. First, the planning horizon for a discretionary fixed cost is short term—usually a single year. By contrast, as we indicated earlier, committed fixed costs have a planning horizon that encompasses many years. Second, discretionary fixed costs can be cut for short periods of time with minimal damage to the long-run goals of the organization. For example, spending on management development programs can be reduced because of poor economic conditions. Although some unfavorable consequences may result from the cutback, it is doubtful that these consequences would be as great as those that would result if the company decided to economize during the year by laying off key personnel.

Whether a particular cost is regarded as committed or discretionary may depend on management's strategy. For example, during recessions when the level of home building is down, many construction companies lay off most of their workers and virtually disband operations. Other construction companies retain large numbers of employees on the payroll, even though the workers have little or no work to do. While these latter companies may be faced with short-term cash flow problems, it will be easier for them to respond quickly when economic conditions improve. And the higher morale and loyalty of their employees may give these companies a significant competitive advantage.

The most important characteristic of discretionary fixed costs is that management is not locked into its decisions regarding such costs. Discretionary costs can be adjusted from year to year or even perhaps during the course of a year if necessary.

A Twist on Fixed and Variable Costs

Mission Controls designs and installs automation systems for food and beverage manufacturers. At most companies, when sales drop and cost cutting is necessary, top managers lay off workers. The founders of Mission Controls decided to do something different when sales drop—they slash their own salaries before they even consider letting any of their employees go. This makes their own salaries somewhat variable, while the wages and salaries of workers act more like fixed costs. The payoff is a loyal and committed workforce.

Source: Christopher Caggiano, "Employment, Guaranteed for Life," *INC*, October 15, 2002, p. 74.

The Trend toward Fixed Costs   The trend in many industries is toward greater fixed costs relative to variable costs. Chores that used to be performed by hand have been taken over by machines. For example, grocery clerks at stores like Safeway and Kroger used to key in prices by hand on cash registers. Now, stores are equipped with barcode readers that enter price and other product information automatically. In general, competition has created pressure to give customers more value for their money—a demand that often can only be satisfied by automating business processes. For example, an H & R Block employee used to fill out tax returns for customers by hand and the advice given to a customer largely depended on the knowledge of that particular employee. Now, sophisticated computer software is used to complete tax returns, and the software provides tax planning and other advice tailored to the customer's needs based on the accumulated knowledge of many experts.

As automation intensifies, the demand for "knowledge" workers—those who work primarily with their minds rather than their muscles—has grown tremendously. Since knowledge workers tend to be salaried, highly trained, and difficult to replace, the costs of compensating these workers are often relatively fixed and are committed rather than discretionary.

Is Labor a Variable or a Fixed Cost?   As the preceding discussion suggests, wages and salaries may be fixed or variable. The behavior of wage and salary costs will differ from one country to another, depending on labor regulations, labor contracts, and custom. In some countries, such as France, Germany, and Japan, management has little flexibility in adjusting the labor force to changes in business activity. In countries such as the United States and the United Kingdom, management typically has much greater latitude. However, even in these less restrictive environments, managers may choose to treat employee compensation as a fixed cost for several reasons.

First, many managers are reluctant to decrease their workforce in response to short-term declines in sales. These managers realize that the success of their businesses hinges on retaining highly skilled and trained employees. If these valuable workers are laid off, it is unlikely that they would ever return or be easily replaced. Furthermore, laying off workers undermines the morale of those employees who remain.

Second, managers do not want to be caught with a bloated payroll in an economic downturn. Therefore, managers are reluctant to add employees in response to short-term increases in sales. Instead, more and more companies rely on temporary and part-time workers to take up the slack when their permanent, full-time employees are unable to handle all of the demand for their products and services. In such companies, labor costs are a complex mixture of fixed and variable costs.

The Regulatory Burden

Peter F. Drucker, a renowned observer of business and society, claims that "the driving force behind the steady growth of temps [and outsourcing of work] . . . is the growing burden of rules and regulations for employers." U.S. laws and regulations concerning employees require companies to file multiple reports—and any breach, even if unintentional, can result in punishment. According to the Small Business Administration, the owner of a small or midsize business spends up to a quarter of his or her time on employment-related paperwork and the cost of complying with government regulations (including tax report preparation) is over $5,000 per employee per year. "No wonder that employers . . . complain bitterly that they have no time to work on products and services. . . . They no longer chant the old mantra 'People are our greatest asset.' Instead, they claim 'People are our greatest liability.'" To the extent that the regulatory burden leads to a decline in permanent full-time employees and an increase in the use of temporary employees and outsourcing, labor costs are converted from fixed to variable costs. While this is not the intent of the regulations, it is a consequence.

Source: Peter F. Drucker, "They're Not Employees, They're People," *Harvard Business Review*, February 2002.

Many major companies have undergone waves of downsizing in recent years in which large numbers of employees, including managers, have lost their jobs. This downsizing may seem to suggest that even management salaries should be regarded as variable costs, but this would not be a valid conclusion. Downsizing has largely been the result of attempts to streamline business processes and cut costs rather than a response to a decline in sales activity. This underscores an important, but subtle, point. Fixed costs can change—they just don't change in response to small changes in activity.

In sum, there is no clear-cut answer to the question "Is labor a variable or fixed cost?" It depends on how much flexibility management has to adjust the workforce and management's strategy. Nevertheless, unless otherwise stated, we will assume in this text that direct labor is a variable cost. This assumption is more likely to be valid for companies in the United States than in countries where employment laws permit much less flexibility.

Labor at Southwest Airlines

IN BUSINESS

Starting with a $10,000 investment in 1966, Herb Kelleher built Southwest Airlines into the most profitable airline in the United States. Prior to stepping down as president and CEO of the airline in 2001, Kelleher wrote: "The thing that would disturb me most to see after I'm no longer CEO is layoffs at Southwest. Nothing kills your company's culture like layoffs. Nobody has ever been furloughed here, and that is unprecedented in the airline industry. It's been a huge strength of ours . . . We could have furloughed at various times and been more profitable, but I always thought that was shortsighted. You want to show your people that you value them and you're not going to hurt them just to get a little money in the short run."

Because of this commitment by management to the company's employees, all wages and salaries are basically committed fixed costs at Southwest Airlines.

Source: Herb Kelleher, "The Chairman of the Board Looks Back," *Fortune*, May 28, 2001, pp. 63–76.

Fixed Costs and the Relevant Range

The concept of the relevant range, which was introduced in the discussion of variable costs, is also important in understanding fixed costs—particularly discretionary fixed costs. The levels of discretionary fixed costs are typically decided at the beginning of the year and depend on the needs of planned programs such as advertising and training. The scope of these programs will depend, in turn, on the overall anticipated level of activity for the year. At very high levels of activity, programs are often broadened or expanded. For example, if the company hopes to increase sales by 25%, it would probably plan for much larger advertising costs than if no sales increase were planned. So the *planned* level of activity might affect total discretionary fixed costs. However, once the total discretionary fixed costs have been budgeted, they are unaffected by the *actual* level of activity. For example, once the advertising budget has been established and spent, it will not be affected by how many units are actually sold. Therefore, the cost is fixed with respect to the *actual* number of units sold.

Discretionary fixed costs are easier to adjust than committed fixed costs. They also tend to be less "lumpy." Committed fixed costs consist of costs such as buildings, equipment, and the salaries of key personnel. It is difficult to buy half a piece of equipment or to hire a quarter of a product-line manager, so the step pattern depicted in Exhibit 5–6 is typical for such costs. The relevant range of activity for a fixed cost is the range of activity over which the graph of the cost is flat as in Exhibit 5–6. As a company expands its level of activity, it may outgrow its present facilities, or the key management team may need to be expanded. The result, of course, will be increased committed fixed costs as larger facilities are built and as new management positions are created.

EXHIBIT 5–6

Fixed Costs and the Relevant Range

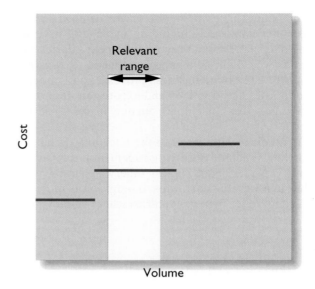

One reaction to the step pattern depicted in Exhibit 5–6 is to conclude that discretionary and committed fixed costs are really just step-variable costs. To some extent this is true, since *almost* all costs can be adjusted in the long run. There are two major differences, however, between the step-variable costs depicted earlier in Exhibit 5–3 and the fixed costs depicted in Exhibit 5–6.

The first difference is that the step-variable costs can often be adjusted quickly as conditions change, whereas once fixed costs have been set, they usually can't be changed easily. A step-variable cost such as maintenance labor, for example, can be adjusted upward or downward by hiring and laying off maintenance workers. By contrast, once a company has signed a lease for a building, it is locked into that level of lease cost for the life of the contract.

The second difference is that the *width of the steps* depicted for step-variable costs is much narrower than the width of the steps depicted for the fixed costs in Exhibit 5–6. The width of the steps relates to volume or level of activity. For step-variable costs, the width of a step might be 40 hours of activity per week if one is dealing, for example, with maintenance labor cost. For fixed costs, however, the width of a step might be *thousands* or even *tens of thousands* of hours of activity. In essence, the width of the steps for step-variable costs is generally so narrow that these costs can be treated essentially as variable costs for most purposes. The width of the steps for fixed costs, on the other hand, is so wide that these costs should be treated as entirely fixed within the relevant range.

Mixed Costs

A **mixed cost** contains both variable and fixed cost elements. Mixed costs are also known as semivariable costs. To continue the Nooksack Expeditions example, the company must pay a license fee of $25,000 per year plus $3 per rafting party to the state's Department of Natural Resources. If the company runs 1,000 rafting parties this year, the total fees paid to the state would be $28,000, made up of $25,000 in fixed cost plus $3,000 in variable cost. Exhibit 5–7 depicts the behavior of this mixed cost.

Even if Nooksack fails to attract any customers, the company still must pay the license fee of $25,000. This is why the cost line in Exhibit 5–7 intersects the vertical cost axis at the $25,000 point. For each rafting party the company organizes, the total cost of the state fees will increase by $3. Therefore, the total cost line slopes upward as the variable cost of $3 per party is added to the fixed cost of $25,000 per year.

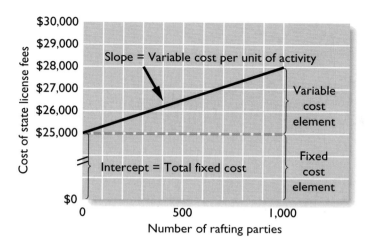

EXHIBIT 5–7

Mixed Cost Behavior

Since the mixed cost in Exhibit 5–7 is represented by a straight line, the following equation for a straight line can be used to express the relationship between a mixed cost and the level of activity:

$$Y = a + bX$$

In this equation,

Y = The total mixed cost
a = The total fixed cost (the vertical intercept of the line)
b = The variable cost per unit of activity (the slope of the line)
X = The level of activity

In the case of the state fees paid by Nooksack Expeditions, the equation is written as follows:

$$Y = \$25,000 + \$3.00X$$

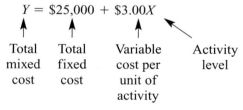

This equation makes it easy to calculate the total mixed cost for any level of activity within the relevant range. For example, suppose that the company expects to organize 800 rafting parties in the next year. The total state fees would be $27,400 calculated as follows:

$Y = \$25,000 + (\$3.00 \text{ per rafting party} \times 800 \text{ rafting parties})$

$= \$27,400$

Cost Analyst

DECISION MAKER

You have been hired to analyze costs for a caterer that provides and serves refreshments for wedding receptions. Costs incurred by the caterer include administrative salaries, rental of the central kitchen, the salary of the full-time chef, wages of part-time cooks, the costs of groceries and kitchen supplies, delivery vehicle depreciation and operating expenses, the wages of part-time food servers, depreciation of silverware and dinnerware, and the costs of cleaning table linens. Which of these costs are likely to be variable with respect to the number of guests at a wedding reception? Which are likely to be fixed? Which are likely to be mixed?

THE ANALYSIS OF MIXED COSTS

In practice, mixed costs are very common. For example, the cost of providing X-ray services to patients at the Harvard Medical School Hospital is a mixed cost. There are substantial fixed costs for equipment depreciation and for the salaries of radiologists and technicians, but there are also variable costs for X-ray film, power, and supplies. At Southwest Airlines, maintenance costs are mixed costs. The company incurs fixed costs for renting maintenance facilities and for keeping skilled mechanics on the payroll, but the costs of replacement parts, lubricating oils, tires, and so forth are variable with respect to how often and how far the company's aircraft are flown.

The fixed portion of a mixed cost represents the minimum cost of having a service *ready and available* for use. The variable portion represents the cost incurred for *actual consumption* of the service, thus it varies in total in proportion to the amount of service actually consumed.

How does management go about actually estimating the fixed and variable components of a mixed cost? The most common methods used in practice are *account analysis* and the *engineering approach.*

In **account analysis,** each account under consideration is classified as either variable or fixed based on the analyst's prior knowledge of how the cost in the account behaves. For example, direct materials would be classified as variable and a building lease cost would be classified as fixed because of the nature of those costs. The total fixed cost of an organization is the sum of the costs for the accounts that have been classified as fixed. The variable cost per unit is estimated by dividing the sum of the costs for the accounts that have been classified as variable by the total activity.

The **engineering approach** to cost analysis involves a detailed analysis of what cost behavior should be, based on an industrial engineer's evaluation of the production methods to be used, the materials specifications, labor requirements, equipment usage, production efficiency, power consumption, and so on. For example, Pizza Hut might use the engineering approach to estimate the cost of preparing and serving a particular take-out pizza. The cost of the pizza would be estimated by carefully costing the specific ingredients used to make the pizza, the power consumed to cook the pizza, and the cost of the container the pizza is delivered in. The engineering approach must be used in those situations where no past experience is available concerning activity and costs. In addition, it is sometimes used together with other methods to improve the accuracy of cost analysis.

Account analysis works best when analyzing costs at a fairly aggregated level, such as the cost of serving patients in the emergency room (ER) of Cook County Hospital. The costs of drugs, supplies, forms, wages, equipment, and so on can be roughly classified as variable or fixed and a mixed cost formula for the overall cost of the emergency room can be estimated fairly quickly. However, this method does not recognize that some of the accounts may contain both fixed and variable costs. For example, the cost of electricity for the ER is a mixed cost. Most of the electricity is used for heating and lighting and is a fixed cost. However, the consumption of electricity increases with activity in the ER since diagnostic equipment, operating theater lights, defibrillators, and so on all consume electricity. The most effective way to estimate the fixed and variable elements of such a mixed cost may be to analyze past records of cost and activity data. These records should reveal whether electrical costs vary significantly with the number of patients and if so, by how much. The remainder of this section explains how to conduct such an analysis of past cost and activity data.

Operations Drive Costs

White Grizzly Adventures is a snowcat skiing and snowboarding company in Meadow Creek, British Columbia, that is owned and operated by Brad and Carole Karafil. The company shuttles 12 guests to the top of the company's steep and tree-covered terrain in a single snowcat. Guests stay as a group at the company's lodge for a fixed number of days and are provided healthful gourmet meals.

Brad and Carole must decide each year when snowcat operations will begin in December and when they will end in early spring, and how many nonoperating days to schedule between groups of guests for maintenance and rest. This decision affects a variety of costs. Examples of costs that are fixed and variable with respect to the number of days of operation at White Grizzly include:

Cost	Cost Behavior—Fixed or Variable with Respect to Days of Operation
Property taxes	Fixed
Summer road maintenance and tree clearing	Fixed
Lodge depreciation	Fixed
Snowcat operator and guides	Variable
Cooks and lodge help	Variable
Snowcat depreciation	Variable
Snowcat fuel	Variable
Food*	Variable

*The costs of food served to guests theoretically depend on the number of guests in residence. However, the lodge is basically always filled to its capacity of 12 persons when the snowcat operation is running, so food costs can be considered to be driven by the days of operation.

Source: Brad & Carole Karafil, owners and operators of White Grizzly Adventures, www.whitegrizzly.com.

1. Which of the following cost behavior assumptions is false? (You may select more than one answer.)
   a. Variable cost per unit increases as the activity increases.
   b. The average fixed cost per unit decreases as the activity increases.
   c. Total variable costs decrease as the activity decreases.
   d. Total fixed costs remain the same as the activity changes (within the relevant range).
2. Which of the following statements is false? (You may select more than one answer.)
   a. The planning horizon for discretionary fixed costs is longer than the planning horizon for committed fixed costs.
   b. Discretionary fixed costs can be cut in the short term if necessary, while committed fixed costs cannot be cut for short periods of time.
   c. As companies increasingly rely on knowledge workers, the labor cost associated with employing these workers is often committed fixed as opposed to discretionary.
   d. A mixed cost contains both committed fixed and discretionary elements.

The chief executive officer of Brentline Hospital has been concerned with the hospital's maintenance costs. This cost had been budgeted for a constant $8,400 per month but has been bouncing around between $7,400 per month and $9,800 per month over the last year. In retrospect, the constant budget was not realistic since at least to some extent maintenance costs can be expected to vary with the overall level of activity in the hospital. In other words, maintenance cost is very likely a mixed cost. Some of this cost consists of fixed costs like salaries and equipment depreciation and some of it consists of variable costs like replacement parts and manufacturer's service calls. To more accurately budget and control maintenance costs, the chief executive officer has requested an analysis that breaks maintenance cost down into its fixed and variable components. After some discussion, it was decided that the appropriate measure of activity for maintenance cost is probably patient-days, where each day a patient is in the hospital counts as one patient-day.

Diagnosing Cost Behavior with a Scattergraph Plot

The analysis of maintenance cost begins by collecting cost and activity data for a number of recent months. The data should be thoroughly checked to make sure they are error-free and contain no distortions. At the very least, the cost data should be based on accruals rather than simply on cash outflows since the latter are affected by when bills happen to be paid. The relevant accrual-based data from Brentline Hospital appear below:

Month	Activity Level: Patient-Days	Maintenance Cost Incurred
January	5,600	$7,900
February	7,100	$8,500
March	5,000	$7,400
April	6,500	$8,200
May	7,300	$9,100
June	8,000	$9,800
July	6,200	$7,800

The first step in analyzing the cost and activity data is to plot the data on a scattergraph. This plot will immediately reveal any nonlinearities or other problems with the data. The scattergraph of maintenance costs versus patient-days at Brentline Hospital is reproduced in the first panel of Exhibit 5–8. Two things should be noted about this scattergraph:

1. The total maintenance cost, Y, is plotted on the vertical axis. Cost is known as the **dependent variable,** since the amount of cost incurred during a period depends on the level of activity for the period. (That is, as the level of activity increases, total cost will also ordinarily increase.)
2. The activity, X (patient-days in this case), is plotted on the horizontal axis. Activity is known as the **independent variable,** since it causes variations in the cost.

From the scattergraph, it is evident that maintenance costs do increase with the number of patient-days. In addition, the scattergraph reveals that the relation between maintenance costs and patient-days is approximately *linear*. Scattergraphs reveal what is called **linear cost behavior** whenever a straight line reasonably approximates the relation between cost and activity. Such a straight line has been drawn using a ruler in the second panel of Exhibit 5–8. Note that the data points do not fall exactly on the straight line. This will almost always happen in practice; the relation is seldom perfectly linear.

Note that the straight line in Exhibit 5–8 has been drawn through the point representing 7,300 patient-days and a total maintenance cost of $9,100. Drawing the straight line through one of the data points helps make a quick-and-dirty estimate of variable and fixed costs. The vertical intercept where the straight line crosses the Y axis—in this case, about $3,300—is the rough estimate of the fixed cost. The variable cost can be quickly

EXHIBIT 5–8

Scattergraph Method of Cost Analysis

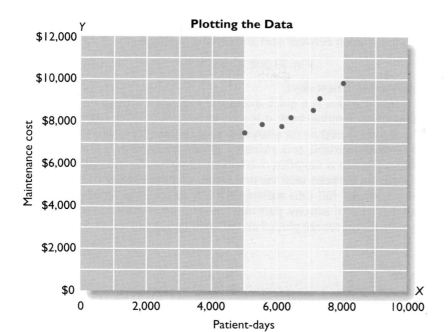

Plotting the Data

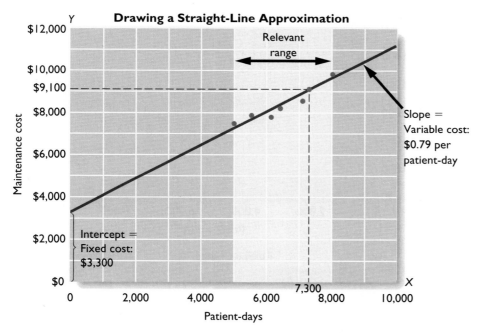

Drawing a Straight-Line Approximation

estimated by subtracting the estimated fixed cost from the total cost at the point lying on the straight line.

Total maintenance cost for 7,300 patient-days (a point falling on the straight line)	$9,100
Less estimated fixed cost (the vertical intercept)	3,300
Estimated total variable cost for 7,300 patient-days	$5,800

The average variable cost per unit at 7,300 patient-days is computed as follows:

$$\text{Variable cost per unit} = \$5,800 \div 7,300 \text{ patient-days}$$

$$= \$0.79 \text{ per patient-day (rounded)}$$

Combining the estimate of the fixed cost and the estimate of the variable cost per patient-day, we can write the relation between cost and activity as follows:

$$Y = \$3,300 + \$0.79X$$

where X is the number of patient-days.

We hasten to add that this *is* a quick-and-dirty method of estimating the fixed and variable cost elements of a mixed cost; it is seldom used in practice when the financial implications of a decision based on the analysis are significant. However, setting aside the estimates of the fixed and variable cost elements, plotting the data on a scattergraph is an essential diagnostic step that is too often overlooked. Suppose, for example, we had been interested in the relation between total nursing wages and the number of patient-days at the hospital. The permanent, full-time nursing staff can handle up to 7,000 patient-days in a month. Beyond that level of activity, part-time nurses must be called in to help out. The cost and activity data for nurses are plotted on the scattergraph in Exhibit 5–9. Looking at

EXHIBIT 5–9

More than One Relevant Range

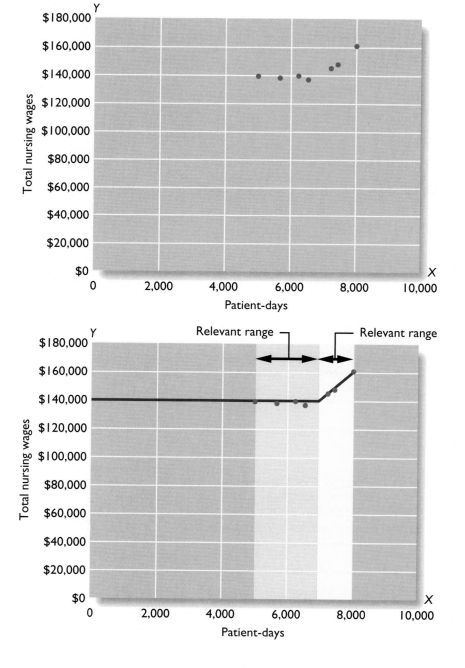

EXHIBIT 5–10

A Diagnostic Scattergraph Plot

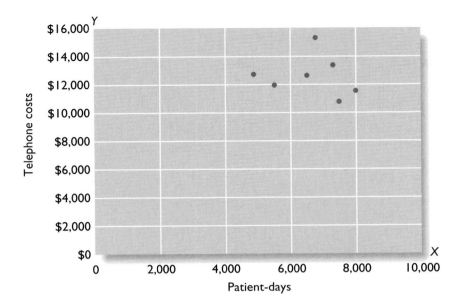

that scattergraph, it is evident that two straight lines would do a much better job of fitting the data than a single straight line. Up to 7,000 patient-days, total nursing wages are essentially a fixed cost. Above 7,000 patient-days, total nursing wages are a mixed cost. This happens because, as stated above, the permanent, full-time nursing staff can handle up to 7,000 patient-days in a month. Above that level, part-time nurses are called in to help, which adds to the cost. Consequently, two straight lines (and two equations) would be used to represent total nursing wages—one for the relevant range of 5,000 to 7,000 patient-days and one for the relevant range of 7,000 to 8,000 patient-days.

As another example, suppose that Brentline Hospital's management is interested in the relation between the hospital's telephone costs and patient-days. Patients are billed directly for their use of telephones, so those costs do not appear on the hospital's cost records. The telephone costs of concern to management are the charges for the staff's use of telephones. The data for this cost are plotted in Exhibit 5–10. It is evident from that plot that while the telephone costs do vary from month to month, they are not related to patient-days. Something other than patient-days is driving the telephone bills. Therefore, it would not make sense to analyze this cost any further by attempting to estimate a variable cost per patient-day for telephone costs. Plotting the data helps the cost analyst to diagnose such situations.

Choosing a Measure of Activity   YOU DECIDE

You are the manager of a for-profit company that helps students prepare for standardized exams such as the SAT. You have been trying to figure out what causes variations in your monthly electrical costs. Electricity is used primarily to run office equipment such as personal computers and to provide lighting for the business office and for classrooms. Below are scattergraphs that show monthly electrical costs plotted against two different possible measures of activity—student-hours and classroom-hours. A student who takes a course involving 10 hours of classroom time would be counted as 10 student-hours. Each hour a classroom is used is counted as one classroom-hour, regardless of the number of students in the classroom at the time.

YOU DECIDE

(continued)

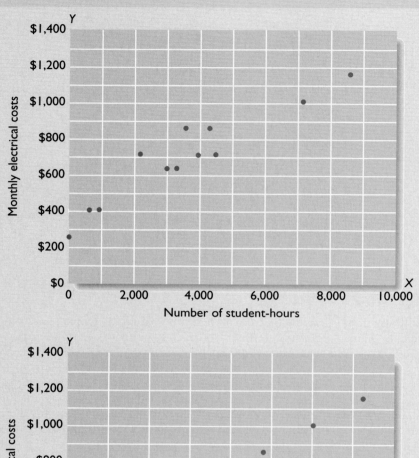

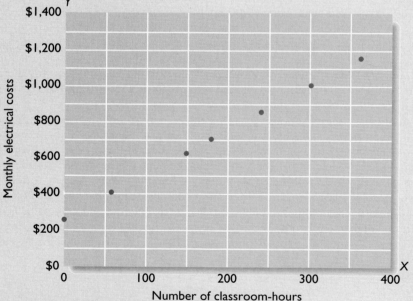

Which measure of activity—student-hours or classroom-hours—best explains variations in monthly electrical costs and should therefore be used to estimate its variable cost component?

The High-Low Method

In addition to the quick-and-dirty method described in the preceding section, more precise methods are available for estimating fixed and variable costs. However, it must be emphasized that fixed and variable costs should be computed only if a scattergraph plot confirms that the relation is approximately linear. In the case of maintenance costs at Brentline Hospital, the relation does appear to be linear. In the case of telephone costs, there isn't any clear relation between telephone costs and patient-days, so there is no point in estimating how much of the cost varies with patient-days.

Assuming that the scattergraph plot indicates a linear relation between cost and activity, the fixed and variable cost elements of a mixed cost can be estimated using the *high-low method* or the *least-squares regression method.* The high-low method is based on the rise-over-run formula for the slope of a straight line. As discussed above, if the relation between cost and activity can be represented by a straight line, then the slope of the straight line is equal to the variable cost per unit of activity. Consequently, the following formula can be used to estimate the variable cost.

$$\text{Variable cost} = \text{Slope of the line} = \frac{\text{Rise}}{\text{Run}} = \frac{Y_2 - Y_1}{X_2 - X_1}$$

To analyze mixed costs with the **high-low method,** you begin by identifying the period with the lowest level of activity and the period with the highest level of activity. The period with the lowest activity is selected as the first point in the above formula and the period with the highest activity is selected as the second point. Consequently, the formula becomes:

$$\frac{\text{Variable}}{\text{cost}} = \frac{Y_2 - Y_1}{X_2 - X_1} = \frac{\text{Cost at the high activity level} - \text{Cost at the low activity level}}{\text{High activity level} - \text{Low activity level}}$$

or

$$\text{Variable cost} = \frac{\text{Change in cost}}{\text{Change in activity}}$$

Therefore, when the high-low method is used, the variable cost is estimated by dividing the difference in cost between the high and low levels of activity by the change in activity between those two points.

Using the high-low method, we first identify the periods with the highest and lowest *activity*—in this case, June and March. We then use the activity and cost data from these two periods to estimate the variable cost component as follows:

	Patient-Days	Maintenance Cost Incurred
High activity level (June)	8,000	$9,800
Low activity level (March)	5,000	7,400
Change	3,000	$2,400

$$\text{Variable cost} = \frac{\text{Change in cost}}{\text{Change in activity}} = \frac{\$2,400}{3,000 \text{ patient-days}} = \$0.80 \text{ per patient-day}$$

Having determined that the variable rate for maintenance cost is 80 cents per patient-day, we can now determine the amount of fixed cost. This is done by taking total cost at *either* the high or the low activity level and deducting the variable cost element. In the computation below, total cost at the high activity level is used in computing the fixed cost element:

$$\text{Fixed cost element} = \text{Total cost} - \text{Variable cost element}$$

$$= \$9,800 - (\$0.80 \text{ per patient-day} \times 8,000 \text{ patient-days})$$

$$= \$3,400$$

Both the variable and fixed cost elements have now been isolated. The cost of maintenance can be expressed as $3,400 per month plus 80 cents per patient-day.

The cost of maintenance can also be expressed in terms of the equation for a straight line as follows:

$$Y = \$3,400 + \$0.80X$$

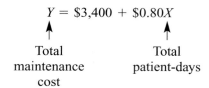

Total maintenance cost	Total patient-days

The data used in this illustration are shown graphically in Exhibit 5–11. Notice that a straight line has been drawn through the points corresponding to the low and high levels of activity. In essence, that is what the high-low method does—it draws a straight line through those two points.

Sometimes the high and low levels of activity don't coincide with the high and low amounts of cost. For example, the period that has the highest level of activity may not have the highest amount of cost. Nevertheless, the highest and lowest levels of *activity* are always used to analyze a mixed cost under the high-low method. The reason is that the analyst would like to use data that reflect the greatest possible variation in activity.

The high-low method is very simple to apply, but it suffers from a major (and sometimes critical) defect—it utilizes only two data points. Generally, two data points are not enough to produce accurate results. Additionally, periods in which the activity level is unusually low or unusually high will tend to produce inaccurate results. A cost formula that is estimated solely using data from these unusual periods may misrepresent the true cost behavior during normal periods. Such a distortion is evident in Exhibit 5–11. The straight line should probably be shifted down somewhat so that it is closer to more of the data points. For these reasons, other methods of cost analysis that utilize a greater number of data points will generally be more accurate than the high-low method. A manager who chooses to use the high-low method should do so with a full awareness of the method's limitations.

Fortunately, computer software makes it very easy to use sophisticated statistical methods, such as *least-squares regression,* that use all of the data and that are capable of

EXHIBIT 5–11

High-Low Method of Cost Analysis

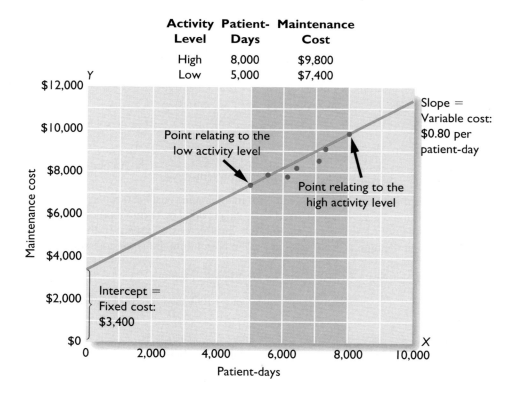

providing much more information than just the estimates of variable and fixed costs. The details of these statistical methods are beyond the scope of this text, but the basic approach is discussed below. Nevertheless, even if the least-squares regression approach is used, it is always a good idea to plot the data in a scattergraph. By simply looking at the scattergraph, you can quickly verify whether it makes sense to fit a straight line to the data using least-squares regression or some other method.

3. Assume a hotel rented 400, 480, and 420 rooms in the months of April, May, and June, respectively; and the total housekeeping costs for the three months in question were $6,000, $6,800, and $6,200. Using the high-low method, what is the amount of monthly fixed housekeeping costs?
   a. $1,000
   b. $1,500
   c. $2,000
   d. $2,500

CONCEPT CHECK

The Least-Squares Regression Method

The **least-squares regression method,** unlike the high-low method, uses all of the data to separate a mixed cost into its fixed and variable components. A *regression line* of the form $Y = a + bX$ is fitted to the data, where a represents the total fixed cost and b represents the variable cost per unit of activity. The basic idea underlying the least-squares regression method is illustrated in Exhibit 5–12 using hypothetical data points. Notice from the exhibit that the deviations from the plotted points to the regression line are measured vertically on the graph. These vertical deviations are called the regression errors. There is nothing mysterious about the least-squares regression method. It simply computes the regression line that minimizes the sum of these squared errors. The formulas that accomplish this are fairly complex and involve numerous calculations, but the principle is simple.

Fortunately, computers are adept at carrying out the computations required by the least-squares regression formulas. The data—the observed values of X and Y—are entered

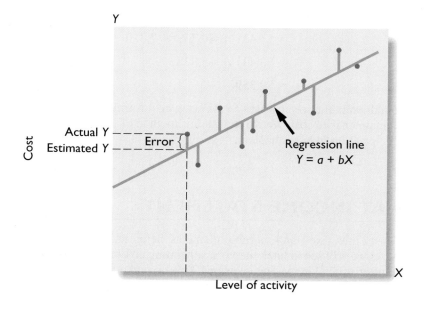

EXHIBIT 5–12

The Concept of Least-Squares Regression

into the computer, and software does the rest. In the case of the Brentline Hospital maintenance cost data, a statistical software package on a personal computer can calculate the following least-squares regression estimates of the total fixed cost (a) and the variable cost per unit of activity (b):

$$a = \$3,431$$

$$b = \$0.759$$

Therefore, using the least-squares regression method, the fixed element of the maintenance cost is $3,431 per month and the variable portion is 75.9 cents per patient-day.

In terms of the linear equation $Y = a + bX$, the cost formula can be written as

$$Y = \$3,431 + \$0.759X$$

where activity (X) is expressed in patient-days.

Notice the least-squares regression estimates (variable cost per patient day = 75.9 cents; fixed cost per month = $3,431) differ from those obtained using the scattergraph method (variable cost per patient-day = 79 cents; fixed cost per month = $3,300) and the high-low method (variable cost per patient-day = 80 cents; fixed cost per month = $3,400). These differences are to be expected given that each method used different amounts of data and in different ways. While any of these three cost formulas can be used to predict costs or establish benchmarks, the method that uses the most data (e.g., least-squares regression) is usually the most accurate. So, if Brentline Hospital wants to esti-mate next month's maintenance costs based on an estimated activity level of 7,800 patient-days, it would most likely rely on the cost formula derived using least-squares re-gression. Rounded to the nearest whole dollar, this formula estimates maintenance costs of $9,351, calculated as follows:

$$Y = \$3,431 + \$0.759X$$

$$= \$3,431 + \$0.759 \times 7,800$$

$$= \$3,431 + \$5,920$$

$$= \$9,351$$

Suppose that it turns out that next month the actual level of activity is 7,810 patient-days and the actual maintenance cost is $9,427. Is this cost too high or too low, given the actual level of activity for the period? According to the cost formula, the maintenance cost should be $9,359 (to the nearest whole dollar), determined as follows:

$$Y = \$3,431 + \$0.759X$$

$$= \$3,431 + \$0.759 \times 7,810$$

$$= \$3,431 + \$5,928$$

$$= \$9,359$$

Since the actual maintenance cost was $9,427, the cost formula suggests that too much was spent on maintenance cost. We will revisit this method of setting benchmarks to com-pare to actual spending in later chapters.

THE CONTRIBUTION FORMAT INCOME STATEMENT

LEARNING OBJECTIVE 4

Prepare an income statement using the contribution format.

Separating costs into fixed and variable elements helps to predict costs and provide benchmarks. As we will see in later chapters, separating costs into fixed and variable ele-ments is also often crucial in making decisions. This crucial distinction between fixed and variable costs is at the heart of the **contribution approach** to the construction of income statements. The unique thing about the contribution approach is that it provides managers with an income statement that clearly distinguishes between fixed and variable costs and therefore facilitates planning, control, and decision making.

Why a New Income Statement Format?

An income statement prepared using the *traditional approach,* as illustrated in Chapter 1, is not organized in terms of cost behavior. Rather, it is organized in a "functional" format—emphasizing the functions of production, administration, and sales. No attempt is made to distinguish between the behavior of costs included under each functional heading. Under the heading "Administrative expense," for example, both variable and fixed costs are lumped together.

Although an income statement prepared in the functional format may be useful for external reporting purposes, it has serious limitations when used for internal purposes. Internally, managers need cost data organized in a format that will facilitate planning, control, and decision making. As we shall see in chapters ahead, these tasks are much easier when cost data are available in a fixed and variable format. The contribution format income statement has been developed in response to these needs.

The Contribution Approach

Exhibit 5–13 uses a simple example to compare the contribution approach to the income statement with the traditional approach discussed in Chapter 1. Notice that the net operating income shown in both income statements in the exhibit is $1,000. In this portion of the chapter, we focus solely on situations where both income statements report the same net operating income. It is possible, and indeed quite common, for a traditional income statement, which is based on absorption costing, and a contribution format income statement, which is based on variable costing, to report different amounts of net operating income. We explore this phenomenon in Appendix 5A: Variable Costing and explain in detail the differences between absorption costing and variable costing.

Concept 5-2

EXHIBIT 5–13 Comparison of the Contribution Income Statement with the Traditional Income Statement

Traditional Approach (costs organized by function)			Contribution Approach (costs organized by behavior)		
Sales		$12,000	Sales		$12,000
Cost of goods sold		6,000*	Less variable expenses:		
Gross margin		6,000	Variable production	$2,000	
Selling and administrative expenses:			Variable selling	600	
Selling	$3,100*		Variable administrative	400	3,000
Administrative	1,900*	5,000	Contribution margin		9,000
Net operating income		$ 1,000	Less fixed expenses:		
			Fixed production	4,000	
			Fixed selling	2,500	
			Fixed administrative	1,500	8,000
			Net operating income		$ 1,000

*Contains both variable and fixed expenses. This is the income statement for a manufacturing company; thus, when the income statement is placed in the contribution format, the "cost of goods sold" figure is divided between variable production costs and fixed production costs. If this were the income statement for a *merchandising* company (which simply purchases completed goods from a supplier), then the cost of goods sold would be *all* variable.

Notice that the contribution approach separates costs into fixed and variable categories, first deducting variable expenses from sales to obtain what is known as the *contribution margin*. The **contribution margin** is the amount remaining from sales revenues after variable expenses have been deducted. This amount *contributes* toward covering fixed expenses and then toward profits for the period.

The contribution approach to the income statement is used as an internal planning, controlling, and decision-making tool. Its emphasis on cost behavior facilitates cost-volume-profit analysis (such as we shall be doing in the next chapter), management performance appraisals, and budgeting. Moreover, the contribution approach helps managers organize data pertinent to all kinds of decisions such as product-line analysis, pricing, use of scarce resources, and make or buy analysis. All of these topics are covered in later chapters.

CONCEPT CHECK

4. A company's contribution approach income statement showed net operating income, variable production expenses, and fixed expenses of $4,000, $15,000, and $10,000, respectively. How much contribution margin did the company earn?
   a. $29,000
   b. $15,000
   c. $19,000
   d. $14,000

SUMMARY

LO1 Understand how fixed and variable costs behave and how to use them to predict costs.
The total amount of a variable cost is proportional to the level of activity within the relevant range. The variable cost per unit of activity is constant as the level of activity changes.

The total amount of a fixed cost is constant as the level of activity changes within the relevant range. The fixed cost per unit of activity decreases as the level of activity increases since a constant amount is divided by a larger number.

To predict costs at a new level of activity, multiply the variable cost per unit by the new level of activity and then add to the result the total fixed cost.

LO2 Use a scattergraph plot to diagnose cost behavior.
A scattergraph plot helps provide insight into the behavior of a cost. In the scattergraph, activity is plotted on the horizontal, X, axis and total cost is plotted on the vertical, Y, axis. If the relation between cost and activity appears to be linear based on the scattergraph plot, then the variable and fixed components of a mixed cost can be estimated using the quick-and-dirty method, the high-low method, or the least-squares regression method.

LO3 Analyze a mixed cost using the high-low method.
To use the high-low method, first identify the periods in which the highest and the lowest levels of activity have occurred. Second, estimate the variable cost element by dividing the change in total cost by the change in activity for these two periods. Third, estimate the fixed cost element by subtracting the total variable cost from the total cost at either the highest or the lowest level of activity.

The high-low method relies on only two, often unusual, data points rather than all of the available data and therefore may provide misleading estimates of variable and fixed costs.

LO4 Prepare an income statement using the contribution format.
Managers use costs organized by behavior in many decisions. To help managers make such decisions, the income statement can be prepared in a contribution format. The traditional income statement format emphasizes the purposes for which costs were incurred (i.e., to manufacture the product, to sell the product, or to administer the organization). In contrast, the contribution format income statement classifies costs by cost behavior (i.e., variable versus fixed).

GUIDANCE ANSWERS TO *DECISION MAKER* AND *YOU DECIDE*

Cost Analyst (p. 209)

Cost	Cost Behavior	Explanation
Administrative salaries	Fixed	Total administrative salaries would be unaffected by the number of guests at a wedding reception.
Rental of the central kitchen	Fixed	The cost of renting the central kitchen would be unaffected by the number of guests at a wedding reception.
Salary of the full-time chef	Fixed	The chef's salary would probably not be affected by the number of guests at a wedding reception.
Wages of part-time cooks	Variable or step-variable	More cooks may need to be hired to prepare meals if the number of guests increases.
Groceries and kitchen supplies	Variable	These costs should be proportional to the number of guests at a reception.
Delivery vehicle depreciation and operating expenses	Fixed or mixed	The cost of operating the vehicle may be affected if more than one trip is necessary due to the number of guests.
Wages of part-time food servers	Variable or step-variable	More food servers may need to be hired if the number of guests increases.
Depreciation of silverware and dinnerware	Fixed or mixed	Wear and breakage should increase with the number of guests, but not depreciation due to obsolescence.
Cleaning of table linens	Variable or step-variable	More table linens may need to be used if the number of guests increases.

Choosing a Measure of Activity (p. 215)

The relation between monthly electrical costs and classroom-hours seems more linear than the relation between monthly electrical costs and student-hours. A straight line drawn through the points on the second scattergraph relating monthly electrical costs to classroom-hours would explain virtually all of the variation in monthly electrical costs—the fit would be almost perfect. In contrast, a straight line drawn through the first scattergraph relating monthly electrical costs to student-hours would leave a lot of unexplained variation in costs—the fit would be far from perfect. On reflection, this makes sense. The cost of lighting a classroom for an hour is the same whether the classroom contains 1 or 20 students, so if the variations in monthly electrical costs are largely due to the costs of lighting classrooms, classroom-hours would be a better measure of activity than student-hours.

GUIDANCE ANSWERS TO CONCEPT CHECKS

1. **Choice a.** Variable cost per unit is constant.
2. **Choices a and d.** The planning horizon is shorter for discretionary fixed costs than for committed fixed costs. A mixed cost includes fixed and variable elements.
3. **Choice c.** The variable cost per room is ($6,800 − $6,000) ÷ (480 − 400) = $10. In April, the total housekeeping cost of $6,000 − (400 rooms × $10 variable cost per room) = $2,000 of fixed costs. A similar calculation can be completed for June.
4. **Choice d.** The net operating income of $4,000 + $10,000 of fixed expenses = Contribution margin of $14,000.

REVIEW PROBLEM I: COST BEHAVIOR

Neptune Rentals offers a boat rental service. Consider the following costs of the company over the relevant range of 5,000 to 8,000 hours of operating time for its boats:

	Hours of Operating Time			
	5,000	6,000	7,000	8,000
Total costs:				
Variable costs	$ 20,000	$?	$?	$?
Fixed costs	168,000	?	?	?
Total costs	$188,000	$?	$?	$?
Cost per hour:				
Variable cost	$?	$?	$?	$?
Fixed cost	?	?	?	?
Total cost per hour	$?	$?	$?	$?

Required:

Compute the missing amounts, assuming that cost behavior patterns remain unchanged within the relevant range of 5,000 to 8,000 hours.

Solution to Review Problem 1

The variable cost per hour can be computed as follows:

$$\$20,000 \div 5,000 \text{ hours} = \$4 \text{ per hour}$$

Therefore, in accordance with the behavior of variable and fixed costs, the missing amounts are as follows:

	Hours of Operating Time			
	5,000	6,000	7,000	8,000
Total costs:				
Variable costs (@$4 per hour)	$ 20,000	$ 24,000	$ 28,000	$ 32,000
Fixed costs	168,000	168,000	168,000	168,000
Total costs	$188,000	$192,000	$196,000	$200,000
Cost per hour:				
Variable cost	$ 4.00	$ 4.00	$ 4.00	$ 4.00
Fixed cost	33.60	28.00	24.00	21.00
Total cost per hour	$ 37.60	$ 32.00	$ 28.00	$ 25.00

Observe that the total variable costs increase in proportion to the number of hours of operating time, but that these costs remain constant at $4 if expressed on a per hour basis.

In contrast, the total fixed costs do not change with changes in the level of activity. They remain constant at $168,000 within the relevant range. With increases in activity, however, the fixed cost per hour decreases, dropping from $33.60 per hour when the boats are operated 5,000 hours a period to only $21.00 per hour when the boats are operated 8,000 hours a period. *Because of this troublesome aspect of fixed costs, they are most easily (and most safely) dealt with on a total basis, rather than on a unit basis, in cost analysis work.*

REVIEW PROBLEM 2: HIGH-LOW METHOD

The administrator of Azalea Hills Hospital would like a cost formula linking the costs involved in admitting patients to the number of patients admitted during a month. The admitting department's costs and the number of patients admitted during the immediately preceding eight months are given in the following table:

Month	Number of Patients Admitted	Admitting Department Costs
May	1,800	$14,700
June	1,900	$15,200
July	1,700	$13,700
August	1,600	$14,000
September	1,500	$14,300
October	1,300	$13,100
November	1,100	$12,800
December	1,500	$14,600

Required:

1. Use the high-low method to establish the fixed and variable components of admitting costs.
2. Express the fixed and variable components of admitting costs as a cost formula in the form $Y = a + bX$.

Solution to Review Problem 2

1. The first step in the high-low method is to identify the periods of the lowest and highest activity. Those periods are November (1,100 patients admitted) and June (1,900 patients admitted). The second step is to compute the variable cost per unit using those two data points:

Month	Number of Patients Admitted	Admitting Department Costs
High activity level (June)	1,900	$15,200
Low activity level (November)	1,100	12,800
Change	800	$ 2,400

$$\text{Variable cost} = \frac{\text{Change in cost}}{\text{Change in activity}} = \frac{\$2,400}{800 \text{ patients admitted}} = \$3 \text{ per patient admitted}$$

The third step is to compute the fixed cost element by deducting the variable cost element from the total cost at either the high or low activity. In the computation below, the high point of activity is used:

Fixed cost element = Total cost − Variable cost element

= $15,200 − ($3 per patient admitted × 1,900 patients admitted)

= $9,500

2. The cost formula is $Y = \$9,500 + \$3X$.

GLOSSARY

Account analysis   A method for analyzing cost behavior in which each account is classified as either variable or fixed based on the analyst's prior knowledge of how the cost in the account behaves. (p. 210)

Activity base   A measure of whatever causes the incurrence of a variable cost. For example, the total cost of X-ray film in a hospital will increase as the number of X-rays taken increases. Therefore, the number of X-rays is the activity base that explains the total cost of X-ray film. (p. 199)

Committed fixed costs   Fixed costs that are difficult to adjust because they relate to the investment in facilities, equipment, and the basic organizational structure of a company. (p. 204)

Contribution approach   An income statement format that is geared to cost behavior. Costs are separated into variable and fixed categories rather than being separated according to the functions of production, sales, and administration. (p. 220)

Contribution margin   The amount remaining from sales revenues after all variable expenses have been deducted. (p. 222)

Cost structure   The relative proportion of fixed, variable, and mixed costs in an organization. (p. 198)

Curvilinear cost   A relation between cost and activity that is a curve rather than a straight line. (p. 202)

Dependent variable   A variable that responds to some causal factor; total cost is the dependent variable, as represented by the letter Y, in the equation $Y = a + bX$. (p. 212)

Discretionary fixed costs   Fixed costs that arise from annual decisions by management to spend in certain fixed cost areas, such as advertising and research. (p. 205)

Engineering approach   A detailed analysis of cost behavior based on an industrial engineer's evaluation of the inputs that are required to carry out a particular activity and of the prices of those inputs. (p. 210)

High-low method   A method of separating a mixed cost into its fixed and variable elements by analyzing the change in cost between the high and low levels of activity. (p. 217)

Independent variable   A variable that acts as a causal factor; activity is the independent variable, as represented by the letter X, in the equation $Y = a + bX$. (p. 212)

Least-squares regression method   A method of separating a mixed cost into its fixed and variable elements by fitting a regression line that minimizes the sum of the squared errors. (p. 219)

Linear cost behavior   Cost behavior is said to be linear when a straight line is a reasonable approximation for the relation between cost and activity. (p. 212)

Mixed cost   A cost that contains both variable and fixed cost elements. (p. 208)

Relevant range   The range of activity within which assumptions about variable and fixed cost behavior are valid. (p. 202)

Step-variable cost   The cost of a resource (such as the cost of a maintenance worker) that is obtainable only in large chunks and that increases and decreases only in response to fairly wide changes in activity. (p. 201)

APPENDIX 5A: VARIABLE COSTING

LEARNING OBJECTIVE 5

Use variable costing to prepare a contribution format income statement and contrast absorption costing and variable costing.

In earlier chapters we discussed *absorption costing,* a system in which *all* manufacturing costs—both fixed and variable—are assigned to products. Absorption costing is generally considered to be required for external reports, but *variable costing* is a different approach to product costing that can be used by managers for internal decision making and reporting. Under **variable costing,** only the variable costs of making a product are assigned to the product. All other costs are treated as period costs and taken directly to the income statement as expenses. As we shall see, variable costing offers managers numerous advantages over absorption costing.

The essential difference between variable costing and absorption costing, as illustrated in Exhibit 5A–1, is how each method accounts for fixed manufacturing overhead costs—all other costs are similarly treated as product costs or period costs under the two methods. In absorption costing, fixed manufacturing overhead costs are initially included as part of the costs of work in process inventories. When units are completed, these costs are transferred to finished goods and only when the units are sold do these costs flow through to the income statement as part of cost of goods sold. In variable costing, fixed manufacturing overhead costs are considered to be period costs—just like selling and administrative costs—and are taken immediately to the income statement as period expenses.

IN BUSINESS   ## The Perverse Effects of Absorption Costing at Nissan

Jed Connelly, the top American executive at Nissan North America, admits: "We had a lot of excess production that we had to force on the market." Nissan liked to run its factories at capacity, regardless of how well the cars were selling, because under its bookkeeping rules (presumably absorption costing), the factories would then generate a profit. As a consequence, Nissan dealers had to slash prices and offer big rebates to sell their cars. According to *Fortune* magazine, "Years of discounting and distress sales seriously undercut the value of the Nissan brand. While Toyota stood for quality, customers came to Nissan to get a better deal."

Source: Alex Taylor III, "The Man Who Wants to Change Japan Inc.," *Fortune,* December 20, 1999, pp. 189–198.

EXHIBIT 5A–1   Variable Costing Versus Absorption Costing

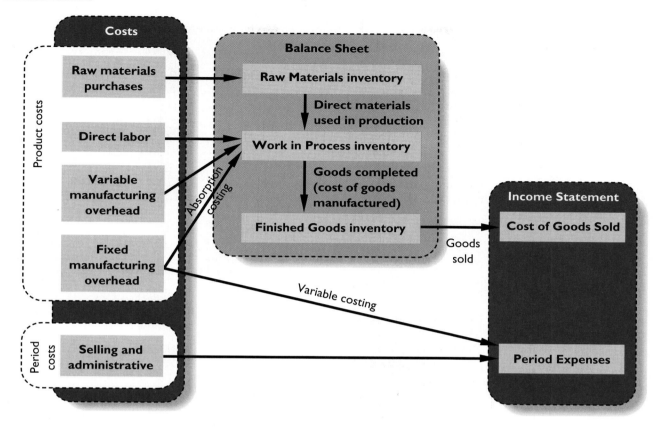

To illustrate the difference between variable costing and absorption costing, consider Weber Light Aircraft, a company that produces light recreational aircraft. Data concerning the company's operations appear below:

	Per Aircraft	Per Month
Selling price	$100,000	
Direct materials	$19,000	
Direct labor	$5,000	
Variable manufacturing overhead	$1,000	
Fixed manufacturing overhead		$70,000
Variable selling and administrative expenses	$10,000	
Fixed selling and administrative expenses		$20,000

	January	February	March
Beginning inventory	0	0	1
Production	1	2	2
Sales	1	1	3
Ending inventory	0	1	0

We will first construct the company's absorption costing income statements for January, February, and March. Then we will show how the company's net operating income would be determined for the same months using variable costing.

Absorption Costing Income Statement

To prepare the company's absorption costing income statements for January, February, and March, we need to determine the company's unit product costs, cost of goods sold, and selling and administrative expenses for each month.

The company's absorption costing unit product costs can be computed as follows[1]:

Absorption Costing Unit Product Cost			
	January	February	March
Direct materials (@ $19,000 per unit produced)...	$19,000	$ 38,000	$ 38,000
Direct labor (@ $5,000 per unit produced).......	5,000	10,000	10,000
Variable manufacturing overhead			
(@ $1,000 per unit produced)	1,000	2,000	2,000
Fixed manufacturing overhead	70,000	70,000	70,000
Total manufacturing cost (a).................	$95,000	$120,000	$120,000
Units produced (b)	1	2	2
Absorption costing unit product cost (a) ÷ (b) ...	$95,000	$ 60,000	$ 60,000

Given these unit product costs, the cost of goods sold under absorption costing in each month would be determined as follows:

Absorption Costing Cost of Goods Sold			
	January	February	March
Absorption costing units product cost (a)	$95,000	$60,000	$60,000
Units sold (b)	1	1	3*
Absorption costing cost of goods sold (a) × (b)	$95,000	$60,000	$180,000

*One of the three units sold in March was produced in February. Since February and March both have unit product costs of $60,000, the March unit product cost of $60,000 can be multiplied by 3.

And the company's selling and administrative expenses would be as follows:

Selling and Administrative Expenses			
	January	February	March
Variable selling and administrative expense			
(@ $10,000 per unit sold)	$10,000	$10,000	$30,000
Fixed selling and administrative expense	20,000	20,000	20,000
Total selling and administrative expense	$30,000	$30,000	$50,000

Putting all of this together, the absorption costing income statements would appear as follows:

Absorption Costing Income Statements			
	January	February	March
Sales	$100,000	$100,000	$300,000
Cost of goods sold......................	95,000	60,000	180,000
Gross margin...........................	5,000	40,000	120,000
Selling and administrative expenses.......	30,000	30,000	50,000
Net operating income....................	$ (25,000)	$ 10,000	$ 70,000

---

[1]For simplicity, we assume in this section that an actual costing system is used in which actual costs are spread over the units produced during the period. If a predetermined overhead rate were used, the analysis would be similar, but more complex.

Note that even though sales were exactly the same in January and February and the cost structure did not change, net operating income was $35,000 higher in February than in January under absorption costing.

The House of Cards at Gillette

IN BUSINESS

Alfred M. Zeien was the successful CEO of Gillette Co. for eight years, leading the company to earnings growth rates of 15% to 20% per year. However, as his successor discovered, some of this profit growth was an illusion based on building inventories. William H. Steele, an analyst with Bank of America Securities, alleges: "There is no question Gillette was making its numbers (in part) by aggressively selling to the trade, and building inventories." Within a three-year period, Gillette's inventories of finished goods had increased by over 40% (to $1.3 billion) even though Gillette's sales had barely increased.

How can building inventories increase profits without any increase in sales? It is called absorption costing. And it can be used to translate increases in production into higher profits even if customers do not buy the units produced.

Source: William C. Symonds, "The Big Trim at Gillette," *BusinessWeek,* November 8, 1999, p. 42.

Variable Costing Contribution Format Income Statement

As discussed earlier, the only reason that absorption costing income differs from variable costing income is that each method accounts for fixed manufacturing overhead differently. Under absorption costing, fixed manufacturing overhead is included in product costs. In variable costing, fixed manufacturing overhead is not included in product costs and instead is treated as a period expense, just like selling and administrative costs.

Under variable costing, product costs consist solely of variable production costs. At Weber Light Aircraft, the variable production cost per unit is $25,000, determined as follows:

Variable Production Cost	
Direct materials	$19,000
Direct labor	5,000
Variable manufacturing overhead	1,000
Variable production cost	$25,000

Since the variable production cost is $25,000 per aircraft, the variable costing cost of goods sold can be easily computed as follows:

Variable Costing Cost of Goods Sold			
	January	February	March
Variable production cost (a)	$25,000	$25,000	$25,000
Units sold (b)	1	1	3
Variable cost of goods sold (a) × (b)	$25,000	$25,000	$75,000

The selling and administrative expenses will exactly equal the amounts reported using absorption costing. The only difference will be how those costs appear on the income statement.

The variable costing income statements for January, February, and March appear below. The contribution approach discussed in the chapter has been used in these income statements.

Variable Costing Contribution Format Income Statements			
	January	February	March
Sales	$100,000	$100,000	$300,000
Less variable expenses:			
Variable cost of goods sold	25,000	25,000	75,000
Variable selling and administrative			
expense	10,000	10,000	30,000
Total variable expenses	35,000	35,000	105,000
Contribution margin	65,000	65,000	195,000
Less fixed expenses:			
Fixed manufacturing overhead	70,000	70,000	70,000
Fixed selling and administrative expense ..	20,000	20,000	20,000
Total fixed expenses	90,000	90,000	90,000
Net operating income	$ (25,000)	$ (25,000)	$105,000

First, note that net operating income is the same in January under absorption costing and variable costing, but differs in the other two months. We will discuss this in some depth shortly.

Second, note that the format of the variable costing income statement differs from the absorption costing income statement. An absorption costing income statement categorizes costs by function—manufacturing versus selling and administrative. All of the manufacturing costs flow through the absorption costing cost of goods sold and all of the selling and administrative costs are listed separately as period expenses. In contrast, in the contribution approach above, costs are categorized according to how they behave. All of the variable expenses are listed together and all of the fixed expenses are listed together. The variable expenses category includes manufacturing costs (i.e., variable cost of goods sold) as well as selling and administrative expenses. The fixed expenses category also includes both manufacturing costs and selling and administrative expenses.

Reconciliation of Variable Costing with Absorption Costing Income

As noted earlier, variable costing and absorption costing net operating incomes may not be the same. In the case of Weber Light Aircraft, the net operating incomes were the same in January, but differed in the other two months. These differences occur because under absorption costing some fixed manufacturing overhead is capitalized in inventories (i.e., included in product costs) rather than currently expensed on the income statement. If inventories increase during a period, under absorption costing some of the fixed manufacturing overhead of the current period will be *deferred* in ending inventories. For example, in February two aircraft were produced and each carried with it $35,000 ($70,000 ÷ 2 aircraft produced) in fixed manufacturing overhead. Since only one aircraft was sold, $35,000 of this fixed manufacturing overhead was on the absorption costing income statement as part of cost of goods sold, but $35,000 would have been on the balance sheet as part of finished goods inventories. In contrast, under variable costing *all* of the $70,000 of fixed manufacturing overhead appeared on the income statement as a period expense. Consequently, net operating income was higher under absorption costing than under variable costing by $35,000 in February. This was reversed in March when two units were produced, but three were sold.

In March, under absorption costing $105,000 of fixed manufacturing overhead was included in cost of goods sold ($35,000 for the unit produced in February and sold in March plus $35,000 for each of the two units produced and sold in March), but only $70,000 was recognized as a period expense under variable costing. Hence, the net operating income in March was $35,000 lower under absorption costing than under variable costing.

In general, when production exceeds sales and hence inventories increase, net operating income is higher under absorption costing than under variable costing. This occurs because some of the fixed manufacturing overhead of the period is *deferred* in inventories under absorption costing. In contrast, when sales exceed production and hence inventories decrease, net operating income is lower under absorption costing than under variable costing. This occurs because some of the fixed manufacturing overhead of previous periods is *released* from inventories under absorption costing. When production and sales are equal, no change in inventories occurs and absorption costing and variable costing net operating incomes are the same.[2]

Variable costing and absorption costing net operating incomes can be reconciled by determining how much fixed manufacturing overhead was deferred in, or released from, inventories during the period.

Fixed Manufacturing Overhead Deferred in, or Released from, Inventories under Absorption Costing			
	January	February	March
Fixed manufacturing overhead in beginning inventories	$0	$ 0	$ 35,000
Fixed manufacturing overhead in ending inventories	0	35,000	0
Fixed manufacturing overhead deferred in (released from) inventories	$0	$35,000	$(35,000)

The reconciliation would then be reported as follows:

Reconciliation of Variable Costing and Absorption Costing Net Operating Incomes			
	January	February	March
Variable costing net operating income	$(25,000)	$(25,000)	$105,000
Add (deduct) fixed manufacturing overhead deferred in (released from) ending inventory under absorption costing	0	35,000	(35,000)
Absorption costing net operating income	$(25,000)	$ 10,000	$ 70,000

Again note that the difference between variable costing net operating income and absorption costing net operating income is entirely due to the amount of fixed manufacturing overhead that is deferred in, or released from, inventories during the period under absorption costing. Changes in inventories affect absorption costing net operating income—they do not affect variable costing net operating income, providing that the cost structure is stable.

---

[2]These general statements about the relation between variable costing and absorption costing net operating income assume LIFO is used to value inventories. Even when LIFO is not used, the general statements tend to be correct.

SUMMARY OF APPENDIX 5A

LO5 **(Appendix) Use variable costing to prepare a contribution format income statement and contrast absorption costing and variable costing.**
Under variable costing, only the variable costs of making a product are assigned to the product. All other costs are treated as period costs and taken directly to the income statement as expenses.

Absorption costing treats fixed manufacturing overhead as a product cost. When units of product are sold these overhead costs flow from finished goods inventory through the income statement as part of cost of goods sold. In variable costing, fixed manufacturing overhead costs are treated as period costs and recorded immediately on the income statement.

GLOSSARY (APPENDIX 5A)

Variable costing   A costing approach under which only the variable costs of making a product are assigned to the product. All other costs are treated as period costs and taken directly to the income statement as expenses. (p. 226)

QUESTIONS

5–1   Distinguish between (a) a variable cost, (b) a fixed cost, and (c) a mixed cost.
5–2   What effect does an increase in volume have on—
   a.   Unit fixed costs?
   b.   Unit variable costs?
   c.   Total fixed costs?
   d.   Total variable costs?
5–3   Define the following terms: (a) cost behavior, and (b) relevant range.
5–4   What is meant by an *activity base* when dealing with variable costs? Give several examples of activity bases.
5–5   Distinguish between (a) a variable cost, (b) a mixed cost, and (c) a step-variable cost. Chart the three costs on a graph, with activity plotted horizontally and cost plotted vertically.
5–6   Managers often assume a strictly linear relationship between cost and volume. How can this practice be defended in light of the fact that many costs are curvilinear?
5–7   Distinguish between discretionary fixed costs and committed fixed costs.
5–8   Classify the following fixed costs as normally being either committed or discretionary:
   a.   Depreciation on buildings.
   b.   Advertising.
   c.   Research.
   d.   Long-term equipment leases.
   e.   Pension payments to the company's retirees.
   f.   Management development and training.
5–9   Does the concept of the relevant range apply to fixed costs? Explain.
5–10   What is the major disadvantage of the high-low method?
5–11   What methods are available for separating a mixed cost into its fixed and variable elements using past records of cost and activity data? Which method is considered to be most accurate? Why?
5–12   Give the general formula for a mixed cost. Which term represents the variable cost? The fixed cost?
5–13   Once a line has been drawn in the quick-and-dirty method, how does one determine the fixed cost element? The variable cost element?
5–14   What is meant by the term *least-squares regression?*
5–15   What is the difference between the contribution approach to the income statement and the traditional approach to the income statement?
5–16   What is the contribution margin?
5–17   (Appendix 5A) What is the basic difference between absorption costing and variable costing?
5–18   (Appendix 5A) Are selling and administrative expenses accounted for as product costs or as period costs under variable costing?
5–19   (Appendix 5A) Explain how fixed manufacturing overhead costs are shifted from one period to another under absorption costing.

5–20 (Appendix 5A) If production exceeds sales, which method would you expect to show the higher net operating income, variable costing or absorption costing? Why?

5–21 (Appendix 5A) If fixed manufacturing overhead costs are released from inventory under absorption costing, what does this tell you about the level of production in relation to the level of sales?

5–22 (Appendix 5A) Under absorption costing, how is it possible to increase net operating income without increasing sales?

BRIEF EXERCISES

BRIEF EXERCISE 5-1   Fixed and Variable Cost Behavior   [LO1]

Espresso Express operates a number of espresso coffee stands in busy suburban malls. The fixed weekly expense of a coffee stand is $1,200 and the variable cost per cup of coffee served is $0.22.

Required:
1. Fill in the following table with your estimates of total costs and cost per cup of coffee at the indicated levels of activity for a coffee stand. Round off the cost of a cup of coffee to the nearest tenth of a cent.

	Cups of Coffee Served in a Week		
	2,000	**2,100**	**2,200**
Fixed cost	?	?	?
Variable cost	?	?	?
Total cost	?	?	?
Cost per cup of coffee served	?	?	?

2. Does the cost per cup of coffee served increase, decrease, or remain the same as the number of cups of coffee served in a week increases? Explain.

BRIEF EXERCISE 5-2   Scattergraph Analysis   [LO2]

Oki Products, Ltd., has observed the following processing costs at various levels of activity over the last 15 months:

Month	Units Produced	Processing Cost
1	4,500	$38,000
2	11,000	$52,000
3	12,000	$56,000
4	5,500	$40,000
5	9,000	$47,000
6	10,500	$52,000
7	7,500	$44,000
8	5,000	$41,000
9	11,500	$52,000
10	6,000	$43,000
11	8,500	$48,000
12	10,000	$50,000
13	6,500	$44,000
14	9,500	$48,000
15	8,000	$46,000

Required:
1. Prepare a scattergraph using the above data. Plot cost on the vertical axis and activity on the horizontal axis. Fit a line to your plotted points using a ruler.
2. Using the quick-and-dirty method, what is the approximate monthly fixed cost? The approximate variable cost per unit processed? Show your computations.

BRIEF EXERCISE 5-3   High-Low Method   [LO3]

The Cheyenne Hotel in Big Sky, Montana, has accumulated records of the total electrical costs of the hotel and the number of occupancy-days over the last year. An occupancy-day represents a room rented out for one day. The hotel's business is highly seasonal, with peaks occurring during the ski season and in the summer.

Month	Occupancy-Days	Electrical Costs
January	1,736	$4,127
February	1,904	$4,207
March	2,356	$5,083
April	960	$2,857
May	360	$1,871
June	744	$2,696
July	2,108	$4,670
August	2,406	$5,148
September	840	$2,691
October	124	$1,588
November	720	$2,454
December	1,364	$3,529

Required:

1. Using the high-low method, estimate the fixed cost of electricity per month and the variable cost of electricity per occupancy-day. Round off the fixed cost to the nearest whole dollar and the variable cost to the nearest whole cent.

2. What other factors other than occupancy-days are likely to affect the variation in electrical costs from month to month?

BRIEF EXERCISE 5-4   Contribution Format Income Statement   [LO4]

The Alpine House, Inc., is a large retailer of winter sports equipment. An income statement for the company's Ski Department for a recent quarter is presented below:

The Alpine House, Inc. Income Statement—Ski Department For the Quarter Ended March 31		
Sales		$150,000
Cost of goods sold		90,000
Gross margin		60,000
Selling and administrative expenses:		
Selling expenses	$30,000	
Administrative expenses	10,000	40,000
Net operating income		$ 20,000

Skis sell, on the average, for $750 per pair. Variable selling expenses are $50 per pair of skis sold. The remaining selling expenses are fixed. The administrative expenses are 20% variable and 80% fixed. The company does not manufacture its own skis; it purchases them from a supplier for $450 per pair.

Required:

1. Prepare an income statement for the quarter using the contribution approach.

2. For every pair of skis sold during the quarter, what was the contribution toward covering fixed expenses and toward earning profits?

BRIEF EXERCISE 5-5   (Appendix 5A) Variable and Absorption Costing Unit Product Costs and Income Statements   [LO5]

Lynch Company manufactures and sells a single product. The following costs were incurred during the company's first year of operations:

Variable costs per unit:	
Manufacturing:	
Direct materials	$6
Direct labor	$9
Variable manufacturing overhead	$3
Variable selling and administrative	$4
Fixed costs per year:	
Fixed manufacturing overhead	$300,000
Fixed selling and administrative	$190,000

During the year, the company produced 25,000 units and sold 20,000 units. The selling price of the company's product is $50 per unit.

Required:
1. Assume that the company uses the absorption costing method:
   a. Compute the unit product cost.
   b. Prepare an income statement for the year.
2. Assume that the company uses the variable costing method:
   a. Compute the unit product cost.
   b. Prepare an income statement for the year.

BRIEF EXERCISE 5-6 (Appendix 5A) Reconciliation of Absorption and Variable Costing Net Operating Incomes [LO5]

Jorgansen Lighting, Inc., manufactures heavy-duty street lighting systems for municipalities. The company uses variable costing for internal management reports and absorption costing for external reports to shareholders, creditors, and the government. The company has provided the following data:

	Year 1	Year 2	Year 3
Inventories:			
Beginning (units)	200	170	180
Ending (units)	170	180	220
Variable costing net operating income	$1,080,400	$1,032,400	$996,400

The company's fixed manufacturing overhead per unit was constant at $560 for all three years.

Required:
1. Determine each year's absorption costing net operating income. Present your answer in the form of a reconciliation report.
2. In Year 4, the company's variable costing net operating income was $984,400 and its absorption costing net operating income was $1,012,400. Did inventories increase or decrease during Year 4? How much fixed manufacturing overhead cost was deferred or released from inventory during Year 4?

EXERCISES

EXERCISE 5-7 High-Low Method; Predicting Cost [LO1, LO3]

The Lakeshore Hotel's guest-days of occupancy and custodial supplies expense over the last seven months were:

Month	Guest-Days of Occupancy	Custodial Supplies Expense
March	4,000	$7,500
April	6,500	$8,250
May	8,000	$10,500
June	10,500	$12,000
July	12,000	$13,500
August	9,000	$10,750
September	7,500	$9,750

Guest-days is a measure of the overall activity at the hotel. For example, a guest who stays at the hotel for three days is counted as three guest-days.

Required:
1. Using the high-low method, estimate a cost formula for custodial supplies expense.
2. Using the cost formula you derived above, what amount of custodial supplies expense would you expect to be incurred at an occupancy level of 11,000 guest-days?

EXERCISE 5-8   Scattergraph Analysis; High-Low Method   [LO2, LO3]
Refer to the data for The Lakeshore Hotel in Exercise 5-7.

Required:
1. Prepare a scattergraph using the data from Exercise 5-7. Plot cost on the vertical axis and activity on the horizontal axis. Using a ruler, fit a line to your plotted points.
2. Using the quick-and-dirty method, what is the approximate monthly fixed cost? The approximate variable cost per guest-day?
3. Scrutinize the points on your graph and explain why the high-low method would or would not yield an accurate cost formula in this situation.

EXERCISE 5-9   Cost Behavior; Contribution Format Income Statement   [LO1, LO4]
Harris Company manufactures and sells a single product. A partially completed schedule of the company's total and per unit costs over the relevant range of 30,000 to 50,000 units produced and sold annually is given below:

	Units Produced and Sold		
	30,000	**40,000**	**50,000**
Total costs:			
Variable costs	$180,000	?	?
Fixed costs	300,000	?	?
Total costs	$480,000	?	?
Cost per unit:			
Variable cost	?	?	?
Fixed cost	?	?	?
Total cost per unit	?	?	?

Required:
1. Complete the schedule of the company's total and unit costs above.
2. Assume that the company produces and sells 45,000 units during the year at a selling price of $16 per unit. Prepare a contribution format income statement for the year.

EXERCISE 5-10   (Appendix 5A) Variable and Absorption Costing Unit Product Costs   [LO5]
Ida Sidha Karya Company is a family-owned company located in the village of Gianyar on the island of Bali in Indonesia. The company produces a handcrafted Balinese musical instrument called a gamelan that is similar to a xylophone. The sounding bars are cast from brass and hand-filed to attain just the right sound. The bars are then mounted on an intricately hand-carved wooden base. The gamelans are sold for 850 (thousand) rupiahs. (The currency in Indonesia is the rupiah, which is denoted by Rp.) Selected data for the company's operations last year follow (all currency values are in thousands of rupiahs):

Units in beginning inventory	0
Units produced	250
Units sold	225
Units in ending inventory	25
Variable costs per unit:	
Direct materials	Rp100
Direct labor	Rp320
Variable manufacturing overhead	Rp40
Variable selling and administrative	Rp20
Fixed costs:	
Fixed manufacturing overhead	Rp60,000
Fixed selling and administrative	Rp20,000

Required:
1. Assume that the company uses absorption costing. Compute the unit product cost for one gamelan.
2. Assume that the company uses variable costing. Compute the unit product cost for one gamelan.

EXERCISE 5-11   (Appendix 5A) Variable Costing Income Statement; Explanation of Difference in Net Operating Income   [LO5]

Refer to the data in Exercise 5-10 for Ida Sidha Karya Company. An absorption costing income statement prepared by the company's accountant appears below (all currency values are in thousands of rupiahs):

Sales (225 units × Rp850 per unit)		Rp191,250
Cost of goods sold (225 units × Rp ? per unit)		157,500
Gross margin		33,750
Selling and administrative expenses:		
Variable selling and administrative	4,500	
Fixed selling and administrative	20,000	24,500
Net operating income		Rp 9,250

Required:
1. Determine how much of the ending inventory consists of fixed manufacturing overhead cost deferred in inventory to the next period.
2. Prepare an income statement for the year using the variable costing method. Explain the difference in net operating income between the two costing methods.

EXERCISE 5-12   Cost Behavior; High-Low Method   [LO1, LO3]

Hoi Chong Transport, Ltd., operates a fleet of delivery trucks in Singapore. The company has determined that if a truck is driven 105,000 kilometers during a year, the average operating cost is 11.4 cents per kilometer. If a truck is driven only 70,000 kilometers during a year, the average operating cost increases to 13.4 cents per kilometer. (The Singapore dollar is the currency used in Singapore.)

Required:
1. Using the high-low method, estimate the variable and fixed cost elements of the annual cost of truck operation.
2. Express the variable and fixed costs in the form $Y = a + bX$.
3. If a truck were driven 80,000 kilometers during a year, what total cost would you expect to be incurred?

EXERCISE 5-13   High-Low Method; Scattergraph Analysis   [LO2, LO3]

The following data relating to units shipped and total shipping expense have been assembled by Archer Company, a wholesaler of large, custom-built air-conditioning units for commercial buildings:

Month	Units Shipped	Total Shipping Expense
January	3	$1,800
February	6	$2,300
March	4	$1,700
April	5	$2,000
May	7	$2,300
June	8	$2,700
July	2	$1,200

Required:
1. Using the high-low method, estimate a cost formula for shipping expense.
2. The president of the company has no confidence in the high-low method and would like you to check out your results using a scattergraph.
   a. Prepare a scattergraph, using the data given above. Plot cost on the vertical axis and activity on the horizontal axis. Use a ruler to fit a straight line to your plotted points.
   b. Using your scattergraph, estimate the approximate variable cost per unit shipped and the approximate fixed cost per month with the quick-and-dirty method.
3. What factors, other than the number of units shipped, are likely to affect the company's total shipping expense? Explain.

EXERCISE 5-14   **High-Low Method; Predicting Cost   [LO1, LO3]**
St. Mark's Hospital contains 450 beds. The average occupancy rate is 80% per month. In other words, on average, 80% of the hospital's beds are occupied by patients. At this level of occupancy, the hospital's operating costs are $32 per occupied bed per day, assuming a 30-day month. This $32 figure contains both variable and fixed cost elements.

During June, the hospital's occupancy rate was only 60%. A total of $326,700 in operating cost was incurred during the month.

Required:
1. Using the high-low method, estimate:
    a.   The variable cost per occupied bed on a daily basis.
    b.   The total fixed operating costs per month.
2. Assume an occupancy rate of 70% per month. What amount of total operating cost would you expect the hospital to incur?

EXERCISE 5-15   **(Appendix 5A) Variable Costing Income Statement; Reconciliation   [LO5]**
Whitman Company has just completed its first year of operations. The company's accountant has prepared an absorption costing income statement for the year:

Whitman Company	
Income Statement	
Sales (35,000 units at $25 per unit)	$875,000
Cost of goods sold (35,000 units at $16 per unit)	560,000
Gross margin	315,000
Selling and administrative expenses	280,000
Net operating income	$ 35,000

The company's selling and administrative expenses consist of $210,000 per year in fixed expenses and $2 per unit sold in variable expenses. The $16 per unit product cost given above is computed as follows:

Direct materials	$ 5
Direct labor	6
Variable manufacturing overhead	1
Fixed manufacturing overhead ($160,000 ÷ 40,000 units)	4
Unit product cost	$16

The company started the year with no inventories. During the year, the company produced 40,000 units, of which 35,000 were sold.

Required:
1. Redo the company's income statement in the contribution format using variable costing.
2. Reconcile any difference between the net operating income on your variable costing income statement and the net operating income on the absorption costing income statement above.

PROBLEMS

PROBLEM 5-16A   **Scattergraph Analysis   [LO2]**
Molina Company is a value-added computer resaler that specializes in providing services to small companies. The company owns and maintains several autos for use by the sales staff. All expenses of operating these autos have been entered into an Automobile Expense account on the company's books. Along with this record of expenses, the company has also kept a careful record of the number of miles the autos have been driven each month.

The company's records of miles driven and total auto expenses over the past 10 months are given below:

Month	Total Mileage (000)	Total Cost
January	4	$3,000
February	8	$3,700
March	7	$3,300
April	12	$4,000
May	6	$3,300
June	11	$3,900
July	14	$4,200
August	10	$3,600
September	13	$4,100
October	15	$4,400

Molina Company's president wants to know the cost of operating the fleet of cars in terms of the fixed monthly cost and the variable cost per mile driven.

Required:

1. Prepare a scattergraph using the data given above. Place cost on the vertical axis and activity (miles driven) on the horizontal axis. Using a ruler, fit a straight line to the plotted points.
2. Estimate the fixed cost per month and the variable cost per mile driven using the quick-and-dirty method.

CHECK FIGURE
(1) $1,000 per month plus
$20 per scan

PROBLEM 5-17A   High-Low and Scattergraph Analysis   [LO2, LO3]

Pleasant View Hospital of British Columbia has just hired a new chief administrator who is anxious to employ sound management and planning techniques in the business affairs of the hospital. Accordingly, she has directed her assistant to summarize the cost structure of the various departments so that data will be available for planning purposes.

The assistant is unsure how to classify the utilities costs in the Radiology Department since these costs do not exhibit either strictly variable or fixed cost behavior. Utilities costs are very high in the department due to a CAT scanner that draws a large amount of power and is kept running at all times. The scanner can't be turned off due to the long warm-up period required for its use. When the scanner is used to scan a patient, it consumes an additional burst of power. The assistant has accumulated the following data on utilities costs and use of the scanner since the first of the year.

Month	Number of Scans	Utilities Cost
January	60	$2,200
February	70	$2,600
March	90	$2,900
April	120	$3,300
May	100	$3,000
June	130	$3,600
July	150	$4,000
August	140	$3,600
September	110	$3,100
October	80	$2,500

The chief administrator has informed her assistant that the utilities cost is probably a mixed cost that will have to be broken down into its variable and fixed cost elements by use of a scattergraph. The assistant feels, however, that if an analysis of this type is necessary, then the high-low method should be used, since it is easier and quicker. The controller has suggested that there may be a better approach.

Required:

1. Using the high-low method, estimate a cost formula for utilities. Express the formula in the form $Y = a + bX$. (The variable rate should be stated in terms of cost per scan.)
2. Prepare a scattergraph using the data above. (The number of scans should be placed on the horizontal axis, and utilities cost should be placed on the vertical axis.) Fit a straight line to the plotted points using a ruler and estimate a cost formula for utilities using the quick-and-dirty method.

PROBLEM 5-18A   Contribution Format versus Traditional Income Statement   [LO4]

Marwick's Pianos, Inc., purchases pianos from a large manufacturer and sells them at the retail level. The pianos cost, on the average, $2,450 each from the manufacturer. Marwick's Pianos, Inc., sells the pianos to its customers at an average price of $3,125 each. The selling and administrative costs that the company incurs in a typical month are presented below:

Costs	Cost Formula
Selling:	
Advertising	$700 per month
Sales salaries and commissions	$950 per month, plus 8% of sales
Delivery of pianos to customers	$30 per piano sold
Utilities	$350 per month
Depreciation of sales facilities	$800 per month
Administrative:	
Executive salaries	$2,500 per month
Insurance	$400 per month
Clerical	$1,000 per month, plus $20 per piano sold
Depreciation of office equipment	$300 per month

During August, Marwick's Pianos, Inc., sold and delivered 40 pianos.

Required:

1. Prepare an income statement for Marwick's Pianos, Inc., for August. Use the traditional format, with costs organized by function.
2. Redo (1) above, this time using the contribution format, with costs organized by behavior. Show costs and revenues on both a total and a per unit basis down through contribution margin.
3. Refer to the income statement you prepared in (2) above. Why might it be misleading to show the fixed costs on a per unit basis?

PROBLEM 5-19A   (Appendix 5A) Variable Costing Income Statement; Reconciliation   [LO5]

During Heaton Company's first two years of operations, the company reported absorption costing net operating income as follows:

	Year 1	Year 2
Sales (@ $25 per unit)	$1,000,000	$1,250,000
Cost of goods sold	720,000	900,000
Gross margin	280,000	350,000
Selling and administrative expenses*	210,000	230,000
Net operating income	$ 70,000	$ 120,000

*$2 per unit variable; $130,000 fixed each year.

The company's $18 unit product cost is computed as follows:

Direct materials	$ 4
Direct labor	7
Variable manufacturing overhead	1
Fixed manufacturing overhead ($270,000 ÷ 45,000 units)	6
Unit product cost	$18

Production and cost data for the two years are:

	Year 1	Year 2
Units produced	45,000	45,000
Units sold	40,000	50,000

Required:

1. Prepare a variable costing income statement for each year.
2. Reconcile the absorption costing and the variable costing net operating income figures for each year.

PROBLEM 5-20A   Identifying Cost Behavior Patterns   [LOI]

A number of graphs displaying cost behavior patterns are shown on the next page. The vertical axis on each graph represents total cost, and the horizontal axis represents level of activity (volume).

Required:

1. For each of the following situations, identify the graph that illustrates the cost behavior pattern involved. Any graph may be used more than once.
    a.   Cost of raw materials used.
    b.   Electricity bill—a flat fixed charge, plus a variable cost after a certain number of kilowatt-hours are used.
    c.   City water bill, which is computed as follows:

First 1,000,000 gallons or less	$1,000 flat fee
Next 10,000 gallons	$0.003 per gallon used
Next 10,000 gallons	$0.006 per gallon used
Next 10,000 gallons	$0.009 per gallon used
Etc.	Etc.

    d.   Depreciation of equipment, where the amount is computed by the straight-line method. When the depreciation rate was established, it was anticipated that the obsolescence factor would be greater than the wear and tear factor.
    e.   Rent on a factory building donated by the city, where the agreement calls for a fixed fee payment unless 200,000 labor-hours or more are worked, in which case no rent need be paid.
    f.   Salaries of maintenance workers, where one maintenance worker is needed for every 1,000 hours of machine-hours or less (that is, 0 to 1,000 hours requires one maintenance worker, 1,001 to 2,000 hours requires two maintenance workers, etc.)
    g.   Cost of raw materials, where the cost starts at $7.50 per unit and then decreases by 5 cents per unit for each of the first 100 units purchased, after which it remains constant at $2.50 per unit.
    h.   Rent on a factory building donated by the county, where the agreement calls for rent of $100,000 less $1 for each direct labor-hour worked in excess of 200,000 hours, but a minimum rental payment of $20,000 must be paid.
    i.   Use of a machine under a lease, where a minimum charge of $1,000 is paid for up to 400 hours of machine time. After 400 hours of machine time, an additional charge of $2 per hour is paid up to a maximum charge of $2,000 per period.

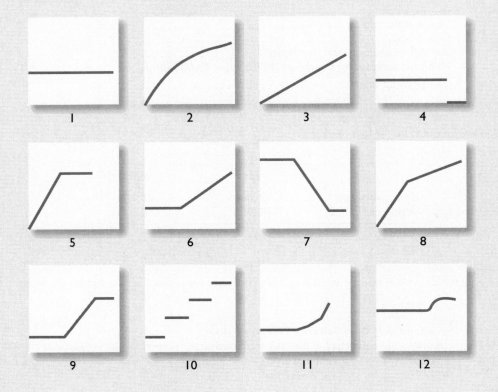

2. How would a knowledge of cost behavior patterns such as those above be of help to a manager in analyzing the cost structure of his or her company?

(CPA, adapted)

PROBLEM 5-21A   Cost Behavior; High-Low Method; Contribution Format Income Statement [LO1, LO3, LO4]

Morrisey & Brown, Ltd., of Sydney is a merchandising company that is the sole distributor of a product that is increasing in popularity among Australian consumers. The company's income statements for the three most recent months follow:

Morrisey & Brown, Ltd. Income Statements For the Three Months Ending September 30			
	July	August	September
Sales in units	4,000	4,500	5,000
Sales revenue	A$400,000	A$450,000	A$500,000
Cost of goods sold	240,000	270,000	300,000
Gross margin	160,000	180,000	200,000
Selling and administrative expenses:			
Advertising expense	21,000	21,000	21,000
Shipping expense	34,000	36,000	38,000
Salaries and commissions	78,000	84,000	90,000
Insurance expense	6,000	6,000	6,000
Depreciation expense	15,000	15,000	15,000
Total selling and administrative expenses. .	154,000	162,000	170,000
Net operating income	A$ 6,000	A$ 18,000	A$ 30,000

(Note: Morrisey & Brown, Ltd.'s Australian-formatted income statement has been recast in the format common in the United States. The Australian dollar is denoted here by A$.)

Required:

1. Identify each of the company's expenses (including cost of goods sold) as either variable, fixed, or mixed.
2. Using the high-low method, separate each mixed expense into variable and fixed elements. State the cost formula for each mixed expense.
3. Redo the company's income statement at the 5,000-unit level of activity using the contribution format.

PROBLEM 5-22A **(Appendix 5A) Variable and Absorption Costing Unit Product Costs and Income Statements; Explanation of Difference in Net Operating Income** **[LO5]**

High Country, Inc., produces and sells many recreational products. The company has just opened a new plant to produce a folding camp cot. The following cost and revenue data relate to May, the first month of the plant's operation:

	File Edit View Insert Format Tools Data Window Help		
	D16		
	A	B	C
1	Beginning inventory	0	
2	Units produced	10,000	
3	Units sold	8,000	
4	Selling price per unit	$75	
5			
6	Selling and administrative expenses:		
7	Variable per unit	$6	
8	Fixed (total)	$200,000	
9	Manufacturing costs:		
10	Direct materials cost per unit	$20	
11	Direct labor cost per unit	$8	
12	Variable manufacturing overhead cost per unit	$2	
13	Fixed manufacturing overhead cost (total)	$100,000	
14			

Management is anxious to see how profitable the new camp cot will be and has asked that an income statement be prepared for May.

Required:

1. Assume the company uses absorption costing.
   a. Determine the unit product cost.
   b. Prepare an income statement for May.
2. Assume the company uses the contribution approach with variable costing.
   a. Determine the unit product cost.
   b. Prepare an income statement for May.
3. Explain the reason for any difference in the ending inventory balance under the two costing methods and the impact of this difference on reported net operating income.

PROBLEM 5-23A **High-Low Method; Predicting Cost** **[LO1, LO3]**

Nova Company's total overhead costs at various levels of activity are presented below:

Month	Machine-Hours	Total Overhead Costs
April	70,000	$198,000
May	60,000	$174,000
June	80,000	$222,000
July	90,000	$246,000

Assume that the total overhead costs above consist of utilities, supervisory salaries, and maintenance. The breakdown of these costs at the 60,000 machine-hour level of activity is:

Utilities (variable)	$ 48,000
Supervisory salaries (fixed)	21,000
Maintenance (mixed)	105,000
Total overhead costs	$174,000

Nova Company's management wants to break down the maintenance cost into its variable and fixed cost elements.

Required:
1. Estimate how much of the $246,000 of overhead cost in July was maintenance cost. (Hint: to do this, it may be helpful to first determine how much of the $246,000 consisted of utilities and supervisory salaries. Think about the behavior of variable and fixed costs!)
2. Using the high-low method, estimate a cost formula for maintenance.
3. Express the company's *total* overhead costs in the linear equation form $Y = a + bX$.
4. What *total* overhead costs would you expect to be incurred at an operating activity level of 75,000 machine-hours?

CHECK FIGURE
(2) $30,000 per month plus $8 per unit

eXcel

PROBLEM 5-24A   High-Low Method; Cost of Goods Manufactured   [LO1, LO3]
Amfac Company manufactures a single product. The company keeps careful records of manufacturing activities from which the following information has been extracted:

	Level of Activity	
	March–Low	June–High
Number of units produced	6,000	9,000
Cost of goods manufactured	$168,000	$257,000
Work in process inventory, beginning	$9,000	$32,000
Work in process inventory, ending	$15,000	$21,000
Direct materials cost per unit	$6.00	$6.00
Direct labor cost per unit	$10.00	$10.00
Manufacturing overhead cost, total	?	?

The company's manufacturing overhead cost consists of both variable and fixed cost elements. To have data available for planning, management wants to determine how much of the overhead cost is variable with units produced and how much of it is fixed per month.

Required:
1. For both March and June, estimate the amount of manufacturing overhead cost added to production. The company had no underapplied or overapplied overhead in either month. (Hint: A useful way to proceed might be to construct a schedule of cost of goods manufactured.)
2. Using the high-low method, estimate a cost formula for manufacturing overhead. Express the variable portion of the formula in terms of a variable rate per unit of product.
3. If 7,000 units are produced during a month, what would the cost of goods manufactured be? (Assume that work in process inventories do not change and that there is no underapplied or overapplied overhead cost for the month.)

CHECK FIGURE
(2) ¥1,500,000 per year plus ¥35 per DLH

PROBLEM 5-25A   High-Low Method; Predicting Cost   [LO1, LO3]
Sawaya Co., Ltd., of Japan is a manufacturing company whose total factory overhead costs fluctuate considerably from year to year according to increases and decreases in the number of direct labor-hours worked in the factory. Total factory overhead costs (in Japanese yen, denoted ¥) at high and low levels of activity for recent years are given below:

	Level of Activity	
	Low	High
Direct labor-hours	50,000	75,000
Total factory overhead costs	¥14,250,000	¥17,625,000

The factory overhead costs above consist of indirect materials, rent, and maintenance. The company has analyzed these costs at the 50,000-hour level of activity as follows:

Indirect materials (variable)	¥ 5,000,000
Rent (fixed)	6,000,000
Maintenance (mixed)	3,250,000
Total factory overhead costs	¥14,250,000

To have data available for planning, the company wants to break down the maintenance cost into its variable and fixed cost elements.

Required:

1. Estimate how much of the ¥17,625,000 factory overhead cost at the high level of activity consists of maintenance cost. (Hint: To do this, it may be helpful to first determine how much of the ¥17,625,000 consists of indirect materials and rent. Think about the behavior of variable and fixed costs!)
2. Using the high-low method, estimate a cost formula for maintenance.
3. What total factory overhead costs would you expect the company to incur at an operating level of 70,000 direct labor-hours?

BUILDING YOUR SKILLS

Communicating in Practice   (LO1, LO4)

Maria Chavez owns a catering company that serves food and beverages at parties and business functions. Chavez's business is seasonal, with a heavy schedule during the summer months and holidays and a lighter schedule at other times.

One of the major events requested by Chavez's customers is a cocktail party. She offers a standard cocktail party and has estimated the total cost per guest as follows:

Food and beverages	$15.00
Labor (0.5 hours @ $10.00 per hour)	5.00
Overhead (0.5 hours @ $13.98 per hour)	6.99
Total cost per guest	$26.99

The standard cocktail party lasts three hours, and she hires one worker for every six guests, which works out to one-half hour of direct labor per guest. The servers work only as needed and are paid only for the hours they actually work.

When bidding on cocktail parties, Chavez adds a 15% markup to yield a price of $31 per guest. Chavez is confident about her estimates of the costs of food and beverages and labor, but is not as comfortable with the estimate of overhead cost. The overhead cost per labor-hour was determined by dividing total overhead expenses for the last 12 months by total labor-hours for the same period. Her overhead includes such costs as annual rent for office space, administrative costs (including those relating to hiring and paying workers), etc.

Chavez has received a request to bid on a large fund-raising cocktail party to be given next month by an important local charity. (The party would last three hours.) She would like to win this contract because the guest list for this charity event includes many prominent individuals that she would like to land as future clients. Other caterers have also been invited to bid on the event, and she believes that one, if not more, of those companies will bid less than $31 per guest. She is not willing to lose money on the event and needs your input before making any decisions.

Required:
Write a memorandum to Ms. Chavez that addresses her concern about her estimate of overhead costs and whether or not she should base her bid on the estimated cost of $26.99 per guest. (Hint: Start by discussing the need to consider cost behavior when estimating costs. You can safely assume that she will not incur any additional fixed costs if she wins the bid on this cocktail party.)

(CMA, adapted)

Teamwork In Action   (LO1)
Assume that your team is going to form a company that will manufacture chocolate chip cookies. The team is responsible for preparing a list of all product components and costs necessary to make this product.

Required:
Prepare a list of all product components and costs necessary to manufacture your cookies and identify each of the product costs as direct materials, direct labor, or factory overhead. Identify each of those costs as variable, fixed, or mixed.

Analytical Thinking   (LO2, LO3)
The Ramon Company manufactures a wide range of products at several locations. The Franklin plant, which manufactures electrical components, has been experiencing difficulties with fluctuating monthly overhead costs. These fluctuations have made it difficult to estimate the level of overhead that will be incurred for a month.

Management wants to be able to estimate overhead costs accurately to better plan its operational and financial needs. A trade publication indicates that for companies manufacturing electrical components, overhead tends to vary with direct labor-hours but may contain both fixed and variable elements.

A member of the accounting staff has suggested that a good starting place for determining the cost behavior of overhead costs would be an analysis of historical data. Data on direct labor-hours and overhead costs have been collected for the past two years. The raw data are as follows:

Month	Prior Year Direct Labor-Hours	Prior Year Overhead Costs	Current Year Direct Labor-Hours	Current Year Overhead Costs
January	20,000	$84,000	21,000	$86,000
February	25,000	$99,000	24,000	$93,000
March	22,000	$89,500	23,000	$93,000
April	23,000	$90,000	22,000	$87,000
May	20,000	$81,500	20,000	$80,000
June	19,000	$75,500	18,000	$76,500
July	14,000	$70,500	12,000	$67,500
August	10,000	$64,500	13,000	$71,000
September	12,000	$69,000	15,000	$73,500
October	17,000	$75,000	17,000	$72,500
November	16,000	$71,500	15,000	$71,000
December	19,000	$78,000	18,000	$75,000

All equipment in the Franklin plant is leased under an arrangement calling for a flat fee up to 19,500 direct labor-hours, after which lease charges are assessed on an hourly basis. Lease expense is a major element of overhead cost.

Required:
1. Using the high-low method, estimate the cost formula for overhead in the Franklin plant.
2. Prepare a scattergraph, including on it all data for the two-year period. Fit a straight line or lines to the plotted points using a ruler. In this part it is not necessary to compute the fixed and variable cost elements.

3. Assume that the Franklin plant works 22,500 direct labor-hours during a month. Compute the expected overhead cost for the month using the cost formulas developed above with:
    a.   The high-low method.
    b.   The scattergraph method [read the expected costs directly off the graph prepared in (2) above].
4. Of the two proposed methods, explain which one the Ramon Company should use to estimate monthly overhead costs in the Franklin plant? Explain why the other method is less desirable.
5. Would a relevant range concept probably be more or less important in the Franklin plant than in most companies?

(CMA, adapted)

Taking It to the Net
As you know, the World Wide Web is a medium that is constantly evolving. Sites come and go and change without notice. To enable periodic updating of site addresses, these problems have been posted to the textbook website (www.mhhe.com/bgn3e). After accessing the site, enter the Student Center and select this chapter to find the Taking It to the Net problems.

6

Cost-Volume-Profit Relationships

CHAPTER OUTLINE

DECISION FEATURE

Forget the Theater—Make Money on Cable TV

"Several years ago, Hollywood experienced a phenomenon known as the 'straight-to-cable' era. What this phrase referred to was a well used (and abused!) movie-making principle that hinted that if anyone (and many times it really was just *anyone*) could produce a movie (quality was never an issue) for under a million dollars, it'd automatically turn a profit from the sale of its cable TV rights. In essence, the 'movie' would bypass the theaters all together [*sic*] and still turn a profit. From a business standpoint, what this money-making scheme illustrates is [that] every product has a break-even point. Make more money than this and you turn a profit. Make less than this, and, well, you get the picture (pardon the pun)."

Source: Ben Chiu, "The Last Big-Budget Combat Sim," *Computer Games,* June 1999, p. 40.

LEARNING OBJECTIVES

After studying Chapter 6, you should be able to:

LO1 Explain how changes in activity affect contribution margin and net operating income.

LO2 Prepare and interpret a cost-volume-profit (CVP) graph.

LO3 Use the contribution margin ratio (CM ratio) to compute changes in contribution margin and net operating income resulting from changes in sales volume.

LO4 Show the effects on contribution margin of changes in variable costs, fixed costs, selling price, and volume.

LO5 Compute the break-even point in unit sales and dollar sales.

LO6 Determine the level of sales needed to achieve a desired target profit.

LO7 Compute the margin of safety and explain its significance.

LO8 Compute the degree of operating leverage at a particular level of sales and explain how it can be used to predict changes in net operating income.

LO9 Compute the break-even point for a multiproduct company and explain the effects of shifts in the sales mix on contribution margin and the break-even point.

C ost-volume-profit (CVP) analysis is a powerful tool that helps managers understand the relationships among cost, volume, and profit. CVP analysis focuses on how profits are affected by the following five factors:

1. Selling prices.
2. Sales volume.
3. Unit variable costs.
4. Total fixed costs.
5. Mix of products sold.

Because CVP analysis helps managers understand how profits are affected by these key factors, it is a vital tool in many business decisions. These decisions include what products and services to offer, what prices to charge, what marketing strategy to use, and what cost structure to implement.

To help understand the role of CVP analysis in business decisions, consider the case of Acoustic Concepts, Inc., a company founded by Prem Narayan, a graduate student in electrical engineering, to market a radically new speaker he has designed for automobile sound systems. The speaker, called the Sonic Blaster, uses an advanced microprocessor to boost amplification to awesome levels. Prem contracted with a Taiwanese electronics manufacturer to produce the speaker. With seed money provided by his family, Prem placed an order with the manufacturer and ran advertisements in auto magazines.

The Sonic Blaster was an immediate success, and sales grew to the point that Prem moved the company's headquarters out of his apartment and into rented office space in a nearby industrial park. He also hired a receptionist, an accountant, a sales manager, and a small sales staff to sell the speakers to retail stores. Prem is concerned about the financial risks of rapidly expanding his company. He also wonders how much sales would have to increase to justify a new marketing campaign proposed by his sales manager. The answers to these and other questions can be found using CVP analysis.

THE BASICS OF COST-VOLUME-PROFIT (CVP) ANALYSIS

To help Prem Narayan answer the questions he has raised, we begin by looking at the contribution format income statement for Acoustic Concepts, Inc. that is shown below. The contribution format income statement classifies costs according to their behavior. Although this type of income statement would not ordinarily be made available to people outside the company, its focus on cost behavior helps managers inside the company by enabling them to judge the impact on profits of changes in selling price, cost, or volume.

Acoustic Concepts, Inc. Contribution Income Statement For the Month of June		
	Total	Per Unit
Sales (400 speakers)	$100,000	$250
Less variable expenses	60,000	150
Contribution margin	40,000	$100
Less fixed expenses	35,000	
Net operating income	$ 5,000	

Notice that sales, variable expenses, and contribution margin are expressed on a per-unit basis as well as in total on this income statement. The per-unit figures will be very helpful in the following pages as we answer some of Prem's questions.

Contribution Margin

As explained in the previous chapter, contribution margin is the amount remaining from sales revenue after variable expenses have been deducted. Thus, it is the amount available to cover fixed expenses and then to provide profits for the period. Notice the sequence here—contribution margin is used *first* to cover the fixed expenses, and then whatever remains goes toward profits. If the contribution margin is not sufficient to cover the fixed expenses, then a loss occurs for the period. To illustrate with an extreme example, assume that Acoustic Concepts sells only one speaker during a particular month. The company's income statement would appear as follows:

LEARNING OBJECTIVE 1

Explain how changes in activity affect contribution margin and net operating income.

	Total	Per Unit
Sales (1 speaker)	$ 250	$250
Less variable expenses	150	150
Contribution margin	100	$100
Less fixed expenses	35,000	
Net operating loss	$(34,900)	

For each additional speaker the company sells during the month, $100 more in contribution margin will become available to help cover the fixed expenses. If a second speaker is sold, for example, then the total contribution margin will increase by $100 (to a total of $200) and the company's loss will decrease by $100, to $34,800:

	Total	Per Unit
Sales (2 speakers)	$ 500	$250
Less variable expenses	300	150
Contribution margin	200	$100
Less fixed expenses	35,000	
Net operating loss	$(34,800)	

If enough speakers can be sold to generate $35,000 in contribution margin, then all of the fixed expenses will be covered and the company will have managed to at least *break even* for the month—that is, it will show neither profit nor loss but just cover all of its costs. To reach the break-even point, the company will have to sell 350 speakers in a month, since each speaker sold yields $100 in contribution margin:

	Total	Per Unit
Sales (350 speakers)	$87,500	$250
Less variable expenses	52,500	150
Contribution margin	35,000	$100
Less fixed expenses	35,000	
Net operating income	$ 0	

Computation of the break-even point is discussed in detail later in the chapter; for the moment, note that the **break-even point** is the level of sales at which profit is zero.

Once the break-even point has been reached, net operating income will increase by the amount of the unit contribution margin for each additional unit sold. For example, if 351 speakers are sold in a month, then the net operating income for the month will be $100, since the company will have sold 1 speaker more than the number needed to break even:

	Total	Per Unit
Sales (351 speakers)	$87,750	$250
Less variable expenses	52,650	150
Contribution margin	35,100	$100
Less fixed expenses	35,000	
Net operating income	$ 100	

If 352 speakers are sold (2 speakers above the break-even point), the net operating income for the month will be $200, and so forth. To estimate the profit at any sales volume above the break-even point, simply multiply the number of units sold over the break-even point by the unit contribution margin. The result represents the anticipated profits for the period. Or, to estimate the effect of a planned increase in sales on profits, simply multiply the increase in units sold by the unit contribution margin. The result will be the expected increase in profits. To illustrate, if Acoustic Concepts is currently selling 400 speakers per month and plans to increase sales to 425 speakers per month, the anticipated impact on profits can be computed as follows:

Increased number of speakers to be sold	25
Contribution margin per speaker	× $100
Increase in net operating income	$2,500

These calculations can be verified as follows:

	Sales Volume			
	400 Speakers	425 Speakers	Difference (25 Speakers)	Per Unit
Sales (@$250 per speaker)	$100,000	$106,250	$6,250	$250
Less variable expenses (@$150 per speaker)	60,000	63,750	3,750	150
Contribution margin	40,000	42,500	2,500	$100
Less fixed expenses	35,000	35,000	0	
Net operating income	$ 5,000	$ 7,500	$2,500	

To summarize these examples, if there were no sales, the company's loss would equal its fixed expenses. Each unit that is sold reduces the loss by the amount of the unit contribution margin. Once the break-even point has been reached, each additional unit sold increases the company's profit by the amount of the unit contribution margin.

CVP Relationships in Graphic Form

LEARNING OBJECTIVE 2

Prepare and interpret a cost-volume-profit (CVP) graph.

The relations among revenue, cost, profit, and volume can be illustrated by a **cost-volume-profit (CVP) graph.** A CVP graph highlights CVP relationships over wide ranges of activity and gives managers a perspective that can be obtained in no other way.

Preparing the CVP Graph   In a CVP graph (sometimes called a *break-even chart*), unit volume is represented on the horizontal (*X*) axis and dollars on the vertical (*Y*) axis. Preparing a CVP graph involves three steps. These steps are keyed to the graph in Exhibit 6–1:

1. Draw a line parallel to the volume axis to represent total fixed expenses. For Acoustic Concepts, total fixed expenses are $35,000.

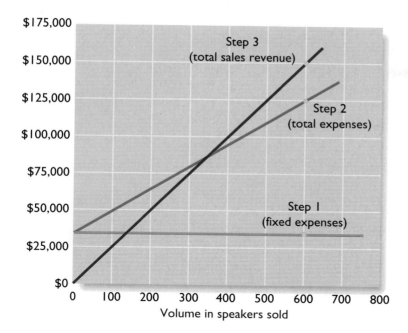

EXHIBIT 6–1

Preparing the CVP Graph

2. Choose some volume of sales and plot the point representing total expenses (fixed and variable) at the activity level you have selected. In Exhibit 6–1, a volume of 600 speakers has been selected. Total expenses at that activity level are:

Fixed expenses	$ 35,000
Variable expenses (600 speakers × $150 per speaker)	90,000
Total expenses	$125,000

After the point has been plotted, draw a line through it back to the point where the fixed expenses line intersects the dollars axis.
3. Again choose some volume of unit sales and plot the point representing total sales dollars at the activity level you have selected. In Exhibit 6–1, a volume of 600 speakers has again been selected. Sales at that activity level total $150,000 (600 speakers × $250 per speaker). Draw a line through this point back to the origin.

The interpretation of the completed CVP graph is given in Exhibit 6–2. The anticipated profit or loss at any given level of sales is measured by the vertical distance between the total revenue line (sales) and the total expenses line (variable expenses plus fixed expenses).

The break-even point is where the total revenue and total expenses lines cross. The break-even point of 350 speakers in Exhibit 6–2 agrees with the break-even point computed earlier.

As discussed earlier, when sales are below the break-even point—in this case, 350 units—the company suffers a loss. Note that the loss (represented by the vertical distance between the total expense and total revenue lines) gets bigger as sales decline. When sales are above the break-even point, the company earns a profit and the size of the profit (represented by the vertical distance between the total revenue and total expense lines) increases as sales increase.

Contribution Margin Ratio (CM Ratio)

In the previous section, we explored how cost-volume-profit relations can be visualized. In this section, we show how the *contribution margin ratio* can be used in cost-volume-profit calculations. As the first step, we have added a column to Acoustic Concepts' contribution

LEARNING OBJECTIVE 3

Use the contribution margin ratio (CM ratio) to compute changes in contribution margin and net operating income resulting from changes in sales volume.

EXHIBIT 6–2

The Completed CVP Graph

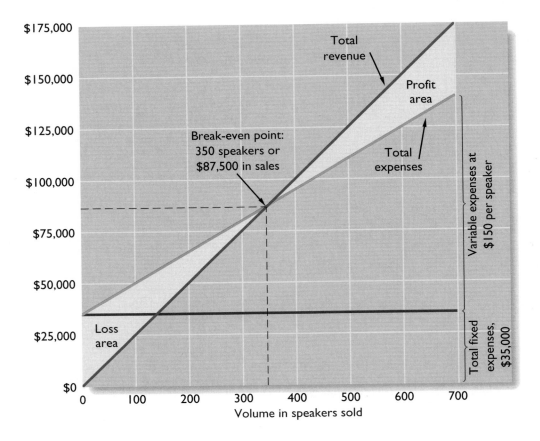

format income statement in which sales revenues, variable expenses, and contribution margin are expressed as a percentage of sales:

	Total	Per Unit	Percent of Sales
Sales (400 speakers)	$100,000	$250	100%
Less variable expenses	60,000	150	60
Contribution margin	40,000	$100	40
Less fixed expenses	35,000		
Net operating income	$ 5,000		

The contribution margin as a percentage of total sales is referred to as the **contribution margin ratio (CM ratio).** This ratio is computed as follows:

$$\text{CM ratio} = \frac{\text{Contribution margin}}{\text{Sales}}$$

For Acoustic Concepts, the computations are:

$$\text{CM ratio} = \frac{\text{Total contribution margin}}{\text{Total sales}} = \frac{\$40,000}{\$100,000} = 40\%$$

In a company such as Acoustic Concepts that has only one product, the CM ratio can also be computed on a per-unit basis as follows:

$$\text{CM ratio} = \frac{\text{Unit contribution margin}}{\text{Unit selling price}} = \frac{\$100}{\$250} = 40\%$$

The CM ratio is extremely useful because it shows how the contribution margin will be affected by a change in total sales. Acoustic Concepts' CM ratio of 40% means that for each dollar increase in sales, total contribution margin will increase by 40 cents ($1 sales × CM ratio of 40%). Net operating income will also increase by 40 cents, assuming that fixed costs are not affected by the increase in sales.

As this illustration suggests, *the impact on net operating income of any given dollar change in total sales can be computed by simply applying the CM ratio to the dollar change.* For example, if Acoustic Concepts plans a $30,000 increase in sales during the coming month, the contribution margin should increase by $12,000 ($30,000 increase in sales × CM ratio of 40%). As we noted above, net operating income will also increase by $12,000 if fixed costs do not change. This is verified by the following table:

| | Sales Volume | | | Percent of Sales |
	Present	Expected	Increase	
Sales	$100,000	$130,000	$30,000	100%
Less variable expenses ..	60,000	78,000*	18,000	60
Contribution margin	40,000	52,000	12,000	40%
Less fixed expenses	35,000	35,000	0	
Net operating income	$ 5,000	$ 17,000	$12,000	

*$130,000 expected sales ÷ $250 per unit = 520 units.
520 units × $150 per unit = $78,000.

The CM ratio is particularly valuable in situations where trade-offs must be made between more dollar sales of one product versus more dollar sales of another. In this situation, products that yield the greatest amount of contribution margin per dollar of sales should be emphasized.

Some Applications of CVP Concepts

The concepts developed on the preceding pages can be used in a variety of decision-making situations such as the five considered below.

Change in Fixed Cost and Sales Volume   Acoustic Concepts is currently selling 400 speakers per month at $250 per speaker for total monthly sales of $100,000. The sales manager feels that a $10,000 increase in the monthly advertising budget would increase monthly sales by $30,000 to a total of 520 units. Should the advertising budget be increased? The following table shows the profit impact of the proposed change in the monthly advertising budget:

LEARNING OBJECTIVE 4
Show the effects on contribution margin of changes in variable costs, fixed costs, selling price, and volume.

Concept 6-1

	Current Sales	Sales with Additional Advertising Budget	Difference	Percent of Sales
Sales	$100,000	$130,000	$30,000	100%
Less variable expenses ...	60,000	78,000*	18,000	60
Contribution margin	40,000	52,000	12,000	40%
Less fixed expenses	35,000	45,000†	10,000	
Net operating income	$ 5,000	$ 7,000	$ 2,000	

*520 units × $150 per unit = $78,000.
†$35,000 + additional $10,000 monthly advertising budget = $45,000.

Assuming no other factors need to be considered, the increase in the advertising budget should be approved since it would increase net operating income by $2,000. There are two shorter ways to arrive at this solution. The first alternative solution follows:

Alternative Solution I

Expected total contribution margin:	
$130,000 × 40% CM ratio	$52,000
Present total contribution margin:	
$100,000 × 40% CM ratio	40,000
Incremental contribution margin	12,000
Change in fixed expenses:	
Less incremental advertising expense	10,000
Increased net operating income	$ 2,000

Since in this case only the fixed costs and the sales volume change, the solution can be presented in an even shorter format, as follows:

Alternative Solution 2

Incremental contribution margin:	
$30,000 × 40% CM ratio	$12,000
Less incremental advertising expense	10,000
Increased net operating income	$ 2,000

Notice that this approach does not depend on knowledge of previous sales. Also note that it is unnecessary under either shorter approach to prepare an income statement. Both of the alternative solutions involve an **incremental analysis**—they consider only those items of revenue, cost, and volume that will change if the new program is implemented. Although in each case a new income statement could have been prepared, the incremental approach is simpler and more direct and focuses attention on the specific changes that would occur as a result of the decision.

Change in Variable Costs and Sales Volume

Refer to the original data. Recall that Acoustic Concepts is currently selling 400 speakers per month. Prem is considering the use of higher-quality components, which would increase his variable costs (and thereby reduce the contribution margin) by $10 per speaker. However, his sales manager predicts that the higher overall quality would increase sales to 480 speakers per month. Should the higher-quality components be used?

The $10 increase in variable costs will decrease the unit contribution margin by $10—from $100 down to $90.

Solution

Expected total contribution margin with higher-quality components:	
480 speakers × $90 per speaker	$43,200
Present total contribution margin:	
400 speakers × $100 per speaker	40,000
Increase in total contribution margin	$ 3,200

According to this analysis, the higher-quality components should be used. Since fixed costs will not change, the $3,200 increase in contribution margin shown above should result in a $3,200 increase in net operating income.

Growing Sales at Amazon.com

Amazon.com was deciding between two tactics for growing sales and profits. The first approach was to invest in television advertising. The second approach was to introduce free shipping on orders over a designated amount of sales. To evaluate the first option, Amazon.com invested in television ads in two markets—Minneapolis, Minnesota, and Portland, Oregon. The company quantified the profit impact of this choice by subtracting the increase in fixed advertising costs from the increase in contribution margin resulting from the advertising campaign. The advertising results paled in comparison to the free "super saver shipping" program, which the company introduced on orders over $99. In fact, the free shipping option proved to be so popular and profitable that within two years Amazon.com dropped its qualifying threshold to $49 and then again to a mere $25. At each stage of this progression, Amazon.com used cost-volume-profit analysis to determine whether the extra revenue from liberalizing the free shipping offer more than offset the associated increase in shipping costs.

Source: Rob Walker, "Because 'Optimism is Essential,'" *Inc.* April 2004, pp. 149–150.

Change in Fixed Cost, Sales Price, and Sales Volume   Refer to the original data and recall again that Acoustics Concepts is currently selling 400 speakers per month. To increase sales, Prem's sales manager would like to cut the selling price by $20 per speaker and increase the advertising budget by $15,000 per month. The sales manager believes that if these two steps are taken, unit sales will increase by 50% to 600 speakers per month. Should the changes be made?

A decrease in the selling price of $20 per speaker will cause the unit contribution margin to decrease from $100 to $80.

Solution

Expected total contribution margin with lower selling price:	
600 speakers × $80 per speaker	$ 48,000
Present total contribution margin:	
400 speakers × $100 per speaker	40,000
Incremental contribution margin	8,000
Change in fixed expenses:	
Less incremental advertising expense	15,000
Reduction in net operating income	$ (7,000)

According to this analysis, the changes should not be made. The $7,000 reduction in net operating income that is shown above can be verified by preparing comparative income statements as follows:

	Present 400 Speakers per Month		Expected 600 Speakers per Month		
	Total	Per Unit	Total	Per Unit	Difference
Sales	$100,000	$250	$138,000	$230	$38,000
Less variable expenses ..	60,000	150	90,000	150	30,000
Contribution margin	40,000	$100	48,000	$ 80	8,000
Less fixed expenses	35,000		50,000*		15,000
Net operating income (loss)	$ 5,000		$ (2,000)		$ (7,000)

*35,000 + Additional monthly advertising budget of $15,000 = $50,000.

Change in Variable Cost, Fixed Cost, and Sales Volume   Refer to Acoustic Concepts' original data. As before, the company is currently selling 400 speakers per month. Prem's sales manager would like to pay a sales commission of $15 per speaker sold, rather than the flat salaries that now total $6,000 per month. The sales manager is confident that the change will increase monthly sales by 15% to 460 speakers per month. Should the change be made?

Solution
Changing the sales staff's compensation from salaries to commissions will affect both fixed and variable expenses. Fixed expenses will decrease by $6,000, from $35,000 to $29,000. Variable expenses will increase by $15, from $150 to $165, and the unit contribution margin will decrease from $100 to $85.

Expected total contribution margin with sales staff on commissions:	
460 speakers × $85 per speaker	$39,100
Present total contribution margin:	
400 speakers × $100 per speaker	40,000
Decrease in total contribution margin	(900)
Change in fixed expenses:	
Add salaries avoided if a commission is paid	6,000
Increase in net operating income	$ 5,100

According to this analysis, the changes should be made. Again, the same answer can be obtained by preparing comparative income statements:

	Present 400 Speakers per Month		Expected 460 Speakers per Month		
	Total	Per Unit	Total	Per Unit	Difference
Sales	$100,000	$250	$115,000	$250	$15,000
Less variable expenses ..	60,000	150	75,900	165	15,900
Contribution margin	40,000	$100	39,100	$ 85	900
Less fixed expenses	35,000		29,000		(6,000)*
Net operating income ...	$ 5,000		$ 10,100		$ 5,100

*Note: A *reduction* in fixed expenses has the effect of *increasing* net operating income.

Change in Regular Sales Price   Refer to the original data where Acoustic Concepts is currently selling 400 speakers per month. The company has an opportunity to make a bulk sale of 150 speakers to a wholesaler if an acceptable price can be negotiated. This sale would not disturb the company's regular sales and would not affect the company's total fixed expenses. What price per speaker should be quoted to the wholesaler if Acoustic Concepts wants to increase its monthly profits by $3,000?

Solution

Variable cost per speaker	$150
Desired profit per speaker:	
$3,000 ÷ 150 speakers	20
Quoted price per speaker	$170

Notice that fixed expenses are not included in the computation. This is because fixed expenses are not affected by the bulk sale, so all of the additional contribution margin increases profits.

The eToys Saga

The company eToys, which sells toys over the Internet, lost $190 million in 1999 on sales of $151 million. One big cost was advertising. eToys spent about $37 on advertising for each $100 of sales. (Other e-tailers were spending even more—in some cases, up to $460 on advertising for each $100 in sales!)

eToys did have some advantages relative to bricks-and-mortar stores such as Toys "R" Us. eToys had much lower inventory costs since it needed to keep on hand only one or two of a slow-moving item, whereas a traditional store has to fully stock its shelves. And bricks-and-mortar retail spaces in malls and elsewhere do cost money—on average, about 7% of sales. However, e-tailers such as eToys have their own set of disadvantages. Customers "pick and pack" their own items at a bricks-and-mortar outlet, but e-tailers have to pay employees to carry out this task. This costs eToys about $33 for every $100 in sales. And the technology to sell over the net is not free. eToys paid about $29 for its website and related technology for every $100 in sales. However, many of these costs of selling over the net are fixed. Toby Lenk, the CEO of eToys, estimated that the company would pass its break-even point somewhere between $750 and $900 million in sales—representing less than 1% of the market for toys. eToys didn't make it and laid off 70% of its employees in January 2001. Subsequently, eToys was acquired by KBtoys.com.

Sources: Erin Kelly, "The Last e-Store on the Block," *Fortune*, September 18, 2000, pp. 214–220; and Jennifer Couzin, *The Industry Standard*, January 4, 2001.

BREAK-EVEN ANALYSIS

CVP analysis is sometimes referred to simply as break-even analysis. This is unfortunate because break-even analysis is only one aspect of CVP analysis—although an important aspect. Break-even analysis is designed to answer questions such as how far could sales drop before the company begins to lose money?

Concept 6-2

Break-Even Computations

Earlier in the chapter we defined the break-even point as the level of sales at which the company's profit is zero. The break-even point can be computed using either the *equation method* or the *contribution margin method*—the two methods are equivalent.

The Equation Method   The **equation method** translates the contribution format income statement illustrated earlier in the chapter into equation form as follows:

$$\text{Profits} = (\text{Sales} - \text{Variable expenses}) - \text{Fixed expenses}$$

Rearranging this equation slightly yields the following equation, which is widely used in CVP analysis:

$$\text{Sales} = \text{Variable expenses} + \text{Fixed expenses} + \text{Profits}$$

At the break-even point, profits are zero. Therefore, the break-even point can be computed by finding that point where sales equal the total of the variable expenses plus the fixed expenses. For Acoustic Concepts, the break-even point in unit sales, Q, can be computed as follows:

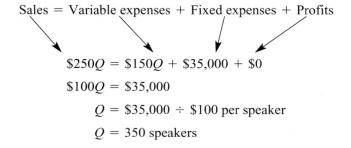

$$\text{Sales} = \text{Variable expenses} + \text{Fixed expenses} + \text{Profits}$$

$$\$250Q = \$150Q + \$35{,}000 + \$0$$
$$\$100Q = \$35{,}000$$
$$Q = \$35{,}000 \div \$100 \text{ per speaker}$$
$$Q = 350 \text{ speakers}$$

where:

Q = Quantity of speakers sold
$\$250$ = Unit selling price
$\$150$ = Unit variable expenses
$\$35{,}000$ = Total fixed expenses

The break-even point in total sales dollars can be computed by multiplying the break-even level of unit sales by the selling price per unit:

$$350 \text{ speakers} \times \$250 \text{ per speaker} = \$87{,}500$$

The break-even point in total sales dollars, X, can also be computed as follows:

$$\text{Sales} = \text{Variable expenses} + \text{Fixed expenses} + \text{Profits}$$
$$X = 0.60X + \$35{,}000 + \$0$$
$$0.40X = \$35{,}000$$
$$X = \$35{,}000 \div 0.40$$
$$X = \$87{,}500$$

where:

X = Total sales dollars
0.60 = Variable expense ratio (Variable expenses $\div$ Sales)
$\$35{,}000$ = Total fixed expenses

Notice that use of ratios in the equation yields a break-even point in sales dollars rather than in units sold. The break-even point in units sold is the following:

$$\$87,500 \div \$250 \text{ per speaker} = 350 \text{ speakers}$$

Recruit

Assume that you are being recruited by the ConneXus Corp. and have an interview scheduled later this week. You are interested in working for this company for a variety of reasons. In preparation for the interview, you did some research at your local library and gathered the following information about the company. ConneXus is a company set up by two young engineers, George Searle and Humphrey Chen, to allow consumers to order music CDs on their cell phones. Suppose you hear on the radio a cut from a CD that you would like to own. If you subscribe to their service, you would pick up your cell phone, punch "*CD," and enter the radio station's frequency and the time you heard the song, and the CD would be on its way to you.

ConneXus charges about $17 for a CD, including shipping. The company pays its supplier about $13, leaving a contribution margin of $4 per CD. Because of the fixed costs of running the service (about $1,850,000 a year), Searle expects the company to lose about $1.5 million in its first year of operations on sales of 88,000 CDs.

What are your initial impressions of this company based on the information you gathered? What other information would you want to obtain during the job interview?

Source: Adapted from Peter Kafka, "Play It Again," *Forbes*, July 26, 1999, p. 94.

The Contribution Margin Method The **contribution margin method** is a shortcut version of the equation method already described. The approach centers on the idea discussed earlier that each unit sold provides a certain amount of contribution margin that goes toward covering fixed costs. To find how many units must be sold to break even, divide the total fixed expenses by the unit contribution margin:

$$\text{Break-even point in units sold} = \frac{\text{Fixed expenses}}{\text{Unit contribution margin}}$$

Each speaker generates a contribution margin of $100 ($250 selling price, less $150 variable expenses). Since the total fixed expenses are $35,000, the break-even point in unit sales is computed as follows:

$$\frac{\text{Fixed expenses}}{\text{Unit contribution margin}} = \frac{\$35,000}{\$100 \text{ per speaker}} = 350 \text{ speakers}$$

A variation of this method uses the CM ratio instead of the unit contribution margin. The result is the break-even point in total sales dollars rather than in total units sold.

$$\text{Break-even point in total sales dollars} = \frac{\text{Fixed expenses}}{\text{CM ratio}}$$

In the Acoustic Concepts example, the calculation is as follows:

$$\frac{\text{Fixed expenses}}{\text{CM ratio}} = \frac{\$35,000}{0.40} = \$87,500$$

This approach, based on the CM ratio, is particularly useful when a company has multiple product lines and wishes to compute a single break-even point for the company as a whole. More is said on this point in a later section.

What Happened to the Profit?

Chip Conley is CEO of Joie de Vivre Hospitality, a company that owns and operates 28 hospitality businesses in northern California. Conley summed up the company's experience after the dot.com crash and 9/11 as follows: "In the history of American hotel markets, no hotel market has ever seen a drop in revenues as precipitous as the one in San Francisco and Silicon Valley in the last two years. On average, hotel revenues . . . dropped 40% to 45%. . . . We've been fortunate that our breakeven point is lower than our competition's. . . . But the problem is that the hotel business is a fixed-cost business. So in an environment where you have those precipitous drops and our costs are moderately fixed, our net incomes—well, they're not incomes anymore, they're losses."

Source: Karen Dillon, "Shop Talk," *Inc*, December 2002, pp. 111–114.

Target Profit Analysis

CVP formulas can be used to determine the sales volume needed to achieve a target profit. Suppose that Acoustic Concepts would like to earn a target profit of $40,000 per month. How many speakers would have to be sold?

The CVP Equation   One approach is to use the equation method. Instead of solving for the unit sales where profits are zero, solve for the unit sales where profits are $40,000.

$$\text{Sales} = \text{Variable expenses} + \text{Fixed expenses} + \text{Profits}$$

$$\$250Q = \$150Q + \$35,000 + \$40,000$$

$$\$100Q = \$75,000$$

$$Q = \$75,000 \div \$100 \text{ per speaker}$$

$$Q = 750 \text{ speakers}$$

where:

$$Q = \text{Quantity of speakers sold}$$
$$\$250 = \text{Unit selling price}$$
$$\$150 = \text{Unit variable expenses}$$
$$\$35,000 = \text{Total fixed expenses}$$
$$\$40,000 = \text{Target profit}$$

Thus, the target profit can be achieved by selling 750 speakers per month, which represents $187,500 in total sales ($250 per speaker × 750 speakers).

The Contribution Margin Approach   A second approach involves expanding the contribution margin formula to include the target profit:

$$\text{Unit sales to attain the target profit} = \frac{\text{Fixed expenses} + \text{Target profit}}{\text{Unit contribution margin}}$$

$$= \frac{\$35,000 + \$40,000}{\$100 \text{ per speaker}}$$

$$= 750 \text{ speakers}$$

This approach gives the same answer as the equation method since it is simply a shortcut version of the equation method. Similarly, the dollar sales needed to attain the target profit can be computed as follows:

$$\text{Dollar sales to attain target profit} = \frac{\text{Fixed expenses} + \text{Target profit}}{\text{CM ratio}}$$

$$= \frac{\$35,000 + \$40,000}{0.40}$$

$$= \$187,500$$

The Margin of Safety

The **margin of safety** is the excess of budgeted (or actual) sales dollars over the break-even volume of sales dollars. It states the amount by which sales can drop before losses are incurred. The higher the margin of safety, the lower the risk of not breaking even and incurring a loss. The formula for its calculation is:

LEARNING OBJECTIVE 7

Compute the margin of safety and explain its significance.

$$\text{Margin of safety} = \text{Total budgeted (or actual) sales} - \text{Break-even sales}$$

The margin of safety can also be expressed in percentage form by dividing the margin of safety in dollars by total dollar sales:

$$\text{Margin of safety percentage} = \frac{\text{Margin of safety in dollars}}{\text{Total budgeted (or actual) sales dollars}}$$

The calculation for the margin of safety for Acoustic Concepts is:

Sales (at the current volume of 400 speakers) (a)	$100,000
Break-even sales (at 350 speakers)	87,500
Margin of safety (in dollars) (b)	$ 12,500
Margin of safety as a percentage of sales, (b) ÷ (a)	12.5%

This margin of safety means that at the current level of sales and with the company's current prices and cost structure, a reduction in sales of $12,500, or 12.5%, would result in just breaking even.

In a single-product company like Acoustic Concepts, the margin of safety can also be expressed in terms of the number of units sold by dividing the margin of safety in dollars by the selling price per unit. In this case, the margin of safety is 50 speakers ($12,500 ÷ $250 per speaker = 50 speakers).

Loan Officer

DECISION MAKER

Sam Calagione owns Dogfish Head Craft Brewery, a microbrewery in Rehoboth Beach, Delaware. He charges his distributors $100 per case for premium beers such as World Wide Stout. The distributors tack on 25% when selling to retailers who in turn add a 30% markup before selling the beer to consumers. In the most recent year, Dogfish's revenue was $7 million and its net operating income was $800,000. Calagione reports that the costs of making one case of World Wide Stout are $30 for raw ingredients, $16 for labor, $6 for bottling and packaging, and $10 for utilities.

Assume that Calagione has approached your bank for a loan. As the loan officer you should consider a variety of factors, including the company's margin of safety. Assuming that the information related to World Wide Stout is representative of all Dogfish microbrews and that other information about the company is favorable, would you consider Dogfish's margin of safety to be comfortable enough to extend a loan?

Source: Patricia Huang, "Château Dogfish," *Forbes,* February 28, 2005, pp. 57–59.

3. Assume a company produces one product that sells for $55, has a variable cost per unit of $35, and has fixed costs of $100,000. How many units must the company sell to earn a target profit of $50,000?
   a.   7,500 units
   b.   10,000 units
   c.   12,500 units
   d.   15,000 units
4. Given the same facts as in question 3 above, if the company exactly meets its target profit, what will be its margin of safety in sales dollars?
   a. $110,000
   b. $127,500
   c. $137,500
   d. $150,000

CVP CONSIDERATIONS IN CHOOSING A COST STRUCTURE

Cost structure refers to the relative proportion of fixed and variable costs in an organization. Managers often have some latitude in trading off between these two types of costs. For example, fixed investments in automated equipment can reduce variable labor costs. In this section, we discuss the choice of a cost structure. We introduce the concept of *operating leverage,* which plays a key role in determining the impact of cost structure on profit stability.

Cost Structure and Profit Stability

When a manager has some latitude in trading off between fixed and variable costs, which cost structure is better—high variable costs and low fixed costs, or the opposite? No single answer to this question is possible; each approach has its advantages. To show what we mean, refer to the income statements given below for two blueberry farms. Bogside Farm depends on migrant workers to pick its berries by hand, whereas Sterling Farm has invested in expensive berry-picking machines. Consequently, Bogside Farm has higher variable costs, but Sterling Farm has higher fixed costs:

	Bogside Farm		Sterling Farm	
	Amount	Percent	Amount	Percent
Sales	$100,000	100%	$100,000	100%
Less variable expenses	60,000	60	30,000	30
Contribution margin	40,000	40%	70,000	70%
Less fixed expenses	30,000		60,000	
Net operating income	$ 10,000		$ 10,000	

Which farm has the better cost structure? The answer depends on many factors, including the long-run trend in sales, year-to-year fluctuations in the level of sales, and the attitude of the owners toward risk. If sales are expected to be above $100,000 in the future, then Sterling Farm probably has the better cost structure. The reason is that its CM ratio is higher, and its profits will therefore increase more rapidly as sales increase. To illustrate, assume that each farm experiences a 10% increase in sales without any increase in fixed costs. The new income statements would be as follows:

	Bogside Farm		Sterling Farm	
	Amount	Percent	Amount	Percent
Sales	$110,000	100%	$110,000	100%
Less variable expenses	66,000	60	33,000	30
Contribution margin	44,000	40%	77,000	70%
Less fixed expenses	30,000		60,000	
Net operating income	$ 14,000		$ 17,000	

Sterling Farm has experienced a greater increase in net operating income due to its higher CM ratio even though the increase in sales was the same for both farms.

What if sales drop below $100,000 from time to time? What are the break-even points of the two farms? What are their margins of safety? The computations needed to answer these questions are shown below using the contribution margin method:

	Bogside Farm	Sterling Farm
Fixed expenses	$ 30,000	$ 60,000
Contribution margin ratio	÷ 0.40	÷ 0.70
Break-even in total sales dollars	$ 75,000	$ 85,714
Total current sales (a)	$100,000	$100,000
Break-even sales	75,000	85,714
Margin of safety in sales dollars (b)	$ 25,000	$ 14,286
Margin of safety as a percentage of sales, (b) ÷ (a)	25.0%	14.3%

This analysis makes it clear that Bogside Farm is less vulnerable to downturns than Sterling Farm. There are two reasons why this is the case. First, due to its lower fixed expenses, Bogside Farm has a lower break-even point and a higher margin of safety. Therefore, it will not incur losses as quickly as Sterling Farm when sales decline. Second, due to its lower CM ratio, Bogside Farm will not lose contribution margin as rapidly as Sterling Farm when sales decline. Thus, Bogside Farm's income will be less volatile. We saw earlier that this is a drawback when sales increase, but it provides more protection when sales drop.

To summarize, without knowing the future, it is not obvious which cost structure is better. Both have advantages and disadvantages. Sterling Farm, with its higher fixed costs

A Losing Cost Structure

Both JetBlue and United Airlines use an Airbus 235 to fly from Dulles International Airport near Washington, DC, to Oakland, California. Both planes have a pilot, copilot, and four flight attendants. That is where the similarity ends. Based on 2002 data, the pilot on the United flight earned $16,350 to $18,000 a month compared to $6,800 per month for the JetBlue pilot. United's senior flight attendants on the plane earned more than $41,000 per year; whereas the JetBlue attendants were paid $16,800 to $27,000 per year. Largely because of the higher labor costs at United, its costs of operating the flight were more than 60% higher than JetBlue's costs. Due to intense fare competition from JetBlue and other low-cost carriers, United was unable to cover its higher operating costs on this and many other flights. Consequently, United went into bankruptcy at the end of 2002.

Source: Susan Carey, "Costly Race in the Sky," *The Wall Street Journal*, September 9, 2002, pp. B1 and B3.

and lower variable costs, will experience wider swings in net operating income as sales fluctuate, with greater profits in good years and greater losses in bad years. Bogside Farm, with its lower fixed costs and higher variable costs, will enjoy greater stability in net operating income and will be more protected from losses during bad years, but at the cost of lower net operating income in good years.

Operating Leverage

A lever is a tool for multiplying force. Using a lever, a massive object can be moved with only a modest amount of force. In business, *operating leverage* serves a similar purpose. **Operating leverage** is a measure of how sensitive net operating income is to a given percentage change in sales. Operating leverage acts as a multiplier. If operating leverage is high, a small percentage increase in sales can produce a much larger percentage increase in net operating income.

Operating leverage can be illustrated by returning to the data for the two blueberry farms. We previously showed that a 10% increase in sales (from $100,000 to $110,000 in each farm) results in a 70% increase in the net operating income of Sterling Farm (from $10,000 to $17,000) and only a 40% increase in the net operating income of Bogside Farm (from $10,000 to $14,000). Thus, for a 10% increase in sales, Sterling Farm experiences a much greater percentage increase in profits than does Bogside Farm. Therefore, Sterling Farm has greater operating leverage than Bogside Farm.

The **degree of operating leverage** at a given level of sales is computed by the following formula:

$$\text{Degree of operating leverage} = \frac{\text{Contribution margin}}{\text{Net operating income}}$$

The degree of operating leverage is a measure, at a given level of sales, of how a percentage change in sales volume will affect profits. To illustrate, the degree of operating leverage for the two farms at a $100,000 sales level would be computed as follows:

$$\text{Bogside Farm:} \frac{\$40,000}{\$10,000} = 4$$

$$\text{Sterling Farm:} \frac{\$70,000}{\$10,000} = 7$$

Since the degree of operating leverage for Bogside Farm is 4, the farm's net operating income grows four times as fast as its sales. Similarly, Sterling Farm's net operating income grows seven times as fast as its sales. Thus, if sales increase by 10%, then we can expect the net operating income of Bogside Farm to increase by four times this amount, or by 40%, and the net operating income of Sterling Farm to increase by seven times this amount, or by 70%.

	(1) Percent Increase in Sales	(2) Degree of Operating Leverage	Percent Increase in Net Operating Income (1) × (2)
Bogside Farm	10%	4	40%
Sterling Farm	10%	7	70%

What is responsible for the higher operating leverage at Sterling Farm? The only difference between the two farms is their cost structure. If two companies have the same total revenue and same total expense but different cost structures, then the company with the higher proportion of fixed costs in its cost structure will have higher operating leverage. Referring back to the original example on page 264, when both farms have sales of $100,000 and total expenses of $90,000, one-third of Bogside Farm's costs are fixed but two-thirds of Sterling Farm's costs are fixed. As a consequence, Sterling's degree of operating leverage is higher than Bogside's.

The degree of operating leverage is not constant; it is greatest at sales levels near the break-even point and decreases as sales and profits rise. This can be seen from the data below, which show the degree of operating leverage for Bogside Farm at various sales levels. (Data used earlier for Bogside Farm are shown in color.)

Sales	$75,000	$80,000	$100,000	$150,000	$225,000
Less variable expenses	45,000	48,000	60,000	90,000	135,000
Contribution margin (a)	30,000	32,000	40,000	60,000	90,000
Less fixed expenses	30,000	30,000	30,000	30,000	30,000
Net operating income (b)	$ 0	$ 2,000	$ 10,000	$ 30,000	$ 60,000
Degree of operating leverage, (a) ÷ (b)	∞	16	4	2	1.5

Thus, a 10% increase in sales would increase profits by only 15% (10% × 1.5) if sales were previously $225,000, as compared to the 40% increase we computed earlier at the $100,000 sales level. The degree of operating leverage will continue to decrease the farther the company moves from its break-even point. At the break-even point, the degree of operating leverage is infinitely large ($30,000 contribution margin ÷ $0 net operating income = ∞).

The degree of operating leverage can be used to quickly estimate what impact various percentage changes in sales will have on profits, without the necessity of preparing detailed income statements. As shown by our examples, the effects of operating leverage can be dramatic. If a company is near its break-even point, then even small percentage increases in sales can yield large percentage increases in profits. *This explains why management will often work very hard for only a small increase in sales volume.* If the degree of operating leverage is 5, then a 6% increase in sales would translate into a 30% increase in profits.

Fan Appreciation   IN BUSINESS

Operating leverage can be a good thing when business is booming but can turn the situation ugly when sales slacken. Jerry Colangelo, the managing partner of the Arizona Diamondbacks professional baseball team, spent over $100 million to sign six free agents—doubling the team's payroll cost—on top of the costs of operating and servicing the debt on the team's new stadium. With annual expenses of about $100 million, the team needs to average 40,000 fans per game to break even.

Faced with a financially risky situation, Colangelo decided to raise ticket prices by 12%. And he did it during Fan Appreciation Weekend! Attendance for the season dropped by 15%, turning what should have been a $20 million profit into a loss of over $10 million for the year. Note that a drop in attendance of 15% did not cut profit by just 15%—that's the magic of operating leverage at work.

Source: Mary Summers, "Bottom of the Ninth, Two Out," *Forbes*, November 1, 1999, pp. 69–70.

STRUCTURING SALES COMMISSIONS

Companies usually compensate salespeople by paying them either a commission based on sales or a salary plus a sales commission. Commissions based on sales dollars can lead to lower profits. To illustrate, consider Pipeline Unlimited, a producer of surfing equipment. Salespeople for the company sell the company's products to retail sporting goods stores throughout North America and the Pacific Basin. Data for two of the company's surf-boards, the XR7 and Turbo models, appear below:

	Model	
	XR7	**Turbo**
Selling price	$695	$749
Less variable expenses	344	410
Contribution margin	$351	$339

Which model will salespeople push hardest if they are paid a commission of 10% of sales revenue? The answer is the Turbo, since it has the higher selling price and hence the larger commission. On the other hand, from the standpoint of the company, profits will be greater if salespeople steer customers toward the XR7 model since it has the higher contribution margin.

To eliminate such conflicts, commissions can be based on contribution margin rather than on selling price. If this is done, the salespersons will want to sell the mix of products that will maximize contribution margin. Providing that fixed costs are not affected by the sales mix, maximizing the contribution margin will also maximize the company's profit. In effect, by maximizing their own compensation, salespersons will also maximize the company's profit.

SALES MIX

Before concluding our discussion of CVP concepts, we need to consider the impact of changes in *sales mix* on a company's profit.

The Definition of Sales Mix

The term **sales mix** refers to the relative proportions in which a company's products are sold. The idea is to achieve the combination, or mix, that will yield the greatest amount of profits. Most companies have many products, and often these products are not equally profitable. Hence, profits will depend to some extent on the company's sales mix. Profits will be greater if high-margin rather than low-margin items make up a relatively large proportion of total sales.

Changes in the sales mix can cause perplexing variations in a company's profits. A shift in the sales mix from high-margin items to low-margin items can cause total profits to decrease even though total sales may increase. Conversely, a shift in the sales mix from low-margin items to high-margin items can cause the reverse effect—total profits may increase even though total sales decrease. It is one thing to achieve a particular sales volume; it is quite another thing to sell the most profitable mix of products.

IN BUSINESS   Kodak: Going Digital

Kodak dominates the film industry in the U.S., selling two out of every three rolls of film. It also processes 40% of all film dropped off for developing. Unfortunately for Kodak, this revenue stream is threatened by digital cameras, which do not use film at all. To counter this threat, Kodak has moved into the digital market with its own line of digital cameras and various services, but sales of digital products undeniably cut into the company's film business. "Chief Financial Officer Robert Brust has 'stress-tested' profit models based on how quickly digital cameras may spread. If half of homes go digital, . . . Kodak's sales would rise 10% a year—but profits would go up only 8% a year. Cost cuts couldn't come fast enough to offset a slide in film sales and the margin pressure from selling cheap digital cameras." The sales mix is moving in the wrong direction, given the company's current cost structure and competitive prices.

Source: Bruce Upbin, "Kodak's Digital Moment," *Forbes*, August 21, 2000, pp. 106–112.

Sales Mix and Break-Even Analysis

If a company sells more than one product, break-even analysis is more complex than discussed earlier in this chapter. The reason is that different products will have different selling prices, different costs, and different contribution margins. Consequently, the break-even point depends on the mix in which the various products are sold. To illustrate, consider Sound Unlimited, a small company that imports DVDs from France for use in personal computers. At present, the company distributes the following DVDs to retail computer stores: the Le Louvre DVD, a multimedia free-form tour of the famous art museum in Paris; and the Le Vin DVD, which features the wines and wine-growing regions of France. Both multimedia products have sound, photos, video clips, and sophisticated software. The company's September sales, expenses, and break-even point are shown in Exhibit 6–3.

As shown in the exhibit, the break-even point is $60,000 in sales. This is computed by dividing the fixed costs by the company's *overall* CM ratio of 45%. The sales mix is currently 20% for the Le Louvre DVD and 80% for the Le Vin DVD. If this sales mix is constant, then at the break-even total sales of $60,000, the sales of the Le Louvre DVD would be $12,000 (20% of $60,000) and the sales of the Le Vin DVD would be $48,000 (80% of $60,000). As shown in Exhibit 6–3, at these levels of sales the company would indeed break even. But $60,000 in sales represents the break-even point for the company only if the sales mix does

EXHIBIT 6–3   Multiproduct Break-Even Analysis

Sound Unlimited
Contribution Income Statement
For the Month of September

	Le Louvre DVD		Le Vin DVD		Total	
	Amount	Percent	Amount	Percent	Amount	Percent
Sales	$20,000	100%	$80,000	100%	$100,000	100%
Less variable expenses	15,000	75	40,000	50	55,000	55
Contribution margin	$ 5,000	25%	$40,000	50%	45,000	45%
Less fixed expenses					27,000	
Net operating income					$ 18,000	

Computation of the break-even point:

$$\frac{\text{Fixed expenses}}{\text{Overall CM ratio}} = \frac{\$27,000}{0.45} = \$60,000$$

Verification of the break-even:

	Le Louvre DVD	Le Vin DVD	Total
Current dollar sales	$20,000	$80,000	$100,000
Percentage of total dollar sales	20%	80%	100%
Sales at break-even	$12,000	$48,000	$ 60,000

	Le Louvre DVD		Le Vin DVD		Total	
	Amount	Percent	Amount	Percent	Amount	Percent
Sales	$12,000	100%	$48,000	100%	$ 60,000	100%
Less variable expenses	9,000	75	24,000	50	33,000	55
Contribution margin	$ 3,000	25%	$24,000	50%	27,000	45%
Less fixed expenses					27,000	
Net operating income					$ 0	

EXHIBIT 6–4 Multiproduct Break-Even Analysis: A Shift in Sales Mix (see Exhibit 6–3)

Sound Unlimited
Contribution Income Statement
For the Month of October

	Le Louvre DVD		Le Vin DVD		Total	
	Amount	Percent	Amount	Percent	Amount	Percent
Sales	$80,000	100%	$20,000	100%	$100,000	100%
Less variable expenses	60,000	75	10,000	50	70,000	70
Contribution margin	$20,000	25%	$10,000	50%	30,000	30%
Less fixed expenses					27,000	
Net operating income					$ 3,000	

Computation of the break-even point:

$$\frac{\text{Fixed expenses}}{\text{Overall CM ratio}} = \frac{\$27,000}{0.30} = \$90,000$$

not change. *If the sales mix changes, then the break-even point will also change.* This is illustrated by the results for October in which the sales mix shifted away from the more profitable Le Vin DVD (which has a 50% CM ratio) toward the less profitable Le Louvre DVD (which has only a 25% CM ratio). These results appear in Exhibit 6–4.

Although sales have remained unchanged at $100,000, the sales mix is exactly the reverse of what it was in Exhibit 6–3, with the bulk of the sales now coming from the less profitable Le Louvre DVD. Notice that this shift in the sales mix has caused both the overall CM ratio and total profits to drop sharply from the prior month—the overall CM ratio has dropped from 45% in September to only 30% in October, and net operating income has dropped from $18,000 to only $3,000. In addition, with the drop in the overall CM ratio, the company's break-even point is no longer $60,000 in sales. Since the company is now realizing less average contribution margin per dollar of sales, it takes more sales to cover the same amount of fixed costs. Thus, the break-even point has increased from $60,000 to $90,000 in sales per year.

In preparing a break-even analysis, some assumption must be made concerning the sales mix. Usually the assumption is that it will not change. However, if the sales mix is expected to change, then this must be explicitly considered in any CVP computations.

IN BUSINESS

Playing the CVP Game

In 2002, General Motors (GM) gave away almost $2,600 per vehicle in customer incentives such as price cuts and 0% financing. "The pricing sacrifices have been more than offset by volume gains, most of which have come from trucks and SUVs, like the Chevy Suburban and the GMC Envoy, which generate far more profit for the company than cars. Lehman Brothers analysts estimate that GM will sell an additional 395,000 trucks and SUVs and an extra 75,000 cars in 2002. The trucks, however, are the company's golden goose, hauling in an average [contribution margin] . . . of about $7,000, compared with just $4,000 for the cars. All told, the volume gains could bring in an additional $3 billion [in profits]."

Source: Janice Revell, "GM's Slow Leak," *Fortune*, October 28, 2002, pp. 105–110.

ASSUMPTIONS OF CVP ANALYSIS

A number of assumptions underlie CVP analysis:

1. Selling price is constant. The price of a product or service will not change as volume changes.
2. Costs are linear and can be accurately divided into variable and fixed elements. The variable element is constant per unit, and the fixed element is constant in total over the entire relevant range.
3. In multiproduct companies, the sales mix is constant.
4. In manufacturing companies, inventories do not change. The number of units produced equals the number of units sold.

While some of these assumptions may be violated in practice, the violations are usually not serious enough to invalidate the CVP analysis. Perhaps the greatest danger lies in relying on simple CVP analysis when a manager is contemplating a large change in volume that lies outside of the relevant range. For example, a manager might contemplate increasing the level of sales far beyond what the company has ever experienced before. However, even in these situations CVP can be used if managers adjust the model as we have done in this chapter to take into account anticipated changes in selling prices, fixed costs, and the sales mix that would otherwise violate the assumptions mentioned above. For example, in a decision that would affect fixed costs, the change in fixed costs can be explicitly taken into account as illustrated earlier in the chapter in the Acoustic Concepts example on page 255.

Assumptions of CVP Analysis

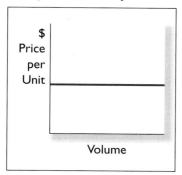

Selling price is constant

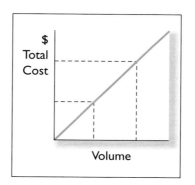

Variable cost per unit is constant

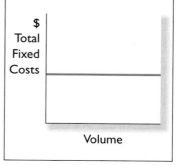

Fixed costs are constant

Sales mix is constant

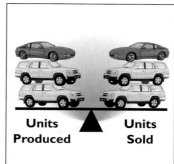

Inventory levels are constant

SUMMARY

LO1   Explain how changes in activity affect contribution margin and net operating income.

The unit contribution margin, which is the difference between a unit's selling price and its variable cost, indicates how net operating income will change as the result of selling one more or one less unit. For example, if a product's unit contribution margin is $10, then selling one more unit will add $10 to the company's profit.

LO2   Prepare and interpret a cost-volume-profit (CVP) graph.

A cost-volume-profit graph displays sales revenues and expenses as a function of unit sales. Revenue is depicted as a straight line slanting upward to the right from the origin. Total expenses include fixed costs and variable costs. The fixed costs are flat on the graph. The variable cost slants upward to the right. The break-even point is the point at which the total sales revenue and total expenses lines intersect on the graph.

LO3   Use the contribution margin ratio (CM Ratio) to compute changes in contribution margin and net operating income resulting from changes in sales volume.

The contribution margin ratio is computed by dividing the unit contribution margin by the unit selling price, or by dividing the total contribution margin by the total sales.

The contribution margin shows how much a dollar increase in sales affects the total contribution margin and net operating income. For example, if a product has a 40% contribution margin ratio, then a $100 increase in sales should result in a $40 increase in contribution margin and in net operating income.

LO4   Show the effects on contribution margin of changes in variable costs, fixed costs, selling price, and volume.

Contribution margin concepts can be used to estimate the effects of changes in various parameters such as variable costs, fixed costs, selling prices, and volume on the total contribution margin and net operating income.

LO5   Compute the break-even point in unit sales and dollar sales.

The break-even point is the level of sales at which profits are zero. It can be computed using several methods. The break-even point in units can be determined by dividing total fixed expenses by the unit contribution margin. The break-even point in sales dollars can be determined by dividing total fixed expenses by the contribution margin ratio.

LO6   Determine the level of sales needed to achieve a desired target profit.

The sales, in units, required to attain a desired target profit can be determined by summing the total fixed expenses and the desired target profit and then dividing the result by the unit contribution margin.

LO7   Compute the margin of safety and explain its significance.

The margin of safety is the difference between the total budgeted (or actual) sales dollars of a period and the break-even sales dollars. It expresses how much cushion there is in the current level of sales above the break-even point.

LO8   Compute the degree of operating leverage at a particular level of sales and explain how it can be used to predict changes in net operating income.

The degree of operating leverage is computed by dividing the total contribution margin by net operating income. The degree of operating leverage can be used to determine the impact a given percentage change in sales would have on net operating income. For example, if a company's degree of operating leverage is 2.5, then a 10% increase in sales from the current level of sales should result in a 25% increase in net operating income.

LO9   Compute the break-even point for a multiproduct company and explain the effects of shifts in the sales mix on contribution margin and the break-even point.

The break-even point for a multiproduct company can be computed by dividing the company's total fixed expenses by the overall contribution margin ratio.

This method for computing the break-even point assumes that the sales mix is constant. If the sales mix shifts toward products with a lower contribution margin ratio, then more total sales are required to attain any given level of profits.

GUIDANCE ANSWERS TO *DECISION MAKER* AND *YOU DECIDE*

Recruit (p. 261)

You can get a feel for the challenges that this company will face by determining its break-even point.

$$Sales = Variable\ expenses + Fixed\ expenses + Profits$$

$$\$17Q = \$13Q + \$1,850,000 + \$0$$

$$\$4Q = \$1,850,000$$

$$Q = 462,500$$

Assuming that its cost structure stays the same, ConneXus needs to increase its sales by 426%—from 88,000 to 462,500 CDs—just to break even. After it reaches that break-even point, net operating income will increase by $4 (the contribution margin) for each additional CD that it sells. Joining the company would be a risky proposition; you should be prepared with some probing questions when you arrive for your interview. (For example, what steps does the company plan to take to increase sales? How might the company reduce its fixed and/or variable expenses so as to lower its break-even point?)

Loan Officer (p. 263)

To determine the company's margin of safety, you need to determine its break-even point. Start by estimating the company's variable expense ratio:

$$Variable\ cost\ per\ unit \div Selling\ price\ per\ unit = Variable\ expense\ ratio$$

$$\$62 \div \$100 = 62\%$$

Then, estimate the company's variable expenses:

$$Sales \times Variable\ expense\ ratio = Estimated\ amount\ of\ variable\ expenses$$

$$\$7,000,000 \times 0.62 = \$4,340,000$$

Next, estimate the company's current level of fixed expenses as follows:

$$Sales = Variable\ expenses + Fixed\ expenses + Profits$$

$$\$7,000,000 = \$4,340,000 + Fixed\ expenses + \$800,000$$

$$Fixed\ expenses = \$7,000,000 - \$4,340,000 - \$800,000$$

$$X = \$1,860,000$$

Use the equation approach to estimate the company's break-even point:

$$Sales = Variable\ expenses + Fixed\ expenses + Profits$$

$$Sales = 0.62\ Sales + \$1,860,000 + \$0$$

$$0.38\ Sales = \$1,860,000$$

$$X = \$4,894,737$$

Finally, compute the company's margin of safety:

$$Margin\ of\ safety = (Sales - Break\text{-}even\ sales) \div Sales$$

$$= (\$7,000,000 - \$4,894,737) \div \$7,000,000$$

$$= 30\%$$

The margin of safety appears to be adequate, so if the other information about the company is favorable, a loan would seem to be justified.

GUIDANCE ANSWERS TO CONCEPT CHECKS

1. **Choice d.** The contribution margin ratio is (1.0 − Variable costs as a percent of sales).
2. **Choice d.** The contribution margin per unit is $12 (40% of $30). Therefore, 5,000 units × $12 contribution margin per unit = Fixed costs of $60,000.
3. **Choice a.** ($100,000 + $50,000) ÷ $20 contribution margin per unit = 7,500 units.
4. **Choice c.** 7,500 units is 2,500 units above the break-even point. Therefore, the margin of safety is 2,500 units × $55 per unit = $137,500.

REVIEW PROBLEM: CVP RELATIONSHIPS

Voltar Company manufactures and sells a specialized cordless telephone for high electromagnetic radiation environments. The company's contribution format income statement for the most recent year is given below:

	Total	Per Unit	Percent of Sales
Sales (20,000 units)	$1,200,000	$60	100%
Less variable expenses	900,000	45	?
Contribution margin	300,000	$15	? %
Less fixed expenses	240,000		
Net operating income	$ 60,000		

Management is anxious to increase the company's profit and has asked for an analysis of a number of items.

Required:
1. Compute the company's CM ratio and variable expense ratio.
2. Compute the company's break-even point in both units and sales dollars. Use the equation method.
3. Assume that sales increase by $400,000 next year. If cost behavior patterns remain unchanged, by how much will the company's net operating income increase? Use the CM ratio to determine your answer.
4. Refer to the original data. Assume that next year management wants the company to earn a minimum profit of $90,000. How many units will have to be sold to meet this target profit?
5. Refer to the original data. Compute the company's margin of safety in both dollar and percentage form.
6. a.   Compute the company's degree of operating leverage at the present level of sales.
   b.   Assume that through a more intense effort by the sales staff the company's sales increase by 8% next year. By what percentage would you expect net income to increase? Use the degree of operating leverage to obtain your answer.
   c.   Verify your answer to part (b) by preparing a new contribution format income statement showing an 8% increase in sales.
7. In an effort to increase sales and profits, management is considering the use of a higher quality speaker. The higher quality speaker would increase variable costs by $3 per unit, but management could eliminate one quality inspector who is paid a salary of $30,000 per year. The sales manager estimates that the higher quality speaker would increase annual sales by at least 20%.
   a.   Assuming that changes are made as described above, prepare a projected contribution format income statement for next year. Show data on a total, per unit, and percentage basis.
   b.   Compute the company's new break-even point in both units and dollars of sales. Use the contribution margin method.
   c.   Would you recommend that the changes be made?

Solution to Review Problem

1.

$$\text{CM ratio} = \frac{\text{Contribution margin}}{\text{Selling price}} = \frac{\$15}{\$60} = 25\%$$

$$\text{Variable expense ratio} = \frac{\text{Variable expense}}{\text{Selling price}} = \frac{\$45}{\$60} = 75\%$$

2.

$$\text{Sales} = \text{Variable expenses} + \text{Fixed expenses} + \text{Profits}$$

$$\$60Q = \$45Q + \$240,000 + \$0$$

$$\$15Q = \$240,000$$

$$Q = \$240,000 \div \$15 \text{ per unit}$$

$$Q = 16,000 \text{ units; or at } \$60 \text{ per unit, } \$960,000$$

Alternative solution:

$$X = 0.75X + \$240,000 + \$0$$

$$0.25X = \$240,000$$

$$X = \$240,000 \div 0.25$$

$$X = \$960,000; \text{ or at } \$60 \text{ per unit, } 16,000 \text{ units}$$

3.

Increase in sales	$400,000
Multiply by the CM ratio	×25%
Expected increase in contribution margin	$100,000

Since the fixed expenses are not expected to change, net operating income will increase by the entire $100,000 increase in contribution margin computed above.

4. Equation method:

$$\text{Sales} = \text{Variable expenses} + \text{Fixed expenses} + \text{Profits}$$

$$\$60Q = \$45Q + \$240,000 + \$90,000$$

$$\$15Q = \$330,000$$

$$Q = \$330,000 \div \$15 \text{ per unit}$$

$$Q = 22,000 \text{ units}$$

Contribution margin method:

$$\frac{\text{Fixed expenses} + \text{Target profit}}{\text{Contribution margin per unit}} = \frac{\$240,000 + \$90,000}{\$15 \text{ per unit}} = 22,000 \text{ units}$$

5.   Margin of safety in dollars = Total sales − Break-even sales

$$= \$1,200,000 - \$960,000 = \$240,000$$

$$\text{Margin of safety percentage} = \frac{\text{Margin of safety in dollars}}{\text{Total sales}} = \frac{\$240,000}{\$1,200,000} = 20\%$$

6. a. $$\text{Degree of operating leverage} = \frac{\text{Contribution margin}}{\text{Net operating income}} = \frac{\$300,000}{\$60,000} = 5$$

b.

Expected increase in sales	8%
Degree of operating leverage	×5
Expected increase in net operating income	40%

c. If sales increase by 8%, then 21,600 units (20,000 × 1.08 = 21,600) will be sold next year. The new contribution format income statement will be as follows:

	Total	Per Unit	Percent of Sales
Sales (21,600 units)	$1,296,000	$60	100%
Less variable expenses	972,000	45	75
Contribution margin	324,000	$15	25%
Less fixed expenses	240,000		
Net operating income	$ 84,000		

Thus, the $84,000 expected net operating income for next year represents a 40% increase over the $60,000 net operating income earned during the current year:

$$\frac{\$84,000 - \$60,000}{\$60,000} = \frac{\$24,000}{\$60,000} = 40\% \text{ increase}$$

Note from the income statement above that the increase in sales from 20,000 to 21,600 units has resulted in increases in *both* total sales and total variable expenses. It is a common error to overlook the increase in variable expenses when preparing a projected contribution format income statement.

7. a.   A 20% increase in sales would result in 24,000 units being sold next year: 20,000 units × 1.20 = 24,000 units.

	Total	Per Unit	Percent of Sales
Sales (24,000 units)	$1,440,000	$60	100%
Less variable expenses	1,152,000	48*	80
Contribution margin	288,000	$12	20%
Less fixed expenses	210,000†		
Net operating income	$ 78,000		

*$45 + $3 = $48; $48 ÷ $60 = 80%.
†$240,000 − $30,000 = $210,000.

Note that the change in per unit variable expenses results in a change in both the per unit contribution margin and the CM ratio.

b. $$\text{Break-even point in unit sales} = \frac{\text{Fixed expenses}}{\text{Contribution margin per unit}}$$

$$= \frac{\$210,000}{\$12 \text{ per unit}} = 17,500 \text{ units}$$

$$\text{Break-even point in dollar sales} = \frac{\text{Fixed expenses}}{\text{CM ratio}}$$

$$= \frac{\$210,000}{0.20} = \$1,050,000$$

c.   Yes, based on these data the changes should be made. The changes will increase the company's net operating income from the present $60,000 to $78,000 per year. Although the changes will also result in a higher break-even point (17,500 units as compared to the present 16,000 units), the company's margin of safety will actually be greater than before:

Margin of safety in dollars = Total sales − Break-even sales

= $1,440,000 − $1,050,000 = $390,000

As shown in (5) above, the company's present margin of safety is only $240,000. Thus, several benefits will result from the proposed changes.

GLOSSARY

Break-even point   The level of sales at which profit is zero. The break-even point can also be defined as the point where total sales equals total expenses or as the point where total contribution margin equals total fixed expenses. (p. 251)

Contribution margin method   A method of computing the break-even point in which the fixed expenses are divided by the contribution margin per unit. (p. 261)

Contribution margin ratio (CM ratio)   The contribution margin as a percentage of total sales. (p. 254)

Cost-volume-profit (CVP) graph   The relationships between an organization's revenues and costs on the one hand and its sales volume on the other hand presented in graphic form. (p. 252)

Degree of operating leverage   A measure, at a given level of sales, of how a percentage change in sales volume will affect profits. The degree of operating leverage is computed by dividing contribution margin by net operating income. (p. 266)

Equation method   A method of computing the break-even point that relies on the equation Sales = Variable expenses + Fixed expenses + Profits. (p. 260)

Incremental analysis   An analytical approach that focuses only on the costs and revenues that change as a result of a decision. (p. 256)

Margin of safety   The excess of budgeted (or actual) dollar sales over the break-even volume of dollar sales. (p. 263)

Operating leverage   A measure of how sensitive net operating income is to a given percentage change in sales. It is computed by dividing the contribution margin by net operating income. (p. 266)

Sales mix   The relative proportions in which a company's products are sold. Sales mix is computed by expressing the sales of each product as a percentage of total sales. (p. 268)

QUESTIONS

6–1   What is meant by a product's contribution margin ratio? How is this ratio useful in planning business operations?

6–2   Often the most direct route to a business decision is to make an incremental analysis based on the information available. What is meant by an *incremental analysis?*

6–3   Company A's cost structure includes costs that are mostly variable, whereas Company B's cost structure includes costs that are mostly fixed. In a time of increasing sales, which company will tend to realize the most rapid increase in profits? Explain.

6–4   What is meant by the term *operating leverage?*

6–5   What is meant by the term *break-even point?*

6–6   Name three approaches to break-even analysis. Briefly explain how each approach works.

6–7   In response to a request from your immediate supervisor, you have prepared a CVP graph portraying the cost and revenue characteristics of your company's product and operations. Explain how the lines on the graph and the break-even point would change if (a) the selling price per unit decreased, (b) the fixed cost increased throughout the entire range of activity portrayed on the graph, and (c) the variable cost per unit increased.

6–8   What is meant by the margin of safety?

6–9   What is meant by the term *sales mix?* What assumption is usually made concerning sales mix in CVP analysis?

6–10   Explain how a shift in the sales mix could result in both a higher break-even point and a lower net operating income.

BRIEF EXERCISES

BRIEF EXERCISE 6–1   Preparing a Contribution Format Income Statement   [LO1]

Whirly Corporation's most recent income statement is shown below:

	Total	Per Unit
Sales (10,000 units)	$350,000	$35.00
Less variable expenses	200,000	20.00
Contribution margin	150,000	$15.00
Less fixed expenses	135,000	
Net operating income	$ 15,000	

Required:

Prepare a new contribution format income statement under each of the following conditions (consider each case independently):

1. The sales volume increases by 100 units.
2. The sales volume decreases by 100 units.
3. The sales volume is 9,000 units.

BRIEF EXERCISE 6–2   Prepare a Cost-Volume-Profit (CVP) Graph   [LO2]

Karlik Enterprises has a single product whose selling price is $24 and whose variable cost is $18 per unit. The company's monthly fixed expense is $24,000.

Required:
1. Prepare a cost-volume-profit graph for the company up to a sales level of 8,000 units.
2. Estimate the company's break-even point in unit sales using your cost-volume-profit graph.

BRIEF EXERCISE 6–3   Computing and Using the CM Ratio   [LO3]
Last month when Holiday Creations, Inc., sold 50,000 units, total sales were $200,000, total variable expenses were $120,000, and total fixed expenses were $65,000.

Required:
1. What is the company's contribution margin (CM) ratio?
2. Estimate the change in the company's net operating income if it were to increase its total sales by $1,000.

BRIEF EXERCISE 6–4   Changes in Variable Costs, Fixed Costs, Selling Price, and Volume   [LO4]
Data for Hermann Corporation are shown below:

	Per Unit	Percent of Sales
Selling price	$90	100%
Less variable expenses	63	70
Contribution margin	$27	30%

Fixed expenses are $30,000 per month and the company is selling 2,000 units per month.

Required:
1. The marketing manager argues that a $5,000 increase in the monthly advertising budget would increase monthly sales by $9,000. Should the advertising budget be increased?
2. Refer to the original data. Management is considering using higher-quality components that would increase the variable cost by $2 per unit. The marketing manager believes the higher-quality product would increase sales by 10% per month. Should the higher-quality components be used?

BRIEF EXERCISE 6–5   Compute the Break-Even Point   [LO5]
Mauro Products has a single product, a woven basket whose selling price is $15 and whose variable cost is $12 per unit. The company's monthly fixed expenses are $4,200.

Required:
1. Solve for the company's break-even point in unit sales using the equation method.
2. Solve for the company's break-even point in sales dollars using the equation method and the CM ratio.
3. Solve for the company's break-even point in unit sales using the contribution margin method.
4. Solve for the company's break-even point in sales dollars using the contribution margin method and the CM ratio.

BRIEF EXERCISE 6–6   Compute the Level of Sales Required to Attain a Target Profit   [LO6]
Lin Corporation has a single product whose selling price is $120 and whose variable cost is $80 per unit. The company's monthly fixed expense is $50,000.

Required:
1. Using the equation method, solve for the unit sales that are required to earn a target profit of $10,000.
2. Using the contribution margin approach, solve for the dollar sales that are required to earn a target profit of $15,000.

BRIEF EXERCISE 6–7   Compute the Margin of Safety   [LO7]
Molander Corporation is a distributor of a sun umbrella used at resort hotels. Data concerning the next month's budget appear below:

Selling price	$30 per unit
Variable expense	$20 per unit
Fixed expense	$7,500 per month
Unit sales	1,000 units per month

Required:

1. Compute the company's margin of safety.
2. Compute the company's margin of safety as a percentage of its sales.

BRIEF EXERCISE 6–8 Compute and Use the Degree of Operating Leverage [LO8]
Engberg Company installs lawn sod in home yards. The company's most recent monthly contribution format income statement follows:

	Amount	Percent of Sales
Sales	$80,000	100%
Less variable expenses	32,000	40%
Contribution margin	48,000	60%
Less fixed expenses	38,000	
Net operating income	$10,000	

Required:

1. Compute the company's degree of operating leverage.
2. Using the degree of operating leverage, estimate the impact on net income of a 5% increase in sales.
3. Verify your estimate from part (2) above by constructing a new contribution format income statement for the company assuming a 5% increase in sales.

BRIEF EXERCISE 6–9 Compute the Break-Even Point for a Multiproduct Company [LO9]
Lucido Products markets two computer games: Claimjumper and Makeover. A contribution format income statement for a recent month for the two games appears below:

	Claimjumper	Makeover	Total
Sales	$30,000	$70,000	$100,000
Less variable expenses	20,000	50,000	70,000
Contribution margin	$10,000	$20,000	30,000
Less fixed expenses			24,000
Net operating income			$ 6,000

Required:

1. Compute the overall contribution margin (CM) ratio for the company.
2. Compute the overall break-even point for the company in sales dollars.
3. Verify the overall break-even point for the company by constructing a contribution format income statement showing the appropriate levels of sales for the two products.

EXERCISES

EXERCISE 6–10 Break-Even Analysis and CVP Graphing [LO2, LO4, LO5]
The Hartford Symphony Guild is planning its annual dinner-dance. The dinner-dance committee has assembled the following expected costs for the event:

Dinner (per person)	$18
Favors and program (per person)	$2
Band	$2,800
Rental of ballroom	$900
Professional entertainment during intermission	$1,000
Tickets and advertising	$1,300

The committee members would like to charge $35 per person for the evening's activities.

Required:
1. Compute the break-even point for the dinner-dance (in terms of the number of persons who must attend).
2. Assume that last year only 300 persons attended the dinner-dance. If the same number attend this year, what price per ticket must be charged in order to break even?
3. Refer to the original data ($35 ticket price per person). Prepare a CVP graph for the dinner-dance from a zero level of activity up to 600 tickets sold. Number of persons should be placed on the horizontal (X) axis, and dollars should be placed on the vertical (Y) axis.

EXERCISE 6–11   Using a Contribution Format Income Statement   [LO1, LO4]
Miller Company's most recent contribution format income statement is shown below:

	Total	Per Unit
Sales (20,000 units)	$300,000	$15.00
Less variable expenses	180,000	9.00
Contribution margin	120,000	$ 6.00
Less fixed expenses	70,000	
Net operating income	$ 50,000	

Required:
Prepare a new contribution format income statement under each of the following conditions (consider each case independently):

1. The sales volume increases by 15%.
2. The selling price decreases by $1.50 per unit, and the sales volume increases by 25%.
3. The selling price increases by $1.50 per unit, fixed expenses increase by $20,000, and the sales volume decreases by 5%.
4. The selling price increases by 12%, variable expenses increase by 60 cents per unit, and the sales volume decreases by 10%.

EXERCISE 6–12   Operating Leverage   [LO4, LO8]
Magic Realm, Inc., has developed a new fantasy board game. The company sold 15,000 games last year at a selling price of $20 per game. Fixed costs associated with the game total $182,000 per year, and variable costs are $6 per game. Production of the game is entrusted to a printing contractor. Variable costs consist mostly of payments to this contractor.

Required:
1. Prepare a contribution format income statement for the game last year and compute the degree of operating leverage.
2. Management is confident that the company can sell 18,000 games next year (an increase of 3,000 games, or 20%, over last year). Compute:
   a.   The expected percentage increase in net operating income for next year.
   b.   The expected total dollar net operating income for next year. (Do not prepare an income statement; use the degree of operating leverage to compute your answer.)

EXERCISE 6–13   Multiproduct Break-Even Analysis   [LO1, LO9]
Olongapo Sports Corporation is the distributor in the Philippines of two premium golf balls—the Flight Dynamic and the Sure Shot. Monthly sales and the contribution margin ratios for the two products follow:

	Product		
	Flight Dynamic	Sure Shot	Total
Sales	P150,000	P250,000	P400,000
CM ratio	80%	36%	?

Fixed expenses total P183,750 per month. (The currency in the Philippines is the peso, which is denoted by P.)

Required:
1. Prepare a contribution format income statement for the company as a whole. Carry computations to one decimal place.
2. Compute the break-even point for the company based on the current sales mix.
3. If sales increase by P100,000 a month, by how much would you expect net operating income to increase? What are your assumptions?

EXERCISE 6–14   Break-Even and Target Profit Analysis   [LO3, LO4, LO5, LO6]

Lindon Company is the exclusive distributor for an automotive product that sells for $40 per unit and has a CM ratio of 30%. The company's fixed expenses are $180,000 per year.

Required:
1. What are the variable expenses per unit?
2. Using the equation method:
   a.   What is the break-even point in units and sales dollars?
   b.   What sales level in units and in sales dollars is required to earn an annual profit of $60,000?
   c.   Assume that by using a more efficient shipper, the company is able to reduce its variable expenses by $4 per unit. What is the company's new break-even point in units and sales dollars?
3. Repeat (2) above using the contribution margin method.

EXERCISE 6–15   Break-Even and Target Profit Analysis   [LO4, LO5, LO6]

Outback Outfitters sells recreational equipment. One of the company's products, a small camp stove, sells for $50 per unit. Variable expenses are $32 per stove, and fixed expenses associated with the stove total $108,000 per month.

Required:
1. Compute the break-even point in number of stoves and in total sales dollars.
2. If the variable expenses per stove increase as a percentage of the selling price, will it result in a higher or a lower break-even point? Why? (Assume that the fixed expenses remain unchanged.)
3. At present, the company is selling 8,000 stoves per month. The sales manager is convinced that a 10% reduction in the selling price would result in a 25% increase in monthly sales of stoves. Prepare two contribution format income statements, one under present operating conditions, and one as operations would appear after the proposed changes. Show both total and per unit data on your statements.
4. Refer to the data in (3) above. How many stoves would have to be sold at the new selling price to yield a minimum net operating income of $35,000 per month?

EXERCISE 6–16   Break-Even Analysis; Target Profit; Margin of Safety; CM Ratio   [LO1, LO3, LO5, LO6, LO7]

Menlo Company manufactures and sells a single product. The company's sales and expenses for last quarter follow:

	Total	Per Unit
Sales	$450,000	$30
Less variable expenses	180,000	12
Contribution margin	270,000	$18
Less fixed expenses	216,000	
Net operating income	$ 54,000	

Required:
1. What is the quarterly break-even point in units sold and in sales dollars?
2. Without resorting to computations, what is the total contribution margin at the break-even point?

3. How many units would have to be sold each quarter to earn a target profit of $90,000? Use the contribution margin method. Verify your answer by preparing a contribution format income statement at the target sales level.
4. Refer to the original data. Compute the company's margin of safety in both dollar and percentage terms.
5. What is the company's CM ratio? If sales increase by $50,000 per quarter and there is no change in fixed expenses, by how much would you expect quarterly net operating income to increase?

EXERCISE 6–17   Interpretive Questions on the CVP Graph   [LO2, LO5]
A CVP graph such as the one shown below is a useful technique for showing relationships between an organization's costs, volume, and profits.

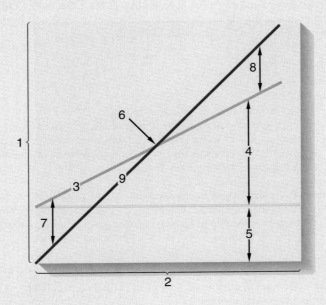

Required:
1. Identify the numbered components in the CVP graph.
2. State the effect of each of the following actions on line 3, line 9, and the break-even point. For line 3 and line 9, state whether the action will cause the line to:

>   Remain unchanged.
>   Shift upward.
>   Shift downward.
>   Have a steeper slope (i.e., rotate upward).
>   Have a flatter slope (i.e., rotate downward).
>   Shift upward *and* have a steeper slope.
>   Shift upward *and* have a flatter slope.
>   Shift downward *and* have a steeper slope.
>   Shift downward *and* have a flatter slope.

In the case of the break-even point, state whether the action will cause the break-even point to:

>   Remain unchanged.
>   Increase.
>   Decrease.
>   Probably change, but the direction is uncertain.

Treat each case independently.

>   x.   *Example.*   Fixed costs are reduced by $5,000 per period.
>   *Answer* (see choices above):   Line 3:   Shift downward.
>   Line 9:   Remain unchanged.
>   Break-even point: Decrease.

a.   The unit selling price is increased from $18 to $20.
b.   Unit variable costs are decreased from $12 to $10.

c. Fixed costs are increased by $3,000 per period.

d. Two thousand more units are sold during the period than were budgeted.

e. Due to paying salespersons a commission rather than a flat salary, fixed costs are reduced by $8,000 per period and unit variable costs are increased by $3.

f. Due to an increase in the cost of materials, both unit variable costs and the selling price are increased by $2.

g. Advertising costs are increased by $10,000 per period, resulting in a 10% increase in the number of units sold.

h. Due to automating an operation previously done by workers, fixed costs are increased by $12,000 per period and unit variable costs are reduced by $4.

PROBLEMS

PROBLEM 6–18A Basics of CVP Analysis [LO1, LO3, LO4, LO5, LO6, LO8]

Feather Friends, Inc., distributes a high-quality wooden birdhouse that sells for $20 per unit. Variable costs are $8 per unit, and fixed costs total $180,000 per year.

Required:

Answer the following independent questions:

CHECK FIGURE
(2) Break-even: $300,000

1. What is the product's CM ratio?

2. Use the CM ratio to determine the break-even point in sales dollars.

3. Due to an increase in demand, the company estimates that sales will increase by $75,000 during the next year. By how much should net operating income increase (or net operating loss decrease) assuming that fixed costs do not change?

4. Assume that the operating results for last year were:

Sales	$400,000
Less variable expenses	160,000
Contribution margin	240,000
Less fixed expenses	180,000
Net operating income	$ 60,000

a. Compute the degree of operating leverage at the current level of sales.

b. The president expects sales to increase by 20% next year. By what percentage should net operating income increase?

5. Refer to the original data. Assume that the company sold 18,000 units last year. The sales manager is convinced that a 10% reduction in the selling price, combined with a $30,000 increase in advertising, would cause annual sales in units to increase by one-third. Prepare two contribution format income statements, one showing the results of last year's operations and one showing the results of operations if these changes are made. Would you recommend that the company do as the sales manager suggests?

6. Refer to the original data. Assume again that the company sold 18,000 units last year. The president does not want to change the selling price. Instead, he wants to increase the sales commission by $1 per unit. He thinks that this move, combined with some increase in advertising, would increase annual sales by 25%. By how much could advertising be increased with profits remaining unchanged? Do not prepare an income statement; use the incremental analysis approach.

PROBLEM 6–19A Basic CVP Analysis; Graphing [LO1, LO2, LO4, LO5]

The Fashion Shoe Company operates a chain of women's shoe shops around the country. The shops carry many styles of shoes that are all sold at the same price. Sales personnel in the shops are paid a substantial commission on each pair of shoes sold (in addition to a small basic salary) in order to encourage them to be aggressive in their sales efforts.

The following worksheet contains cost and revenue data for Shop 48 and is typical of the company's many outlets:

| File | Edit | View | Insert | Format | Tools | Data | Window | Help |

	A	B	C
		Per Pair of Shoes	
1			
2	Selling price	$ 30.00	
3			
4	Variable expenses:		
5	Invoice cost	$ 13.50	
6	Sales commission	4.50	
7	Total variable expenses	$ 18.00	
8			
9		*Annual*	
10	Fixed expenses:		
11	Advertising	$ 30,000	
12	Rent	20,000	
13	Salaries	100,000	
14	Total fixed expenses	$ 150,000	
15			

Sheet1 / Sheet2 / Sheet3

Required:

1. Calculate the annual break-even point in dollar sales and in unit sales for Shop 48.
2. Prepare a CVP graph showing cost and revenue data for Shop 48 from a zero level of activity up to 17,000 pairs of shoes sold each year. Clearly indicate the break-even point on the graph.
3. If 12,000 pairs of shoes are sold in a year, what would be Shop 48's net operating income or loss?
4. The company is considering paying the store manager of Shop 48 an incentive commission of 75 cents per pair of shoes (in addition to the salesperson's commission). If this change is made, what will be the new break-even point in dollar sales and in unit sales?
5. Refer to the original data. As an alternative to (4) above, the company is considering paying the store manager 50 cents commission on each pair of shoes sold in excess of the break-even point. If this change is made, what will be the shop's net operating income or loss if 15,000 pairs of shoes are sold?
6. Refer to the original data. The company is considering eliminating sales commissions entirely in its shops and increasing fixed salaries by $31,500 annually. If this change is made, what will be the new break-even point in dollar sales and in unit sales for Shop 48? Would you recommend that the change be made? Explain.

PROBLEM 6–20A   Sales Mix; Multiproduct Break-Even Analysis   [LO5, LO9]
Gold Star Rice, Ltd., of Thailand exports Thai rice throughout Asia. The company grows three varieties of rice—Fragrant, White, and Loonzain. (The currency in Thailand is the baht, which is denoted by B.) Budgeted sales by product and in total for the coming month are shown below:

	Product							Total	
	White		Fragrant		Loonzain				
Percentage of total sales . .	20%		52%		28%			100%	
Sales.	B150,000	100%	B390,000	100%	B210,000	100%		B750,000	100%
Less variable expenses . .	108,000	72%	78,000	20%	84,000	40%		270,000	36%
Contribution margin	B 42,000	28%	B312,000	80%	B126,000	60%		480,000	64%
Less fixed expenses								449,280	
Net operating income . . .								B 30,720	

$$\text{Break-even point in sales dollars} = \frac{\text{Fixed expenses}}{\text{CM ratio}} = \frac{\text{B}449,280}{0.64} = \text{B}702,000$$

As shown by these data, net operating income is budgeted at B30,720 for the month and break-even sales at B702,000.

Assume that actual sales for the month total B750,000 as planned. Actual sales by product are: White, B300,000; Fragrant, B180,000; and Loonzain, B270,000.

Required:
1. Prepare a contribution format income statement for the month based on actual sales data. Present the income statement in the format shown above.
2. Compute the break-even point in sales dollars for the month based on your actual data.
3. Considering the fact that the company met its B750,000 sales budget for the month, the president is shocked at the results shown on your income statement in (1) above. Prepare a brief memo for the president explaining why both the operating results and the break-even point in sales dollars are different from what was budgeted.

PROBLEM 6–21A Missing Data; Basic CVP Concepts [LO1, LO9]
Fill in the missing amounts in each of the eight case situations below. Each case is independent of the others. (Hint: One way to find the missing amounts would be to prepare a contribution format income statement for each case, enter the known data, and then compute the missing items.)

a. Assume that only one product is being sold in each of the four following case situations:

Case	Units Sold	Sales	Variable Expenses	Contribution Margin per Unit	Fixed Expenses	Net Operating Income (Loss)
1	15,000	$180,000	$120,000	?	$50,000	?
2	?	$100,000	?	$10	$32,000	$8,000
3	10,000	?	$70,000	$13	?	$12,000
4	6,000	$300,000	?	?	$100,000	$(10,000)

b. Assume that more than one product is being sold in each of the four following case situations:

Case	Sales	Variable Expenses	Average Contribution Margin (Percent)	Fixed Expenses	Net Operating Income (Loss)
1	$500,000	?	20%	?	$7,000
2	$400,000	$260,000	?	$100,000	?
3	?	?	60%	$130,000	$20,000
4	$600,000	$420,000	?	?	$(5,000)

PROBLEM 6–22A Basics of CVP Analysis; Cost Structure [LO1, LO3, LO4, LO5, LO6]
Due to erratic sales of its sole product—a high-capacity battery for laptop computers—PEM, Inc., has been experiencing difficulty for some time. The company's contribution format income statement for the most recent month is given below:

Sales (19,500 units × $30 per unit)	$585,000
Less variable expenses	409,500
Contribution margin	175,500
Less fixed expenses	180,000
Net operating loss	$ (4,500)

Required:

1. Compute the company's CM ratio and its break-even point in both units and dollars.
2. The president believes that a $16,000 increase in the monthly advertising budget, combined with an intensified effort by the sales staff, will result in an $80,000 increase in monthly sales. If the president is right, what will be the effect on the company's monthly net operating income or loss? (Use the incremental approach in preparing your answer.)
3. Refer to the original data. The sales manager is convinced that a 10% reduction in the selling price, combined with an increase of $60,000 in the monthly advertising budget, will cause unit sales to double. What will the new contribution format income statement look like if these changes are adopted?
4. Refer to the original data. The Marketing Department thinks that a fancy new package for the laptop computer battery would help sales. The new package would increase packaging costs by 75 cents per unit. Assuming no other changes, how many units would have to be sold each month to earn a profit of $9,750?
5. Refer to the original data. By automating certain operations, the company could reduce variable costs by $3 per unit. However, fixed costs would increase by $72,000 each month.
   a. Compute the new CM ratio and the new break-even point in both units and dollars.
   b. Assume that the company expects to sell 26,000 units next month. Prepare two contribution format income statements, one assuming that operations are not automated and one assuming that they are. (Show data on a per unit and percentage basis, as well as in total, for each alternative.)
   c. Would you recommend that the company automate its operations? Explain.

PROBLEM 6–23A   Sales Mix; Break-Even Analysis; Margin of Safety   [LO1, LO5, LO7, LO9]
Island Novelties, Inc., of Palau makes two products, Hawaiian Fantasy and Tahitian Joy. Present revenue, cost, and sales data for the two products follow:

CHECK FIGURE
(1b) Break-even: $732,000
(2b) Margin of safety: 22%

	Hawaiian Fantasy	Tahitian Joy
Selling price per unit	$15	$100
Variable expenses per unit	$9	$20
Number of units sold annually	20,000	5,000

Fixed expenses total $475,800 per year. The Republic of Palau uses the U.S. dollar as its currency.

Required:

1. Assuming the sales mix given above, do the following:
   a. Prepare a contribution format income statement showing both dollar and percent columns for each product and for the company as a whole.
   b. Compute the break-even point in dollars for the company as a whole and the margin of safety in both dollars and percent.
2. The company has developed a new product to be called Samoan Delight. Assume that the company could sell 10,000 units at $45 each. The variable expenses would be $36 each. The company's fixed expenses would not change.
   a. Prepare another contribution format income statement, including sales of the Samoan Delight (sales of the other two products would not change).
   b. Compute the company's new break-even point in dollars and the new margin of safety in both dollars and percent.
3. The president of the company examines your figures and says, "There's something strange here. Our fixed costs haven't changed and you show greater total contribution margin if we add the new product, but you also show our break-even point going up. With greater contribution margin, the break-even point should go down, not up. You've made a mistake somewhere." Explain to the president what has happened.

PROBLEM 6–24A   Graphing; Incremental Analysis; Operating Leverage   [LO2, LO4, LO5, LO6, LO8]
Angie Silva has recently opened The Sandal Shop in Brisbane, Australia, a store that specializes in fashionable sandals. Angie has just received a degree in business and she is anxious to apply the principles she has learned to her business. In time, she hopes to open a chain of sandal shops. As a first step, she has prepared the following analysis for her new store:

Sales price per pair of sandals	$40
Variable expenses per pair of sandals	16
Contribution margin per pair of sandals	$24
Fixed expenses per year:	
Building rental	$15,000
Equipment depreciation	7,000
Selling	20,000
Administrative	18,000
Total fixed expenses	$60,000

CHECK FIGURE
(1)   Break-even: 2,500 pairs
(5a)   Leverage: 6

Required:

1. How many pairs of sandals must be sold each year to break even? What does this represent in total sales dollars?
2. Prepare a CVP graph for the store from a zero level of activity up to 4,000 pairs of sandals sold each year. Indicate the break-even point on your graph.
3. Angie has decided that she must earn at least $18,000 the first year to justify her time and effort. How many pairs of sandals must be sold to reach this target profit?
4. Angie now has two salespersons working in the store—one full time and one part time. It will cost her an additional $8,000 per year to convert the part-time position to a full-time position. Angie believes that the change would bring in an additional $25,000 in sales each year. Should she convert the position? Use the incremental approach. (Do not prepare an income statement.)
5. Refer to the original data. During the first year, the store sold only 3,000 pairs of sandals and reported the following operating results:

Sales (3,000 pairs)	$120,000
Less variable expenses	48,000
Contribution margin	72,000
Less fixed expenses	60,000
Net operating income	$ 12,000

   a.   What is the store's degree of operating leverage?
   b.   Angie is confident that with a more intense sales effort and with a more creative advertising program she can increase sales by 50% next year. What would be the expected percentage increase in net operating income? Use the degree of operating leverage to compute your answer.

PROBLEM 6–25A   **Changes in Fixed and Variable Costs; Break-Even and Target Profit Analysis [LO4, LO5, LO6]**

CHECK FIGURE
(1) Break-even: 21,000 units

Neptune Company produces toys and other items for use in beach and resort areas. A small, inflatable toy has come onto the market that the company is anxious to produce and sell. The new toy will sell for $3 per unit. Enough capacity exists in the company's plant to produce 16,000 units of the toy each month. Variable costs to manufacture and sell one unit would be $1.25, and fixed costs associated with the toy would total $35,000 per month.

The company's Marketing Department predicts that demand for the new toy will exceed the 16,000 units that the company is able to produce. Additional manufacturing space can be rented from another company at a fixed cost of $1,000 per month. Variable costs in the rented facility would total $1.40 per unit, due to somewhat less efficient operations than in the main plant.

Required:

1. Compute the monthly break-even point for the new toy in units and in total sales dollars. Show all computations in good form.
2. How many units must be sold each month to make a monthly profit of $12,000?
3. If the sales manager receives a bonus of 10 cents for each unit sold in excess of the break-even point, how many units must be sold each month to earn a return of 25% on the monthly investment in fixed costs?

PROBLEM 6–26A   Break-Even and Target Profit Analysis   [LO5, LO6]
The Shirt Works sells a large variety of tee shirts and sweatshirts. Steve Hooper, the owner, is thinking of expanding his sales by hiring local high school students, on a commission basis, to sell sweatshirts bearing the name and mascot of the local high school.

CHECK FIGURE
(1) 300 sweatshirts

These sweatshirts would have to be ordered from the manufacturer six weeks in advance, and they could not be returned because of the unique printing required. The sweatshirts would cost Mr. Hooper $8 each with a minimum order of 75 sweatshirts. Any additional sweatshirts would have to be ordered in increments of 75.

Since Mr. Hooper's plan would not require any additional facilities, the only costs associated with the project would be the costs of the sweatshirts and the costs of the sales commissions. The selling price of the sweatshirts would be $13.50 each. Mr. Hooper would pay the students a commission of $1.50 for each sweatshirt sold.

Required:
1. To make the project worthwhile, Mr. Hooper would require a $1,200 profit for the first three months of the venture. What level of sales in units and in dollars would be required to reach this target net operating income? Show all computations.
2. Assume that the venture is undertaken and an order is placed for 75 sweatshirts. What would be Mr. Hooper's break-even point in units and in sales dollars? Show computations and explain the reasoning behind your answer.

BUILDING YOUR SKILLS

Analytical Thinking   [LO5, LO9]
Cheryl Montoya picked up the phone and called her boss, Wes Chan, the vice president of marketing at Piedmont Fasteners Corporation: "Wes, I'm not sure how to go about answering the questions that came up at the meeting with the president yesterday."

"What's the problem?"

"The president wanted to know the break-even point for each of the company's products, but I am having trouble figuring them out."

"I'm sure you can handle it, Cheryl. And, by the way, I need your analysis on my desk tomorrow morning at 8:00 sharp in time for the follow-up meeting at 9:00."

Piedmont Fasteners Corporation makes three different clothing fasteners in its manufacturing facility in North Carolina. Data concerning these products appear below:

	Velcro	Metal	Nylon
Normal annual sales volume	100,000	200,000	400,000
Unit selling price	$1.65	$1.50	$0.85
Variable cost per unit	$1.25	$0.70	$0.25

Total fixed expenses are $400,000 per year.

All three products are sold in highly competitive markets, so the company is unable to raise its prices without losing unacceptable numbers of customers.

The company has an extremely effective just-in-time manufacturing system, so there are no beginning or ending work in process or finished goods inventories.

Required:
1. What is the company's over-all break-even point in total sales dollars?
2. Of the total fixed costs of $400,000, $20,000 could be avoided if the Velcro product were dropped, $80,000 if the Metal product were dropped, and $60,000 if the Nylon product were dropped. The remaining fixed costs of $240,000 consist of common fixed costs such as administrative salaries and rent on the factory building that could be avoided only by going out of business entirely.
   a. What is the break-even point in units for each product?
   b. If the company sells exactly the break-even quantity of each product, what will be the overall profit of the company? Explain this result.

Communicating in Practice   [LO4, LO5, LO6, LO8]

Pittman Company is a small but growing manufacturer of telecommunications equipment. The company has no sales force of its own; rather, it relies completely on independent sales agents to market its products. These agents are paid a commission of 15% of selling price for all items sold.

Barbara Cheney, Pittman's controller, has just prepared the company's budgeted income statement for next year. The statement follows:

CHECK FIGURE
(1a) Break-even:
$12,000,000

Pittman Company		
Budgeted Income Statement		
For the Year Ended December 31		
Sales		$16,000,000
Manufacturing costs:		
Variable	$7,200,000	
Fixed overhead	2,340,000	9,540,000
Gross margin		6,460,000
Selling and administrative costs:		
Commissions to agents	2,400,000	
Fixed marketing costs	120,000*	
Fixed administrative costs	1,800,000	4,320,000
Net operating income		2,140,000
Less fixed interest cost		540,000
Income before income taxes		1,600,000
Less income taxes (30%)		480,000
Net income		$ 1,120,000

*Primarily depreciation on storage facilities.

As Barbara handed the statement to Karl Vecci, Pittman's president, she commented, "I went ahead and used the agents' 15% commission rate in completing these statements, but we've just learned that they refuse to handle our products next year unless we increase the commission rate to 20%."

"That's the last straw," Karl replied angrily. "Those agents have been demanding more and more, and this time they've gone too far. How can they possibly defend a 20% commission rate?"

"They claim that after paying for advertising, travel, and the other costs of promotion, there's nothing left over for profit," replied Barbara.

"I say it's just plain robbery," retorted Karl. "And I also say it's time we dumped those guys and got our own sales force. Can you get your people to work up some cost figures for us to look at?"

"We've already worked them up," said Barbara. "Several companies we know about pay a 7.5% commission to their own salespeople, along with a small salary. Of course, we would have to handle all promotion costs, too. We figure our fixed costs would increase by $2,400,000 per year, but that would be more than offset by the $3,200,000 (20% × $16,000,000) that we would avoid on agents' commissions."

The breakdown of the $2,400,000 cost follows:

Salaries:	
Sales manager	$ 100,000
Salespersons	600,000
Travel and entertainment	400,000
Advertising	1,300,000
Total	$2,400,000

"Super," replied Karl. "And I noticed that the $2,400,000 is just what we're paying the agents under the old 15% commission rate."

"It's even better than that," explained Barbara. "We can actually save $75,000 a year because that's what we're having to pay the auditing firm now to check out the agents' reports. So our overall administrative costs would be less."

"Pull all of these numbers together and we'll show them to the executive committee tomorrow," said Karl. "With the approval of the committee, we can move on the matter immediately."

Required:

1. Compute Pittman Company's break-even point in sales dollars for next year assuming:
    a.   That the agents' commission rate remains unchanged at 15%.
    b.   That the agents' commission rate is increased to 20%.
    c.   That the company employs its own sales force.

2. Assume that Pittman Company decides to continue selling through agents and pays the 20% commission rate. Determine the volume of sales that would be required to generate the same net income as contained in the budgeted income statement for next year.

3. Determine the volume of sales at which net income would be equal regardless of whether Pittman Company sells through agents (at a 20% commission rate) or employs its own sales force.

4. Compute the degree of operating leverage that the company would expect to have on December 31 at the end of next year assuming:
    a.   That the agents' commission rate remains unchanged at 15%.
    b.   That the agents' commission rate is increased to 20%.
    c.   That the company employs its own sales force.
    Use income *before* income taxes in your operating leverage computation.

5. Based on the data in (1) through (4) above, make a recommendation as to whether the company should continue to use sales agents (at a 20% commission rate) or employ its own sales force. Give reasons for your answer.

(CMA, adapted)

Teamwork in Action   (LO1, LO4)

Revenue from major intercollegiate sports is an important source of funds for many colleges. Most of the costs of putting on a football or basketball game may be fixed and may increase very little as the size of the crowd increases. Thus, the revenue from every extra ticket sold may be almost pure profit.

Choose a sport played at your college or university, such as football or basketball, that generates significant revenue. Talk with the business manager of your college's sports programs before answering the following questions:

Required:

1. What is the maximum seating capacity of the stadium or arena in which the sport is played? During the past year, what was the average attendance at the games? On average, what percentage of the stadium or arena capacity was filled?

2. The number of seats sold often depends on the opponent. The attendance for a game with a traditional rival (e.g., Nebraska vs. Colorado, University of Washington vs. Washington State, or Texas vs. Texas A&M) is usually substantially above the average. Also, games against conference foes may draw larger crowds than other games. As a consequence, the number of tickets sold for a game is somewhat predictable. What implications does this have for the nature of the costs of putting on a game? Are most of the costs really fixed with respect to the number of tickets sold?

3. Estimate the variable cost per ticket sold.

4. Estimate the total additional revenue that would be generated in an average game if all of the tickets were sold at their normal prices. Estimate how much profit is lost because these tickets are not sold.

5. Estimate the ancillary revenue (parking and concessions) per ticket sold. Estimate how much profit is lost in an average game from these sources of revenue as a consequence of not having a sold-out game.

6. Estimate how much additional profit would be generated for your college if every game were sold out for the entire season.

Skills Challenger   [LO5, LO6]

The Pediatric Department at Wymont General Hospital has a capacity of 90 beds and operates 24 hours a day every day. The measure of activity in the department is patient-days, where one patient-day represents one patient occupying a bed for one day. The average revenue per patient-day is $130 and the average variable cost per patient-day is $50. The fixed cost of the department (not including personnel costs) is $454,000.

The only personnel directly employed by the Pediatric Department are aides, nurses, and supervising nurses. The hospital has minimum staffing requirements for the department based on total annual patient-days in Pediatrics. Hospital requirements, beginning at the minimum expected level of activity, follow:

CHECK FIGURE
(2) 16,325 patient-days

Annual Patient-Days	Aides	Nurses	Supervising Nurses
10,000–14,000	21	11	4
14,001–17,000	22	12	4
17,001–23,725	22	13	4
23,726–25,550	25	14	5
25,551–27,375	26	14	5
27,376–29,200	29	16	6

These staffing levels represent full-time equivalents, and it should be assumed that the Pediatric Department always employs only the minimum number of required full-time equivalent personnel.

Average annual salaries for each class of employee are: aides, $18,000; nurses, $26,000; and supervising nurses, $36,000.

Required:

1. Compute the total fixed costs (including the salaries of aides, nurses, and supervising nurses) in the Pediatric Department for each level of activity shown above (i.e., total fixed costs at the 10,000–14,000 patient-day level of activity, total fixed costs at the 14,001–17,000 patient-day level of activity, etc.).
2. Compute the minimum number of patient-days required for the Pediatric Department to break even.
3. Determine the minimum number of patient-days required for the Pediatric Department to earn an annual "profit" of $200,000.

(CPA, adapted)

Taking It to the Net

As you know, the World Wide Web is a medium that is constantly evolving. Sites come and go and change without notice. To enable periodic updating of site addresses, these problems have been posted to the textbook website (www.mhhe.com/bgn3e). After accessing the site, enter the Student Center and select this chapter to find the Taking It to the Net problems.

7 Profit Planning

CHAPTER OUTLINE

DECISION FEATURE

Lilo & Stitch on Budget

The full-length feature cartoon *Tarzan* grossed about $450 million worldwide for The Walt Disney Company. However, production costs got out of control. The company traditionally manages film production by focusing on meeting the planned release date—paying little attention to costs. In the case of *Tarzan*, production fell behind schedule due to the tendency of animation teams to add more eye-dazzling complexity to each production. At one point, it was estimated that 190,000 individual drawings would be needed to complete the film in contrast to the 130,000 drawings needed to complete *The Lion King*. To meet *Tarzan*'s release date, workers were pulled off other productions and were often paid at overtime rates. The size of the film crew eventually reached 573, which was nearly twice the size of the crew that had made *The Lion King*. With animators earning salaries in the hundreds of thousands of dollars, the cost implications were staggering.

Thomas S. Schumacher, Disney's feature-animation chief, was charged with dramatically reducing the cost of future films while making sure that the audience wouldn't notice any decline in quality. *Lilo & Stitch* was the first film to be produced with this goal in mind. The process began by prioritizing where the money was to be spent. The budget for music was kept generous; animation costs were cut by controlling the small details that add big costs with little effect on the quality of the film. For example, animators wanted to draw cute designs on the shirts worn by Nani, Lilo's big sister. However, adding this level of detail on every frame in which Nani appears in the film would have added about $250,000 in cost. By controlling such details, *Lilo & Stitch* was finished on time and at a cost of about $80 million. This contrasted with a cost of more than $150 million for *Tarzan*.

Source: Bruce Orwall, "Comics Stripped: At Disney, String of Weak Cartoons Leads to Cost Cuts," *The Wall Street Journal,* June 18, 2002, pp. A1 and A8.

In this chapter, we focus on the steps taken by businesses to achieve their planned levels of profits—a process called *profit planning.* Profit planning is accomplished by preparing a number of budgets, which, when brought together, form an integrated business plan known as the *master budget.* The master budget is an essential management tool that communicates management's plans throughout the organization, allocates resources, and coordinates activities.

THE BASIC FRAMEWORK OF BUDGETING

LEARNING OBJECTIVE 1

Understand why organizations budget and the processes they use to create budgets.

A **budget** is a detailed plan for acquiring and using financial and other resources over a specified time period. It represents a plan for the future expressed in formal quantitative terms. The act of preparing a budget is called *budgeting.* The use of budgets to control an organization's activities is known as *budgetary control.*

The **master budget** is a summary of a company's plans that sets specific targets for sales, production, and financing activities. It culminates in a cash budget, a budgeted income statement, and a budgeted balance sheet. In short, it represents a comprehensive expression of management's financial plans for the future.

Personal Budgets

Nearly everyone budgets to some extent, even though many of the people who use budgets do not recognize what they are doing as budgeting. For example, many people make estimates of their income and plan expenditures for food, clothing, housing, and so on. As a result of this planning, people restrict their spending to some predetermined, allowable amount. These people clearly go through a budgeting process. Income is estimated, expenditures are planned, and spending is restricted in accordance with the plan. Individuals also use budgets for purposes such as purchasing a home, financing college education, or setting aside funds for retirement.

The budgets of a business or other organization serve much the same functions as the budgets prepared informally by individuals. Business budgets tend to be more detailed and to involve more work, but they are similar to the budgets prepared by individuals in most other respects. Like personal budgets, they assist in planning and controlling expenditures; they also assist in predicting operating results and financial condition in future periods.

Difference Between Planning and Control

Concept 7-1

The terms *planning* and *control* are often confused, and occasionally are used as though they mean the same thing. Actually, planning and control are two quite distinct concepts. **Planning** involves developing objectives and preparing various budgets to achieve these objectives. **Control** involves the steps taken by management to increase the likelihood that the objectives set down at the planning stage are attained and that all parts of the organization are working together toward that goal. To be completely effective, a good budgeting system must provide for *both* planning and control. Good planning without effective control is time wasted.

Advantages of Budgeting

Organizations realize many benefits from budgeting including the following:

1. Budgets *communicate* management's plans throughout the organization.
2. Budgets force managers to *think about* and plan for the future. In the absence of the necessity to prepare a budget, too many managers would spend all of their time dealing with daily emergencies.

3. The budgeting process provides a means of *allocating resources* to those parts of the organization where they can be used most effectively.
4. The budgeting process can uncover potential *bottlenecks* before they occur.
5. Budgets *coordinate* the activities of the entire organization by *integrating* the plans of its various parts. Budgeting helps to ensure that everyone in the organization is pulling in the same direction.
6. Budgets define goals and objectives that can serve as *benchmarks* for evaluating subsequent performance.

Responsibility Accounting

Most of what we say in this chapter and in the next three chapters is concerned with *responsibility accounting*. The basic idea underlying **responsibility accounting** is that a manager should be held responsible for those items—and *only* those items—that the manager can actually control to a significant extent. Each line item (i.e., revenue or cost) in the budget is made the responsibility of a manager, and that manager is held responsible for subsequent deviations between budgeted goals and actual results. In effect, responsibility accounting *personalizes* accounting information by looking at revenues and costs from a *personal control* standpoint. This concept is central to any effective profit planning and control system. Someone must be held responsible for each cost or else no one will be responsible, and the cost will inevitably grow out of control.

Being held responsible for financial performance does not mean that the manager is penalized if the actual results do not measure up to the budgeted goals. However, the manager should take the initiative to correct any unfavorable discrepancies, should understand the source of significant favorable or unfavorable discrepancies, and should be prepared to explain the reasons for discrepancies to higher management. The point of an effective responsibility accounting system is to make sure that nothing "falls through the cracks," that the organization reacts quickly and appropriately to deviations from its plans, and that the organization learns from the feedback it gets by comparing budgeted goals to actual results. The point is *not* to penalize individuals for missing targets.

Planning and Control

Planning

Control

Choosing a Budget Period

Operating budgets ordinarily cover the company's fiscal year. Many companies divide their budget year into four quarters. The first quarter is then subdivided into months, and monthly budgets are developed. The last three quarters are carried in the budget as quarterly totals only. As the year progresses, the figures for the second quarter are broken down into monthly amounts, then the third-quarter figures are broken down, and so forth. This approach has the advantage of requiring periodic review and reappraisal of budget data throughout the year.

In this chapter, we will focus on one-year operating budgets. However, using basically the same techniques, operating budgets can be prepared for periods that extend over many years. It may be difficult to accurately forecast sales and costs much beyond a year, but even rough estimates can be invaluable in uncovering potential problems and opportunities.

The Self-Imposed Budget

The success of a budget program will largely be determined by the way in which the budget is developed. In the most successful budget programs, managers actively participate in preparing their own budgets. This is in contrast to the approach in which budgets are imposed from above. The participative approach to preparing budgets is particularly important if the budget is to be used to control and evaluate a manager's performance. If a budget is imposed on a manager from above, it will probably generate resentment rather than cooperation and commitment.

The budgeting approach in which managers prepare their own budget estimates—called a *self-imposed budget*—is generally considered to be the most effective method of budget preparation. A **self-imposed budget** or **participative budget,** as illustrated in Exhibit 7–1, is a budget that is prepared with the full cooperation and participation of managers at all levels.

EXHIBIT 7–1

The Initial Flow of Budget Data in a Participative Budgeting System

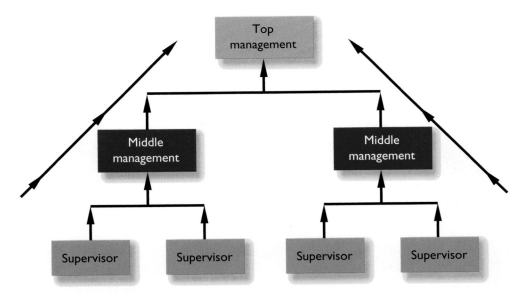

The initial flow of budget data in a participative system is from lower levels of responsibility to higher levels of responsibility. Each person with responsibility for cost control will prepare his or her own budget estimates and submit them to the next higher level of management. These estimates are reviewed and consolidated as they move upward in the organization.

A number of advantages are commonly cited for self-imposed budgets:

1. Individuals at all levels of the organization are recognized as members of the team whose views and judgments are valued by top management.
2. Budget estimates prepared by front-line managers are often more accurate and reliable than estimates prepared by top managers who have less intimate knowledge of markets and day-to-day operations.
3. Motivation is generally higher when individuals participate in setting their own goals than when management imposes the goals. Self-imposed budgets create commitment.
4. A manager who is not able to meet a budget that has been imposed from above can always say that the budget was unrealistic and was impossible to meet. With a self-imposed budget, this excuse is not available.

Realistically, there is always the danger that self-imposed budgets prepared by lower-level managers may be too loose and allow too much "budgetary slack." Since the manager will be held accountable for deviations of actual results from the budget, there is a natural tendency for the manager to try to influence the budgetary goals so that they can be easier rather than harder to attain. For this reason, if no other, budgets prepared by lower-level managers should be scrutinized by higher levels of management. Without such a review, self-imposed budgets may be too slack, resulting in inefficiency and waste. Therefore, before budgets are accepted, they should be carefully reviewed by immediate superiors. If changes from the budget seem desirable, the items in question should be discussed and modified as appropriate.

In essence, all levels of an organization should work together to produce the budget. Since top management is generally unfamiliar with detailed, day-to-day operations, it should rely on subordinates to provide detailed budget data. On the other hand, top management has an overall strategic perspective that is also vital. Each level of responsibility in an organization should contribute its unique knowledge and perspective in a *cooperative* effort to develop an integrated budget.

We have described an ideal budgetary process that involves self-imposed budgets prepared by the managers who are directly responsible for revenues and costs. Most organizations deviate from this ideal. Typically, top managers initiate the budget process by issuing broad guidelines for overall target profits or sales. Lower-level managers are directed to prepare budgets that meet those targets. The difficulty is that the targets set by top managers may be unrealistically high or may allow too much slack. If the targets are too high and employees know they are unrealistic, motivation will suffer. If the targets allow too much slack, waste will occur. And unfortunately top managers are often not in a position to know whether the targets are appropriate. Admittedly, however, a pure self-imposed budgeting system may lack sufficient strategic direction and lower-level managers may be tempted to build slack into their budgets. Nevertheless, because of the motivational advantages of self-imposed budgets, top managers should be cautious about imposing inflexible targets from above.

Human Factors in Budgeting

The success of a budget program also depends on: (1) the degree to which top management accepts the budget program as a vital part of the company's activities, and (2) the way in which top management uses budgeted data.

If a budget program is to be successful, it must have the complete acceptance and support of the persons who occupy key management positions. If lower or middle management personnel sense that top management is lukewarm about budgeting, or if they sense that top management simply tolerates budgeting as a necessary evil, then their own attitudes will reflect a similar lack of enthusiasm. Budgeting is hard work, and if top management is not enthusiastic about and committed to the budget program, then it is unlikely that anyone else in the organization will be either.

In administering the budget program, it is particularly important that top management not use the budget to pressure or blame employees. Using budgets in such negative ways will simply breed hostility, tension, and mistrust rather than greater cooperation and productivity. Unfortunately, the budget is too often used as a pressure device and excessive emphasis is placed on "meeting the budget" under all circumstances. Rather than being used as a weapon, the budget should be used as a positive instrument to assist in establishing goals, measuring operating results, and isolating areas that need attention.

Management must recognize that the human aspects of budgeting are extremely important. It is easy to become preoccupied with the technical aspects of the budget to the exclusion of the human aspects. Indeed, the use of budget data in a rigid and inflexible manner is the greatest single complaint of persons whose performance is evaluated using budgets. Management should remember that the purposes of the budget are to motivate employees and to coordinate their efforts. Preoccupation with the dollars and cents in the budget, or being rigid and inflexible, is usually counterproductive.

In establishing a budget, how challenging should budget targets be? Some experts argue that budget targets should be very challenging and should require managers to stretch to meet goals. Even the most capable managers may have to scramble to meet such a "stretch budget" and they may not always succeed. In practice, most companies set their budget targets at a "highly achievable" level. A highly achievable budget may be challenging, but it can almost always be met by competent managers exerting reasonable effort.

Bonuses based on meeting and exceeding budgets are often a key element of management compensation. Typically, no bonus is paid unless the budget is met. The bonus often increases when the budget target is exceeded, but the bonus is usually capped out at some level. For obvious reasons, managers who have such a bonus plan or whose performance is evaluated based on meeting budget targets usually prefer to be evaluated based on highly achievable budgets than on stretch budgets. Moreover, highly achievable budgets may help build a manager's confidence and generate greater commitment to the budget. And finally, highly achievable budgets may result in less undesirable behavior at the end of budgetary periods by managers who are intent on earning their bonuses. Examples of such undesirable behaviors are presented in several of the In Business boxes in this chapter.

Zero-Based Budgeting

The traditional approach to budgeting starts with the previous year's budget and then adds to it (or subtracts from it) according to anticipated needs. This is an incremental approach to budgeting in which the previous year's budget is taken for granted as a baseline.

Zero-based budgeting is an alternative approach. Under a **zero-based budget,** managers are required to justify *all* budgeted expenditures, not just changes in the budget from the previous year. The baseline is zero rather than last year's budget.

A zero-based budget requires considerable documentation. In addition to all of the schedules in the usual master budget, the manager must prepare a series of "decision packages" in which all of the activities of the department are ranked according to their relative importance and their costs are identified. Higher-level managers can then review the decision packages and cut back in those areas that are less critical or whose costs do not appear to be justified.

Zero-based budgeting sounds like a good idea. However, critics of zero-based budgeting charge that properly executed zero-based budgeting is too time-consuming and too costly to justify on an annual basis. In addition, it is argued that annual reviews soon become mechanical and that the whole purpose of zero-based budgeting is then lost.

Whether or not an organization should use an annual review is a matter of judgment. In some situations, annual zero-based reviews may be justified; in other situations, they may not.

The Budget Committee

A standing **budget committee** is usually responsible for overall policy relating to the budget program and for coordinating the preparation of the budget. This committee may consist of the president; vice presidents in charge of various functions such as sales, production, and purchasing; and the controller. Difficulties and disputes relating to the budget are resolved by the budget committee. In addition, the budget committee approves the final budget and receives periodic reports on the progress of the organization in attaining budgeted goals.

Disputes can (and do) erupt over budget matters. Because budgets allocate resources, the budgeting process to a large extent determines which departments get relatively more resources and which get less. Also, the budget sets the benchmarks by which managers and their departments will be at least partially evaluated. Therefore, it should not be surprising that managers take the budgeting process very seriously and invest considerable energy and emotion in ensuring that their interests, and those of their departments, are protected. Because of this, the budgeting process can easily degenerate into an interoffice brawl in which the ultimate goal of working together toward common goals is forgotten.

Running a successful budgeting program that avoids interoffice battles requires considerable interpersonal skills in addition to purely technical skills. But even the best interpersonal skills will fail if, as discussed earlier, top management uses the budget process to inappropriately pressure employees or to assign blame.

Better than Budgets?

Borealis is a company headquartered in Copenhagen, Denmark, that produces polymers for the plastics industry. Thomas Boesen, the company's financial controller, felt that the traditional budgeting process had outlived its usefulness—markets were changing so fast that the budget was out of date within weeks of its publication. Moreover, since budgets were used to control and evaluate the performance of managers, they were subject to considerable gaming behavior that reduced their accuracy and usefulness. So over a five-year period the company phased out its traditional budgets and replaced them with rolling forecasts and several other management tools. Instead of holding managers to a budget, targets based on competitors' performance were set for variable costs, fixed costs, and operating margins. Managers were given the freedom to spend money as needed to meet these competitive benchmarks. Since the rolling forecasts of financial results were not used to control spending or to evaluate managers' performance, managers had little incentive to "game the system," and hence the forecasts were more accurate than those obtained through the traditional budgeting process.

Source: Professor Bjorn Jorgensen, *Borealis,* Harvard Business School Case 9-102-048, Rev: May 9, 2002.

An Overview of the Master Budget

The master budget consists of a number of separate but interdependent budgets. Exhibit 7–2 provides an overview of the various parts of the master budget and how they are related.

The Sales Budget   A **sales budget** is a detailed schedule showing the expected sales for the budget period; typically, it is expressed in both dollars and units. An accurate sales budget is the key to the entire budgeting process. All other parts of the master budget are dependent on the sales budget, as illustrated in Exhibit 7–2. Thus, if the sales budget is inaccurate, then the rest of the budgeting process is largely a waste of time.

The sales budget helps determine how many units need to be produced. Thus, the production budget is prepared after the sales budget. The production budget in turn is used to determine the direct materials budget, the direct labor budget, and the manufacturing overhead budget. These budgets are then combined with data from the sales budget and the selling and administrative expense budget to determine the cash budget. In essence, the sales budget triggers a chain reaction that leads to the development of the other budgets.

EXHIBIT 7–2

The Master Budget Interrelationships

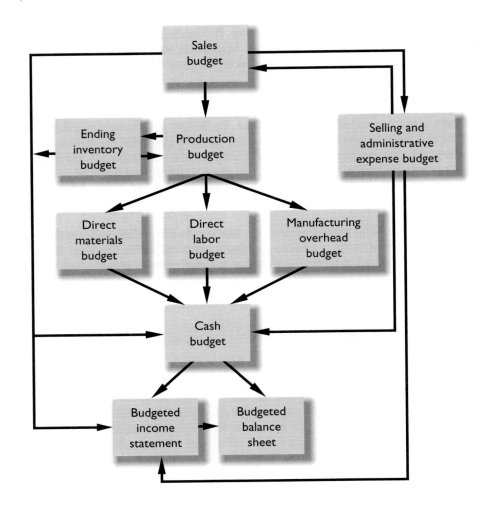

As shown in Exhibit 7–2, the selling and administrative expense budget is both dependent on and a determinant of the sales budget. This reciprocal relationship arises because sales will in part be determined by the funds committed to marketing and sales promotion.

The Cash Budget   Once the operating budgets (sales, production, and so on) have been established, the cash budget and other financial budgets can be prepared. A **cash budget** is a detailed plan showing how cash resources will be acquired and used over the budget period. Observe from Exhibit 7–2 that all of the operating budgets have an impact on the cash budget. In the case of the sales budget, the impact comes from the planned cash collections to be received from sales. In the case of the other budgets, the impact comes from the planned cash expenditures within the budgets themselves.

Sales Forecasting—A Critical Step

The sales budget is based on the company's *sales forecast.* Sales from prior years are commonly used as a starting point in preparing the sales forecast. In addition, the analyst may examine the company's unfilled back orders, the company's pricing policy and marketing plans, trends in the industry, and general economic conditions. Sophisticated statistical tools may be used to analyze the data and to build models that are helpful in predicting key factors influencing the company's sales. Some companies use computer simulations to enhance their sales forecasts. We will not, however, go into the details of sales forecasting. This subject is more appropriately covered in marketing courses.

Biasing Forecasts

A manager's compensation is often tied to the budget. Typically, no bonus is paid unless a minimum performance hurdle such as 80% of the budget target is attained. Once that hurdle is passed, the manager's bonus increases until a cap is reached. That cap is often set at 120% of the budget target.

This common method of tying a manager's compensation to the budget has some serious negative side effects. For example, a marketing manager for a big beverage company intentionally grossly understated demand for the company's products for an upcoming major holiday so that the budget target for revenues would be low and easy to beat. Unfortunately, the company tied its production to this biased forecast and ran out of products to sell during the height of the holiday selling season.

As another example, near the end of the year another group of managers announced a price increase of 10% effective January 2 of the following year. Why would they do this? By announcing this price increase, managers hoped that customers would order before the end of the year, helping managers meet their sales targets for the current year. Sales in the following year would, of course, drop. What trick would managers pull to meet their sales targets next year in the face of this drop in demand?

Sources: Michael C. Jensen, "Corporate Budgeting Is Broken—Let's Fix It," *Harvard Business Review,* November, 2001; and Michael C. Jensen, "Why Pay People to Lie?" *The Wall Street Journal,* January 8, 2001, p. A32.

Predicting Demand

O'Reilly Auto Parts uses sophisticated demand software from Nonstop Solutions to forecast seasonal variations in sales. For example, monthly sales of windshield wiper blades vary from 25,000 in the summer to 50,000 in the winter. Demand software uses weather data, economic trends, and other information to make forecasts and can even learn from its past mistakes.

Source: Chana R. Schoenberger, "The Weakest Link," *Forbes,* October 1, 2001, pp. 114–115.

PREPARING THE MASTER BUDGET

Hampton Freeze is a company that was started in 2004 to make premium popsicles using only natural ingredients and featuring exotic flavors such as tangy tangerine and minty mango. The company's business is highly seasonal, with most of the sales occurring in the spring and summer.

In 2005, the company's second year of operations, a major cash crunch in the first and second quarters almost forced the company into bankruptcy. In spite of this cash crunch, 2005 turned out to be a very successful year in terms of overall cash flow and net income. Partly as a result of that harrowing experience, the president of the company decided toward the end of 2005 to hire a professional financial manager. The new financial manager quickly diagnosed the problem as an unfortunate mismatch in the timing of the company's major expenses and receipts. Generally speaking, the company must make its products and pay its suppliers before its products are sold and its customers pay for their purchases. This gap between cash inflows and cash outflows could be bridged by borrowing. A common way to arrange for such short-term borrowing is a *line of credit* provided by a bank. Under a line of credit, a bank agrees to make loans to an organization up to a specified limit at a specified rate of interest over a specified period of time with specified repayment terms. If the line of credit is not needed, no money is borrowed and no interest is paid. If the line of credit *is* needed, the organization borrows the amount needed at the time, within the credit limit, and then pays interest and principal as specified in the credit line's contract. To arrange for a line of credit, the company will need to forecast how much it will need to borrow and when. Since this would be a natural by-product of creating a cash budget, the new financial manager suggested that Hampton Freeze institute a formal budgeting process. By budgeting, the company may be able to arrange for an adequate line of credit that would enable it to avoid a repeat of the financial problems of 2005.

With the full backing of the president, the new financial manager set out to create a master budget for the year 2006. In her planning for the budgeting process, the new financial manager drew up the following list of documents that would together make up the master budget:

1. A sales budget, including a schedule of expected cash collections.
2. A production budget (a merchandise purchases budget would be used in a merchandising company).
3. A direct materials budget, including a schedule of expected cash disbursements for purchases of materials.
4. A direct labor budget.
5. A manufacturing overhead budget.
6. An ending finished goods inventory budget.
7. A selling and administrative expense budget.
8. A cash budget.
9. A budgeted income statement.
10. A budgeted balance sheet.

The new financial manager felt it was important to have everyone's cooperation in the budgeting process, so she asked the president to call a companywide meeting in which the budgeting process would be explained. At the meeting there was initially some grumbling, but the president was able to convince nearly everyone of the necessity for planning and getting better control over spending. It helped that the cash crisis earlier in the year was still fresh in everyone's minds. As much as some people disliked the idea of budgets, they liked their jobs even more. In the months that followed, the new financial manager worked closely with all of the company's other managers involved in the master budget, gathering data from them and making sure that they understood and fully supported the parts of the master budget that would affect them. In subsequent years, the new financial manager hoped to turn the whole budgeting process over to the company's other managers and to take a more advisory role.

The interdependent documents making up Hampton Freeze's 2006 master budget are explained in the remaining part of this section, beginning with the sales budget.

The Sales Budget

LEARNING OBJECTIVE 2

Prepare a sales budget, including a schedule of expected cash collections.

The sales budget is the starting point in preparing the master budget. As shown earlier in Exhibit 7–2, all other items in the master budget, including production, purchases, inventories, and expenses, depend on it.

The sales budget is constructed by multiplying budgeted unit sales by the selling price. Schedule 1 on the next page contains the quarterly sales budget for Hampton Freeze for the year 2006. Notice from the schedule that the company plans to sell 100,000 cases of popsicles during the year, with sales peaking in the third quarter.

A schedule of expected cash collections, such as the one that appears in Schedule 1 for Hampton Freeze, is prepared after the sales budget. This schedule will be needed later to prepare the cash budget. Cash collections consist of collections on credit sales made to customers in prior periods plus collections on sales made in the current budget period. At Hampton Freeze, experience has shown that 70% of sales are collected in the quarter in which the sale is made and the remaining 30% are collected in the following quarter. For example, 70% of the first quarter sales of $200,000 (or $140,000) are collected during the first quarter and 30% (or $60,000) are collected during the second quarter.

SCHEDULE 1

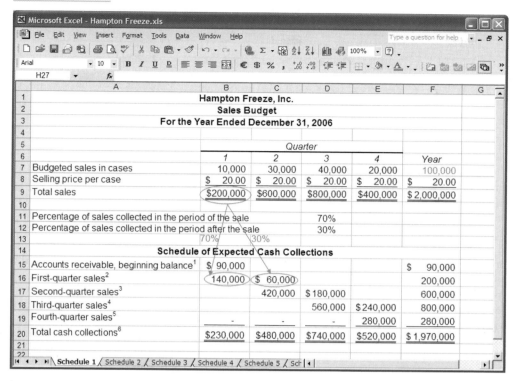

[1]Cash collections from last year's fourth-quarter sales. See the beginning-of-year balance sheet on page 316.

[2]$200,000 × 70%; $200,000 × 30%.

[3]$600,000 × 70%; $600,000 × 30%.

[4]$800,000 × 70%; $800,000 × 30%.

[5]$400,000 × 70%.

[6]Uncollected fourth-quarter sales appear as accounts receivable on the company's end-of-year balance sheet (see Schedule 10 on page 317).

Be Realistic

Gillette, the company that makes razors and other consumer products, got into trouble trying to meet increasingly unrealistic sales targets. The buyer at one of the company's big retail customers told Gillette's new CEO, Jim Kilts, that "he always waited until the last week of the quarter to order anything from Gillette 'because I know that you will always cut a deal.' To hit their numbers each quarter, [the Gillette salepersons] were willing to do anything—offer cut-rate deals, rearrange product packaging—whatever it took to make the sale." This resulted in artificially large sales at the end of the quarter—disrupting production schedules and loading the retail stores with excess inventory at discounted prices that would have to be sold off before more inventory would be ordered from Gillette.

Source: Katrina Brooker, "Jim Kilts Is an Old-School Curmudgeon," *Fortune,* December 30, 2002, pp. 95–102.

The Production Budget

The production budget is prepared after the sales budget. The **production budget** lists the number of units that must be produced during each budget period to meet sales needs and to provide for the desired ending inventory. Production needs can be determined as follows:

Budgeted unit sales	XXXX
Add desired ending inventory	XXXX
Total needs	XXXX
Less beginning inventory	XXXX
Required production	XXXX

Note that production requirements for a quarter are influenced by the desired level of the ending inventory. Inventories should be carefully planned. Excessive inventories tie up funds and create storage problems. Insufficient inventories can lead to lost sales or last-minute, high cost crash production efforts. At Hampton Freeze, management believes that an ending inventory equal to 20% of the next quarter's sales strikes the appropriate balance.

Schedule 2 contains the production budget for Hampton Freeze. The first row in the production budget contains the budgeted sales, which have been taken directly from the sales budget (Schedule 1). The total needs for the first quarter are determined by adding together the budgeted sales of 10,000 cases for the quarter and the desired ending inventory of 6,000 cases. As discussed above, the ending inventory is intended to provide some cushion in case problems develop in production or sales increase unexpectedly. Since the budgeted sales for the second quarter are 30,000 cases and management would like the ending inventory in each quarter to equal 20% of the following quarter's sales, the desired ending inventory is 6,000 cases (20% of 30,000 cases). Consequently, the

SCHEDULE 2

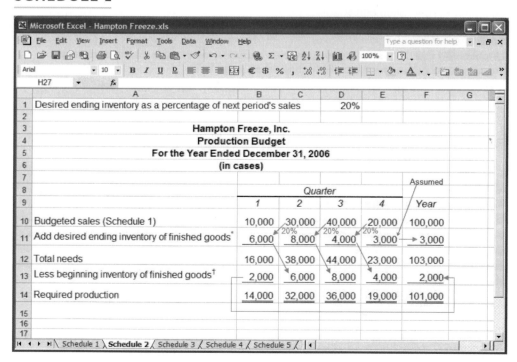

*Twenty percent of the next quarter's sales. The ending inventory of 3,000 cases is assumed.

†The beginning inventory in each quarter is the same as the prior quarter's ending inventory.

total needs for the first quarter are 16,000 cases. However, since the company already has 2,000 cases in beginning inventory, only 14,000 cases need to be produced in the first quarter.

Pay particular attention to the Year column to the right of the production budget in Schedule 2. In some cases (e.g., budgeted sales and required production), the amount listed for the year is the sum of the quarterly amounts for the item. In other cases (e.g., desired inventory of finished goods and beginning inventory of finished goods), the amount listed for the year is not simply the sum of the quarterly amounts. From the standpoint of the entire year, the beginning finished goods inventory is the same as the beginning finished goods inventory for the first quarter—it is *not* the sum of the beginning finished goods inventories for all quarters. Similarly, from the standpoint of the entire year, the ending finished goods inventory is the same as the ending finished goods inventory for the fourth quarter—it is *not* the sum of the ending finished goods inventories for all four quarters. It is important to pay attention to such distinctions in all of the schedules that follow.

Inventory Purchases—Merchandising Company

Hampton Freeze prepares a production budget, since it is a *manufacturing* company. If it were a *merchandising* company, it would instead prepare a **merchandise purchases budget** showing the amount of goods to be purchased from its suppliers during the period. The merchandise purchases budget follows the same basic format as the production budget, as shown below:

Budgeted sales	XXXXX
Add desired ending merchandise inventory	XXXXX
Total needs	XXXXX
Less beginning merchandise inventory	XXXXX
Required purchases	XXXXX

A merchandising company would prepare a merchandise purchases budget such as the one above for each item carried in stock. The merchandise purchases budget can be expressed in terms of either units or the purchase cost of those units. So, for example, the Budgeted sales shown in the table above can be expressed in terms of either the number of units sold or the purchase cost of the units sold.

The Direct Materials Budget

Returning to Hampton Freeze, after the production requirements have been computed, a *direct materials budget* can be prepared. The **direct materials budget** details the raw materials that must be purchased to fulfill the production budget and to provide for adequate inventories. The required purchases of raw materials are computed as follows:

Raw materials needed to meet the production schedule	XXXXX
Add desired ending inventory of raw materials	XXXXX
Total raw materials needs	XXXXX
Less beginning inventory of raw materials	XXXXX
Raw materials to be purchased	XXXXX

LEARNING OBJECTIVE 4

Prepare a direct materials budget, including a schedule of expected cash disbursements for purchases of materials.

Schedule 3 contains the direct materials budget for Hampton Freeze. The only raw material included in that budget is high fructose sugar, which is the major ingredient in

SCHEDULE 3

	Microsoft Excel - Hampton Freeze.xls						
	File Edit View Insert Format Tools Data Window Help					Type a question for help	
	Arial — 10 — B I U						
	M38						

	A	B	C	D	E	F	G
1	Desired ending inventory of raw materials as percentage of the next period's production needs.					10%	
2							
3	Hampton Freeze, Inc.						
4	Direct Materials Budget						
5	For the Year Ended December 31, 2006						
6						Assumed	
7				Quarter			
8		1	2	3	4	Year	
9	Required production in cases (Schedule 2)	14,000	32,000	36,000	19,000	101,000	
10	Raw materials needed per case (pounds)	15	15	15	15	15	
11	Production needs (pounds)	210,000	480,000	540,000	285,000	1,515,000	
12	Add desired ending inventory of raw materials[1]	48,000	54,000	28,500	22,500	22,500	
13	Total needs	258,000	534,000	568,500	307,500	1,537,500	
14	Less beginning inventory of raw materials	21,000	48,000	54,000	28,500	21,000	
15	Raw materials to be purchased	237,000	486,000	514,500	279,000	1,516,500	
16	Cost of raw materials per pound	$ 0.20	$ 0.20	$ 0.20	$ 0.20	$ 0.20	
17	Cost of raw materials to be purchased	$ 47,400	$ 97,200	$ 102,900	$ 55,800	$ 303,300	
18							
19	Percentage of purchases paid for in the period of the purchase			50%			
20	Percentage of purchases paid for in the period after purchase			50%			
21		50%	50%				
22	Schedule of Expected Cash Disbursements for Materials						
23							
24	Accounts payable, beginning balance[2]	$ 25,800				$ 25,800	
25	First-quarter purchases[3]	23,700	$ 23,700			47,400	
26	Second-quarter purchases[4]		48,600	$ 48,600		97,200	
27	Third-quarter purchases[5]			51,450	$ 51,450	102,900	
28	Fourth-quarter purchases[6]	-	-	-	27,900	27,900	
29	Total cash disbursements	$ 49,500	$ 72,300	$ 100,050	$ 79,350	$ 301,200	
30							

Schedule 1 / Schedule 2 \ **Schedule 3** / Schedule 4 / Schedule 5 / Schedu

[1]Ten percent of the next quarter's production needs. For example, the second-quarter production needs are 480,000 pounds. Therefore, the desired ending inventory for the first quarter would be 10% × 480,000 pounds = 48,000 pounds. The ending inventory of 22,500 pounds for the fourth quarter is assumed.

[2]Cash payments for last year's fourth-quarter material purchases. See the beginning-of-year balance sheet on page 316.

[3]$47,400 × 50%; $47,400 × 50%.

[4]$97,200 × 50%; $97,200 × 50%.

[5]$102,900 × 50%; $102,900 × 50%.

[6]$55,800 × 50%. Unpaid fourth-quarter purchases appear as accounts payable on the company's end-of-year balance sheet.

popsicles other than water. The remaining raw materials are relatively insignificant and are included in variable manufacturing overhead. As with finished goods, management would like to maintain a cushion of raw materials inventory that in this case equals 10% of the following quarter's production needs.

The first line in the direct materials budget contains the required production for each quarter, which is taken directly from the production budget (Schedule 2). Looking at the first quarter, since the production schedule calls for production of 14,000 cases of popsicles and each case requires 15 pounds of sugar, the total production needs are 210,000 pounds of sugar (14,000 cases × 15 pounds per case). In addition, management wants to have ending inventories of 48,000 pounds of sugar, which is 10% of the following quarter's needs of 480,000 pounds. Consequently, the total needs are 258,000 pounds (210,000 pounds for the current quarter's production plus 48,000 pounds for the desired ending inventory). However, since the company already has 21,000 pounds in beginning inventory, only 237,000 pounds of sugar (258,000 pounds − 21,000 pounds) will need to be purchased. Finally, the cost of the raw materials purchases is determined by multiplying the amount of raw material to be purchased by its unit cost. In this case, since 237,000 pounds of sugar need to be purchased during the first quarter and sugar costs $0.20 per pound, the total cost will be $47,400 (237,000 pounds × $0.20 per pound).

As with the production budget, the amounts listed under the Year column are not always the sum of the quarterly amounts. The desired ending raw materials inventory for the year is the same as the desired ending raw materials inventory for the fourth quarter. Likewise, the beginning raw materials inventory for the year is the same as the beginning raw materials inventory for the first quarter.

The direct materials budget (and the merchandise purchases budget for a merchandising company) is usually accompanied by a schedule of expected cash disbursements for raw materials (or merchandise purchases). This schedule is needed to prepare the overall cash budget. Disbursements for raw materials (or merchandise purchases) consist of payments for purchases on account in prior periods plus any payments for purchases in the current budget period. Schedule 3 contains such a schedule of cash disbursements for Hampton Freeze.

Ordinarily, companies do not immediately pay their suppliers. At Hampton Freeze, the policy is to pay for 50% of purchases in the quarter in which the purchase is made and 50% in the following quarter, so while the company intends to purchase $47,400 worth of sugar in the first quarter, the company will only pay for half, $23,700, in the first quarter and the other half will be paid in the second quarter. The company will also pay $25,800 in the first quarter for sugar that was purchased on account in the previous quarter, but not yet paid for. This is the beginning balance in the accounts payable. Therefore, the total cash disbursements for sugar in the first quarter are $49,500—the $25,800 payment for sugar acquired in the previous quarter plus the $23,700 payment for sugar acquired during the first quarter.

The Direct Labor Budget

The **direct labor budget** is also developed from the production budget. Direct labor requirements must be computed so that the company will know whether sufficient labor time is available to meet production needs. By knowing in advance how much labor time will be needed throughout the budget year, the company can develop plans to adjust the labor force as the situation requires. Companies that neglect to budget run the risk of facing labor shortages or having to hire and lay off workers at awkward times. Erratic labor policies lead to insecurity, low morale, and inefficiency.

The direct labor budget for Hampton Freeze is shown in Schedule 4. The first line in the direct labor budget consists of the required production for each quarter, which is taken directly from the production budget (Schedule 2). The direct labor requirement for each quarter is computed by multiplying the number of units to be produced in that quarter by the number of direct labor-hours required to make a unit. For example, 14,000 cases are to be produced in the first quarter and each case requires 0.40 direct labor-hour, so a total of 5,600 direct labor-hours (14,000 cases × 0.40 direct labor-hour per case) will be required in the first quarter. The direct labor requirements can then be translated into budgeted direct labor costs. How this is done will depend on the company's labor policy. In Schedule 4, Hampton Freeze has assumed that the direct labor force will be adjusted as the work requirements change from quarter to quarter. In that case, the direct labor cost is computed by simply multiplying the direct labor-hour requirements by the direct labor rate per hour. For example, the direct labor cost in the first quarter is $84,000 (5,600 direct labor-hours × $15 per direct labor-hour).

However, many companies have employment policies or contracts that prevent them from laying off and rehiring workers as needed. Suppose, for example, that Hampton Freeze has 25 workers who are classified as direct labor and each of them is guaranteed

LEARNING OBJECTIVE 5

Prepare a direct labor budget.

SCHEDULE 4

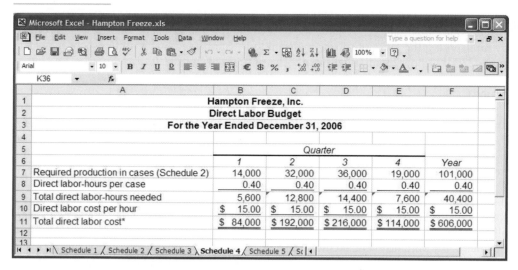

*This schedule assumes that the direct labor work force will be fully adjusted to the total direct labor-hours needed each quarter.

at least 480 hours of pay each quarter at a rate of $15 per hour. In that case, the minimum direct labor cost for a quarter would be as follows:

25 workers × 480 hours per worker × $15 per hour = $180,000

Note that in Schedule 4 the direct labor costs for the first and fourth quarters would have to be increased to $180,000 if Hampton Freeze guarantees each of its workers 480 hours of pay each quarter.

The Manufacturing Overhead Budget

The **manufacturing overhead budget** lists all costs of production other than direct materials and direct labor. Schedule 5 shows the manufacturing overhead budget for Hampton Freeze. At Hampton Freeze, manufacturing overhead is separated into variable and fixed components. The variable component is $4 per direct labor-hour and the fixed component is $60,600 per quarter. Because the variable component of manufacturing overhead depends on direct labor, the first line in the manufacturing overhead budget consists of the budgeted direct labor-hours from the direct labor budget (Schedule 4). The budgeted direct labor-hours in each quarter are multiplied by the variable rate to determine the variable component of manufacturing overhead. For example, the variable manufacturing overhead for the first quarter is $22,400 (5,600 direct labor-hours × $4.00 per direct labor-hour). This is added to the fixed manufacturing overhead for the quarter to determine the total manufacturing overhead for the quarter of $83,000 ($22,400 + $60,600).

A few words about fixed costs and the budgeting process are in order. In most cases, fixed costs are the costs of supplying capacity to make products, process purchase orders, handle customer calls, and so on. The amount of capacity that will be required depends on the expected level of activity for the period. If the expected level of activity is greater than the company's current capacity, then fixed costs may have to be increased. Or, if the expected level of activity is appreciably below the company's current capacity, then it may be desirable to decrease fixed costs if possible. However, once the level of the fixed costs has been determined in the budget, the costs really are fixed. The time to adjust fixed costs is during the budgeting process. An activity-based costing system can help to

SCHEDULE 5

Microsoft Excel - Hampton Freeze.xls

	A	B	C	D	E	F	G
1		Hampton Freeze, Inc.					
2		Manufacturing Overhead Budget					
3		For the Year Ended December 31, 2006					
4							
5				Quarter			
6		1	2	3	4	Year	
7	Budgeted direct labor-hours (Schedule 4)	5,600	12,800	14,400	7,600	40,400	
8	Variable overhead rate	$ 4.00	$ 4.00	$ 4.00	$ 4.00	$ 4.00	
9	Variable manufacturing overhead	$ 22,400	$ 51,200	$ 57,600	$ 30,400	$ 161,600	
10	Fixed manufacturing overhead	60,600	60,600	60,600	60,600	242,400	
11	Total manufacturing overhead	83,000	111,800	118,200	91,000	404,000	
12	Less depreciation	15,000	15,000	15,000	15,000	60,000	
13	Cash disbursements for manufacturing overhead	$ 68,000	$ 96,800	$ 103,200	$ 76,000	$ 344,000	
14							
15	Total manufacturing overhead (a)					$ 404,000	
16	Budgeted direct labor-hours (b)					40,400	
17	Predetermined overhead rate for the year (a)÷(b)					$ 10.00	
18							

Schedule 1 / Schedule 2 / Schedule 3 / Schedule 4 \ **Schedule 5** / Schedul

determine the appropriate level of fixed costs at budget time by answering questions like, "How many clerks will we need to hire to process the anticipated number of purchase orders next year?" For simplicity, all of the budgeting examples in this book assume that the appropriate levels of fixed costs have already been determined for the budget with the aid of activity-based costing or some other method.

The last line of Schedule 5 for Hampton Freeze shows its budgeted cash disbursements for manufacturing overhead. Since some of the overhead costs are not cash outflows, the total budgeted manufacturing overhead costs must be adjusted to determine the cash disbursements for manufacturing overhead. At Hampton Freeze, the only significant noncash manufacturing overhead cost is depreciation, which is $15,000 per quarter. These noncash depreciation charges are deducted from the total budgeted manufacturing overhead to determine the expected cash disbursements. Hampton Freeze pays all overhead costs involving cash disbursements in the quarter incurred. Note that the company's predetermined overhead rate for the year is $10 per direct labor-hour, which is determined by dividing the total budgeted manufacturing overhead for the year by the total budgeted direct labor-hours for the year.

The Ending Finished Goods Inventory Budget

After completing Schedules 1–5, all of the data needed to compute unit product costs have been compiled. The unit product costs are needed for two reasons: first, to determine cost of goods sold on the budgeted income statement; and second, to determine the value of ending inventory on the balance sheet. The carrying cost of unsold units is computed on the **ending finished goods inventory budget.**

The new financial manager considered using variable costing to prepare Hampton Freeze's budget statements, but she decided to use absorption costing instead because the bank would very likely require absorption costing financial statements. She also knew that it would be easy to convert the absorption costing financial statements to a variable costing basis later. At this point, the primary concern was to determine what financing, if any, would be required in the year 2006 and then to arrange for that financing from the bank.

SCHEDULE 6

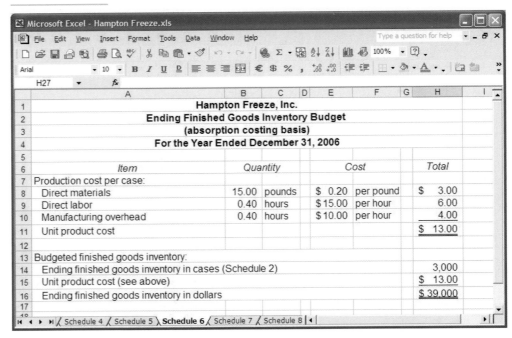

Microsoft Excel - Hampton Freeze.xls

	A	B	C	D	E	F	G	H	I
1			Hampton Freeze, Inc.						
2			Ending Finished Goods Inventory Budget						
3			(absorption costing basis)						
4			For the Year Ended December 31, 2006						
5									
6		Item	Quantity			Cost		Total	
7	Production cost per case:								
8	Direct materials	15.00	pounds		$ 0.20	per pound		$ 3.00	
9	Direct labor	0.40	hours		$15.00	per hour		6.00	
10	Manufacturing overhead	0.40	hours		$10.00	per hour		4.00	
11	Unit product cost							$ 13.00	
12									
13	Budgeted finished goods inventory:								
14	Ending finished goods inventory in cases (Schedule 2)							3,000	
15	Unit product cost (see above)							$ 13.00	
16	Ending finished goods inventory in dollars							$ 39,000	
17									

Schedule 4 / Schedule 5 \ **Schedule 6** / Schedule 7 / Schedule 8

The unit product cost computations are shown in Schedule 6. For Hampton Freeze, the absorption costing unit product cost is $13 per case of popsicles—consisting of $3 of direct materials, $6 of direct labor, and $4 of manufacturing overhead. Manufacturing overhead is applied to units of product at the rate of $10 per direct labor-hour. The budgeted carrying cost of the ending inventory is $39,000.

The Selling and Administrative Expense Budget

The **selling and administrative expense budget** lists the budgeted expenses for areas other than manufacturing. In large organizations, this budget would be a compilation of many smaller, individual budgets submitted by department heads and other persons responsible for selling and administrative expenses. For example, the marketing manager in a large organization would submit a budget detailing the advertising expenses for each budget period.

Schedule 7 contains the selling and administrative expense budget for Hampton Freeze. Like the manufacturing overhead budget, the selling and administrative expense budget is divided into variable and fixed cost components. In the case of Hampton Freeze, the variable selling and administrative expense is $1.80 per case. Consequently, budgeted sales in cases for each quarter are entered at the top of the schedule. These data are taken from the sales budget (Schedule 1). The budgeted variable selling and administrative expenses are determined by multiplying the budgeted cases sold by the variable selling and administrative expense per case. For example, the budgeted variable selling and administrative expense for the first quarter is $18,000 (10,000 cases × $1.80 per case). The fixed selling and administrative expenses (all given data) are then added to the variable selling and administrative expenses to arrive at the total budgeted selling and administrative expenses. Finally, to determine the cash disbursements for selling and administrative expenses, the total budgeted selling and administrative expense is adjusted by subtracting any noncash selling and administrative expenses (in this case, just depreciation).

SCHEDULE 7

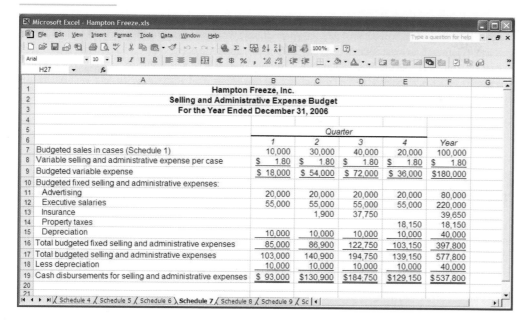

Hampton Freeze, Inc. Selling and Administrative Expense Budget For the Year Ended December 31, 2006					
	Quarter				
	1	2	3	4	Year
Budgeted sales in cases (Schedule 1)	10,000	30,000	40,000	20,000	100,000
Variable selling and administrative expense per case	$ 1.80	$ 1.80	$ 1.80	$ 1.80	$ 1.80
Budgeted variable expense	$ 18,000	$ 54,000	$ 72,000	$ 36,000	$180,000
Budgeted fixed selling and administrative expenses:					
Advertising	20,000	20,000	20,000	20,000	80,000
Executive salaries	55,000	55,000	55,000	55,000	220,000
Insurance		1,900	37,750		39,650
Property taxes				18,150	18,150
Depreciation	10,000	10,000	10,000	10,000	40,000
Total budgeted fixed selling and administrative expenses	85,000	86,900	122,750	103,150	397,800
Total budgeted selling and administrative expenses	103,000	140,900	194,750	139,150	577,800
Less depreciation	10,000	10,000	10,000	10,000	40,000
Cash disbursements for selling and administrative expenses	$ 93,000	$130,900	$184,750	$129,150	$537,800

Budget Analyst

YOU DECIDE

You have been hired as a budget analyst by a regional chain of Italian restaurants with attached bars. Management has had difficulty in the past predicting some of its costs; the assumption has always been that all operating costs are variable with respect to gross restaurant sales. What would you suggest doing to improve the accuracy of the budget forecasts?

---

1. If a company has a beginning merchandise inventory of $50,000, a desired ending merchandise inventory of $30,000, and a budgeted cost of goods sold of $300,000, what is the amount of required inventory purchases?
    a. $320,000
    b. $280,000
    c. $380,000
    d. $300,000
2. Budgeted unit sales for March, April, and May are 75,000, 80,000, and 90,000 units. Management desires to maintain an ending inventory equal to 30% of the next month's unit sales. How many units should be produced in April?
    a. 80,000 units
    b. 83,000 units
    c. 77,000 units
    d. 85,000 units

CONCEPT CHECK

Keeping Current

Jim Bell, Hunstman Corp.'s director of corporate finance, says that his company must frequently update its budgets and its forecasts to meet the demands of investors, creditors, and others. The company updates its annual budget each month, using the most recent data, to provide greater accuracy as the year unfolds. The budget is also used together with sophisticated modeling software to evaluate what effects decisions and various changes in input prices and other parameters might have on future results.

Source: Tim Reason, "Partial Clearing," *CFO*, December 2002, pp. 73–76.

LEARNING OBJECTIVE 8

Prepare a cash budget.

Concept 7-2

The Cash Budget

As illustrated in Exhibit 7–2, the cash budget pulls together much of the data developed in the preceding steps. It is a good idea to review Exhibit 7–2 to get the big picture firmly in mind before moving on.

The cash budget is composed of four major sections:

1. The receipts section.
2. The disbursements section.
3. The cash excess or deficiency section.
4. The financing section.

The receipts section lists all of the cash inflows, except from financing, expected during the budget period. Generally, the major source of receipts will be from sales.

The disbursements section summarizes all cash payments that are planned for the budget period. These payments will include raw materials purchases, direct labor payments, manufacturing overhead costs, and so on, as contained in their respective budgets. In addition, other cash disbursements such as equipment purchases and dividends are listed.

The cash excess or deficiency section is computed as follows:

Cash balance, beginning	XXXX
Add receipts	XXXX
Total cash available	XXXX
Less disbursements	XXXX
Excess (deficiency) of cash available over disbursements	XXXX

If a cash deficiency exists during any budget period, the company will need to borrow funds. If there is a cash excess during any budget period, funds borrowed in previous periods can be repaid or the excess funds can be invested.

The financing section details the borrowings and repayments projected to take place during the budget period. It also lists interest payments that will be due on money borrowed.[1]

Since cash balances can fluctuate widely from day to day, the cash budget should be broken down into time periods that are as short as feasible. While a monthly cash budget is most common, some organizations budget cash on a weekly or even daily basis. A quarterly cash budget for Hampton Freeze that can be further refined as necessary appears in Schedule 8.

---

[1]The format for the statement of cash flows, which is discussed in Chapter 13, may also be used for the cash budget.

SCHEDULE 8

```
Microsoft Excel - Hampton Freeze.xls
File  Edit  View  Insert  Format  Tools  Data  Window  Help          Type a question for help
Arial        10    B I U ...
L39         fx
```

	A	B	C	D	E	F	G	H
1	Interest rate on borrowings		10%					
2								
3			Hampton Freeze, Inc.					
4			Cash Budget					
5			For the Year Ended December 31, 2006					
6								
7					Quarter			
8		Schedule	1	2	3	4	Year	
9	Cash balance, beginning		$42,500	$40,000	$40,000	$40,500	$42,500	
10	Add receipts:							
11	Collections from customers	1	230,000	480,000	740,000	520,000	1,970,000	
12	Total cash available		272,500	520,000	780,000	560,500	2,012,500	
13	Less disbursements:							
14	Direct materials	3	49,500	72,300	100,050	79,350	301,200	
15	Direct labor	4	84,000	192,000	216,000	114,000	606,000	
16	Manufacturing overhead	5	68,000	96,800	103,200	76,000	344,000	
17	Selling and administrative	7	93,000	130,900	184,750	129,150	537,800	
18	Equipment purchases		50,000	40,000	20,000	20,000	130,000	
19	Dividends		8,000	8,000	8,000	8,000	32,000	
20	Total disbursements		352,500	540,000	632,000	426,500	1,951,000	
21	Excess (deficiency) of cash available over disbursements		(80,000)	(20,000)	148,000	134,000	61,500	
22	Financing:							
23	Borrowings (at beginning)*		120,000	60,000	-	-	180,000	
24	Repayments (at ending)		-	-	(100,000)	(80,000)	(180,000)	
25	Interest†		-	-	(7,500)	(6,500)	(14,000)	
26	Total financing		120,000	60,000	(107,500)	(86,500)	(14,000)	
27	Cash balance, ending		$40,000	$40,000	$40,500	$47,500	$47,500	
28								
29								

```
◄ ◄ ► ►◄ Schedule 4 / Schedule 5 / Schedule 6 / Schedule 7 \ Schedule 8 / Schedule 9 / Sched ◄
```

*The company requires a minimum cash balance of $40,000. Therefore, borrowing must be sufficient to cover the cash deficiency of $80,000 in quarter 1 and to provide for the minimum cash balance of $40,000. All borrowings and repayments of principal are in round $1,000 amounts.

†The interest payments relate only to the principal being repaid at the time it is repaid. For example, the interest in quarter 3 relates only to the interest due on the $100,000 principal being repaid from quarter 1 borrowing: $100,000 × 10% per year × ¾ year = $7,500. The interest paid in quarter 4 is computed as follows:

$20,000 × 10% per year × 1 year $2,000
$60,000 × 10% per year × ¾ year 4,500
Total interest paid $6,500

The cash budget builds on the earlier schedules and on additional data that are provided below:

- The beginning cash balance is $42,500.
- Management plans to spend $130,000 during the year on equipment purchases: $50,000 in the first quarter; $40,000 in the second quarter; $20,000 in the third quarter; and $20,000 in the fourth quarter.
- The board of directors has approved cash dividends of $8,000 per quarter.

- Management would like to have a cash balance of at least $40,000 at the beginning of each quarter for contingencies.
- It has been assumed that Hampton Freeze has arranged with a bank for a line of credit that would enable the company to borrow at an interest rate of 10% per year. All borrowing and repayments are in round $1,000 amounts. All borrowing occurs at the beginning of quarters and all repayments are made at the end of quarters. Interest is due when repayments are made and only on the amount of principal that is repaid.

The cash budget is prepared one quarter at a time, starting with the first quarter. The cash budget was begun by entering the beginning balance of cash for the first quarter of $42,500—a number that is given above. Receipts—in this case, just the $230,000 in cash collections from customers—are added to the beginning balance to arrive at the total cash available of $272,500. Since the total disbursements are $352,500 and the total cash available is only $272,500, there is a shortfall of $80,000. Since management would like to have a beginning cash balance of at least $40,000 for the second quarter, the company will need to borrow $120,000.

Required Borrowings at the End of the First Quarter	
Desired ending cash balance	$ 40,000
Plus deficiency of cash available over disbursements	80,000
Required borrowings	$120,000

The second quarter of the cash budget is handled similarly. Note that the ending cash balance for the first quarter is brought forward as the beginning cash balance for the second quarter. Also note that additional borrowing is required in the second quarter because of the continued cash shortfall.

Required Borrowings at the End of the Second Quarter	
Desired ending cash balance	$40,000
Plus deficiency of cash available over disbursements	20,000
Required borrowings	$60,000

In the third quarter, the cash flow situation improves dramatically and the excess of cash available over disbursements is $148,000. This makes it possible for the company to repay part of its loan from the bank, which now totals $180,000. How much can be repaid? The total amount of the principal *and* interest that can be repaid is determined as follows:

Total Maximum Feasible Loan Payments at the End of the Third Quarter	
Excess of cash available over disbursements	$148,000
Less desired ending cash balance	40,000
Maximum feasible principal and interest payment	$108,000

The next step—figuring out the exact amount of the loan payment—is tricky since interest must be paid on the principal amount that is repaid. In this case, the principal amount that is repaid must be less than $108,000, so we know that we would be paying off part of the loan that was taken out at the beginning of the first quarter. Since the repayment would be made at the end of the third quarter, interest would have accrued for three quarters. So the interest owed would be ¾ of 10%, or 7.5%. Either a trial-and-error or an algebraic approach will lead to the conclusion that the maximum principal repayment that can be made is $100,000.[2] The interest payment would be 7.5% of this amount, or $7,500—making the total payment $107,500.

In the fourth quarter, all of the loan and accumulated interest are paid off. If all loans are not repaid at the end of the year and budgeted financial statements are prepared, then interest must be accrued on the unpaid loans. This interest will not appear on the cash budget (since it has not yet been paid), but it will appear as interest expense on the budgeted income statement and as a liability on the budgeted balance sheet.

As with the production and raw materials budgets, the amounts under the Year column in the cash budget are not always the sum of the amounts for the four quarters. In particular, the beginning cash balance for the year is the same as the beginning cash balance for the first quarter and the ending cash balance for the year is the same as the ending cash balance for the fourth quarter. Also note the beginning cash balance in any quarter is the same as the ending cash balance for the previous quarter.

Concentrating on the Cash Flow

IN BUSINESS

Burlington Northern Santa Fe (BNSF) operates the second largest railroad in the United States. The company's senior vice president, CFO, and treasurer is Tom Hunt, who reports that "As a general theme, we've become very cash-flow-oriented." After the merger of the Burlington Northern and Santa Fe railroads, the company went through a number of years in which they were investing heavily and consequently had negative cash flows. To keep on top of the company's cash position, Hunt has a cash forecast prepared every month. "Everything falls like dominoes from free cash flow," Hunt says. "It provides us with alternatives. Right now, the alternative of choice is buying back our own stock . . . [b]ut it could be increasing dividends or making acquisitions. All those things are not even on the radar screen if you don't have free cash flow."

Source: Randy Myers, "Cash Crop: The 2000 Working Capital Survey," *CFO,* August 2000, pp. 59–82.

The Budgeted Income Statement

A budgeted income statement can be prepared from the data developed in Schedules 1–8. *The budgeted income statement is one of the key schedules in the budget process.* It shows the company's planned profit, and serves as a benchmark to compare to subsequent performance.

Schedule 9 contains the budgeted income statement for Hampton Freeze.

---

[2]The algebraic approach to determining the amount that can be repaid on the loan follows:
Let X be the amount of the principal repayment. Then $10\% \times \frac{3}{4} \times X$ is the amount of interest owed on that principal amount. Since the company can afford to pay at most $108,000 to the bank, the sum of the principal repayment and the interest payment cannot exceed $108,000.

$$X + 10\% \times \tfrac{3}{4} \times X \le \$108,000, \text{ or}$$

$$X \le \$100,465$$

Since all repayments must be in round $1,000 amounts, the appropriate principal repayment is $100,000.

SCHEDULE 9

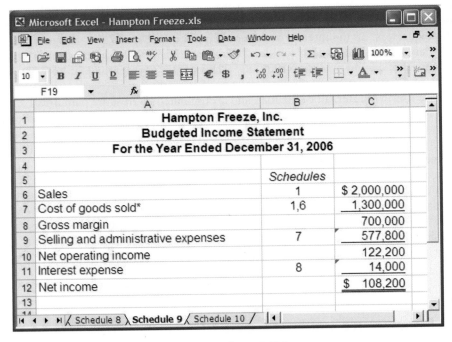

*100,000 cases sold × $13 per case = $1,300,000.

The Budgeted Balance Sheet

The budgeted balance sheet is developed from the balance sheet from the beginning of the
budget period and data contained in the various schedules. Hampton Freeze's budgeted balance
sheet is presented in Schedule 10. Some of the data on the budgeted balance sheet have
been taken from the company's previous end-of-year balance sheet, which appears below:

Hampton Freeze, Inc.
Balance Sheet
December 31, 2005

Assets

Current assets:		
Cash	$ 42,500	
Accounts receivable	90,000	
Raw materials inventory (21,000 pounds)	4,200	
Finished goods inventory (2,000 cases)	26,000	
Total current assets		$162,700
Plant and equipment:		
Land	80,000	
Buildings and equipment	700,000	
Accumulated depreciation	(292,000)	
Plant and equipment, net		488,000
Total assets		$650,700
Liabilities and Stockholders' Equity		
Current liabilities:		
Accounts payable (raw materials)		$ 25,800
Stockholders' equity:		
Common stock, no par	$175,000	
Retained earnings	449,900	
Total stockholders' equity		624,900
Total liabilities and stockholders' equity		$650,700

SCHEDULE 10

Microsoft Excel - Hampton Freeze.xls

File   Edit   View   Insert   Format   Tools   Data   Window   Help   Type a question for help

12   B I U

H27

	A	B	C	D	E
1	Hampton Freeze, Inc.				
2	Budgeted Balance Sheet				
3	December 31, 2006				
4					
5	Assets				
6	Current assets:				
7	Cash	$ 47,500	(a)		
8	Accounts receivable	120,000	(b)		
9	Raw materials inventory	4,500	(c)		
10	Finished goods inventory	39,000	(d)		
11	Total current assets			$ 211,000	
12	Plant and equipment:				
13	Land	80,000	(e)		
14	Buildings and equipment	830,000	(f)		
15	Accumulated depreciation	(392,000)	(g)		
16	Plant and equipment, net			518,000	
17	Total assets			$ 729,000	
18					
19	Liabilities and Stockholders' Equity				
20	Current liabilities:				
21	Accounts payable (raw materials)			$ 27,900	(h)
22	Stockholders' equity:				
23	Common stock, no par	$ 175,000	(i)		
24	Retained earnings	526,100	(j)		
25	Total stockholders' equity			701,100	
26	Total liabilities and stockholders' equity			$ 729,000	
27					

Schedule 8 / Schedule 9 / **Schedule 10**

Explanation of December 31, 2006, balance sheet figures:

(a) The ending cash balance, as projected by the cash budget in Schedule 8.
(b) Thirty percent of fourth-quarter sales, from Schedule 1 ($400,000 × 30% = $120,000).
(c) From Schedule 3, the ending raw materials inventory will be 22,500 pounds. This material costs $0.20 per pound. Therefore, the ending inventory in dollars will be 22,500 pounds × $0.20 = $4,500.
(d) From Schedule 6.
(e) From the December 31, 2005 balance sheet (no change).
(f) The December 31, 2005 balance sheet indicated a balance of $700,000. During 2006, $130,000 of additional equipment will be purchased (see Schedule 8), bringing the December 31, 2006 balance to $830,000.
(g) The December 31, 2005 balance sheet indicated a balance of $292,000. During 2006, $100,000 of depreciation will be taken ($60,000 on Schedule 5 and $40,000 on Schedule 7), bringing the December 31, 2006 balance to $392,000.
(h) One-half of the fourth-quarter raw materials purchases, from Schedule 3.
(i) From the December 31, 2005 balance sheet (no change).

(j)

December 31, 2005, balance	$449,900
Add net income, from Schedule 9	108,200
	558,100
Deduct dividends paid, from Schedule 8	32,000
December 31, 2006, balance	$526,100

CONCEPT CHECK

3. March, April, and May sales are $100,000, $120,000, and $125,000, respectively. A total of 80% of all sales are credit sales and 20% are cash sales. A total of 60% of credit sales are collected in the month of the sale and 40% are collected in the next month. There are no bad debt expenses. What is the amount of cash collections for April?
   a. $89,600
   b. $111,600
   c. $113,600
   d. $132,600

4. Referring to the facts in question 3 above, what is the accounts receivable balance at the end of May?
   a. $40,000
   b. $50,000
   c. $72,000
   d. $80,000

Assuming that the company's plans unfold as expected, the master budget indicates that the company will be profitable, its balance sheet will be sound, but that the company will need to borrow in the short term to make payments to employees and suppliers. Armed with this data, the company can approach a bank to arrange for a line of credit or other form of loan. It is much easier to arrange for a loan before it is needed than to show up at the bank begging for a loan in an emergency situation. With the master budget, the company can show the bank a solid plan for repaying any loans. This is not the primary purpose of budgeting. As discussed previously, the primary purposes of budgeting include communicating plans, coordinating efforts, allocating resources, and setting benchmarks. Nevertheless, budgets also help managers uncover potential problems such as cash shortfalls.

DECISION MAKER

Bank Manager

You are the manager of a branch of a state bank located in a medium-sized community. The owner of a small manufacturing company in the community wants to apply for an unsecured line of credit for the upcoming year. The company has been in business for several years but has experienced seasonal cash shortages as it has grown. What documents would you request from the owner to back up the loan request and what tests would you apply to the documents to ensure that they are realistic?

IN BUSINESS

Automating the Budgeting Process

A number of companies, including Texaco, Fujitsu, Sprint, Nationwide Financial Services, Nortel Networks, Owens Corning, and Xilinx have been attempting to streamline and automate the budgeting process. The goal is to eliminate the conventional iterative budgeting process that often finds preliminary budgets being passed up and down the management hierarchy many times before final agreement is reached—wasting much time and resulting in budgets that often don't reconcile. Apart from the tremendous technical challenges of integrating diverse budgets from many different operations, automation faces a high behavioral hurdle. As Greg Vesey of Texaco states, "Planning is the most political of all processes to fall under the finance function." Consequently, as many as half of all automation efforts fail. Companies such as National Semiconductor Corp. have given up entirely and have returned to their old budgeting methods.

Source: Russ Banham, "The Revolution in Planning," *CFO*, August 1999, pp. 46–56.

SUMMARY

LO1   Understand why organizations budget and the processes they use to create budgets.

Organizations budget for a variety of reasons, including to communicate management's plans throughout the organization, to force managers to think about and plan for the future, to allocate resources within the organization, to identify bottlenecks before they occur, to coordinate activities, and to provide benchmarks for evaluating subsequent performance.

Budgets should be developed with the full participation of all managers who will be subject to budgetary controls.

LO2   Prepare a sales budget, including a schedule of expected cash collections.

The sales budget forms the foundation for the master budget. It provides details concerning the anticipated unit and dollar sales.

The schedule of expected cash collections is based on the sales budget, the expected breakdown between cash and credit sales, and the expected pattern of collections on credit sales.

LO3   Prepare a production budget.

The production budget details how many units must be produced each budget period to satisfy expected sales and to provide for adequate levels of finished goods inventories.

LO4   Prepare a direct materials budget, including a schedule of expected cash disbursements for purchases of materials.

The direct materials budget shows the materials that must be purchased each budget period to meet anticipated production requirements and to provide for adequate levels of materials inventories.

Cash disbursements for purchases of materials will depend on the amount of materials purchased in each budget period and the company's policies concerning payments to suppliers for materials bought on credit.

LO5   Prepare a direct labor budget.

The direct labor budget shows the direct labor-hours that are required to meet the production schedule as detailed in the production budget. The direct labor-hour requirements are used to determine the direct labor cost in each budget period.

LO6   Prepare a manufacturing overhead budget.

Manufacturing overhead consists of both variable and fixed manufacturing overhead. The variable manufacturing overhead ultimately depends on the number of units produced from the production budget. The variable and fixed manufacturing overhead costs are combined to determine the total manufacturing overhead. Any noncash manufacturing overhead such as depreciation is deducted from the total manufacturing overhead to determine the cash disbursements for manufacturing overhead.

LO7   Prepare a selling and administrative expense budget.

Like manufacturing overhead, selling and administrative expenses consist of both variable and fixed expenses. The variable expenses depend on the number of units sold or some other measure of activity. The variable and fixed expenses are combined to determine the total selling and administrative expense. Any noncash selling and administrative expenses such as depreciation are deducted from the total to determine the cash disbursements for selling and administrative expenses.

LO8   Prepare a cash budget.

The cash budget is a critical piece of the master budget. It permits managers to anticipate and plan for cash shortfalls.

The cash budget is organized into a receipts section, a disbursements section, a cash excess or deficiency section, and a financing section. The cash budget draws on information taken from nearly all of the other budgets and schedules including the schedule of cash collections, the schedule of cash disbursements for purchases of materials, the direct labor budget, the manufacturing overhead budget, and the selling and administrative expense budget.

LO9   Prepare a budgeted income statement.

The budgeted income statement is constructed using data from the sales budget, the ending finished goods inventory budget, the manufacturing overhead budget, the selling and administrative budget, and the cash budget.

LO10   Prepare a budgeted balance sheet.

The budgeted balance sheet is constructed using data from virtually all other parts of the master budget.

GUIDANCE ANSWERS TO *DECISION MAKER* AND *YOU DECIDE*

Budget Analyst (p. 311)

Not all costs are variable with respect to gross restaurant sales. For example, assuming no change in the number of restaurant sites, rental costs are probably fixed. To more accurately forecast costs for the budget, costs should be separated into variable and fixed components. Furthermore, more appropriate activity measures should be selected for the variable costs. For example, gross restaurant sales may be divided into food sales and bar sales—each of which could serve as an activity measure for some costs. In addition, some costs (such as the costs of free dinner rolls) may be variable with respect to the number of diners rather than with respect to food or bar sales. Other activity measures may permit even more accurate cost predictions.

Bank Manager (p. 318)

At minimum, you should request a cash budget with supporting documents including a sales budget, production budget, direct materials budget, direct labor budget, manufacturing overhead budget, selling and administrative expense budget, budgeted income statement, and budgeted balance sheet. You should check that the cash budget provides for repayment of the loan, plus interest, and that it leaves the company with sufficient cash reserves to start the new year. You should also check that assumptions concerning sales growth and fixed and variable costs are consistent with the company's recent experience.

GUIDANCE ANSWERS TO CONCEPT CHECKS

1. **Choice b.** Required inventory purchases are calculated as follows: Cost of goods sold of $300,000 + Ending inventory of $30,000 − Beginning inventory of $50,000 = $280,000.
2. **Choice b.** 80,000 units sold in April + 27,000 units of desired ending inventory − 24,000 units of beginning inventory = 83,000 units.
3. **Choice c.** Cash collections for April are calculated as follows: ($100,000 × 80% × 40%) + ($120,000 × 20%) + ($120,000 × 80% × 60%) = $113,600.
4. **Choice a.** The May 31 accounts receivable balance is $125,000 × 80% × 40% = $40,000.

REVIEW PROBLEM: BUDGET SCHEDULES

Mynor Corporation manufactures and sells a product that has seasonal variations in demand, with peak sales coming in the third quarter. The following information concerns operations for Year 2—the coming year—and for the first two quarters of Year 3:

a. The company's single product sells for $8 per unit. Budgeted sales in units for the next six quarters are as follows (all sales are on credit):

	Year 2 Quarter				Year 3 Quarter	
	1	2	3	4	1	2
Budgeted unit sales	40,000	60,000	100,000	50,000	70,000	80,000

b. Sales are collected in the following pattern: 75% in the quarter the sales are made, and the remaining 25% in the following quarter. On January 1, Year 2, the company's balance sheet showed $65,000 in accounts receivable, all of which will be collected in the first quarter of the year. Bad debts are negligible and can be ignored.

c. The company desires an ending finished goods inventory at the end of each quarter equal to 30% of the budgeted unit sales for the next quarter. On December 31, Year 1, the company had 12,000 units on hand.

d. Five pounds of raw materials are required to complete one unit of product. The company requires ending raw materials inventory at the end of each quarter equal to 10% of the following quarter's production needs. On December 31, Year 1, the company had 23,000 pounds of raw materials on hand.

e. The raw material costs $0.80 per pound. Raw material purchases are paid for in the following pattern: 60% paid in the quarter the purchases are made, and the remaining 40% paid in the following quarter. On January 1, Year 2, the company's balance sheet showed $81,500 in accounts payable for raw material purchases, all of which will be paid for in the first quarter of the year.

Required:

Prepare the following budgets and schedules for the year, showing both quarterly and total figures:

1. A sales budget and a schedule of expected cash collections.
2. A production budget.
3. A direct materials budget and a schedule of expected cash payments for purchases of materials.

Solution to Review Problem

1. The sales budget is prepared as follows:

| | Year 2 Quarter | | | | |
	1	2	3	4	Year
Budgeted unit sales........	40,000	60,000	100,000	50,000	250,000
Selling price per unit	× $8	× $8	× $8	× $8	× $8
Total sales	$320,000	$480,000	$800,000	$400,000	$2,000,000

Based on the budgeted sales above, the schedule of expected cash collections is prepared as follows:

| | Year 2 Quarter | | | | |
	1	2	3	4	Year
Accounts receivable, beginning balance.............	$ 65,000				$ 65,000
First-quarter sales ($320,000 × 75%, 25%)...........	240,000	$ 80,000			320,000
Second-quarter sales ($480,000 × 75%, 25%)		360,000	$120,000		480,000
Third-quarter sales ($800,000 × 75%, 25%)			600,000	$200,000	800,000
Fourth-quarter sales ($400,000 × 75%).............				300,000	300,000
Total cash collections	$305,000	$440,000	$720,000	$500,000	$1,965,000

2. Based on the sales budget in units, the production budget is prepared as follows:

| | Year 2 Quarter | | | | | Year 3 Quarter | |
	1	2	3	4	Year 2	1	2
Budgeted unit sales.......................	40,000	60,000	100,000	50,000	250,000	70,000	80,000
Add desired ending inventory of finished goods*....	18,000	30,000	15,000	21,000†	21,000	24,000	
Total needs......................	58,000	90,000	115,000	71,000	271,000	94,000	
Less beginning inventory of finished goods	12,000	18,000	30,000	15,000	12,000	21,000	
Required production......................	46,000	72,000	85,000	56,000	259,000	73,000	

*30% of the following quarter's budgeted sales in units.
†30% of the budgeted Year 3 first-quarter sales.

3. Based on the production budget, raw materials will need to be purchased during the year as follows:

	Year 2 Quarter					Year 3 Quarter
	1	2	3	4	Year 2	1
Required production (units)	46,000	72,000	85,000	56,000	259,000	73,000
Raw materials needed per unit (pounds)	× 5	× 5	× 5	× 5	× 5	× 5
Production needs (pounds)......................	230,000	360,000	425,000	280,000	1,295,000	365,000
Add desired ending inventory of raw materials (pounds)*......................	36,000	42,500	28,000	36,500†	36,500	
Total needs (pounds)............................	266,000	402,500	453,000	316,500	1,331,500	
Less beginning inventory of raw materials (pounds)............................	23,000	36,000	42,500	28,000	23,000	
Raw materials to be purchased (pounds)	243,000	366,500	410,500	288,500	1,308,500	

*10% of the following quarter's production needs in pounds.
†10% of the Year 3 first-quarter production needs in pounds.

Based on the raw material purchases above, expected cash payments are computed as follows:

	Year 2 Quarter				Year
	1	2	3	4	
Cost of raw materials to be purchased at $0.80 per pound	$194,400	$293,200	$328,400	$230,800	$1,046,800
Accounts payable, beginning balance	$ 81,500				$ 81,500
First-quarter purchases ($194,400 × 60%, 40%).........	116,640	$ 77,760			194,400
Second-quarter purchases ($293,200 × 60%, 40%)		175,920	$117,280		293,200
Third-quarter purchases ($328,400 × 60%, 40%)			197,040	$131,360	328,400
Fourth-quarter purchases ($230,800 × 60%)............				138,480	138,480
Total cash disbursements	$198,140	$253,680	$314,320	$269,840	$1,035,980

GLOSSARY

Budget   A detailed plan for acquiring and using financial and other resources over a specified time period. (p. 294)

Budget committee   A group of key managers who are responsible for overall policy matters relating to the budget program and for coordinating the preparation of the budget. (p. 298)

Cash budget   A detailed plan showing how cash resources will be acquired and used over some specific time period. (p. 300)

Control   Those steps taken by management to increase the likelihood that the objectives set down at the planning stage are attained and that all parts of the organization are working together toward that goal. (p. 294)

Direct labor budget   A detailed plan showing labor requirements over some specific time period. (p. 307)

Direct materials budget   A detailed plan showing the amount of raw materials that must be purchased during a period to meet both production and inventory needs. (p. 305)

Ending finished goods inventory budget   A budget showing the dollar amount of unsold finished goods inventory that will appear on the ending balance sheet. (p. 309)

Manufacturing overhead budget   A detailed plan showing the production costs, other than direct materials and direct labor, that will be incurred over a specified time period. (p. 308)

Master budget   A summary of a company's plans in which specific targets are set for sales, production, and financing activities and that generally culminates in a cash budget, budgeted income statement, and budgeted balance sheet. (p. 294)

Merchandise purchases budget   A budget used by a merchandising company that shows the amount of goods that must be purchased from suppliers during the period. (p. 305)

Participative budget   See *self-imposed budget.* (p. 296)

Planning   Developing objectives and preparing budgets to achieve these objectives. (p. 294)

Production budget   A detailed plan showing the number of units that must be produced during a period in order to meet both sales and inventory needs. (p. 303)

Responsibility accounting   A system of accountability in which managers are held responsible for those items of revenue and cost—and only those items—over which the manager can exert significant control. The managers are held responsible for differences between budgeted goals and actual results. (p. 295)

Sales budget   A detailed schedule showing the expected sales for coming periods; these sales are typically expressed in both dollars and units. (p. 299)

Self-imposed budget   A method of preparing budgets in which managers prepare their own budgets. These budgets are then reviewed by the manager's supervisor, and any issues are resolved by mutual agreement. (p. 296)

Selling and administrative expense budget   A detailed schedule of planned expenses that will be incurred in areas other than manufacturing during a budget period. (p. 310)

Zero-based budget   A method of budgeting in which managers are required to justify all costs as if the programs involved were being proposed for the first time. (p. 298)

QUESTIONS

7–1   What is a budget? What is budgetary control?

7–2   What are some of the major benefits to be gained from budgeting?

7–3   What is meant by the term *responsibility accounting?*

7–4   What is a master budget? Briefly describe its contents.

7–5   Why is the sales forecast the starting point in budgeting?

7–6   "As a practical matter, planning and control mean exactly the same thing." Do you agree? Explain.

7–7   What is a self-imposed budget? What are the major advantages of self-imposed budgets? What caution must be exercised in their use?

7–8   How can budgeting assist a company in its employment policies?

7–9   "The principal purpose of the cash budget is to see how much cash the company will have in the bank at the end of the year." Do you agree? Explain.

BRIEF EXERCISES

BRIEF EXERCISE 7–1   Budget Process   (LO1)
The following terms pertain to the budgeting process:

Benchmarks	Bottlenecks
Budget	Budget committee
Control	Imposed from above
Motivation	Planning
Responsibility accounting	Self-imposed budget

Required:
Fill in the blanks with the most appropriate word or phrase from the above list.

1. _____ is generally higher when an individual participates in setting his or her own goals than when the goals are imposed from above.

2. If a manager is not able to meet the budget and it has been _____, the manager can always say that the budget was unreasonable or unrealistic to start with, and therefore was impossible to meet.

3. A _____ is a detailed plan for acquiring and using financial and other resources over a specified time period.

4. _____ involves developing objectives and preparing various budgets to achieve those objectives.

5. The budgeting process can uncover potential _____ before they occur.
6. _____ involves the steps taken by management to increase the likelihood that the objectives set down at the planning stage are attained.
7. Budgets define goals and objectives that can serve as _____ for evaluating subsequent performance.
8. In _____, a manager is held accountable for those items, and only those items, over which he or she has significant control.
9. A _____ is one that is prepared with the full cooperation and participation of managers at all levels of the organization.
10. A _____ is usually responsible for overall policy matters relating to the budget program and for coordinating the preparation of the budget itself.

BRIEF EXERCISE 7–2   Schedule of Expected Cash Collections   [LO2]
Silver Company sells a product that is very popular as a Mother's Day gift. Thus, peak sales occur in May of each year. These peak sales are shown in the company's sales budget for the second quarter given below (all sales are on account):

	April	May	June	Total
Budgeted sales	$300,000	$500,000	$200,000	$1,000,000

From past experience, the company has learned that 20% of a month's sales are collected in the month of sale, another 70% are collected in the month following sale, and the remaining 10% are collected in the second month following sale. Bad debts are negligible and can be ignored. February sales totaled $230,000, and March sales totaled $260,000.

Required:
1. Prepare a schedule of expected cash collections from sales, by month and in total, for the second quarter.
2. Assume that the company will prepare a budgeted balance sheet as of June 30. Compute the accounts receivable as of that date.

BRIEF EXERCISE 7–3   Production Budget   [LO3]
Down Under Products, Ltd., of Australia has budgeted sales of its popular boomerang for the next four months as follows:

	Sales in Units
April	50,000
May	75,000
June	90,000
July	80,000

The company is now in the process of preparing a production budget for the second quarter. Past experience has shown that end-of-month inventory levels must equal 10% of the following month's sales. The inventory at the end of March was 5,000 units.

Required:
Prepare a production budget for the second quarter; in your budget, show the number of units to be produced each month and for the quarter in total.

BRIEF EXERCISE 7–4   Direct Materials Budget   [LO4]
Three grams of musk oil are required for each bottle of Mink Caress, a very popular perfume made by a small company in western Siberia. The cost of the musk oil is 150 roubles per kilogram. (Siberia is located in Russia, whose currency is the rouble.) Budgeted production of Mink Caress is given below by quarters for Year 2 and for the first quarter of Year 3.

	Year 2 Quarter				Year 3 Quarter
	First	Second	Third	Fourth	First
Budgeted production, in bottles	60,000	90,000	150,000	100,000	70,000

Musk oil has become so popular as a perfume ingredient that it has become necessary to carry large inventories as a precaution against stock-outs. For this reason, the inventory of musk oil at the end of a quarter must be equal to 20% of the following quarter's production needs. Some 36,000 grams of musk oil will be on hand to start the first quarter of Year 2.

Required:

Prepare a direct materials budget for musk oil, by quarter and in total, for Year 2. At the bottom of your budget, show the amount of purchases in roubles for each quarter and for the year in total.

BRIEF EXERCISE 7–5   Direct Labor Budget   [LO5]

The production department of Rordan Corporation has submitted the following forecast of units to be produced by quarter for the upcoming fiscal year.

	1st Quarter	2nd Quarter	3rd Quarter	4th Quarter
Units to be produced	8,000	6,500	7,000	7,500

Each unit requires 0.35 direct labor-hours, and direct laborers are paid $12.00 per hour.

Required:

1. Construct the company's direct labor budget for the upcoming fiscal year, assuming that the direct labor work force is adjusted each quarter to match the number of hours required to produce the forecasted number of units produced.
2. Construct the company's direct labor budget for the upcoming fiscal year, assuming that the direct labor work force is not adjusted each quarter. Instead, assume that the company's direct labor work force consists of permanent employees who are guaranteed to be paid for at least 2,600 hours of work each quarter. If the number of required direct labor-hours is less than this number, the workers are paid for 2,600 hours anyway. Any hours worked in excess of 2,600 hours in a quarter are paid at the rate of 1.5 times the normal hourly rate for direct labor.

BRIEF EXERCISE 7–6   Manufacturing Overhead Budget   [LO6]

The direct labor budget of Yuvwell Corporation for the upcoming fiscal year contains the following details concerning budgeted direct labor-hours.

	1st Quarter	2nd Quarter	3rd Quarter	4th Quarter
Budgeted direct labor-hours	8,000	8,200	8,500	7,800

The company's variable manufacturing overhead rate is $3.25 per direct labor-hour and the company's fixed manufacturing overhead is $48,000 per quarter. The only noncash item included in the fixed manufacturing overhead is depreciation, which is $16,000 per quarter.

Required:

1. Construct the company's manufacturing overhead budget for the upcoming fiscal year.
2. Compute the company's manufacturing overhead rate (including both variable and fixed manufacturing overhead) for the upcoming fiscal year. Round off to the nearest whole cent.

BRIEF EXERCISE 7–7   Selling and Administrative Expense Budget   [LO7]

The budgeted unit sales of Weller Company for the upcoming fiscal year are provided below:

	1st Quarter	2nd Quarter	3rd Quarter	4th Quarter
Budgeted unit sales	15,000	16,000	14,000	13,000

The company's variable selling and administrative expense per unit is $2.50. Fixed selling and administrative expenses include advertising expenses of $8,000 per quarter, executive salaries of $35,000 per quarter, and depreciation of $20,000 per quarter. In addition, the company will make insurance payments of $5,000 in the first quarter and $5,000 in the third quarter. Finally, property taxes of $8,000 will be paid in the second quarter.

Required:
Prepare the company's selling and administrative expense budget for the upcoming fiscal year.

BRIEF EXERCISE 7–8   Cash Budget   (LO8)
Garden Depot is a retailer that is preparing its budget for the upcoming fiscal year. Management has prepared the following summary of its budgeted cash flows:

	1st Quarter	2nd Quarter	3rd Quarter	4th Quarter
Total cash receipts	$180,000	$330,000	$210,000	$230,000
Total cash disbursements	$260,000	$230,000	$220,000	$240,000

The company's beginning cash balance for the upcoming fiscal year will be $20,000. The company requires a minimum cash balance of $10,000 and may borrow any amount needed from a local bank at an annual interest rate of 12%. The company may borrow any amount at the beginning of any quarter and may repay its loans, or any part of its loans, at the end of any quarter. Interest payments are due on any principal at the time it is repaid.

Required:
Prepare the company's cash budget for the upcoming fiscal year.

BRIEF EXERCISE 7–9   Budgeted Income Statement   (LO9)
Gig Harbor Boating is the wholesale distributor of a small recreational catamaran sailboat. Management has prepared the following summary data to use in its annual budgeting process:

Budgeted unit sales	460
Selling price per unit	$1,950
Cost per unit	$1,575
Variable selling and administrative expenses (per unit)	$75
Fixed selling and administrative expenses (per year)	$105,000
Interest expense for the year	$14,000

Required:
Prepare the company's budgeted income statement. Use the absorption costing income statement format shown in schedule?

BRIEF EXERCISE 7–10   Budgeted Balance Sheet   (LO10)
The management of Mecca Copy, a photocopying center located on University Avenue, has compiled the following data to use in preparing its budgeted balance sheet for next year:

	Ending Balances
Cash	?
Accounts receivable	$8,100
Supplies inventory	$3,200
Equipment	$34,000
Accumulated depreciation	$16,000
Accounts payable	$1,800
Common stock	$5,000
Retained earnings	?

The beginning balance of retained earnings was $28,000, net income is budgeted to be $11,500, and dividends are budgeted to be $4,800.

Required:
Prepare the company's budgeted balance sheet.

EXERCISES

EXERCISE 7–11 Sales and Production Budgets (LO2, LO3)

The marketing department of Jessi Corporation has submitted the following sales forecast for the upcoming fiscal year.

	1st Quarter	2nd Quarter	3rd Quarter	4th Quarter
Budgeted unit sales	11,000	12,000	14,000	13,000

The selling price of the company's product is $18.00 per unit. Management expects to collect 65% of sales in the quarter in which the sales are made, 30% in the following quarter, and 5% of sales are expected to be uncollectible. The beginning balance of accounts receivable, all of which is expected to be collected in the first quarter, is $70,200.

The company expects to start the first quarter with 1,650 units in finished goods inventory. Management desires an ending finished goods inventory in each quarter equal to 15% of the next quarter's budgeted sales. The desired ending finished goods inventory for the fourth quarter is 1,850 units.

Required:

1. Prepare the company's sales budget and schedule of expected cash collections.
2. Prepare the company's production budget for the upcoming fiscal year.

EXERCISE 7–12 Production and Direct Materials Budgets (LO3, LO4)

The marketing department of Gaeber Industries has submitted the following sales forecast for the upcoming fiscal year.

	1st Quarter	2nd Quarter	3rd Quarter	4th Quarter
Budgeted unit sales	8,000	7,000	6,000	7,000

The company expects to start the first quarter with 1,600 units in finished goods inventory. Management desires an ending finished goods inventory in each quarter equal to 20% of the next quarter's budgeted sales. The desired ending finished goods inventory for the fourth quarter is 1,700 units.

In addition, the beginning raw materials inventory for the first quarter is budgeted to be 3,120 pounds and the beginning accounts payable for the first quarter is budgeted to be $14,820.

Each unit requires 2 pounds of raw material that costs $4.00 per pound. Management desires to end each quarter with an inventory of raw materials equal to 20% of the following quarter's production needs. The desired ending inventory for the fourth quarter is 3,140 pounds. Management plans to pay for 75% of raw material purchases in the quarter acquired and 25% in the following quarter.

Required:

1. Prepare the company's production budget for the upcoming fiscal year.
2. Prepare the company's direct materials budget and schedule of expected cash disbursements for materials for the upcoming fiscal year.

EXERCISE 7–13 Direct Materials and Direct Labor Budgets (LO4, LO5)

The production department of Hareston Company has submitted the following forecast of units to be produced by quarter for the upcoming fiscal year.

	1st Quarter	2nd Quarter	3rd Quarter	4th Quarter
Units to be produced	7,000	8,000	6,000	5,000

In addition, the beginning raw materials inventory for the first quarter is budgeted to be 1,400 pounds and the beginning accounts payable for the first quarter is budgeted to be $2,940.

Each unit requires 2 pounds of raw material that costs $1.40 per pound. Management desires to end each quarter with an inventory of raw materials equal to 10% of the following quarter's production needs. The desired ending inventory for the fourth quarter is 1,500 pounds. Management plans to pay for 80% of raw material purchases in the quarter acquired and 20% in the following quarter. Each unit requires 0.60 direct labor-hours and direct labor-hour workers are paid $14.00 per hour.

Required:
1. Prepare the company's direct materials budget and schedule of expected cash disbursements for materials for the upcoming fiscal year.
2. Prepare the company's direct labor budget for the upcoming fiscal year, assuming that the direct labor work force is adjusted each quarter to match the number of hours required to produce the forecasted number of units produced.

EXERCISE 7–14   Direct Labor and Manufacturing Overhead Budgets   (LO5, LO6)
The production department of Raredon Corporation has submitted the following forecast of units to be produced by quarter for the upcoming fiscal year.

	1st Quarter	2nd Quarter	3rd Quarter	4th Quarter
Units to be produced	12,000	14,000	13,000	11,000

Each unit requires 0.70 direct labor-hours, and direct labor-hour workers are paid $10.50 per hour.

In addition, the variable manufacturing overhead rate is $1.50 per direct labor-hour. The fixed manufacturing overhead is $80,000 per quarter. The only noncash element of manufacturing overhead is depreciation, which is $22,000 per quarter.

Required:
1. Prepare the company's direct labor budget for the upcoming fiscal year, assuming that the direct labor work force is adjusted each quarter to match the number of hours required to produce the forecasted number of units produced.
2. Prepare the company's manufacturing overhead budget.

EXERCISE 7–15   Schedules of Expected Cash Collections and Disbursements; Cash Budget [LO2, LO4, LO8]
You have been asked to prepare a December cash budget for Ashton Company, a distributor of exercise equipment. The following information is available about the company's operations:

CHECK FIGURE
(3) Ending cash balance:
$20,000

a.   The cash balance on December 1 is $40,000.
b.   Actual sales for October and November and expected sales for December are as follows:

	October	November	December
Cash sales	$65,000	$70,000	$83,000
Sales on account	$400,000	$525,000	$600,000

Sales on account are collected over a three-month period as follows: 20% collected in the month of sale, 60% collected in the month following sale, and 18% collected in the second month following sale. The remaining 2% is uncollectible.

c.   Purchases of inventory will total $280,000 for December. Thirty percent of a month's inventory purchases are paid during the month of purchase. The accounts payable remaining from November's inventory purchases total $161,000, all of which will be paid in December.

d.   Selling and administrative expenses are budgeted at $430,000 for December. Of this amount, $50,000 is for depreciation.

e.   A new web server for the Marketing Department costing $76,000 will be purchased for cash during December, and dividends totaling $9,000 will be paid during the month.

f.   The company maintains a minimum cash balance of $20,000. An open line of credit is available from the company's bank to bolster the cash position as needed.

Required:
1. Prepare a schedule of expected cash collections for December.
2. Prepare a schedule of expected cash disbursements for merchandise purchases for December.
3. Prepare a cash budget for December. Indicate in the financing section any borrowing that will be needed during the month.

EXERCISE 7–16   Cash Budget Analysis   [LO8]

A cash budget, by quarters, is given below for a retail company. (000 omitted). The company requires a minimum cash balance of at least $5,000 to start each quarter.

			Quarter		
	1	2	3	4	Year
Cash balance, beginning	$ 6	$?	$?	$?	$?
Add collections from customers	?	?	96	?	323
Total cash available	71	?	?	?	?
Less disbursements:					
Purchases of inventory	35	45	?	35	?
Operating expenses	?	30	30	?	113
Equipment purchases	8	8	10	?	36
Dividends	2	2	2	2	?
Total disbursements	?	85	?	?	?
Excess (deficiency) of cash available over disbursements	(2)	?	11	?	?
Financing:					
Borrowings	?	15	—	—	?
Repayments (including interest)*	—	—	(?)	(17)	(?)
Total financing	?	?	?	?	?
Cash balance, ending	$?	$?	$?	$?	$?

*Interest will total $1,000 for the year.

Required:
Fill in the missing amounts in the above table.

PROBLEMS

PROBLEM 7–17A   Production and Direct Materials Budgets   [LO3, LO4]

Pearl Products Limited of Shenzhen, China, manufactures and distributes toys throughout Southeast Asia. Three cubic centimeters (cc) of solvent H300 are required to manufacture each unit of Supermix, one of the company's products. The company is now planning raw materials needs for the third quarter, the quarter in which peak sales of Supermix occur. To keep production and sales moving smoothly, the company has the following inventory requirements:

CHECK FIGURE
(1) July: 36,000 units

a. The finished goods inventory on hand at the end of each month must be equal to 3,000 units of Supermix plus 20% of the next month's sales. The finished goods inventory on June 30 is budgeted to be 10,000 units.

b. The raw materials inventory on hand at the end of each month must be equal to one-half of the following month's production needs for raw materials. The raw materials inventory on June 30 is budgeted to be 54,000 cc of solvent H300.

c. The company maintains no work in process inventories.
    A sales budget for Supermix for the last six months of the year follows.

	Budgeted Unit Sales
July	35,000
August	40,000
September	50,000
October	30,000
November	20,000
December	10,000

Required:
1. Prepare a production budget for Supermix for July, August, September, and October.
2. Examine the production budget that you prepared in (1) above. Why will the company produce more units than it sells in July and August, and fewer units than it sells in September and October?
3. Prepare a direct materials budget showing the quantity of solvent H300 to be purchased for July, August, and September, and for the quarter in total.

CHECK FIGURE
(1) July: $317,500
(2) July 31 cash balance: $28,000

PROBLEM 7–18A   Schedule of Expected Cash Collections; Cash Budget   [LO2, LO8]
Herbal Care Corp., a distributor of herb-based sunscreens, is ready to begin its third quarter, in which peak sales occur. The company has requested a $40,000, 90-day loan from its bank to help meet cash requirements during the quarter. Since Herbal Care has experienced difficulty in paying off its loans in the past, the loan officer at the bank has asked the company to prepare a cash budget for the quarter. In response to this request, the following data have been assembled:

a. On July 1, the beginning of the third quarter, the company will have a cash balance of $44,500.
b. Actual sales for the last two months and budgeted sales for the third quarter follow (all sales are on account):

May (actual)	$250,000
June (actual)	$300,000
July (budgeted)	$400,000
August (budgeted)	$600,000
September (budgeted)	$320,000

Past experience shows that 25% of a month's sales are collected in the month of sale, 70% in the month following sale, and 3% in the second month following sale. The remainder is uncollectible.

c. Budgeted merchandise purchases and budgeted expenses for the third quarter are given below:

	July	August	September
Merchandise purchases	$240,000	$350,000	$175,000
Salaries and wages	$45,000	$50,000	$40,000
Advertising	$130,000	$145,000	$80,000
Rent payments	$9,000	$9,000	$9,000
Depreciation	$10,000	$10,000	$10,000

Merchandise purchases are paid in full during the month following purchase. Accounts payable for merchandise purchases on June 30, which will be paid during July, total $180,000.
d. Equipment costing $10,000 will be purchased for cash during July.
e. In preparing the cash budget, assume that the $40,000 loan will be made in July and repaid in September. Interest on the loan will total $1,200.

Required:
1. Prepare a schedule of expected cash collections for July, August, and September and for the quarter in total.
2. Prepare a cash budget, by month and in total, for the third quarter.
3. If the company needs a minimum cash balance of $20,000 to start each month, can the loan be repaid as planned? Explain.

CHECK FIGURE
(2a) May purchases: $574,000
(3) June 30 cash balance: $57,100

PROBLEM 7–19A   Cash Budget with Supporting Schedules   [LO2, LO4, LO8]
Garden Sales, Inc., sells garden supplies. Management is planning its cash needs for the second quarter. The company usually has to borrow money during this quarter to support peak sales of lawn care equipment, which occur during May. The following information has been assembled to assist in preparing a cash budget for the quarter:

a. Budgeted monthly absorption costing income statements for April–July are:

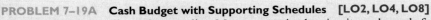

	April	May	June	July
Sales	$600,000	$900,000	$500,000	$400,000
Cost of goods sold	420,000	630,000	350,000	280,000
Gross margin	180,000	270,000	150,000	120,000
Selling and administrative expenses:				
Selling expense	79,000	120,000	62,000	51,000
Administrative expense*	45,000	52,000	41,000	38,000
Total selling and administrative expenses	124,000	172,000	103,000	89,000
Net operating income	$ 56,000	$ 98,000	$ 47,000	$ 31,000

*Includes $20,000 of depreciation each month.

b. Sales are 20% for cash and 80% on account.
c. Sales on account are collected over a three-month period with 10% collected in the month of sale; 70% collected in the first month following the month of sale; and the remaining 20% collected in the second month following the month of sale. February's sales totaled $200,000, and March's sales totaled $300,000.
d. Inventory purchases are paid for within 15 days. Therefore, 50% of a month's inventory purchases are paid for in the month of purchase. The remaining 50% is paid in the following month. Accounts payable at March 31 for inventory purchases during March total $126,000.
e. Each month's ending inventory must equal 20% of the cost of the merchandise to be sold in the following month. The merchandise inventory at March 31 is $84,000.
f. Dividends of $49,000 will be declared and paid in April.
g. Land costing $16,000 will be purchased for cash in May.
h. The cash balance at March 31 is $52,000; the company must maintain a cash balance of at least $40,000.
i. The company can borrow from its bank as needed to bolster the Cash account. Borrowings and repayments must be in multiples of $1,000. All borrowings take place at the beginning of a month, and all repayments are made at the end of a month. The annual interest rate is 12%. Compute interest on whole months ($1/12$, $2/12$, and so forth).

Required:

1. Prepare a schedule of expected cash collections for April, May, and June, and for the quarter in total.
2. Prepare the following for merchandise inventory:
   a. A merchandise purchases budget for April, May, and June.
   b. A schedule of expected cash disbursements for merchandise purchases for April, May, and June, and for the quarter in total.
3. Prepare a cash budget for April, May, and June as well as in total for the quarter. Show borrowings from the company's bank and repayments to the bank as needed to maintain the minimum cash balance.

PROBLEM 7–20A **Integration of the Sales, Production, and Direct Materials Budgets [LO2, LO3, LO4]**

CHECK FIGURE
(2) July: 36,000 units

Milo Company manufactures beach umbrellas. The company is preparing detailed budgets for the third quarter and has assembled the following information to assist in the budget preparation:

a. The Marketing Department has estimated unit sales as follows for the remainder of the year:

July	30,000	October	20,000
August	70,000	November	10,000
September	50,000	December	10,000

The selling price of the beach umbrellas is $12 per unit.

b. All sales are on account. Based on past experience, sales are collected in the following pattern:

30% in the month of sale
65% in the month following sale
5% uncollectible

Sales for June totaled $300,000.

c. The company maintains finished goods inventories equal to 15% of the following month's sales. This requirement will be met at the end of June.

d. Each beach umbrella requires 4 feet of Gilden, a material that is sometimes hard to acquire. Therefore, the company requires that the ending inventory of Gilden be equal to 50% of the following month's production needs. The inventory of Gilden on hand at the beginning and end of the quarter will be:

June 30	72,000 feet
September 30	? feet

e. Gilden costs $0.80 per foot. One-half of a month's purchases of Gilden is paid for in the month of purchase; the remainder is paid for in the following month. The accounts payable on July 1 for purchases of Gilden during June will be $76,000.

Required:
1. Prepare a sales budget, by month and in total, for the third quarter. (Show your budget in both units and dollars.) Also prepare a schedule of expected cash collections, by month and in total, for the third quarter.
2. Prepare a production budget for each of the months July, August, September, and October.
3. Prepare a direct materials budget for Gilden, by month and in total, for the third quarter. Also prepare a schedule of expected cash disbursements for Gilden, by month and in total, for the third quarter.

PROBLEM 7–21A   Cash Budget; Income Statement; Balance Sheet   [LO4, LO8, LO9, LO10]
Minden Company is a wholesale distributor of premium European chocolates. The company's balance sheet as of April 30 is given below:

CHECK FIGURE
(1) Ending cash balance:
$8,900

Minden Company Balance Sheet April 30	
Assets	
Cash	$ 9,000
Accounts receivable	54,000
Inventory	30,000
Buildings and equipment, net of depreciation	207,000
Total assets	$300,000
Liabilities and Stockholders' Equity	
Accounts payable	$ 63,000
Note payable	14,500
Capital stock, no par	180,000
Retained earnings	42,500
Total liabilities and stockholders' equity	$300,000

The company is in the process of preparing budget data for May. A number of budget items have already been prepared, as stated below:

a. Sales are budgeted at $200,000 for May. Of these sales, $60,000 will be for cash; the remainder will be credit sales. One-half of a month's credit sales are collected in the month the sales are made, and the remainder is collected in the following month. All of the April 30 accounts receivable will be collected in May.

b. Purchases of inventory are expected to total $120,000 during May. These purchases will all be on account. Forty percent of all purchases are paid for in the month of purchase; the remainder are paid in the following month. All of the April 30 accounts payable to suppliers will be paid during May.

c. The May 31 inventory balance is budgeted at $40,000.

d. Selling and administrative expenses for May are budgeted at $72,000, exclusive of depreciation. These expenses will be paid in cash. Depreciation is budgeted at $2,000 for the month.

e. The note payable on the April 30 balance sheet will be paid during May, with $100 in interest. (All of the interest relates to May.)

f. New refrigerating equipment costing $6,500 will be purchased for cash during May.

g. During May, the company will borrow $20,000 from its bank by giving a new note payable to the bank for that amount. The new note will be due in one year.

Required:

1. Prepare a cash budget for May. Support your budget with a schedule of expected cash collections from sales and a schedule of expected cash disbursements for merchandise purchases.

2. Prepare a budgeted income statement for May. Use the absorption costing income statement format as shown in Schedule 9.

3. Prepare a budgeted balance sheet as of May 31.

PROBLEM 7–22A Completing a Master Budget [LO2, LO4, LO7, LO8, LO9, LO10]

Hillyard Company, an office supplies specialty store, prepares its master budget on a quarterly basis. The following data have been assembled to assist in preparing the master budget for the first quarter:

a. As of December 31 (the end of the prior quarter), the company's general ledger showed the following account balances:

CHECK FIGURE
(2a) February purchases: $315,000
(4) February ending cash balance: $30,800

	Debits	Credits
Cash	$ 48,000	
Accounts Receivable	224,000	
Inventory	60,000	
Buildings and Equipment (net)	370,000	
Accounts Payable		$ 93,000
Capital Stock		500,000
Retained Earnings		109,000
	$702,000	$702,000

b. Actual sales for December and budgeted sales for the next four months are as follows:

December (actual)	$280,000
January	$400,000
February	$600,000
March	$300,000
April	$200,000

c. Sales are 20% for cash and 80% on credit. All payments on credit sales are collected in the month following sale. The accounts receivable at December 31 are a result of December credit sales.

d. The company's gross margin is 40% of sales. (In other words, cost of goods sold is 60% of sales.)

e. Monthly expenses are budgeted as follows: salaries and wages, $27,000 per month: advertising, $70,000 per month; shipping, 5% of sales; other expenses, 3% of sales. Depreciation, including depreciation on new assets acquired during the quarter, will be $42,000 for the quarter.

f. Each month's ending inventory should equal 25% of the following month's cost of goods sold.

g. One-half of a month's inventory purchases is paid for in the month of purchase; the other half is paid in the following month.

h. During February, the company will purchase a new copy machine for $1,700 cash. During March, other equipment will be purchased for cash at a cost of $84,500.

i. During January, the company will declare and pay $45,000 in cash dividends.

j. The company must maintain a minimum cash balance of $30,000. An open line of credit is available at a local bank for any borrowing that may be needed during the quarter. All borrowing is done at the beginning of a month, and all repayments are made at the end of a month. Borrowings and repayments of principal must be in multiples of $1,000. Interest is paid only at the time of payment of principal. The annual interest rate is 12%. (Figure interest on whole months, e.g., 1/12, 2/12.)

Required:

Using the data above, complete the following statements and schedules for the first quarter:

1. Schedule of expected cash collections:

	January	February	March	Quarter
Cash sales	$ 80,000			
Credit sales	224,000			
Total cash collections	$304,000			

2. a. Merchandise purchases budget:

	January	February	March	Quarter
Budgeted cost of goods sold	$240,000*	$360,000		
Add desired ending inventory	90,000†			
Total needs	330,000			
Less beginning inventory	60,000			
Required purchases	$270,000			

*$400,000 sales × 60% cost ratio = $240,000.
†$360,000 × 25% = $90,000.

b. Schedule of expected cash disbursements for merchandise purchases:

	January	February	March	Quarter
December purchases	$ 93,000			$ 93,000
January purchases	135,000	$135,000		270,000
February purchases				
March purchases				
Total cash disbursements for purchases	$228,000			

3. Schedule of expected cash disbursements for selling and administrative expenses:

	January	February	March	Quarter
Salaries and wages	$ 27,000			
Advertising	70,000			
Shipping	20,000			
Other expenses	12,000			
Total cash disbursements for selling and administrative expenses	$129,000			

4. Cash budget:

	January	February	March	Quarter
Cash balance, beginning	$ 48,000			
Add cash collections	304,000			
Total cash available	352,000			

(continued)

(concluded)

	January	February	March	Quarter
Less cash disbursements:				
Purchases of inventory.........	228,000			
Selling and administrative				
expenses..................	129,000			
Purchases of equipment				
Cash dividends...............	45,000			
Total cash disbursements	402,000			
Excess (deficiency) of cash.......	(50,000)			
Financing:				
Etc.				

5. Prepare an absorption costing income statement for the quarter ending March 31 as shown in Schedule 9 in the chapter.
6. Prepare a balance sheet as of March 31.

PROBLEM 7–23A   Cash Budget with Supporting Schedules   [LO2, LO4, LO7, LO8]

Westex Products is a wholesale distributor of industrial cleaning products. When the treasurer of Westex Products approached the company's bank late in the current year seeking short-term financing, he was told that money was very tight and that any borrowing over the next year would have to be supported by a detailed statement of cash collections and disbursements. The treasurer also was told that it would be very helpful to the bank if borrowers would indicate the quarters in which they would be needing funds, as well as the amounts that would be needed, and the quarters in which repayments could be made.

Since the treasurer is unsure as to the particular quarters in which bank financing will be needed, he has assembled the following information to assist in preparing a detailed cash budget:

a. Budgeted sales and merchandise purchases for next year, as well as actual sales and purchases for the last quarter of the current year, are:

CHECK FIGURE
(2) First quarter disbursements: $75,000
(3) First quarter ending cash balance: $12,000

	Sales	Merchandise Purchases
Current year:		
Fourth quarter actual	$200,000	$126,000
Next year:		
First quarter estimated	$300,000	$186,000
Second quarter estimated	$400,000	$246,000
Third quarter estimated	$500,000	$305,000
Fourth quarter estimated	$200,000	$126,000

b. The company normally collects 65% of a quarter's sales before the quarter ends and another 33% in the following quarter. The remainder is uncollectible. This pattern of collections is now being experienced in the current year's fourth-quarter actual data.

c. Eighty percent of a quarter's merchandise purchases are paid for within the quarter. The remainder is paid for in the following quarter.

d. Selling and administrative expenses for next year are budgeted at $50,000 per quarter plus 15% of sales. Of the fixed amount, $20,000 each quarter is depreciation.

e. The company will pay $10,000 in dividends each quarter.

f. Equipment purchases of $75,000 will be made in the second quarter, and purchases of $48,000 will be made in the third quarter. These purchases will be for cash.

g. The Cash account contained $10,000 at the end of the current year. The treasurer feels that this represents a minimum balance that must be maintained.

h. Any borrowing will take place at the beginning of a quarter, and any repayments will be made at the end of a quarter at an annual interest rate of 10%. Interest is paid only when principal is repaid. All borrowings and all repayments of principal must be in round $1,000 amounts. Interest payments can be in any amount. (Compute interest on whole months, e.g., $1/12$, $2/12$.)

i. At present, the company has no loans outstanding.

Required:
1. Prepare the following by quarter and in total for next year:
    a. A schedule of expected cash collections.
    b. A schedule of expected cash disbursements for merchandise purchases.
2. Compute the expected cash disbursements for selling and administrative expenses, by quarter and in total, for next year.
3. Prepare a cash budget, by quarter and in total, for next year. Show clearly in your budget the quarter(s) in which borrowing will be necessary and the quarter(s) in which repayments can be made, as requested by the company's bank.

PROBLEM 7–24A   Completing a Master Budget   [LO2, LO4, LO7, LO8, LO9, LO10]
The following data relate to the operations of Shilow Company, a wholesale distributor of consumer goods:

Current assets as of March 31:	
Cash	$8,000
Accounts receivable	$20,000
Inventory	$36,000
Building and equipment, net	$120,000
Accounts payable	$21,750
Capital stock........................	$150,000
Retained earnings	$12,250

a. The gross margin is 25% of sales.
b. Actual and budgeted sales data:

March (actual)	$50,000
April	$60,000
May	$72,000
June	$90,000
July	$48,000

c. Sales are 60% for cash and 40% on credit. Credit sales are collected in the month following sale. The accounts receivable at March 31 are a result of March credit sales.

d. Each month's ending inventory should equal 80% of the following month's budgeted cost of goods sold.

e. One-half of a month's inventory purchases is paid for in the month of purchase; the other half is paid for in the following month. The accounts payable at March 31 are the result of March purchases of inventory.

f.   Monthly expenses are as follows: commissions, 12% of sales; rent, $2,500 per month; other expenses (excluding depreciation), 6% of sales. Assume that these expenses are paid monthly. Depreciation is $900 per month (includes depreciation on new assets).
g.   Equipment costing $1,500 will be purchased for cash in April.
h.   The company must maintain a minimum cash balance of $4,000. An open line of credit is available at a local bank. All borrowing is done at the beginning of a month, and all repayments are made at the end of a month; borrowing must be in multiples of $1,000. The annual interest rate is 12%. Interest is paid only at the time of repayment of principal; figure interest on whole months ($\frac{1}{12}$, $\frac{2}{12}$, and so forth).

Required:
Using the preceding data:

1. Complete the following schedule:

Schedule of Expected Cash Collections

	April	May	June	Quarter
Cash sales	$36,000			
Credit sales	20,000			
Total collections...............	$56,000			

2. Complete the following:

Merchandise Purchases Budget

	April	May	June	Quarter
Budgeted cost of goods sold	$45,000*	$54,000		
Add desired ending inventory	43,200†			
Total needs	88,200			
Less beginning inventory	36,000			
Required purchases	$52,200			

*$60,000 sales × 75% cost ratio = $45,000.
†$54,000 × 80% = $43,200

Schedule of Expected Cash Disbursements—Merchandise Purchases

	April	May	June	Quarter
March purchases	$21,750			$21,750
April purchases	26,100	$26,100		52,200
May purchases				
June purchases				
Total disbursements	$47,850			

3. Complete the following:

Schedule of Expected Cash Disbursements—Selling and Administrative Expenses

	April	May	June	Quarter
Commissions	$ 7,200			
Rent	2,500			
Other expenses	3,600			
Total disbursements	$13,300			

4. Complete the following cash budget:

Cash Budget	April	May	June	Quarter
Cash balance, beginning	$ 8,000			
Add cash collections	56,000	———	———	———
Total cash available	64,000	———	———	———
Less cash disbursements:				
For inventory	47,850			
For expenses	13,300			
For equipment	1,500	———	———	———
Total cash disbursements	62,650	———	———	———
Excess (deficiency) of cash	1,350			
Financing:				
Etc.				

5. Prepare an absorption costing income statement similar to Schedule 9 for the quarter ended June 30.
6. Prepare a balance sheet as of June 30.

BUILDING YOUR SKILLS

Communicating in Practice   (LO8)
Risky Rolling, Inc. is a rapidly expanding manufacturer of skateboards that have been modified for use on ski slopes during the off-season. This year's sales are considerably higher than last year's sales, and sales are expected to double next year. The unexpected growth in sales has presented numerous challenges to the company's management team and the stress is really starting to show. Laura Dennan, the company's president, believes that the management time required to prepare a cash budget should be devoted to other, more pressing matters.

Required:
Write a memorandum to the president that states why cash budgeting is particularly important to a rapidly expanding company such as Risky Rolling.

Teamwork in Action   (LO1)
Tom Emory and Jim Morris strolled back to their plant from the administrative offices of Ferguson & Son Mfg. Company. Tom is manager of the machine shop in the company's factory; Jim is the manager of the equipment maintenance department.

The men had just attended the monthly performance evaluation meeting for plant department heads. These meetings had been held on the third Tuesday of each month since Robert Ferguson, Jr., the president's son, had become plant manager a year earlier.

As they were walking, Tom Emory spoke: "Boy, I hate those meetings! I never know whether my department's accounting reports will show good or bad performance. I'm beginning to expect the worst. If the accountants say I saved the company a dollar, I'm called 'Sir,' but if I spend even a little too much—boy, do I get in trouble. I don't know if I can hold on until I retire."

Tom had just been given the worst evaluation he had ever received in his long career with Ferguson & Son. He was the most respected of the experienced machinists in the company. He had been with Ferguson & Son for many years and was promoted to supervisor of the machine shop when the company expanded and moved to its present location. The president (Robert Ferguson, Sr.) had often stated that the company's success was due to the high quality of the work of machinists like Tom. As supervisor, Tom stressed the importance of craftsmanship and told his workers that he wanted no sloppy work coming from his department.

When Robert Ferguson, Jr., became the plant manager, he directed that monthly performance comparisons be made between actual and budgeted costs for each department. The departmental budgets were intended to encourage the supervisors to reduce inefficiencies and to seek cost reduction opportunities. The company controller was instructed to have his staff "tighten" the budget slightly whenever a department attained its budget in a given month; this was done to reinforce the plant manager's desire to reduce costs.

The young plant manager often stressed the importance of continued progress toward attaining the budget; he also made it known that he kept a file of these performance reports for future reference when he succeeded his father.

Tom Emory's conversation with Jim Morris continued as follows:

Emory: I really don't understand. We've worked so hard to meet the budget, and the minute we do so they tighten the budget on us. We can't work any faster and still maintain quality. I think my men are ready to quit trying. Besides, those reports don't tell the whole story. We always seem to be interrupting the big jobs for all those small rush orders. All that setup and machine adjustment time is killing us. And quite frankly, Jim, you were no help. When our hydraulic press broke down last month, your people were nowhere to be found. We had to take it apart ourselves and got stuck with all that idle time.

Morris: I'm sorry about that, Tom, but you know my department has had trouble making budget, too. We were running well behind at the time of that problem, and if we'd spent a day on that old machine, we would never have made it up. Instead we made the scheduled inspections of the forklift trucks because we knew we could do those in less than the budgeted time.

Emory: Well, Jim, at least you have some options. I'm locked into what the scheduling department assigns to me and you know they're being harassed by sales for those special orders. Incidentally, why didn't your report show all the supplies you guys wasted last month when you were working in Bill's department?

Morris: We're not out of the woods on that deal yet. We charged the maximum we could to other work and haven't even reported some of it yet.

Emory: Well, I'm glad you have a way of getting out of the pressure. The accountants seem to know everything that's happening in my department, sometimes even before I do. I thought all that budget and accounting stuff was supposed to help, but it just gets me into trouble. It's all a big pain. I'm trying to put out quality work; they're trying to save pennies.

Required:

The team should discuss and then respond to the following two questions. All team members should agree with and understand the answers and be prepared to explain the solutions in class. (Each teammate can assume responsibility for a different part of the presentation.)

1. Identify the problems that appear to exist in Ferguson & Son Mfg. Company's budgetary control system and explain how the problems are likely to reduce the effectiveness of the system.
2. Explain how Ferguson & Son Mfg. Company's budgetary control system could be revised to improve its effectiveness.

(CMA, adapted)

Ethics Challenge [LO1]

Norton Company, a manufacturer of infant furniture and carriages, is in the initial stages of preparing the annual budget for next year. Scott Ford has recently joined Norton's accounting staff and is interested to learn as much as possible about the company's budgeting process. During a recent lunch with Marge Atkins, sales manager, and Pete Granger, production manager, Ford initiated the following conversation.

Ford: Since I'm new around here and am going to be involved with the preparation of the annual budget, I'd be interested to learn how the two of you estimate sales and production numbers.

Atkins: We start out very methodically by looking at recent history, discussing what we know about current accounts, potential customers, and the general state of consumer spending. Then, we add that usual dose of intuition to come up with the best forecast we can.

Granger: I usually take the sales projections as the basis for my projections. Of course, we have to make an estimate of what this year's ending inventories will be, which is sometimes difficult.

Ford: Why does that present a problem? There must have been an estimate of ending inventories in the budget for the current year.

Granger: Those numbers aren't always reliable since Marge makes some adjustments to the sales numbers before passing them on to me.

Ford: What kind of adjustments?

Atkins: Well, we don't want to fall short of the sales projections so we generally give ourselves a little breathing room by lowering the initial sales projection anywhere from 5% to 10%.

Granger: So, you can see why this year's budget is not a very reliable starting point. We always have to adjust the projected production rates as the year progresses and, of course, this changes the ending inventory estimates. By the way, we make similar adjustments to expenses by adding at least 10% to the estimates; I think everyone around here does the same thing.

Required:

1. Marge Atkins and Pete Granger have described the use of what is sometimes called *budgetary slack.*
   a. Explain why Atkins and Granger behave in this manner and describe the benefits they expect to realize from the use of budgetary slack.
   b. Explain how the use of budgetary slack can adversely affect Atkins and Granger.
2. As a management accountant, Scott Ford believes that the behavior described by Marge Atkins and Pete Granger may be unethical. By referring to the Institute of Management Accountants' Standards of Ethical Conduct in Chapter 1, explain why the use of budgetary slack may be unethical.

(CMA, adapted)

CHECK FIGURE
(1c) April purchases: 79,000 units
(2) June 30 cash balance: $94,700

Analytical Thinking   [LO2, LO4, LO8, LO9, LO10]

You have just been hired as a new management trainee by Earrings Unlimited, a distributor of earrings to various retail outlets located in shopping malls across the country. In the past, the company has done very little in the way of budgeting and at certain times of the year has experienced a shortage of cash.

Since you are well trained in budgeting, you have decided to prepare comprehensive budgets for the upcoming second quarter in order to show management the benefits that can be gained from an integrated budgeting program. To this end, you have worked with accounting and other areas to gather the information assembled below.

The company sells many styles of earrings, but all are sold for the same price—$10 per pair. Actual sales of earrings for the last three months and budgeted sales for the next six months follow (in pairs of earrings):

January (actual)	20,000	June (budget)	50,000
February (actual)	26,000	July (budget)	30,000
March (actual)	40,000	August (budget)	28,000
April (budget)	65,000	September (budget)	25,000
May (budget)	100,000		

The concentration of sales before and during May is due to Mother's Day. Sufficient inventory should be on hand at the end of each month to supply 40% of the earrings sold in the following month.

Suppliers are paid $4 for a pair of earrings. One-half of a month's purchases is paid for in the month of purchase; the other half is paid for in the following month. All sales are on credit, with no discount, and payable within 15 days. The company has found, however, that only 20% of a month's sales are collected in the month of sale. An additional 70% is collected in the following month, and the remaining 10% is collected in the second month following sale. Bad debts have been negligible.

Monthly operating expenses for the company are given below:

Variable:	
Sales commissions	4% of sales
Fixed:	
Advertising	$200,000
Rent	$18,000
Salaries	$106,000
Utilities	$7,000
Insurance	$3,000
Depreciation	$14,000

Insurance is paid on an annual basis, in November of each year.

The company plans to purchase $16,000 in new equipment during May and $40,000 in new equipment during June; both purchases will be for cash. The company declares dividends of $15,000 each quarter, payable in the first month of the following quarter.

A listing of the company's ledger accounts as of March 31 is given below:

Assets	
Cash	$ 74,000
Accounts receivable ($26,000 February sales;	
$320,000 March sales)	346,000
Inventory	104,000
Prepaid insurance	21,000
Property and equipment (net)	950,000
Total assets	$1,495,000
Liabilities and Stockholders' Equity	
Accounts payable	$ 100,000
Dividends payable	15,000
Capital stock	800,000
Retained earnings	580,000
Total liabilities and stockholders' equity	$1,495,000

The company maintains a minimum cash balance of $50,000. All borrowing is done at the beginning of a month; any repayments are made at the end of a month.

The annual interest rate is 12%. Interest is computed and paid at the end of each quarter on all loans outstanding during the quarter.

Required:

Prepare a master budget for the three-month period ending June 30. Include the following detailed budgets:

1. a. A sales budget, by month and in total.
    b. A schedule of expected cash collections from sales, by month and in total.
    c. A merchandise purchases budget in units and in dollars. Show the budget by month and in total.
    d. A schedule of expected cash disbursements for merchandise purchases, by month and in total.
2. A cash budget. Show the budget by month and in total. Determine any borrowing that would be needed to maintain the minimum cash balance of $50,000.
3. A budgeted income statement for the three-month period ending June 30. Use the contribution approach.
4. A budgeted balance sheet as of June 30.

Taking It to the Net

As you know, the World Wide Web is a medium that is constantly evolving. Sites come and go and change without notice. To enable periodic updating of site addresses, these problems have been posted to the textbook website (www.mhhe.com/bgn3e). After accessing the site, enter the Student Center and select this chapter to find the Taking It to the Net problems.

8

Standard Costs

CHAPTER OUTLINE

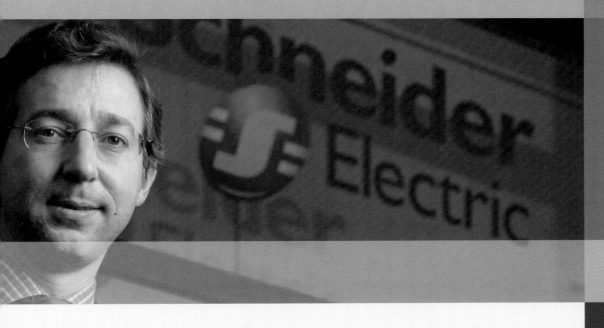

DECISION FEATURE

Managing Materials and Labor

Schneider Electric's Oxford, Ohio, plant manufactures metal-housed units (Busways) that transport electricity from its point of entry into a building to remote locations throughout the building. The plant's managers pay close attention to direct material costs because they constitute the majority of the plant's total manufacturing costs. To help control scrap rates for direct material inputs, such as copper, steel, and aluminum, the accounting department prepares direct materials quantity variances. These variances compare the standard quantity of direct materials that should have been used to make a product (according to computations made by the plant's engineers) to the amount of direct materials that were actually used. Quantifying these differences helps employees identify and deal with the causes of excessive scrap, such as an inadequately trained machine operator, poor quality raw material inputs, or a malfunctioning machine.

Because direct labor is also a significant component of the plant's total manufacturing costs, the management team also keeps daily tabs on its direct labor efficiency variance. This variance compares the standard amount of labor time allowed to make a product to the actual amount of labor time used. When idle workers cause an unfavorable labor efficiency variance, managers react to this information by temporarily moving workers from departments experiencing slack to those that are constraining production.

———

Source: Conversation with Doug Taylor, Plant Controller, Schneider Electric's Oxford, Ohio, plant.

LEARNING OBJECTIVES

*After studying Chapter 8,
you should be able to:*

LO1 Explain how direct materials standards and direct labor standards are set.

LO2 Compute the direct materials price and quantity variances and explain their significance.

LO3 Compute the direct labor rate and efficiency variances and explain their significance.

LO4 Compute the variable manufacturing overhead spending and efficiency variances.

LO5 (Appendix 8A) Prepare journal entries to record standard costs and variances.

In this chapter we begin our study of management control and performance measures. As explained in the following quotation, performance measurement serves a vital function in both personal life and in organizations:

> Imagine you want to improve your basketball shooting skill. You know that practice will help, so you [go] to the basketball court. There you start shooting toward the hoop, but as soon as the ball gets close to the rim your vision goes blurry for a second, so that you cannot observe where the ball ended up in relation to the target (left, right, in front, too far back, inside the hoop?). It would be pretty difficult to improve under those conditions . . . (And by the way, how long would [shooting baskets] sustain your interest if you couldn't observe the outcome of your efforts?)
>
> Or imagine someone engaging in a weight loss program. A normal step in such programs is to purchase a scale to be able to track one's progress: Is this program working? Am I losing weight? A positive answer would be encouraging and would motivate me to keep up the effort, while a negative answer might lead me to reflect on the process: Am I working on the right diet and exercise program? Am I doing everything I am supposed to? etc. Suppose you don't want to set up a sophisticated measurement system and decide to forgo the scale. You would still have some idea of how well you are doing from simple methods such as clothes feeling looser, a belt that fastens at a different hole, or simply via observation in a mirror! Now, imagine trying to sustain a weight loss program without *any* feedback on how well you are doing.
>
> In these . . . examples, availability of quantitative measures of performance can yield two types of benefits: First, performance feedback can help improve the "production process" through a better understanding of what works and what doesn't; e.g., shooting this way works better than shooting that way. Secondly, feedback on performance can sustain motivation and effort, because it is encouraging and/or because it suggests that more effort is required for the goal to be met.[1]

In the same way, performance measurement can be helpful in an organization. It can provide feedback concerning what works and what does not work, and it can help motivate people to sustain their efforts.

Focusing on the Numbers

Joe Knight is the CEO of Setpoint, a company that designs and builds factory-automation equipment. Knight uses a large whiteboard, with about 20 rows and 10 columns, to focus worker attention on key factors involved in managing projects. A visitor to the plant, Steve Petersen, asked Knight to explain the board, but Knight instead motioned one of his workers to come over. The young man, with a baseball cap turned backward on his head, proceeded to walk the visitor through the board, explaining the calculation of gross margin and other key indicators on the board.

"'I was just amazed,' Petersen recalls. 'He knew that board inside and out. He knew every number on it. He knew exactly where the company was and where they had to focus their attention. There was no hesitation . . . . I was so impressed . . . that the people on the shop floor had it down like that. It was their scoreboard. It was the way they could tell if they were winning or losing. I talked to several of them, and I just couldn't get over the positive attitude they had and their understanding of the numbers.'"

Source: Bo Burlingham, "What's Your Culture Worth?," *Inc.*, September 2001, pp. 124–133.

---

[1]Soumitra Dutta and Jean-François Manzoni, *Process Reengineering, Organizational Change and Performance Improvement* (New York: McGraw-Hill, 1999), Chapter IV.

Companies in highly competitive industries like FedEx, Southwest Airlines, Dell, Shell Oil, and Toyota must be able to provide high-quality goods and services at low cost. If they do not, their customers will go elsewhere. Stated in the starkest terms, managers must obtain inputs such as raw materials and electricity at the lowest possible prices and must use them as effectively as possible—while maintaining or increasing the quality of what they sell. If inputs are purchased at prices that are too high or more input is used than is really necessary, higher costs will result.

How do managers control the prices that are paid for inputs and the quantities that are used? They could examine every transaction in detail, but this obviously would be an inefficient use of management time. For many companies, the answer to this control problem lies at least partially in *standard costs.*

STANDARD COSTS—MANAGEMENT BY EXCEPTION

A *standard* is a benchmark or "norm" for measuring performance. Standards are found everywhere. Your doctor evaluates your weight using standards for individuals of your age, height, and gender. The food we eat in restaurants must be prepared under specified standards of cleanliness. The buildings we live in must conform to standards set in building codes. Standards are also widely used in managerial accounting where they relate to the *quantity* and *cost* (or acquisition price) of inputs used in manufacturing goods or providing services.

Standards in the Spanish Royal Tobacco Factory   IN BUSINESS

Standards have been used for centuries. For example, the Spanish Royal Tobacco Factory in Seville used standards to control costs in the 1700s. The Royal Tobacco Factory had a monopoly over snuff and cigar production in Spain and was the largest industrial building in Europe. Employee theft of tobacco was a particular problem, due to its high value. Careful records were maintained for each worker of the amount of tobacco leaf issued to the worker, the number of cigars expected to be made based on standards, and the actual production. The worker was not paid if the actual production was less than expected. To minimize theft, tobacco was weighed after each production step to determine the amount of waste.

Source: Salvador Carmona, Mahmoud Ezzamel, and Fernando Gutiérrez, "Control and Cost Accounting Practices in the Spanish Royal Tobacco Factory," *Accounting Organizations and Society,* Vol. 22, pp. 411–446.

Managers—often assisted by engineers and accountants—set quantity and cost standards for each major input such as raw materials and labor time. *Quantity standards* specify how much of an input should be used to make a product or provide a service. *Cost (price) standards* specify how much should be paid for each unit of the input. Actual quantities and actual costs of inputs are compared to these standards. If either the quantity or the cost of inputs departs significantly from the standards, managers investigate the discrepancy to find the cause of the problem and eliminate it. This process is called **management by exception.**

In our daily lives, we operate in a management by exception mode most of the time. Consider what happens when you sit down in the driver's seat of your car. You put the key in the ignition, you turn the key, and your car starts. Your expectation (standard) that the car will start is met; you do not have to open the car hood and check the battery, the connecting cables, the fuel lines, and so on. If you turn the key and the car does not start, then you have a discrepancy (variance). Your expectations are not met, and you need to investigate why. Note that even if the car starts after a second try, it still would be wise to investigate. The fact that the expectation was not met should be viewed as an opportunity to uncover the cause of the problem rather than as simply an annoyance. If the underlying cause is not discovered and corrected, the problem may recur and become much worse.

Management by Exception

This basic approach to identifying and solving problems is the essence of the *variance analysis cycle,* which is illustrated in Exhibit 8–1. The cycle begins with the preparation of standard cost performance reports in the accounting department. These reports highlight the *variances,* which are the differences between actual results and what should have occurred according to the standards. The variances raise questions. Why did this variance occur? Why is this variance larger than it was last period? The significant variances are investigated to discover their root causes. Corrective actions are taken. And then next period's operations are carried out. The cycle begins again with the preparation of a new standard cost performance report for the latest period. The emphasis should be on highlighting problems, finding their root causes, and then taking corrective action. The goal is to improve operations—not to assign blame.

IN BUSINESS   ## Standard Costing at Parker Brass

The Brass Products Division at Parker Hannifin Corporation, known as Parker Brass, is a world-class manufacturer of tube and brass fittings, valves, hose, and hose fittings. Management at the company uses variances from its standard costing system to target problem areas for improvement. If a production variance exceeds 5% of sales, the responsible manager is required to explain the variance and propose a plan of action to correct the detected problems. In the past, variances were reported at the end of the month—often several weeks after a particular job had been completed. Now, a variance report is generated the day after a job is completed and summary variance reports are prepared weekly. These more frequent reports help managers take more timely corrective action.

Source: David Johnsen and Parvez Sopariwala, "Standard Costing Is Alive and Well at Parker Brass," *Management Accounting Quarterly,* Winter 2000, pp. 12–20.

Who Uses Standard Costs?

Manufacturing, service, food, and not-for-profit organizations all make use of standards to some extent. Auto service centers like Firestone and Sears, for example, often set specific labor time standards for the completion of certain work tasks, such as installing a carburetor or doing a valve job, and then measure actual performance against these standards. Fast-food outlets such as McDonald's have exacting standards for the quantity of meat going into a sandwich, as well as standards for the cost of the meat. Hospitals have

Variance Analysis Cycle

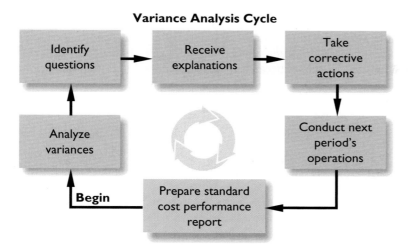

EXHIBIT 8–1

The Variance Analysis Cycle

standard costs for food, laundry, and other items, as well as standard time allowances for certain routine activities, such as laboratory tests. In short, you are likely to run into standard costs in virtually any line of business.

Manufacturing companies often have highly developed standard costing systems in which standards for direct materials, direct labor, and overhead are created for each product. A **standard cost card** shows the standard quantities and costs of the inputs required to produce a unit. In the following section, we provide a detailed example of setting standard costs and preparing a standard cost card.

SETTING STANDARD COSTS

Setting price and quantity standards requires the combined expertise of everyone who has responsibility for purchasing and using inputs. In a manufacturing setting, this might include accountants, purchasing managers, engineers, production supervisors, line managers, and production workers. Past records of purchase prices and input usage can be helpful in setting standards. However, the standards should be designed to encourage efficient *future* operations, not just a repetition of past operations that may or may not have been efficient.

Ideal versus Practical Standards

Should standards be attainable all of the time, part of the time, or almost none of the time? Opinions vary, but standards tend to fall into one of two categories—either ideal or practical.

Ideal standards can be attained only under the best circumstances. They allow for no machine breakdowns or other work interruptions, and they call for a level of effort that can be attained only by the most skilled and efficient employees working at peak effort 100% of the time. Some managers feel that such standards spur continual improvement. These managers argue that even though employees know they will rarely meet the standard, it is a constant reminder of the need for ever-increasing efficiency and effort. Few organizations use ideal standards. Most managers feel that ideal standards tend to discourage even the most diligent workers. Moreover, variances from ideal standards are difficult to interpret. Large variances from the ideal are normal and it is therefore difficult to "manage by exception."

Practical standards are standards that are "tight but attainable." They allow for normal machine downtime and employee rest periods, and they can be attained through reasonable, though highly efficient, efforts by the average worker. Variances from practical standards typically signal a need for management attention because they represent deviations that fall outside of normal operating conditions. Furthermore, practical standards can serve multiple purposes. In addition to signaling abnormal conditions, they can also be used in forecasting cash flows and in planning inventory. By contrast, ideal standards cannot be used for these purposes because they do not allow for normal inefficiencies and result in unrealistic forecasts.

Throughout the remainder of this chapter, we will assume that practical rather than ideal standards are in use.

YOU DECIDE

Owner of a Painting Company

Having painted a relative's house last summer, you have decided to start your own housepainting company this summer and have hired several of your friends. An uncle who is in the construction business has suggested that you use time standards for various tasks such as preparing wood siding, painting wood trim, and painting wood siding. A table of such standards for professional painters has been published in a recent issue of a trade magazine for painting contractors. What advantages and disadvantages do you see in using such standards? How do you think they should be used in your business, if at all?

We now turn our attention to a one-year-old company called the Colonial Pewter Company to explain many of the key concepts in this chapter. The company's only product is a reproduction of an 18th-century pewter bookend that is made largely by hand, using traditional metalworking tools. Consequently, the manufacturing process is labor intensive and requires a high level of skill.

Colonial Pewter has recently expanded its workforce to take advantage of unexpected demand for the bookends. The company started with a small group of experienced pewter workers but has had to hire less experienced workers as a result of the expansion. Recently, production problems have been encountered with iron-contaminated pewter that was acquired several months ago by the purchasing department for a bargain price. The combination of inexperienced workers and contaminated raw materials seems to have caused an unusual amount of waste and higher than expected costs. To better understand the root causes of his company's problems, the president has directed his controller to install a standard costing system.

Setting Direct Materials Standards

The controller's first task was to prepare price and quantity standards for the company's only significant raw material, pewter ingots. The **standard price per unit** for direct materials should reflect the final, delivered cost of the materials, net of any discounts taken. After consulting with the purchasing manager, the controller calculated the following standard price of a pound of pewter in ingot form:

Purchase price, top-grade pewter ingots, in 40-pound ingots	$3.60
Freight, by truck, from the supplier's warehouse	0.44
Receiving and handling	0.05
Less purchase discount	(0.09)
Standard price per pound	$4.00

Notice that the standard price reflects a particular grade of material (top grade), purchased in particular lot sizes (40-pound ingots), and delivered by a particular type of carrier (truck). Allowances have also been made for handling and discounts. If everything proceeds according to these expectations, the net cost of a pound of pewter should be $4.00.

The **standard quantity per unit** for direct materials should reflect the amount of material required for each unit of finished product, as well as an allowance for unavoidable waste, spoilage, and other normal inefficiencies. After consulting with the production manager, the controller prepared the following documentation for the standard quantity of pewter in a pair of bookends:

Material requirements as specified in the bill of materials for a pair of bookends, in pounds	2.7
Allowance for waste and spoilage, in pounds	0.2
Allowance for rejects, in pounds	0.1
Standard quantity per pair of bookends, in pounds	3.0

A **bill of materials** lists the quantity of each type of material going into a unit of finished product. It is a handy source for determining the basic material input per unit, but it should be adjusted for waste and other factors, as shown above, when determining the standard quantity per unit of product. "Waste and spoilage" in the table above refers to materials that are wasted as a normal part of the production process or that spoil before they are used. "Rejects" refers to the direct material contained in units that are defective and must be scrapped.

Although allowances for waste, spoilage, and rejects are often built into standards, this practice is often criticized because it contradicts the zero defects goal that underlies improvement programs such as Six Sigma. If allowances for waste, spoilage, and rejects *are* built into the standard cost, those allowances should be periodically reviewed and reduced over time to reflect improved processes, better training, and better equipment.

Once the price and quantity standards have been set, the standard cost of material per unit of finished product can be computed as follows:

$$3.0 \text{ pounds per unit} \times \$4.00 \text{ per pound} = \$12 \text{ per unit}$$

This $12 cost will appear as one item on the product's standard cost card.

Setting Direct Labor Standards

Direct labor price and quantity standards are usually expressed in terms of a labor rate and labor-hours. The **standard rate per hour** for direct labor should include wages, fringe benefits, and other labor costs. Using last month's wage records and in consultation with the production manager, the controller determined the standard rate per direct labor-hour at the Colonial Pewter Company as follows:

Basic wage rate per hour	$10
Employment taxes at 10% of the basic rate	1
Fringe benefits at 30% of the basic rate	3
Standard rate per direct labor-hour	$14

Many companies prepare a single standard rate per hour for all employees in a department. This standard rate reflects the expected "mix" of workers, even though the actual wage rates may vary somewhat from individual to individual due to differing skills or seniority. According to the standard computed above, the direct labor rate for Colonial Pewter should average $14 per hour.

The standard direct labor time required to complete a unit of product (called the **standard hours per unit**) is perhaps the single most difficult standard to determine. One approach is to break down each operation performed on the product into elemental body movements (such as reaching, pushing, and turning over). Published tables of standard times for such movements can be used to estimate the total time required to execute a sequence of movements to complete a task. Another approach is for an industrial engineer to do a time and motion study, actually clocking the time required for each task. As stated earlier, the standard time should include allowances for breaks, personal needs of employees, cleanup, and machine downtime.

After consulting with the production manager, the controller prepared the following documentation for the standard hours per unit:

Basic labor time per unit, in hours	1.9
Allowance for breaks and personal needs	0.1
Allowance for cleanup and machine downtime	0.3
Allowance for rejects	0.2
Standard labor-hours per unit of product	2.5

Once the rate and time standards have been set, the standard labor cost per unit of product can be computed as follows:

$$2.5 \text{ hours per unit} \times \$14 \text{ per hour} = \$35 \text{ per unit}$$

This $35 per unit standard labor cost appears along with direct materials on the standard cost card for a pair of pewter bookends.

Watching the Pennies

Industrie Natuzzi SpA, founded and run by Pasquale Natuzzi, produces handmade leather furniture for the world market in Santaeramo Del Colle in southern Italy. Natuzzi is export-oriented and has, for example, about 25% of the U.S. leather furniture market. The company's furniture is handmade by craftsmen, each of whom has a networked computer at his or her workstation. The computer provides precise instructions on how to accomplish a particular task and keeps track of how quickly the craftsman completes the task. If the craftsman beats the standard time for the task, the computer adds a bonus to the craftsman's pay.

The company's computers know exactly how much thread, screws, foam, leather, labor, and so on is required for every model. "Should the price of Argentinean hides or German dyes rise one day, employees in Santaeramo enter the new prices into the computer, and the costs for all sofas with that leather and those colors are immediately recalculated. 'Everything has to be clear for me,' says Natuzzi. 'Why this penny? Where is it going?'"

Source: Richard C. Morais, "A Methodical Man," *Forbes,* August 11, 1997, pp. 70–72.

Setting Variable Manufacturing Overhead Standards

As with direct labor, the price and quantity standards for variable manufacturing overhead are usually expressed in terms of rate and hours. The rate represents *the variable portion of the predetermined overhead rate* discussed in Chapter 2; the hours represent whatever base is used to apply overhead to units of product (usually machine-hours or direct labor-hours, as we learned in Chapter 2). At Colonial Pewter, the variable portion of the predetermined overhead rate is $3 per direct labor-hour. Therefore, the standard variable manufacturing overhead cost per unit is computed as follows:

$$2.5 \text{ hours per unit} \times \$3 \text{ per hour} = \$7.50 \text{ per unit}$$

This $7.50 per unit cost for variable manufacturing overhead appears along with direct materials and direct labor on the standard cost card in Exhibit 8–2. Observe that the **standard cost per unit** for direct materials, direct labor, and variable manufacturing overhead is computed the same way—by multiplying the standard quantity or hours by the standard price or rate.

Inputs	(1) Standard Quantity or Hours	(2) Standard Price or Rate	(3) Standard Cost (1) × (2)
Direct materials	3.0 pounds	$4.00 per pound	$12.00
Direct labor	2.5 hours	$14.00 per hour	35.00
Variable manufacturing overhead	2.5 hours	$3.00 per hour	7.50
Total standard cost per unit			$54.50

EXHIBIT 8–2

Standard Cost Card—Variable
Manufacturing Costs

Are Standards the Same as Budgets?

Standards and budgets are very similar. The major distinction between the two terms is that a standard is a *unit* amount, whereas a budget is a *total* amount. The standard cost for direct materials at Colonial Pewter is $12 per pair of bookends. If 1,000 pairs of bookends are to be made, then the budgeted cost of direct materials would be $12,000. In effect, *a standard can be viewed as the budgeted cost for one unit of product.*

A GENERAL MODEL FOR VARIANCE ANALYSIS

Two important reasons for separating standards into two categories—price and quantity—are that different managers are usually responsible for buying and for using inputs and that these two activities occur at different points in time. In the case of raw materials, for example, the purchasing manager is responsible for the price, and this responsibility is exercised at the time of purchase. In contrast, the production manager is responsible for the amount of the raw material used, and this responsibility is exercised when the materials are used in production, which may occur considerably after the purchase date. Because of these differences, it is important to clearly distinguish between deviations from price standards and deviations from quantity standards. Differences between *standard* prices and *actual* prices and between *standard* quantities and *actual* quantities are called **variances.** The act of computing and interpreting variances is called *variance analysis.*

Price and Quantity Variances

Exhibit 8–3 presents a general model for computing standard cost variances for variable costs. This model isolates price variances from quantity variances and shows how each of these variances is computed.[2] We will be using this model throughout the chapter to compute variances for direct materials, direct labor, and variable manufacturing overhead.

Three things should be noted from Exhibit 8–3. First, a price variance and a quantity variance can be computed for all three variable costs—direct materials, direct labor, and variable manufacturing overhead—even though the variances have different names. For example, a price variance is called a *materials price variance* in the case of direct materials but a *labor rate variance* in the case of direct labor and an *overhead spending variance* in the case of variable manufacturing overhead.

Second, even though a price variance may be called by different names, it is computed exactly the same way for direct materials, direct labor, and variable manufacturing overhead. The same is true of the quantity variance.

Third, the input represents the actual quantity of direct materials, direct labor, and variable manufacturing overhead used; the output represents the good production of the period, expressed in terms of the *standard quantity (or the standard hours) allowed for the actual output* (see column 3 in Exhibit 8–3). The **standard quantity allowed** or **standard**

---

[2]Variance analysis of fixed costs is discussed in the next chapter.

EXHIBIT 8–3

A General Model for Variance Analysis—Variable Manufacturing Costs

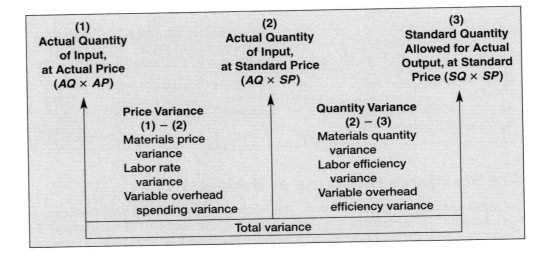

hours allowed means the amount of direct materials, direct labor, or variable manufacturing overhead *that should have been used* to produce the actual output of the period. This could be more or less than the actual materials, labor, or overhead, depending on the efficiency or inefficiency of operations. The standard quantity allowed is computed by multiplying the actual output in units by the standard input allowed per unit.

With this general model as the foundation, we will now calculate Colonial Pewter's price and quantity variances.

USING STANDARD COSTS—DIRECT MATERIALS VARIANCES

LEARNING OBJECTIVE 2

Compute the direct materials price and quantity variances and explain their significance.

Concept 8-1

After determining Colonial Pewter Company's standard costs for direct materials, direct labor, and variable manufacturing overhead, the next step was to compute the company's variances for June, the most recent month. As discussed in the preceding section, variances are computed by comparing standard costs to actual costs. To facilitate this comparison, the controller referred to the standard cost data contained in Exhibit 8–2. This exhibit shows that the standard cost of direct materials per unit of product (i.e., per pair of bookends) is as follows:

3.0 pounds per unit × $4.00 per pound = $12 per unit

Colonial Pewter's records for June showed that 6,500 pounds of pewter were purchased at a cost of $3.80 per pound. This cost included freight and handling and was net of a quantity purchase discount. All of the material purchased was used during June to manufacture 2,000 pairs of pewter bookends. Using these data and the standard costs from Exhibit 8–2, the controller computed the price and quantity variances shown in Exhibit 8–4.

The three arrows in Exhibit 8–4 point to three different total cost figures. The first, $24,700, refers to the actual total cost of the pewter that was purchased during June. The second, $26,000, refers to what the pewter would have cost if it had been purchased at the standard price of $4.00 a pound rather than the actual price of $3.80 a pound. The difference between these two amounts, $1,300 ($26,000 − $24,700), is the price variance. It exists because the actual purchase price was $0.20 per pound less than the standard purchase price. Since 6,500 pounds were purchased, the total amount of the variance is $1,300 ($0.20 per pound × 6,500 pounds). This variance is labeled favorable (denoted by F), since the actual purchase price was less than the standard purchase price. A price variance is labeled unfavorable (denoted by U) if the actual purchase price exceeds the standard purchase price.

The third arrow in Exhibit 8–4 points to $24,000—the cost if the pewter had been purchased at the standard price *and* only the standard quantity allowed per unit had been used. The standards call for 3 pounds of pewter per unit. Since 2,000 units were produced,

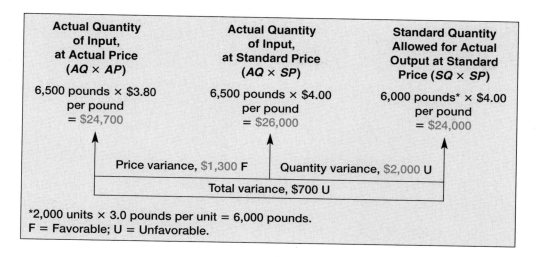

EXHIBIT 8–4

Variance Analysis—Direct Materials

Actual Quantity of Input, at Actual Price (AQ × AP)	Actual Quantity of Input, at Standard Price (AQ × SP)	Standard Quantity Allowed for Actual Output at Standard Price (SQ × SP)
6,500 pounds × $3.80 per pound = $24,700	6,500 pounds × $4.00 per pound = $26,000	6,000 pounds* × $4.00 per pound = $24,000

Price variance, $1,300 F | Quantity variance, $2,000 U

Total variance, $700 U

*2,000 units × 3.0 pounds per unit = 6,000 pounds.
F = Favorable; U = Unfavorable.

6,000 pounds of pewter should have been used. This is referred to as the standard quantity allowed for the actual output. If this 6,000 pounds of pewter had been purchased at the standard price of $4.00 per pound, the company would have spent $24,000. The difference between this amount, $24,000, and the amount at the end of the middle arrow in Exhibit 8–4, $26,000, is the quantity variance of $2,000.

To understand this quantity variance, note that the actual amount of pewter used in production was 6,500 pounds. However, the standard amount of pewter allowed for the actual output is 6,000 pounds. Therefore, a total of 500 pounds too much pewter was used to produce the actual output. To express this in dollar terms, the 500 pounds is multiplied by the standard price of $4.00 per pound to yield the quantity variance of $2,000. Why is the standard price, rather than the actual price, of the pewter used in this calculation? The production manager is ordinarily responsible for the quantity variance. If the actual price were used in the calculation of the quantity variance, the production manager would be held responsible for the efficiency or inefficiency of the purchasing manager. Apart from being unfair, fruitless arguments between the production manager and purchasing manager would occur every time the actual price of an input is above its standard price. To avoid these arguments, the standard price is used when computing the quantity variance.

The quantity variance in Exhibit 8–4 is labeled unfavorable (denoted by U). This is because more pewter was used to produce the actual output than the standard allows. A quantity variance is labeled unfavorable (U) if the actual quantity exceeds the standard quantity and is labeled favorable (F) if the actual quantity is less than the standard quantity.

The computations in Exhibit 8–4 reflect the fact that all of the material purchased during June was also used during June. How are the variances computed if the amount of material purchased differs from the amount used? To illustrate, assume that during June the company purchased 6,500 pounds of materials, as before, but that it used only 5,000 pounds of material during the month and produced only 1,600 units. In this case, the price variance and quantity variance would be computed as shown in Exhibit 8–5.

Most companies compute the materials price variance when materials are *purchased* rather than when they are used in production. There are two reasons for this practice. First, delaying the computation of the price variance until the materials are used would result in less timely variance reports. Second, computing the price variance when the materials are purchased allows the materials to be carried in the inventory accounts at their standard cost. This greatly simplifies bookkeeping. (See Appendix 8A at the end of the chapter for an explanation of how the bookkeeping works in a standard costing system.)

Note from the exhibit that the price variance is computed on the entire amount of material purchased (6,500 pounds), as before, whereas the quantity variance is computed only on the portion of this material used in production during the month (5,000 pounds). What about the other 1,500 pounds of material that were purchased during the period, but that have not yet been used? When those materials are used in future periods, a quantity

EXHIBIT 8–5

Variance Analysis—Direct Materials, When the Amount Purchased Differs from the Amount Used

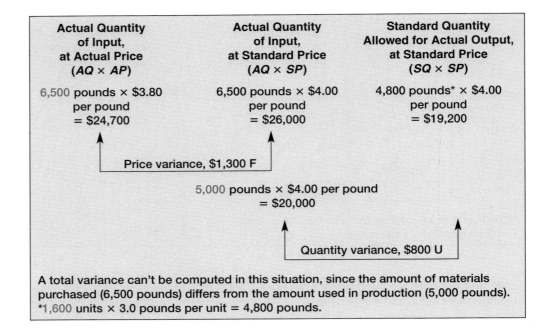

Actual Quantity of Input, at Actual Price (AQ × AP)	Actual Quantity of Input, at Standard Price (AQ × SP)	Standard Quantity Allowed for Actual Output, at Standard Price (SQ × SP)
6,500 pounds × $3.80 per pound = $24,700	6,500 pounds × $4.00 per pound = $26,000	4,800 pounds* × $4.00 per pound = $19,200

Price variance, $1,300 F

5,000 pounds × $4.00 per pound = $20,000

Quantity variance, $800 U

A total variance can't be computed in this situation, since the amount of materials purchased (6,500 pounds) differs from the amount used in production (5,000 pounds).
*1,600 units × 3.0 pounds per unit = 4,800 pounds.

variance will be computed. However, a price variance will not be computed when the materials are finally used since the price variance was computed when the materials were purchased. The situation illustrated in Exhibit 8–5 is common for companies that purchase materials well before they are used in production.

Materials Price Variance—A Closer Look

A **materials price variance** measures the difference between what is paid for a given quantity of materials and what should have been paid according to the standard. From Exhibit 8–4, this difference can be expressed by the following formula:

$$\text{Materials price variance} = (AQ \times AP) - (AQ \times SP)$$

Actual quantity   Actual price   Standard price

The formula can be factored as follows:

$$\text{Materials price variance} = AQ(AP - SP)$$

Some managers prefer this simpler formula, since it permits variance computations to be made very quickly. Using the data from Exhibit 8–4 in this formula, we have the following:

$$6,500 \text{ pounds } (\$3.80 \text{ per pound} - \$4.00 \text{ per pound}) = \$1,300 \text{ F}$$

Notice that the answer is the same as that shown in Exhibit 8–4. Also note that when using this formula approach, a negative variance is always labeled as favorable (F) and a positive variance is always labeled as unfavorable (U). This will be true of all variance formulas in this and later chapters.

Variance reports are often organized in a tabular format. An excerpt from Colonial Pewter's variance report is shown below along with the purchasing manager's explanation for the materials price variance.

	(1)	(2)	(3)	(4) Difference in Price	(5) Total Price Variance	
Colonial Pewter Company Performance Report—Purchasing Department						
Item Purchased	Quantity Purchased	Actual Price	Standard Price	(2) − (3)	(1) × (4)	Explanation
Pewter	6,500 pounds	$3.80	$4.00	$0.20	$1,300 F	Bargained for an especially good price
F = Favorable; U = Unfavorable.						

Isolation of Variances   Variances should be isolated and brought to the attention of management as quickly as possible. The sooner deviations from standard are brought to the attention of management, the sooner problems can be evaluated and corrected.

What should management do with the variance data? The most significant variances should be viewed as red flags that call attention to the fact that an exception has occurred that will require explanation by the responsible manager and perhaps follow-up effort. The performance report itself may contain explanations for the variances, as illustrated above. In the case of Colonial Pewter Company, the purchasing manager, said that the favorable price variance resulted from bargaining for an especially good price.

Responsibility for the Variance   Who is responsible for the materials price variance? Generally speaking, the purchasing manager has control over the price paid for goods and is therefore responsible for the materials price variance. Many factors influence the prices paid for goods, including how many units are ordered, how the order is delivered, whether the order is a rush order, and the quality of materials purchased. A deviation in any of these factors from what was assumed when the standards were set can result in a price variance. For example, purchase of second-grade materials rather than top-grade materials may result in a favorable price variance, since the lower-grade materials would generally be less costly (but perhaps less suitable for production).

However, someone other than the purchasing manager could be responsible for a materials price variance. Production may be scheduled in such a way, for example, that the purchasing manager must request express delivery. In these cases, the production manager should be held responsible for the resulting price variances.

A word of caution is in order. Variance analysis should not be used to assign blame. The emphasis must be on *supporting* the line managers and *assisting* them in meeting the goals that they have participated in setting for the company. In short, the emphasis should be positive rather than negative. Excessive dwelling on what has already happened, particularly in terms of trying to find someone to blame, can destroy morale and kill any cooperative spirit.

Materials Quantity Variance—A Closer Look

The **materials quantity variance** measures the difference between the quantity of materials used in production and the quantity that should have been used according to the standard. Although the variance is concerned with the physical usage of materials, as shown in Exhibit 8–4, it is generally stated in dollar terms to help judge its importance.

The formula for the materials quantity variance is as follows:

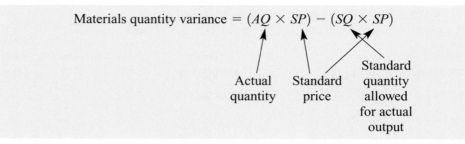

$$\text{Materials quantity variance} = (AQ \times SP) - (SQ \times SP)$$

Actual quantity   Standard price   Standard quantity allowed for actual output

Again, the formula can be factored as follows:

$$\text{Materials quantity variance} = SP(AQ - SQ)$$

Using the data from Exhibit 8–4 in the formula, we have the following:

$$\$4.00 \text{ per pound } (6,500 \text{ pounds} - 6,000 \text{ pounds*}) = \$2,000 \text{ U}$$

*2,000 units × 3.0 pounds per unit = 6,000 pounds.

The answer, of course, is the same as that shown in Exhibit 8–4. The data might appear as follows if a formal performance report were prepared:

Colonial Pewter Company
Performance Report—Production Department

Type of Materials	(1) Standard Price	(2) Actual Quantity	(3) Standard Quantity Allowed	(4) Difference in Quantity (2) − (3)	(5) Total Quantity Variance (1) × (4)	Explanation
Pewter	$4.00	6,500 pounds	6,000 pounds	500 pounds	$2,000 U	Low-quality materials unsuitable for production

F = Favorable; U = Unfavorable.

The materials quantity variance is best isolated when materials are used in production. Materials are drawn for the number of units to be produced, according to the standard bill of materials for each unit. Any additional materials are usually drawn with an excess materials requisition slip, which is different in color from the normal requisition slips. This procedure calls attention to the excessive usage of materials *while production is still in process* and provides an opportunity to correct any developing problem.

Excessive materials usage can result from many factors, including faulty machines, inferior materials quality, untrained workers, and poor supervision. Generally speaking, it is the responsibility of the production department to see that material usage is kept in line with standards. There may be times, however, when the *purchasing* department may be responsible for an unfavorable materials quantity variance. For example, if the purchasing department obtains inferior quality materials in an effort to economize on price, the materials may be unsuitable for use and may result in excessive waste. Thus, purchasing rather than production would be responsible for the quantity variance. At Colonial Pewter, the production manager claimed that low-quality materials were the cause of the unfavorable materials quantity variance for June on the Production Department's Performance Report.

CONCEPT
CHECK ✓

1. The standard and actual prices per pound of raw material are $4.00 and $4.50, respectively. A total of 10,500 pounds of raw material was purchased and then used to produce 5,000 units. The quantity standard allows two pounds of the raw material per unit produced. What was the materials quantity variance?
   a. $5,000 unfavorable
   b. $5,000 favorable
   c. $2,000 favorable
   d. $2,000 unfavorable
2. Referring to the facts in question 1 above, what was the material price variance?
   a. $5,250 favorable
   b. $5,250 unfavorable
   c. $5,000 unfavorable
   d. $5,000 favorable

What Happened to the Raisins?

IN BUSINESS

Management at an unnamed breakfast cereal company became concerned about the apparent waste of raisins in one of its products. A box of the product was supposed to contain 10 ounces of cereal and 2 ounces of raisins. However, the production process had been using an average of 2.5 ounces of raisins per box. To correct the problem, a bonus was offered to employees if the consumption of raisins dropped to 2.1 ounces per box or less—which would allow for about 5% waste. Within a month, the target was hit and bonuses were distributed. However, another problem began to appear. Market studies indicated that customers had become dissatisfied with the amount of raisins in the product. Workers had hit the 2.1-ounce per box target by drastically reducing the amount of raisins in rush orders. Boxes of the completed product are ordinarily weighed and if the weight is less than 12 ounces, the box is rejected. However, rush orders aren't weighed since that would slow down the production process. Consequently, workers were reducing the raisins in rush orders so as to hit the overall target of 2.1 ounces of raisins per box. This resulted in substandard boxes of cereal in rush orders and customer complaints. Clearly, managers need to be very careful when they set targets and standards. They may not get what they bargained for. Subsequent investigation by an internal auditor revealed that, due to statistical fluctuations, an average of about 2.5 ounces of raisins must be used to ensure that every box contains at least 2 ounces of raisins.

Source: Harper A. Roehm and Joseph R. Castellano, "The Danger of Relying on Accounting Numbers Alone," *Management Accounting Quarterly*, Fall 1999, pp. 4–9.

USING STANDARD COSTS—DIRECT LABOR VARIANCES

The next step in determining Colonial Pewter's variances for June is to compute the direct labor variances for the month. Recall from Exhibit 8–2 that the standard direct labor cost per unit of product is $35, computed as follows:

LEARNING OBJECTIVE 3
Compute the direct labor rate and efficiency variances and explain their significance.

$$2.5 \text{ hours per unit} \times \$14.00 \text{ per hour} = \$35 \text{ per unit}$$

During June, the company paid its direct labor workers $74,250, including employment taxes and fringe benefits, for 5,400 hours of work. This was an average of $13.75 per hour. Using these data and the standard costs from Exhibit 8–2, the direct labor rate and efficiency variances are computed in Exhibit 8–6.

Notice that the column headings in Exhibit 8–6 are the same as those used in the prior two exhibits, except that in Exhibit 8–6 the terms *hours* and *rate* are used in place of the terms *quantity* and *price*.

Concept 8-2

EXHIBIT 8–6

Variance Analysis—Direct Labor

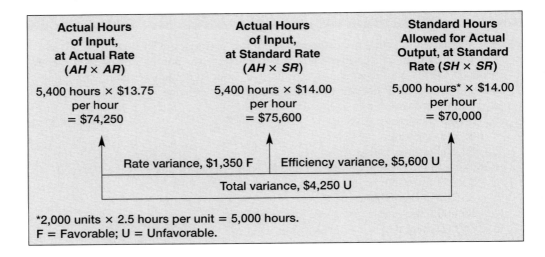

*2,000 units × 2.5 hours per unit = 5,000 hours.
F = Favorable; U = Unfavorable.

Labor Rate Variance—A Closer Look

As explained earlier, the price variance for direct labor is commonly termed a **labor rate variance.** This variance measures any deviation from standard in the average hourly rate paid to direct labor workers. The formula for the labor rate variance is expressed as follows:

$$\text{Labor rate variance} = (AH \times AR) - (AH \times SR)$$

$$
\begin{array}{ccc}
\text{Actual} & \text{Actual} & \text{Standard} \\
\text{hours} & \text{rate} & \text{rate}
\end{array}
$$

The formula can be factored as follows:

$$\text{Labor rate variance} = AH(AR - SR)$$

Using the data from Exhibit 8–6 in the formula, the labor rate variance can be computed as follows:

$$5,400 \text{ hours} (\$13.75 \text{ per hour} - \$14.00 \text{ per hour}) = \$1,350 \text{ F}$$

In most companies, the wage rates paid to workers are quite predictable. Nevertheless, rate variances can arise because of the way labor is used. Skilled workers with high hourly rates of pay may be given duties that require little skill and call for lower hourly rates of pay. This will result in an unfavorable labor rate variance, since the actual hourly rate of pay will exceed the standard rate specified for the particular task. In contrast, a favorable rate variance would result when workers who are paid at a rate lower than specified in the standard are assigned to the task. However, the lower paid workers may not be as efficient. Finally, overtime work at premium rates will result in an unfavorable rate variance if the overtime premium is charged to the direct labor account.

Who is responsible for controlling the labor rate variance? Since labor rate variances generally arise as a result of how labor is used, production supervisors bear responsibility for seeing that labor rate variances are kept under control.

Labor Efficiency Variance—A Closer Look

The **labor efficiency variance** attempts to measure the productivity of direct labor. No variance is more closely watched by management, since it is widely believed that increasing direct labor productivity is vital to reducing costs. The formula for the labor efficiency variance is expressed as follows:

$$\text{Labor efficiency variance} = (AH \times SR) - (SH \times SR)$$

Actual   Standard   Standard hours
hours   rate   allowed for
                        actual output

The formula can be factored as follows:

$$\text{Labor efficiency variance} = SR(AH - SH)$$

Using the data from Exhibit 8–6 in the formula, we have the following:

$$\$14.00 \text{ per hour } (5{,}400 \text{ hours } - 5{,}000 \text{ hours*}) = \$5{,}600 \text{ U}$$

*2,000 units × 2.5 hours per unit = 5,000 hours.

Possible causes of an unfavorable labor efficiency variance include poorly trained or motivated workers; poor quality materials, requiring more labor time; faulty equipment, causing breakdowns and work interruptions; poor supervision of workers; and inaccurate standards. The managers in charge of production would usually be responsible for control of the labor efficiency variance. However, purchasing could be held responsible if acquisition of poor materials resulted in excessive labor processing time.

Another important cause of an unfavorable labor efficiency variance may be insufficient demand for the company's products. Managers in some companies argue that it is difficult, and perhaps unwise, to constantly adjust the workforce in response to changes in the amount of work that needs to be done. In such companies, the direct labor workforce is essentially fixed in the short run. If demand is insufficient to keep everyone busy, workers are not laid off. In this case, if demand falls below the level needed to keep everyone busy, an unfavorable labor efficiency variance will often be recorded.

If customer orders are insufficient to keep the workers busy, the work center manager has two options—either accept an unfavorable labor efficiency variance or build inventory.[3] A central lesson of lean production is that building inventory with no immediate prospect of sale is a bad idea. Excessive inventory—particularly work in process inventory—leads to high defect rates, obsolete goods, and generally inefficient operations. As a consequence, when the workforce is basically fixed in the short term, managers must be cautious about how labor efficiency variances are used. Some experts advocate eliminating labor efficiency variances entirely in such situations—at least for the purposes of motivating and controlling workers on the shop floor.

Department Resources Manager

DECISION MAKER

You are the manager of the computer-generated special effects department for a company that produces special effects for high-profile films. You receive a copy of this month's performance report for your department and discover a large labor efficiency variance that is unfavorable. What factors might have contributed to this unfavorable variance?

---

[3]For further discussion, see Eliyahu M. Goldratt and Jeff Cox, *The Goal,* 2nd rev. ed. (Croton-on-Hudson, NY: North River Press, 1992).

USING STANDARD COSTS—VARIABLE MANUFACTURING OVERHEAD VARIANCES

The final step in the analysis of Colonial Pewter's variances for June is to compute the variable manufacturing overhead variances. The variable portion of manufacturing overhead can be analyzed using the same basic formulas that are used to analyze direct materials and direct labor. Recall from Exhibit 8–2 that the standard variable manufacturing overhead is $7.50 per unit of product, computed as follows:

$$2.5 \text{ hours per unit} \times \$3.00 \text{ per hour} = \$7.50 \text{ per unit}$$

Colonial Pewter's cost records showed that the total actual variable manufacturing overhead cost for June was $15,390. Recall from the earlier discussion of the direct labor variances that 5,400 hours of direct labor time were recorded during the month and that the company produced 2,000 pairs of bookends. The analysis of this overhead data appears in Exhibit 8–7.

Notice the similarities between Exhibits 8–6 and 8–7. These similarities arise from the fact that direct labor-hours are being used as the base for allocating overhead cost to units of product; thus, the same hourly figures appear in Exhibit 8–7 for variable manufacturing overhead as in Exhibit 8–6 for direct labor. The main difference between the two exhibits is in the standard hourly rate being used, which in this company is much lower for variable manufacturing overhead than for direct labor.

Manufacturing Overhead Variances—A Closer Look

The formula for the **variable overhead spending variance** is expressed as follows:

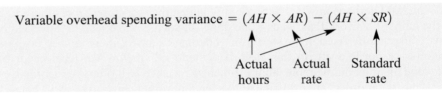

$$\text{Variable overhead spending variance} = (AH \times AR) - (AH \times SR)$$

Actual hours   Actual rate   Standard rate

This formula can be factored as follows:

$$\text{Variable overhead spending variance} = AH(AR - SR)$$

EXHIBIT 8–7

Variance Analysis—Variable Manufacturing Overhead

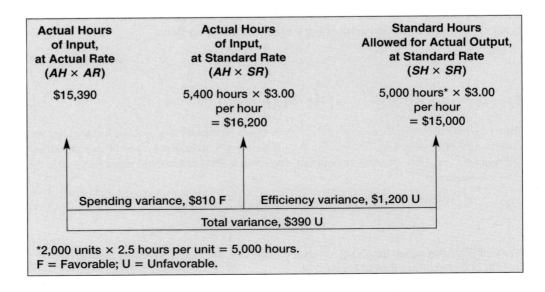

Actual Hours of Input, at Actual Rate (AH × AR)	Actual Hours of Input, at Standard Rate (AH × SR)	Standard Hours Allowed for Actual Output, at Standard Rate (SH × SR)
$15,390	5,400 hours × $3.00 per hour = $16,200	5,000 hours* × $3.00 per hour = $15,000

Spending variance, $810 F   Efficiency variance, $1,200 U

Total variance, $390 U

*2,000 units × 2.5 hours per unit = 5,000 hours.
F = Favorable; U = Unfavorable.

Using the data from Exhibit 8–7 in the formula, the variable overhead spending variance can be computed as follows:

$$5{,}400 \text{ hours } (\$2.85 \text{ per hour* } - \$3.00 \text{ per hour}) = \$810 \text{ F}$$

*$15,390 ÷ 5,400 hours = $2.85 per hour.

The formula for the **variable overhead efficiency variance** is expressed as follows:

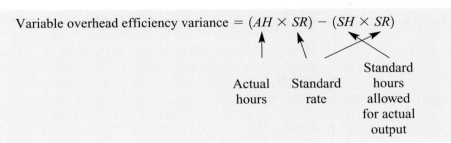

Variable overhead efficiency variance $= (AH \times SR) - (SH \times SR)$

| | Actual hours | Standard rate | Standard hours allowed for actual output |

This formula can be factored as follows:

Variable overhead efficiency variance $= SR(AH - SH)$

Again using the data from Exhibit 8–7, the variance can be computed as follows:

$$\$3.00 \text{ per hour } (5{,}400 \text{ hours } - 5{,}000 \text{ hours*}) = \$1{,}200 \text{ U}$$

*2,000 units × 2.5 hours per unit = 5,000 hours.

We will reserve further discussion of the variable overhead spending and efficiency variances until the next chapter, where overhead analysis is discussed in depth.

Before proceeding further, we suggest that you pause at this point and go back and review the data contained in Exhibits 8–2 through 8–7. These exhibits and the accompanying text discussion provide a comprehensive, integrated illustration of standard setting and variance analysis.

---

3. The actual direct labor wage rate is $8.50 and 4,500 direct labor hours were actually worked during the month. The standard direct labor wage rate is $8.00 and the standard quantity of hours allowed for the actual level of output was 5,000 direct labor hours. What was the direct labor efficiency variance?
   a. $4,000 favorable
   b. $4,000 unfavorable
   c. $4,500 unfavorable
   d. $4,500 favorable
4. Referring to the facts in question 3 above, what is the variable overhead efficiency variance if the standard variable overhead per direct labor hour is $5.00?
   a. $5,000 favorable
   b. $5,000 unfavorable
   c. $2,500 unfavorable
   d. $2,500 favorable

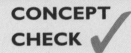

CONCEPT CHECK ✔

To review Colonial Pewter's standard cost variances, the largest variances are the unfavorable materials quantity variance of $2,000 and the unfavorable labor efficiency variance of $5,600. These variances were thoroughly discussed by the responsible managers, with the conclusion that the variances were probably due to the new inexperienced workers. The unfavorable labor efficiency variance was probably due to the inability of the inexperienced workers to work as fast or as effectively as the company's seasoned workforce. The materials quantity variance was traced to an unusually large number of rejected bookends that resulted from faulty workmanship. The production manager reported that efforts were already underway to correct these problems. The newer workers were being teamed with more experienced workers to show them more efficient and effective ways of doing their jobs.

VARIANCE ANALYSIS AND MANAGEMENT BY EXCEPTION

Variance analysis and performance reports are important elements of *management by exception*. Simply put, management by exception means that the manager's attention is directed to areas where goals are not being met. Time and effort should not be wasted focusing on things that are going smoothly.

The budgets and standards discussed in this chapter and in the preceding chapter reflect management's plans. If all goes according to plan, there will be little difference between actual results and the results that would be expected according to the budgets and standards. If this happens, managers can concentrate on other issues. However, if actual results do not conform to the budget and to standards, the performance reporting system sends a signal to the manager that an "exception" has occurred. This signal is in the form of a variance from the budget or standards.

However, are all variances worth investigating? The answer is no. Differences between actual results and what was expected will almost always occur. If every variance were investigated, management would waste a great deal of time tracking down nickel-and-dime differences. Variances may occur for a variety of reasons—only some of which are worthy of management's attention. For example, hotter-than-normal weather in the summer may result in higher-than-expected electrical bills for air conditioning. Or, workers may work slightly faster or slower on a particular day. Because of unpredictable random factors, one can expect that virtually every cost category will produce a variance of some kind.

How should managers decide which variances are worth investigating? One clue is the size of the variance. A variance of $5 is probably not big enough to warrant attention, whereas a variance of $5,000 might well be worth tracking down. Another clue is the size of the variance relative to the amount of spending. A variance that is only 0.1% of spending on an item is likely to be well within the bounds one would normally expect due to random factors. On the other hand, a variance of 10% of spending is much more likely to be a signal that something is wrong.

In addition to watching for unusually large variances, the pattern of the variances should be monitored. For example, a run of steadily mounting variances should trigger an investigation even though none of the variances is large enough by itself to warrant investigation.

EVALUATION OF CONTROLS BASED ON STANDARD COSTS

Advantages of Standard Costs

Standard cost systems have a number of advantages.

1. Standard costs are a key element in a management by exception approach. If costs remain within the standards, managers can focus on other issues. When costs fall significantly outside the standards, managers are alerted that there may be problems requiring attention. This approach helps managers focus on important issues.
2. Standards that are viewed as reasonable by employees can promote economy and efficiency. They provide benchmarks that individuals can use to judge their own performance.
3. Standard costs can greatly simplify bookkeeping. Instead of recording actual costs for each job, the standard costs for direct materials, direct labor, and overhead can be charged to jobs.

4. Standard costs fit naturally in an integrated system of "responsibility accounting." The standards establish what costs should be, who should be responsible for them, and whether actual costs are under control.

Potential Problems with the Use of Standard Costs

The improper use of standard costs can present a number of potential problems.

1. Standard cost variance reports are usually prepared on a monthly basis and often are released days or even weeks after the end of the month. As a consequence, the information in the reports may be so outdated that it is almost useless. Timely, frequent reports that are approximately correct are better than infrequent reports that are very precise but out of date by the time they are released. Some companies are now reporting variances and other key operating data daily or even more frequently.

2. If managers are insensitive and use variance reports as a club, morale will suffer. Employees should receive positive reinforcement for work well done. Management by exception, by its nature, tends to focus on the negative. If variances are used as a club, subordinates may be tempted to cover up unfavorable variances or take actions that are not in the best interests of the company to make sure the variances are favorable. For example, workers may put on a crash effort to increase output at the end of the month to avoid an unfavorable labor efficiency variance. In the rush to produce more output, quality may suffer.

3. Labor quantity standards and efficiency variances make two important assumptions. First, they assume that the production process is labor-paced; if labor works faster, output will go up. However, output in many companies is not determined by how fast labor works; rather, it is determined by the processing speed of machines. Second, the computations assume that labor is a variable cost. However, direct labor may be essentially fixed. If labor is fixed, then an undue emphasis on labor efficiency variances creates pressure to build excess inventories.

4. In some cases, a "favorable" variance can be as bad or worse than an "unfavorable" variance. For example, McDonald's has a standard for the amount of hamburger meat that should be in a Big Mac. A "favorable" variance would mean that less meat was used than the standard specifies. The result is a substandard Big Mac and possibly a dissatisfied customer.

5. Too much emphasis on meeting the standards may overshadow other important objectives such as maintaining and improving quality, on-time delivery, and customer satisfaction. This tendency can be reduced by using supplemental performance measures that focus on these other objectives.

6. Just meeting standards may not be sufficient; continual improvement may be necessary to survive in a competitive environment. For this reason, some companies focus on the trends in the standard cost variances—aiming for continual improvement rather than just meeting the standards. In other companies, engineered standards are replaced either by a rolling average of actual costs, which is expected to decline, or by very challenging target costs.

In sum, managers should exercise considerable care when using a standard cost system. It is particularly important that managers go out of their way to focus on the positive, rather than just on the negative, and to be aware of possible unintended consequences.

Nevertheless, standard costs are found in the vast majority of manufacturing companies and in many service companies, although their use is changing. For evaluating performance, standard cost variances may be supplanted in the future by a particularly interesting development known as the *balanced scorecard,* which is discussed in the next section. The balanced scorecard concept has been eagerly embraced by a wide variety of organizations, including Analog Devices, KPMG, Tenneco, Allstate, AT&T, Elf Atochem, Conair-Franklin, CIGNA Corporation, London Life Insurance Co., Southern Gardens Citrus Processing, Duke Children's Hospital, JP Morgan Chase, 3COM, Rockwater, Apple Computer, Advanced Micro Devices (AMD), FMC, the Bank of Montreal, the

Massachusetts Special Olympics, United Way of Southeastern New England, Boston Lyric Opera, Bridgeport Hospital and Healthcare Services, and the Housing Authority of Fiji.

BALANCED SCORECARD

A **balanced scorecard** consists of an integrated set of performance measures that are derived from and support the company's strategy.[4,5] A strategy is essentially a theory about how to achieve the organization's goals. For example, Southwest Airlines' strategy is to offer passengers low prices and fun on short-haul jet service. The low prices result from the absence of costly frills such as meals, assigned seating, and interline baggage checking. The friendly service is provided by flight attendants who go out of their way to entertain passengers with their antics. This is an interesting strategy. Southwest Airlines consciously hires people who have a sense of humor and who enjoy their work. Hiring and retaining such employees probably costs no more—and may cost less—than retaining grumpy flight attendants who view their jobs as a chore. Southwest Airlines' strategy is to build loyal customers through a combination of "fun"—which does not cost anything to provide—and low prices that are possible because of the lack of costly frills offered by competing airlines. The theory is that low prices and fun will lead to loyal customers, which, in combination with low costs, will lead to high profits. So far, this theory has worked.

---

[4]The balanced scorecard concept was developed by Robert Kaplan and David Norton. For further details, see their articles "The Balanced Scorecard—Measures that Drive Performance," *Harvard Business Review,* January/February 1992, pp. 71–79; "Using the Balanced Scorecard as a Strategic Management System," *Harvard Business Review,* January/February 1996, pp. 75–85; "Why Does a Business Need a Balanced Scorecard?" *Journal of Cost Management,* May/June 1997, pp. 5–10; and their book *Translating Strategy into Action: The Balanced Scorecard* (Boston, MA: Harvard Business School Press, 1996).

[5]In the 1960s, the French developed a concept similar to the balanced scorecard called Tableau de Bord or "dashboard." For details, see Michel Lebas, "Managerial Accounting in France: Overview of Past Tradition and Current Practice," *The European Accounting Review,* 1994, 3, no. 3, pp. 471–487; and Marc Epstein and Jean-François Manzoni, "The Balanced Scorecard and the Tableau de Bord: Translating Strategy into Action," *Management Accounting,* August 1997, pp. 28–36.

Under the balanced scorecard approach, top management translates its strategy into performance measures that employees can understand and influence. For example, the amount of time passengers have to wait in line to have their baggage checked might be a performance measure for the supervisor in charge of the Southwest Airlines check-in counter at the Phoenix airport. This performance measure is easily understood by the supervisor and can be improved by the supervisor's actions. Under the balanced scorecard approach, nonfinancial measures of performance—such as the amount of time passengers must wait to check bags—are used in addition to financial measures of performance such as standard cost variances. Nonfinancial measures of performance of quality and customer satisfaction are particularly important since they typically tie directly to the company's strategy in a cause-and-effect manner and they serve as leading indicators of the company's success.

The Balanced Scorecard at the City of Charlotte

IN BUSINESS

Governmental and nonprofit organizations as well as businesses can use the balanced scorecard approach to performance measurement. The City of Charlotte, North Carolina, developed a balanced scorecard with four major goals: (1) increase perception of safety; (2) strengthen neighborhoods; (3) promote economic opportunity; and (4) improve service quality. To strengthen neighborhoods, the city's managers set goals to: (a) promote safe, decent housing; (b) increase home ownership; and (c) increase job placements. The corresponding performance measures are: (a) the number of code compliances in housing; (b) the number of assisted purchases of homes; and (c) the number of adult job placements.

Pam Syfert, Charlotte's City Manager, states: "The Scorecard is a communication, information, and learning system. Building a scorecard helps managers link today's actions with the achievement of today's priorities. It encourages accountability. And, today, we define accountability by results."

Source: Robert S. Kaplan, *City of Charlotte (A),* Harvard Business School case 9-199-036, December 15, 1998.

SUMMARY

LO1   Explain how direct materials standards and direct labor standards are set.

Each direct cost has both a price and a quantity standard. The standard price for an input is the price that should be paid for a single unit of the input. In the case of direct materials, the price should include shipping and receiving costs and should be net of quantity and other discounts. In the case of direct labor, the standard rate should include wages, fringe benefits, and employment taxes.

LO2   Compute the direct materials price and quantity variances and explain their significance.

The materials price variance is the difference between the actual price paid for materials and the standard price, multiplied by the quantity purchased. An unfavorable variance occurs whenever the actual price exceeds the standard price. A favorable variance occurs when the actual price is less than the standard price for the input.

The materials quantity variance is the difference between the amount of materials actually used and the amount that should have been used to produce the actual good output of the period, multiplied by the standard price per unit of the input. An unfavorable materials quantity variance occurs when the amount of materials actually used exceeds the amount that should have been used according to the materials quantity standard. A favorable variance occurs when the amount of materials actually used is less than the amount that should have been used according to the standard.

LO3   Compute the direct labor rate and efficiency variances and explain their significance.

The direct labor rate variance is the difference between the actual wage rate paid and the standard wage rate, multiplied by the hours worked. An unfavorable variance occurs whenever the actual wage rate exceeds the standard wage rate. A favorable variance occurs when the actual wage rate is less than the standard wage rate.

The labor efficiency variance is the difference between the hours actually worked and the hours that should have been used to produce the actual good output of the period, multiplied by the standard wage rate. An unfavorable labor efficiency variance occurs when the hours actually worked exceed the hours allowed for the actual output. A favorable variance occurs when the hours actually worked are less than hours allowed for the actual output.

LO4 Compute the variable manufacturing overhead spending and efficiency variances.
The variable manufacturing overhead spending variance is the difference between the actual variable manufacturing overhead cost incurred and the actual hours worked multiplied by the variable manufacturing overhead rate. The variable manufacturing overhead efficiency variance is the difference between the hours actually worked and the hours that should have been used to produce the actual good output of the period, multiplied by the standard variable manufacturing overhead rate.

GUIDANCE ANSWERS TO *DECISION MAKER* AND *YOU DECIDE*

Owner of a Painting Company (p. 348)
The standards published in the trade magazine are for professional painters; at least initially, they would not be realistic for your painting crew, which is inexperienced. Therefore, the standards would not be particularly useful for bidding on jobs or for setting budgets. Nevertheless, the standards would provide important feedback about how well the painting crew is performing relative to the professional competition. Setting a goal of beating the professional painters (as represented by the standards) might energize your painting crew and motivate them to work harder and to think of innovative ways of improving the painting process.

Psychologically, it might be best not to use the labels *unfavorable* and *favorable* for the variances since almost all of them will initially be unfavorable. Instead, you might focus on the ratio of the actual time to the standard time, with the idea that this ratio should decline over time and eventually should be less than 1.0. This ratio could be plotted on a weekly or daily basis and displayed in a prominent location so that everyone in the painting crew can see how well the crew is doing relative to professional painters.

Department Resources Manager (p. 359)
An unfavorable labor efficiency variance in the computer-generated special effects department might have been caused by inexperienced, poorly trained, or unmotivated employees, faulty hardware and/or software that may have caused work interruptions, and/or poor supervision of the employees in this department. In addition, it is possible that there was insufficient demand for the output of this department—resulting in idle time—or that the standard (or benchmark) for this department is inaccurate.

GUIDANCE ANSWERS TO CONCEPT CHECKS

1. **Choice d.** The materials quantity variance is (10,500 pounds used − 10,000 pounds allowed) × $4.00 per pound = $2,000 unfavorable.
2. **Choice b.** The materials price variance is ($4.50 actual price per pound − $4.00 standard price per pound) × 10,500 pounds purchased = $5,250 unfavorable.
3. **Choice a.** The direct labor efficiency variance is (4,500 hours − 5,000 hours) × $8.00 standard hourly rate = $4,000 favorable.
4. **Choice d.** The variable overhead efficiency variance is (4,500 hours − 5,000 hours) × $5.00 per hour = $2,500 favorable.

REVIEW PROBLEM: STANDARD COSTS

Xavier Company produces a single product. Variable manufacturing overhead is applied to products on the basis of direct labor-hours. The standard costs for one unit of product are as follows:

Direct material: 6 ounces at $0.50 per ounce	$ 3
Direct labor: 1.8 hours at $10 per hour	18
Variable manufacturing overhead: 1.8 hours at $5 per hour	9
Total standard variable cost per unit	$30

During June, 2,000 units were produced. The costs associated with June's operations were as follows:

Material purchased: 18,000 ounces at $0.60 per ounce	$10,800
Material used in production: 14,000 ounces	—
Direct labor: 4,000 hours at $9.75 per hour	$39,000
Variable manufacturing overhead costs incurred	$20,800

Required:

Compute the direct materials, direct labor, and variable manufacturing overhead variances.

Solution to Review Problem

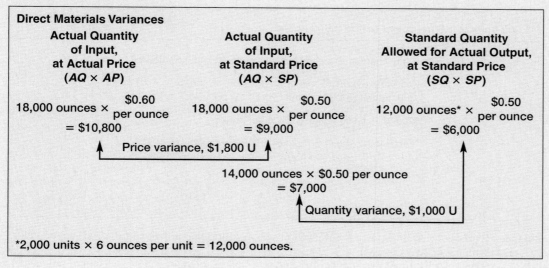

Direct Materials Variances

Actual Quantity of Input, at Actual Price (AQ × AP)	Actual Quantity of Input, at Standard Price (AQ × SP)	Standard Quantity Allowed for Actual Output, at Standard Price (SQ × SP)
18,000 ounces × $0.60 per ounce = $10,800	18,000 ounces × $0.50 per ounce = $9,000	12,000 ounces* × $0.50 per ounce = $6,000

Price variance, $1,800 U

14,000 ounces × $0.50 per ounce = $7,000

Quantity variance, $1,000 U

*2,000 units × 6 ounces per unit = 12,000 ounces.

Using the formulas in the chapter, the same variances would be computed as follows:

$$\text{Materials price variance} = AQ(AP - SP)$$
$$18{,}000 \text{ ounces } (\$0.60 \text{ per ounce} - \$0.50 \text{ per ounce}) = \$1{,}800 \text{ U}$$

$$\text{Materials quantity variance} = SP(AQ - SQ)$$
$$\$0.50 \text{ per ounce } (14{,}000 \text{ ounces} - 12{,}000 \text{ ounces}) = \$1{,}000 \text{ U}$$

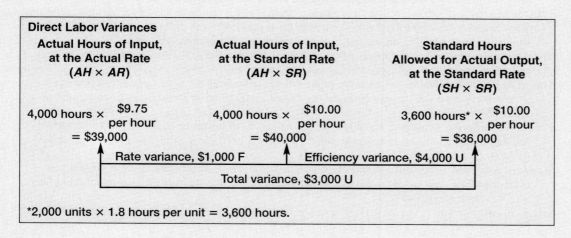

Direct Labor Variances

Actual Hours of Input, at the Actual Rate (AH × AR)	Actual Hours of Input, at the Standard Rate (AH × SR)	Standard Hours Allowed for Actual Output, at the Standard Rate (SH × SR)
4,000 hours × $9.75 per hour = $39,000	4,000 hours × $10.00 per hour = $40,000	3,600 hours* × $10.00 per hour = $36,000

Rate variance, $1,000 F   Efficiency variance, $4,000 U

Total variance, $3,000 U

*2,000 units × 1.8 hours per unit = 3,600 hours.

Using the formulas in the chapter, the same variances would be computed as follows:

$$\text{Labor rate variance} = AH(AR - SR)$$
$$4{,}000 \text{ hours } (\$9.75 \text{ per hour} - \$10.00 \text{ per hour}) = \$1{,}000 \text{ F}$$

$$\text{Labor efficiency variance} = SR(AH - SH)$$
$$\$10.00 \text{ per hour } (4{,}000 \text{ hours} - 3{,}600 \text{ hours}) = \$4{,}000 \text{ U}$$

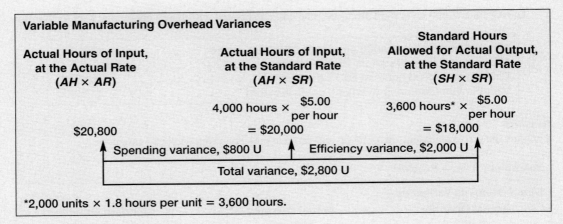

Using the formulas in the chapter, the same variances would be computed as:

Variable overhead spending variance = $AH(AR - SR)$
4,000 hours ($5.20 per hour* − $5.00 per hour) = $800 U

*$20,800 ÷ 4,000 hours = $5.20 per hour.

Variable overhead efficiency variance = $SR(AH - SH)$
$5.00 per hour (4,000 hours − 3,600 hours) = $2,000 U

GLOSSARY

Balanced scorecard   An integrated set of performance measures that is derived from and supports the organization's strategy. (p. 364)

Bill of materials   A listing of the amount of each type of material required to make a unit of product. (p. 349)

Ideal standards   Standards that allow for no machine breakdowns or other work interruptions and that require peak efficiency at all times. (p. 347)

Labor efficiency variance   A measure of the difference between the actual hours taken to complete a task and the standard hours allowed, multiplied by the standard hourly labor rate. (p. 358)

Labor rate variance   A measure of the difference between the actual hourly labor rate and the standard rate, multiplied by the number of hours worked during the period. (p. 358)

Management by exception   A system of management in which standards are set for various operating activities, with actual results then compared to these standards. Any differences that are deemed significant are brought to the attention of management as "exceptions." (p. 345)

Materials price variance   A measure of the difference between the actual unit price paid for an item and the standard price, multiplied by the quantity purchased. (p. 354)

Materials quantity variance   A measure of the difference between the actual quantity of materials used in production and the standard quantity allowed, multiplied by the standard price per unit of materials. (p. 355)

Practical standards   Standards that allow for normal machine downtime and other work interruptions and that can be attained through reasonable, though highly efficient, efforts by the average worker. (p. 347)

Standard cost card   A detailed listing of the standard amounts of direct materials, direct labor, and overhead that should go into a unit of product, multiplied by the standard price or rate that has been set for each input. (p. 347)

Standard cost per unit   The standard cost of a unit of product as shown on the standard cost card; it is computed by multiplying the standard quantity or hours by the standard price or rate for each cost input. (p. 350)

Standard hours allowed   The time that should have been taken to complete the period's output as computed by multiplying the actual number of units produced by the standard hours allowed per unit. (p. 352)

Standard hours per unit   The amount of labor time that should be required to complete a single unit of product, including allowances for breaks, machine downtime, cleanup, rejects, and other normal inefficiencies. (p. 349)

Standard price per unit   The price that should be paid for a single unit of a material, including allowances for quality, quantity purchased, shipping, receiving, and other such costs, net of any discounts allowed. (p. 348)

Standard quantity allowed   The amount of materials that should have been used to complete the period's actual output. It is computed by multiplying the actual number of units produced by the standard quantity per unit. (p. 351)

Standard quantity per unit   The amount of materials that should be required to complete a single unit of product, including allowances for normal waste, spoilage, rejects, and similar inefficiencies. (p. 349)

Standard rate per hour   The labor rate that should be incurred per hour of labor time, including employment taxes, fringe benefits, and other such labor costs. (p. 349)

Variable overhead efficiency variance   The difference between the actual level of activity (direct labor-hours, machine-hours, or some other base) and the standard activity allowed, multiplied by the variable part of the predetermined overhead rate. (p. 361)

Variable overhead spending variance   The difference between the actual variable overhead cost incurred during a period and the standard cost that should have been incurred based on the actual activity of the period. (p. 360)

Variance   The difference between standard prices and quantities on the one hand and actual prices and quantities on the other hand. (p. 351)

APPENDIX 8A: GENERAL LEDGER ENTRIES TO RECORD VARIANCES

Although standard costs and variances can be computed and used without being formally entered into the accounting records, many organizations prefer to make formal journal entries. Formal entry tends to give variances a greater emphasis than informal, off-the-record computations. This emphasis signals management's desire to keep costs within the limits that have been set. In addition, formal use of standard costs simplifies the bookkeeping process enormously. Inventories and cost of goods sold can be valued at their standard costs—eliminating the need to keep track of the actual cost of each unit.

> **LEARNING OBJECTIVE 5**
>
> Prepare journal entries to record standard costs and variances.

Direct Materials Variances

To illustrate the general ledger entries needed to record standard cost variances, we will return to the data contained in the review problem at the end of the chapter. The entry to record the purchase of direct materials would be as follows:

Raw Materials (18,000 ounces at $0.50 per ounce)	9,000	
Materials Price Variance (18,000 ounces at		
$0.10 per ounce U)	1,800	
Accounts Payable (18,000 ounces at $0.60 per ounce) . . .		10,800

Notice that the price variance is recognized when purchases are made, rather than when materials are actually used in production and that the materials are carried in the inventory account at standard cost. As direct materials are later drawn from inventory and used in production, the quantity variance is recorded as follows:

Work in Process (12,000 ounces at $0.50 per ounce)	6,000	
Materials Quantity Variance (2,000 ounces U at		
$0.50 per ounce)	1,000	
Raw Materials (14,000 ounces at $0.50 per ounce)		7,000

Thus, direct materials are added to the Work in Process account at the standard cost of the materials that should have been used to produce the actual output.

Notice that both the price variance and the quantity variance above are unfavorable and are debit entries. If either of these variances had been favorable, it would have appeared as a credit entry.

Direct Labor Variances

Referring again to the cost data in the review problem at the end of the chapter, the general ledger entry to record the incurrence of direct labor cost would be:

Work in Process (3,600 hours at $10.00 per hour)	36,000	
Labor Efficiency Variance (400 hours U at $10.00 per hour). .	4,000	
Labor Rate Variance (4,000 hours at $0.25 per hour F) . .		1,000
Wages Payable (4,000 hours at $9.75 per hour).		39,000

Thus, as with direct materials, direct labor costs enter into the Work in Process account at standard, both in terms of the rate and in terms of the hours allowed for the actual production of the period. Note that the unfavorable labor efficiency variance is a debit entry whereas the favorable labor rate variance is a credit entry.

Variable Manufacturing Overhead Variances

Variable manufacturing overhead variances are usually not recorded in the accounts separately but rather are determined as part of the general analysis of overhead, which is discussed in the next chapter.

Cost Flows in a Standard Cost System

The flows of costs through the company's accounts are illustrated in Exhibit 8A–1. Note that entries into the various inventory accounts are made at standard cost—not actual cost. The differences between actual and standard costs are entered into special accounts that accumulate the various standard cost variances. Ordinarily, these standard cost variance accounts are closed out to Cost of Goods Sold at the end of the period. Unfavorable variances increase Cost of Goods Sold, and favorable variances decrease Cost of Goods Sold.

EXHIBIT 8A–1

Cost Flows in a Standard Cost System*

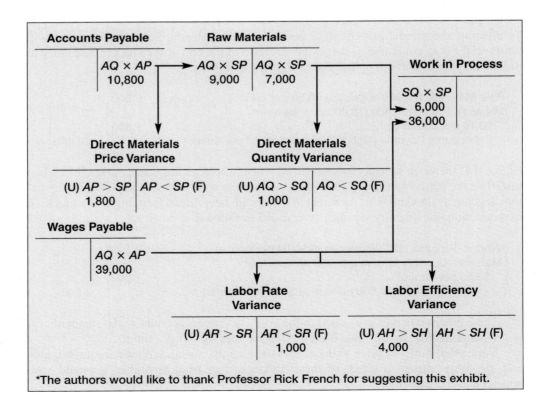

*The authors would like to thank Professor Rick French for suggesting this exhibit.

SUMMARY FOR APPENDIX 8A

LO5 **(Appendix 8A) Prepare journal entries to record standard costs and variances.**
Raw materials, work in process, and finished goods inventories are all carried at their standard costs. Differences between actual and standard costs are recorded as variances. Favorable variances are credit entries and unfavorable variances are debit entries.

QUESTIONS

8–1 What is a quantity standard? What is a price standard?

8–2 Distinguish between ideal and practical standards.

8–3 What is meant by the term *variance*?

8–4 What is meant by the term *management by exception*?

8–5 Who is generally responsible for the materials price variance? The materials quantity variance? The labor efficiency variance?

8–6 The materials price variance can be computed at what two different points in time? Which is better? Why?

8–7 What are the dangers of using standards as punitive tools?

8–8 What effect, if any, would you expect poor quality materials to have on direct labor variances?

8–9 If variable manufacturing overhead is applied to production on the basis of direct labor-hours and the direct labor efficiency variance is unfavorable, will the variable overhead efficiency variance be favorable or unfavorable, or could it be either? Explain.

8–10 Why can undue emphasis on labor efficiency variances lead to excess work in process inventories?

8–11 (Appendix 8A) What are the advantages of making formal journal entries in the accounting records for variances?

BRIEF EXERCISES

BRIEF EXERCISE 8–1 Setting Standards [LO1]
Victoria Chocolates, Ltd., makes premium handcrafted chocolate confections in London. The owner of the company is setting up a standard cost system and has collected the following data for one of the company's products, the Empire Truffle. This product is made with the finest white chocolate and various fillings. The data below pertain only to the white chocolate used in the product (the currency is stated in pounds, denoted here as £):

Material requirements, kilograms of white chocolate per dozen truffles	0.70 kilograms
Allowance for waste, kilograms of white chocolate per dozen truffles	0.03 kilograms
Allowance for rejects, kilograms of white chocolate per dozen truffles	0.02 kilograms
Purchase price, finest grade white chocolate	£7.50 per kilogram
Purchase discount	8% of purchase price
Shipping cost from the supplier in Belgium	£0.30 per kilogram
Receiving and handling cost	£0.04 per kilogram

Required:
1. Determine the standard price of a kilogram of white chocolate.
2. Determine the standard quantity of white chocolate for a dozen truffles.
3. Determine the standard cost of the white chocolate in a dozen truffles.

BRIEF EXERCISE 8–2 Direct Materials Variances [LO2]
Bandar Industries Berhad of Malaysia manufactures sporting equipment. One of the company's products, a football helmet for the North American market, requires a special plastic. During the quarter ending June 30, the company manufactured 35,000 helmets, using 22,500 kilograms of plastic. The plastic cost the company RM 171,000. (The currency in Malaysia is the ringgit, which is denoted here by RM.)

According to the standard cost card, each helmet should require 0.6 kilograms of plastic, at a cost of RM 8 per kilogram.

Required:
1. What cost for plastic should have been incurred to make 35,000 helmets? How much greater or less is this than the cost that was incurred?
2. Break down the difference computed in (1) above into a materials price variance and a materials quantity variance.

BRIEF EXERCISE 8–3   Direct Labor Variances   [LO3]

SkyChefs, Inc., prepares in-flight meals for a number of major airlines. One of the company's products is grilled salmon in dill sauce with baby new potatoes and spring vegetables. During the most recent week, the company prepared 4,000 of these meals using 960 direct labor-hours. The company paid these direct labor workers a total of $9,600 for this work, or $10.00 per hour.

According to the standard cost card for this meal, it should require 0.25 direct labor-hours at a cost of $9.75 per hour.

Required:
1. What direct labor cost should have been incurred to prepare 4,000 meals? How much does this differ from the actual direct labor cost?
2. Break down the difference computed in (1) above into a labor rate variance and a labor efficiency variance.

BRIEF EXERCISE 8–4   Variable Overhead Variances   [LO4]

Logistics Solutions provides order fulfillment services for dot.com merchants. The company maintains warehouses that stock items carried by its dot.com clients. When a client receives an order from a customer, the order is forwarded to Logistics Solutions, which pulls the item from storage, packs it, and ships it to the customer. The company uses a predetermined variable overhead rate based on direct labor-hours.

In the most recent month, 120,000 items were shipped to customers using 2,300 direct labor-hours. The company incurred a total of $7,360 in variable overhead costs.

According to the company's standards, 0.02 direct labor-hours are required to fulfill an order for one item and the variable overhead rate is $3.25 per direct labor-hour.

Required:
1. What variable overhead cost should have been incurred to fill the orders for the 120,000 items? How much does this differ from the actual variable overhead cost?
2. Break down the difference computed in (1) above into a variable overhead spending variance and a variable overhead efficiency variance.

BRIEF EXERCISE 8–5   (Appendix 8A) Recording Variances in the General Ledger   [LO5]

Bliny Corporation makes a product with the following standard costs for direct material and direct labor:

Direct material: 2.00 meters at $3.25 per meter	$6.50
Direct labor: 0.40 hours at $12.00 per hour	$4.80

During the most recent month, 5,000 units were produced. The costs associated with the month's production of this product were as follows:

Material purchased: 12,000 meters at $3.15 per meter	$37,800
Material used in production: 10,500 meters	—
Direct labor: 1,975 hours at $12.20 per hour	$24,095

The standard cost variances for direct material and direct labor are:

Materials price variance: 12,000 meters at $0.10 per meter F . .	$1,200 F
Materials quantity variance: 500 meters at $3.25 per meter U . .	$1,625 U
Labor rate variance: 1,975 hours at $0.20 per hour U	$395 U
Labor efficiency variance: 25 hours at $12.00 per hour F	$300 F

Required:
1. Prepare the general ledger entry to record the purchase of materials on account for the month.
2. Prepare the general ledger entry to record the use of materials for the month.
3. Prepare the general ledger entry to record the incurrence of direct labor cost for the month.

EXERCISES

EXERCISE 8–6   Setting Standards; Preparing a Standard Cost Card   [LO1]
Martin Company manufactures a powerful cleaning solvent. The main ingredient in the solvent is a raw material called Echol. Information concerning the purchase and use of Echol follows:

a. *Purchase of Echol*   Echol is purchased in 15-gallon containers at a cost of $115 per container. A discount of 2% is offered by the supplier for payment within 10 days, and Martin Company takes all discounts. Shipping costs, which Martin Company must pay, amount to $130 for an average shipment of 100 15-gallon containers of Echol.

b. *Use of Echol*   The bill of materials calls for 7.6 quarts of Echol per bottle of cleaning solvent. (Each gallon contains four quarts.) About 5% of all Echol used is lost through spillage or evaporation (the 7.6 quarts above is the *actual* content per bottle). In addition, statistical analysis has shown that every 41st bottle is rejected at final inspection because of contamination.

Required:
1. Compute the standard purchase price for one quart of Echol.
2. Compute the standard quantity of Echol (in quarts) per salable bottle of cleaning solvent.
3. Using the data from (1) and (2) above, prepare a standard cost card showing the standard cost of Echol per bottle of cleaning solvent.

EXERCISE 8–7   Direct Materials and Direct Labor Variances   [LO2, LO3]
Huron Company produces a commercial cleaning compound known as Zoom. The direct materials and direct labor standards for one unit of Zoom are given below:

	Standard Quantity or Hours	Standard Price or Rate	Standard Cost
Direct materials	4.6 pounds	$2.50 per pound	$11.50
Direct labor	0.2 hours	$12.00 per hour	$2.40

During the most recent month, the following activity was recorded:

a. Twenty thousand pounds of material were purchased at a cost of $2.35 per pound.
b. All of the material purchased was used to produce 4,000 units of Zoom.
c. 750 hours of direct labor time were recorded at a total labor cost of $10,425.

Required:
1. Compute the direct materials price and quantity variances for the month.
2. Compute the direct labor rate and efficiency variances for the month.

EXERCISE 8–8   Direct Materials Variances   [LO2]
Refer to the data in Exercise 8–7. Assume that instead of producing 4,000 units during the month, the company produced only 3,000 units, using 14,750 pounds of material. (The rest of the material purchased remained in raw materials inventory.)

Required:
Compute the direct materials price and quantity variances for the month.

EXERCISE 8–9   Direct Labor and Variable Manufacturing Overhead Variances   [LO3, LO4]
Erie Company manufactures a small CD player called the Jogging Mate. The company uses standards to control its costs. The labor standards that have been set for one Jogging Mate CD player are as follows:

Standard Hours	Standard Rate per Hour	Standard Cost
18 minutes	$12.00	$3.60

During August, 5,750 hours of direct labor time were needed to make 20,000 units of the Jogging Mate. The direct labor cost totaled $73,600 for the month.

Required:
1. What direct labor cost should have been incurred to make 20,000 units of the Jogging Mate? By how much does this differ from the cost that was incurred?
2. Break down the difference in cost from (1) above into a labor rate variance and a labor efficiency variance.
3. The budgeted variable manufacturing overhead rate is $4 per direct labor-hour. During August, the company incurred $21,850 in variable manufacturing overhead cost. Compute the variable overhead spending and efficiency variances for the month.

EXERCISE 8–10   (Appendix 8A) Direct Materials and Direct Labor Variances; Journal Entries [LO2, LO3, LO5]
Genola Fashions began production of a new product on June 1. The company uses a standard cost system and has established the following standards for one unit of the new product:

	Standard Quantity or Hours	Standard Price or Rate	Standard Cost
Direct materials	2.5 yards	$14 per yard	$35.00
Direct labor	1.6 hours	$8 per hour	$12.80

During June, the following activity was recorded regarding the new product:

a.   Purchasing acquired 10,000 yards of material at a cost of $13.80 per yard.
b.   Production used 8,000 yards of the material to manufacture 3,000 units of the new product.
c.   Production reported that 5,000 direct labor-hours were worked on the new product at a cost of $43,000.

Required:
1. For direct materials:
   a.   Compute the direct materials price and quantity variances.
   b.   Prepare journal entries to record the purchase of materials and the use of materials in production.
2. For direct labor:
   a.   Compute the direct labor rate and efficiency variances.
   b.   Prepare a journal entry to record the incurrence of direct labor cost for the month.
3. Post the entries you have prepared to the following T-accounts:

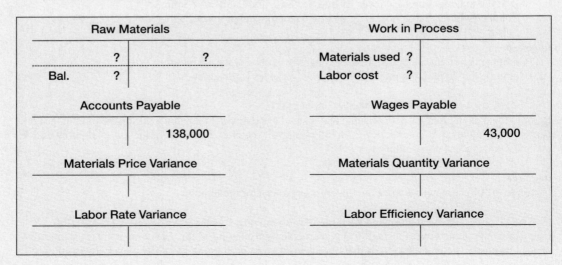

EXERCISE 8–11   Direct Materials and Direct Labor Variances   [LO2, LO3]

Dawson Toys, Ltd., produces a toy called the Maze. The company has recently established a standard cost system to help control costs and has established the following standards for the Maze toy:

> Direct materials: 6 microns per toy at $0.50 per micron
> Direct labor: 1.3 hours per toy at $8 per hour

During July, the company produced 3,000 Maze toys. Production data for the month on the toy follow:

a. *Direct materials:* 25,000 microns were purchased at a cost of $0.48 per micron. 5,000 of these microns were still in inventory at the end of the month.

b. *Direct labor:* 4,000 direct labor-hours were worked at a cost of $36,000.

Required:

1. Compute the following variances for July:
   a.   Direct materials price and quantity variances.
   b.   Direct labor rate and efficiency variances.
2. Prepare a brief explanation of the possible causes of each variance.

PROBLEMS

PROBLEM 8–12A   Comprehensive Variance Analysis   [LO2, LO3, LO4]

Miller Toy Company manufactures a plastic swimming pool at its Westwood Plant. The plant has been experiencing problems as shown by its June contribution format income statement below:

CHECK FIGURE
(1a) Materials price
      variance: $3,000 F
(2)   Net variance: $16,290 U

	Budgeted	Actual
Sales (15,000 pools)	$450,000	$450,000
Less variable expenses:		
Variable cost of goods sold*	180,000	196,290
Variable selling expenses	20,000	20,000
Total variable expenses	200,000	216,290
Contribution margin	250,000	233,710
Less fixed expenses:		
Manufacturing overhead	130,000	130,000
Selling and administrative	84,000	84,000
Total fixed expenses	214,000	214,000
Net operating income	$ 36,000	$ 19,710

*Contains direct materials, direct labor, and variable manufacturing overhead.

Janet Dunn, who has just been appointed general manager of the Westwood Plant, has been given instructions to "get things under control." Upon reviewing the plant's income statement, Ms. Dunn has concluded that the major problem lies in the variable cost of goods sold. She has been provided with the following standard cost per swimming pool:

	Standard Quantity or Hours	Standard Price or Rate	Standard Cost
Direct materials	3.0 pounds	$2.00 per pound	$ 6.00
Direct labor	0.8 hour	$6.00 per hour	4.80
Variable manufacturing overhead	0.4 hour*	$3.00 per hour	1.20
Total standard cost			$12.00

*Based on machine-hours.

Ms. Dunn has determined that during June the plant produced 15,000 pools and incurred the following costs:

a. Purchased 60,000 pounds of materials at a cost of $1.95 per pound.
b. Used 49,200 pounds of materials in production. (Finished goods and work in process inventories are insignificant and can be ignored.)
c. Worked 11,800 direct labor-hours at a cost of $7.00 per hour.
d. Incurred variable manufacturing overhead cost totaling $18,290 for the month. A total of 5,900 machine-hours was recorded.

It is the company's policy to close all variances to cost of goods sold on a monthly basis.

Required:

1. Compute the following variances for June:
    a. Direct materials price and quantity variances.
    b. Direct labor rate and efficiency variances.
    c. Variable overhead spending and efficiency variances.
2. Summarize the variances that you computed in (1) above by showing the net overall favorable or unfavorable variance for the month. What impact did this figure have on the company's income statement? Show computations.
3. Pick out the two most significant variances that you computed in (1) above. Explain to Ms. Dunn possible causes of these variances.

PROBLEM 8–13A   Basic Variance Analysis   [LO2, LO3, LO4]
Becton Labs, Inc., produces various chemical compounds for industrial use. One compound, called Fludex, is prepared using an elaborate distilling process. The company has developed standard costs for one unit of Fludex, as follows:

CHECK FIGURE
(1a) Materials price
variance: $15,000 F
(2a) Labor efficiency
variance: $4,375 U

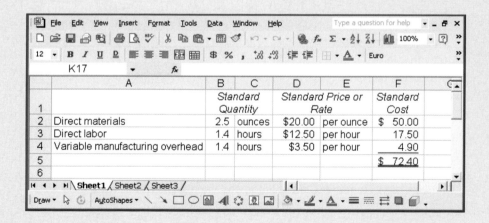

	A	B	C	D	E	F
1		Standard Quantity		Standard Price or Rate		Standard Cost
2	Direct materials	2.5	ounces	$20.00	per ounce	$ 50.00
3	Direct labor	1.4	hours	$12.50	per hour	17.50
4	Variable manufacturing overhead	1.4	hours	$3.50	per hour	4.90
5						$ 72.40
6						

During November, the following activity was recorded by the company relative to production of Fludex:

a. Materials purchased, 12,000 ounces at a cost of $225,000.
b. There was no beginning inventory of materials; however, at the end of the month, 2,500 ounces of material remained in ending inventory.
c. The company employs 35 lab technicians to work on the production of Fludex. During November, each worked an average of 160 hours at an average rate of $12 per hour.
d. Variable manufacturing overhead is assigned to Fludex on the basis of direct labor-hours. Variable manufacturing overhead costs during November totaled $18,200.
e. During November, 3,750 good units of Fludex were produced.

The company's management is anxious to determine the efficiency of the Fludex production activities.

Required:

1. For direct materials:
   a. Compute the price and quantity variances.
   b. The materials were purchased from a new supplier who is anxious to enter into a long-term purchase contract. Would you recommend that the company sign the contract? Explain.
2. For direct labor:
   a. Compute the rate and efficiency variances.
   b. In the past, the 35 technicians employed in the production of Fludex consisted of 20 senior technicians and 15 assistants. During November, the company experimented with fewer senior technicians and more assistants in order to save costs. Would you recommend that the new labor mix be continued? Explain.
3. Compute the variable overhead spending and efficiency variances. What relation can you see between this efficiency variance and the labor efficiency variance?

PROBLEM 8–14A   Variance Analysis in a Hospital   [LO2, LO3, LO4]

John Fleming, chief administrator for Valley View Hospital, is concerned about the costs for tests in the hospital's lab. Charges for lab tests are consistently higher at Valley View than at other hospitals and have resulted in many complaints. Also, because of strict regulations on amounts reimbursed for lab tests, payments received from insurance companies and governmental units have not been high enough to cover lab costs.

Mr. Fleming has asked you to evaluate costs in the hospital's lab for the past month. The following information is available:

a. Two types of tests are performed in the lab—blood tests and smears. During the past month, 1,800 blood tests and 2,400 smears were performed in the lab.
b. Small glass plates are used in both types of tests. During the past month, the hospital purchased 12,000 plates at a cost of $28,200. This cost is net of a 6% quantity discount. 1,500 of these plates were unused at the end of the month; no plates were on hand at the beginning of the month.
c. During the past month, 1,150 hours of labor time were recorded in the lab at a cost of $13,800.
d. The lab's variable overhead cost last month totaled $7,820.

CHECK FIGURE
(1) Materials quantity variance: $5,250 U
(2a) Labor rate variance: $2,300 F

Valley View Hospital has never used standard costs. By searching industry literature, however, you have determined the following nationwide averages for hospital labs:

a. *Plates:* Two plates are required per lab test. These plates cost $2.50 each and are disposed of after the test is completed.
b. *Labor:* Each blood test should require 0.3 hours to complete, and each smear should require 0.15 hours to complete. The average cost of this lab time is $14 per hour.
c. *Overhead:* Overhead cost is based on direct labor-hours. The average rate for variable overhead is $6 per hour.

Required:

1. Compute a materials price variance for the plates purchased last month and a materials quantity variance for the plates used last month.
2. For labor cost in the lab:
   a. Compute a labor rate variance and a labor efficiency variance.
   b. In most hospitals, one-half of the workers in the lab are senior technicians and one-half are assistants. In an effort to reduce costs, Valley View Hospital employs only one-fourth senior technicians and three-fourths assistants. Would you recommend that this policy be continued? Explain.
3. Compute the variable overhead spending and efficiency variances. Is there any relation between the variable overhead efficiency variance and the labor efficiency variance? Explain.

PROBLEM 8–15A   **(Appendix 8A) Comprehensive Variance Analysis; Journal Entries**
[LO2, LO3, LO4, LO5]

Trueform Products, Inc., produces a broad line of sports equipment and uses a standard cost system for control purposes. Last year the company produced 8,000 varsity footballs. The standard costs associated with this football, along with the actual costs incurred last year, are given below (per football):

	Standard Cost	Actual Cost
Direct materials:		
Standard: 3.7 feet at $5.00 per foot	$18.50	
Actual: 4.0 feet at $4.80 per foot		$19.20
Direct labor:		
Standard: 0.9 hour at $7.50 per hour	6.75	
Actual: 0.8 hour at $8.00 per hour		6.40
Variable manufacturing overhead:		
Standard: 0.9 hour at $2.50 per hour	2.25	
Actual: 0.8 hour at $2.75 per hour		2.20
Total cost per football	$27.50	$27.80

The president was elated when he saw that actual costs exceeded standard costs by only $0.30 per football. He stated, "I was afraid that our unit cost might get out of hand when we gave out those raises last year in order to stimulate output. But it's obvious our costs are well under control."

There was no inventory of materials on hand to start the year. During the year, 32,000 feet of materials were purchased and used in production.

Required:

1. For direct materials:
   a. Compute the price and quantity variances for the year.
   b. Prepare journal entries to record all activity relating to direct materials for the year.
2. For direct labor:
   a. Compute the rate and efficiency variances.
   b. Prepare a journal entry to record the incurrence of direct labor cost for the year.
3. Compute the variable overhead spending and efficiency variances.
4. Was the president correct in his statement that "our costs are well under control"? Explain.
5. State possible causes of each variance that you have computed.

PROBLEM 8–16A   **Setting Standards**   **[LO1]**

Danson Company is a chemical manufacturer that supplies various products to industrial users. The company plans to introduce a new chemical solution, called Nysap, for which it needs to develop a standard product cost. The following information is available on the production of Nysap:

a. Nysap is made by combining a chemical compound (nyclyn) and a solution (salex), and boiling the mixture. A 20% loss in volume occurs for both the salex and the nyclyn during boiling. After boiling, the mixture consists of 9.6 liters of salex and 12 kilograms of nyclyn per 10-liter batch of Nysap.

b. After the boiling process is complete, the solution is cooled slightly before 5 kilograms of protet are added per 10-liter batch of Nysap. The addition of the protet does not affect the total liquid volume. The resulting solution is then bottled in 10-liter containers.

c. The finished product is highly unstable, and one 10-liter batch out of five is rejected at final inspection. Rejected batches have no commercial value and are thrown out.

d. It takes a worker 35 minutes to process one 10-liter batch of Nysap. Employees work an eight-hour day, including one hour per day for rest breaks and cleanup.

Required:

1. Determine the standard quantity for each of the raw materials needed to produce an acceptable 10-liter batch of Nysap.
2. Determine the standard labor time allowed to produce an acceptable 10-liter batch of Nysap.
3. Assuming the following purchase prices and costs, prepare a standard cost card for direct materials and direct labor for one acceptable 10-liter batch of Nysap:

Salex	$1.50 per liter	
Nyclyn	$2.80 per kilogram	
Protet	$3.00 per kilogram	
Direct labor cost	$9.00 per hour	

(CMA, adapted)

PROBLEM 8–17A   Comprehensive Variance Analysis   [LO1, LO2, LO3, LO4]

Highland Company produces a lightweight backpack that is popular with college students. Standard variable costs relating to a single backpack are given below:

CHECK FIGURE
(1) Standard cost: $31.50
(3) 2.8 yards

	Standard Quantity or Hours	Standard Price or Rate	Standard Cost
Direct materials	?	$6 per yard	$?
Direct labor	?	?	?
Variable manufacturing overhead	?	$3 per direct labor-hour	?
Total standard cost			$?

Overhead is applied to production on the basis of direct labor-hours. During March, 1,000 backpacks were manufactured and sold. Selected information relating to the month's production is given below:

	Materials Used	Direct Labor	Variable Manufacturing Overhead
Total standard cost allowed*	$16,800	$10,500	$4,200
Actual costs incurred	$15,000	?	$3,600
Materials price variance	?		
Materials quantity variance	$1,200 U		
Labor rate variance		?	
Labor efficiency variance		?	
Variable overhead spending variance ...			?
Variable overhead efficiency variance ...			?

*For the month's production.

The following additional information is available for March's production:

Actual direct labor-hours	1,500
Standard overhead rate per direct labor-hour	$3.00
Standard price of one yard of materials	$6.00
Difference between standard and actual cost per backpack produced during March	$0.15 F

Required:
1. What is the standard cost of a single backpack?
2. What was the actual cost per backpack produced during March?
3. How many yards of material are required at standard per backpack?
4. What was the materials price variance for March?
5. What is the standard direct labor rate per hour?
6. What was the labor rate variance for March? The labor efficiency variance?
7. What was the variable overhead spending variance for March? The variable overhead efficiency variance?
8. Prepare a standard cost card for one backpack.

PROBLEM 8–18A   Working Backwards from Labor Variances   [LO3]
The auto repair shop of Quality Motor Company uses standards to control the labor time and labor cost in
the shop. The standard labor cost for a motor tune-up is given below:

Job	Standard Hours	Standard Rate	Standard Cost
Motor tune-up	2.5 labor-hours	$9 per labor-hour	$22.50

The record showing the time spent in the shop last week on motor tune-ups has been misplaced. However,
the shop supervisor recalls that 50 tune-ups were completed during the week, and the controller recalls the
following variance data relating to tune-ups:

Labor rate variance	$87 F
Total labor variance	$93 U

Required:
1. Determine the number of actual labor-hours spent on tune-ups during the week.
2. Determine the actual hourly rate of pay for tune-ups last week.

(Hint: A useful way to proceed would be to work from known to unknown data either by using the variance
formulas or by using the columnar format shown in Exhibit 8–6.)

**PROBLEM 8–19A   (Appendix 8A) Comprehensive Variance Analysis with Incomplete Data;
Journal Entries   [LO1, LO2, LO3, LO4, LO5]**
Maple Products, Ltd., manufactures a super-strong hockey stick. The standard cost of one hockey stick is:

	Standard Quantity or Hours	Standard Price or Rate	Standard Cost
Direct materials	? feet	$3.00 per foot	$?
Direct labor	2 hours	? per hour	?
Variable manufacturing overhead	? hours	$1.30 per hour	?
Total standard cost			$27.00

Last year, 8,000 hockey sticks were produced and sold. Selected cost data relating to last year's operations
follow:

	Dr.	Cr.
Accounts payable—direct materials purchased (60,000 feet) ...		$174,000
Wages payable (? hours)		$79,200*
Work in process—direct materials	$115,200	
Direct labor rate variance		$3,300
Variable overhead efficiency variance	$650	
*Relates to the actual direct labor cost for the year.		

The following additional information is available for last year's operations:

a.   No materials were on hand at the start of last year. Some of the materials purchased during the year
     were still on hand in the warehouse at the end of the year.
b.   The variable manufacturing overhead rate is based on direct labor-hours. Total actual variable manu-
     facturing overhead cost for last year was $19,800.
c.   Actual direct materials usage for last year exceeded the standard by 0.2 feet per stick.

Required:

1. For direct materials:
   a. Compute the price and quantity variances for last year.
   b. Prepare journal entries to record all activities relating to direct materials for last year.
2. For direct labor:
   a. Using the rate variance given above, calculate the standard hourly wage rate and compute the efficiency variance for last year.
   b. Prepare a journal entry to record activity relating to direct labor for last year.
3. Compute the variable overhead spending variance for last year and verify the variable overhead efficiency variance given above.
4. State possible causes of each variance that you have computed.
5. Prepare a standard cost card for one hockey stick.

PROBLEM 8–20A Variance Analysis with Multiple Lots [LO2, LO3]

Hillcrest Leisure Wear, Inc., manufactures men's clothing. The company has a single line of slacks that is produced in lots, with each lot representing an order from a customer. As a lot is completed, the customer's store label is attached to the slacks before shipment.

Hillcrest has a standard cost system and has established the following standards for a dozen slacks:

CHECK FIGURE
(2b) Total quantity variance: $216 U
(4b) Total labor efficiency variance: $3,900 U

	Standard Quantity or Hours	Standard Price or Rate	Standard Cost
Direct materials ...	32 yards	$2.40 per yard	$76.80
Direct labor	6 hours	$7.50 per hour	$45.00

During October, Hillcrest worked on three orders for slacks. The company's job cost records for the month reveal the following:

Lot	Units in Lot (dozens)	Materials Used (yards)	Hours Worked
48	1,500	48,300	8,900
49	950	30,140	6,130
50	2,100	67,250	10,270

The following additional information is available:

a. Hillcrest purchased 180,000 yards of material during October at a cost of $424,800.
b. Direct labor cost incurred during the month for production of slacks amounted to $192,280.
c. There was no work in process inventory on October 1. During October, lots 48 and 49 were completed, and lot 50 was 100% complete with respect to materials and 80% complete with respect to labor.

Required:

1. Compute the materials price variance for the materials purchased during October.
2. Determine the materials quantity variance for October in both yards and dollars:
   a. For each lot worked on during the month.
   b. For the company as a whole.
3. Compute the labor rate variance for October.
4. Determine the labor efficiency variance for the month in both hours and dollars:
   a. For each lot worked on during the month.
   b. For the company as a whole.
5. In what situations might it be better to express variances in units (hours, yards, and so on) rather than in dollars? In dollars rather than in units?

(CPA, adapted)

PROBLEM 8–21A Developing Standard Costs [LO1]

ColdKing Company is a small producer of fruit-flavored frozen desserts. For many years, ColdKing's products have had strong regional sales on the basis of brand recognition; however, other companies have begun marketing similar products in the area, and price competition has become increasingly intense. John Wake-field, the company's controller, is planning to implement a standard cost system for ColdKing and has gath-ered considerable information from his co-workers on production and material requirements for ColdKing's products. Wakefield believes that the use of standard costing will allow ColdKing to improve cost control and make better pricing decisions.

   ColdKing's most popular product is raspberry sherbet. The sherbet is produced in 10-gallon batches, and each batch requires 6 quarts of good raspberries. The fresh raspberries are sorted by hand before they enter the production process. Because of imperfections in the raspberries and normal spoilage, 1 quart of berries is discarded for every 4 quarts of acceptable berries. Three minutes is the standard direct labor time for the sorting that is required to obtain 1 quart of acceptable raspberries. The acceptable raspberries are then blended with the other ingredients; blending requires 12 minutes of direct labor time per batch. After blend-ing, the sherbet is packaged in quart containers. Wakefield has gathered the following pricing information:

a. ColdKing purchases raspberries at a cost of $0.80 per quart. All other ingredients cost a total of $0.45 per gallon of sherbet.
b. Direct labor is paid at the rate of $9.00 per hour.
c. The total cost of direct material and direct labor required to package the sherbet is $0.38 per quart.

Required:
1. Develop the standard cost for the direct cost components (materials, labor, and packaging) of a 10-gallon batch of raspberry sherbet. The standard cost should identify the standard quantity, standard rate, and standard cost per batch for each direct cost component of a batch of raspberry sherbet.
2. As part of the implementation of a standard cost system at ColdKing, John Wakefield plans to train those responsible for maintaining the standards on how to use variance analysis. Wakefield is particularly concerned with the causes of unfavorable variances.
   a. Discuss possible causes of unfavorable materials price variances and identify the individual(s) who should be held responsible for these variances.
   b. Discuss possible causes of unfavorable labor efficiency variances and identify the individual(s) who should be held responsible for these variances.

(CMA, adapted)

PROBLEM 8–22A   Direct Materials and Direct Labor Variances; Computations from Incomplete Data   [LO1, LO2, LO3]
Sharp Company manufactures a product for which the following standards have been set:

	Standard Quantity or Hours	Standard Price or Rate	Standard Cost
Direct materials	3 feet	$5 per foot	$15
Direct labor	? hours	? per hour	?

During March, the company purchased direct materials at a cost of $55,650, all of which were used in the production of 3,200 units of product. In addition, 4,900 hours of direct labor time were worked on the product during the month. The cost of this labor time was $36,750. The following variances have been computed for the month:

Materials quantity variance	$4,500 U
Total labor variance	$1,650 F
Labor efficiency variance	$800 U

Required:
1. For direct materials:
   a. Compute the actual cost per foot for materials for March.
   b. Compute the materials price variance and a total variance for materials.
2. For direct labor:
   a. Compute the standard direct labor rate per hour.
   b. Compute the standard hours allowed for the month's production.
   c. Compute the standard hours allowed per unit of product.

(Hint: In completing the problem, it may be helpful to move from known to unknown data either by using the columnar format shown in Exhibits 8–4 and 8–6 or by using the variance formulas.)

BUILDING YOUR SKILLS

Communicating in Practice   (LO1)

Make an appointment to meet with the manager of an auto repair shop that uses standards. In most cases, this would be an auto repair shop that is affiliated with a national chain such as Firestone or Sears or the service department of a new-car dealer.

Required:

At the scheduled meeting, find out the answers to the following questions and write a memo to your instructor describing the information obtained during your meeting.

1. How are standards set?
2. Are standards practical or ideal?
3. Is the actual time taken to complete a task compared to the standard time?
4. What are the consequences of unfavorable variances? Of favorable variances?
5. Do the standards and variances create any potential problems?

Analytical Thinking (Appendix 8A)   [LO2, LO3, LO5]

You are employed by Olster Company, which manufactures products for the senior citizen market. As a rising young executive in the company, you are scheduled to make a presentation in a few hours to your superior. This presentation relates to last week's production of Maxitol, a popular health tonic that is manufactured by Olster Company. Unfortunately, while studying ledger sheets and variance summaries by poolside in the company's fitness area, you were bumped and dropped the papers into the pool. In desperation, you fished the papers from the water, but you have discovered that only the following fragments are readable:

CHECK FIGURE
(1) 120 batches
(3d) Materials price
variance: $560 U

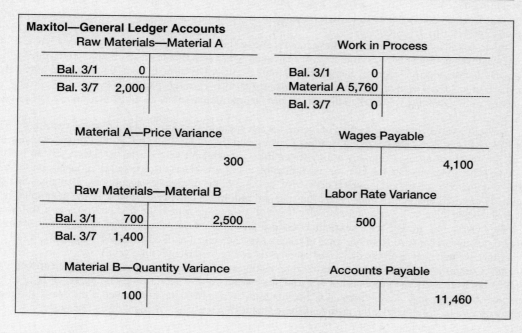

You remember that the accounts payable are for purchases of both Material A and Material B. You also remember that only 10 direct labor workers are involved in the production of Maxitol and that each worked 40 hours last week. The wages payable above are for wages earned by these workers.

You realize that to be ready for your presentation, you must reconstruct all data relating to Maxitol very quickly. As a start, you have called purchasing and found that 1,000 gallons of Material A and 800 pounds of Material B were purchased last week.

Required:
1. How many batches of Maxitol were produced last week? (This is a key figure; be sure it's right before going on.)
2. For Material A:
   a. What was the cost of Material A purchased last week?
   b. How many gallons were used in production last week?
   c. What was the quantity variance?
   d. Prepare journal entries to record all activity relating to Material A for last week.
3. For Material B:
   a. What is the standard cost per pound for Material B?
   b. How many pounds of Material B were used in production last week? How many pounds should have been used at standard?
   c. What is the standard quantity of Material B per batch?
   d. What was the price variance for Material B last week?
   e. Prepare journal entries to record all activity relating to Material B for last week.
4. For direct labor:
   a. What is the standard rate per direct labor-hour?
   b. What are the standard hours per batch?
   c. What were the standard hours allowed for last week's production?
   d. What was the labor efficiency variance for last week?
   e. Prepare a journal entry to record all activity relating to direct labor for last week.
5. Complete the standard cost card shown above for one batch of Maxitol.

Ethics Case   [LO1]

Stacy Cummins, the newly hired controller at Merced Home Products, Inc., was disturbed by what she had discovered about the standard costs at the Home Security Division. In looking over the past several years of quarterly earnings reports at the Home Security Division, she noticed that the first-quarter earnings were always poor, the second-quarter earnings were slightly better, the third-quarter earnings were again slightly better, and the fourth quarter always ended with a spectacular performance in which the Home Security Division managed to meet or exceed its target profit for the year. She also was concerned to find letters from the company's external auditors to top management warning about an unusual use of standard costs at the Home Security Division.

When Ms. Cummins ran across these letters, she asked the assistant controller, Gary Farber, if he knew what was going on at the Home Security Division. Gary said that it was common knowledge in the company that the vice president in charge of the Home Security Division, Preston Lansing, had rigged the standards at his division in order to produce the same quarterly earnings pattern every year. According to company policy, variances are taken directly to the income statement as an adjustment to cost of goods sold.

Favorable variances have the effect of increasing net operating income, and unfavorable variances have the effect of decreasing net operating income. Lansing had rigged the standards so that there were always large favorable variances. Company policy was a little vague about when these variances have to be reported on the divisional income statements. While the intent was clearly to recognize variances on the income statement in the period in which they arise, nothing in the company's accounting manuals actually explicitly required this. So for many years Lansing had followed a practice of saving up the favorable variances and using them to create a nice smooth pattern of earnings growth in the first three quarters, followed by a big "Christmas present" of an extremely good fourth quarter. (Financial reporting regulations forbid carrying variances forward from one year to the next on the annual audited financial statements, so all of the variances must appear on the divisional income statement by the end of the year.)

Ms. Cummins was concerned about these revelations and attempted to bring up the subject with the president of Merced Home Products but was told that "we all know what Lansing's doing, but as long as he continues to turn in such good reports, don't bother him." When Ms. Cummins asked if the board of directors was aware of the situation, the president somewhat testily replied, "Of course they are aware."

Required:
1. How did Preston Lansing probably "rig" the standard costs—are the standards set too high or too low? Explain.

2. Should Preston Lansing be permitted to continue his practice of managing reported earnings?
3. What should Stacy Cummins do in this situation?

Teamwork in Action   (LO1)

Terry Travers is the manufacturing supervisor of Aurora Manufacturing Company, which produces a variety of plastic products. Some of these products are standard items that are listed in the company's catalog, while others are made to customer specifications. Each month, Travers receives a performance report showing the budget for the month, the actual activity, and the variance between budget and actual. Part of Travers' annual performance evaluation is based on his department's performance against budget. Aurora's purchasing manager, Sally Christensen, also receives monthly performance reports and she, too, is evaluated in part on the basis of these reports.

The monthly reports for June had just been distributed when Travers met Christensen in the hallway outside their offices. Scowling, Travers began the conversation, "I see we have another set of monthly performance reports hand-delivered by that not very nice junior employee in the budget office. He seemed pleased to tell me that I'm in trouble with my performance again."

Christensen: I got the same treatment. All I ever hear about are the things I haven't done right. Now I'll have to spend a lot of time reviewing the report and preparing explanations. The worst part is that it's now the 21st of July so the information is almost a month old, and we have to spend all this time on history.

Travers: My biggest gripe is that our production activity varies a lot from month to month, but we're given an annual budget that's written in stone. Last month we were shut down for three days when a strike delayed delivery of the basic ingredient used in our plastic formulation, and we had already exhausted our inventory. You know about that problem, though, because we asked you to call all over the country to find an alternate source of supply. When we got what we needed on a rush basis, we had to pay more than we normally do.

Christensen: I expect problems like that to pop up from time to time—that's part of my job—but now we'll both have to take a careful look at our reports to see where the charges are reflected for that rush order. Every month I spend more time making sure I should be charged for each item reported than I do making plans for my department's daily work. It's really frustrating to see charges for things I have no control over.

Travers: The way we get information doesn't help, either. I don't get copies of the reports you get, yet a lot of what I do is affected by your department, and by most of the other departments we have. Why do the budget and accounting people assume that I should be told only about my operations even though the president regularly gives us pep talks about how we all need to work together as a team?

Christensen: I seem to get more reports than I need, and I am never asked to comment on them until top management calls me on the carpet about my department's shortcomings. Do you ever hear comments when your department shines?

Travers: I guess they don't have time to review the good news. One of my problems is that all the reports are in dollars and cents. I work with people, machines, and materials. I need information to help me *this* month to solve *this* month's problems—not another report of the dollars expended *last* month or the month before.

Required:

Your team should discuss and then respond to the following questions. All team members should agree with and understand the answers and be prepared to report on those answers in class. (Each teammate can assume responsibility for a different part of the presentation.)

1. Based on the conversation between Terry Travers and Sally Christensen, describe the likely motivation and behavior of these two employees as a result of the standard cost and variance reporting system that is used by Aurora Manufacturing Company.
2. List the recommendations that your team would make to Aurora Manufacturing Company to enhance employee motivation as it relates to the company's standard cost and variance reporting system.

(CMA, adapted)

Taking It to the Net

As you know, the World Wide Web is a medium that is constantly evolving. Sites come and go and change without notice. To enable periodic updating of site addresses, these problems have been posted to the textbook website (www.mhhe.com/bgn3e). After accessing the site, enter the Student Center and select this chapter to find the Taking It to the Net problems.

9

Flexible Budgets and Overhead Analysis

CHAPTER OUTLINE

A LOOK BACK

We discussed budgeting in Chapter 7—the process that is used by organizations to plan the financial aspects of their operations. We introduced management control and performance measures in Chapter 8 with a discussion of standard costs and variance analysis.

A LOOK AT THIS CHAPTER

Chapter 9 continues our coverage of the budgeting process by presenting the flexible approach to budgeting, including the use of a flexible budget to control overhead costs.

A LOOK AHEAD

We continue the discussion of management control and performance measures in Chapter 10 by focusing on how decentralized organizations are managed.

Flexible Budgets

- Characteristics of a Flexible Budget
- Deficiencies of the Static Budget
- How a Flexible Budget Works
- Using the Flexible Budgeting Concept in Performance Evaluation
- The Measure of Activity—A Critical Choice

Variable Overhead Variances—A Closer Look

- Actual versus Standard Hours
- Spending Variance Alone
- Both Spending and Efficiency Variances
- Activity-Based Costing and the Flexible Budget

Overhead Rates and Fixed Overhead Analysis

- Flexible Budgets and Overhead Rates
- Overhead Application in a Standard Cost System
- The Fixed Overhead Variances
- The Budget Variance—A Closer Look
- The Volume Variance—A Closer Look
- Graphic Analysis of Fixed Overhead Variances
- Cautions in Fixed Overhead Analysis
- Overhead Variances and Under- or Overapplied Overhead Cost

Chapter Nine

DECISION FEATURE

NASA Reduces Its Overhead Costs

NASA (www.nasa.gov) is the agency responsible for all civilian aeronautical and space activities sponsored by the United States. An online newsletter (today@nasa.gov) provides daily updates about the activities of NASA. During the six-year period from 1994 to 2000, NASA's budget decreased from $14.5 billion to $13.6 billion. Comparing fiscal 1990 through 1994 to fiscal 1995 through 1999, the average spacecraft development cost declined by 65%, the average development time decreased from 8 to 5 years, and the number of flights per year increased from 2 to 7.

NASA was able to achieve more with less during the 1990s by significantly reducing its overhead costs. By way of illustration, it took a crew of 1,000 to send Viking to Mars. Just under 20 years later, a crew of 50 sent the Pathfinder to Mars. Part of NASA's success can be attributed to its decision to outsource support activities. Contractors aggressively bid against each other to perform the work. This example of NASA's determination to control its overhead costs relates to a cost management program that was instituted by NASA in 1995.

The multiyear initiative encompasses NASA's management, budgeting, and accounting processes. In part, the program is expected to reduce the cost of missions, inspire the agency's managers to perform efficiently, benchmark activities, support the decision-making process, provide justification for NASA's budget requests, and further enhance NASA's accountability to the taxpayers.

Source: NASA website; and John Rhea, "Cutting the Fat: DOD Can Learn How from NASA," *Military & Aerospace Electronics,* March 1998, p. 3 (3 pages).

LEARNING OBJECTIVES

After studying Chapter 9, you should be able to:

LO1 Prepare a flexible budget and explain the advantages of the flexible budget approach over the static budget approach.

LO2 Prepare a performance report for both variable and fixed overhead costs using the flexible budget approach.

LO3 Use a flexible budget to prepare a variable overhead performance report containing only a spending variance.

LO4 Use a flexible budget to prepare a variable overhead performance report containing both a spending and an efficiency variance.

LO5 Compute the predetermined overhead rate and apply overhead to products in a standard cost system.

LO6 Compute and interpret the fixed overhead budget and volume variances.

Controlling overhead costs is a major preoccupation of managers in business, in government, and in not-for-profit organizations. Overhead is a major cost, if not *the* major cost, in many organizations. For example, it costs Microsoft very little to make copies of its software for sale to customers; almost all of Microsoft's costs are in research and development and marketing—elements of overhead. Or consider Disney World. The only direct cost of serving a particular guest is the cost of the food the guest consumes at the park; virtually all of the other costs of running the amusement park are overhead. Even Boeing, a manufacturer, has huge amounts of overhead in the form of engineering salaries, buildings, insurance, administrative salaries, and marketing costs.

Since overhead is usually made up of many separate costs, including everything from disposable coffee cups in the visitors' waiting area to the president's salary, it is more difficult to control than direct materials and direct labor. Overhead control is further complicated by the fact that overhead costs can be variable, fixed, or a mixture of variable and fixed. However, these complications can be largely overcome by using flexible budgets. In this chapter, we study flexible budgets in detail and learn how they can be used to control costs. We also expand the study of overhead variances that we started in Chapter 8.

Before getting into the detailed computations involved with flexible budgeting, let's start with a simple example. Imagine for a moment that you work as a baggage handler for an airline. Your boss has said that you should be able to unload 20 pieces of luggage from an airplane per minute. Yesterday when flight 2707 arrived at your airport from Boston, it had 300 pieces of luggage on it. Today flight 2707 is due to arrive from Boston and your boss has decided that the flight is likely to contain 300 pieces of luggage just like yesterday; therefore, you should be able to unload all the luggage in 15 minutes (300 pieces of luggage ÷ 20 pieces per minute). When you finish unloading the luggage, your boss yells at you for taking 20 minutes instead of 15 minutes. However, the flight actually contained 460 pieces of luggage. How would you feel? Chances are that you would complain. You might do some quick math in your head as follows. If there were 460 pieces of luggage on this flight and you are expected to unload 20 pieces per minute, then you should have been expected to unload the luggage on this flight in 23 minutes (460 ÷ 20). You did it in just 20 minutes instead of 23 minutes. Therefore, you should be getting a pat on the back, not yelled at! Notice, your natural inclination was to "flex" the budget of 15 minutes, which was based on 300 pieces of luggage, to reflect what the budget should be for 460 pieces of luggage—23 minutes. Congratulations, you have just instinctively applied the basics of flexible budgeting. Now, let's proceed by applying dollars and cents to this concept.

FLEXIBLE BUDGETS

Characteristics of a Flexible Budget

The budgets that we studied in Chapter 7 were *static budgets*. A **static budget** is prepared at the beginning of the budgeting period and is valid for only the planned level of activity. A static budget is suitable for planning but is inappropriate for evaluating how well costs are controlled. If the actual level of activity during a period differs from what was planned, it would be misleading to simply compare actual costs to the static budget. If activity is higher than expected, variable costs should be higher than expected; and if activity is lower than expected, variable costs should be lower than expected.

Flexible budgets take into account how changes in activity affect costs. A **flexible budget** makes it easy to estimate what costs should be for any level of activity within a specified range. When a flexible budget is used in performance evaluation, actual costs are compared to what the *costs should have been for the actual level of activity during the period* rather than to the budgeted costs from the original budget. This is a very important distinction—particularly for variable costs. If adjustments for the level of activity are not made, it is very difficult to interpret discrepancies between budgeted and actual costs.

Deficiencies of the Static Budget

To illustrate the difference between a static budget and a flexible budget, consider the case of Rick's Hairstyling, an upscale hairstyling salon located in Beverly Hills that is owned and managed by Rick Manzi. The salon has very loyal customers—many of whom are associated with the film industry. Despite the glamour associated with his salon, Rick is a very shrewd businessman. Recently he has been attempting to get better control of his overhead costs by preparing monthly budgets.

At the end of February, Rick carefully prepared the March budget for overhead items that appears in Exhibit 9–1. Rick believes that the number of customers served in a month is the best way to measure the overall level of activity in his salon. Rick refers to these visits as client-visits. A customer who comes into the salon and has his or her hair styled is counted as one client-visit. Rick identified three major categories of variable overhead costs—hairstyling supplies, client gratuities, and electricity—and four major categories of fixed costs—support staff wages and salaries, rent, insurance, and utilities other than electricity. Client gratuities consist of flowers, candies, and glasses of champagne that Rick gives to his customers while they are in the salon. Rick considers electricity to be a variable cost, since almost all of the electricity in the salon is consumed by running blow-dryers, curling irons, and other hairstyling equipment.

To develop the budget for variable overhead, Rick estimated that the average cost per client-visit should be $1.20 for hairstyling supplies, $4.00 for client gratuities, and $0.20 for electricity. Based on his estimate of 5,000 client-visits in March, Rick budgeted for $6,000 ($1.20 per client-visit × 5,000 client-visits) in hairstyling supplies, $20,000

Static vs. Flexible Budgets

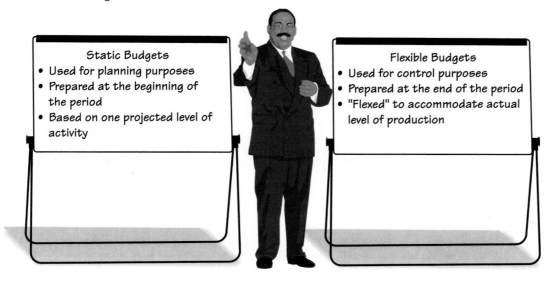

Static Budgets
- Used for planning purposes
- Prepared at the beginning of the period
- Based on one projected level of activity

Flexible Budgets
- Used for control purposes
- Prepared at the end of the period
- "Flexed" to accommodate actual level of production

EXHIBIT 9–1

RICK'S
hairstyling salon

> **Rick's Hairstyling**
> **Static Budget**
> **For the Month Ended March 31**
>
> | | |
> |---|---:|
> | Budgeted number of client-visits .... | 5,000 |
> | Budget variable overhead costs: | |
> | Hairstyling supplies (@ $1.20 per client-visit) .... | $ 6,000 |
> | Client gratuities (@ $4.00 per client-visit) .... | 20,000 |
> | Electricity (@ $0.20 per client-visit) .... | 1,000 |
> | Total variable overhead cost .... | 27,000 |
> | Budgeted fixed overhead costs: | |
> | Support staff wages and salaries .... | 8,000 |
> | Rent .... | 12,000 |
> | Insurance .... | 1,000 |
> | Utilities other than electricity .... | 500 |
> | Total fixed overhead cost .... | 21,500 |
> | Total budgeted overhead cost .... | $48,500 |

($4.00 per client-visit × 5,000 client-visits) in client gratuities, and $1,000 ($0.20 per client-visit × 5,000 client-visits) in electricity.

Rick's fixed overhead budget was based on records of how much he had spent on these items in the past. The budget included $8,000 for support staff wages and salaries, $12,000 for rent, $1,000 for insurance, and $500 for utilities other than electricity.

At the end of March, Rick prepared a report comparing actual to budgeted costs. That report appears in Exhibit 9–2. The problem with that report, as Rick immediately realized, is that it compares costs at one level of activity (5,200 client-visits) to costs at a different level of activity (5,000 client-visits). Since Rick had 200 more client-visits than expected, his variable costs *should* be higher than budgeted. From Rick's standpoint, although the increase in client-visits is desirable, it is having a negative impact on the variable overhead variances shown in his report. He knows that to make the report more meaningful he

EXHIBIT 9–2

> **Rick's Hairstyling**
> **Static Budget Performance Report**
> **For the Month Ended March 31**
>
> | | Actual | Budgeted | Variance |
> |---|---:|---:|---:|
> | Client-visits............................... | 5,200 | 5,000 | 200 F |
> | Variable overhead costs: | | | |
> | Hairstyling supplies .... | $ 6,400 | $ 6,000 | $ 400 U* |
> | Client gratuities .... | 22,300 | 20,000 | 2,300 U* |
> | Electricity .... | 1,020 | 1,000 | 20 U* |
> | Total variable overhead cost .... | 29,720 | 27,000 | 2,720 U* |
> | Fixed overhead costs: | | | |
> | Support staff wages and salaries .... | 8,100 | 8,000 | 100 U |
> | Rent.................................... | 12,000 | 12,000 | 0 |
> | Insurance .... | 1,000 | 1,000 | 0 |
> | Utilities other than electricity............. | 470 | 500 | 30 F |
> | Total fixed overhead cost .... | 21,570 | 21,500 | 70 U |
> | Total overhead cost...................... | $51,290 | $48,500 | $2,790 U* |
>
> *The cost variances for variable costs and for total overhead are useless for evaluating how well costs were controlled since they have been derived by comparing actual costs at one level of activity to budgeted costs at a different level of activity.

needs to separate the portion of his variable overhead variances that is caused by the extra 200 client-visits from the portion that relates to his cost control efforts.

How a Flexible Budget Works

Exhibit 9–3 illustrates how flexible budgets work. It shows how overhead costs can be expected to change, depending on the monthly level of activity. Within the activity range of 4,900 to 5,200 client-visits, the fixed costs are expected to remain the same. For the variable overhead costs, the per client costs ($1.20 for hairstyling supplies, $4.00 for client gratuities, and $0.20 for electricity) are multiplied by the appropriate number of client-visits in each column. For example, the $1.20 cost of hairstyling supplies was multiplied by 4,900 client-visits to give the total cost of $5,880 for hairstyling supplies at that level of activity.

> **LEARNING OBJECTIVE 2**
> Prepare a performance report for both variable and fixed overhead costs using the flexible budget approach.

Using the Flexible Budgeting Concept in Performance Evaluation

To get a better idea of how well variable overhead costs were controlled in March, the flexible budgeting concept was used to create a new performance report based on the *actual* number of client-visits for the month (Exhibit 9–4). The budget is prepared by multiplying the actual level of activity by the cost formula for each of the variable cost categories. For example, using the $1.20 per client-visit for hairstyling supplies, the total cost for this item *should be* $6,240 for 5,200 client-visits ($1.20 per client-visit × 5,200 client-visits). Since the actual cost for hairstyling supplies was $6,400, the unfavorable variance was $160.

Contrast the flexible budget performance report in Exhibit 9–4 with the static budget approach in Exhibit 9–2. The variance for hairstyling supplies was $400 unfavorable using the static budget approach. However, actual costs at one level of activity were being compared to budgeted costs at a different level of activity. This is like comparing apples to oranges. Because actual activity was higher by 200 client-visits than budgeted activity,

EXHIBIT 9–3   Illustration of the Flexible Budgeting Concept

	Rick's Hairstyling Flexible Budget For the Month Ended March 31				
Budgeted number of client-visits............	5,000				
Overhead Costs	Cost Formula (per client-visit)	Activity (in client-visits)			
		4,900	5,000	5,100	5,200
Variable overhead costs:					
Hairstyling supplies....................	$1.20	$ 5,880	$ 6,000	$ 6,120	$ 6,240
Client gratuities	4.00	19,600	20,000	20,400	20,800
Electricity (variable)...................	0.20	980	1,000	1,020	1,040
Total variable overhead cost	$5.40	26,460	27,000	27,540	28,080
Fixed overhead costs:					
Support staff wages and salaries.........		8,000	8,000	8,000	8,000
Rent.....................................		12,000	12,000	12,000	12,000
Insurance...............................		1,000	1,000	1,000	1,000
Utilities other than electricity		500	500	500	500
Total fixed overhead cost.................		21,500	21,500	21,500	21,500
Total overhead cost		$47,960	$48,500	$49,040	$49,580

EXHIBIT 9–4

Rick's Hairstyling
Flexible Budget Performance Report
For the Month Ended March 31

Budgeted number of client-visits 5,000
Actual number of client-visits 5,200

Overhead Costs	Cost Formula (per client-visit)	Actual Costs Incurred for 5,200 Client-Visits	Budget Based on 5,200 Client-Visits	Variance
Variable overhead costs:				
Hairstyling supplies	$1.20	$ 6,400	$ 6,240	$ 160 U
Client gratuities.	4.00	22,300	20,800	1,500 U
Electricity (variable)	0.20	1,020	1,040	20 F
Total variable overhead cost	$5.40	29,720	28,080	1,640 U
Fixed overhead costs:				
Support staff wages and salaries		8,100	8,000	100 U
Rent.		12,000	12,000	0
Insurance		1,000	1,000	0
Utilities other than electricity		470	500	30 F
Total fixed overhead cost		21,570	21,500	70 U
Total overhead cost		$51,290	$49,580	$1,710 U

the total cost of hairstyling supplies *should* have been $240 ($1.20 per client-visit × 200 client-visits) higher than budgeted. As a result, $240 of the $400 "unfavorable" variance in the static budget performance report in Exhibit 9–2 was spurious.

In contrast, the flexible budget performance report in Exhibit 9–4 provides a more valid assessment of performance. Apples are compared to apples. Actual costs are compared to what costs should have been at the actual level of activity. When this is done, we see that the variance is $160 unfavorable rather than $400 unfavorable as it was in the original static budget performance report. In some cases, as with electricity, an unfavorable variance may be transformed into a favorable variance when an increase in activity is properly taken into account.

CONCEPT CHECK

1. Which of the following statements is false? (You may select more than one answer.)
   a. A flexible budget is used for control purposes and a static budget is used for planning purposes.
   b. A flexible budget is prepared at the end of the period and a static budget is prepared at the beginning of the period.
   c. A flexible budget is most useful for controlling fixed costs.
   d. A static budget provides budgeted estimates for one level of activity.
2. A company's static budget estimate of total overhead costs was $100,000 based on the assumption that 10,000 units would be produced and sold. The company estimates that 30% of its overhead is variable and the remainder is fixed. What would be the total overhead cost according to the flexible budget if 12,000 units were produced and sold?
   a. $96,000
   b. $100,000
   c. $106,000
   d. $116,000

Focus on Opportunities

Legendary management guru Peter F. Drucker cautions managers that "almost without exception, the first page of the [monthly] report presents the areas in which results fall below expectations or in which expenditures exceed the budget. It focuses on problems. Problems cannot be ignored. But . . . enterprises have to focus on opportunities. That requires a small but fundamental procedural change: a new first page to the monthly report, one that precedes the page that shows the problems. The new page should focus on where results are better than expected. As much time should be spent on that new first page as traditionally was spent on the problem page."

Source: Peter F. Drucker, "Change Leaders," *Inc.*, June 1999, pp. 65–72.

The largest variance on the flexible budget performance report is the $1,500 unfavorable variance for client gratuities. Rick had suspected that these expenses had gotten a little out of control, and the report confirmed those suspicions. He resolved to watch these expenses more closely in the coming months.

Confusion often arises concerning the fixed costs on a performance report. Actual fixed costs can differ from budgeted fixed costs. Costs are called fixed because they shouldn't be affected by changes in the level of activity within the relevant range. However, that does not mean that fixed costs can't change for other reasons. For example, Rick's utility bill, which includes natural gas for heating, varies with the weather. Additionally, the use of the term *fixed* may suggest that the cost can't be controlled, but that isn't true. It is often easier to control fixed costs than variable costs. For example, it would be fairly easy for Rick to control his insurance costs, which are fixed, by adjusting the amount of his insurance protection. It would be much more difficult for Rick to have much impact on the variable cost of electricity, which is a necessary cost of serving customers.

To reiterate, it is important to remember that a cost is variable if it is proportional to activity; it is fixed if it does not depend on the level of activity. However, fixed costs can change for reasons having nothing to do with changes in the level of activity. And controllability has little to do with whether a cost is variable or fixed. Fixed costs are often more controllable than variable costs.

Using the flexible budget approach, Rick Manzi now has a better way of assessing whether overhead costs are under control. The analysis is not so simple, however, in companies that provide a variety of products and services. The number of units produced or customers served may not be an adequate measure of overall activity. For example, does it make sense to count a Sony CD player, worth less than $50, as equivalent to a large-screen high-definition Sony TV? If the number of units produced is used as a measure of overall activity, then the CD player and the large-screen TV would be counted as equivalent. Clearly, the number of units produced (or customers served) may not be appropriate as an overall measure of activity when the organization has a variety of products or services; a common denominator may be needed.

The Measure of Activity—A Critical Choice

What should be used as the measure of activity when the company produces a variety of products and services? At least three factors are important in selecting an activity base for an overhead flexible budget:

1. The variable overhead costs should be related to the activity base on a cause-and-effect basis. Changes in the activity base should cause, or at least be highly correlated with, changes in the variable overhead costs in the flexible budget. Ideally, the variable overhead costs in the flexible budget should vary in direct proportion to changes in the activity base. For example, in a carpentry shop specializing in handmade wood furniture, the costs of miscellaneous supplies such as glue, wooden dowels, and sandpaper can be expected to vary with the number of direct

labor-hours. Direct labor-hours would therefore be a good measure of activity to use in a flexible budget for the costs of such supplies.

2. The activity base should not be expressed in dollars or other currency. For example, direct labor cost is usually a poor choice for an activity base in flexible budgets. Changes in wage rates affect the activity base but do not usually result in a proportionate change in overhead. For example, we would not ordinarily expect to see a 5% increase in the consumption of glue in a carpentry shop if the workers receive a 5% increase in pay. Therefore, it is normally best to use physical rather than financial measures of activity in flexible budgets.

3. The activity base should be simple and easily understood. A base that is not easily understood will probably result in confusion and misunderstanding. It is difficult to control costs if people don't understand the reports or do not accept them as valid.

IN BUSINESS

Gas Stations

Generally, convenience store and car wash sales are directly related to the volume of gas sold by a gas station. Consequently, the gas sales budget would be the starting point for the entire budgeting process. Factors that should be considered when forecasting gas sales might include: the prior year's sales, changes in the volume of traffic in the area, changes in the environment that impact access to the station (for example, road construction or the installation of median barriers that impede access), and changes in the number or type of gas stations that are operating in the immediate vicinity.

    When a flexible budgeting approach is used, the manager of a gas station might choose to prepare one overhead budget or separate overhead budgets for each of its segments (gas station, convenience store, and car wash). The decision would be based on whether or not the same activity base could be used for the three segments.

Source: Steven P. Smalley, "Measuring the Convenience of Gas Stations," *Appraisal Journal,* October 1999, p. 339.

VARIABLE OVERHEAD VARIANCES—A CLOSER LOOK

Concept 9-2

When the flexible budget is based on *hours* of activity (such as direct labor-hours) rather than on units of product or number of customers served, the flexible budget on the performance report can be based on either the actual hours used *or* the standard hours allowed for the actual output. Which should be used?

Actual versus Standard Hours

The nature of the problem can best be seen through a specific example. MicroDrive Corporation makes precision computer disk-drive motors for military applications. Data concerning the company's variable manufacturing overhead costs are shown in Exhibit 9–5.

    MicroDrive Corporation uses machine-hours as the activity base in its flexible budget because the company's managers believe most of the overhead costs are driven by machine-hours. Based on the budgeted production of 25,000 motors and the standard of 2 machine-hours per motor, the budgeted level of activity was 50,000 machine-hours. However, actual production for the year was only 20,000 motors, and 42,000 hours of machine time were used to produce these motors. According to the standard, only 40,000 hours of machine time should have been used (40,000 machine-hours = 2 machine-hours per motor × 20,000 motors).

Budgeted production	25,000	motors
Actual production	20,000	motors
Standard machine-hours per motor	2	machine-hours per motor
Budgeted machine-hours (2 × 25,000)	50,000	machine-hours
Standard machine-hours allowed		
for the actual output (2 × 20,000)	40,000	machine-hours
Actual machine-hours	42,000	machine-hours
Variable overhead costs per machine-hour:		
Indirect labor	$0.80	per machine-hour
Lubricants	$0.30	per machine-hour
Power	$0.40	per machine-hour
Actual total variable overhead costs:		
Indirect labor	$36,000	
Lubricants	11,000	
Power	24,000	
Total actual variable overhead cost	$71,000	

EXHIBIT 9–5

MicroDrive Corporation Data

In preparing an overhead performance report for the year, MicroDrive could use the 42,000 machine-hours actually worked during the year *or* the 40,000 machine-hours that should have been worked according to the standard. If the actual hours are used, only a spending variance will be computed. If the standard hours are used, both a spending *and* an efficiency variance will be computed. Both of these approaches are illustrated in the following sections.

Spending Variance Alone

If MicroDrive Corporation bases its overhead performance report on the 42,000 machine-hours actually worked during the year, then the performance report will show only a spending variance for variable overhead. A performance report prepared in this way is shown in Exhibit 9–6.

The formula for the spending variance was introduced in the preceding chapter. That formula is:

LEARNING OBJECTIVE 3

Use a flexible budget to prepare a variable overhead performance report containing only a spending variance.

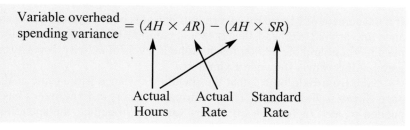

$$\begin{array}{l}\text{Variable overhead} \\ \text{spending variance}\end{array} = (AH \times AR) - (AH \times SR)$$

Actual Hours   Actual Rate   Standard Rate

Or, in factored form:

$$\begin{array}{l}\text{Variable overhead} \\ \text{spending variance}\end{array} = AH(AR - SR)$$

The report in Exhibit 9–6 is structured around the first, or unfactored, format.

Interpreting the Spending Variance   The variable overhead spending variance is useful only to the extent that the cost driver for variable overhead really is the actual hours worked. Then the flexible budget based on the actual hours worked is a valid benchmark that tells us how much *should* have been spent in total on variable overhead items

EXHIBIT 9–6

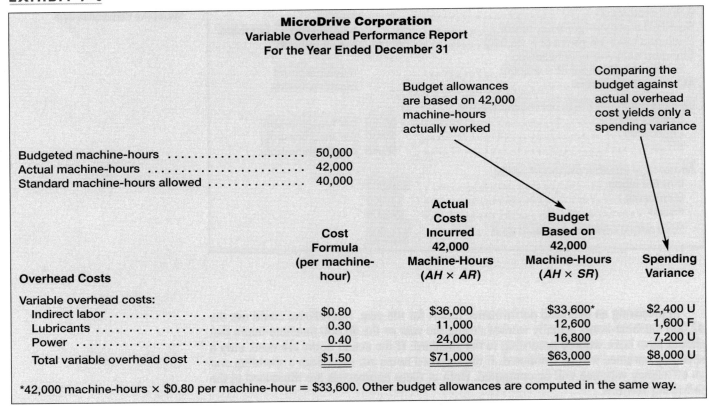

MicroDrive Corporation
Variable Overhead Performance Report
For the Year Ended December 31

Budget allowances are based on 42,000 machine-hours actually worked

Comparing the budget against actual overhead cost yields only a spending variance

Budgeted machine-hours	50,000
Actual machine-hours	42,000
Standard machine-hours allowed	40,000

Overhead Costs	Cost Formula (per machine-hour)	Actual Costs Incurred 42,000 Machine-Hours (AH × AR)	Budget Based on 42,000 Machine-Hours (AH × SR)	Spending Variance
Variable overhead costs:				
Indirect labor	$0.80	$36,000	$33,600*	$2,400 U
Lubricants	0.30	11,000	12,600	1,600 F
Power	0.40	24,000	16,800	7,200 U
Total variable overhead cost	$1.50	$71,000	$63,000	$8,000 U

*42,000 machine-hours × $0.80 per machine-hour = $33,600. Other budget allowances are computed in the same way.

during the period. The actual overhead costs would be larger than this benchmark, resulting in an unfavorable variance, if either (1) the variable overhead items cost more to purchase than the standards allow or (2) more variable overhead items were used than the standards allow. So the spending variance includes both price and quantity variances.

Both Spending and Efficiency Variances

If management of MicroDrive Corporation wants both a spending and an efficiency variance for variable overhead, then it should compute budget allowances for *both* the 40,000 machine-hour and the 42,000 machine-hour levels of activity. A performance report prepared in this way is shown in Exhibit 9–7.

Note from Exhibit 9–7 that the spending variance is the same as the spending variance shown in Exhibit 9–6. The performance report in Exhibit 9–7 has simply been expanded to also include an efficiency variance. Together, the spending and efficiency variances make up the total variance.

Interpreting the Efficiency Variance   Like the variable overhead spending variance, the variable overhead efficiency variance is useful only to the extent that the cost driver for variable overhead really is the actual hours worked. Then any increase in hours actually worked should result in additional variable overhead costs. Consequently, if too many hours were used to create the actual output, this is likely to result in an increase in variable overhead. The variable overhead efficiency variance is an estimate of the effect on variable overhead costs of inefficiency in the use of the base (i.e., hours). In a sense, the term *variable overhead efficiency variance* is a misnomer. It seems to suggest that it measures the efficiency with which variable overhead resources were used. It does not. It is an estimate of the indirect effect on variable overhead costs of inefficiency in the use of the activity base.

Recall from the preceding chapter that the variable overhead efficiency variance is a function of the difference between the actual hours incurred and the hours that should have been used to produce the period's output:

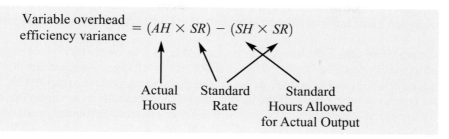

$$\text{Variable overhead efficiency variance} = (AH \times SR) - (SH \times SR)$$

Or, in factored form:

$$\text{Variable overhead efficiency variance} = SR(AH - SH)$$

If more hours are worked than are allowed at standard, then the overhead efficiency variance will be unfavorable. However, as discussed above, the inefficiency is not in the use of overhead *but rather in the use of the base itself.*

This point can be illustrated by looking again at Exhibit 9–7. Two thousand more machine-hours were used during the period than should have been used to produce the period's

EXHIBIT 9–7

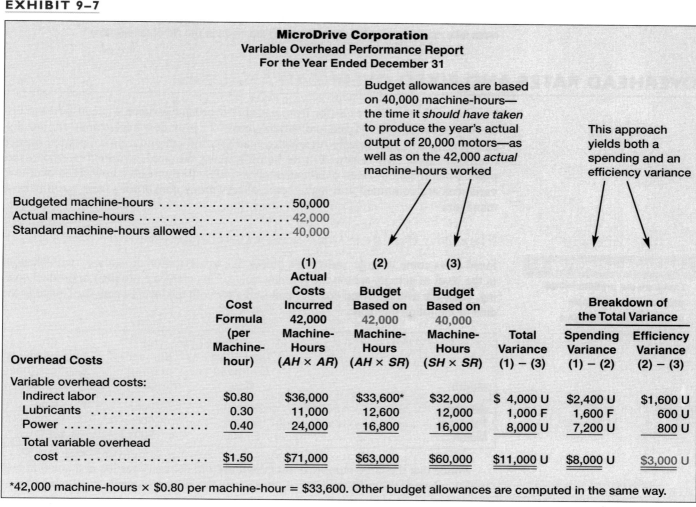

MicroDrive Corporation
Variable Overhead Performance Report
For the Year Ended December 31

Budget allowances are based on 40,000 machine-hours—the time it *should have taken* to produce the year's actual output of 20,000 motors—as well as on the 42,000 *actual* machine-hours worked

This approach yields both a spending and an efficiency variance

Budgeted machine-hours 50,000
Actual machine-hours 42,000
Standard machine-hours allowed 40,000

		(1) Actual Costs Incurred 42,000 Machine-Hours (AH × AR)	(2) Budget Based on 42,000 Machine-Hours (AH × SR)	(3) Budget Based on 40,000 Machine-Hours (SH × SR)		Breakdown of the Total Variance	
Overhead Costs	Cost Formula (per Machine-hour)				Total Variance (1) − (3)	Spending Variance (1) − (2)	Efficiency Variance (2) − (3)
Variable overhead costs:							
Indirect labor	$0.80	$36,000	$33,600*	$32,000	$ 4,000 U	$2,400 U	$1,600 U
Lubricants	0.30	11,000	12,600	12,000	1,000 F	1,600 F	600 U
Power	0.40	24,000	16,800	16,000	8,000 U	7,200 U	800 U
Total variable overhead cost	$1.50	$71,000	$63,000	$60,000	$11,000 U	$8,000 U	$3,000 U

*42,000 machine-hours × $0.80 per machine-hour = $33,600. Other budget allowances are computed in the same way.

output. Each of these hours presumably required the incurrence of $1.50 of variable over-head cost, resulting in an unfavorable variance of $3,000 (2,000 machine-hours × $1.50 per machine-hour = $3,000). Although this $3,000 variance is called an overhead efficiency variance, it could better be called a machine-hours efficiency variance, since it results from using too many machine-hours rather than from inefficient use of overhead resources.

Control of the Efficiency Variance   Who is responsible for control of the overhead efficiency variance? Since the variance really reflects efficiency in the utilization of the base underlying the flexible budget, whoever is responsible for control of this base is responsible for control of the variance. If the base is direct labor-hours, then the supervisor responsible for the use of labor time will be responsible for any overhead efficiency variance.

Activity-Based Costing and the Flexible Budget

It is unlikely that all of the variable overhead in a complex organization is driven by a single factor such as the number of units produced or the number of labor-hours or machine-hours. Activity-based costing provides a way of recognizing a variety of overhead cost drivers and thereby increasing the accuracy of the costing system. In activity-based costing, each over-head cost pool has its own measure of activity. The actual spending in each overhead cost pool can be independently evaluated using the techniques discussed in this chapter. The only difference is that the cost formulas for variable overhead costs will be stated in terms of dif-ferent kinds of activities instead of all being stated in terms of units or a common measure of activity such as direct labor-hours or machine-hours. If done properly, activity-based cost-ing can greatly enhance the usefulness of overhead performance reports by recognizing mul-tiple causes of overhead costs. In general, the usefulness of overhead performance reports depends on how carefully the reports are designed and prepared. In particular, managers must take care to separate variable from fixed costs in the flexible budgets.

OVERHEAD RATES AND FIXED OVERHEAD ANALYSIS

Fixed overhead variances differ from variable overhead variances because of the dif-ference in the nature of fixed and variable costs. To provide a background for our dis-cussion, we will first briefly review the need for, and computation of, predetermined overhead rates. This review will be helpful, since the predetermined overhead rate plays a major role in fixed overhead analysis. We will then show how fixed overhead variances are computed and make some observations concerning their usefulness to managers.

Flexible Budgets and Overhead Rates

LEARNING OBJECTIVE 5

Compute the predetermined overhead rate and apply overhead to products in a standard cost system.

Fixed costs come in large, indivisible pieces that by definition do not vary with changes in the level of activity within the relevant range. This creates a problem in product cost-ing, since the average fixed cost per unit will vary with the level of activity. Consider the data in the following table:

Month	(1) Total Fixed Overhead Cost	(2) Number of Units Produced	(3) Average Fixed Cost per Unit (1) ÷ (2)
January	$6,000	1,000	$6.00
February	$6,000	1,500	$4.00
March	$6,000	800	$7.50

Notice that the large number of units produced in February results in a low unit cost ($4.00), whereas the small number of units produced in March results in a high unit cost

($7.50). This phenomenon occurs only in connection with the fixed portion of overhead, since by definition the variable portion of overhead remains constant on a per unit basis, rising and falling in total proportionately with changes in the activity level. Most managers feel that the fixed portion of unit cost should be stabilized so that a single unit cost can be used throughout the year. As we learned in Chapter 2, this stability can be accomplished through use of the predetermined overhead rate.

Throughout the remainder of this chapter, we will be analyzing the fixed overhead costs of MicroDrive Corporation. To assist us in that task, the flexible budget of the company—including fixed costs—is displayed in Exhibit 9–8. Note that the total fixed overhead costs amount to $300,000 within the range of activity in the flexible budget.

Denominator Activity The formula that we used in Chapter 2 to compute the predetermined overhead rate was:

$$\text{Predetermined overhead rate} = \frac{\text{Estimated total manufacturing overhead cost}}{\text{Estimated total amount of the base (MH, DLH, etc.)}}$$

The estimated total amount of the base in the formula for the predetermined overhead rate is called the **denominator activity.** Recall from our discussion in Chapter 2 that once an estimated activity level (denominator activity) has been chosen, it remains unchanged throughout the year, even if the actual level of activity turns out to be different from what was estimated. The reason for not changing the denominator is to keep the amount of overhead applied to each unit of product the same regardless of when it is produced during the year.

Computing the Overhead Rate When we discussed predetermined overhead rates in Chapter 2, we didn't explain how the estimated total manufacturing cost was determined. This figure can be derived from the flexible budget. Once the denominator level of activity has been chosen, the flexible budget can be used to determine the total amount of overhead cost that should be incurred at that level of activity. The predetermined overhead

EXHIBIT 9–8

MicroDrive Corporation
Flexible Budgets at Various Levels of Activity

Overhead Costs	Cost Formula (per machine-hour)	40,000	45,000	50,000	55,000
Variable overhead costs:					
Indirect labor	$0.80	$ 32,000	$ 36,000	$ 40,000	$ 44,000
Lubricants	0.30	12,000	13,500	15,000	16,500
Power	0.40	16,000	18,000	20,000	22,000
Total variable overhead cost	$1.50	60,000	67,500	75,000	82,500
Fixed overhead costs:					
Depreciation		100,000	100,000	100,000	100,000
Supervisory salaries		160,000	160,000	160,000	160,000
Insurance		40,000	40,000	40,000	40,000
Total fixed overhead cost		300,000	300,000	300,000	300,000
Total overhead cost		$360,000	$367,500	$375,000	$382,500

Activity (in machine-hours)

rate can then be computed using the following variation on the basic formula for the pre-determined overhead rate:

$$\text{Predetermined overhead rate} = \frac{\text{Overhead from the flexible budget at the denominator level of activity}}{\text{Denominator level of activity}}$$

To illustrate, refer to MicroDrive Corporation's flexible budget for manufacturing overhead in Exhibit 9–8. Suppose that the budgeted activity level for the year is 50,000 machine-hours and that this will be used as the denominator activity in the formula for the predetermined overhead rate. The numerator in the formula is the estimated total overhead cost of $375,000 when the level of activity is 50,000 machine-hours. This amount is taken from the flexible budget in Exhibit 9–8. Thus, the predetermined overhead rate for MicroDrive Corporation will be computed as follows:

$$\frac{\$375,000}{50,000 \text{ MHs}} = \$7.50 \text{ per machine-hour (MH)}$$

Or the company can break its predetermined overhead rate down into variable and fixed elements rather than using a single combined figure:

$$\text{Variable element: } \frac{\$75,000}{50,000 \text{ MHs}} = \$1.50 \text{ per machine-hour (MH)}$$

$$\text{Fixed element: } \frac{\$300,000}{50,000 \text{ MHs}} = \$6 \text{ per machine-hour (MH)}$$

For every standard machine-hour of operation, work in process will be charged with $7.50 of overhead, of which $1.50 is variable overhead and $6.00 is fixed overhead. Since a disk-drive motor should take two machine-hours to complete, its cost will include $3 of variable overhead and $12 of fixed overhead, as shown on the following standard cost card:

Standard Cost Card—Per Motor	
Direct materials (assumed)	$14
Direct labor (assumed)	6
Variable overhead (2 machine-hours at $1.50 per machine-hour)	3
Fixed overhead (2 machine-hours at $6 per machine-hour)	12
Total standard cost per motor	$35

In sum, the flexible budget provides the estimated overhead cost needed to compute the predetermined overhead rate. Thus, the flexible budget plays a key role in determining the amount of fixed and variable overhead cost that will be charged to units of product.

IN BUSINESS   Know Your Costs

Understanding the difference between fixed and variable costs can be critical. Kennard T. Wing, of OMG Center for Collaborative Learning, reports that a large health care system made the mistake of classifying all of its costs as variable. As a consequence, when volume dropped, managers felt that costs should be cut proportionately and more than 1,000 people were laid off—even though "the workload of most of them had no direct relation to patient volume. The result was that morale of the survivors plummeted and within a year the system was scrambling to replace not only those it had let go, but many others who had quit. The point is, the accounting systems we design and implement really do affect management decisions in significant ways. A system built on a bad model of the business will either not be used or, if used, will lead to bad decisions."

Source: Kennard T. Wing, "Using Enhanced Cost Models in Variance Analysis for Better Control and Decision Making," *Management Accounting Quarterly,* Winter 2000, pp. 27–35.

Overhead Application in a Standard Cost System

To understand fixed overhead variances, we first have to understand how overhead is applied to work in process in a standard cost system. Recall from Chapter 2 that we applied overhead to work in process on the basis of actual hours of activity (multiplied by the predetermined overhead rate). This procedure was correct, since at the time we were dealing with a normal cost system.[1] However, we are now dealing with a standard cost system. In such a system, overhead is applied to work in process on the basis of the *standard hours allowed for the output of the period* rather than on the basis of the actual number of hours worked. This point is illustrated in Exhibit 9–9. In a standard cost system, every unit of product is charged with the same amount of overhead cost, regardless of how much time the unit actually requires for processing.

The Fixed Overhead Variances

To illustrate the computation of fixed overhead variances, we will refer again to the data for MicroDrive Corporation.

Denominator activity in machine-hours	50,000	
Budgeted fixed overhead costs	$300,000	
Fixed portion of the predetermined overhead rate (computed earlier)		$6 per machine-hour

> **LEARNING OBJECTIVE 6**
>
> Compute and interpret the fixed overhead budget and volume variances.

Let's assume that the following actual operating results were recorded for the year:

Actual machine-hours	42,000
Standard machine-hours allowed*	40,000
Actual fixed overhead costs:	
Depreciation	$100,000
Supervisory salaries	172,000
Insurance	36,000
Total actual fixed overhead cost	$308,000
*For the actual production of the year.	

From these data, two variances can be computed for fixed overhead—a *budget variance* and a *volume variance*. The variances are shown in Exhibit 9–10.

Notice from the exhibit that overhead has been applied to work in process on the basis of 40,000 standard hours allowed for the actual output of the year rather than on the basis of 42,000 actual hours worked. As stated earlier, this keeps unit costs from being affected by variations in efficiency.

Normal Cost System		Standard Cost System	
Manufacturing Overhead		Manufacturing Overhead	
Actual overhead costs incurred	Applied overhead costs: Actual hours × Predetermined overhead rate	Actual overhead costs incurred	Applied overhead costs: Standard hours allowed for actual output × Predetermined overhead rate
Under- or overapplied overhead		Under- or overapplied overhead	

EXHIBIT 9–9

Applied Overhead Costs: Normal Cost System versus Standard Cost System

---

[1]Normal cost systems are discussed in Chapter 2.

EXHIBIT 9–10

Computation of the Fixed
Overhead Variances

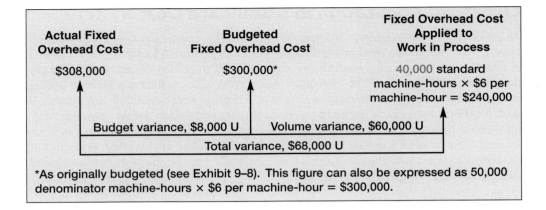

*As originally budgeted (see Exhibit 9–8). This figure can also be expressed as 50,000 denominator machine-hours × $6 per machine-hour = $300,000.

The Budget Variance—A Closer Look

The **budget variance** is the difference between the actual fixed overhead costs incurred during the period and the original budgeted fixed overhead costs for the period. It can be computed as shown in Exhibit 9–10 or by using the following formula:

$$\text{Budget variance} = \text{Actual fixed overhead cost} - \text{Budgeted fixed overhead cost}$$

Applying this formula to MicroDrive Corporation, the budget variance would be computed as follows:

$$\$308,000 - \$300,000 = \$8,000 \text{ U}$$

The variances computed for the fixed costs at Rick's Hairstyling in Exhibit 9–4 are all budget variances, since they represent the difference between the actual fixed overhead cost and the budgeted fixed overhead cost.

An expanded overhead performance report for MicroDrive Corporation appears in Exhibit 9–11. This report includes the budget variances for fixed overhead as well as the spending variances for variable overhead from Exhibit 9–6.

The budget variances for fixed overhead can be very useful, since they represent the difference between how much *should* have been spent (according to the original budget) and how much was actually spent. For example, supervisory salaries has a $12,000 unfavorable variance. There should be some explanation for this large variance. Was it due to an increase in salaries? Was it due to overtime? Was another supervisor hired? If so, why was another supervisor hired?

EXHIBIT 9–11

Fixed Overhead Costs on the
Overhead Performance Report

MicroDrive Corporation
Overhead Performance Report
For the Year Ended December 31

Budgeted machine-hours.................. 50,000
Actual machine-hours..................... 42,000
Standard machine-hours allowed 40,000

Overhead Costs	Cost Formula (per machine-hour)	Actual Costs 42,000 Machine-Hours	Budget Based on 42,000 Machine-Hours	Spending or Budget Variance
Variable overhead costs:				
Indirect labor	$0.80	$ 36,000	$ 33,600	$ 2,400 U
Lubricants	0.30	11,000	12,600	1,600 F
Power	0.40	24,000	16,800	7,200 U
Total variable				
overhead cost	$1.50	71,000	63,000	8,000 U
Fixed overhead costs:				
Depreciation		100,000	100,000	0
Supervisory salaries		172,000	160,000	12,000 U
Insurance		36,000	40,000	4,000 F
Total fixed overhead cost ...		308,000	300,000	8,000 U
Total overhead cost		$379,000	$363,000	$16,000 U

The Volume Variance—A Closer Look

The **volume variance** is a measure of facility utilization. The variance arises whenever the standard hours allowed for the output of a period are different from the denominator activity level that was planned when the period began. It can be computed as shown in Exhibit 9–10 or by using the following formula:

$$\frac{\text{Volume}}{\text{variance}} = \begin{array}{c}\text{Fixed portion of} \\ \text{the predetermined} \\ \text{overhead rate}\end{array} \times \left(\begin{array}{c}\text{Denominator} \\ \text{hours}\end{array} - \begin{array}{c}\text{Standard hours} \\ \text{allowed}\end{array}\right)$$

Applying this formula to MicroDrive Corporation, the volume variance would be computed as follows:

$6 per MH (50,000 MHs − 40,000 MHs) = $60,000 U

Note that this computation agrees with the volume variance as shown in Exhibit 9–10. As stated earlier, the volume variance is a measure of facility utilization. An unfavorable variance, as above, means that the company operated at an activity level *below* that planned for the period. A favorable variance would mean that the company operated at an activity level *greater* than that planned for the period.

It is important to note that the volume variance does not measure over- or underspending. A company normally would incur the same dollar amount of fixed overhead cost regardless of whether the period's activity was above or below the planned (denominator) level. In short, the volume variance is an activity-related variance. It is explainable only by activity and is controllable only through activity.

To summarize:

1. If the denominator activity and the standard hours allowed for the output of the period are the same, the volume variance is zero.

2. If the denominator activity is greater than the standard hours allowed for the output
   of the period, then the volume variance is unfavorable. This indicates that facilities
   were utilized less than was planned.
3. If the denominator activity is less than the standard hours allowed for the output of
   the period, then the volume variance is favorable. This indicates that facilities were
   utilized more than was planned.

DECISION MAKER   **Vice President of Production**

One of the company's factories produces a single product. The factory recently reported a significant unfavorable volume variance for the year. Sales for that product were less than anticipated. What should you do?

Graphic Analysis of Fixed Overhead Variances

Graphic analysis can provide insights into the budget and volume variances. A graph containing these variances is presented in Exhibit 9–12.

As shown in the graph, fixed overhead cost is applied to work in process at the predetermined rate of $6 for each standard hour of activity. (The applied-cost line is the upward-sloping line on the graph.) Since a denominator level of 50,000 machine-hours was used in computing the $6 rate, the applied-cost line crosses the budget-cost line at exactly 50,000 machine-hours. If the denominator hours and the standard hours allowed for the output are the same, there can be no volume variance. It is only when the standard hours differ from the denominator hours that a volume variance can arise.

In the case at hand, the standard hours allowed for the actual output (40,000 hours) are less than the denominator hours (50,000 hours). The result is an unfavorable volume variance, since less cost was applied to production than was originally budgeted. If the

EXHIBIT 9–12

Graphic Analysis of Fixed
Overhead Variances

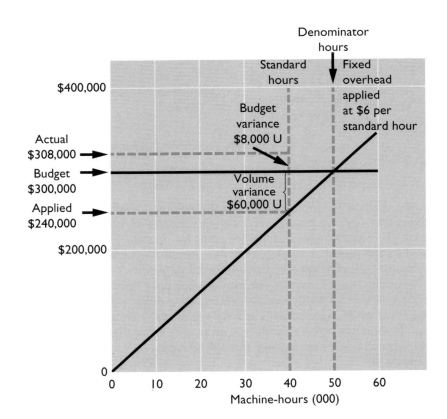

situation had been reversed and the standard hours allowed for the actual output had exceeded the denominator hours, then the volume variance on the graph would have been favorable.

3. A company's actual and budgeted fixed overhead are $220,000 and $200,000, respectively. The fixed portion of the predetermined overhead rate is $8 per unit. How many units was the predetermined overhead rate based on?
   a.   20,000 units
   b.   25,000 units
   c.   30,000 units
   d.   35,000 units
4. Referring to the facts in question 3 above, what is the fixed overhead volume variance if 32,000 units were actually produced?
   a. $56,000 favorable
   b. $56,000 unfavorable
   c. $75,000 unfavorable
   d. $75,000 favorable

Cautions in Fixed Overhead Analysis

A volume variance for fixed overhead arises because when applying the costs to work in process, we act *as if* the fixed costs were variable and depended on activity. This point can be seen from the graph in Exhibit 9–12. Notice from the graph that the fixed overhead costs are applied to work in process at a rate of $6 per hour *as if* they were variable. Treating these costs as if they were variable is necessary for product costing purposes, but some real dangers lurk here. Managers can easily be misled into thinking that fixed costs are *in fact* variable.

Keep clearly in mind that fixed overhead costs come in large, indivisible pieces. Expressing fixed costs on a unit or per hour basis, though necessary for product costing for external reports, is artificial. Increases or decreases in activity in fact have no effect on total fixed costs within the relevant range of activity. Even though fixed costs are expressed on a unit or per hour basis, they are *not* proportional to activity. In a sense, the volume variance is the error that occurs as a result of treating fixed costs as variable costs in the costing system.

Overhead Variances and Under- or Overapplied Overhead Cost

Four variances relating to overhead cost have been computed for MicroDrive Corporation in this chapter. These four variances are as follows:

Variable overhead spending variance (p. 396)	$ 8,000 U
Variable overhead efficiency variance (p. 397)	3,000 U
Fixed overhead budget variance (p. 402)	8,000 U
Fixed overhead volume variance (p. 402)	60,000 U
Total overhead variance	$79,000 U

Recall from Chapter 2 that under- or overapplied overhead is the difference between the amount of overhead applied to products and the actual overhead costs incurred during a period. Basically, the overhead variances we have computed in this chapter break the under- or overapplied overhead down into variances that can be used by managers for control purposes. *The sum of the overhead variances equals the under- or overapplied overhead cost for a period.*

Furthermore, in a standard cost system, unfavorable variances are equivalent to underapplied overhead and favorable variances are equivalent to overapplied overhead. Unfavorable variances occur because more was spent on overhead than the standards allow. Underapplied overhead occurs when more was spent on overhead than was applied to products during the period. But in a standard costing system, the standard amount of overhead allowed is exactly the same as the amount of overhead applied to products. Therefore, in a standard costing system, unfavorable variances and underapplied overhead are the same thing, as are favorable variances and overapplied overhead.

For MicroDrive Corporation, the total overhead variance was $79,000 unfavorable. Therefore, its overhead cost was underapplied by $79,000 for the year. To solidify this point in your mind, *carefully study the review problem at the end of the chapter!* This review problem provides a comprehensive summary of overhead analysis, including the computation of under- or overapplied overhead cost in a standard cost system.

Overhead Accounts: Fertile Ground for Fraud

Particularly in small companies, no one but the controller may understand concepts such as overhead variances and overapplied and underapplied overhead. Furthermore, a small company controller may be able to both authorize cash disbursements and account for them. Since small, closely held companies often do not hire external auditors, these circumstances create an ideal environment for fraud.

Such was the case in a small manufacturing company with 100 employees and $30 million in annual sales. The controller embezzled nearly $1 million from the company over three years by writing checks to himself. The consultant who uncovered the fraud was tipped off by the unusually high overhead variances that resulted from the controller recording fictitious expenses in the overhead accounts to offset the fraudulent cash disbursements. After the fraud was exposed, the company implemented various controls to reduce the risk of future problems, such as hiring an internal auditor and requiring periodic review of overhead variances to identify and explain significant discrepancies.

Source: John B. MacArthur, Bobby E. Waldrup, and Gary R. Fane, "Caution: Fraud Overhead," *Strategic Finance*, October 2004, pp. 28–32.

YOU DECIDE   Production Manager

You are the production manager at a factory that makes decorator ceramic tiles. Your company's top management has adopted lean production as a guiding principle. During the last month, you filled all orders for tiles completely with no defects and on time, and you started and ended the month with no work-in-process inventories. You feel that the factory was working extremely effectively during the month and were surprised to be asked by top management to explain a very large unfavorable volume variance. What would have caused the unfavorable volume variance? How can such an unfavorable volume variance be avoided in the future?

SUMMARY

LO1   Prepare a flexible budget and explain the advantages of the flexible budget approach over the static budget approach.

A flexible budget shows what costs should be as a function of the level of activity. A flexible budget provides a better benchmark for evaluating how well costs have been controlled than the static budget approved at the beginning of the period. Some costs should be different from the amounts budgeted at the beginning of the period simply because the level of activity is different from what was expected. The flexible budget takes this fact into account, whereas the static budget does not.

LO2   Prepare a performance report for both variable and fixed overhead costs using the flexible budget approach.

A flexible budget performance report compares actual costs to what the costs should have been, given the actual level of activity for the period. Variable costs are flexed (i.e., adjusted) for the actual level of activity. This is done by multiplying the cost per unit of activity by the actual level of activity. Fixed costs, at least within the relevant range, are not adjusted for the level of activity. The total cost for a fixed cost item is carried over from the static budget without adjustment.

LO3   Use a flexible budget to prepare a variable overhead performance report containing only a spending variance.

The spending variance for a variable overhead expense is computed by comparing the actual cost incurred to the amount that should have been spent, based on the actual direct labor-hours or machine-hours of the period.

LO4   Use a flexible budget to prepare a variable overhead performance report containing both a spending and an efficiency variance.

As stated above, the spending variance for a variable overhead expense is computed by comparing the actual cost incurred to the amount that should have been spent, based on the actual direct labor-hours or machine-hours of the period. The efficiency variance is computed by comparing the cost that should have been incurred for the actual direct labor-hours or machine-hours of the period to the cost that should have been incurred for the actual level of *output* of the period.

LO5   Compute the predetermined overhead rate and apply overhead to products in a standard cost system.

In a standard cost system, overhead is applied to products based on the standard hours allowed for the actual output of the period. This differs from a normal cost system in which overhead is applied to products based on the actual hours of the period.

LO6   Compute and interpret the fixed overhead budget and volume variances.

The fixed overhead budget variance is the difference between the actual total fixed overhead costs incurred for the period and the budgeted total fixed overhead costs. This variance measures how well fixed overhead costs were controlled.

    The fixed overhead volume variance is the difference between the fixed overhead applied to production using the predetermined overhead rate and the budgeted total fixed overhead. A favorable variance occurs when the standard hours allowed for the actual output exceed the hours assumed when the predetermined overhead rate was computed. An unfavorable variance occurs when the standard hours allowed for the actual output are less than the hours assumed when the predetermined overhead rate was computed.

GUIDANCE ANSWERS TO *DECISION MAKER* AND *YOU DECIDE*

Vice President of Production (p. 404)

An unfavorable fixed overhead volume variance means that the factory is operating below the activity level that was planned for the year. You should meet with the vice president of sales to determine why demand was less than planned. Was production part of the problem? Were orders delivered late? Were customers quoted lead times that were too long? Could production help increase demand by improving the quality of the product and the services provided to customers? If sales are declining and are not expected to rebound, you should consider how to make use of the excess capacity in this factory. You might consider whether the factory could be reconfigured to produce another product or if a section of the factory could be leased to another company.

Production Manager (p. 406)

The unfavorable volume variance was caused by the actual level of activity in the factory being less than the denominator level of activity. Since the factory produced only what was ordered, which is exactly what it should do in a lean production environment, the production manager should not be held responsible for this variance. Given the denominator level of activity, the production manager could have avoided the unfavorable volume variance only by producing more than was ordered—which would have violated lean production principles.

The easiest way to avoid an unfavorable volume variance is to set the denominator level of activity at a much lower level so that it is unlikely that it would exceed the actual level of activity. Unfortunately, the production manager is unlikely to have the authority to change the denominator level of activity. If the denominator level of activity is not changed, then the only way to avoid an unfavorable volume variance is to produce at a higher level than the denominator level of activity—which again would be a violation of lean principles if sales are less than the denominator level of activity.

GUIDANCE ANSWERS TO CONCEPT CHECKS

1. **Choice c.** A flexible budget is most useful for controlling variable costs, not fixed costs.
2. **Choice c.** The flexible budget at 12,000 units would be (12,000 units × $3 per unit variable overhead) + $70,000 of fixed overhead = $106,000.
3. **Choice b.** Budgeted fixed overhead of $200,000 ÷ $8 per unit fixed overhead rate = 25,000 units.
4. **Choice a.** The fixed overhead volume variance is (32,000 units − 25,000 units) × $8 per unit = $56,000 favorable.

REVIEW PROBLEM: OVERHEAD ANALYSIS

(This problem provides a comprehensive review of Chapter 9, including the computation of under- or over-applied overhead and its breakdown into the four overhead variances.)

Data for the manufacturing overhead of Aspen Company are given below:

Overhead Costs	Cost Formula (per machine-hour)	Machine-Hours 5,000	6,000	7,000
Variable overhead costs:				
Supplies	$0.20	$ 1,000	$ 1,200	$ 1,400
Indirect labor	0.30	1,500	1,800	2,100
Total variable overhead cost	$0.50	2,500	3,000	3,500
Fixed overhead costs:				
Depreciation		4,000	4,000	4,000
Supervision		5,000	5,000	5,000
Total fixed overhead cost		9,000	9,000	9,000
Total overhead cost		$11,500	$12,000	$12,500

Five hours of machine time are required per unit of product. The company has set its denominator activity for the coming period at 6,000 machine-hours (or 1,200 units). The predetermined overhead rate is computed as follows:

$$\text{Total: } \frac{\$12,000}{6,000 \text{ MHs}} = \$2.00 \text{ per machine-hour}$$

$$\text{Variable element: } \frac{\$3,000}{6,000 \text{ MHs}} = \$0.50 \text{ per machine-hour}$$

$$\text{Fixed element: } \frac{\$9,000}{6,000 \text{ MHs}} = \$1.50 \text{ per machine-hour}$$

Assume the following *actual* results for the period:

Number of units produced	1,300 units
Actual machine-hours	6,800 machine-hours
Standard machine-hours allowed*	6,500 machine-hours
Actual variable overhead cost	$4,200
Actual fixed overhead cost	$9,400

*1,300 units × 5 machine-hours per unit.

Therefore, the company's Manufacturing Overhead account would appear as follows at the end of the period:

Manufacturing Overhead

Actual overhead costs	13,600*	13,000†	Applied overhead costs
Underapplied overhead	600		

*$4,200 variable + $9,400 fixed = $13,600.
†6,500 standard machine-hours × $2 per machine-hour = $13,000.
In a standard cost system, overhead is applied on the basis of standard hours, not actual hours.

Required:

Analyze the $600 underapplied overhead in terms of:

1. A variable overhead spending variance.
2. A variable overhead efficiency variance.
3. A fixed overhead budget variance.
4. A fixed overhead volume variance.

Solution to Review Problem

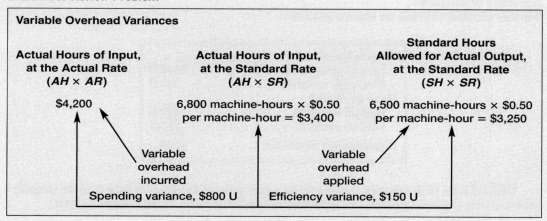

These same variances in the alternative format would be computed as follows:

Variable overhead spending variance:

$$\text{Spending variance} = (AH \times AR) - (AH \times SR)$$

($4,200*) − (6,800 machine-hours × $0.50 per machine-hour) = $800 U

*AH × AR equals the total actual cost for the period.

Variable overhead efficiency variance:

$$\text{Efficiency variance} = SR(AH - SH)$$

$0.50 per machine-hour (6,800 machine-hours $-$ 6,500 machine-hours) = $150 U

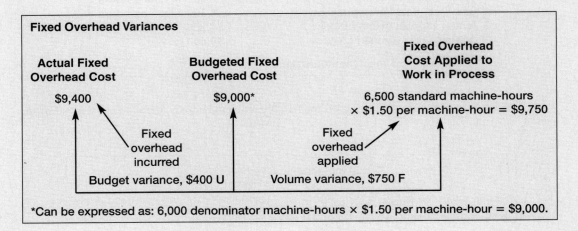

Fixed Overhead Variances

Actual Fixed Overhead Cost	Budgeted Fixed Overhead Cost	Fixed Overhead Cost Applied to Work in Process
$9,400	$9,000*	6,500 standard machine-hours × $1.50 per machine-hour = $9,750

Fixed overhead incurred

Fixed overhead applied

Budget variance, $400 U   Volume variance, $750 F

*Can be expressed as: 6,000 denominator machine-hours × $1.50 per machine-hour = $9,000.

These same variances in the alternative format would be computed as follows:

Fixed overhead budget variance:

$$\frac{\text{Budget}}{\text{variance}} = \frac{\text{Actual fixed}}{\text{overhead cost}} - \frac{\text{Budgeted}}{\text{fixed overhead cost}}$$

$$= \$9,400 - \$9,000 = \$400 \text{ U}$$

Fixed overhead volume variance:

$$\text{Volume variance} = \begin{matrix}\text{Fixed portion} \\ \text{of the predetermined} \\ \text{overhead rate}\end{matrix} \times \left(\begin{matrix}\text{Denominator} \\ \text{hours}\end{matrix} - \begin{matrix}\text{Standard} \\ \text{hours}\end{matrix}\right)$$

$$= \$1.50 \text{ per machine-hour } (6,000 \text{ machine-hours} - 6,500 \text{ machine-hours}) = \$750 \text{ F}$$

Summary of Variances

The four overhead variances are summarized below:

Variable overhead:	
Spending variance............	$800 U
Efficiency variance............	150 U
Fixed overhead:	
Budget variance..............	400 U
Volume variance..............	750 F
Underapplied overhead..........	$600

Notice that the $600 summary variance figure agrees with the underapplied balance in the company's Manufacturing Overhead account. This agreement verifies the accuracy of our variance analysis.

GLOSSARY

Budget variance   A measure of the difference between the actual fixed overhead costs incurred during the period and budgeted fixed overhead costs as contained in the flexible budget. (p. 402)

Denominator activity   The activity figure used to compute the predetermined overhead rate. (p. 399)

Flexible budget   A budget that is designed to cover a range of activity and that can be used to develop budgeted costs at any point within that range to compare to actual costs incurred. (p. 389)

Static budget A budget created at the beginning of the budgeting period that is valid only for the planned level of activity. (p. 388)

Volume variance The variance that arises whenever the standard hours allowed for the actual output of a period are different from the denominator activity level that was used to compute the predetermined overhead rate. (p. 403)

QUESTIONS

9–1 What is a static budget?

9–2 What is a flexible budget and how does it differ from a static budget?

9–3 In comparing flexible budget data with actual data in a performance report for variable overhead, what variance(s) will be produced if the flexible budget data are based on actual hours worked? On both actual hours worked and standard hours allowed?

9–4 What is meant by the term *standard hours allowed?*

9–5 How does the variable manufacturing overhead spending variance differ from the materials price variance?

9–6 Why is the term *overhead efficiency variance* a misnomer?

9–7 What is meant by the term *denominator level of activity?*

9–8 Why do we apply overhead to work in process on the basis of standard hours allowed in this chapter when we applied it on the basis of actual hours in Chapter 2? What is the difference in costing systems between the two chapters?

9–9 What does the fixed overhead budget variance measure?

9–10 Under what circumstances would you expect the volume variance to be favorable? Unfavorable? Does the variance measure deviations in spending for fixed overhead items? Explain.

9–11 Underapplied or overapplied overhead can be broken down into what four variances?

9–12 If factory overhead is overapplied for August, would you expect the total of the overhead variances to be favorable or unfavorable?

BRIEF EXERCISES

BRIEF EXERCISE 9–1 Preparing a Flexible Budget [LO1]

An incomplete flexible budget is given below for Lavage Rapide, a Swiss company that owns and operates a large automatic carwash facility near Geneva. The Swiss currency is the Swiss franc, which is denoted by SFr.

Lavage Rapide **Flexible Budget** **For the Month Ended August 31**				
Overhead Costs	**Cost Formula (per car)**	**Activity (cars)**		
		8,000	**9,000**	**10,000**
Variable overhead costs:				
Cleaning supplies	?	?	7,200 SFr	?
Electricity	?	?	2,700	?
Maintenance	?	?	1,800	?
Total variable overhead cost	?	?	?	?
Fixed overhead costs:				
Operator wages		?	9,000	?
Depreciation		?	6,000	?
Rent		?	8,000	?
Total fixed overhead cost		?	?	?
Total overhead cost		?	? SFr	?

Required:

Fill in the missing data.

BRIEF EXERCISE 9–2   Using a Flexible Budget   [LO1]
Refer to the data in Brief Exercise 9–1. Lavage Rapide's owner-manager would like to prepare a budget for August assuming an activity level of 8,800 cars.

Required:
Prepare a static budget for August. Use Exhibit 9–1 in the chapter as your guide.

BRIEF EXERCISE 9–3   Flexible Budget Performance Report   [LO2]
Refer to the data in Brief Exercise 9–1. Lavage Rapide's actual level of activity during August was 8,900 cars, although the owner had constructed his static budget for the month assuming the level of activity would be 8,800 cars. The actual overhead costs incurred during August are given below:

	Actual Costs Incurred for 8,900 Cars
Variable overhead costs:	
Cleaning supplies	7,080 SFr
Electricity	2,460 SFr
Maintenance	1,550 SFr
Fixed overhead costs:	
Operator wages	9,100 SFr
Depreciation	7,000 SFr
Rent	8,000 SFr

Required:
Prepare a flexible budget performance report for both the variable and fixed overhead costs for August. Use Exhibit 9–4 in the chapter as your guide.

BRIEF EXERCISE 9–4   Variable Overhead Performance Report with Just a Spending Variance [LO3]
Yung Corporation bases its variable overhead performance report on the actual direct labor-hours of the period. Data concerning the most recent year that ended on December 31 appear below:

Budgeted direct labor-hours	38,000
Actual direct labor-hours	34,000
Standard direct labor-hours allowed	35,000

Cost formula (per direct labor-hour):

Indirect labor	$0.60
Supplies	$0.10
Electricity	$0.05

Actual costs incurred:

Indirect labor	$21,200
Supplies	$3,200
Electricity	$1,600

Required:
Prepare a variable overhead performance report using the format in Exhibit 9–6. Compute just the variable overhead spending variances (do not compute the variable overhead efficiency variances).

BRIEF EXERCISE 9–5   Variable Overhead Performance Report with Both Spending and Efficiency Variances   [LO4]

Refer to the data for Yung Corporation in Brief Exercise 9–4. Management would like to compute both spending and efficiency variances for variable overhead in the company's variable overhead performance report.

Required:

Prepare a variable overhead performance report using the format in Exhibit 9–7. Compute both the variable overhead spending variances and the overhead efficiency variances.

BRIEF EXERCISE 9–6   Applying Overhead in a Standard Costing System   [LO5]

Privack Corporation has a standard cost system in which it applies overhead to products based on the standard direct labor-hours allowed for the actual output of the period. Data concerning the most recent year appear below:

Variable overhead cost per direct labor-hour	$2.00
Total fixed overhead cost per year	$250,000
Budgeted standard direct labor-hours (denominator level of activity)	40,000
Actual direct labor-hours	39,000
Standard direct labor-hours allowed for the actual output	38,000

Required:

1. Compute the predetermined overhead rate for the year.
2. Determine the amount of overhead that would be applied to the output of the period.

BRIEF EXERCISE 9–7   Fixed Overhead Variances   [LO6]

Primara Corporation has a standard cost system in which it applies overhead to products based on the standard direct labor-hours allowed for the actual output of the period. Data concerning the most recent year appear below:

Total budgeted fixed overhead cost for the year	$250,000
Actual fixed overhead cost for the year	$254,000
Budgeted standard direct labor-hours (denominator level of activity)	25,000
Actual direct labor-hours	27,000
Standard direct labor-hours allowed for the actual output	26,000

Required:

1. Compute the fixed portion of the predetermined overhead rate for the year.
2. Compute the fixed overhead budget variance and volume variance.

EXERCISES

EXERCISE 9–8   Prepare a Flexible Budget   [LO1]

The cost formulas for Emory Company's manufacturing overhead costs are given below. These cost formulas cover a relevant range of 15,000 to 25,000 machine-hours each year.

Overhead Costs	Cost Formula
Utilities	$0.30 per machine-hour
Indirect labor	$52,000 plus $1.40 per machine-hour
Supplies	$0.20 per machine-hour
Maintenance	$18,000 plus $0.10 per machine-hour
Depreciation	$90,000

Required:
Prepare a flexible budget in increments of 5,000 machine-hours. Include all costs in your budget.

EXERCISE 9–9   **Variable Overhead Performance Report**   **[LO3]**
The variable portion of Murray Company's flexible budget for manufacturing overhead is given below:

Variable Overhead Costs	Cost Formula (per machine-hour)	Machine-Hours 10,000	12,000	14,000
Supplies	$0.20	$ 2,000	$ 2,400	$ 2,800
Maintenance	0.80	8,000	9,600	11,200
Utilities	0.10	1,000	1,200	1,400
Rework	0.40	4,000	4,800	5,600
Total variable overhead cost	$1.50	$15,000	$18,000	$21,000

During a recent period, the company recorded 11,500 machine-hours of activity. The variable overhead costs incurred were:

Supplies	$2,400
Maintenance	$8,000
Utilities	$1,100
Rework time	$5,300

The budgeted activity for the period had been 12,000 machine-hours.

Required:
1. Prepare a variable overhead performance report for the period. Indicate whether variances are favorable (F) or unfavorable (U). Show only a spending variance on your report.
2. Discuss the significance of the variances. Might some variances be the result of others? Explain.

EXERCISE 9–10   **Variable Overhead Performance Report**   **[LO4]**
The cost formulas for variable overhead costs in a machine shop are given below:

Variable Overhead Cost	Cost Formula (per machine-hour)
Power	$0.30
Setup time	0.20
Polishing wheels	0.16
Maintenance	0.18
Total variable overhead cost	$0.84

During August, the machine shop was scheduled to work 11,250 machine-hours and to produce 4,500 units of product. The standard machine time per unit of product is 2.5 hours. A strike near the end of the month forced a cutback in production. Actual results for the month were:

Actual machine-hours worked	9,250
Actual number of units produced	3,600

Actual costs for the month were:

Variable Overhead Cost	Total Actual Costs	Per Machine-Hour
Power	$2,405	$0.26
Setup time	2,035	0.22
Polishing wheels	1,110	0.12
Maintenance	925	0.10
Total variable overhead cost	$6,475	$0.70

Required:

Prepare an overhead performance report for the machine shop for August. Use column headings in your report as shown below:

Overhead Item	Cost Formula (per machine-hour)	Actual Costs Incurred 9,250 Machine-Hours	Budget Based on ? Machine-Hours	Budget Based on ? Machine-Hours	Total Variance	Breakdown of the Total Variance	
						Spending Variance	Efficiency Variance

EXERCISE 9–11   Predetermined Overhead Rate; Overhead Variances   [LO4, LO5, LO6]

Norwall Company's flexible budget for manufacturing overhead (in condensed form) is given below:

Overhead Costs	Cost Formula (per machine-hour)	Machine-Hours		
		50,000	60,000	70,000
Variable costs	$3	$150,000	$180,000	$210,000
Fixed costs		300,000	300,000	300,000
Total overhead cost		$450,000	$480,000	$510,000

The following information is available for a recent period:

a. The denominator activity of 60,000 machine-hours is used to compute the predetermined overhead rate.

b. At the 60,000 standard machine-hours level of activity, the company should produce 40,000 units of product.

c. The company's actual operating results were:

Number of units produced	42,000
Actual machine-hours	64,000
Actual variable overhead costs	$185,600
Actual fixed overhead costs	$302,400

Required:

1. Compute the predetermined overhead rate and break it down into variable and fixed cost elements.
2. Compute the standard hours allowed for the actual production.
3. Compute the variable overhead spending and efficiency variances and the fixed overhead budget and volume variances.

EXERCISE 9–12   Variable Overhead Performance Report with Both Spending and Efficiency Variances   [LO4]

The check-clearing office of Columbia National Bank is responsible for processing all checks that come to the bank for payment. Managers at the bank believe that variable overhead costs are essentially proportional to the number of labor-hours worked in the office, so labor-hours are used as the activity base when preparing variable overhead budgets and performance reports. Data for September, the most recent month, appear below:

Budgeted labor-hours	3,080	
Actual labor-hours	3,100	
Standard labor-hours allowed for the actual number of checks processed	3,200	

	Cost Formula (per labor-hour)	Actual Costs Incurred in September
Variable overhead costs:		
Office supplies	$0.10	$ 365
Staff coffee lounge	0.20	520
Indirect labor	0.90	2,710
Total variable overhead cost	$1.20	$3,595

Required:

Prepare a variable overhead performance report for September for the check-clearing office that includes both spending and efficiency variances. Use Exhibit 9–7 as a guide.

EXERCISE 9–13   Predetermined Overhead Rate   [LO5]

Operating at a normal level of 30,000 direct labor-hours, Lasser Company produces 10,000 units of product each period. The direct labor wage rate is $12 per hour. Two and one-half yards of direct materials go into each unit of product; the material costs $8.60 per yard. The flexible budget used to plan and control manufacturing overhead costs is given below (in condensed form):

	Cost Formula (per direct labor-hour)	Direct Labor-Hours		
Overhead Costs		20,000	30,000	40,000
Variable costs	$1.90	$ 38,000	$ 57,000	$ 76,000
Fixed costs		168,000	168,000	168,000
Total overhead cost		$206,000	$225,000	$244,000

Required:

1. Using 30,000 direct labor-hours as the denominator activity, compute the predetermined overhead rate and break it down into variable and fixed elements.
2. Complete the standard cost card below for one unit of product:

Direct materials, 2.5 yards at $8.60 per yard	$21.50
Direct labor, ?	?
Variable overhead, ?	?
Fixed overhead, ?	?
Total standard cost per unit	$?

EXERCISE 9–14   Fixed Overhead Variances   [LO6]

Selected operating information on three different companies for a recent year is given below:

	Company		
	A	**B**	**C**
Full-capacity machine-hours	10,000	18,000	20,000
Budgeted machine-hours*	9,000	17,000	20,000
Actual machine-hours	9,000	17,800	19,000
Standard machine-hours allowed for actual production	9,500	16,000	20,000

*Denominator activity for computing the predetermined overhead rate.

Required:

For each company, state whether the company would have a favorable or unfavorable volume variance and why.

PROBLEMS

PROBLEM 9–15A   Preparing a Performance Report   [LO2, LO3]

The St. Lucia Blood Bank, a private charity partly supported by government grants, is located on the Caribbean island of St. Lucia. The Blood Bank has just finished its operations for September, which was a particularly busy month due to a powerful hurricane that hit neighboring islands causing many injuries. The hurricane largely bypassed St. Lucia, but residents of St. Lucia willingly donated their blood to help people on other islands. As a consequence, the blood bank collected and processed over 20% more blood than had been originally planned for the month.

CHECK FIGURE
(1) Flexible budget total cost at 620 liters: $32,290

A report prepared by a government official comparing actual costs to budgeted costs for the Blood Bank appears below. (The currency on St. Lucia is the East Caribbean dollar.) Continued support from the government depends on the Blood Bank's ability to demonstrate control over its costs.

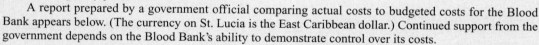

St. Lucia Blood Bank Cost Control Report For the Month Ended September 30			
	Actual	**Budget**	**Variance**
Liters of blood collected	620	500	120
Variable costs:			
Medical supplies	$ 9,350	$ 7,500	$1,850 U
Lab tests	6,180	6,000	180 U
Refreshments for donors	1,340	1,000	340 U
Administrative supplies	400	250	150 U
Total variable cost	17,270	14,750	2,520 U
Fixed costs:			
Staff salaries	10,000	10,000	0
Equipment depreciation	2,800	2,500	300 U
Rent	1,000	1,000	0
Utilities	570	500	70 U
Total fixed cost	14,370	14,000	370 U
Total cost	$31,640	$28,750	$2,890 U

The managing director of the Blood Bank was very unhappy with this report, claiming that his costs were higher than expected due to the emergency on the neighboring islands. He also pointed out that the additional costs had been fully covered by payments from grateful recipients on the other islands. The government official who prepared the report countered that all of the figures had been submitted by the Blood

Bank to the government; he was just pointing out that actual costs were a lot higher than promised in the budget.

Required:

1. Prepare a new performance report for September using the flexible budget approach. (Note: Even though some of these costs might be classified as direct costs rather than as overhead, the flexible budget approach can still be used to prepare a flexible budget performance report.)
2. Do you think any of the variances in the report you prepared should be investigated? Why?

PROBLEM 9–16A　Preparing an Overhead Performance Report　[LO2, LO3, LO6]

Several years ago, Westmont Company developed a comprehensive budgeting system for profit planning and control purposes. The line supervisors have been very happy with the system and with the reports being prepared on their performance, but both middle and upper management have expressed considerable dissatisfaction with the information being generated by the system. A typical manufacturing overhead performance report for a recent period follows:

CHECK FIGURE
(3) Total of spending and budget variances: $5,700 U

Westmont Company Overhead Performance Report—Assembly Department For the Quarter Ended March 31			
	Actual	**Budget**	**Variance**
Machine-hours	35,000	40,000	
Variable overhead costs:			
Indirect materials	$ 29,700	$ 32,000	$2,300 F
Rework	7,900	8,000	100 F
Utilities	51,800	56,000	4,200 F
Machine setup	11,600	12,000	400 F
Total variable overhead cost	101,000	108,000	7,000 F
Fixed overhead costs:			
Maintenance	79,200	80,000	800 F
Inspection	60,000	60,000	0
Total fixed overhead cost	139,200	140,000	800 F
Total overhead cost	$240,200	$248,000	$7,800 F

After receiving a copy of this overhead performance report, the supervisor of the Assembly Department stated, "These reports are super. It makes me feel really good to see how well things are going in my department. I can't understand why those people upstairs complain so much."

The budget data above are for the original planned level of activity for the quarter.

Required:

1. The company's vice president is uneasy about the performance reports being prepared and would like you to evaluate their usefulness to the company.
2. What changes, if any, should be made in the overhead performance report to give better insight into how well the supervisor is controlling costs?
3. Prepare a new overhead performance report for the quarter, incorporating any changes you suggested in (2) above. (Include both the variable and the fixed costs in your report.)

PROBLEM 9–17A　Applying Overhead; Overhead Variances　[LO4, LO5, LO6]

Chilczuk, S.A., of Gdansk, Poland, is a major producer of classic Polish sausage. The company uses a standard cost system to help control costs. Manufacturing overhead is applied to production on the basis of standard direct labor-hours. According to the company's flexible budget, the following manufacturing overhead costs should be incurred at an activity level of 35,000 labor-hours (the denominator activity level):

CHECK FIGURE
(3) Spending variance: €3,000 U Budget variance: €600 F

Variable manufacturing overhead costs	€ 87,500
Fixed manufacturing overhead costs	210,000
Total manufacturing overhead cost	€297,500

The currency in Poland is the euro, which is denoted here by €.

During the most recent year, the following operating results were recorded:

Activity:	
Actual labor-hours worked	30,000
Standard labor-hours allowed for output	32,000
Cost:	
Actual variable manufacturing overhead cost incurred ...	€78,000
Actual fixed manufacturing overhead cost incurred	€209,400

At the end of the year, the company's Manufacturing Overhead account contained the following data:

Manufacturing Overhead			
Actual	287,400	Applied	272,000
	15,400		

Management would like to determine the cause of the €15,400 underapplied overhead.

Required:

1. Compute the predetermined overhead rate. Break the rate down into variable and fixed cost elements.
2. Show how the €272,000 Applied figure in the Manufacturing Overhead account was computed.
3. Analyze the €15,400 underapplied overhead figure in terms of the variable overhead spending and efficiency variances and the fixed overhead budget and volume variances.
4. Explain the meaning of each variance that you computed in (3) above.

PROBLEM 9–18A   Comprehensive Standard Cost Variances   [LO4, LO5, LO6]

Flandro Company uses a standard cost system and sets predetermined overhead rates on the basis of direct labor-hours. The following data are taken from the company's budget for the current year:

Denominator activity (direct labor-hours)	5,000
Variable manufacturing overhead cost	$25,000
Fixed manufacturing overhead cost	$59,000

CHECK FIGURE
(2) Materials quantity
variance: $2,200 U
(3) Volume variance:
$11,800 F

The standard cost card for the company's only product is given below:

Direct materials, 3 yards at $4.40 per yard	$13.20
Direct labor, 1 DLH at $12 per DLH	12.00
Manufacturing overhead, 1 DLH at $16.80 per DLH ..	16.80
Standard cost per unit	$42.00

During the year, the company produced 6,000 units of product and incurred the following costs:

Materials purchased, 24,000 yards at $4.80 per yard	$115,200
Materials used in production (in yards)	18,500
Direct labor cost incurred, 5,800 DLHs at $13 per DLH	$75,400
Variable manufacturing overhead cost incurred	$29,580
Fixed manufacturing overhead cost incurred	$60,400

Required:

1. Redo the standard cost card in a clearer, more usable format by detailing the variable and fixed overhead cost elements.
2. Prepare an analysis of the variances for materials and labor for the year.

3. Prepare an analysis of the variances for variable and fixed overhead for the year.
4. What effect, if any, does the choice of a denominator activity level have on unit standard costs? Is the volume variance a controllable variance from a spending point of view? Explain.

CHECK FIGURE
(1) Standard DLHs allowed:
38,000 hours

PROBLEM 9–19A   Using Fixed Overhead Variances   [LO6]

The standard cost card for the single product manufactured by Cutter, Inc., is given below:

Standard Cost Card—per Unit	
Direct materials, 3 yards at $6 per yard	$ 18
Direct labor, 4 DLHs at $15.50 per DLH	62
Variable overhead, 4 DLHs at $1.50 per DLH	6
Fixed overhead, 4 DLHs at $5 per DLH	20
Total standard cost per unit	$106

Manufacturing overhead is applied to production on the basis of standard direct labor-hours. During the year, the company worked 37,000 hours and manufactured 9,500 units of product. Selected data relating to the company's fixed manufacturing overhead cost for the year are shown below:

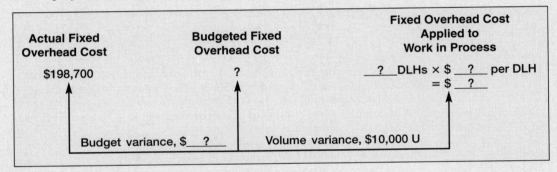

Required:

1. What were the standard direct labor-hours allowed for the year's production?
2. What was the amount of fixed overhead cost contained in the flexible budget for the year?
3. What was the fixed overhead budget variance for the year?
4. What denominator activity level did the company use in setting the predetermined overhead rate for the year?

PROBLEM 9–20A   Comprehensive Standard Cost Variances   [LO4, LO6]

"Wonderful! Not only did our salespeople do a good job in meeting the sales budget this year, but our production people did a good job in controlling costs as well," said Kim Clark, president of Martell Company. "Our $18,300 overall manufacturing cost variance is only 1.2% of the $1,536,000 standard cost of products made during the year. That's well within the 3% parameter set by management for acceptable variances. It looks like everyone will be in line for a bonus this year."

The company produces and sells a single product. The standard cost card for the product follows:

CHECK FIGURE
(3a) Efficiency variance:
$3,750 U
(3b) Volume variance:
$42,000 F

Standard Cost Card—per Unit of Product	
Direct materials, 2 feet at $8.45 per foot	$16.90
Direct labor, 1.4 direct labor hours at $16 per direct labor-hour	22.40
Variable overhead, 1.4 direct labor-hours at $2.50 per direct labor-hour	3.50
Fixed overhead, 1.4 direct labor-hours at $6 per direct labor-hour	8.40
Standard cost per unit	$51.20

The following additional information is available for the year just completed:

a. The company manufactured 30,000 units of product during the year.
b. A total of 64,000 feet of material was purchased during the year at a cost of $8.55 per foot. All of this material was used to manufacture the 30,000 units. There were no beginning or ending inventories for the year.

c. The company worked 43,500 direct labor-hours during the year at a direct labor cost of $15.80 per hour.
d. Overhead is applied to products on the basis of standard direct labor-hours. Data relating to manufacturing overhead costs follow:

Denominator activity level (direct labor-hours)	35,000
Budgeted fixed overhead costs (from the overhead flexible budget)	$210,000
Actual variable overhead costs incurred	$108,000
Actual fixed overhead costs incurred	$211,800

Required:

1. Compute the direct materials price and quantity variances for the year.
2. Compute the direct labor rate and efficiency variances for the year.
3. For manufacturing overhead compute:
    a. The variable overhead spending and efficiency variances for the year.
    b. The fixed overhead budget and volume variances for the year.
4. Total the variances you have computed, and compare the net amount with the $18,300 mentioned by the president. Do you agree that bonuses should be given to everyone for good cost control during the year? Explain.

PROBLEM 9–21A Relations Among Fixed Overhead Variances [LO5, LO6]

Selected information relating to Yost Company's operations for the most recent year is given below:

CHECK FIGURE
(3) Volume variance:
$18,000 U

Activity:	
Denominator activity (machine-hours)	45,000
Standard hours allowed per unit	3
Number of units produced	14,000
Costs:	
Actual fixed overhead costs incurred	$267,000
Fixed overhead budget variance	$3,000 F

The company applies overhead cost to products on the basis of standard machine-hours.

Required:

1. What were the standard machine-hours allowed for the actual production?
2. What was the fixed portion of the predetermined overhead rate?
3. What was the volume variance?

PROBLEM 9–22A Applying Overhead; Overhead Variances [LO4, LO5, LO6]

Lane Company manufactures a single product that requires a great deal of hand labor. Overhead cost is applied on the basis of standard direct labor-hours. The company's condensed flexible budget for manufacturing overhead is given below:

CHECK FIGURE
(2) Standard cost: $54
(4) Volume variance:
$24,000 F

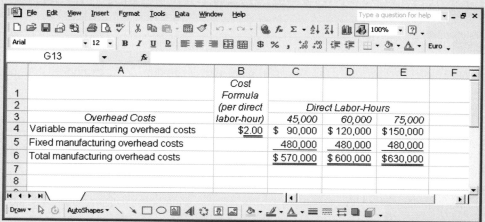

	Cost Formula (per direct labor-hour)	Direct Labor-Hours		
Overhead Costs		45,000	60,000	75,000
Variable manufacturing overhead costs	$2.00	$ 90,000	$ 120,000	$150,000
Fixed manufacturing overhead costs		480,000	480,000	480,000
Total manufacturing overhead costs		$ 570,000	$ 600,000	$630,000

The company's product requires 3 pounds of material that has a standard cost of $7 per pound and 1.5 hours of direct labor time that has a standard rate of $12 per hour.

The company planned to operate at a denominator activity level of 60,000 direct labor-hours and to produce 40,000 units of product during the most recent year. Actual activity and costs for the year were as follows:

Number of units produced	42,000
Actual direct labor-hours worked	65,000
Actual variable manufacturing overhead cost incurred	$123,500
Actual fixed manufacturing overhead cost incurred	$483,000

Required:

1. Compute the predetermined overhead rate for the year. Break the rate down into variable and fixed elements.
2. Prepare a standard cost card for the company's product; show the details for all manufacturing costs on your standard cost card.
3. Do the following:
   a. Compute the standard direct labor-hours allowed for the year's production.
   b. Complete the following Manufacturing Overhead T-account for the year:

Manufacturing Overhead	
?	?
?	?

4. Determine the reason for any underapplied or overapplied overhead for the year by computing the variable overhead spending and efficiency variances and the fixed overhead budget and volume variances.
5. Suppose the company had chosen 65,000 direct labor-hours as the denominator activity rather than 60,000 hours. State which, if any, of the variances computed in (4) above would have changed, and explain how the variance(s) would have changed. No computations are necessary.

PROBLEM 9–23A   Evaluating an Overhead Performance Report   [LO2, LO4]
Frank Western, supervisor of the Machining Department for Freemont Company, was visibly upset after being reprimanded for his department's poor performance over the prior month. The department's performance report is given below:

CHECK FIGURE
(2) Total variance: $6,500 F

Freemont Company
Performance Report—Machining Department

	Cost Formula (per machine-hour)	Actual	Budget	Variance
Machine-hours		38,000	35,000	
Variable overhead costs:				
Utilities	$0.40	$ 15,700	$ 14,000	$ 1,700 U
Indirect labor	2.30	86,500	80,500	6,000 U
Supplies	0.60	26,000	21,000	5,000 U
Maintenance	1.20	44,900	42,000	2,900 U
Total variable overhead cost	$4.50	173,100	157,500	15,600 U
Fixed overhead costs:				
Supervision		38,000	38,000	0
Maintenance		92,400	92,000	400 U
Depreciation		80,000	80,000	0
Total fixed overhead cost		210,400	210,000	400 U
Total overhead cost		$383,500	$367,500	$16,000 U

"I just can't understand all the red ink," said Western to Sarah Mason, supervisor of another department. "When the boss called me in, I thought he was going to give me a pat on the back because I know for a fact that my department worked more efficiently last month than it has ever worked before. Instead, he tore me apart. I thought for a minute that it might be over the supplies that were stolen out of our warehouse last month. But they only amounted to a couple of thousand dollars, and just look at this report. *Everything* is unfavorable."

The budget for the Machining Department had called for production of 14,000 units last month, which is equal to a budgeted activity level of 35,000 machine-hours (at a standard time of 2.5 machine-hours per unit). Actual production in the Machining Department for the month was 16,000 units.

Required:

1. Evaluate the overhead performance report given above and explain why the variances are all unfavorable.
2. Prepare a new overhead performance report that will help Mr. Western's superiors assess efficiency and cost control in the Machining Department. (Hint: Exhibit 9–7 may be helpful in structuring your report; however, the report you prepare should include both variable and fixed costs.)
3. Would the supplies stolen out of the warehouse be included as part of the variable overhead spending variance or as part of the variable overhead efficiency variance for the month? Explain.

PROBLEM 9–24A Flexible Budget and Overhead Performance Report [LO1, LO2, LO3, LO4]
You have just been hired by FAB Company, the manufacturer of a revolutionary new garage door opening device. John Foster, the president, has asked that you review the company's costing system and "do what you can to help us get better control of our manufacturing overhead costs." You find that the company has never used a flexible budget, and you suggest that preparing such a budget would be an excellent first step in overhead planning and control.

After much effort and analysis, you are able to determine the following cost formulas for the company's normal operating range of 20,000 to 30,000 machine-hours each month:

eXcel

CHECK FIGURE
(2) Total of spending and budget variances: $800 U

Overhead Costs	Cost Formula
Utilities	$0.90 per machine-hour
Maintenance	$1.60 per machine-hour plus $40,000 per month
Machine setup	$0.30 per machine-hour
Indirect labor	$0.70 per machine-hour plus $130,000 per month
Depreciation	$70,000 per month

To show the president how the flexible budget concept works, you have gathered the following actual manufacturing overhead cost data for the most recent month, March, in which the company worked 26,000 machine-hours and produced 15,000 units:

Utilities.......................................	$ 24,200
Maintenance...................................	78,100
Machine setup	8,400
Indirect labor.................................	149,600
Depreciation	71,500
Total manufacturing overhead cost..............	$331,800

The only variance in the fixed costs for the month was with depreciation, which increased as a result of purchasing new equipment.

The company had originally planned to work 30,000 machine-hours during March.

Required:

1. Prepare a flexible budget for the company in increments of 5,000 machine-hours.
2. Prepare an overhead performance report for the company for March. (Use the format illustrated in Exhibit 9–11.)
3. What additional information would you need to compute an overhead efficiency variance for the company?

BUILDING YOUR SKILLS

Communicating in Practice   (LOI)

Use an online yellow pages directory such as www.switchboard.com to find a manufacturer in your area that has a website. Make an appointment with the controller or chief financial officer of the company. Before your meeting, find out as much as you can about the organization's operations from its website.

Required:

After asking the following questions, write a brief memorandum to your instructor that summarizes the information obtained from the company's website and addresses what you found out during your interview.

1. Are actual overhead costs compared to a static budget, to a flexible budget, or to something else?
2. Does the organization distinguish between variable and fixed overhead costs in its performance reports?
3. What are the consequences of unfavorable variances? Of favorable variances?

Ethics Challenge   [LO2]

Tom Kemper is the controller of the Wichita manufacturing facility of Prudhom Enterprises, Incorporated. Among the many reports that must be filed with corporate headquarters is the annual overhead performance report. The report covers the year ended December 31, and is due at corporate headquarters shortly after the beginning of the New Year. Kemper does not like putting work off to the last minute, so just before Christmas he put together a preliminary draft of the overhead performance report. Some adjustments would later be required for transactions that occur between Christmas and New Year's Day, but there are generally very few of these. A copy of the preliminary draft report, which Kemper completed on December 21, follows:

Wichita Manufacturing Facility
Overhead Performance Report
December 21 Preliminary Draft

Budgeted machine-hours 200,000
Actual machine-hours 180,000

Overhead Costs	Cost Formula (per machine-hour)	Actual Costs 180,000 Machine-Hours	Budget Based on 180,000 Machine-Hours	Spending or Budget Variance
Variable overhead costs:				
Power.......................	$0.10	$ 19,750	$ 18,000	$ 1,750 U
Supplies....................	0.25	47,000	45,000	2,000 U
Abrasives...................	0.30	58,000	54,000	4,000 U
Total variable overhead cost	$0.65	124,750	117,000	7,750 U
Fixed overhead costs:				
Depreciation		345,000	332,000	13,000 U
Supervisory salaries		273,000	275,000	2,000 F
Insurance....................		37,000	37,000	0
Industrial engineering		189,000	210,000	21,000 F
Factory building lease...........		60,000	60,000	0
Total fixed overhead cost.........		904,000	914,000	10,000 F
Total overhead cost		$1,028,750	$1,031,000	$ 2,250 F

Melissa Ilianovitch, the general manager at the Wichita facility, asked to see a copy of the preliminary draft report at 4:45 P.M. on December 23. Kemper carried a copy of the report to her office where the following discussion took place:

Ilianovitch: Ouch! Almost all of the variances on the report are unfavorable. The only thing that looks good at all are the favorable variances for supervisory salaries and for industrial engineering. How did we have an unfavorable variance for depreciation?

Kemper: Do you remember that milling machine that broke down because the wrong lubricant was used by the machine operator?

Ilianovitch: Only vaguely.

Kemper: It turned out we couldn't fix it. We had to scrap the machine and buy a new one.

Ilianovitch: This report doesn't look good. I was raked over the coals last year when we had just a few unfavorable variances.

Kemper: I'm afraid the final report is going to look even worse.

Ilianovitch: Oh?

Kemper: The line item for industrial engineering on the report is for work we hired Ferguson Engineering to do for us on a contract basis. The original contract was for $210,000, but we asked them to do some additional work that was not in the contract. Under the terms of the contract, we have to reimburse Ferguson Engineering for the costs of the additional work. The $189,000 in actual costs that appear on the preliminary draft report reflects only their billings up through December 21. The last bill they had sent us was on November 28, and they completed the project just last week. Yesterday I got a call from Laura Sunder over at Ferguson and she said they would be sending us a final bill for the project before the end of the year. The total bill, including the reimbursements for the additional work, is going to be . . .

Ilianovitch: I am not sure I want to hear this.

Kemper: $225,000.

Ilianovitch: Ouch! Ouch! Ouch!

Kemper: The additional work we asked them to do added $15,000 to the cost of the project.

Ilianovitch: No way can I turn in a performance report with an overall unfavorable variance. They'll kill me at corporate headquarters. Call up Laura at Ferguson and ask her not to send the bill until after the first of the year. We have to have that $21,000 favorable variance for industrial engineering on the performance report.

Required:

What should Tom Kemper do? Explain.

Teamwork in Action   [LO2]

Boyne University offers an extensive continuing education program in many cities throughout the state. For the convenience of its faculty and administrative staff and to save costs, the university employs a supervisor to operate a motor pool. The motor pool operated with 20 vehicles until February, when an additional automobile was acquired. The motor pool furnishes gasoline, oil, and other supplies for its automobiles. A mechanic does routine maintenance and minor repairs. Major repairs are done at a nearby commercial garage.

CHECK FIGURE
(1) Total cost variance: $294 F

Each year, the supervisor prepares an operating budget that informs the university administration of the funds needed for operating the motor pool. Depreciation (straight line) on the automobiles is recorded in the budget in order to determine the cost per mile of operating the vehicles.

The following schedule presents the operating budget for the current year, which has been approved by the university. The schedule also shows actual operating costs for March of the current year compared to one-twelfth of the annual operating budget.

University Motor Pool Budget Report for March			
	Annual Operating Budget	Monthly Budget*	March Actual	(Over) Under Budget
Gasoline	$ 42,000	$ 3,500	$ 4,300	$(800)
Oil, minor repairs, parts	3,600	300	380	(80)
Outside repairs	2,700	225	50	175
Insurance	6,000	500	525	(25)
Salaries and benefits	30,000	2,500	2,500	0
Depreciation of vehicles	26,400	2,200	2,310	(110)
Total cost	$110,700	$ 9,225	$10,065	$(840)
Total miles	600,000	50,000	63,000	
Cost per mile	$ 0.1845	$0.1845	$0.1598	
Number of automobiles in use	20	20	21	

*Annual operating budget ÷ 12 months.

The annual operating budget was constructed on the following assumptions:

a.   Twenty automobiles in the motor pool.
b.   Thirty thousand miles driven per year per automobile.
c.   Twenty-five miles per gallon per automobile.
d. $1.75 per gallon of gasoline.
e. $0.006 cost per mile for oil, minor repairs, and parts.
f. $135 cost per automobile per year for outside repairs.
g. $300 cost per automobile per year for insurance.

The supervisor of the motor pool is unhappy with the monthly report comparing budget and actual costs for March, claiming it presents an unfair picture of performance. A previous employer used flexible budgeting to compare actual costs to budgeted amounts.

Required:
1.   Using a flexible budgeting approach, prepare a new performance report for March showing budgeted costs, actual costs, and variances. All team members should understand how the revised performance report was prepared.
2.   The team should discuss and then write up brief answers to the questions listed below. All team members should agree with and understand the answers.
    a.   What are the deficiencies in the performance report that was prepared by the budget analyst?
    b.   How does the revised performance report, which was prepared using a flexible budget approach, overcome these deficiencies?

(CMA, adapted)

Analytical Thinking   (LO4, LO5, LO6)
A company that uses a standard cost system has provided the following data. The company's flexible budget for manufacturing overhead is based on standard machine-hours.

CHECK FIGURE
(5) $210,000 fixed
(14) $1.75/hour

1. Denominator activity in hours	?
2. Standard hours allowed for units produced	32,000
3. Actual hours worked	30,000
4. Flexible budget variable overhead per machine-hour	?
5. Flexible budget fixed overhead (total)	?
6. Actual variable overhead cost incurred	$54,000
7. Actual fixed overhead cost incurred	$209,400
8. Variable overhead cost applied to production*	?
9. Fixed overhead cost applied to production*	$192,000
10. Variable overhead spending variance	?
11. Variable overhead efficiency variance	$3,500 F
12. Fixed overhead budget variance	?
13. Fixed overhead volume variance	$18,000 U
14. Variable portion of the predetermined overhead rate	?
15. Fixed portion of the predetermined overhead rate	?
16. Underapplied (or overapplied) overhead	?

*Based on standard hours allowed for units produced.

Required:
Compute the unknown amounts. (Hint: One way to proceed would be to use the format for variance analysis found in Exhibit 8–7 for variable overhead and in Exhibit 9–10 for fixed overhead.)

Taking It to the Net
As you know, the World Wide Web is a medium that is constantly evolving. Sites come and go and change without notice. To enable periodic updating of site addresses, these problems have been posted to the textbook website (www.mhhe.com/bgn3e). After accessing the site, enter the Student Center and select this chapter to find the Taking It to the Net problems.

10

Decentralization

CHAPTER OUTLINE

A LOOK BACK

We introduced management control and performance measures in Chapter 8 with a discussion of standard costs and variance analysis. Chapter 9 extended that discussion to overhead costs.

A LOOK AT THIS CHAPTER

Chapter 10 continues our coverage of performance measurement by introducing return on investment and residual income measures to motivate managers and monitor progress toward achieving the company's goals.

A LOOK AHEAD

After introducing the concept of relevant costs and benefits, we discuss in Chapter 11 how effective decision making depends on the correct use of relevant data.

DECISION FEATURE

DECISION FEATURE

Centralizing Communications

Ingersoll-Rand, a global conglomerate that traces its roots to the early 1870s, has about 46,000 employees. The company has received numerous recognitions and awards, including being named the *Industryweek* Best Managed Company for several years in a row. Even so, the company decided that it needed to restructure its organization to effectively compete in the current economic environment.

Previously comprising 8 autonomous companies, Ingersoll-Rand now operates as 13 separate business units. To improve communications, its computer systems were integrated to provide information to managers and headquarters in real time. The company continues to operate in a decentralized fashion. Even though many of its functions have been centralized, such as purchasing, payroll, and accounts receivable and payable, decision making is still spread throughout the organization. For example, factory managers continue to be responsible for deciding what must be purchased. However, instead of directly issuing purchase orders to vendors, requisitions are communicated to headquarters, which then issues the purchase orders. As a result of this centralized approach to purchasing, the company has been able to negotiate better discounts with suppliers.

Analysts estimate the cost of the restructuring at $50 million. Don Janson, director of common administrative resources implementations at Ingersoll-Rand, predicts that the changes will pay for themselves within three years.

Sources: Ingersoll-Rand Company website; and Steve Konicki, "A Company Merges Its Many Units—Successfully," *Informationweek*, May 8, 2000, pp. 174–178.

LEARNING OBJECTIVES

After studying Chapter 10, you should be able to:

LO1 Compute the return on investment (ROI) and show how changes in sales, expenses, and assets affect an organization's ROI.

LO2 Compute residual income and understand the strengths and weaknesses of this method of measuring performance.

Once an organization grows beyond a few people, it becomes impossible for the top manager to make decisions about everything. For example, the CEO of the Hyatt Hotel chain cannot be expected to decide whether a particular hotel guest at the Hyatt Hotel on Maui should be allowed to check out later than the normal checkout time. It makes sense for the CEO to authorize employees at Maui to make this decision. As in this example, managers in large organizations have to delegate some decisions to those who are at lower levels in the organization.

DECENTRALIZATION IN ORGANIZATIONS

In a **decentralized organization,** decision-making authority is not confined to a few top executives; rather, decision-making authority is spread throughout the organization. All large organizations are decentralized to some extent out of necessity. At one extreme, strongly decentralized organizations empower even the lowest-level managers and employees to make decisions. At the other extreme, strongly centralized organizations provide lower-level managers with little freedom to make decisions. Although most organizations fall somewhere between these two extremes, the trend is towards decentralization.

Advantages and Disadvantages of Decentralization

The major advantages of decentralization include:

1. Delegating day-to-day problem solving to lower-level managers allows top management to concentrate on bigger issues such as overall strategy.
2. Lower-level managers often have more detailed and up-to-date information about their areas of responsibility than top management, and therefore, they are better able to make day-to-day operating decisions.
3. By eliminating layers of decision making and approvals, organizations can respond more quickly to customers and to changes in the operating environment.
4. Granting decision-making authority to lower-level managers helps train them for higher-level positions.
5. Empowering lower-level managers to make decisions can increase their motivation and job satisfaction.

The major disadvantages of decentralization include:

1. Lower-level managers may make decisions without fully understanding the big picture.
2. Coordination may be lacking among lower-level managers.
3. Lower-level managers may have objectives that clash with the objectives of the entire organization.[1] For example, a manager may be more interested in increasing the size of his or her department, bringing with it more power and prestige, than in increasing its effectiveness.

---

[1]Similar problems exist with top-level managers as well. The shareholders of the company delegate their decision-making authority to the top managers. Unfortunately, top managers may abuse that trust by rewarding themselves and their friends too generously, spending too much company money on palatial offices, and so on. The issue of how to ensure that top managers act in the best interests of the company's owners continues to puzzle experts. To a large extent, the owners rely on performance evaluation using return on investment and residual income measures as discussed later in the chapter and on bonuses and stock options. The stock market is also an important disciplining mechanism. If top managers squander the company's resources, the price of the company's stock will almost surely fall—resulting in a loss of prestige, bonuses, and possibly a job. And, of course, particularly outrageous self-dealing may land a CEO in court, as recent events have demonstrated.

4. Spreading innovative ideas may be difficult. Someone in one part of the organization may have a terrific idea that would benefit other parts of the organization, but without strong central direction, the idea may not be shared with, and adopted by, other parts of the organization.

The disadvantages of decentralization cited above can be reduced by the effective use of performance measures, such as those discussed later in this chapter, that tend to align the manager's interests with those of the overall organization and by the effective use of technology such as intranet systems that make it easier for information to be shared across departments.

Decentralization: A Delicate Balance

IN BUSINESS

Decentralization has its advantages and disadvantages. Bed Bath & Beyond, a specialty retailer headquartered in Union, New Jersey, benefits from decentralizing its merchandise stocking decisions to local store managers, who choose 70% of their store's merchandise based on local customer tastes. For example, the company's Manhattan stores stock wall paint, but its suburban stores do not because home improvement giants in the suburbs, such as Home Depot, meet this customer need.

On the other hand, Nestle, a consumer food products company with $60 billion in annual sales, has been working to overcome glaring inefficiencies arising from its decentralized management structure. For example, in Switzerland "each candy and ice cream factory was ordering its own sugar. Moreover, different factories were using different names for the identical grade of sugar, making it almost impossible for bosses at headquarters to track costs." Nestle hopes to significantly reduce costs and simplify recordkeeping by centralizing its raw materials purchases.

Sources: Nanette Byrnes, "What's Beyond for Bed Bath & Beyond?" *BusinessWeek*, January 19, 2004, pp. 44–50, and Carol Matlack, "Nestle Is Starting to Slim Down at Last," *BusinessWeek*, October 27, 2003, pp. 56–57.

RESPONSIBILITY ACCOUNTING

Since decentralized organizations delegate decision-making responsibility to lower-level managers, they need *responsibility accounting systems* that link lower-level managers' decision-making authority with accountability for the outcomes of those decisions. The term **responsibility center** is used for any part of an organization whose manager has control over and is accountable for cost, profit, or investments. The three primary types of responsibility centers are *cost centers, profit centers,* and *investment centers.*[2]

Cost, Profit, and Investment Centers

Cost Center   The manager of a **cost center** has control over costs, but not over revenue or investment funds. Service departments such as accounting, finance, general administration, legal, and personnel are usually classified as cost centers. In addition, manufacturing facilities are often considered to be cost centers. The managers of cost centers are expected to minimize costs while providing the level of products and services demanded by other parts of the organization. For example, the manager of a manufacturing facility would be evaluated at least in part by comparing actual costs to how much

---

[2]Some companies classify business segments that are responsible mainly for generating revenue, such as an insurance sales office, as *revenue centers.* Other companies would consider this to be just another type of profit center, since costs of some kind (salaries, rent, utilities) are usually deducted from the revenues in the segment's income statement.

costs should have been for the actual level of output during the period. Standard cost variances and flexible budget variances, such as those discussed in Chapters 8 and 9, are often used to evaluate cost center performance.

 Profit Center   The manager of a **profit center** has control over both costs and revenue. Like a cost center manager, a profit center manager does not have control over investment funds. For example, the manager in charge of a Six Flags amusement park would be responsible for both the revenues and costs, and hence the profits, of the amusement park, but may not have control over major investments in the park. Profit center managers are often evaluated by comparing actual profit to targeted or budgeted profit.

Investment Center   The manager of an **investment center** has control over cost, revenue, and investments in operating assets. For example, the vice president of the Truck Division at General Motors would have a great deal of discretion over investments in the division. This vice president would be responsible for initiating investment proposals, such as funding research into more fuel-efficient engines for sport-utility vehicles. Once the proposal has been approved by General Motor's top-level managers and board of directors, the vice president of the Truck Division would then be responsible for making sure that the investment pays off. Investment center managers are usually evaluated using return on investment (ROI) or residual income measures, as discussed later in the chapter.

IN BUSINESS

(continued)

years ago . . . identified just such extreme incentives as a red flag. 'If you're right under the target, there's a tremendous economic interest to accelerate earnings," says David F. Larcker, a professor of accounting at the Wharton School. 'If you're right over it, there is an incentive to push earnings into the next period.'"

Sources: *Reuters,* "Tyco Says to Restate Several Years of Results," June 16, 2003; Jeanne King, *Reuters,* "New York Trial of ex-Tyco CEO Kozlowski Can Proceed," June 23, 2003; and, William C. Symonds, Diane Brady, Geoffrey Smith, and Lorraine Woellert, "Tyco: Aggressive or Out of Line?" *BusinessWeek,* November 1, 1999, pp. 160–165.

An Organizational View of Responsibility Centers

Superior Foods Corporation provides an example of the various kinds of responsibility centers that exist in an organization. Superior Foods manufactures and distributes snack foods and beverages. Exhibit 10–1 shows a partial organization chart for Superior Foods that displays its cost, profit, and investment centers. Note that the departments and work centers that do not generate significant revenues by themselves are classified as cost centers. These are staff departments, such as finance, legal, and personnel, and operating units, such as the bottling plant, warehouse, and beverage distribution center. The profit centers generate revenues, and they include the salty snacks, beverages, and confections product families. The vice president of operations oversees the allocation of investment funds across the product families and is responsible for the profits of those product families. And finally, corporate headquarters is an investment center, since it is responsible for all revenues, costs, and investments.

EXHIBIT 10–1   Business Segments Classified as Cost, Profit, and Investment Centers

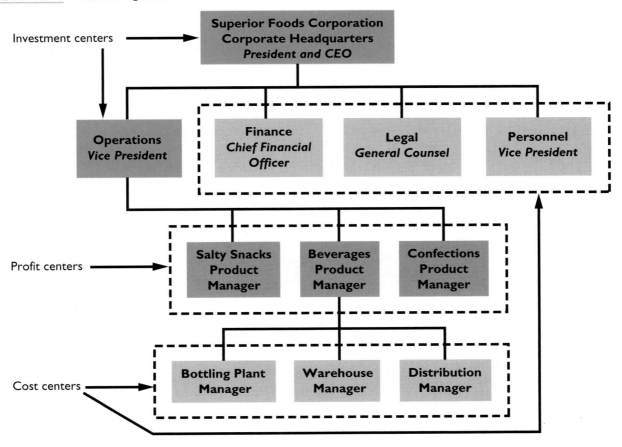

Meeting Targets the Wrong Way

Putting too much emphasis on meeting financial targets can lead to undesirable behavior. Michael C. Jensen reports, "I once watched the management of a manufacturing company struggle to reach their year-end targets. In late fall, they announced a price increase of 10% effective January 2. Now it may be that a price increase was needed, but it was not in line with the competition, nor was it likely that January 2, of all dates, was the best time for the increase. A price increase on January 2, would, however, cause customers to order before year-end and thereby help managers reach their targets." The short-term boost in sales comes at the cost of lost future sales and possible customer ill will.

Source: Michael C. Jensen, "Why Pay People to Lie?" *The Wall Street Journal*, January 8, 2001, p. A32.

Decentralization and Segment Reporting

Effective decentralization requires *segmented reporting.* In addition to the companywide income statement, reports are needed for individual segments of the organization. A **segment** is a part or activity of an organization about which managers would like cost, revenue, or profit data. Cost, profit, and investment centers are segments as are sales territories, individual stores, service centers, manufacturing plants, marketing departments, individual customers, and product lines. A company's operations can be segmented in many ways. For example, a grocery store chain like Safeway or Kroger can segment its business by geographic region, by individual store, by the nature of the merchandise (i.e., green groceries, canned goods, paper goods), by brand name, and so on.

Segmenting a Company

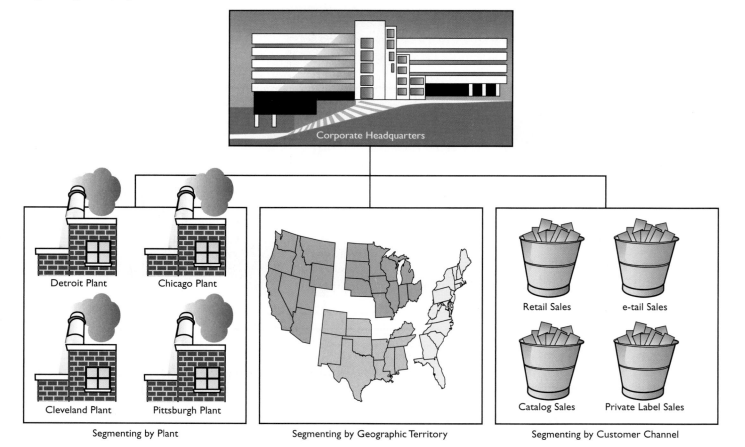

Corporate Headquarters

Detroit Plant   Chicago Plant

Cleveland Plant   Pittsburgh Plant

Segmenting by Plant

Segmenting by Geographic Territory

Retail Sales   e-tail Sales

Catalog Sales   Private Label Sales

Segmenting by Customer Channel

Traceable and Common Fixed Costs

In segment reports, *traceable fixed costs* should be distinguished from *common fixed costs*. A **traceable fixed cost** of a segment is a fixed cost that is incurred because of the existence of the segment and would disappear if the segment were eliminated. Examples of traceable fixed costs include the following:

- The salary of the Fritos product manager at PepsiCo is a traceable fixed cost of the Fritos business segment of PepsiCo.
- The maintenance cost for the building in which Boeing 747s are assembled is a traceable fixed cost of the 747 business segment of Boeing.
- The liability insurance at Disney World is a traceable fixed cost of the Disney World business segment of the Disney Corporation.

A **common fixed cost** is a fixed cost that supports the operations of more than one segment, but is not traceable in whole or in part to any one segment. Even if the segment were entirely eliminated, there would be no change in a common fixed cost. Examples of common fixed costs include the following:

- The salary of the CEO of General Motors is a common fixed cost of the various divisions of General Motors.
- The cost of the checkout equipment at a Safeway or Kroger grocery store is a common fixed cost of the various departments—such as groceries, produce, bakery—in the store.
- The cost of the receptionist's salary at an office shared by a number of doctors is a common fixed cost of the doctors. The cost is traceable to the office, but not to individual doctors.

In general, traceable costs should be assigned to segments, but common fixed costs should not. Assigning common fixed costs to segments would overstate the costs that are actually caused by the segments and that could be avoided by eliminating the segments. The details of how to deal with traceable and common fixed costs in segment reports are covered in more advanced texts. For example, see Chapter 12 of Ray Garrison, Eric Noreen, and Peter Brewer, *Managerial Accounting,* 11th edition, McGraw-Hill/Irwin, 2006.

1. Managers in which of the following responsibility centers are held responsible for profits? (You may select more than one answer.)
   a. Revenue centers
   b. Cost centers
   c. Profit centers
   d. Investment centers
2. Which of the following statements is false? (You may select more than one answer.)
   a. The same cost can be traceable or common depending on how the segment is defined.
   b. In general, common fixed costs should be assigned to segments.
   c. If a company eliminates a segment of its business, the costs that were traceable to that segment should disappear.
   d. If four segments share $1 million in common fixed costs and one segment is eliminated, the common fixed costs will decrease by $250,000.

CONCEPT CHECK ✓

RATE OF RETURN FOR MEASURING MANAGERIAL PERFORMANCE

When a company is truly decentralized, managers are given a great deal of autonomy. Profit and investment centers are often virtually independent businesses, with their managers having about the same control over decisions as if they were in fact running their own independent companies. With this autonomy, fierce competition often develops among managers, with each striving to make his or her segment the "best" in the company.

Competition between investment centers is particularly keen for investment funds. How do top managers in corporate headquarters go about deciding who gets new investment funds as they become available, and how do these managers decide which investment centers are most profitably using the funds that they have already been given? One of the most popular ways of making these judgments is to measure the rate of return that investment center managers are able to generate on their assets. This rate of return is called the *return on investment (ROI).*

The Return on Investment (ROI) Formula

Concept 10-1

The **return on investment (ROI)** is defined as net operating income divided by average operating assets:

$$\text{ROI} = \frac{\text{Net operating income}}{\text{Average operating assets}}$$

The higher the return on investment (ROI) of a business segment, the greater the profit earned per dollar invested in the segment's operating assets.

Net Operating Income and Operating Assets Defined

Note that *net operating income,* rather than net income, is used in the ROI formula. **Net operating income** is income before interest and taxes and is sometimes referred to as EBIT (earnings before interest and taxes). Net operating income is used in the formula because the base (i.e., denominator) consists of *operating assets.* Thus, to be consistent we use net operating income in the numerator.

Operating assets include cash, accounts receivable, inventory, plant and equipment, and all other assets held for operating purposes. Examples of assets that are not included in operating assets (i.e., examples of nonoperating assets) include land held for future use, an investment in another company, or a building rented to someone else. These assets are not held for operating purposes and therefore are excluded from operating assets. The operating assets base used in the formula is typically computed as the average of the operating assets between the beginning and the end of the year.

Most companies use the net book value (i.e., acquisition cost less accumulated depreciation) of depreciable assets to calculate average operating assets. This approach has drawbacks. An asset's net book value decreases over time as the accumulated depreciation increases. This decreases the denominator in the ROI calculation, thus increasing ROI. Consequently, ROI mechanically increases over time. Moreover, replacing old depreciated equipment with new equipment increases the book value of depreciable assets and decreases ROI. Hence, it is argued that using net book value in the calculation of average operating assets results in a predictable pattern of increasing ROI over time as accumulated depreciation grows and discourages replacing old equipment with new, updated equipment. An alternative to the net book value is the gross cost of the asset, which ignores accumulated depreciation. Gross cost stays constant over time because depreciation is ignored; therefore, ROI does not grow automatically over time, and replacing a fully depreciated asset with a comparably priced new asset will not adversely affect ROI.

Nevertheless, most companies use the net book value approach to computing average operating assets because it is consistent with their financial reporting practices of recording the net book value of assets on the balance sheet and including depreciation as an operating expense on the income statement. In this text, we will use the net book value approach unless a specific exercise or problem directs otherwise.

Understanding ROI

The equation for ROI, net operating income divided by average operating assets, does not provide much help to managers interested in taking actions to improve their ROI. It only offers two levers for improving performance—net operating income and average operating assets. Fortunately, ROI can also be expressed in terms of **margin** and **turnover** as follows:

$$ROI = Margin \times Turnover$$

where

$$Margin = \frac{Net\ operating\ income}{Sales}$$

and

$$Turnover = \frac{Sales}{Average\ operating\ assets}.$$

Note that the sales terms in the margin and turnover formulas cancel out when they are multiplied together, yielding the original formula for ROI stated in terms of net operating income and average operating assets. So either formula for ROI will always give the same answer. However, the margin and turnover formulation provides some additional insights.

From a manager's perspective, margin and turnover are very important concepts. Margin is improved by increasing sales or reducing operating expenses, including cost of goods sold and selling and administrative expenses. The lower the operating expenses per dollar of sales, the higher the margin earned. Some managers tend to focus too much on margin and ignore turnover. However, turnover incorporates a crucial area of a manager's responsibility—the investment in operating assets. Excessive funds tied up in operating assets (e.g., cash, accounts receivable, inventories, plant and equipment, and other assets) depress turnover and lower ROI. In fact, inefficient use of operating assets can be just as much of a drag on profitability as excessive operating expenses, which depress margin.

The E.I. du Pont de Nemours and Company (better know as DuPont) pioneered the use of ROI and recognized the importance of looking at both margin and turnover in assessing a manager's performance. ROI is now widely used as the key measure of investment center performance. ROI reflects in a single figure many aspects of the manager's responsibilities. It can be compared to the returns of other investment centers in the organization, the returns of other companies in the industry, and to the past returns of the investment center itself.

Insuring the Bottom Line

Insurance companies have begun to offer managers a radical way to avoid some of the risk of having to report bad financial results. For example, the Reliance Group has created a product called Enterprise Earnings Protection Insurance that covers any operating earnings shortfall due to events beyond management's control. If a company buys an insurance policy guaranteeing $5 million in profits, but it posted only a $3 million profit, then Reliance would have to make up the difference of $2 million. Reliance reports that a company may have to pay as little as 5% of its estimated profit to insure against a 20% shortfall.

Source: Diane Brady, "Is Your Bottom Line Covered?" *BusinessWeek*, February 8, 1999, pp. 85–86.

DuPont also developed the diagram that appears in Exhibit 10–2. This exhibit helps managers understand how they can work to improve ROI. Any increase in ROI must involve at least one of the following:

1. Increased sales
2. Reduced operating expenses
3. Reduced operating assets

Many actions involve combinations of changes in sales, expenses, and operating assets. For example, a manager may make an investment in (i.e., increase) operating assets to reduce operating expenses or increase sales. Whether the net effect is favorable or not is judged in terms of its overall impact on ROI.

To illustrate how ROI is impacted by various actions, we will use the Monthaven outlet of the Burger Grill chain as an example. Burger Grill is a small chain of upscale casual restaurants that has been rapidly adding outlets via franchising. The Monthaven franchise is owned by a group of local surgeons who have little time to devote to management and little expertise in business matters. Therefore, they delegate operating decisions—including decisions concerning investment in operating assets such as inventories—to a professional manager they have hired. The manager is evaluated largely based on the ROI the franchise generates.

The following data represent the results of operations for the most recent month:

Sales	$100,000
Operating expenses	$90,000
Net operating income	$10,000
Average operating assets	$50,000

EXHIBIT 10–2　Elements of Return on Investment (ROI)

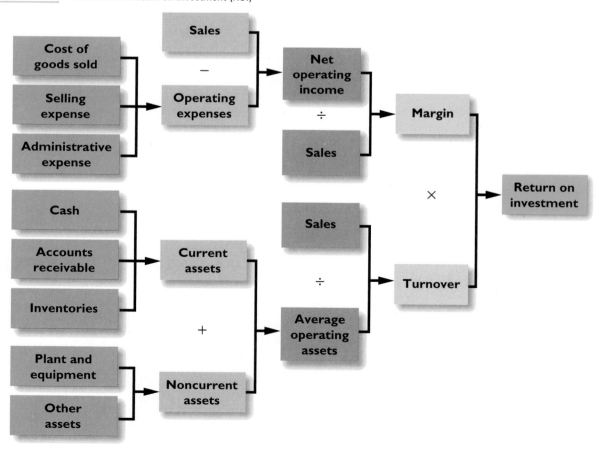

The rate of return generated by the Monthaven Burger Grill investment center is as follows:

$$\text{ROI} = \text{Margin} \times \text{Turnover}$$

$$= \frac{\text{Net operating income}}{\text{Sales}} \times \frac{\text{Sales}}{\text{Average operating assets}}$$

$$= \frac{\$10,000}{\$100,000} \times \frac{\$100,000}{\$50,000}$$

$$= 10\% \times 2 = 20\%$$

Example 1: Increased Sales without Any Increase in Operating Assets   Assume that the manager of the Monthaven Burger Grill is able to increase sales by 10% without any increase in operating assets. The increase in sales will require additional operating expenses, but as long as fixed costs are not affected by the increase in sales and the manager exercises effective control over costs, operating expenses will increase by less than 10%. Assume that the increase in operating expenses will be 7.8%. The new net operating income would therefore be $12,980, determined as follows:

Sales (1.10 × $100,000)	$110,000
Operating expenses (1.078 × $90,000)	97,020
Net operating income	$ 12,980

In this case, the new ROI will be:

$$\text{ROI} = \frac{\text{Net operating income}}{\text{Sales}} \times \frac{\text{Sales}}{\text{Average operating assets}}$$

$$= \frac{\$12,980}{\$110,000} \times \frac{\$110,000}{\$50,000}$$

$$= 11.8\% \times 2.2 = 25.96\% \text{ (as compared to 20\% originally)}$$

Note that the key to improved ROI in the case of an increase in sales is that the percentage increase in operating expenses must be less than the percentage increase in sales.

Example 2: Decreased Operating Expenses with No Change in Sales or Operating Assets   Assume that by improving business processes, the manager of the Monthaven Burger Grill is able to reduce operating expenses by $1,000 without any effect on sales or operating assets. This reduction in operating expenses will result in increasing net operating income by $1,000, from $10,000 to $11,000. The new ROI will be:

$$\text{ROI} = \frac{\text{Net operating income}}{\text{Sales}} \times \frac{\text{Sales}}{\text{Average operating assets}}$$

$$= \frac{\$11,000}{\$100,000} \times \frac{\$100,000}{\$50,000}$$

$$= 11\% \times 2 = 22\% \text{ (as compared to 20\% originally)}$$

When margins are being squeezed, cutting expenses is often the first line of attack adopted by a manager. Discretionary fixed costs (i.e., fixed costs that arise from annual decisions by management) usually come under scrutiny first, and various programs are either curtailed or eliminated in an effort to cut costs. Managers must be careful, however, not to cut too much or in the wrong place. That may have the effect of decreasing sales or indirectly causing increased costs elsewhere. Also, managers must remember that indiscriminate cost-cutting can destroy morale.

Example 3: Decreased Operating Assets with No Change in Sales or Operating Expenses   Assume that the manager of the Monthaven Burger Grill is able to reduce inventories by $10,000 using the principles of lean production. This might actually have a positive effect on sales (through fresher ingredients) and on operating expenses (through reduced inventory spoilage), but for the sake of illustration, suppose the reduction in inventories has no effect on sales or operating expenses. The reduction in inventories will reduce average operating assets by $10,000, from $50,000 down to $40,000. The new ROI will be:

$$\text{ROI} = \frac{\text{Net operating income}}{\text{Sales}} \times \frac{\text{Sales}}{\text{Average operating assets}}$$

$$= \frac{\$10,000}{\$100,000} \times \frac{\$100,000}{\$40,000}$$

$$= 10\% \times 2.5 = 25\% \text{ (as compared to 20\% originally)}$$

In this example, lean production was used to reduce operating assets. Another common tactic for reducing operating assets is to speed up the collection of accounts receivable. For example, many companies encourage customers to pay electronically rather than by mail.

Example 4: Invest in Operating Assets to Increase Sales   Assume that the manager of the Monthaven Burger Grill invests $2,000 in a state-of-the-art soft-serve ice cream machine that is capable of dispensing a number of different flavors. This new machine will result in additional sales of $4,000 and additional operating expenses of $1,000. Thus, net operating income will increase by $3,000, to $13,000. The new ROI will be:

$$\text{ROI} = \frac{\text{Net operating income}}{\text{Sales}} \times \frac{\text{Sales}}{\text{Average operating assets}}$$

$$= \frac{\$13,000}{\$104,000} \times \frac{\$104,000}{\$52,000}$$

$$= 12.5\% \times 2 = 25\% \text{ (as compared to 20\% originally)}$$

In this particular example, the investment had no effect on turnover, which remained at 2, so there had to be an increase in margin in order to improve the ROI.

IN BUSINESS

McDonald Chic

McDonald's France has been spending lavishly to remodel its restaurants to blend with local architecture and to make their interiors less uniform and sterile. For example, some outlets in the Alps have wood-and-stone interiors similar to those of alpine chalets. The idea is to defuse the negative feelings many of the French people have toward McDonald's as a symbol of American culture and, perhaps more importantly, to try to entice customers to linger over their meals and spend more. This investment in operating assets has apparently been successful—even though a Big Mac costs about the same in Paris as in New York, the average French customer spends about $9 per visit versus only about $4 in the U.S.

Source: Carol Matlack and Pallavi Gogoi, "What's This? The French Love McDonald's?" *BusinessWeek*, January 13, 2003, p. 50.

ROI and the Balanced Scorecard

Simply exhorting managers to increase ROI is not sufficient. Managers who are told to increase ROI will naturally wonder how this is to be accomplished. The Du Pont scheme, which is illustrated in Exhibit 10–2, provides managers with *some* guidance. Generally speaking, ROI can be increased by increasing sales, decreasing costs, and/or decreasing investments in operating assets. However, it may not be obvious to managers how they are supposed to increase sales, decrease costs, and decrease investments in a way that is consistent with the company's strategy. For example, a manager who is given inadequate guidance may cut back on investments that are critical to implementing the company's strategy.

For that reason, as discussed in Chapter 8, when managers are evaluated based on ROI, a balanced scorecard approach is advised. And indeed, ROI, or residual income (discussed below), is typically included as one of the financial performance measures on a company's balanced scorecard. As briefly discussed in Chapter 8, the balanced scorecard provides a way of communicating a company's strategy to managers throughout the organization. The scorecard indicates *how* the company intends to improve its financial performance. A well-constructed balanced scorecard should answer questions like: "What internal business processes should be improved?" and "Which customer should be targeted and how will they be attracted and retained at a profit?" In short, a well-constructed balanced scorecard can provide managers with a road map that indicates how the company intends to increase its ROI. In the absence of such a road map of the company's strategy, managers may have difficulty understanding what they are supposed to do to increase ROI and they may work at cross-purposes rather than in harmony with the overall strategy of the company.

Criticisms of ROI

Although ROI is widely used in evaluating performance, it is subject to the following criticisms:

1. Just telling managers to increase ROI may not be enough. Managers may not know how to increase ROI; they may increase ROI in a way that is inconsistent with the company's strategy; or they may take actions that increase ROI in the short run but harm the company in the long run (such as cutting back on research and development). This is why ROI is best used as part of a balanced scorecard as discussed above. A balanced scorecard can provide concrete guidance to managers, making it more likely that actions taken are consistent with the company's strategy, and reducing the likelihood that short-run performance will be enhanced at the expense of long-term performance.
2. A manager who takes over a business segment typically inherits many committed costs over which the manager has no control. These committed costs make it difficult to fairly assess the performance of the manager relative to other managers.
3. As discussed in the next section, a manager who is evaluated based on ROI may reject investment opportunities that are profitable for the company as a whole but that would negatively impact the division's ROI.

Let the Buyer Beware

Those who sell products and services to businesses are well aware that many potential customers look very carefully at the impact the purchase would have on ROI before making a purchase. Unfortunately, some salespersons make extravagant ROI claims. For example, businesspeople complain that software salespersons routinely exaggerate the impact that new software will have on ROI. Some of the tricks used by salespersons include: inflating the salaries of workers who are made redundant by productivity gains; omitting costs such as training costs and implementation costs; inflating expected sales increases; and using former clients as examples of ROI gains when the clients were given the software for free or for nominal cost. The message? Be skeptical of salespersons' claims with respect to ROI gains from purchasing their products and services.

Source: Scott Leibs, "All Hail the ROI," *CFO*, April 2002, pp. 27–28.

Jewelry Store Manager

DECISION MAKER

You were recently hired as the manager of a chain of jewelry stores that are located in downtown Chicago. You are excited about the high level of autonomy that you have been given to run the stores but are nervous because you've heard rumors that the previous manager was let go because the return on investment (ROI) of the stores was unacceptable. What steps should you consider to improve ROI?

RESIDUAL INCOME—ANOTHER MEASURE OF PERFORMANCE

Concept 10-2

Residual income is another approach to measuring an investment center's performance. **Residual income** is the net operating income that an investment center earns above the minimum required return on its operating assets. In equation form, residual income is calculated as follows:

$$\frac{\text{Residual}}{\text{income}} = \frac{\text{Net operating}}{\text{income}} - \left(\frac{\text{Average operating}}{\text{assets}} \times \frac{\text{Minimum required}}{\text{rate of return}}\right)$$

Economic Value Added (EVA®) is an adaptation of residual income that has been adopted by many companies.[3] Under EVA, companies often modify their accounting principles in various ways. For example, funds used for research and development are often treated as investments rather than as expenses under EVA.[4] These complications are best dealt with in a more advanced course; in this text we will focus on the basics and will not draw any distinction between residual income and EVA.

When residual income or EVA is used to measure performance, the objective is to maximize the total amount of residual income or EVA, not to maximize ROI. This is an important distinction. If the objective were to maximize ROI, then every company should divest all of its products except the single product with the highest ROI. A wide variety of organizations have embraced some version of residual income or EVA, including Bausch & Lomb, Best Buy, Boise Cascade, Coca-Cola, Dun and Bradstreet, Eli Lilly, Federated Mogul, Georgia-Pacific, Guidant Corporation, Hershey Foods, Husky Injection Molding, J.C. Penney, Kansas City Power & Light, Olin, Quaker Oats, Silicon Valley Bank, Sprint, Toys R Us, Tupperware, and the United States Postal Service. In addition, financial institutions such as Credit Suisse First Boston now use EVA—and its allied concept, market value added—to evaluate potential investments in other companies.

IN BUSINESS

Heads I Win, Tails You Lose

A number of companies, including AT&T, Armstrong Holdings, and Baldwin Technology, have stopped using residual income measures of performance after trying them. Why? Reasons differ, but "bonus evaporation is often seen as the Achilles' heel of value-based metrics [like residual income and EVA]—and a major cause of plans being dropped." Managers tend to love residual income and EVA when their bonuses are big, but clamor for changes in performance measures when bonuses shrink.

Source: Bill Richard and Alix Nyberg, "Do EVA and Other Value Metrics Still Offer a Good Mirror of Company Performance?" *CFO*, March 2001, pp. 56–64.

For purposes of illustration, consider the following data for an investment center—the Ketchikan Division of Alaskan Marine Services Corporation.

---

[3]The basic idea underlying residual income and economic value added has been around for over 100 years. In recent years, economic value added has been popularized and trademarked by the consulting firm Stern, Stewart & Co.
[4]Over 100 different adjustments could be made for deferred taxes, LIFO reserves, provisions for future liabilities, mergers and acquisitions, gains or losses due to changes in accounting rules, operating leases, and other accounts, but most companies make only a few. For further details, see John O'Hanlon and Ken Peasnell, "Wall Street's Contribution to Management Accounting: The Stern Stewart EVA® Financial Management System," *Management Accounting Research* 9 (1998), pp. 421–444.

```
        Alaskan Marine Services Corporation
                 Ketchikan Division
          Basic Data for Performance Evaluation

Average operating assets  ...........................  $100,000
Net operating income .................................  $20,000
Minimum required rate of return  .....................     15%
```

Alaskan Marine Services Corporation has long had a policy of evaluating investment center managers based on ROI, but it is considering a switch to residual income. The controller of the company, who is in favor of the change to residual income, has provided the following table that shows how the performance of the division would be evaluated under each of the two methods:

```
              Alaskan Marine Services Corporation
                       Ketchikan Division
```

	ROI	Residual Income
	Alternative Performance Measures	
Average operating assets (a)	$100,000	$100,000
Net operating income (b)	$ 20,000	$ 20,000
ROI, (b) ÷ (a)	20%	
Minimum required return (15% × $100,000)........		15,000
Residual income		$ 5,000

The reasoning underlying the residual income calculation is straightforward. The company is able to earn a rate of return of at least 15% on its investments. Since the company has invested $100,000 in the Ketchikan Division in the form of operating assets, the company should be able to earn at least $15,000 (15% × $100,000) on this investment. Since the Ketchikan Division's net operating income is $20,000, the residual income above and beyond the minimum required return is $5,000. If residual income is adopted as the performance measure to replace ROI, the manager of the Ketchikan Division would be evaluated based on the growth in residual income from year to year.

Motivation and Residual Income

One of the primary reasons why the controller of Alaskan Marine Services Corporation would like to switch from ROI to residual income has to do with how managers view new investments under the two performance measurement schemes. The residual income approach encourages managers to make investments that are profitable for the entire company but that would be rejected by managers who are evaluated by the ROI formula.

To illustrate this problem with ROI, suppose that the manager of the Ketchikan Division is considering purchasing a computerized diagnostic machine to aid in servicing marine diesel engines. The machine would cost $25,000 and is expected to generate additional operating income of $4,500 a year. From the standpoint of the company, this would be a good investment since it promises a rate of return of 18% ($4,500 ÷ $25,000), which exceeds the company's minimum required rate of return of 15%.

If the manager of the Ketchikan Division is evaluated based on residual income, she would be in favor of the investment in the diagnostic machine as shown below:

Alaskan Marine Services Corporation
Ketchikan Division
Performance Evaluated Using Residual Income

	Present	New Project	Overall
Average operating assets.	$100,000	$25,000	$125,000
Net operating income.	$ 20,000	$ 4,500	$ 24,500
Minimum required return	15,000	3,750*	18,750
Residual income	$ 5,000	$ 750	$ 5,750

*$25,000 × 15% = $3,750.

Since the project would increase the residual income of the Ketchikan Division by $750, the manager would want to invest in the new diagnostic machine.

Now suppose that the manager of the Ketchikan Division is evaluated based on ROI. The effect of the diagnostic machine on the division's ROI is computed below:

Alaskan Marine Services Corporation
Ketchikan Division
Performance Evaluated Using ROI

	Present	New Project	Overall
Average operating assets (a)	$100,000	$25,000	$125,000
Net operating income (b)	$20,000	$4,500	$24,500
ROI, (b) ÷ (a)	20%	18%	19.6%

The new project reduces the division's ROI from 20% to 19.6%. This happens because the 18% rate of return on the new diagnostic machine, while above the company's 15% minimum required rate of return, is below the division's present ROI of 20%. Therefore, the new diagnostic machine would drag the division's ROI down even though it would be a good investment from the standpoint of the company as a whole. If the manager of the division is evaluated based on ROI, she will be reluctant to even propose such an investment.

Generally, a manager who is evaluated based on ROI will reject any project whose rate of return is below the division's current ROI even if the rate of return on the project is above the minimum required rate of return for the entire company. In contrast, any project whose rate of return is above the minimum required rate of return for the company will result in an increase in residual income. Since it is in the best interests of the company as a whole to accept any project whose rate of return is above the minimum required rate of return, managers who are evaluated based on residual income will tend to make better decisions concerning investment projects than managers who are evaluated based on ROI.

IN BUSINESS

Shoring Up Return on Capital

Manitowic Co. is located in Manitowic, Wisconsin, on the shores of Lake Michigan. The company makes construction cranes, ice machines, and Great Lakes shipping vessels. Over the past four years, the company's share price has increased over 500%. Part of this increase is attributed to the company's adoption of EVA. The company has slashed headquarters staff from 127 to 30 people. Inventories have been cut by $50 million—from $84 million down to $34 million. Divisions that fail to cut excess assets get no bonus. Before the adoption of EVA, the company's return on total capital was 10.5%. It is now 22%.

Source: Michelle Conlin, "Hoisting Job," *Forbes*, April 19, 1999, pp. 152, 156.

Shoe Store Manager

You are the manager of a shoe store in a busy shopping mall. The store is part of a national chain that evaluates its store managers on the basis of return on investment (ROI). As the manager of the store, you have control over costs, pricing, and the inventory you carry. The ROI of your store was 17.21% last year and is projected to be 17.00% this year unless some action is taken. The projected ROI has been computed as follows:

Average operating assets (a)	$2,000,000
Net operating income (b)	$340,000
ROI, (b) ÷ (a)	17.00%

Your bonus this year will depend on improving your ROI performance over last year. The minimum required rate of return on investment for the national chain is 15%.

You are considering two alternatives for improving this year's ROI:

a. Cut inventories (and average operating assets) by $500,000. This will unfortunately result in a reduction in sales, with a negative impact on net operating income of $79,000.

b. Add a new product line that would increase average operating inventories by $200,000, but would increase net operating income by $33,000.

Which alternative would result in you earning a bonus for the year? Which alternative is in the best interests of the national chain?

Divisional Comparison and Residual Income

The residual income approach has one major disadvantage. It can't be used to compare the performance of divisions of different sizes. You would expect larger divisions to have more residual income than smaller divisions, not necessarily because they are better managed but simply because they are bigger.

As an example, consider the following residual income computations for the Wholesale Division and the Retail Division of Sisal Marketing Corporation:

	Wholesale Division	Retail Division
Average operating assets (a)	$1,000,000	$250,000
Net operating income	$ 120,000	$ 40,000
Minimum required return: 10% × (a)	100,000	25,000
Residual income	$ 20,000	$ 15,000

Observe that the Wholesale Division has slightly more residual income than the Retail Division, but that the Wholesale Division has $1,000,000 in operating assets as compared to only $250,000 in operating assets for the Retail Division. Thus, the Wholesale Division's greater residual income is probably more a result of its size than the quality of its management. In fact, it appears that the smaller division may be better managed, since it has been able to generate nearly as much residual income with only one-fourth as much in operating assets to work with. When comparing investment centers, it is probably better to focus on the percentage change in residual income from year to year rather than on the absolute amount of the residual income.

CONCEPT CHECK

3. Last year sales were $300,000, net operating income was $75,000, and average operating assets were $500,000. If sales next year remain the same as last year and expenses and average operating assets are reduced by 5%, what will be the return on investment next year?
   a. 12.2%
   b. 18.2%
   c. 20.2%
   d. 25.2%
4. Referring to the facts in question 3 above, if the minimum required return is 12%, what will be the residual income next year?
   a. $26,250
   b. $27,250
   c. $28,250
   d. $29,250

Transfer Prices

A problem arises in evaluating segments of a company when one segment provides a good or service to another segment. For example, the truck division of Ford provides trucks to the passenger car division to use in its operations. If both the truck and passenger car divisions are evaluated based on their profits, disputes are likely to arise over the *transfer price* charged for the trucks used by the passenger car division. A **transfer price** is the price charged when one segment of an organization provides a good or service to another segment in the organization. The selling segment, in this case the truck division, would naturally like the transfer price to be as high as possible whereas the buying segment, in this case the passenger car division, would like the price to be as low as possible.

The question of what transfer price to charge is one of the most difficult problems in managerial accounting. The objective in transfer pricing should be to motivate the segment managers to do what is in the best interests of the overall organization. For example, if we want the manager of the passenger car division of Ford to make decisions that are in the best interests of the overall organization, the transfer price charged to the passenger car division for trucks must be the cost incurred by the entire organization up to the point of transfer—including any opportunity costs. If the transfer price is less than this cost, then the manager of the passenger car division will think that the cost of the trucks is lower than it really is and will tend to demand more trucks than would be optimal for the entire company. If the transfer price is greater than the cost incurred by the entire organization up to the point of the transfer, then the passenger car division manager will think the cost of the trucks is higher than it really is and will tend to demand fewer trucks than would be optimal for the entire organization. While this principle may seem clear-cut, as a practical matter, implementing it is very difficult for a variety of reasons. In practice, companies usually adopt a simplified transfer pricing policy based on variable cost, absorption cost, or market prices. All of these approaches have flaws, which are covered in more advanced texts.

SUMMARY

LO1 Compute the return on investment (ROI) and show how changes in sales, expenses, and assets affect an organization's ROI.
Return on investment (ROI) is defined as net operating income divided by average operating assets. Alternatively, it can be defined as the product of margin and turnover, where margin is net operating income divided by sales and turnover is sales divided by average operating assets.

The relations among sales, expenses, assets, and ROI are complex. The effect of a change in any one variable on the others will depend on the specific circumstances. Nevertheless, an increase in sales often leads to an increase in ROI via the effect of sales on net operating income. If the organization has significant fixed costs, then a given percentage increase in sales is likely to have an even larger percentage effect on net operating income.

LO2 **Compute residual income and understand the strengths and weaknesses of this method of measuring performance.**

Residual income is the difference between net operating income and the minimum required return on average operating assets. The minimum required return on average operating assets is computed by applying the minimum rate of return to the average operating assets.

A major advantage of residual income over ROI is that it encourages investment in projects whose rates of return are above the minimum required rate of return for the entire organization, but below the segment's current ROI.

GUIDANCE ANSWERS TO *DECISION MAKER* AND *YOU DECIDE*

Jewelry Store Manager (p. 441)

Three approaches can be used to increase ROI:

1. Increase sales—An increase in sales will positively impact the margin if expenses increase proportionately less than sales. An increase in sales will also favorably affect turnover if there is not a proportionate increase in operating assets.
2. Reduce expenses—This approach is often the first path selected by managers to increase profitability and ROI. You should start by reviewing the stores' discretionary fixed costs (such as advertising). It may be possible to cut some discretionary fixed costs with minimal damage to the long-run goals of the organization. You should also investigate whether there are adequate physical controls over the inventory of jewelry items. Thefts result in an increase in cost of goods sold without a corresponding increase in sales!
3. Reduce operating assets—An excessive investment in operating assets (such as inventory) reduces turnover and hurts ROI. Given the nature of the operations of retail jewelry stores, inventory must be in sufficient quantities at specific times during the year (such as Christmas, Valentine's Day, and Mother's Day) or sales will suffer. However, those levels do not need to be maintained throughout the year.

Shoe Store Manager (p. 445)

The effects of the two alternatives on your store's ROI for the year can be computed as follows:

	Present	Alternative (a)	Overall
Average operating assets (a)	$2,000,000	$(500,000)	$1,500,000
Net operating income (b)	$340,000	$(79,000)	$261,000
ROI, (b) ÷ (a)	17.00%	15.80%	17.40%

	Present	Alternative (b)	Overall
Average operating assets (a)	$2,000,000	$200,000	$2,200,000
Net operating income (b)	$340,000	$33,000	$373,000
ROI, (b) ÷ (a)	17.00%	16.50%	16.95%

Alternative (a) would increase your store's ROI to 17.40%—beating last year's ROI and hence earning you a bonus. Alternative (b) would actually decrease your store's ROI and would result in no bonus for the year. So to earn the bonus, you would select Alternative (a). However, this alternative is not in the best interests of the national chain since the ROI of the lost sales is 15.8%, which exceeds the national chain's minimum required rate of return of 15%. Rather, it would be in the national chain's interests to adopt Alternative (b)—the addition of a new product line. The ROI on these sales would be 16.5%, which exceeds the minimum required rate of return of 15%.

GUIDANCE ANSWERS TO CONCEPT CHECKS

1. **Choices c and d.** Both profit and investment center managers are held responsible for profits. In addition, an investment center manager is held responsible for earning an adequate return on investment or residual income.
2. **Choices b and d.** Common fixed costs should not be assigned to segments. Common fixed costs will not decrease if a segment is discontinued.
3. **Choice b.** The profit would be $300,000 − ($225,000 × 95%) = $86,250. The return on investment would be ($86,250 ÷ ($500,000 × 95%) = 18.2%.
4. **Choice d.** The residual income would be $86,250 − ($475,000 × 12%) = $29,250.

REVIEW PROBLEM: RETURN ON INVESTMENT (ROI) AND RESIDUAL INCOME

The Magnetic Imaging Division of Medical Diagnostics, Inc., has reported the following results for last year's operations:

Sales.........................	$25 million
Net operating income	$3 million
Average operating assets	$10 million

Required:
1. Compute the margin, turnover, and ROI for the Magnetic Imaging Division.
2. Top management of Medical Diagnostics, Inc., has set a minimum required rate of return on average operating assets of 25%. What is the Magnetic Imaging Division's residual income for the year?

Solution to Review Problem
1. The required calculations appear below:

$$\text{Margin} = \frac{\text{Net operating income}}{\text{Sales}}$$

$$= \frac{\$3,000,000}{\$25,000,000}$$

$$= 12\%$$

$$\text{Turnover} = \frac{\text{Sales}}{\text{Average operating assets}}$$

$$= \frac{\$25,000,000}{\$10,000,000}$$

$$= 2.5$$

$$\text{ROI} = \text{Margin} \times \text{Turnover}$$

$$= 12\% \times 2.5$$

$$= 30\%$$

2. The residual income for the Magnetic Imaging Division is computed as follows:

Average operating assets...........................	$10,000,000
Net operating income...............................	$ 3,000,000
Minimum required return (25% × $10,000,000)	2,500,000
Residual income....................................	$ 500,000

GLOSSARY

Common fixed cost A fixed cost that supports more than one business segment, but is not traceable in whole or in part to any one of the business segments. (p. 435)

Cost center A business segment whose manager has control over cost but has no control over revenue or the use of investment funds. (p. 431)

Decentralized organization An organization in which decision making authority is not confined to a few top executives but rather is spread throughout the organization. (p. 430)

Economic Value Added (EVA) A concept similar to residual income in which a variety of adjustments may be made to GAAP financial statements for performance evaluation purposes. (p. 442)

Investment center A business segment whose manager has control over cost, revenue, and the use of investment funds. (p. 432)

Margin Net operating income divided by sales. (p. 437)

Net operating income Income before interest and income taxes have been deducted. (p. 436)

Operating assets Cash, accounts receivable, inventory, plant and equipment, and all other assets held for productive use in an organization. (p. 436)

Profit center A business segment whose manager has control over cost and revenue but has no control over the use of investment funds. (p. 432)

Residual income The net operating income that an investment center earns above the required return on its operating assets. (p. 442)

Responsibility center Any business segment whose manager has control over cost, revenue, or the use of investment funds. (p. 431)

Return on investment (ROI) Net operating income divided by average operating assets. It also equals margin multiplied by turnover. (p. 436)

Segment Any part or activity of an organization about which the manager seeks cost, revenue, or profit data. (p. 434)

Traceable fixed cost A fixed cost that is incurred because of the existence of a particular business segment and that would be eliminated if the segment were eliminated. (p. 435)

Transfer price The price charged when one division or segment provides goods or services to another division or segment of an organization. (p. 446)

Turnover Sales divided by the average operating assets. (p. 437)

QUESTIONS

10–1 What is meant by the term *decentralization?*

10–2 What benefits result from decentralization?

10–3 Distinguish between a cost center, a profit center, and an investment center.

10–4 Define a segment of an organization. Give several examples of segments.

10–5 What is meant by the terms *margin* and *turnover?*

10–6 What is meant by residual income?

10–7 In what way can the use of ROI as a performance measure for investment centers lead to bad decisions? How does the residual income approach overcome this problem?

10–8 What is meant by the term *transfer price,* and why are transfer prices needed?

BRIEF EXERCISES

BRIEF EXERCISE 10–1   Compute the Return on Investment (ROI)   [LO1]

Alyeska Services Company, a division of a major oil company, provides various services to the operators of the North Slope oil field in Alaska. Data concerning the most recent year appear below:

Sales.................................	$7,500,000
Net operating income	$600,000
Average operating assets	$5,000,000

Required:

1. Compute the margin for Alyeska Services Company.
2. Compute the turnover for Alyeska Services Company.
3. Compute the return on investment (ROI) for Alyeska Services Company.

BRIEF EXERCISE 10–2   Effects of Changes in Sales, Expenses, and Assets on ROI   [LO1]
CommercialServices.com Corporation provides business-to-business services on the Internet. Data concerning the most recent year appear below:

Sales......................................	$3,000,000
Net operating income	$150,000
Average operating assets	$750,000

Required:
Consider each question below independently. Carry out all computations to two decimal places.

1. Compute the company's return on investment (ROI).
2. The entrepreneur who founded the company is convinced that sales will increase next year by 50% and that net operating income will increase by 200%, with no increase in average operating assets. What would be the company's ROI?
3. The chief financial officer of the company believes a more realistic scenario would be a $1,000,000 increase in sales, requiring a $250,000 increase in average operating assets, with a resulting $200,000 increase in net operating income. What would be the company's ROI in this scenario?

BRIEF EXERCISE 10–3   Residual Income   [LO2]
Juniper Design Ltd. of Manchester, England, is a company specializing in providing design services to residential developers. Last year the company had net operating income of £600,000 on sales of £3,000,000. The company's average operating assets for the year were £2,800,000 and its minimum required rate of return was 18%. (The currency used in England is the pound sterling, denoted by £.)

Required:
Compute the company's residual income for the year.

EXERCISES

EXERCISE 10–4   Computing and Interpreting Return on Investment (ROI)   [LO1]
Selected operating data for two divisions of Outback Brewing, Ltd., of Australia are given below:

	Division	
	Queensland	**New South Wales**
Sales...	$4,000,000	$7,000,000
Average operating assets	$2,000,000	$2,000,000
Net operating income.........................	$360,000	$420,000
Property, plant, and equipment (net).............	$950,000	$800,000

Required:
1. Compute the rate of return for each division using the return on investment (ROI) formula stated in terms of margin and turnover.
2. Which divisional manager seems to be doing the better job? Why?

EXERCISE 10–5   Evaluating New Investments Using Return on Investment (ROI) and Residual Income   [LO1, LO2]
Selected sales and operating data for three divisions of different structural engineering firms are given below:

	Division A	Division B	Division C
Sales	$12,000,000	$14,000,000	$25,000,000
Average operating assets.................	$3,000,000	$7,000,000	$5,000,000
Net operating income	$600,000	$560,000	$800,000
Minimum required rate of return	14%	10%	16%

Required:

1. Compute the return on investment (ROI) for each division using the formula stated in terms of margin and turnover.
2. Compute the residual income for each division.
3. Assume that each division is presented with an investment opportunity that would yield a 15% rate of return.
   a. If performance is being measured by ROI, which division or divisions will probably accept the opportunity? Reject? Why?
   b. If performance is being measured by residual income, which division or divisions will probably accept the opportunity? Reject? Why?

EXERCISE 10–6 Contrasting Return on Investment (ROI) and Residual Income [LO1, LO2]

Meiji Isetan Corp. of Japan has two consulting offices with headquarters in Osaka and Yokohama. Selected data on the two offices follow (in millions of yen, denoted by ¥):

	Office	
	Osaka	**Yokohama**
Sales................................	¥3,000,000	¥9,000,000
Net operating income..................	¥210,000	¥720,000
Average operating assets	¥1,000,000	¥4,000,000

Required:

1. For each office, compute the return on investment (ROI) in terms of margin and turnover. Where necessary, carry computations to two decimal places.
2. Assume that the company evaluates performance using residual income and that the minimum required rate of return for any office is 15%. Compute the residual income for each office.
3. Is Yokohama's greater amount of residual income an indication that it is better managed? Explain.

EXERCISE 10–7 Cost-Volume Profit Analysis and Return on Investment (ROI) [LO1]

Posters.com is a small Internet retailer of high-quality posters. The company has $1,000,000 in operating assets and fixed expenses of $150,000 per year. With this level of operating assets and fixed expenses, the company can support sales of up to $3,000,000 per year. The company's contribution margin ratio is 25%, which means that an additional dollar of sales results in additional contribution margin, and net operating income, of 25 cents.

Required:

1. Complete the following table showing the relation between sales and return on investment (ROI).

Sales	Net Operating Income	Average Operating Assets	ROI
$2,500,000	$475,000	$1,000,000	?
$2,600,000	$?	$1,000,000	?
$2,700,000	$?	$1,000,000	?
$2,800,000	$?	$1,000,000	?
$2,900,000	$?	$1,000,000	?
$3,000,000	$?	$1,000,000	?

2. What happens to the company's return on investment (ROI) as sales increase? Explain.

EXERCISE 10–8 Effects of Changes in Profits and Assets on Return on Investment (ROI) [LO1]

Pecs Alley is a regional chain of health clubs. The managers of the clubs, who have authority to make investments as needed, are evaluated based largely on return on investment (ROI). The Springfield Club reported the following results for the past year:

Sales..........................	$1,400,000
Net operating income............	$70,000
Average operating assets	$350,000

Required:

The following questions are to be considered independently. Carry out all computations to two decimal places.

1. Compute the club's return on investment (ROI).
2. Assume that the manager of the club is able to increase sales by $70,000 and that, as a result, net operating income increases by $18,200. Further assume that this is possible without any increase in operating assets. What would be the club's return on investment (ROI)?
3. Assume that the manager of the club is able to reduce expenses by $14,000 without any change in sales or operating assets. What would be the club's return on investment (ROI)?
4. Assume that the manager of the club is able to reduce operating assets by $70,000 without any change in sales or net operating income. What would be the club's return on investment (ROI)?

PROBLEMS

CHECK FIGURE
(1b) Total ROI: 19.2%

PROBLEM 10–9A   Return on Investment (ROI) and Residual Income   [LO1, LO2]
"I know headquarters wants us to add that new product line," said Dell Havasi, manager of Billings Company's Office Products Division. "But I want to see the numbers before I make any move. Our division's return on investment (ROI) has led the company for three years, and I don't want any let-down."

Billings Company is a decentralized wholesaler with five autonomous divisions. The divisions are evaluated on the basis of ROI, with year-end bonuses given to the divisional managers who have the highest ROIs. Operating results for the company's Office Products Division for the most recent year are given below:

Sales............................	$10,000,000
Less variable expenses..............	6,000,000
Contribution margin.................	4,000,000
Less fixed expenses	3,200,000
Net operating income	$ 800,000
Divisional operating assets...........	$ 4,000,000

The company had an overall return on investment (ROI) of 15% last year (considering all divisions). The Office Products Division has an opportunity to add a new product line that would require an additional investment in operating assets of $1,000,000. The cost and revenue characteristics of the new product line per year would be:

Sales	$2,000,000
Variable expenses	60% of sales
Fixed expenses	$640,000

Required:

1. Compute the Office Products Division's ROI for the most recent year; also compute the ROI as it would appear if the new product line is added.
2. If you were in Dell Havasi's position, would you accept or reject the new product line? Explain.

3. Why do you suppose headquarters is anxious for the Office Products Division to add the new product line?

4. Suppose that the company's minimum required rate of return on operating assets is 12% and that performance is evaluated using residual income.

   a. Compute the Office Products Division's residual income for the most recent year; also compute the residual income as it would appear if the new product line is added.

   b. Under these circumstances, if you were in Dell Havasi's position, would you accept or reject the new product line? Explain.

PROBLEM 10–10A   Return on Investment (ROI) and Residual Income   [LO1, LO2]
Financial data for Joel de Paris, Inc., for last year follow:

CHECK FIGURE
(1) ROI: 25%

Joel de Paris, Inc.
Balance Sheet

	Ending Balance	Beginning Balance
Assets		
Cash	$ 120,000	$ 140,000
Accounts receivable	530,000	450,000
Inventory	380,000	320,000
Plant and equipment, net	620,000	680,000
Investment in Buisson, S.A.	280,000	250,000
Land (undeveloped)	170,000	180,000
Total assets	$2,100,000	$2,020,000
Liabilities and Stockholders' Equity		
Accounts payable	$ 310,000	$ 360,000
Long-term debt	1,500,000	1,500,000
Stockholders' equity	290,000	160,000
Total liabilities and stockholders' equity	$2,100,000	$2,020,000

Joel de Paris, Inc.
Income Statement

Sales		$4,050,000
Less operating expenses		3,645,000
Net operating income		405,000
Less interest and taxes:		
Interest expense	$150,000	
Tax expense	110,000	260,000
Net income		$ 145,000

The company paid dividends of $15,000 last year. The "Investment in Buisson, S.A.," on the balance sheet represents an investment in the stock of another company.

Required:

1. Compute the company's margin, turnover, and return on investment (ROI) for last year.
2. The board of directors of Joel de Paris, Inc., has set a minimum required rate of return of 15%. What was the company's residual income last year?

PROBLEM 10–11A   Return on Investment (ROI) Analysis   [LO1]
The contribution format income statement for Huerra Company for last year is given below:

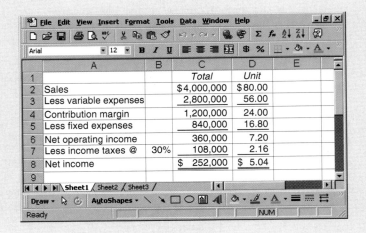

A	B	C	D	E
1		*Total*	*Unit*	
2 Sales		$4,000,000	$80.00	
3 Less variable expenses		2,800,000	56.00	
4 Contribution margin		1,200,000	24.00	
5 Less fixed expenses		840,000	16.80	
6 Net operating income		360,000	7.20	
7 Less income taxes @	30%	108,000	2.16	
8 Net income		$ 252,000	$ 5.04	
9				

The company had average operating assets of $2,000,000 during the year.

Required:
1. Compute the company's return on investment (ROI) for the period using the ROI formula stated in terms of margin and turnover.
   For each of the following questions, indicate whether the margin and turnover will increase, decrease, or remain unchanged as a result of the events described, and then compute the new ROI figure. Consider each question separately, starting in each case from the data used to compute the original ROI in (1) above.
2. Using just-in-time (JIT), the company is able to reduce the average level of inventory by $400,000. (The released funds are used to pay off short-term creditors.)
3. The company achieves a cost savings of $32,000 per year by using less costly materials.
4. The company issues bonds and uses the proceeds to purchase $500,000 in machinery and equipment at the beginning of the period. Interest on the bonds is $60,000 per year. Sales remain unchanged. The new, more efficient equipment reduces production costs by $20,000 per year.
5. As a result of a more intense effort by salespeople, sales are increased by 20%; operating assets remain unchanged.
6. At the beginning of the period, obsolete inventory carried on the books at a cost of $40,000 is scrapped and written off as a loss.
7. At the beginning of the period, the company uses $200,000 of cash (received on accounts receivable) to repurchase and retire some of its common stock.

PROBLEM 10–12A   Return on Investment (ROI) and Residual Income; Decentralization [LO1, LO2]
Raddington Industries produces tool and die machinery for manufacturers. The company expanded vertically several years ago by acquiring Reigis Steel Company, one of its suppliers of alloy steel plates. Raddington decided to maintain Reigis' separate identity and therefore established the Reigis Steel Division as one of its investment centers.

Raddington evaluates its divisions on the basis of ROI. Management bonuses are also based on ROI. All investments in operating assets are expected to earn a minimum required rate of return of 11%.

Reigis' ROI has ranged from 14% to 17% since it was acquired by Raddington. During the past year, Reigis had an investment opportunity that would yield an estimated rate of return of 13%. Reigis' management decided against the investment because it believed the investment would decrease the division's overall ROI.

Last year's absorption costing income statement for Reigis Steel Division is given below. The division's operating assets employed were $12,960,000 at the end of the year, which represents an 8% increase over the previous year-end balance.

Reigis Steel Division		
Divisional Income Statement		
For the Year Ended December 31		
Sales.........................		$31,200,000
Cost of goods sold		16,500,000
Gross margin		14,700,000
Selling and administrative expenses:		
Selling expenses	$5,620,000	
Administrative expenses	7,208,000	12,828,000
Net operating income		$ 1,872,000

Required:

1. Compute the following performance measures for the Reigis Steel Division:
   a. ROI. (Remember, ROI is based on the *average* operating assets, computed from the beginning-of-year and end-of-year balances.) State ROI in terms of margin and turnover.
   b. Residual income.
2. Would the management of Reigis Steel Division have been more likely to accept the investment opportunity it had last year if residual income were used as a performance measure instead of ROI? Explain.
3. The Reigis Steel Division is a separate investment center within Raddington Industries. Identify the items Reigis must be free to control if it is to be evaluated fairly by either the ROI or residual income performance measures.

(CMA, adapted)

PROBLEM 10–13A   Comparison of Performance Using Return on Investment (ROI)   [LO1]
Comparative data on three companies in the same service industry are given below:

CHECK FIGURE
(2) Company A
margin: 14%

	Company		
	A	**B**	**C**
Sales	$600,000	$500,000	$?
Net operating income...........	$84,000	$70,000	$?
Average operating assets	$300,000	$?	$1,000,000
Margin.......................	?	?	3.5%
Turnover	?	?	2
ROI	?	7%	?

Required:

1. What advantages are there to breaking down the ROI computation into two separate elements, margin and turnover?
2. Fill in the missing information above, and comment on the relative performance of the three companies in as much detail as the data permit. Make *specific recommendations* about how to improve the return on investment.

(Adapted from National Association of Accountants,
Research Report No. 35, p. 34)

PROBLEM 10–14A   **Return on Investment (ROI) and Residual Income Relations**   **[LO1, LO2]**

A family friend has asked for your help in analyzing the operations of three anonymous companies operating in the same service sector industry. Supply the missing data in the table below:

	Company		
	A	B	C
Sales	$9,000,000	$7,000,000	$4,500,000
Net operating income	$?	$280,000	$?
Average operating assets...........	$3,000,000	$?	$1,800,000
Return on investment (ROI)	18%	14%	?
Minimum required rate of return:			
Percentage......................	16%	?	15%
Dollar amount	$?	$320,000	$?
Residual income	$?	$?	$90,000

PROBLEM 10–15A   **Return on Investment (ROI)**   **[LO1]**

Provide the missing data in the following table for a distributor of martial arts products:

	Division		
	Alpha	Bravo	Charlie
Sales..................................	$?	$11,500,000	$?
Net operating income..................	$?	$920,000	$210,000
Average operating assets	$800,000	$?	$?
Margin................................	4%	?	7%
Turnover	5	?	?
Return on investment (ROI)	?	20%	14%

BUILDING YOUR SKILLS

Teamwork in Action   **(LO2)**

Divide your team into two groups—one will play the part of the managers of the Consumer Products Division of Highstreet Enterprises, Inc., and the other will play the part of the managers of the Industrial Products Division of the same company.

    The Consumer Products Division would like to acquire an advanced electric motor from the Industrial Products Division that would be used to make a state-of-the-art sorbet maker. At the expected selling price of $89, the Consumer Products Division would sell 50,000 sorbet makers per year. Each sorbet maker would require one of the advanced electric motors. The only possible source for the advanced electric motor is the Industrial Products Division, which holds a critical patent. The variable cost of the sorbet maker (not including the cost of the electric motor) would be $54. The sorbet maker project would require additional fixed costs of $180,000 per year and additional operating assets of $3,000,000.

    The Industrial Products Division has plenty of spare capacity to make the electric motors requested by the Consumer Products Division. The variable cost of producing the motors would be $13 per unit. The additional fixed costs that would have to be incurred to fill the order from the Consumer Products Division would amount to $30,000 per year and the additional operating assets would be $400,000.

    The division managers of Highstreet Enterprises are evaluated based on residual income, with a minimum required rate of return of 20%.

Required:

The two groups—those representing the managers of the Consumer Products Division and those representing the managers of the Industrial Products Division—should negotiate concerning the transfer price for the 50,000 advanced electric motors per year. (The groups may or may not be able to come to an agreement.) Whatever the outcome of the negotiations, each group should write a memo to the instructor justifying the outcome in terms of what would be in the best interests of their division.

Analytical Thinking   **[LO1, LO2]**

The Valve Division of Bendix, Inc., produces a small valve that is used by various companies as a component part in their products. Bendix, Inc., operates its divisions as autonomous units, giving its divisional managers great discretion in pricing and other decisions. Each division is expected to generate a minimum required rate of return of at least 14% on its operating assets. The Valve Division has average operating assets of $700,000. The valves are sold for $5 each. Variable costs are $3 per valve, and fixed costs total $462,000 per year. The division has a capacity of 300,000 valves each year.

Required:

1. How many valves must the Valve Division sell each year to generate the desired rate of return on its assets?
   a. What is the margin earned at this level of sales?
   b. What is the turnover at this level of sales?
2. Assume that the Valve Division's current ROI equals the minimum required rate of 14%. In order to increase the division's ROI, the divisional manager wants to increase the selling price per valve by 4%. Market studies indicate that an increase in the selling price would cause sales to drop by 20,000 units each year. However, operating assets could be reduced by $50,000 due to decreased needs for accounts receivable and inventory. Compute the margin, turnover, and ROI if these changes are made.
3. Refer to the original data. Assume again that the Valve Division's current ROI equals the minimum required rate of 14%. Rather than increase the selling price, the sales manager wants to reduce the selling price per valve by 4%. Market studies indicate that this would fill the plant to capacity. In order to carry the greater level of sales, however, operating assets would increase by $50,000. Compute the margin, turnover, and ROI if these changes are made.
4. Refer to the original data. Assume that the normal volume of sales is 280,000 valves each year at a price of $5 per valve. Another division of the company is currently purchasing 20,000 valves each year from an overseas supplier, at a price of $4.25 per valve. The manager of the Valve Division has refused to meet this price, pointing out that it would result in a loss for his division:

Selling price per valve		$4.25
Cost per valve:		
Variable	$3.00	
Fixed ($462,000 ÷ 300,000 valves)	1.54	4.54
Net loss per valve		$(0.29)

The manager of the Valve Division also points out that the normal $5 selling price barely allows his division to earn the required 14% rate of return. "If we take on some business at only $4.25 per unit, then our ROI is obviously going to suffer," he reasons, "and maintaining that ROI figure is the key to my future. Besides, taking on these extra units would require us to increase our operating assets by at least $50,000 due to the larger inventories and accounts receivable we would be carrying." Would you recommend that the Valve Division sell to the other division at $4.25? Show ROI computations to support your answer.

Communicating in Practice (LO1, LO2)

How do the performance measurement and compensation systems of service companies compare with those of manufacturers? Ask the manager of your local McDonald's, Wendy's, Burger King, or other fast-food chain if he or she could spend some time discussing the performance measures that the company uses to evaluate store managers and how the performance measures tie in with their compensation.

Required:

After asking the following questions, write a brief memorandum to your instructor that summarizes what you discovered during your interview with the manager of the franchise.

1. What are the national chain's goals, that is, the broad, long-range plans of the company (e.g., to increase market share)?
2. What performance measures are used to help motivate the store managers and monitor progress toward achieving the corporation's goals?
3. Are the performance measures consistent with the store manager's compensation plan?

Taking It to the Net

As you know, the World Wide Web is a medium that is constantly evolving. Sites come and go and change without notice. To enable periodic updating of site addresses, these problems have been posted to the textbook website (www.mhhe.com/bgn3e). After accessing the site, enter the Student Center and select this chapter to find the Taking It to the Net problems.

11

Relevant Costs for Decision Making

CHAPTER OUTLINE

Chapter Eleven

DECISION FEATURE

Massaging the Numbers

Building and expanding convention centers appears to be an obsession with politicians. Indeed, in 44 cities across the United States, billions of dollars are being spent to build or expand convention centers—adding more than 7 million square feet of convention space to the 64 million square feet that already exists. Given that trade show attendance across the country has been steadily declining, how do politicians justify these enormous investments? Politicians frequently rely on consultants who produce studies that purport to show the convention center will have a favorable economic impact on the area.

These economic impact studies are bogus in two respects. First, a large portion of the so-called favorable economic impact that is cited by consultants would be realized by a city even if it did not invest in a new or expanded convention center. For example, Portland, Oregon, voters overwhelmingly opposed spending $82 million to expand their city's convention center. Nonetheless, local politicians proceeded with the project. After completing the expansion, more than 70% of the people spending money at trade shows in Portland were from the Portland area. How much of the money spent by these locals would have been spent in Portland anyway if the convention center had not been expanded? We don't know, but in all likelihood much of this money would have been spent anyway at the zoo, the art museum, the theater, local restaurants, and so on. This portion of the "favorable" economic impact cited by consultants and used by politicians to justify expanding convention centers should be ignored because of its irrelevance. Second, since the supply of convention centers throughout the United States substantially exceeds demand, convention centers must offer substantial economic incentives, such as waiving rental fees, to attract trade shows. The cost of these concessions, although often excluded from consultants' projections, further erodes the genuine economic viability of building or expanding a convention center.

Source: Victoria Murphy, "The Answer Is Always Yes," *Forbes,* February, 28, 2005, pp. 82–84.

Managers are constantly faced with problems of deciding what products to sell, whether to make or buy component parts, what prices to charge, what channels of distribution to use, whether to accept special orders at special prices, and so forth. Making such decisions is often a difficult task that is complicated by numerous alternatives and massive amounts of data, only some of which may be relevant.

Every decision involves choosing from among at least two alternatives. In making a decision, the costs and benefits of one alternative must be compared to the costs and benefits of other alternatives. Costs that differ between alternatives are called **relevant costs.** Distinguishing between relevant and irrelevant cost and benefit data is critical for two reasons. First, irrelevant data can be ignored—saving decision makers tremendous amounts of time and effort. Second, bad decisions can easily result from erroneously including irrelevant costs and benefits when analyzing alternatives. To be successful in decision making, managers must be able to tell the difference between relevant and irrelevant data and must be able to correctly use the relevant data in analyzing alternatives. The purpose of this chapter is to develop these skills by illustrating their use in a wide range of decision-making situations. We hasten to add that these decision-making skills are as important in your personal life as they are to managers. After completing your study of this chapter, you should be able to think more clearly about decisions in many facets of your life.

COST CONCEPTS FOR DECISION MAKING

Four cost terms discussed in Chapter 1 are particularly applicable to this chapter. These terms are *differential costs, incremental costs, opportunity costs,* and *sunk costs.* You may find it helpful to turn back to Chapter 1 and refresh your memory concerning these terms before reading on.

Identifying Relevant Costs and Benefits

LEARNING OBJECTIVE 1

Identify relevant and irrelevant costs and benefits in a decision.

Only those costs and benefits that differ in total between alternatives are relevant in a decision. If the total amount of a cost will be the same regardless of the alternative selected, then the decision has no effect on the cost and it can be ignored. For example, if you are trying to decide whether to go to a movie or to rent a videotape for the evening, the rent on your apartment is irrelevant. Whether you go to a movie or rent a videotape, the rent on your apartment will be exactly the same and is therefore irrelevant to the decision. On the other hand, the cost of the movie ticket and the cost of renting the videotape would be relevant in the decision since they are *avoidable costs*.

An **avoidable cost** is a cost that can be eliminated in whole or in part by choosing one alternative over another. By choosing the alternative of going to the movie, the cost of renting the videotape can be avoided. By choosing the alternative of renting the videotape, the cost of the movie ticket can be avoided. Therefore, the cost of the movie ticket and the cost of renting the videotape are both avoidable costs. On the other hand, the rent on the apartment is not an avoidable cost of either alternative. You would continue to rent your apartment under either alternative. Avoidable costs are relevant costs. Unavoidable costs are irrelevant costs.

Two broad categories of costs are never relevant in decisions. These irrelevant costs are:

1. Sunk costs.
2. Future costs that do not differ between the alternatives.

As we learned in Chapter 1, a **sunk cost** is a cost that has already been incurred and cannot be avoided regardless of what a manager decides to do. In the example above, the rent on your apartment would be a sunk cost assuming that you signed a lease that cannot be broken. Sunk costs are always the same no matter what alternatives are being considered; therefore, they are irrelevant and should be ignored when making decisions. Future costs that do *not* differ between alternatives should also be ignored when making decisions. Continuing with the example above, if you intend to order a pizza after either going to the movie theater or renting a video, the cost of the pizza would be irrelevant when deciding between the movie theater and the video. Whether you return home from the movie theater and order a pizza or order a pizza after your video ends, the cost of the pizza will be the same. Notice, the cost of the pizza is not a sunk cost because you could decide later in the evening to save some money by not ordering the pizza. Nonetheless, the cost of the pizza is irrelevant to the decision at hand because it is a future cost that does not differ between the alternatives.

Along with sunk cost, the term **differential cost** was introduced in Chapter 1. In managerial accounting, the terms *avoidable cost, differential cost, incremental cost,* and *relevant cost* are often used interchangeably. To identify the costs that are avoidable in a particular decision and are therefore relevant, these steps should be followed:

1. Eliminate costs and benefits that do not differ between alternatives. These irrelevant costs consist of (a) sunk costs and (b) future costs that do not differ between alternatives.
2. Use the remaining costs and benefits that do differ between alternatives in making the decision. The costs that remain are the differential, or avoidable, costs.

The Sunk Cost Trap

IN BUSINESS

Hal Arkes, a psychologist at Ohio University, asked 61 college students to assume they had mistakenly purchased tickets for both a $50 and a $100 ski trip for the same weekend. They could go on only one of the ski trips and would have to throw away the unused ticket. He further asked them to assume that they would actually have more fun on the $50 trip. Most of the students reported that they would go on the less enjoyable $100 trip. The larger cost mattered more to the students than having more fun. However, the sunk costs of the tickets should have been totally irrelevant in this decision. No matter which trip was selected, the actual total cost was $150—the cost of both tickets. And since this cost does not differ between the alternatives, it should be ignored. Like these students, most people have a great deal of difficulty ignoring sunk costs when making decisions.

Source: John Gourville and Dilip Soman, "Pricing and the Psychology of Consumption," *Harvard Business Review*, September 2002, pp. 92–93.

Different Costs for Different Purposes

We need to recognize a fundamental concept of managerial accounting from the outset of our discussion—costs that are relevant in one decision situation are not necessarily relevant in another. In other words, *managers need different costs for different purposes.* For one purpose, a particular group of costs may be relevant; for another purpose, an entirely different group of costs may be relevant. Thus, in *each* decision situation the data must be carefully analyzed to isolate the relevant costs. Otherwise, there is the risk of being misled by irrelevant data.

The concept of "different costs for different purposes" is basic to managerial accounting; we shall see its application frequently in the pages that follow.

An Example of Identifying Relevant Costs and Benefits

Cynthia is currently a student in an MBA program in Boston and would like to visit a friend in New York City over the weekend. She is trying to decide whether to drive or take the train. Because she is on a tight budget, she wants to carefully consider the costs of the two alternatives. If one alternative is far less expensive than the other, that may be decisive in her choice. By car, the distance between her apartment in Boston and her friend's apartment in New York City is 230 miles. Cynthia has compiled the following list of items to consider:

Automobile Costs		
Item	Annual Cost of Fixed Items	Cost per Mile (based on 10,000 miles per year)
(a) Annual straight-line depreciation on car [($24,000 original cost − $10,000 estimated resale value in 5 years)/5 years]	$2,800	$0.280
(b) Cost of gasoline ($1.60 per gallon ÷ 32 miles per gallon)		0.050
(c) Annual cost of auto insurance and license	$1,380	0.138
(d) Maintenance and repairs		0.065
(e) Parking fees at school ($45 per month × 8 months) ..	$360	0.036
(f) Total average cost per mile		$0.569
Other Data		
(g) Reduction in the resale value of car due solely to wear and tear	$0.026 per mile	
(h) Cost of round-trip Amtrak ticket from Boston to New York City	$104	
(i) Benefit of relaxing and being able to study during the train ride rather than having to drive	?	
(j) Cost of putting the dog in a kennel while gone	$40	
(k) Benefit of having a car available in New York City ...	?	
(l) Hassle of parking the car in New York City	?	
(m) Cost of parking the car in New York City	$25 per day	

Which costs and benefits are relevant in this decision? Remember, only those costs and benefits that differ between alternatives are relevant. Everything else is irrelevant and can be ignored.

Start at the top of the list with item (a): the original cost of the car is a sunk cost. This cost has already been incurred and therefore can never differ between alternatives. Consequently, it is irrelevant and can be ignored. The same is true of the accounting depreciation of $2,800 per year, which simply spreads the sunk cost across five years.

Move down the list to item (b): the cost of gasoline consumed by driving to New York City is a relevant cost in this decision. If Cynthia takes the train, this cost would not be incurred. Hence, the cost differs between alternatives and is therefore relevant.

Item (c), the annual cost of auto insurance and license, is not relevant. Whether Cynthia takes the train or drives on this particular trip, her annual auto insurance premium and her auto license fee will remain the same.[1]

Item (d), the cost of maintenance and repairs, is relevant. While maintenance and repair costs have a large random component, over the long run they should be more or less proportional to the number of miles the car is driven. Thus, the average cost of $0.065 per mile is a reasonable estimate to use.

---

[1]If Cynthia has an accident while driving to New York City or back, this might affect her insurance premium when the policy is renewed. The increase in the insurance premium would be a relevant cost of this particular trip, but the normal amount of the insurance premium is not relevant in any case.

Item (e), the monthly fee that Cynthia pays to park at her school during the academic year is not relevant. Regardless of which alternative she selects—driving or taking the train—she will still need to pay for parking at school.

Item (f) is the total average cost of $0.569 per mile. As discussed above, some elements of this total are relevant, but some are not relevant. Since it contains some irrelevant costs, it would be incorrect to estimate the cost of driving to New York City and back by simply multiplying the $0.569 by 460 miles (230 miles each way × 2). This erroneous approach would yield a cost of driving of $261.74. Unfortunately, such mistakes are often made in both personal life and in business. Since the total cost is stated on a per-mile basis, people are easily misled. Often people think that if the cost is stated as $0.569 per mile, the cost of driving 100 miles is $56.90. But it is not. Many of the costs included in the $0.569 cost per mile are sunk and/or fixed and will not increase if the car is driven another 100 miles. The $0.569 is an average cost, not an incremental cost. Beware of such unitized costs (i.e., costs stated in terms of a dollar amount per unit, per mile, per direct labor-hour, per machine-hour, and so on)—they are often misleading.

Item (g), the decline in the resale value of the car that occurs as a consequence of driving more miles, is relevant in the decision. Because she uses the car, its resale value declines. This reduction in resale value is a real cost of using the car that should be taken into account. Cynthia estimates this cost by accessing the *Kelly Blue Book* website at www.kbb.com. The reduction in resale value of an asset through use or over time is often called *real* or *economic depreciation*. This is different from accounting depreciation, which attempts to match the sunk cost of an asset with the periods that benefit from that cost.

Item (h), the $104 cost of a round-trip ticket on Amtrak, is relevant in this decision. If she drives, she would not have to buy the ticket.

Item (i) is relevant to the decision, even if it is difficult to put a dollar value on relaxing and being able to study while on the train. It is relevant because it is a benefit that is available under one alternative but not under the other.

Item (j), the cost of putting Cynthia's dog in the kennel while she is gone, is irrelevant in this decision. Whether she takes the train or drives to New York City, she will still need to put her dog in a kennel.

Like item (i), items (k) and (l) are relevant to the decision even if it is difficult to measure their dollar impacts.

Item (m), the cost of parking in New York City, is relevant to the decision.

Bringing together all of the relevant data, Cynthia would estimate the relevant costs of driving and taking the train as follows:

Relevant financial cost of driving to New York City:	
Gasoline (460 miles at $0.050 per mile)	$23.00
Maintenance and repairs (460 miles @ $0.065 per mile)	29.90
Reduction in the resale value of car due solely to wear and tear (460 miles @ $0.026 per mile)	11.96
Cost of parking the car in New York City (2 days @ $25 per day)	50.00
Total	$114.86

Relevant financial cost of taking the train to New York City:	
Cost of round-trip Amtrak ticket from Boston to New York City	$104.00

What should Cynthia do? From a purely financial standpoint, it would be cheaper by $10.86 ($114.86 − $104.00) to take the train than to drive. Cynthia has to decide if the convenience of having a car in New York City outweighs the additional cost and the disadvantages of being unable to relax and study on the train and the hassle of finding parking in the city.

In this example, we focused on identifying the relevant costs and benefits—everything else was ignored. In the next example, we will begin the analysis by including all of the costs and benefits—relevant or not. We will see that if we are very careful, we will still get the correct answer because the irrelevant costs and benefits will cancel out when we compare the alternatives.

IN BUSINESS

Cruising on the Cheap

Cruise ship operators such as Princess Cruises sometimes offer deep discounts on popular cruises. For example, a 10-day Mediterranean cruise on the Norwegian Dream was once offered at up to 75% off the list price. A seven-day cruise to Alaska could be booked for a $499–$700 discount. The cause? "An ambitious fleet expansion left the cruise industry grappling with a tidal wave of capacity . . . Most cruise costs are fixed whether all the ship's berths are filled or not, so it is better to sell cheap than not at all . . . In the current glut, discounting has made it possible for the cruise lines to keep berths nearly full."

Source: Martin Brannigan, *The Wall Street Journal,* July 17, 2000, pp. B1 and B4.

Reconciling the Total and Differential Approaches

Oak Harbor Woodworks is considering a new labor-saving machine that rents for $3,000 per year. The machine will be used on the company's butcher block production line. Data concerning the company's annual sales and costs of butcher blocks with and without the new machine are shown below:

	Current Situation	Situation with the New Machine
Units produced and sold	5,000	5,000
Selling price per unit	$40	$40
Direct materials cost per unit	$14	$14
Direct labor cost per unit	$8	$5
Variable overhead cost per unit	$2	$2
Fixed costs, other	$62,000	$62,000
Fixed costs, rental of new machine	—	$3,000

Given the annual sales and the price and cost data above, the net operating income for the product under the two alternatives can be computed as shown in Exhibit 11–1.

Note that the net operating income is $12,000 higher with the new machine, so that is the better alternative. Note also that the $12,000 advantage for the new machine can be obtained in two different ways. It is the difference between the $30,000 net operating income with the new machine and the $18,000 net operating income for the current situation. It is also the sum of the differential costs and benefits as shown in the last column of Exhibit 11–1. A positive number in the Differential Costs and Benefits column indicates that the difference between the alternatives favors the new machine; a negative number indicates that the difference favors the current situation. A zero in that column simply means that the total amount for the item is exactly the same for both alternatives. Thus, since the difference in the net operating incomes equals the sum of the differences for the individual items, any cost or benefit that is the same for both alternatives will have no impact on which alternative is preferred. This is the reason that costs and benefits that do not differ between alternatives are irrelevant and can be ignored. If we properly account for them, they will cancel out when we compare the alternatives.

We could have arrived at the same solution much more quickly by ignoring altogether the irrelevant costs and benefits.

EXHIBIT 11–1

Total and Differential Costs

	Current Situation	Situation with New Machine	Differential Costs and Benefits
Sales (5,000 units @ $40 per unit)	$200,000	$200,000	$ 0
Less variable expenses:			
Direct materials (5,000 units @ $14 per unit)	70,000	70,000	0
Direct labor (5,000 units @ $8 and $5 per unit)	40,000	25,000	15,000
Variable overhead (5,000 units @ $2 per unit)	10,000	10,000	0
Total variable expenses	120,000	105,000	
Contribution margin	80,000	95,000	
Less fixed expenses:			
Other	62,000	62,000	0
Rent of new machine	0	3,000	(3,000)
Total fixed expenses	62,000	65,000	
Net operating income	$ 18,000	$ 30,000	$12,000

- The selling price per unit and the number of units sold do not differ between the alternatives. Therefore, the total sales revenues are exactly the same for the two alternatives as shown in Exhibit 11–1. Since the sales revenues are exactly the same, they have no effect on the difference in net operating income between the two alternatives. That is shown in the last column in Exhibit 11–1, which shows a $0 differential benefit.

- The direct materials cost per unit, the variable overhead cost per unit, and the number of units produced and sold do not differ between the alternatives. Consequently, the total direct materials cost and the total variable overhead cost will be the same for the two alternatives and can be ignored.

- The "other" fixed expenses do not differ between the alternatives, so they can be ignored as well.

Indeed, the only costs that do differ between the alternatives are direct labor costs and the fixed rental cost of the new machine. Hence, the two alternatives can be compared based only on these relevant costs:

Net advantage to renting the new machine:	
Decrease in direct labor costs (5,000 units at a cost savings of $3 per unit)	$15,000
Increase in fixed expenses	(3,000)
Net annual cost savings from renting the new machine	$12,000

If we focus on just the relevant costs and benefits, we get exactly the same answer as when we listed all of the costs and benefits—including those that do not differ between the alternatives and hence are irrelevant. We get the same answer because the only costs and benefits that matter in the final comparison of the net operating incomes are those that differ between the two alternatives and hence are not zero in the last column of Exhibit 11–1. Those two relevant costs are both listed in the above analysis showing the net advantage of renting the new machine.

Why Isolate Relevant Costs?

In the preceding example, we used two different approaches to analyze the alternatives. First, we considered all costs, both those that were relevant and those that were not; and second, we considered only the relevant costs. We obtained the same answer under both approaches. It would be natural to ask, "Why bother to isolate relevant costs when total costs will do the job just as well?" Isolating relevant costs is desirable for at least two reasons.

First, only rarely will enough information be available to prepare a detailed income statement for both alternatives. Assume, for example, that you are called on to make a decision relating to a portion of a *single operation* of a multidepartmental, multiproduct company. Under these circumstances, it would be virtually impossible to prepare an income statement of any type. You would have to rely on your ability to recognize which costs are relevant and which are not in order to assemble the data necessary to make a decision.

Second, mingling irrelevant costs with relevant costs may cause confusion and distract attention from the information that is really critical. Furthermore, the danger always exists that an irrelevant piece of data may be used improperly, resulting in an incorrect decision. The best approach is to ignore irrelevant data and base the decision entirely on relevant data.

Relevant cost analysis, combined with the contribution approach to the income statement, provides a powerful tool for making decisions. We will investigate various uses of this tool in the remaining sections of this chapter.

IN BUSINESS

Environmental Costs Add Up

A decision analysis can be flawed by incorrectly including irrelevant costs such as sunk costs and future costs that do not differ between alternatives. It can also be flawed by omitting future costs that *do* differ between alternatives. This is particularly a problem with environmental costs because they have dramatically increased in recent years and are often overlooked by managers.

Consider the environmental complications posed by a decision of whether to install a solvent-based or powder-based system for spray-painting parts. In a solvent painting system, parts are sprayed as they move along a conveyor. The paint that misses the part is swept away by a wall of water, called a water curtain. The excess paint accumulates in a pit as sludge that must be removed each month. Environmental regulations classify this sludge as hazardous waste. As a result, the company must obtain a permit to produce the waste and must maintain meticulous records of how the waste is transported, stored, and disposed of. The annual costs of complying with these regulations can easily exceed $140,000 in total for a painting facility that initially costs only $400,000 to build. The costs of complying with environmental regulations include the following:

- The waste sludge must be hauled to a special disposal site. The typical disposal fee is about $300 per barrel, or $55,000 per year for a modest solvent-based painting system.
- Workers must be specially trained to handle the paint sludge.
- The company must carry special insurance.
- The company must pay substantial fees to the state for releasing pollutants (i.e., the solvent) into the air.
- The water in the water curtain must be specially treated to remove contaminants. This can cost tens of thousands of dollars per year.

In contrast, a powder-based painting system avoids almost all of these environmental costs. Excess powder used in the painting process can be recovered and reused without creating a hazardous waste. Additionally, the powder-based system does not release contaminants into the atmosphere. Therefore, even though the cost of building a powder-based system may be higher than the cost of building a solvent-based system, over the long run the costs of the powder-based system may be far lower due to the high environmental costs of a solvent-based system. Managers need to be aware of such environmental costs and take them fully into account when making decisions.

Source: Germain Böer, Margaret Curtin, and Louis Hoyt, "Environmental Cost Management," *Management Accounting,* September 1998, pp. 28–38.

1. Which of the following statements is false? (You may select more than one answer.)
   a. Under some circumstances, a sunk cost may be a relevant cost.
   b. Future costs that do not differ between alternatives are irrelevant.
   c. The same cost may be relevant or irrelevant depending on the decision context.
   d. Only variable costs are relevant costs. Fixed costs cannot be relevant costs.
2. Assume that in October you bought a $450 nonrefundable airline ticket to Telluride, Colorado, for a 5-day/4-night winter ski vacation. You now have an opportunity to buy an airline ticket for a 5-day/4-night winter ski vacation in Stowe, Vermont, for $400 that includes a free ski lift ticket. The price of your lift ticket for the Telluride vacation would be $300. The price of a hotel room in Telluride is $180 per night. The price of a hotel room in Stowe is $150 per night. Which of the following costs is not relevant in a decision of whether to proceed with the planned trip to Telluride or to change to a trip to Stowe?
   a. The $450 airline ticket to Telluride.
   b. The $400 airline ticket to Stowe.
   c. The $300 lift ticket for the Telluride vacation.
   d. The $180 per night hotel room in Telluride.
3. Based on the facts in question 2 above, does a differential cost analysis favor Telluride or Stowe, and by how much?
   a. Stowe by $470.
   b. Stowe by $20.
   c. Telluride by $70.
   d. Telluride $20.

ADDING AND DROPPING PRODUCT LINES AND OTHER SEGMENTS

Decisions relating to whether product lines or other segments of a company should be dropped and new ones added are among the most difficult that a manager has to make. In such decisions, many qualitative and quantitative factors must be considered. Ultimately, however, any final decision to drop a business segment or to add a new one is going to hinge primarily on the impact the decision will have on net operating income. To assess this impact, costs must be carefully analyzed.

LEARNING OBJECTIVE 2

Prepare an analysis showing whether a product line or other business segment should be dropped or retained.

An Illustration of Cost Analysis

Consider the three major product lines of the Discount Drug Company—drugs, cosmetics, and housewares. Sales and cost information for the preceding month for each separate product line and for the store in total are given in Exhibit 11–2.

Concept 11-1

What can be done to improve the company's overall performance? One product line—housewares—shows a net operating loss for the month. Perhaps dropping this line would increase the company's profits. However, the report in Exhibit 11–2 may be misleading. No attempt has been made in Exhibit 11–2 to distinguish between fixed expenses that may be avoidable if a product line is dropped and fixed expenses that cannot be avoided by dropping any particular product line. The two alternatives are keeping the housewares product line and dropping the housewares product line. Only those costs that differ between these two alternatives (i.e., that can be avoided by dropping the housewares product line) are relevant. In deciding whether to drop a product line, it is crucial for managers to clearly identify which costs can be avoided, and hence are relevant to the decision, and which costs cannot be avoided, and hence are irrelevant. The decision should be approached as follows:

If the housewares line is dropped, then the company will lose $20,000 per month in contribution margin, but by dropping the line it may be possible to avoid some fixed costs.

EXHIBIT 11–2

Discount Drug Company
Product Lines

	Product Line			
	Drugs	**Cosmetics**	**Housewares**	**Total**
Sales	$125,000	$75,000	$ 50,000	$250,000
Less variable expenses	50,000	25,000	30,000	105,000
Contribution margin	75,000	50,000	20,000	145,000
Less fixed expenses:				
Salaries	29,500	12,500	8,000	50,000
Advertising	1,000	7,500	6,500	15,000
Utilities	500	500	1,000	2,000
Depreciation—fixtures	1,000	2,000	2,000	5,000
Rent	10,000	6,000	4,000	20,000
Insurance	2,000	500	500	3,000
General administrative	15,000	9,000	6,000	30,000
Total fixed expenses	59,000	38,000	28,000	125,000
Net operating income (loss)	$ 16,000	$12,000	$ (8,000)	$ 20,000

It may be possible, for example, to discharge certain employees, or it may be possible to reduce advertising costs. If by dropping the housewares line the company is able to avoid more in fixed costs than it loses in contribution margin, then it will be better off if the product line is eliminated, since overall net operating income should improve. On the other hand, if the company is not able to avoid as much in fixed costs as it loses in contribution margin, then the housewares line should be kept. In short, the manager should ask, "What costs can I avoid if I drop this product line?"

As we have seen from our earlier discussion, not all costs are avoidable. For example, some of the costs associated with a product line may be sunk costs. Other costs may be allocated fixed costs that will not differ in total regardless of whether the product line is dropped or retained.

To show how to proceed in a product-line analysis, suppose that the management of the Discount Drug Company has analyzed the fixed costs being charged to the three product lines and has determined the following:

1. The salaries expense represents salaries paid to employees working directly on the product. All of the employees working in housewares would be discharged if the product line is dropped.
2. The advertising expense represents product advertising specific to each product line and is avoidable if the line is dropped.
3. The utilities expense represents utilities costs for the entire company. The amount charged to each product line is an allocation based on space occupied and is not avoidable if the product line is dropped.
4. The depreciation expense represents depreciation on fixtures used for display of the various product lines. Although the fixtures are nearly new, they are custom-built and will have no resale value if the housewares line is dropped.
5. The rent expense represents rent on the entire building housing the company; it is allocated to the product lines on the basis of sales dollars. The monthly rent of $20,000 is fixed under a long-term lease agreement.
6. The insurance expense represents insurance carried on inventories within each of the three product lines.
7. The general administrative expense represents the costs of accounting, purchasing, and general management, which are allocated to the product lines on the basis of sales dollars. These costs will not change if the housewares line is dropped.

With this information, management can determine that $15,000 of the fixed expenses assigned to housewares are avoidable and $13,000 are not.

Fixed Expenses	Total Cost Assigned to Housewares	Not Avoidable*	Avoidable
Salaries	$ 8,000		$ 8,000
Advertising	6,500		6,500
Utilities	1,000	$ 1,000	
Depreciation—fixtures	2,000	2,000	
Rent	4,000	4,000	
Insurance	500		500
General administrative	6,000	6,000	
Total	$28,000	$13,000	$15,000

*These fixed costs represent either (1) sunk costs or (2) future costs that will not change whether the housewares line is retained or discontinued.

To determine how dropping the housewares product line will affect the overall profits of the company, we can compare the contribution margin that will be lost to the fixed costs that can be avoided if the line is dropped:

Contribution margin lost if the housewares line is discontinued (see Exhibit 11–2)	$(20,000)
Less fixed costs that can be avoided if the housewares line is discontinued (see above)	15,000
Decrease in overall company net operating income	$ (5,000)

In this case, the fixed costs that can be avoided by dropping the product line ($15,000) are less than the contribution margin that will be lost ($20,000). Therefore, based on the data given, the housewares line should not be discontinued unless a more profitable use can be found for the floor and counter space that it is occupying.

A Comparative Format

Decisions such as dropping a product line can also be approached by preparing comparative income statements showing the effects on the company as a whole of either keeping or dropping the product line as in Exhibit 11–1. A comparative analysis of this type for the Discount Drug Company is shown in Exhibit 11–3.

As shown in the last column of the exhibit, overall company net operating income will decrease by $5,000 each period if the housewares line is dropped. This is the same answer, of course, as we obtained when we focused just on the lost contribution margin and avoidable fixed costs.

Beware of Allocated Fixed Costs

Our conclusion that the housewares line should not be dropped seems to conflict with the data shown earlier in Exhibit 11–2, which suggest that the housewares line is showing an $8,000 loss. Why keep a product line that is showing a loss? The explanation for this apparent inconsistency lies in part with the *common fixed costs* that are being allocated to the product lines. A **common fixed cost** is a fixed cost that supports the operations of more than one segment of an organization and that is not avoidable in whole or in part by eliminating any one segment. For example, the salary of the CEO of a company ordinarily would not be cut if any one product line were dropped, so it is a common fixed cost of the product lines. In fact, if dropping a product line is a good idea that results in higher profits for the company, the compensation of the CEO is likely to

EXHIBIT 11–3

A Comparative Format for
Product-Line Analysis

	Keep Housewares	Drop Housewares	Difference: Net Operating Income Increase (or Decrease)
Sales	$50,000	$ 0	$(50,000)
Less variable expenses	30,000	0	30,000
Contribution margin	20,000	0	(20,000)
Less fixed expenses:			
Salaries	8,000	0	8,000
Advertising	6,500	0	6,500
Utilities	1,000	1,000	0
Depreciation—fixtures	2,000	2,000	0
Rent	4,000	4,000	0
Insurance	500	0	500
General administrative	6,000	6,000	0
Total fixed expenses	28,000	13,000	15,000
Net operating income (loss)	$ (8,000)	$(13,000)	$ (5,000)

increase, rather than decrease. One of the great dangers in allocating common fixed costs is that such allocations can make a product line (or other segment of a business) *look* less profitable than it really is. In the case of the Discount Drug Company, allocating the common fixed costs among all product lines caused the housewares product line to *look* unprofitable, whereas, in fact, dropping the line would result in a decrease in overall company net operating income. This point can be shown by recasting the data in Exhibit 11–2 to eliminate the allocation of the common fixed costs. This recasting of data is shown in Exhibit 11–4.

Notice that the common fixed expenses have not been allocated to the product lines in Exhibit 11–4. Only the fixed expenses that are traceable to the product lines and that could be avoided by dropping the product lines are assigned to them. For example, the fixed expenses of advertising the housewares product line can be traced to that product line and can be eliminated if that product line is dropped. However, the general administrative expenses, such as the CEO's salary, cannot be traced to the individual product lines and would not be eliminated if any one product line were dropped. Consequently, these common fixed expenses are not allocated to the product lines in Exhibit 11–4 as they were in Exhibit 11–2. The allocations in Exhibit 11–2 provide a misleading picture that suggests that portions of the fixed common expenses can be eliminated by dropping individual product lines—which is not the case.

Exhibit 11–4 gives us a much different perspective of the housewares line than does Exhibit 11–2. As shown in Exhibit 11–4, the housewares line is covering all of its own traceable fixed costs and is generating a $3,000 *segment margin* toward covering the common fixed costs of the company. The **segment margin** is the difference between the revenue generated by a segment and its own traceable costs. However, the segment margin must be adjusted before making a decision such as dropping a product line. The segment margin may include costs and benefits that, while traceable to the segment, are not avoidable in the specific decision at hand. For example, the traceable fixed expenses of the housewares product line include $2,000 of fixtures depreciation. These costs can be traced to the housewares segment, but they are sunk costs and therefore should be ignored when deciding whether to drop the product line. Adding back this $2,000 of sunk costs to the segment margin of $3,000 yields the $5,000 in net operating income that would be foregone if the housewares product line were dropped.

	Product Line			
	Drugs	Cosmetics	Housewares	Total
Sales	$125,000	$75,000	$50,000	$250,000
Less variable expenses	50,000	25,000	30,000	105,000
Contribution margin	75,000	50,000	20,000	145,000
Less traceable fixed expenses:				
Salaries	29,500	12,500	8,000	50,000
Advertising	1,000	7,500	6,500	15,000
Depreciation—fixtures	1,000	2,000	2,000	5,000
Insurance.	2,000	500	500	3,000
Total traceable fixed expenses.	33,500	22,500	17,000	73,000
Product-line segment margin	$ 41,500	$27,500	$ 3,000*	72,000
Less common fixed expenses:				
Utilities.				2,000
Rent.				20,000
General administrative				30,000
Total common fixed expenses. .				52,000
Net operating income.				$ 20,000

*If the housewares line is dropped, this $3,000 in segment margin will be lost to the company. In addition, the $2,000 depreciation on the fixtures is a sunk cost that cannot be avoided. The sum of these two figures ($3,000 + $2,000 = $5,000) would be the decrease in the company's overall profits if the housewares line were discontinued.

Additionally, we should note that managers may rationally choose to retain an unprofitable product—particularly if selling such a product helps the company sell other products. For example, a company like Hewlett Packard or Lexmark may choose to sell printers for personal computers at a loss in order to sell more of its highly profitable proprietary ink cartridges.

The Trap Laid by Fully Allocated Costs

IN BUSINESS

A bakery distributed its products through route salespersons, each of whom loaded a truck with an assortment of products in the morning and spent the day calling on customers in an assigned territory. Believing that some items were more profitable than others, management asked for an analysis of product costs and sales. The accountants to whom the task was assigned allocated all manufacturing and marketing costs to products to obtain a net profit for each product. The resulting figures indicated that some of the products were being sold at a loss, and management discontinued these products. However, when this change was put into effect, the company's overall profit declined. It was then seen that by dropping some products, sales revenues had been reduced without commensurate reduction in costs because the common manufacturing costs and route sales costs had to be continued in order to make and sell the remaining products.

THE MAKE OR BUY DECISION

A decision whether to produce a part internally or to buy the part externally from a supplier is called a **make or buy decision.** To provide an illustration of a make or buy decision, consider Mountain Goat Cycles. The company is now producing the heavy-duty

LEARNING OBJECTIVE 3

Prepare a make or buy analysis.

gear shifters used in its most popular line of mountain bikes. The company's Accounting Department reports the following annual costs of producing 8,000 units of the shifter internally:

	Per Unit	8,000 Units
Direct materials	$ 6	$ 48,000
Direct labor	4	32,000
Variable overhead	1	8,000
Supervisor's salary	3	24,000
Depreciation of special equipment	2	16,000
Allocated general overhead	5	40,000
Total cost	$21	$168,000

An outside supplier has offered to sell 8,000 shifters a year to Mountain Goat Cycles at a price of only $19 each. Should the company stop producing the shifters internally and start purchasing them from the outside supplier? As always, the focus should be on the relevant costs. As we have seen, relevant (i.e., differential or avoidable) costs can be obtained by eliminating those costs that are not avoidable—that is, by eliminating (1) the sunk costs and (2) the future costs that will continue regardless of whether the shifters are produced internally or purchased outside. The costs that remain are avoidable by purchasing outside. If these avoidable costs are less than the outside purchase price, then the company should continue to manufacture its own shifters and reject the outside supplier's offer. That is, the company should purchase outside only if the outside purchase price is less than the costs that can be avoided internally as a result of stopping production of the shifters.

Looking at the cost data, note that depreciation of special equipment is listed as one of the costs of producing the shifters internally. Since the equipment has already been purchased, this depreciation is a sunk cost and is therefore irrelevant. If the equipment could be sold, its salvage value would be relevant. Or if the machine could be used to make other products, this could be relevant as well. However, we will assume that the equipment has no salvage value and that it has no other use except making the heavy-duty gear shifters.

Also note that the company is allocating a portion of its general overhead costs to the shifters. Any portion of this general overhead cost that would actually be eliminated if the gear shifters were purchased rather than made would be relevant in the analysis. However, it is likely that the general overhead costs allocated to the gear shifters are in fact common to all items produced in the factory and would continue unchanged even if the shifters are purchased from the outside. Such allocated common costs are not relevant costs (since they do not differ between the make or buy alternatives) and should be eliminated from the analysis along with the sunk costs.

The variable costs of producing the shifters (direct materials, direct labor, and variable overhead) are relevant costs, since they can be avoided by buying the shifters from the outside supplier. If the supervisor can be discharged and his or her salary avoided by buying the shifters, then it too is relevant to the decision. Assuming that both the variable costs and the supervisor's salary can be avoided by buying from the outside supplier, then the analysis takes the form shown in Exhibit 11–5.

Since it costs $40,000 less to continue to make the shifters internally than to buy them from the outside supplier, Mountain Goat Cycles should reject the outside supplier's offer. However, management may wish to consider one additional factor before coming to a final decision. This factor is the opportunity cost of the space now being used to produce the shifters.

EXHIBIT 11–5

Mountain Goat Cycles Make or Buy Analysis

	Total Relevant Costs—8,000 units	
	Make	Buy
Direct materials (8,000 units @ $6 per unit)	$ 48,000	
Direct labor (8,000 units @ $4 per unit)	32,000	
Variable overhead (8,000 units @ $1 per unit)	8,000	
Supervisor's salary	24,000	
Depreciation of special equipment (not relevant)	—	
Allocated general overhead (not relevant)	—	
Outside purchase price.		$152,000
Total cost	$112,000	$152,000
Difference in favor of continuing to make	$40,000	

Employee Health Benefits—Make or Buy?

IN BUSINESS

With health care insurance premiums rising by over 10% per year, companies have been searching for ways to reduce the costs of providing health care to their employees. Some companies have adopted the unconventional approach of providing health care services in-house. Quad/Graphics, a printing company with 14,000 employees, hired its own doctors and nurses to provide primary health care on-site. By "making" its own health care for employees rather than "buying" it through the purchase of insurance, the company claims that its health care costs have risen just 6% annually and that their spending on health care is now 17% less than the industry average.

Source: Kimberly Weisul, "There's a Doctor in the House," *BusinessWeek*, December 16, 2002, p. 8.

OPPORTUNITY COST

If the space now being used to produce the shifters *would otherwise be idle,* then Mountain Goat Cycles should continue to produce its own shifters and the supplier's offer should be rejected, as stated above. Idle space that has no alternative use has an opportunity cost of zero.

But what if the space now being used to produce shifters could be used for some other purpose? In that case, the space would have an opportunity cost equal to the segment margin that could be derived from the best alternative use of the space.

To illustrate, assume that the space now being used to produce shifters could be used to produce a new cross-country bike that would generate a segment margin of $60,000 per year. Under these conditions, Mountain Goat Cycles would be better off accepting the supplier's offer and using the available space to produce the new product line:

	Make	Buy
Total annual cost (see Exhibit 11–5)	$112,000	$152,000
Opportunity cost—segment margin forgone on a potential new product line	60,000	
Total cost	$172,000	$152,000
Difference in favor of purchasing from the outside supplier . . .	20,000	

Opportunity costs are not recorded in the organization's general ledger because they do not represent actual dollar outlays. Rather, they represent economic benefits that are *forgone* as a result of pursuing some course of action. The opportunity cost for Mountain Goat Cycles is sufficiently large in this case to change the decision.

IN BUSINESS

The Other Side of the Coin

This section of the chapter focuses on a company's decision to make or buy a part. However, we can also look at this situation from the standpoint of the potential supplier for the part. It isn't always easy to be a supplier. Steven Keller, founder and CEO of Keller Design, a small maker of pet accessories, found this out the hard way after landing a contract with Target, the big retailing chain. Eventually, sales to Target grew to be 80% of Keller Design's business. "Then reality bit. Target suddenly decided to drop . . . four kinds of can lids and food scoops . . . Later, an unexpected $100,000 charge for airfreighting devoured Keller's profits on a $300,000 shipment. Target also changed its mind about 6,000 specially made ceramic dog bowls, which will probably have to be dumped on a close-out firm for a fraction of Keller's investment . . . The odds are pretty well stacked against you. Contracts with large customers tend to be boilerplate, shifting most of the risk to the supplier." The moral of the story for Keller Design—protect yourself by having your own lawyer go over all contracts, contest unreasonable charges, and don't rely too much on one big customer.

Source: Leigh Gallagher, "Holding the Bag," *Forbes,* June 14, 1999, pp. 164 and 168.

IN BUSINESS

Tough Choices

Brad and Carole Karafil own and operate White Grizzly Adventures, a snowcat skiing and snowboarding company in Meadow Creek, British Columbia. While rare, it does sometimes happen that the company is unable to operate due to bad weather. Guests are housed and fed, but no one can ski. The contract signed by each guest stipulates that no refund is given in the case of an unavoidable cancellation that is beyond the control of the operators. So technically, Brad and Carole are not obligated to provide any refund if they must cancel operations due to bad weather. However, 70% of their guests are repeat customers and a guest who has paid roughly $300 a day to ski is likely to be unhappy if skiing is cancelled even though it is no fault of White Grizzly.

What costs, if any, are saved if skiing is cancelled and the snowcat does not operate? Not much. Guests are still housed and fed and the guides, who are independent contractors, are still paid. Some snowcat operating costs are avoided, but little else. Therefore, there would be little cost savings to pass on to guests.

Brad and Carole could issue a credit to be used for one day of skiing at another time. If a customer with such a credit occupied a seat on a snowcat that would otherwise be empty, the only significant cost to Brad and Carole would be the cost of feeding the customer. However, an empty seat basically doesn't exist—the demand for seats far exceeds the supply and the schedule is generally fully booked far in advance of the ski season. Consequently, the real cost of issuing a credit for one day of skiing is high. Brad and Carole would be giving up $300 from a paying customer for every guest they issue a credit voucher to. Issuing a credit voucher involves an opportunity cost of $300 in forgone sales revenues.

What would you do if you had to cancel skiing due to bad weather? Would you issue a refund or a credit voucher, losing money in the process, or would you risk losing customers? It's a tough choice.

Source: Brad and Carole Karafil, owners and operators of White Grizzly Adventures, www.whitegrizzly.com.

DECISION MAKER

Vice President of Production

You are faced with a make or buy decision. The company currently makes a component for one of its products but is considering whether it should instead purchase the component. If the offer from an outside supplier were accepted, the company would no longer need to rent the machinery that is currently being used to manufacture the component. You realize that the annual rental cost is a fixed cost, but recall some sort of warning about fixed costs. Is the annual rental cost relevant to this make or buy decision?

SPECIAL ORDERS

Managers must often evaluate whether a *special order* should be accepted, and if the order is accepted, the price that should be charged. A **special order** is a one-time order that is not considered part of the company's normal ongoing business. To illustrate, Mountain Goat Cycles has just received a request from the Seattle Police Department to produce 100 specially modified mountain bikes at a price of $179 each. The bikes would be used to patrol some of the more densely populated residential sections of the city. Mountain Goat Cycles can easily modify its City Cruiser model to fit the specifications of the Seattle Police. The normal selling price of the City Cruiser bike is $249, and its unit product cost is $182 as shown below:

Direct materials	$ 86
Direct labor	45
Manufacturing overhead	51
Unit product cost	$182

The variable portion of the above manufacturing overhead is $6 per unit. The order would have no effect on the company's total fixed manufacturing overhead costs.

The modifications requested by the Seattle Police Department consist of welded brackets to hold radios, nightsticks, and other gear. These modifications would require $17 in incremental variable costs. In addition, the company would have to pay a graphics design studio $1,200 to design and cut stencils that would be used for spray-painting the Seattle Police Department's logo and other identifying marks on the bikes.

This order should have no effect on the company's other sales. The production manager says that she can handle the special order without disrupting any of the company's regular scheduled production.

What effect would accepting this order have on the company's net operating income?

Only the incremental costs and benefits are relevant. Since the existing fixed manufacturing overhead costs would not be affected by the order, they are not relevant. The incremental net operating income can be computed as follows:

	Per Unit	Total 100 Bikes
Incremental revenue	$179	$17,900
Incremental costs:		
Variable costs:		
Direct materials	86	8,600
Direct labor	45	4,500
Variable manufacturing overhead	6	600
Special modifications	17	1,700
Total variable cost	$154	15,400
Fixed cost:		
Purchase of stencils		1,200
Total incremental cost		16,600
Incremental net operating income		$ 1,300

Therefore, even though the $179 price on the special order is below the normal $182 unit product cost and the order would require additional costs, the order would increase net operating income. In general, a special order is profitable if the incremental revenue from the special order exceeds the incremental costs of the order. We must note, however, that it is important to make sure that there is indeed idle capacity and that the special order does not cut into normal unit sales or undercut prices on normal sales. If the company was operating at capacity, opportunity costs would have to be taken into account as well as the incremental costs that have already been detailed above.

PRICING NEW PRODUCTS

When offering a new product or service for the first time, a company must decide on its selling price. A cost-based approach is often followed in practice. In this approach, the product is first designed and produced, then its cost is determined and its price is computed by adding a mark-up to the cost. This *cost-plus* approach to pricing suffers from a number of drawbacks—the most obvious being that customers may not be willing to pay the price set by the company. If the price is too high, customers may decide to purchase a similar product from a competitor or, if no similar competing product exists, they may decide not to buy the product at all.

Target costing provides an alternative, market-based approach to pricing new products. In the **target costing** approach, management estimates how much the market will be willing to pay for the new product even before the new product has been designed. The company's required profit margin is subtracted from the estimated selling price to determine the target cost for the new product. A cross-functional team consisting of designers, engineers, cost accountants, marketing personnel, and production personnel is charged with the responsibility of ensuring that the cost of the product is ultimately less than the target cost. If at some point in the product development process it becomes clear that the target cost is unattainable, the new product is abandoned.

The target costing approach to pricing has a number of advantages over the cost-plus approach. First, the target costing approach is focused on the market and the customer. A product is not made unless the company is reasonably confident that customers will buy the product at a price that provides the company with an adequate profit. Second, the target costing approach instills a much higher level of cost-consciousness than the cost-plus approach and probably results in less expensive products that are more attractive to customers. In essence, target costing holds managers accountable for ensuring that actual product costs do not exceed a preestablished ceiling. In the cost-plus approach, there is no preestablished ceiling—higher costs simply result in higher prices. This lack of cost accountability allows designers and engineers to create products with expensive features without considering whether the added costs of these features would result in a selling price that exceeds what customers would be willing to pay. Not surprisingly, some companies are abandoning the cost-plus approach to new product pricing in favor of target costing.

Target Costing

Step 1: What will customers pay for this product?

Step 2: What is our target cost?

Step 3: How can we design the product to meet the target cost?

Step 4: Let's manufacture the product!

Market Research Department

Finance Department

Project Engineering Department

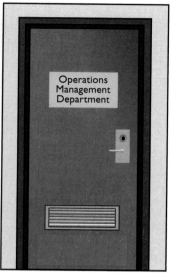

Operations Management Department

Tutor

YOU DECIDE

Your financial accounting instructor has suggested that you should consider working with selected students in her class as a tutor. Should you adopt a cost-plus or target costing approach to setting your hourly fee?

UTILIZATION OF A CONSTRAINED RESOURCE

Managers are routinely faced with the problem of deciding how constrained resources should be utilized. A department store, for example, has a limited amount of floor space and therefore cannot stock every product that may be available. A manufacturer has a limited number of machine-hours and a limited number of direct labor-hours at its disposal. When a limited resource of some type restricts the company's ability to satisfy demand, the company has a **constraint.** Since the company cannot fully satisfy demand, the manager must decide how the constrained resource should be used. Fixed costs are usually unaffected by such choices, so the course of action that will maximize the company's *total* contribution margin should usually be selected.

> **LEARNING OBJECTIVE 5**
>
> Determine the most profitable use of a constrained resource and the value of obtaining more of the constrained resource.

Contribution Margin per Unit of the Constrained Resource

To maximize total contribution margin, a company should not necessarily promote those products that have the highest *unit* contribution margins. Rather, total contribution margin will be maximized by promoting those products or accepting those orders that provide the highest *contribution margin per unit of the constrained resource.* To illustrate, Mountain Goat Cycles makes a line of paniers—a saddlebag for bicycles. There are two models of paniers—a touring model and a mountain model. Cost and revenue data for the two models of paniers are given below:

| | Model | |
	Mountain Panier	Touring Panier
Selling price per unit	$25	$30
Variable cost per unit	10	18
Contribution margin per unit	$15	$12
Contribution margin (CM) ratio	60%	40%

The mountain panier appears to be much more profitable than the touring panier. It has a $15 per unit contribution margin as compared to only $12 per unit for the touring model, and it has a 60% CM ratio as compared to only 40% for the touring model.

But now let us add one more piece of information—the plant that makes the paniers is operating at capacity. This does not mean that every machine and every person in the plant is working at the maximum possible rate. Because machines have different capacities, some machines will be operating at less than 100% of capacity. However, if the plant as a whole cannot produce any more units, some machine or process must be operating at capacity. The machine or process that is limiting overall output is called the **bottleneck**—it is the constraint.

At Mountain Goat Cycles, the bottleneck is a stitching machine. The mountain panier requires two minutes of stitching time, and the touring panier requires one minute of stitching time. Since the stitching machine already has more work than it can handle, some orders for the mountain panier or for the touring panier will have to be turned down. Naturally, managers will want to know which product is less profitable. To answer this question, focus on the contribution margin per unit of the constrained resource. This figure is computed by dividing the contribution margin by the amount of the constrained resource a unit of product requires. These calculations are carried out below for the mountain and touring paniers.

| | Model | |
	Mountain Panier	Touring Panier
Contribution margin per unit (above) (a)	$15.00	$12.00
Stitching machine time required to produce one unit (b)	2 minutes	1 minute
Contribution margin per unit of the constrained resource, (a) ÷ (b)	$7.50 per minute	$12.00 per minute

It is now easy to decide which product is less profitable and should be deemphasized. Each minute on the stitching machine that is devoted to the touring panier results in an increase of $12 in contribution margin and profits. The comparable figure for the mountain panier is only $7.50 per minute. Therefore, the touring model should be emphasized. Even though the mountain model has the larger contribution margin per unit and the larger CM ratio, the touring model provides the larger contribution margin in relation to the constrained resource.

To verify that the touring model is indeed the more profitable product, suppose an hour of additional stitching time is available and that unfilled orders exist for both products. The additional hour on the stitching machine could be used to make either 30 mountain paniers (60 minutes ÷ 2 minutes per mountain panier) or 60 touring paniers (60 minutes ÷ 1 minute per touring panier), with the following profit implications:

	Model	
	Mountain Panier	**Touring Panier**
Contribution margin per unit (above)	$ 15	$ 12
Additional units that can be processed in one hour	× 30	× 60
Additional contribution margin	$450	$720

Since the additional contribution margin would be $720 for the touring paniers and only $450 for the mountain paniers, the touring paniers make the most profitable use of the company's constrained resource—the stitching machine.

This example clearly shows that looking at unit contribution margins alone is not enough; the contribution margin must be viewed in relation to the amount of the constrained resource each product requires.

Theory of Constraints Software

Indalex Aluminum Solutions Group is the largest producer of soft alloy extrusions in North America. The company has installed a new generation of business intelligence software created by pVelocity, Inc., of Toronto, Canada. The software "provides decision makers across our entire manufacturing enterprise with time-based financial metrics using TOC concepts to identify bottlenecks." And, it "shifts the focus of a manufacturing company from traditional cost accounting measurements to measuring the generation of dollars per unit of time." For example, instead of emphasizing products with the largest gross margins or contribution margins, the software helps managers to identify and emphasize the products that maximize the contribution margin per unit of the constrained resource.

Source: Mike Alger, "Managing a Business as a Portfolio of Customers," *Strategic Finance*, June 2003, pp. 54–57.

Managing Constraints

Profits can be increased by effectively managing an organization's constraints. One aspect of managing a constraint is to decide how to best utilize it. As discussed above, if the constraint is a bottleneck in the production process, the manager should select the product mix that maximizes the total contribution margin. In addition, the manager should take an active role in managing the constraint itself. Management should focus efforts on increasing the efficiency of the bottleneck operation and on increasing its capacity. Such efforts directly increase the output of finished goods and will often pay off in an almost immediate increase in profits.

It is often possible for a manager to increase the capacity of the bottleneck, which is called **relaxing (or elevating) the constraint.** For example, the stitching machine operator could be asked to work overtime. This would result in more available stitching time and hence the production of more finished goods that can be sold. The benefits from relaxing the constraint in such a manner are often enormous and can be easily quantified. The manager should first ask, "What would I do with additional capacity at the bottleneck if it were available?" In our example, if unfilled orders exist for both the touring and mountain paniers, the additional capacity would be used to process more touring paniers, since they earn a contribution margin of $12 per minute, or $720 per hour. Since overtime pay for the operator is likely to be much less than $720 per hour, running the stitching machine on overtime would be an excellent way to increase the profits of the company while at the same time satisfying customers.

To reinforce this concept, suppose that there are only unfilled orders for the mountain panier. How much would it be worth to the company to run the stitching machine overtime in this situation? Since the additional capacity would be used to make the mountain panier, the value of that additional capacity would drop to $7.50 per minute or $450 per hour. Nevertheless, the value of relaxing the constraint would still be quite high.

These calculations indicate that managers should pay great attention to the bottleneck operation. If a bottleneck machine breaks down or is ineffectively utilized, the losses to the company can be quite large. In our example, for every minute the stitching machine is down due to breakdowns or setups, the company loses between $7.50 and $12.00. The losses on an hourly basis are between $450 and $720! In contrast, there is no such loss of contribution margin if time is lost on a machine that is not a bottleneck—such machines have excess capacity anyway.

The implications are clear. Managers should focus much of their attention on managing the bottleneck. As we have discussed, managers should emphasize products that most profitably utilize the constrained resource. They should also make sure that products are processed smoothly through the bottleneck, with minimal lost time due to breakdowns and setups. And they should try to find ways to increase the capacity at the bottleneck.

The capacity of a bottleneck can be effectively increased in a number of ways, including:

- Working overtime on the bottleneck.
- Subcontracting some of the processing that would be done at the bottleneck.
- Investing in additional machines at the bottleneck.
- Shifting workers from processes that are not the bottleneck to the process that is the bottleneck.
- Focusing business process improvement efforts such as Six Sigma on the bottleneck.
- Reducing defective units. Each defective unit that is processed through the bottleneck and subsequently scrapped takes the place of a good unit that could be sold.

The last three methods of increasing the capacity of the bottleneck are particularly attractive, since they are essentially free and may even yield additional cost savings.

The methods and ideas discussed in this section are all part of the Theory of Constraints, which was introduced in the Prologue. A number of organizations have successfully used the Theory of Constraints to improve their performance, including Avery Dennison, Bethlehem Steel, Binney & Smith, Boeing, Champion International, Ford Motor Company, General Motors, ITT, National Semiconductor, Pratt and Whitney Canada, Pretoria Academic Hospital, Procter and Gamble, Texas Instruments, United Airlines, United Electrical Controls, the United States Air Force Logistics Command, and the United States Navy Transportation Corps.

CONCEPT CHECK ✓

4. A company has received a special order from a customer to make 5,000 units of a customized product. The direct material cost per unit of the customized product is $15, the direct labor cost per unit is $5, and the manufacturing overhead per unit is $18, including $6 of variable manufacturing overhead. If the company has sufficient available manufacturing capacity, what is the minimum price that can be accepted for the special order?
   a. $24
   b. $26
   c. $32
   d. $38
5. Refer to the facts from question 4 above; however, in answering this question assume that the company is operating at 100% of its capacity without the special

order. If the company normally manufactures only one product that has a contribution margin of $20 per unit and that consumes 2 minutes of the constrained resource per unit, what is the opportunity cost (stated in terms of forgone contribution margin) of taking the special order? Assume the special order would require 1.5 minutes of the constrained resource per unit.

a. $25,000
b. $50,000
c. $75,000
d. $100,000

CONCEPT CHECK ✓

(continued)

Elevating a Constraint

IN BUSINESS

The Odessa, Texas, Police Department was having trouble hiring new employees. Its eight-step hiring process was taking 117 days to complete; therefore, the best qualified job applicants were accepting other employment offers before the Odessa Police Department could finish evaluating their candidacy. The Theory of Constraints revealed that the constraint in the eight-step hiring process was the background investigation—which took an average of 104 days. The other seven steps—filling out an application and completing a written exam, an oral interview, a polygraph exam, a medical exam, a psychological exam and a drug screen—took a combined total of 13 days. The Odessa Police Department elevated its constraint by hiring additional background checkers. This resulted in slashing its application processing time from 117 days to 16 days.

Source: Lloyd J. Taylor III, Brian J. Moersch, and Geralyn McClure Franklin, "Applying the Theory of Constraints to a Public Safety Hiring Process," *Public Personnel Management*, Fall 2003, pp. 367–382.

SUMMARY

LO1   Identify relevant and irrelevant costs and benefits in a decision.

Every decision involves a choice from among at least two alternatives. Only those costs and benefits that differ in total between the alternatives are relevant; costs and benefits that are the same for all alternatives are not affected by the decision and can be ignored. Only future costs that differ between alternatives are relevant. Costs that have already been incurred are sunk costs and are always irrelevant. Future costs that do not differ between alternatives are not relevant.

LO2   Prepare an analysis showing whether a product line or other business segment should be dropped or retained.

A decision of whether a product line or other segment should be dropped should focus on the differences in the costs and benefits between dropping or retaining the product line or segment. Caution should be exercised when using reports in which common fixed costs have been allocated among segments. If these common fixed costs are unaffected by the decision of whether to drop or retain the segment, they are irrelevant and should be removed before determining the real profitability of a segment.

LO3   Prepare a make or buy analysis.

A make or buy decision should focus on the costs and benefits that differ between the alternatives of making or buying a component. As in other decisions, sunk costs—such as the depreciation on old equipment—should be ignored. Future costs that do not differ between alternatives—such as allocations of common fixed costs like general overhead—should be ignored.

LO4   Prepare an analysis showing whether a special order should be accepted.

When deciding whether to accept or reject a special order, focus on the benefits and costs that differ between those two alternatives. Specifically, a special order should be accepted when the incremental revenue from the sale exceeds the incremental cost. As always, sunk costs and future costs that do not differ between the alternatives are irrelevant.

LO5 Determine the most profitable use of a constrained resource and the value of obtaining more of the constrained resource.

When demand for a company's products and services exceeds its ability to supply them, the company has a bottleneck. The bottleneck, whether it is a particular material, skilled labor, or a specific machine, is a constrained resource. Since the company is unable to make everything it could sell, managers must decide what the company will make and what the company will not make. In this situation, the profitability of a product is best measured by its contribution margin per unit of the constrained resource. The products with the highest contribution margin per unit of the constrained resource should be favored.

Managers should focus their attention on effectively managing the constraint. This involves making the best use possible of the constrained resource and increasing the amount of the constrained resource that is available. The value of relaxing the constraint is determined by the contribution margin per unit of the constrained resource for the work that would be done if more of the resource were available.

GUIDANCE ANSWERS TO *DECISION MAKER* AND *YOU DECIDE*

Vice President of Production (p. 474)

The warning that you may recall about fixed costs in decisions relates to *allocated* fixed costs. Allocated fixed costs often make a product line or other segment of a business appear less profitable than it really is. However, in this situation, the annual rental cost for the machinery is an *avoidable* fixed cost rather than an allocated fixed cost. An avoidable fixed cost is a cost that can be eliminated in whole or in part by choosing one alternative over another. Because the annual rental cost of the machinery can be avoided if the company purchases the components from an outside supplier, it is relevant to this decision.

Tutor (p. 477)

Individuals who provide services to others often struggle to decide how to charge for their services. As a tutor, you probably will not incur any significant costs, unless you agree to provide supplies (such as paper, pencils, calculators, or study guides) or software. As such, a cost-plus approach may not be a practical way to set the hourly fee (or price) for your services. On the other hand, if you use a target costing approach, you would estimate how much students would be willing to pay for the tutoring services. If your institution offers tutoring services to its students, you should inquire about the fee and you should check the student newspaper (or local newspapers) to determine the going rate for tutors. If you plan to tutor instead of working at a part-time job, you should consider the opportunity cost (that is, the hourly wage that you will be forgoing).

GUIDANCE ANSWERS TO CONCEPT CHECKS

1. **Choices a and d.** Sunk costs are always irrelevant. Fixed costs can be relevant costs.
2. **Choice a.** The cost of the airline ticket to Telluride is a sunk cost; it has already been incurred and the ticket is nonrefundable.
3. **Choice b.** The cost of going to Stowe would be $1,000 [$400 + ($150 per night × 4 nights)] whereas the incremental cost of going to Telluride would be $1,020 [$300 + ($180 per night × 4 nights)]. Note that the $450 cost of flying to Telluride is irrelevant at this point because it is a sunk cost. The analysis favors Stowe by $20.
4. **Choice b.** The minimum price would be $15 direct materials + $5 direct labor + $6 variable manufacturing overhead = $26.
5. **Choice c.** The special order requires 7,500 minutes (5,000 units × 1.5 minutes per unit). Taking the special order would require sacrificing 3,750 units (7,500 minutes ÷ 2 minutes per unit) of the regular product. The forgone contribution margin would be 3,750 units × $20 per unit = $75,000.

REVIEW PROBLEM: RELEVANT COSTS

Charter Sports Equipment manufactures round, rectangular, and octagonal trampolines. Sales and expense data for the past month follow:

	Trampoline			
	Round	Rectangular	Octagonal	Total
Sales	$ 140,000	$500,000	$360,000	$1,000,000
Less variable expenses	60,000	200,000	150,000	410,000
Contribution margin	80,000	300,000	210,000	590,000
Less fixed expenses:				
Advertising—traceable	41,000	110,000	65,000	216,000
Depreciation of special equipment.................	20,000	40,000	35,000	95,000
Line supervisors' salaries	6,000	7,000	6,000	19,000
General factory overhead*	28,000	100,000	72,000	200,000
Total fixed expenses	95,000	257,000	178,000	530,000
Net operating income (loss)	$ (15,000)	$ 43,000	$ 32,000	$ 60,000

*A common fixed cost that is allocated on the basis of sales dollars.

Management is concerned about the continued losses shown by the round trampolines and wants a recommendation as to whether or not the line should be discontinued. The special equipment used to produce the trampolines has no resale value. If the round trampoline model is dropped, the two line supervisors assigned to the model would be discharged.

Required:

1. Should production and sale of the round trampolines be discontinued? The company has no other use for the capacity now being used to produce the round trampolines. Show computations to support your answer.
2. Recast the above data in a format that would be more useful to management in assessing the profitability of the various product lines.

Solution to Review Problem

1. No, production and sale of the round trampolines should not be discontinued. Computations to support this answer follow:

Contribution margin lost if the round trampolines are discontinued ...		$(80,000)
Less fixed costs that can be avoided:		
Advertising—traceable	$41,000	
Line supervisors' salaries	6,000	47,000
Decrease in net operating income for the company as a whole		$(33,000)

The depreciation of the special equipment represents a sunk cost, and therefore it is not relevant to the decision. The general factory overhead is allocated and will presumably continue regardless of whether or not the round trampolines are discontinued; thus, it is not relevant.

2. If management wants a clearer picture of the profitability of the segments, the general factory overhead should not be allocated. It is a common fixed cost and therefore should be deducted from the

total product-line segment margin, as shown in Exhibit 11–4. A more useful income statement format would be as follows:

	Trampoline			Total
	Round	Rectangular	Octagonal	
Sales	$140,000	$500,000	$360,000	$1,000,000
Less variable expenses	60,000	200,000	150,000	410,000
Contribution margin	80,000	300,000	210,000	590,000
Less traceable fixed expenses:				
Advertising—traceable	41,000	110,000	65,000	216,000
Depreciation of special equipment . .	20,000	40,000	35,000	95,000
Line supervisors' salaries	6,000	7,000	6,000	19,000
Total traceable fixed expenses	67,000	157,000	106,000	330,000
Product-line segment margin	$ 13,000	$143,000	$104,000	260,000
Less common fixed expenses				200,000
Net operating income (loss)				$ 60,000

GLOSSARY

Avoidable cost   A cost that can be eliminated (in whole or in part) by choosing one alternative over another in a decision. This term is synonymous with *relevant cost* and *differential cost*. (p. 460)

Bottleneck   A machine or some other part of a process that limits the output of the entire process. (p. 478)

Common fixed cost   A fixed cost that supports the operations of more than one segment of an organization and is not avoidable in whole or in part by eliminating any one segment. (p. 469)

Constraint   A limitation under which a company must operate, such as limited available machine time or limited raw materials available that restricts the company's ability to satisfy demand. (p. 477)

Differential cost   Any cost that differs between alternatives in a decision. This term is synonymous with *avoidable cost* and *relevant cost*. (p. 461)

Make or buy decision   A decision concerning whether an item should be produced internally or purchased from an outside supplier. (p. 471)

Relaxing (or elevating) the constraint   An action that increases the amount of a constrained resource. (p. 479)

Relevant cost   A cost that differs between alternatives in a particular decision. This term is synonymous with *avoidable cost* and *differential cost*. (p. 460)

Segment margin   The difference between the revenue generated by a segment and its own traceable cost. (p. 470)

Special order   A one-time order that is not considered part of the company's normal ongoing business. (p. 475)

Sunk cost   Any cost that has already been incurred and that cannot be changed by any decision made now or in the future. (p. 460)

Target costing   Before launching a new product, management estimates how much the market will be willing to pay for the product and then takes steps to ensure that the cost of the product will be low enough to provide an adequate profit margin. (p. 476)

QUESTIONS

11–1   What is a *relevant cost*?

11–2   Define the following terms: *incremental cost, opportunity cost,* and *sunk cost.*

11–3   Are variable costs always relevant costs? Explain.

11–4   Why is the original cost of a machine the company already owns irrelevant in decisions?

11–5 "Sunk costs are easy to spot—they're simply the fixed costs associated with a decision." Do you agree? Explain.

11–6 "Variable costs and differential costs mean the same thing." Do you agree? Explain.

11–7 "All future costs are relevant in decision making." Do you agree? Why?

11–8 Prentice Company is considering dropping one of its product lines. What costs of the product line would be relevant to this decision? Irrelevant?

11–9 "If a product line is generating a loss, then that's pretty good evidence that the product line should be discontinued." Do you agree? Explain.

11–10 What is the danger in allocating common fixed costs among product lines or other segments of an organization?

11–11 How does opportunity cost enter into the make or buy decision?

11–12 Give four examples of possible constraints.

11–13 How does relating product contribution margins to the amount of the constrained resource they require help a company ensure that profits are maximized?

BRIEF EXERCISES

BRIEF EXERCISE 11–1 Identifying Relevant Costs [LO1]

A number of costs are listed below that may be relevant in decisions faced by the management of Svahn, AB, a Swedish manufacturer of sailing yachts:

Item	Case 1 Relevant	Case 1 Not Relevant	Case 2 Relevant	Case 2 Not Relevant
a. Sales revenue				
b. Direct materials				
c. Direct labor				
d. Variable manufacturing overhead				
e. Depreciation—Model B100 machine				
f. Book value—Model B100 machine				
g. Disposal value—Model B100 machine				
h. Market value—Model B300 machine (cost)				
i. Fixed manufacturing overhead (general)				
j. Variable selling expense				
k. Fixed selling expense				
l. General administrative overhead				

Required:

Copy the information above onto your answer sheet and place an X in the appropriate column to indicate whether each item is relevant or not relevant in the following situations. Requirement 1 relates to Case 1 above, and requirement 2 relates to Case 2.

1. The company chronically has no idle capacity and the old Model B100 machine is the company's constraint. Management is considering purchasing a Model B300 machine to use in addition to the company's present Model B100 machine. The old Model B100 machine will continue to be used to capacity as before, with the new Model B300 machine being used to expand production. This will increase the company's production and sales. The increase in volume will be large enough to require increases in fixed selling expenses and in general administrative overhead, but not in fixed manufacturing overhead.

2. The old Model B100 machine is not the company's constraint, but management is considering replacing it with a new Model B300 machine because of the potential savings in direct materials with the new machine. The Model B100 machine would be sold. This change will have no effect on production or sales, other than some savings in direct materials costs due to less waste.

BRIEF EXERCISE 11–2   Dropping or Retaining a Segment   [LO2]

Bed & Bath, a retailing company, has two departments, Hardware and Linens. A recent monthly contribution format income statement for the company follows:

	Department		Total
	Hardware	Linens	
Sales	$3,000,000	$1,000,000	$4,000,000
Less variable expenses	900,000	400,000	1,300,000
Contribution margin	2,100,000	600,000	2,700,000
Less fixed expenses	1,400,000	800,000	2,200,000
Net operating income (loss)	$ 700,000	$ (200,000)	$ 500,000

A study indicates that $340,000 of the fixed expenses being charged to Linens are sunk costs or allocated costs that will continue even if the Linens Department is dropped. In addition, the elimination of the Linens Department will result in a 10% decrease in the sales of the Hardware Department.

Required:

If the Linens Department is dropped, what will be the effect on the net operating income of the company as a whole?

BRIEF EXERCISE 11–3   Make or Buy a Component   [LO3]

For many years Futura Company has purchased the starters that it installs in its standard line of farm tractors. Due to a reduction in output, the company has idle capacity that could be used to produce the starters. The chief engineer has recommended against this move, however, pointing out that the cost to produce the starters would be greater than the current $8.40 per unit purchase price:

	Per Unit	Total
Direct materials	$3.10	
Direct labor	2.70	
Supervision	1.50	$60,000
Depreciation	1.00	$40,000
Variable manufacturing overhead	0.60	
Rent	0.30	$12,000
Total production cost	$9.20	

A supervisor would have to be hired to oversee production of the starters. However, the company has sufficient idle tools and machinery that no new equipment would have to be purchased. The rent charge above is based on space utilized in the plant. The total rent on the plant is $80,000 per period. Depreciation is due to obsolescence rather than wear and tear.

Required:

Prepare computations showing how much profits will increase or decrease as a result of making the starters.

BRIEF EXERCISE 11–4   Special Order   [LO4]

Delta Company produces a single product. The cost of producing and selling a single unit of this product at the company's normal activity level of 60,000 units per year is:

Direct materials	$5.10
Direct labor	$3.80
Variable manufacturing overhead	$1.00
Fixed manufacturing overhead	$4.20
Variable selling and administrative expense	$1.50
Fixed selling and administrative expense	$2.40

The normal selling price is $21 per unit. The company's capacity is 75,000 units per year. An order has been received from a mail-order house for 15,000 units at a special price of $14 per unit. This order would not affect regular sales.

Required:

1. If the order is accepted, by how much will annual profits be increased or decreased? (The order will not change the company's total fixed costs.)
2. Assume the company has 1,000 units of this product left over from last year that are vastly inferior to the current model. The units must be sold through regular channels at reduced prices. What unit cost figure is relevant for establishing a minimum selling price for these units? Explain.

BRIEF EXERCISE 11–5   **Utilization of a Constrained Resource   [LO5]**
Benoit Company produces three products, A, B, and C. Data concerning the three products follow (per unit):

	Product		
	A	**B**	**C**
Selling price	$80	$56	$70
Less variable expenses:			
Direct materials	24	15	9
Other variable expenses	24	27	40
Total variable expenses	48	42	49
Contribution margin	$32	$14	$21
Contribution margin ratio	40%	25%	30%

Demand for the company's products is very strong, with far more orders each month than the company has raw materials available to produce. The same material is used in each product. The material costs $3 per pound with a maximum of 5,000 pounds available each month.

Required:
Which orders would you advise the company to accept first, those for A, for B, or for C? Which orders second? Third?

EXERCISES

EXERCISE 11–6   **Identification of Relevant Costs   (LO1)**
Kristen Lu purchased a used automobile for $8,000 at the beginning of last year and incurred the following operating costs:

Depreciation ($8,000 ÷ 5 years)	$1,600
Insurance	$1,200
Garage rent	$360
Automobile tax and license	$40
Variable operating cost	14¢ per mile

The variable operating costs consist of gasoline, oil, tires, maintenance, and repairs. Kristen estimates that, at her current rate of usage, the car will have zero resale value in five years, so the annual straight-line depreciation is $1,600. The car is kept in a garage for a monthly fee.

Required:
1. Kristen drove the car 10,000 miles last year. Compute the average cost per mile of owning and operating the car.
2. Kristen is unsure about whether she should use her own car or rent a car to go on an extended cross-country trip for two weeks during spring break. What costs above are relevant in this decision? Explain.

3. Kristen is thinking about buying an expensive sports car to replace the car she bought last year. She would drive the same number of miles regardless of which car she owns and would rent the same parking space. The sports car's variable operating costs would be roughly the same as the variable operating costs of her old car. However, her insurance and automobile tax and license costs would go up. What costs are relevant in estimating the incremental cost of owning the more expensive car? Explain.

EXERCISE 11–7   Identification of Relevant Costs   [LO1]
Bill has just returned from a duck hunting trip. He has brought home eight ducks. Bill's friend, John, disapproves of duck hunting, and to discourage Bill from further hunting, John has presented him with the following cost estimate per duck:

Camper and equipment:	
Cost, $12,000; usable for eight seasons; 10 hunting trips per season	$150
Travel expense (pickup truck):	
100 miles at $0.31 per mile (gas, oil, and tires—$0.21 per mile; depreciation	
and insurance—$0.10 per mile)	31
Shotgun shells (two boxes)	20
Boat:	
Cost, $2,320, usable for eight seasons; 10 hunting trips per season	29
Hunting license:	
Cost, $30 for the season; 10 hunting trips per season	3
Money lost playing poker:	
Loss, $24 (Bill plays poker every weekend)	24
Bottle of whiskey:	
Cost, $15 (used to ward off the cold)	15
Total cost	$272
Cost per duck ($272 ÷ 8 ducks)	$ 34

Required:
1. Assuming that the duck hunting trip Bill has just completed is typical, what costs are relevant to a decision as to whether Bill should go duck hunting again this season?
2. Suppose that Bill gets lucky on his next hunting trip and shoots 10 ducks in the amount of time it took him to shoot 8 ducks on his last trip. How much would it have cost him to shoot the last two ducks? Explain.
3. Which costs are relevant in a decision of whether Bill should give up hunting? Explain.

EXERCISE 11–8   Dropping or Retaining a Segment   [LO2]
Thalassines Kataskeves, S.A., of Greece makes marine equipment. The company has been experiencing losses on its bilge pump product line for several years. The most recent quarterly contribution format income statement for the bilge pump product line follows:

Thalassines Kataskeves, S.A.
Income Statement—Bilge Pump
For the Quarter Ended March 31

Sales		€850,000
Less variable expenses:		
Variable manufacturing expenses	€330,000	
Sales commissions	42,000	
Shipping	18,000	
Total variable expenses		390,000
Contribution margin		460,000
		(continued)

(concluded)

Thalassines Kataskeves, S.A.
Income Statement—Bilge Pump
For the Quarter Ended March 31

Less fixed expenses:

Advertising	270,000
Depreciation of equipment (no resale value)	80,000
General factory overhead	105,000*
Salary of product-line manager	32,000
Insurance on inventories	8,000
Purchasing department expenses	45,000†
Total fixed expenses	540,000
Net operating loss	€(80,000)

*Common costs allocated on the basis of machine-hours.
†Common costs allocated on the basis of sales dollars.

The currency in Greece is the euro, denoted here by €. Discontinuing the bilge pump product line would not affect sales of other product lines and would have no effect on the company's total general factory overhead or total Purchasing Department expenses.

Required:

Would you recommend that the bilge pump product line be discontinued? Support your answer with appropriate computations.

EXERCISE 11–9 Make or Buy a Component [LO3]

Han Products manufactures 30,000 units of part S-6 each year for use on its production line. At this level of activity, the cost per unit for part S-6 is as follows:

Direct materials	$ 3.60
Direct labor	10.00
Variable manufacturing overhead	2.40
Fixed manufacturing overhead	9.00
Total cost per part	$25.00

An outside supplier has offered to sell 30,000 units of part S-6 each year to Han Products for $21 per part. If Han Products accepts this offer, the facilities now being used to manufacture part S-6 could be rented to another company at an annual rental of $80,000. However, Han Products has determined that two-thirds of the fixed manufacturing overhead being applied to part S-6 would continue even if part S-6 were purchased from the outside supplier.

Required:

Prepare computations showing how much profits will increase or decrease if the outside supplier's offer is accepted.

EXERCISE 11–10 Evaluating a Special Order [LO4]

Imperial Jewelers is considering a special order for 20 handcrafted gold bracelets to be given as gifts to members of a wedding party. The normal selling price of a gold bracelet is $189.95 and its unit product cost is $149.00 as shown below:

Direct materials	$ 84.00
Direct labor	45.00
Manufacturing overhead	20.00
Unit product cost	$149.00

Most of the manufacturing overhead is fixed and unaffected by variations in how much jewelry is produced in any given period. However, $4.00 of the overhead is variable with respect to the number of bracelets produced. The customer who is interested in the special bracelet order would like special filigree applied to the bracelets. This filigree would require additional materials costing $2.00 per bracelet and would also require acquisition of a special tool costing $250 that would have no other use once the special order is completed. This order would have no effect on the company's regular sales and the order could be fulfilled using the company's existing capacity without affecting any other order.

Required:
What effect would accepting this order have on the company's net operating income if a special price of $169.95 per bracelet is offered for this order? Should the special order be accepted at this price?

EXERCISE 11–11   Utilization of a Constrained Resource   [LO5]
Barlow Company manufactures three products: A, B, and C. The selling price, variable costs, and contribution margin for one unit of each product follow:

	Product		
	A	**B**	**C**
Selling price	$180	$270	$240
Less variable expenses:			
Direct materials	24	72	32
Other variable expenses	102	90	148
Total variable expenses	126	162	180
Contribution margin	$ 54	$108	$ 60
Contribution margin ratio	30%	40%	25%

The same raw material is used in all three products. Barlow Company has only 5,000 pounds of raw material on hand and will not be able to obtain any more of it for several weeks due to a strike in its supplier's plant. Management is trying to decide which product(s) to concentrate on next week in filling its backlog of orders. The material costs $8 per pound.

Required:
1. Compute the amount of contribution margin that will be obtained per pound of material used in each product.
2. Which orders would you recommend that the company work on next week—the orders for product A, product B, or product C? Show computations.
3. A foreign supplier could furnish Barlow with additional stocks of the raw material at a substantial premium over the usual price. If there is unfilled demand for all three products, what is the highest price that Barlow Company should be willing to pay for an additional pound of materials? Explain.

PROBLEMS

CHECK FIGURE
(1) Decrease in profits:
$3,200

PROBLEM 11–12A   Dropping or Retaining a Flight   [LO2]
Profits have been decreasing for several years at Pegasus Airlines. In an effort to improve the company's performance, consideration is being given to dropping several flights that appear to be unprofitable.
     A typical income statement for one such flight (flight 482) is given below (per flight):

Ticket revenue (175 seats × 40% occupancy × $200 ticket price)	$14,000	100.0%
Less variable expenses ($15 per person)	1,050	7.5
Contribution margin	12,950	92.5%

(continued)

(concluded)

Less flight expenses:	
Salaries, flight crew	1,800
Flight promotion	750
Depreciation of aircraft	1,550
Fuel for aircraft	5,800
Liability insurance	4,200
Salaries, flight assistants	1,500
Baggage loading and flight preparation	1,700
Overnight costs for flight crew and assistants at destination	300
Total flight expenses	17,600
Net operating loss	$ (4,650)

The following additional information is available about flight 482:

a. Members of the flight crew are paid fixed annual salaries, whereas the flight assistants are paid by the flight.

b. One-third of the liability insurance is a special charge assessed against flight 482 because in the opinion of the insurance company, the destination of the flight is in a "high-risk" area. The remaining two-thirds would be unaffected by a decision to drop flight 482.

c. The baggage loading and flight preparation expense is an allocation of ground crews' salaries and depreciation of ground equipment. Dropping flight 482 would have no effect on the company's total baggage loading and flight preparation expenses.

d. If flight 482 is dropped, Pegasus Airlines has no authorization at present to replace it with another flight.

e. Aircraft depreciation is due entirely to obsolescence. Depreciation due to wear and tear is negligible.

f. Dropping flight 482 would not allow Pegasus Airlines to reduce the number of aircraft in its fleet or the number of flight crew on its payroll.

Required:

1. Prepare an analysis showing what impact dropping flight 482 would have on the airline's profits.
2. The airline's scheduling officer has been criticized because only about 50% of the seats on Pegasus' flights are being filled compared to an industry average of 60%. The scheduling officer has explained that Pegasus' average seat occupancy could be improved considerably by eliminating about 10% of its flights, but that doing so would reduce profits. Explain how this could happen.

PROBLEM 11–13A Dropping or Retaining a Segment [LO2]
The Regal Cycle Company manufactures three types of bicycles—a dirt bike, a mountain bike, and a racing bike. Data on sales and expenses for the past quarter follow:

CHECK FIGURE
(1) Discontinuing the racing bikes would decrease net operating income by $11,000

	Dirt Bikes	Mountain Bikes	Racing Bikes	Total
Sales	$90,000	$150,000	$60,000	$300,000
Less variable manufacturing and selling expenses	27,000	60,000	33,000	120,000
Contribution margin	63,000	90,000	27,000	180,000
Less fixed expenses:				
Advertising, traceable	10,000	14,000	6,000	30,000
Depreciation of special equipment	6,000	9,000	8,000	23,000
Salaries of product-line managers	12,000	13,000	10,000	35,000
Allocated common fixed expenses*	18,000	30,000	12,000	60,000
Total fixed expenses	46,000	66,000	36,000	148,000
Net operating income (loss)	$17,000	$ 24,000	$ (9,000)	$ 32,000

*Allocated on the basis of sales dollars.

Management is concerned about the continued losses shown by the racing bikes and wants a recommendation as to whether or not the line should be discontinued. The special equipment used to produce racing bikes has no resale value and does not wear out.

Required:
1. Should production and sale of the racing bikes be discontinued? Explain. Show computations to support your answer.
2. Recast the above data in a format that would be more usable to management in assessing the long-run profitability of the various product lines.

CHECK FIGURE
(1) The part can be made inside the company for $6 less per unit

PROBLEM 11–14A   Make or Buy a Component   [LO3]

Troy Engines, Ltd., manufactures a variety of engines for use in heavy equipment. The company has always produced all of the necessary parts for its engines, including all of the carburetors. An outside supplier has offered to sell one type of carburetor to Troy Engines, Ltd., for a cost of $35 per unit. To evaluate this offer, Troy Engines, Ltd., has gathered the following information relating to its own cost of producing the carburetor internally:

	Per Unit	15,000 Units per Year
Direct materials	$14	$210,000
Direct labor	10	150,000
Variable manufacturing overhead	3	45,000
Fixed manufacturing overhead, traceable	6*	90,000
Fixed manufacturing overhead, allocated	9	135,000
Total cost	$42	$630,000

*One-third supervisory salaries; two-thirds depreciation of special equipment (no resale value).

Required:
1. Assuming that the company has no alternative use for the facilities that are now being used to produce the carburetors, should the outside supplier's offer be accepted? Show all computations.
2. Suppose that if the carburetors were purchased, Troy Engines, Ltd., could use the freed capacity to launch a new product. The segment margin of the new product would be $150,000 per year. Should Troy Engines, Ltd., accept the offer to buy the carburetors for $35 per unit? Show all computations.

CHECK FIGURE
(1) Dropping housekeeping would decrease overall net operating income by $28,000.

PROBLEM 11–15A   Dropping or Retaining a Segment   (LO2)

Jackson County Senior Services is a nonprofit organization devoted to providing essential services to seniors who live in their own homes within the Jackson County area. Three services are provided for seniors—home nursing, meals on wheels, and housekeeping. In the home nursing program, nurses visit seniors on a regular basis to check on their general health and to perform tests ordered by their physicians. The meals on wheels program delivers a hot meal once a day to each senior enrolled in the program. The housekeeping service provides weekly housecleaning and maintenance services. Data on revenue and expenses for the past year follow:

	Home Nursing	Meals on Wheels	House-keeping	Total
Revenues	$260,000	$400,000	$240,000	$900,000
Less variable expenses	120,000	210,000	160,000	490,000
Contribution margin	140,000	190,000	80,000	410,000
Less fixed expenses:				
Depreciation	8,000	40,000	20,000	68,000
Liability insurance	20,000	7,000	15,000	42,000
Program administrators' salaries	40,000	38,000	37,000	115,000
General administrative overhead*	52,000	80,000	48,000	180,000
Total fixed expenses	120,000	165,000	120,000	405,000
Net operating income (loss)	$ 20,000	$ 25,000	$ (40,000)	$ 5,000

*Allocated on the basis of program revenues.

The head administrator of Jackson County Senior Services, Judith Miyama, is concerned about the organization's finances and considers the net operating income of $5,000 last year to be razor-thin. (Last year's results were very similar to the results for previous years and are representative of what would be expected in the future.) She feels that the organization should be building its financial reserves at a more rapid rate in order to prepare for the next inevitable recession. After seeing the above report, Ms. Miyama asked for more information about the financial advisability of perhaps discontinuing the housekeeping program.

The depreciation in housekeeping is for a small van that is used to carry the housekeepers and their equipment from job to job. If the program were discontinued, the van would be donated to a charitable organization. None of the general administrative overhead would be avoided if the housekeeping program were dropped, but the liability insurance and the salary of the program administrator would be avoided.

Required:

1. Should the housekeeping program be discontinued? Explain. Show computations to support your answer.
2. Recast the above data in a format that would be more useful to management in assessing the long-run financial viability of the various services.

PROBLEM 11-16A Shutting Down or Continuing to Operate a Plant [LO2]
(Note: This type of decision is similar to dropping a product line.)
Birch Company normally produces and sells 30,000 units of RG-6 each month. RG-6 is a small electrical relay used as a component part in the automotive industry. The selling price is $22 per unit, variable costs are $14 per unit, fixed manufacturing overhead costs total $150,000 per month, and fixed selling costs total $30,000 per month.

Employment-contract strikes in the companies that purchase the bulk of the RG-6 units have caused Birch Company's sales to temporarily drop to only 8,000 units per month. Birch Company estimates that the strikes will last for two months, after which time sales of RG-6 should return to normal. Due to the current low level of sales, Birch Company is thinking about closing down its own plant during the strike, which would reduce its fixed manufacturing overhead costs by $45,000 per month and its fixed selling costs by 10%. Start-up costs at the end of the shutdown period would total $8,000. Since Birch Company uses lean production methods, no inventories are on hand.

CHECK FIGURE
(1) $40,000 disadvantage to close

Required:

1. Assuming that the strikes continue for two months, would you recommend that Birch Company close its own plant? Explain. Show computations in good form.
2. At what level of sales (in units) for the two-month period should Birch Company be indifferent between closing the plant or keeping it open? Show computations. (Hint: This is a type of break-even analysis, except that the fixed cost portion of your break-even computation should include only those fixed costs that are relevant [i.e., avoidable] over the two-month period.)

PROBLEM 11-17A Make or Buy Analysis [LO3]
"In my opinion, we ought to stop making our own drums and accept that outside supplier's offer," said Wim Niewindt, managing director of Antilles Refining, N.V., of Aruba. "At a price of 18 florins per drum, we would be paying 5 florins less than it costs us to manufacture the drums in our own plant. (The currency in Aruba is the florin, denoted below by fl.) Since we use 60,000 drums a year, that would be an annual cost savings of 300,000 florins." Antilles Refining's present cost to manufacture one drum is given below (based on 60,000 drums per year):

CHECK FIGURE
(1) fl36,000 advantage to buy

Direct materials	fl10.35
Direct labor	6.00
Variable overhead	1.50
Fixed overhead (fl2.80 general company overhead, fl1.60 depreciation, and fl0.75 supervision)	5.15
Total cost per drum	fl23.00

A decision about whether to make or buy the drums is especially important at this time since the equipment being used to make the drums is completely worn out and must be replaced. The choices facing the company are:

Alternative 1: Rent new equipment and continue to make the drums. The equipment would be rented for fl135,000 per year.

Alternative 2: Purchase the drums from an outside supplier at fl18 per drum.

The new equipment would be more efficient than the equipment that Antilles Refining has been using and, according to the manufacturer, would reduce direct labor and variable overhead costs by 30%. The old equipment has no resale value. Supervision cost (fl45,000 per year) and direct materials cost per drum would not be affected by the new equipment. The new equipment's capacity would be 90,000 drums per year.

The company's total general company overhead would be unaffected by this decision.

Required:

1. To assist the managing director in making a decision, prepare an analysis showing the total cost and the cost per drum for each of the two alternatives given above. Assume that 60,000 drums are needed each year. Which course of action would you recommend to the managing director?
2. Would your recommendation in (1) above be the same if the company's needs were: (a) 75,000 drums per year or (b) 90,000 drums per year? Show computations to support your answer, with costs presented on both a total and a per unit basis.
3. What other factors would you recommend that the company consider before making a decision?

CHECK FIGURE
(1) Increased profit:
$65,000

eXcel

PROBLEM 11–18A   Accept or Reject a Special Order   [LO4]

Polaski Company manufactures and sells a single product called a Ret. Operating at capacity, the company can produce and sell 30,000 Rets per year. Costs associated with this level of production and sales are given below:

	Unit	Total
Direct materials............................	$15	$ 450,000
Direct labor	8	240,000
Variable manufacturing overhead	3	90,000
Fixed manufacturing overhead	9	270,000
Variable selling expense....................	4	120,000
Fixed selling expense......................	6	180,000
Total cost.................................	$45	$1,350,000

The Rets normally sell for $50 each. Fixed manufacturing overhead is constant at $270,000 per year within the range of 25,000 through 30,000 Rets per year.

Required:

1. Assume that due to a recession, Polaski Company expects to sell only 25,000 Rets through regular channels next year. A large retail chain has offered to purchase 5,000 Rets if Polaski is willing to accept a 16% discount off the regular price. There would be no sales commissions on this order; thus, variable selling expenses would be slashed by 75%. However, Polaski Company would have to purchase a special machine to engrave the retail chain's name on the 5,000 units. This machine would cost $10,000. Polaski Company has no assurance that the retail chain will purchase additional units in the future. Determine the impact on profits next year if this special order is accepted.
2. Refer to the original data. Assume again that Polaski Company expects to sell only 25,000 Rets through regular channels next year. The U.S. Army would like to make a one-time-only purchase of 5,000 Rets. The Army would pay a fixed fee of $1.80 per Ret, and it would reimburse Polaski Company for all costs of production (variable and fixed) associated with the units. Since the Army would pick up the Rets with its own trucks, there would be no variable selling expenses associated with this order. If Polaski Company accepts the order, by how much will profits increase or decrease for the year?
3. Assume the same situation as that described in (2) above, except that the company expects to sell 30,000 Rets through regular channels next year. Thus, accepting the U.S. Army's order would require giving up regular sales of 5,000 Rets. If the Army's order is accepted, by how much will profits increase or decrease from what they would be if the 5,000 Rets were sold through regular channels?

PROBLEM 11-19A Utilization of a Constrained Resource [LO5]

The Walton Toy Company manufactures a line of dolls and a doll dress sewing kit. Demand for the dolls is increasing, and management requests assistance from you in determining an economical sales and production mix for the coming year. The company has provided the following data:

	File Edit View Insert Format Tools Data Window Help						
	B I U D ≣ ≣ $ % , .00 .00 ≡ ≡ ✓ ⊞ ▾ A ▾ Euro						
	H10 fx						
	A	B	C	D	E	F	
1	Product	Demand Next Year (units)	Selling Price per Unit	Direct Materials	Direct Labor		
2	Debbie	50,000	$13.50	$4.30	$3.20		
3	Trish	42,000	$5.50	$1.10	$2.00		
4	Sarah	35,000	$21.00	$6.44	$5.60		
5	Mike	40,000	$10.00	$2.00	$4.00		
6	Sewing kit	325,000	$8.00	$3.20	$1.60		
7							

The following additional information is available:

a. The company's plant has a capacity of 130,000 direct labor-hours per year on a single-shift basis. The company's present employees and equipment can produce all five products.
b. The direct labor rate of $8 per hour is expected to remain unchanged during the coming year.
c. Fixed costs total $520,000 per year. Variable overhead costs are $2 per direct labor-hour.
d. All of the company's nonmanufacturing costs are fixed.
e. The company's finished goods inventory is negligible and can be ignored.

Required:

1. Determine the contribution margin per direct labor-hour expended on each product.
2. Prepare a schedule showing the total direct labor-hours that will be required to produce the units estimated to be sold during the coming year.
3. Examine the data you have computed in (1) and (2) above. How would you allocate the 130,000 direct labor hours of capacity to Walton Toy Company's various products?
4. What is the highest price, in terms of a rate per hour, that Walton Toy Company would be willing to pay for additional capacity (that is, for added direct labor time)?
5. Assume again that the company does not want to reduce sales of any product. Identify ways in which the company could obtain the additional output.

(CPA, adapted)

PROBLEM 11-20A Relevant Cost Analysis in a Variety of Situations [LO2, LO3, LO4]

Andretti Company has a single product called a Dak. The company normally produces and sells 60,000 Daks each year at a selling price of $32 per unit. The company's unit costs at this level of activity are given below:

Direct materials	$10.00	
Direct labor	4.50	
Variable manufacturing overhead	2.30	
Fixed manufacturing overhead	5.00	($300,000 total)
Variable selling expenses	1.20	
Fixed selling expenses	3.50	($210,000 total)
Total cost per unit	$26.50	

A number of questions relating to the production and sale of Daks follow. Each question is independent.

Required:

1. Assume that Andretti Company has sufficient capacity to produce 90,000 Daks each year without any increase in fixed manufacturing overhead costs. The company could increase its sales by 25% above the present 60,000 units each year if it were willing to increase the fixed selling expenses by $80,000. Would the increased fixed selling expenses be justified?

2. Assume again that Andretti Company has sufficient capacity to produce 90,000 Daks each year. A customer in a foreign market wants to purchase 20,000 Daks. Import duties on the Daks would be $1.70 per unit, and costs for permits and licenses would be $9,000. The only selling costs that would be associated with the order would be $3.20 per unit shipping cost. Compute the per unit break-even price on this order.

3. The company has 1,000 Daks on hand that have some irregularities and are therefore considered to be "seconds." Due to the irregularities, it will be impossible to sell these units at the normal price through regular distribution channels. What unit cost figure is relevant for setting a minimum selling price? Explain.

4. Due to a strike in its supplier's plant, Andretti Company is unable to purchase more material for the production of Daks. The strike is expected to last for two months. Andretti Company has enough material on hand to operate at 30% of normal levels for the two-month period. As an alternative, Andretti could close its plant down entirely for the two months. If the plant were closed, fixed manufacturing overhead costs would continue at 60% of their normal level during the two-month period and the fixed selling expenses would be reduced by 20%. What would be the impact on profits of closing the plant for the two-month period?

5. An outside manufacturer has offered to produce Daks and ship them directly to Andretti's customers. If Andretti Company accepts this offer, the facilities that it uses to produce Daks would be idle; however, fixed manufacturing overhead costs would be reduced by 75%. Since the outside manufacturer would pay for all shipping costs, the variable selling expenses would be only two-thirds of their present amount. Compute the unit cost that is relevant for comparison to the price quoted by the outside manufacturer.

BUILDING YOUR SKILLS

Teamwork in Action   (LO3, LO5)

Sportway, Inc., is a wholesale distributor supplying a wide range of moderately priced sporting equipment to large chain stores. About 60% of Sportway's products are purchased from other companies while the remainder of the products are manufactured by Sportway. The company has a Plastics Department that is currently manufacturing molded fishing tackle boxes. Sportway is able to manufacture and sell 8,000 tackle boxes annually, making full use of its direct labor capacity at available workstations. Presented below are the selling price and costs associated with Sportway's tackle boxes.

Selling price per box		$86.00
Cost per box:		
Molded plastic	$ 8.00	
Hinges, latches, handle	9.00	
Direct labor ($15 per hour)	18.75	
Manufacturing overhead	12.50	
Selling and administrative cost	17.00	65.25
Net operating income per box		$20.75

Because Sportway believes it could sell 12,000 tackle boxes if it had sufficient manufacturing capacity, the company has looked into the possibility of purchasing the tackle boxes for distribution. Maple Products, a steady supplier of quality products, would be able to provide up to 9,000 tackle boxes per year at a price of $68 per box delivered to Sportway's facility.

Traci Kader, Sportway's production manager, has suggested that the company could make better use of its Plastics Department by manufacturing skateboards. To support her position, Traci has a market study that indicates an expanding market for skateboards. Traci believes that Sportway could expect to sell 17,500 skateboards annually at a price of $45 per skateboard. Traci's estimate of the costs to manufacture the skateboards is presented below.

Selling price per skateboard		$45.00
Cost per skateboard:		
Molded plastic	$5.50	
Wheels, hardware	7.00	
Direct labor ($15 per hour)	7.50	
Manufacturing overhead	5.00	
Selling and administrative cost	9.00	34.00
Net operating income per skateboard		$11.00

In the Plastics Department, Sportway uses direct labor-hours as the allocation base for manufacturing overhead. Included in the manufacturing overhead for the current year is $50,000 of fixed overhead costs, of which 40% is traceable to the Plastics Department and 60% is allocated factorywide manufacturing overhead cost. The remaining manufacturing overhead cost is variable with respect to direct labor-hours. The skateboards could be produced with existing equipment and personnel in the Plastics Department.

For each unit of product that Sportway sells, regardless of whether the product has been purchased or is manufactured by Sportway, there is an allocated $6 fixed cost per unit for distribution. This $6 per unit is included in the selling and administrative cost for all products. The remaining amount of selling and administrative cost for all products—purchased or manufactured—is variable. The total selling and administrative cost figure for the purchased tackle boxes would be $10 per unit.

Required:
Your team should discuss and then respond to the following questions. All team members should agree with and understand the answers (including the calculations supporting the answers) and be prepared to report to the class. (Each teammate can assume responsibility for a different part of the presentation.)

1. Determine the number of direct labor-hours per year being used to manufacture tackle boxes.
2. Compute the contribution margin per unit for:
   a. Purchased tackle boxes.
   b. Manufactured tackle boxes.
   c. Manufactured skateboards.
3. Determine the number of tackle boxes (if any) that Sportway should purchase and the number of tackle boxes and/or skateboards that it should manufacture, and compute the improvement in net operating income that will result from this product mix over current operations.

(CMA, adapted)

Ethics Challenge   [LO2]

Haley Romeros had just been appointed vice president of the Rocky Mountain Region of the Bank Services Corporation (BSC). The company provides check processing services for small banks. The banks send checks presented for deposit or payment to BSC, which records the data on each check in a computerized database. BSC then sends the data electronically to the nearest Federal Reserve Bank check-clearing center where the appropriate transfers of funds are made between banks. The Rocky Mountain Region has three check processing centers, which are located in Billings, Montana; Great Falls, Montana; and Clayton, Idaho. Prior to her promotion to vice president, Ms. Romeros had been the manager of a check processing center in New Jersey.

Immediately upon assuming her new position, Ms. Romeros requested a complete financial report for the just-ended fiscal year from the region's controller, John Littlebear. Ms. Romeros specified that the financial report should follow the standardized format required by corporate headquarters for all regional performance reports. That report follows:

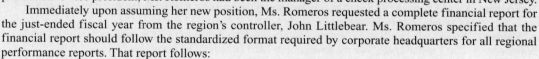

Bank Services Corporation (BSC)
Rocky Mountain Region
Financial Performance

| | Check Processing Centers | | | |
	Billings	Great Falls	Clayton	Total
Sales	$20,000,000	$18,000,000	$12,000,000	$50,000,000
Operating expenses:				
Direct labor	12,500,000	11,000,000	8,500,000	32,000,000
Variable overhead	350,000	310,000	190,000	850,000
Equipment depreciation	1,300,000	1,400,000	1,200,000	3,900,000
Facility expense	900,000	800,000	1,100,000	2,800,000
Local administrative expense*	140,000	160,000	150,000	450,000
Regional administrative expense†	600,000	540,000	360,000	1,500,000
Corporate administrative expense‡	1,900,000	1,710,000	1,140,000	4,750,000
Total operating expense	17,690,000	15,920,000	12,640,000	46,250,000
Net operating income	$ 2,310,000	$ 2,080,000	$ (640,000)	$ 3,750,000

*Local administrative expenses are the administrative expenses incurred at the check processing centers.
†Regional administrative expenses are allocated to the check processing centers based on sales.
‡Corporate administrative expenses are charged to segments of the company such as the Rocky Mountain Region and the check processing centers at the rate of 9.5% of their sales.

Upon seeing this report, Ms. Romeros summoned John Littlebear for an explanation.

Romeros: What's the story on Clayton? It didn't have a loss the previous year did it?

Littlebear: No, the Clayton facility has had a nice profit every year since it was opened six years ago, but Clayton lost a big contract this year.

Romeros: Why?

Littlebear: One of our national competitors entered the local market and bid very aggressively on the contract. We couldn't afford to meet the bid. Clayton's costs—particularly their facility expenses—are just too high. When Clayton lost the contract, we had to lay off a lot of employees, but we could not reduce the fixed costs of the Clayton facility.

Romeros: Why is Clayton's facility expense so high? It's a smaller facility than either Billings or Great Falls and yet its facility expense is higher.

Littlebear: The problem is that we are able to rent suitable facilities very cheaply at Billings and Great Falls. No such facilities were available at Clayton; we had them built. Unfortunately, there were big cost overruns. The contractor we hired was inexperienced at this kind of work and in fact went bankrupt before the project was completed. After hiring another contractor to finish the work, we were way over budget. The large depreciation charges on the facility didn't matter at first because we didn't have much competition at the time and could charge premium prices.

Romeros: Well we can't do that anymore. The Clayton facility will obviously have to be shut down. Its business can be shifted to the other two check processing centers in the region.

Littlebear: I would advise against that. The $1,200,000 in depreciation at the Clayton facility is misleading. That facility should last indefinitely with proper maintenance. And it has no resale value; there is no other commercial activity around Clayton.

Romeros: What about the other costs at Clayton?

Littlebear: If we shifted Clayton's business over to the other two processing centers in the region, we wouldn't save anything on direct labor or variable overhead costs. We might save $90,000 or so in local administrative expense, but we would not save any regional administrative expense and corporate headquarters would still charge us 9.5% of our sales as corporate administrative expense.

In addition, we would have to rent more space in Billings and Great Falls in order to handle the work transferred from Clayton; that would probably cost us at least $600,000 a year. And don't forget that it will cost us something to move the equipment from Clayton to Billings and Great Falls. And the move will disrupt service to customers.

Romeros: I understand all of that, but a money-losing processing center on my performance report is completely unacceptable.

Littlebear: And if you shut down Clayton, you are going to throw some loyal employees out of work.

Romeros: That's unfortunate, but we have to face hard business realities.

Littlebear: And you would have to write off the investment in the facilities at Clayton.

Romeros: I can explain a write-off to corporate headquarters; hiring an inexperienced contractor to build the Clayton facility was my predecessor's mistake. But they'll have my head at headquarters if I show operating losses every year at one of my processing centers. Clayton has to go. At the next corporate board meeting, I am going to recommend that the Clayton facility be closed.

Required:

1. From the standpoint of the company as a whole, should the Clayton processing center be shut down and its work redistributed to other processing centers in the region? Explain.
2. Do you think Haley Romeros's decision to shut down the Clayton facility is ethical? Explain.
3. What influence should the depreciation on the facilities at Clayton have on prices charged by Clayton for its services?

CHECK FIGURE
(1) $0.20 savings per box to make

Communicating in Practice (LO3)

Silven Industries, which manufactures and sells a highly successful line of summer lotions and insect repellents, has decided to diversify in order to stabilize sales throughout the year. A natural area for the company to consider is the production of winter lotions and creams to prevent dry and chapped skin.

After considerable research, a winter products line has been developed. However, Bob Murdock, Silven's president, has decided to introduce only one of the new products for this coming winter. If the product is a success, further expansion in future years will be initiated.

The product selected (called Chap-Off) is a lip balm that will be sold in a lipstick-type tube. The product will be sold to wholesalers in boxes of 24 tubes for $8 per box. Because of excess capacity, no additional fixed manufacturing overhead costs will be incurred to produce the product. However, a $90,000 charge for fixed manufacturing overhead will be absorbed by the product under the company's absorption costing system.

Using the production and sales estimates of 100,000 boxes of Chap-Off, the Accounting Department has developed the following cost per box:

Direct material	$3.60
Direct labor	2.00
Manufacturing overhead	1.40
Total cost	$7.00

The costs above include costs for producing both the lip balm and the tube that contains it. As an alternative to making the tubes, Silven has approached a supplier to discuss the possibility of purchasing the tubes for Chap-Off. The purchase price of the empty tubes from the supplier would be $1.35 per box of 24 tubes. If Silven Industries accepts the purchase proposal, direct labor and variable manufacturing overhead costs per box of Chap-Off would be reduced by 10% and direct materials costs would be reduced by 25%.

Required:

Write a memorandum to the president that answers the following questions. Use headings to organize the information presented in the memorandum. Include computations to support your answers where appropriate.

1. Should Silven Industries make the tubes for the lip balm or buy them from the supplier? How much would be saved by making this decision?
2. What is the maximum purchase price that would be acceptable to Silven Industries if the tubes for the lip balm were bought from a supplier?
3. As noted above, the Accounting Department assumed that 100,000 boxes of Chap-Off would be produced and sold. However, the vice president of sales estimates that 120,000 boxes of Chap-Off can be sold. This higher volume would require additional equipment at an annual rental of $40,000. Assuming the company buys the tubes from the supplier at $1.35 per box of 24 tubes and that the supplier will not accept an order for less than 100,000 boxes of tubes, should Silven Industries make the tubes for the lip balm or buy them from the supplier? What are the total costs of producing 120,000 boxes of Chap-Off assuming that the company makes the tubes? What are the total costs assuming that the company buys the tubes? How much would be saved by buying the tubes rather than making them internally?
4. Refer to the information in (3) above. Assume that a different supplier will accept an order of any size for the tubes at $1.35 per box of 24 tubes. Should Silven Industries make the tubes for the lip balm or buy them from the supplier?
5. What qualitative factors should be considered in this make or buy decision?

(CMA, heavily adapted)

Analytical Thinking   [LO2]

Tracey Douglas is the owner and managing director of Heritage Garden Furniture, Ltd., a South African company that makes museum-quality reproductions of antique outdoor furniture. Ms. Douglas would like advice concerning the advisability of eliminating the model C3 lawnchair. These lawnchairs have been among the company's best-selling products, but they seem to be unprofitable.

A condensed absorption costing income statement for the company and for the model C3 lawnchair for the quarter ended June 30 follows:

CHECK FIGURE
(2) Minimum sales: R60,000

	All Products	Model C3 Lawnchair
Sales...	R2,900,000	R300,000
Cost of goods sold:		
Direct materials......................................	759,000	122,000
Direct labor...	680,000	72,000
Fringe benefits (20% of direct labor)....................	136,000	14,400
Variable manufacturing overhead	28,000	3,600
Building rent and maintenance	30,000	4,000
Depreciation	75,000	19,100
Total cost of goods sold...........................	1,708,000	235,100
Gross margin	1,192,000	64,900

(continued)

(concluded)		Model C3
	All Products	**Lawnchair**
Selling and administrative expenses:		
Product managers' salaries	75,000	10,000
Sales commissions (5% of sales)	145,000	15,000
Fringe benefits (20% of salaries and commissions)	44,000	5,000
Shipping	120,000	10,000
General administrative expenses	464,000	48,000
Total selling and administrative expenses	848,000	88,000
Net operating income (loss).	R 344,000	R (23,100)
The currency in South Africa is the rand, denoted here by R.		

The following additional data have been supplied by the company:

a. Direct labor is a variable cost.
b. All of the company's products are manufactured in the same facility and use the same equipment. Building rent and maintenance and depreciation are allocated to products using various bases. The equipment does not wear out through use; it eventually becomes obsolete.
c. There is ample capacity to fill all orders.
d. Dropping the model C3 lawnchair would have no effect on sales of other product lines.
e. Work in process and finished goods inventories are insignificant.
f. Shipping costs are traced directly to products.
g. General administrative expenses are allocated to products on the basis of sales dollars. There would be no effect on the total general administrative expenses if the model C3 lawnchair were dropped.
h. If the model C3 lawnchair were dropped, the product manager would be laid off.

Required:
1. Given the current level of sales, would you recommend that the model C3 lawnchair be dropped? Prepare appropriate computations to support your answer.
2. What would sales of the model C3 lawnchair have to be, at minimum, in order to justify retaining the product? Explain. (Hint: Set this up as a break-even problem but include only the relevant costs.)

Taking It to the Net
As you know, the World Wide Web is a medium that is constantly evolving. Sites come and go and change without notice. To enable periodic updating of site addresses, these problems have been posted to the textbook website (www.mhhe.com/bgn3e). After accessing the site, enter the Student Center and select this chapter to find the Taking It to the Net problems.

12

Capital Budgeting Decisions

CHAPTER OUTLINE

DECISION FEATURE

Invest Less, Make More

Steven Burd became the CEO of Safeway, one of the largest food and drug retailers in North America, in 1992. At the time, Safeway was operating approximately 1,100 stores, which occupied approximately 39 million square feet of retail space. Burd immediately slashed annual capital spending from $550 million to $290 million. He justified the decision as follows: "We had projects that were not returning the cost of money. So we cut spending back, which made the very best projects come to the surface."

Safeway set a minimum 22.5% pretax return on investment in all new store and remodeling projects. In addition to opening new stores, Burd felt that the company could increase sales by expanding existing stores that are in excellent locations. With its new approach to capital budgeting firmly in place, Safeway started to steadily increase its capital spending on both new stores and remodeling projects. Ten years after implementing the new decision-making process, Safeway's 1,782 stores occupied 78.8 million square feet of retail space.

———

Sources: Safeway, Inc., website; and Robert Berner, "Safeway's Resurgence Is Built on Attention to Detail," *The Wall Street Journal,* October 2, 1998, p. B4.

The term **capital budgeting** is used to describe how managers plan significant outlays on projects that have long-term implications, such as the purchase of new equipment and the introduction of new products. Most companies have many more potential projects than can actually be funded. Hence, managers must carefully select those projects that promise the greatest future return. How well managers make these capital budgeting decisions is a critical factor in the long-run profitability of the company.

Capital budgeting involves *investment*—a company must commit funds now in order to receive a return in the future. Investments are not limited to stocks and bonds. Purchase of inventory or equipment is also an investment. For example, Tri-Con Global Restaurants Inc. makes an investment when it opens a new Pizza Hut restaurant. L. L. Bean makes an investment when it installs a new computer to handle customer billing. DaimlerChrysler makes an investment when it redesigns a product such as the Jeep Eagle and must retool its production lines. Merck & Co. invests in medical research. Amazon.com makes an investment when it redesigns its website. All of these investments require committing funds today with the expectation of earning a return on these funds in the future in the form of additional cash inflows or reduced cash outflows.

CAPITAL BUDGETING—PLANNING INVESTMENTS

Typical Capital Budgeting Decisions

Virtually any decision that involves an outlay now in order to obtain some future return is a capital budgeting decision. Typical capital budgeting decisions include:

1. Cost reduction decisions: Should new equipment be purchased to reduce costs?
2. Expansion decisions: Should a new plant, warehouse, or other facility be acquired to increase capacity and sales?
3. Equipment selection decisions: Which of several available machines should be purchased?
4. Lease or buy decisions: Should new equipment be leased or purchased?
5. Equipment replacement decisions: Should old equipment be replaced now or later?

Capital budgeting decisions fall into two broad categories—*screening decisions* and *preference decisions.* **Screening decisions** relate to whether a proposed project passes a preset hurdle. For example, a company may have a policy of accepting projects only if they promise a return of 20% on the investment. The required rate of return is the minimum rate of return a project must yield to be acceptable.

Preference decisions, by contrast, relate to selecting from among several *competing* courses of action. To illustrate, a company may be considering several different machines to replace an existing machine on the assembly line. The choice of which machine to purchase is a *preference* decision.

In this chapter, we initially discuss ways of making screening decisions. Preference decisions are discussed toward the end of the chapter.

The Time Value of Money

As stated earlier, capital investments usually earn returns that extend over fairly long periods of time. Therefore, when evaluating investment proposals, methods should be used that recognize *the time value of money.* A dollar today is worth more than a dollar a year from now because you can put the dollar you own today in a bank and have more than a dollar a year from now. Therefore, projects that promise earlier returns are preferable to those that promise later returns.

Capital budgeting techniques that recognize the time value of money use *discounted cash flows.* We will spend most of this chapter showing how to use discounted cash flow methods in making capital budgeting decisions. If you are not already familiar with discounting and the use of present value tables, you should read Appendix 12A, The Concept of Present Value, at the end of this chapter before proceeding any further.

Several approaches can be used to evaluate investments using discounted cash flows. The easiest method to use is the *net present value method,* which is the subject of the next several sections.

Screening versus Preference Decisions

Screening Decisions   **Preference Decisions**

IN BUSINESS

Choosing a Cat

Sometimes a long-term decision does not have to involve present value calculations or any other sophisticated analytical technique. White Grizzly Adventures of Meadow Creek, British Columbia, needs two snowcats for its powder skiing operations—one for shuttling guests to the top of the mountain and one to be held in reserve in case of mechanical problems with the first. Bombardier of Canada sells new snowcats for $250,000 and used, reconditioned snowcats for $150,000. In either case, the snowcats are good for about 5,000 hours of operation before they need to be reconditioned. From White Grizzly's perspective, the choice is clear. Since both new and reconditioned snowcats last about 5,000 hours, but the reconditioned snowcats cost $100,000 less, the reconditioned snowcats are the obvious choice. They may not have all of the latest bells and whistles, but they get the job done at a price a small operation can afford.

Bombardier snowcats do not have passenger cabs as standard equipment. To save money, White Grizzly builds its own custom-designed passenger cab for about $15,000, using recycled Ford Escort seats and industrial-strength aluminum for the frame and siding. If purchased retail, a passenger cab would cost about twice as much and would not be as well-suited for snowcat skiing.

Source: Brad & Carole Karafil, owners and operators of White Grizzly Adventures, www.whitegrizzly.com.

THE NET PRESENT VALUE METHOD

Concept 12-1

Under the net present value method, the present value of a project's cash inflows is compared to the present values of the project's cash outflows. The difference between the present values of these cash flows, called the **net present value,** determines whether or not the project is an acceptable investment. To illustrate, consider the following data:

> **Example A** Harper Company is contemplating the purchase of a machine capable of performing certain operations that are now performed manually. The machine will cost $50,000, and it will last for five years. At the end of the five-year period, the machine will have a zero scrap value. Use of the machine will reduce labor costs by $18,000 per year. Harper Company requires a minimum pretax return of 20% on all investment projects.[1]

Should the machine be purchased? Harper Company must determine whether a cash investment now of $50,000 can be justified if it will result in an $18,000 reduction in cost each year over the next five years. It may appear that the answer is obvious since the total cost savings is $90,000 ($18,000 per year × 5 years). However, the company can earn a 20% return by investing its money elsewhere. It is not enough that the cost reductions cover just the original cost of the machine; they must also yield a return of at least 20% or the company would be better off investing the money elsewhere.

To determine whether the investment is desirable, the stream of annual $18,000 cost savings should be discounted to its present value and then compared to the cost of the new machine. Since Harper Company requires a minimum return of 20% on all investment projects, this rate is used in the discounting process and is called the *discount rate.* Exhibit 12–1 shows how to compute the net present value of this investment opportunity.

According to the analysis, Harper Company should purchase the new machine. The present value of the cost savings is $53,838, whereas the present value of the required

---

[1]For simplicity, we ignore inflation and taxes. The impact of inflation and income taxes on capital budgeting decisions is discussed in Appendices 14B and 14D of Ray Garrison, Eric Noreen, and Peter Brewer, *Managerial Accounting,* 11th edition, McGraw-Hill, 2006.

Initial cost			$50,000	
Life of the project			5 years	
Annual cost savings			$18,000	
Salvage value			$0	
Required rate of return			20%	

Item	Year(s)	Amount of Cash Flow	20% Factor	Present Value of Cash Flows
Annual cost savings........	1–5	$18,000	2.991*	$53,838
Initial investment	Now	$(50,000)	1.000	(50,000)
Net present value.........				$ 3,838

*From Table 12B–4 in Appendix 12B at the end of this chapter.

EXHIBIT 12–1

Net Present Value Analysis of a Proposed Project

investment (cost of the machine) is only $50,000. Deducting the present value of the required investment from the present value of the cost savings gives the *net present value* of $3,838. Whenever the net present value is zero or greater, as in our example, an investment project is acceptable. Whenever the net present value is negative (the present value of the cash outflows exceeds the present value of the cash inflows), an investment project is not acceptable. In sum:

If the Net Present Value Is ...	Then the Project Is ...
Positive	Acceptable, since it promises a return greater than the required rate of return.
Zero	Acceptable, since it promises a return equal to the required rate of return.
Negative	Not acceptable, since it promises a return less than the required rate of return.

There is another way to interpret the net present value. The new machine promises more than the required 20% rate of return. This is evident from the positive net present value of $3,838. Harper Company could spend up to $53,838 for the new machine and still obtain the minimum required 20% rate of return. The net present value of $3,838, therefore, shows the amount of "cushion" or "margin of error." One way to look at this is that the company could underestimate the cost of the new machine by up to $3,838, or overestimate the net present value of the future cash savings by up to $3,838, and the project would still be financially attractive.

Emphasis on Cash Flows

In capital budgeting decisions, the focus is on cash flows and not on accounting net income. The reason is that accounting net income is based on accrual concepts that ignore the timing of cash flows into and out of an organization. From a capital budgeting standpoint, the timing of cash flows is important, since a dollar received today is more valuable than a dollar received in the future. Therefore, even though accounting net income is useful for many things, it is not ordinarily used in discounted cash flow analysis.[2] Instead of focusing on accounting net income, the analyst should concentrate on identifying the specific cash flows of the investment project.

[2]Under certain conditions, capital budgeting decisions can be correctly made by discounting appropriately defined accounting net income. However, this approach requires advanced techniques that are beyond the scope of this book.

What kinds of cash flows should the analyst look for? Although they will vary from project to project, certain types of cash flows tend to recur as explained in the following paragraphs.

Typical Cash Outflows   Most projects will have an immediate cash outflow in the form of an initial investment in equipment or other assets. Any salvage value realized from the sale of old equipment can be recognized as a cash inflow or as a reduction in the required investment. In addition, some projects require that a company expand its working capital. **Working capital** is current assets (cash, accounts receivable, and inventory) less current liabilities. When a company takes on a new project, the balances in the current asset accounts will often increase. For example, opening a new Nordstrom's department store would require additional cash in sales registers and more inventory. These additional working capital needs should be treated as part of the initial investment in a project. Also, many projects require periodic outlays for repairs and maintenance and for additional operating costs. These should all be treated as cash outflows for capital budgeting purposes.

Typical Cash Inflows   On the cash inflow side, a project will normally either increase revenues or reduce costs. Either way, the amount involved should be treated as a cash inflow for capital budgeting purposes. Notice that, from the standpoint of cash flows, *a reduction in costs is equivalent to an increase in revenues.* Cash inflows are also frequently realized from selling equipment for its salvage value when a project ends, although in some cases the company may actually have to pay to dispose of low-value or hazardous items. In addition, any working capital that was tied up in the project can be released for use elsewhere at the end of the project and should be treated as a cash inflow. Working capital is released, for example, when a company sells off its inventory or collects its accounts receivable.

In summary, the following types of cash flows are common in business investment projects:

Cash outflows:
  Initial investment (including installation costs).
  Increased working capital needs.
  Repairs and maintenance.
  Incremental operating costs.
Cash inflows:
  Incremental revenues.
  Reduction in costs.
  Salvage value.
  Release of working capital.

IN BUSINESS

Hazardous PCs

Disposing of old equipment can be difficult and costly—particularly when disposal is governed by environmental regulations. For example, computer equipment often contains lead and other substances that could contaminate the air, soil, or groundwater. Cindy Brethauer, the network administrator for 1st Choice Bank, in Greeley, Colorado, was faced with the mounting problem of storing old monitors, printers, and personal computers that could not be simply thrown away. These bulky items were constantly being shuttled back and forth from one storage space to another. For help, she turned to Technology Recycling LLC, which hauls away old computers and peripherals for $35 per component. Technology LLC strips the machines, recycling some of the materials and taking environmentally sensitive materials to disposal facilities approved by the Environmental Protection Agency. Technology LLC handles the complicated paperwork for its customers.

Source: Jill Hecht Maxwell, *Inc. Tech,* 2000, 1, p. 25.

Simplifying Assumptions

Two simplifying assumptions are usually made in net present value analysis.

The first assumption is that all cash flows other than the initial investment occur at the end of periods. This is somewhat unrealistic in that cash flows typically occur *throughout* a period rather than just at its end. The purpose of this assumption is to simplify computations. The second assumption is that all cash flows generated by an investment project are immediately reinvested at a rate of return equal to the discount rate. Unless these conditions are met, the net present value computed for the project will not be accurate.

A Return on Investment of 100%

During negotiations to build a replacement for the old Fenway Park in Boston, the Red Sox offered the city approximately $2 million per year over 30 years in exchange for an investment of $150 million by the city for land acquisition and cleanup. In May 2000, after denying his lack of support for the project, Boston Mayor Thomas M. Menino stated that his goal is a 100% rate of return on any investment that is made by the city. Some doubt that the Red Sox would be able to pay players' salaries if the team were required to meet the mayor's goal. The mayor has countered with a list of suggestions for raising private funds (such as selling shares to the public, as the city's pro basketball team the Celtics did in 1986). Private funds would reduce the investment that would need to be made by the city and, as a result, reduce the future payments made to the city by the Red Sox.

Source: Meg Vaillancourt, "Boston Mayor Wants High Return on Investment in New Ballpark," *Knight-Ridder/Tribune Business News,* May 11, 2000, pITEM00133018.

Choosing a Discount Rate

A positive net present value indicates that the project's return exceeds the discount rate. A negative net present value indicates that the project's return is less than the discount rate. Therefore, if the company's minimum required rate of return is used as the discount rate, a project with a positive net present value is acceptable and a project with a negative net present value is unacceptable.

The company's *cost of capital* is usually regarded as the minimum required rate of return. The **cost of capital** is the average rate of return the company must pay to its long-term creditors and to shareholders for using their funds. The cost of capital is the minimum required rate of return because if a project's rate of return is less than the cost of capital, the company does not earn enough of a return to compensate its creditors and shareholders. Therefore, any project with a rate of return less than the cost of capital should be rejected.

The cost of capital serves as a *screening device* in net present value analysis. When the cost of capital is used as the discount rate, any project with a negative net present value does not cover the company's cost of capital and should be discarded as unacceptable.

Negotiator for the Red Sox

As stated in the In Business above, Boston Mayor Thomas M. Menino's goal is a 100% rate of return on any investment that is made by the city to build a new park for the Red Sox. How would you respond to the mayor?

An Extended Example of the Net Present Value Method

Example B presents an extended example of how the net present value method is used to analyze an investment proposal. This example helps to tie together (and reinforce) many of the ideas developed thus far.

Example B   Under a special licensing arrangement, Swinyard Company has an opportunity to market a new product for a five-year period. The product would be purchased from the manufacturer, with Swinyard Company responsible for promotion and distribution costs. The licensing arrangement could be renewed at the end of the five-year period. After careful study, Swinyard Company has estimated the following costs and revenues for the new product:

Cost of equipment needed	$60,000
Working capital needed	$100,000
Overhaul of the equipment in four years	$5,000
Salvage value of the equipment in five years	$10,000
Annual revenues and costs:	
Sales revenues	$200,000
Cost of goods sold	$125,000
Out-of-pocket operating costs (for salaries,	
advertising, and other direct costs)	$35,000

At the end of the five-year period, if Swinyard decides not to renew the licensing arrangement, the working capital would be released for investment elsewhere. Swinyard Company uses a 14% discount rate. Would you recommend that the new product be introduced?

This example involves a variety of cash inflows and cash outflows. The solution is given in Exhibit 12–2.

EXHIBIT 12–2   The Net Present Value Method—An Extended Example

Sales revenues	$200,000
Less cost of goods sold	125,000
Less out-of-pocket costs for	
salaries, advertising, etc.	35,000
Annual net cash inflows	$ 40,000

Item	Year(s)	Amount of Cash Flows	14% Factor	Present Value of Cash Flows
Purchase of equipment	Now	$(60,000)	1.000	$ (60,000)
Working capital needed	Now	$(100,000)	1.000	(100,000)
Overhaul of equipment	4	$(5,000)	0.592*	(2,960)
Annual net cash inflows from sales				
of the product line	1–5	$40,000	3.433†	137,320
Salvage value of the equipment	5	$10,000	0.519*	5,190
Working capital released	5	$100,000	0.519*	51,900
Net present value				$ 31,450

*From Table 12B–3 in Appendix 12B.
†From Table 12B–4 in Appendix 12B.

Notice how the working capital is handled in this exhibit. It is counted as a cash outflow at the beginning of the project and as a cash inflow when it is released at the end of the project. Also notice how the sales revenues, cost of goods sold, and out-of-pocket costs are handled. **Out-of-pocket costs** are actual cash outlays for salaries, advertising, and other operating expenses. Depreciation is not an out-of-pocket cost because it involves no current cash outlay.

Since the net present value is positive, the new product should be added assuming the company has no better use for the investment funds.

EXPANDING THE NET PRESENT VALUE METHOD

So far, our examples have involved only a single investment alternative. We will now expand our discussion of the net present value method to include two alternatives. In addition, we will integrate the concept of relevant costs into the discounted cash flow analysis.

The net present value method can be used to compare competing investment projects in two ways. One is the *total-cost approach,* and the other is the *incremental-cost approach.* Each approach is illustrated in the next few pages.

The Total-Cost Approach

The total-cost approach is the most flexible method for comparing projects. To illustrate the mechanics of the approach, consider the following data:

Example C   Harper Ferry Company provides a ferry service across the Mississippi River. One of its small ferryboats is in poor condition. This ferry can be renovated at an immediate cost of $200,000. Further repairs and an overhaul of the motor will be needed five years from now at a cost of $80,000. In all, the ferry will be usable for 10 years if this work is done. At the end of 10 years, the ferry will have to be scrapped at a salvage value of approximately $60,000. The scrap value of the ferry right now is $70,000. It will cost $300,000 each year to operate the ferry, and revenues will total $400,000 annually.

As an alternative, Harper Ferry Company can purchase a new ferryboat at a cost of $360,000. The new ferry will have a life of 10 years, but it will require some repairs costing $30,000 at the end of 5 years. At the end of 10 years, the ferry will have a scrap value of $60,000. It will cost $210,000 each year to operate the ferry, and revenues will total $400,000 annually.

Harper Ferry Company requires a return of at least 14% before taxes on all investment projects.

Should the company purchase the new ferry or renovate the old ferry? Exhibit 12–3 gives the solution using the total-cost approach.

Two points should be noted from the exhibit. First, *all* cash inflows and *all* cash outflows are included in the solution under each alternative. No effort has been made to isolate those cash flows that are relevant to the decision and those that are not relevant. The inclusion of all cash flows associated with each alternative gives the approach its name—the *total-cost* approach.

Second, notice that the net present value is computed for each of the two alternatives. This is a distinct advantage of the total-cost approach in that an unlimited number of alternatives can be compared side by side to determine the best option. For example, another alternative for Harper Ferry Company would be to get out of the ferry business entirely. If management desired, the net present value of this alternative could be computed to compare with the alternatives shown in Exhibit 12–3. Still other alternatives might be open to the company. Once management has determined the net

EXHIBIT 12–3   The Total-Cost Approach to Project Selection

		New Ferry	Old Ferry
Annual revenues		$400,000	$400,000
Annual cash operating costs		210,000	300,000
Net annual cash inflows		$190,000	$100,000

Item	Year(s)	Amount of Cash Flows	14% Factor*	Present Value of Cash Flows
Buy the new ferry:				
Initial investment	Now	$(360,000)	1.000	$(360,000)
Salvage value of the old ferry	Now	$70,000	1.000	70,000
Repairs in five years	5	$(30,000)	0.519	(15,570)
Net annual cash inflows	1–10	$190,000	5.216	991,040
Salvage value of the new ferry	10	$60,000	0.270	16,200
Net present value				701,670
Keep the old ferry:				
Renovation	Now	$(200,000)	1.000	(200,000)
Repairs in five years	5	$(80,000)	0.519	(41,520)
Net annual cash inflows	1–10	$100,000	5.216	521,600
Salvage value of the old ferry	10	$60,000	0.270	16,200
Net present value				296,280
Net present value in favor of buying the new ferry				$ 405,390

*All present value factors are from Tables 12B–3 and 12B–4 in Appendix 12B.

present value of each alternative, it can select the option that promises to be the most profitable. In the case at hand, given only two alternatives, the best alternative is to purchase the new ferry.[3]

Does It Really Need to Be New?

Tom Copeland, the director of Corporate Finance Practice at the consulting firm Monitor Group, observes: "If they could afford it, most people would like to drive a new car. Managers are no different . . . [I]n my experience, . . . [managers] routinely spend millions of dollars on new machines years earlier than they need to. In most cases, the overall cost (including the cost of breakdowns) is 30% to 40% lower if a company continues servicing an existing machine for five more years instead of buying a new one. In order to fight impulsive acquisitions of new machinery, companies should require unit managers to run the numbers on all alternative investment options open to them—including maintaining the existing assets or buying used ones."

Source: Tom Copeland, "Cutting Costs Without Drawing Blood," *Harvard Business Review*, September–October 2000, pp. 3–7.

The Incremental-Cost Approach

When only two alternatives are being considered, the incremental-cost approach offers a simpler and more direct route to a decision. Unlike the total-cost approach, it includes in the discounted cash flow analysis only those costs and revenues that *differ* between the

---

[3]The alternative with the highest net present value is not always the best choice, although it is the best choice in this case. For further discussion, see the section Preference Decisions—The Ranking of Investment Projects.

EXHIBIT 12–4   The Incremental-Cost Approach to Project Selection

Item	Year(s)	Amount of Cash Flows	14% Factor*	Present Value of Cash Flows
Incremental investment to buy the new ferry	Now	$(160,000)	1.000	$(160,000)
Salvage value of the old ferry now	Now	$70,000	1.000	70,000
Difference in repairs in five years	5	$50,000	0.519	25,950
Increase in net annual cash inflows	1–10	$90,000	5.216	469,440
Difference in salvage value in 10 years	10	$0	0.270	0
Net present value in favor of buying the new ferry				$ 405,390

*All present value factors are from Tables 12B–3 and 12B–4 in Appendix 12B.

two alternatives being considered. To illustrate, refer again to the data in Example C relating to Harper Ferry Company. The solution using only differential costs is presented in Exhibit 12–4.[4]

Two things should be noted from the data in this exhibit. First, the net present value in favor of buying the new ferry of $405,390 shown in Exhibit 12–4 agrees with the net present value shown under the total-cost approach in Exhibit 12–3. The two approaches are just different roads to the same destination.

Second, notice that the costs used in Exhibit 12–4 are just the differences between the costs shown for the two alternatives in the prior exhibit. For example, the $160,000 incremental investment required to purchase the new ferry in Exhibit 12–4 is the difference between the $360,000 cost of the new ferry and the $200,000 cost required to renovate the old ferry from Exhibit 12–3. The other figures in Exhibit 12–4 have been computed in the same way.

Least-Cost Decisions

Revenues (and cash inflows) are not directly involved in some decisions. For example, a company that does not charge for delivery service may need to replace an old delivery truck, or a company may be trying to decide whether to lease or buy its fleet of company cars. In situations such as these, where no revenues are involved, the most desirable alternative is the one that promises the *least total cost* from the present value perspective. Hence, these are known as least-cost decisions. To illustrate a least-cost decision, assume the following data:

Example D   Val-Tek Company is considering replacing an old threading machine. A new threading machine is available that would substantially reduce annual operating costs. Selected data relating to the old and the new machines are presented below:

	Old Machine	New Machine
Purchase cost when new	$200,000	$250,000
Salvage value now	$30,000	—
Annual cash operating costs	$150,000	$90,000
Overhaul needed immediately	$40,000	—
Salvage value in six years	$0	$50,000
Remaining life	6 years	6 years

Val-Tek Company uses a 10% discount rate.

---

[4]Technically, the incremental-cost approach is misnamed, since it focuses on differential costs (that is, on both cost increases and decreases) rather than just on incremental costs. As used here, the term *incremental costs* should be interpreted broadly to include both cost increases and cost decreases.

EXHIBIT 12–5   The Total-Cost Approach (Least-Cost Decision)

Item	Year(s)	Amount of Cash Flows	10% Factor*	Present Value of Cash Flows
Buy the new machine:				
Initial investment	Now	$(250,000)	1.000	$(250,000)†
Salvage value of the old machine	Now	$30,000	1.000	30,000†
Annual cash operating costs	1–6	$(90,000)	4.355	(391,950)
Salvage value of the new machine	6	$50,000	0.564	28,200
Present value of net cash outflows				(583,750)
Keep the old machine:				
Overhaul needed now	Now	$(40,000)	1.000	(40,000)
Annual cash operating costs	1–6	$(150,000)	4.355	(653,250)
Present value of net cash outflows				(693,250)
Net present value in favor of				
buying the new machine				$ 109,500

*All factors are from Tables 12B–3 and 12B–4 in Appendix 12B.
†These two items could be netted into a single $220,000 incremental-cost figure ($250,000 − $30,000 = $220,000).

Exhibit 12–5 analyzes the alternatives using the total-cost approach.

As shown in the exhibit, the new machine has the lowest total cost in terms of the present value of the net cash outflows. An analysis of the two alternatives using the incremental-cost approach is presented in Exhibit 12–6. As before, the data in this exhibit represent the differences between the alternatives as shown under the total-cost approach.

CONCEPT CHECK

1. Which of the following statements is false? (You may select more than one answer.)
   a. The total-cost and incremental-cost approaches to net present value analysis can occasionally lead to conflicting results.
   b. The cost of capital is a screening mechanism for net present value analysis.
   c. The present value of a dollar increases as the time of receipt extends further into the future.
   d. The higher the cost of capital, the lower the present value of a dollar received in the future.

EXHIBIT 12–6   The Incremental-Cost Approach (Least-Cost Decision)

Item	Year(s)	Amount of Cash Flows	10% Factor*	Present Value of Cash Flows
Incremental investment required to				
purchase the new machine	Now	$(210,000)	1.000	$(210,000)†
Salvage value of the old machine	Now	$30,000	1.000	30,000†
Savings in annual cash operating costs	1–6	$60,000	4.355	261,300
Difference in salvage value in six years	6	$50,000	0.564	28,200
Net present value in favor of buying				
the new machine				$ 109,500

*All factors are from Tables 12B–3 and 12B–4 in Appendix 12B.
†These two items could be netted into a single $180,000 incremental-cost figure ($210,000 − $30,000 = $180,000).

Trading In That Old Car?

Consumer Reports magazine provides the following data concerning the alternatives of keeping a four-year-old Ford Taurus for three years or buying a similar new car to replace it. The illustration assumes the car would be purchased and used in suburban Chicago.

	Keep the Old Taurus	Buy a New Taurus
Annual maintenance	$1,180	$650
Annual insurance	$370	$830
Annual license	$15	$100
Trade-in value in three years	$605	$7,763
Purchase price, including sales tax		$17,150

Consumer Reports is ordinarily extremely careful in its analysis, but it has omitted in this instance one financial item that differs substantially between the alternatives. What is it? To check your answer, go to the textbook website at www.mhhe.com/bgn3e. After accessing the site, click on the link to the Internet Exercises and then the link to this chapter.

Source: "When to Give Up on Your Clunker," *Consumer Reports,* August 2000, pp. 12–16.

Financing the Sports Car

Assume you would like to buy a new Mazda Miata sports car. The car can be purchased for $21,495 in cash or it can be acquired from the dealer via a leasing arrangement. Under the terms of the lease, you would have to make a payment of $2,078 when the lease is signed and then monthly payments of $300 for 24 months. At the end of the 24-month lease, you can choose to buy the car you have leased for an additional payment of $13,776. If you do not make that final payment, the car reverts to the dealer.

You have enough cash to make the initial payment on the lease, but not enough to buy the car for cash. However, you could borrow the additional cash from a credit union for 1% per month. Do you think you should borrow money from a credit union to purchase the car or should you sign a lease with the dealer?

Hints: The net present value of the cash purchase option, including any payments to the credit union, is $21,495 using 1% per month as the discount rate. (Accept this statement as true; don't try to do the computations to verify it.) Determine the net present value of the lease, using 1% per month as the discount rate. The present value of an annuity of $1 for 24 periods at 1% per period is 21.243 and the present value of a single payment of $1 at the end of 24 periods at 1% per period is 0.788.

PREFERENCE DECISIONS—THE RANKING OF INVESTMENT PROJECTS

Recall that when considering investment opportunities, managers must make two types of decisions—screening decisions and preference decisions. Screening decisions, which come first, pertain to whether or not a proposed investment is acceptable. Preference decisions come *after* screening decisions and attempt to answer the following question: "How do the remaining investment proposals, all of which have been screened and provide an acceptable rate of return, rank in terms of preference? That is, which one(s) would be *best* for the company to accept?"

Sometimes preference decisions are called rationing decisions or ranking decisions because they ration limited investment funds among many competing alternatives. Hence, the alternatives must be ranked.

LEARNING OBJECTIVE 2

Rank investment projects in order of preference.

Unfortunately, the net present value of one project cannot be directly compared to the net present value of another project unless the investments are equal. For example, assume that a company is considering two competing investments, as shown below:

	Investment	
	A	**B**
Investment required	$(10,000)	$(5,000)
Present value of cash inflows	11,000	6,000
Net present value	$ 1,000	$ 1,000

Although each project has a net present value of $1,000, the projects are not equally desirable if the funds available for investment are limited. The project requiring an investment of only $5,000 is much more desirable than the project requiring an investment of $10,000. This fact can be highlighted by dividing the net present value of the project by the investment required. The result, shown below in equation form, is called the **project profitability index.**

$$\text{Project profitability index } = \frac{\text{Net present value of the project}}{\text{Investment required}} \qquad (1)$$

The project profitability indexes for the two investments above would be computed as follows:

	Investment	
	A	**B**
Net present value (a)	$1,000	$1,000
Investment required (b)	$10,000	$5,000
Project profitability index, (a) ÷ (b)	0.10	0.20

When using the project profitability index to rank competing investments projects, the preference rule is: *The higher the project profitability index, the more desirable the project.*[5] Applying this rule to the two investments above, investment B should be chosen over investment A.

The project profitability index is an application of the techniques for utilizing constrained resources discussed in Chapter 11. In this case, the constrained resource is the limited funds available for investment, and the project profitability index is similar to the contribution margin per unit of the constrained resource.

A few details should be clarified with respect to the computation of the project profitability index. The "Investment required" refers to any cash outflows that occur at the beginning of the project, reduced by any salvage value recovered from the sale of old equipment. The "Investment required" also includes any investment in working capital that the project may need.

---

[5]Because of the "lumpiness" of projects, the project profitability index ranking may not be perfect. Nevertheless, it is a good starting point. For further details, see the Profitability Analysis Appendix at the end of Ray Garrison, Eric Noreen, and Peter Brewer, *Managerial Accounting,* 11th edition, McGraw-Hill, 2006.

THE INTERNAL RATE OF RETURN METHOD

The *internal rate of return* method is a popular alternative to the net present value method. The **internal rate of return** is the rate of return promised by an investment over its useful life. It is computed by finding the discount rate at which the net present value of the investment is zero. The internal rate of return can be used either to screen projects or to rank them. Any project whose internal rate of return is less than the cost of capital is rejected and in general, the higher a project's rate of return, the more desirable it is.

For technical reasons that are discussed in more advanced texts, the net present value method is generally considered to be more reliable than the internal rate of return method for both screening and ranking projects.

THE NET PRESENT VALUE METHOD AND INCOME TAXES

Our discussion of the net present value method has assumed that there are no income taxes. In most countries—including the United States—income taxes, both on individual income and on business income, are a fact of life.

Income taxes affect net present value analysis in two ways. First, income taxes affect the cost of capital in that the cost of capital should reflect the *after-tax* cost of long-term debt and of equity. Second, net present value analysis should focus on *after-tax cash flows*. The effects of income taxes on both revenues and expenses should be fully reflected in the analysis. This includes taking into account the tax deductibility of depreciation. Whereas depreciation is not itself a cash flow, it reduces taxable income and therefore income taxes, which *are* a cash flow. The techniques for adjusting the cost of capital and cash flows for income taxes are beyond the scope of this book and are covered in more advanced texts.

OTHER APPROACHES TO CAPITAL BUDGETING DECISIONS

The net present value and internal rate of return methods are widely used as decision-making tools. Other methods of making capital budgeting decisions are also used, however, and are preferred by some managers. In this section, we discuss two such methods known as *payback* and *simple rate of return*. Both methods have been used for many years, but have been declining in popularity.

The Payback Method

The payback method focuses on the *payback period*. The **payback period** is the length of time that it takes for a project to recoup its initial cost from the cash receipts that it generates. This period is sometimes referred to as "the time that it takes for an investment to pay for itself." The basic premise of the payback method is that the more quickly the cost of an investment can be recovered, the more desirable is the investment.

The payback period is expressed in years. *When the net annual cash inflow is the same every year,* the following formula can be used to compute the payback period:

$$\text{Payback period} = \frac{\text{Investment required}}{\text{Net annual cash inflow}} \qquad (2)$$

> **LEARNING OBJECTIVE 3**
>
> Determine the payback period for an investment.

Concept 12-2

To illustrate the payback method, consider the following data:

Example E   York Company needs a new milling machine. The company is considering two machines: machine A and machine B. Machine A costs $15,000 and will reduce operating costs by $5,000 per year. Machine B costs only $12,000 but will also reduce operating costs by $5,000 per year.

Required:
Which machine should be purchased according to the payback method?

$$\text{Machine A payback period} = \frac{\$15,000}{\$5,000} = 3.0 \text{ years}$$

$$\text{Machine B payback period} = \frac{\$12,000}{\$5,000} = 2.4 \text{ years}$$

According to the payback calculations, York Company should purchase machine B because it has a shorter payback period than machine A.

Investing in an MBA

The financial benefit of earning an MBA degree is enhanced earning power; the costs include both tuition and the opportunity cost of lost salary for two years. *Forbes* magazine computed both the net present value and the payback period for 80 full-time MBA programs. *Forbes* looked at the first five years of enhanced earnings after the degree is granted and the costs of getting the degree. The net present value of an MBA varies a great deal—ranging from over $100,000 at Harvard to $1,000 or less at some institutions. The payback periods show less variation. The quickest paybacks are at Harvard and Ohio State—3.3 years. The slowest payback is about five years. Earnings that extend beyond the five-year horizon are ignored in the *Forbes* analysis. If these earnings had been included, the net present values of degrees at even the lowest-ranked schools would have increased substantially.

Source: Kurt Brandenhausen, "The Bottom Line on B-Schools," *Forbes,* February 7, 2000, pp. 100–104.

Evaluation of the Payback Method

The payback method is not a true measure of the profitability of an investment. Rather, it simply tells a manager how many years will be required to recover the original investment. Unfortunately, a shorter payback period does not always mean that one investment is more desirable than another.

To illustrate, again consider the two machines used in Example E. Since machine B has a shorter payback period than machine A, it *appears* that machine B is more desirable than machine A. But if we add one more piece of information, this illusion quickly disappears. Machine A has a projected 10-year life, and machine B has a projected 5-year life. It would take two purchases of machine B to provide the same length of service as would be provided by a single purchase of machine A. Under these circumstances, machine A would be a much better investment than machine B, even though machine B has a shorter payback period. Unfortunately, the payback method ignores differences in useful life between investments. Such differences can be very important, and relying on payback alone may result in incorrect decisions.

A further criticism of the payback method is that it does not consider the time value of money. A cash inflow to be received several years in the future is weighed the same as a cash inflow received right now. To illustrate, assume that for an investment of $8,000 you can purchase either of the two following streams of cash inflows:

Year	0	1	2	3	4	5	6	7	8
Stream 1. .					$8,000	$2,000	$2,000	$2,000	$2,000
Stream 2. .		$2,000	$2,000	$2,000	$2,000	$8,000			

Which stream of cash inflows would you prefer to receive in return for your $8,000 investment? Each stream has a payback period of 4.0 years. Therefore, if payback alone is used to make the decision, the streams would be considered equally desirable. However, from a time value of money perspective stream 2 is much more desirable than stream 1.

On the other hand, under certain conditions the payback method can be very useful. For one thing, it can help identify which investment proposals are in the "ballpark." That is, it can be used as a screening tool to help answer the question, "Should I consider this proposal further?" If a proposal doesn't provide a payback within some specified period, it can be dropped without further analysis. In addition, the payback period is often of great importance to new companies that are "cash poor." When a company is cash poor, a project with a short payback period but a low rate of return might be preferred over another project with a high rate of return but a long payback period. The reason is that the company may simply need a faster return of its cash investment. And finally, the payback method is sometimes used in industries where products become obsolete very rapidly—such as consumer electronics. Since products may last only a year or two, the payback period on investments must be very short.

Conservation Is Not Self-Denial

IN BUSINESS

Amory Lovins, the director of the Rocky Mountain Institute in Snowmass, Colorado, is a passionate advocate of energy efficiency as a means of conserving natural resources and reducing pollution. Rather than cutting energy consumption by adopting more austere lifestyles, Lovins believes that energy consumption can be radically cut by using energy more efficiently. This approach has the virtues of combining energy conservation with cash savings and better living standards. He claims that America's annual electric bill of $220 billion could be cut in half by making investments with a payback period of one year or less. To illustrate his point, Lovins designed the institute's headquarters to require no furnace or air conditioning. During the cold winters, daytime solar heat enters the building through a built-in greenhouse, is soaked up by massive stone walls and foundations, and is then released at night. The institute is hardly a chilling, austere structure. Its passive heating system supports a small stand of tropical fruit trees, a mini fish farm, an indoor waterfall, and a hot tub. Lovins claims that the building's efficient design added only $6,000 to its construction costs and the payback period on this investment was only 10 months.

Source: David Stipp, "Can This Man Solve America's Energy Crisis?" *Fortune*, May 13, 2002, pp. 100–110.

An Extended Example of Payback

As shown by formula (2) given earlier, the payback period is computed by dividing the investment in a project by the net annual cash inflows that the project will generate. If new equipment is replacing old equipment, then any salvage value to be received when disposing of the old equipment should be deducted from the cost of the new equipment, and only the *incremental* investment should be used in the payback computation. In addition, any depreciation deducted in arriving at the project's net operating income must be added back to obtain the project's expected net annual cash inflow. To illustrate, consider the following data:

Example F Goodtime Fun Centers, Inc., operates amusement parks. Some of the vending machines in one of its parks provide very little revenue, so the company is considering removing the machines and installing equipment to dispense soft ice cream. The equipment would cost $80,000 and have an eight-year useful life. Incremental annual revenues and costs associated with the sale of ice cream would be as follows:

Sales	$150,000
Less cost of ingredients	90,000
Contribution margin	60,000
Less fixed expenses:	
Salaries	27,000
Maintenance	3,000
Depreciation	10,000
Total fixed expenses	40,000
Net operating income	$ 20,000

The vending machines can be sold for a $5,000 scrap value. The company will not purchase equipment unless it has a payback of three years or less. Does the equipment to dispense ice cream pass this hurdle?

Exhibit 12–7 computes the payback period of the proposed equipment. Several things should be noted from this exhibit. First, depreciation is added back to net operating income to obtain the net annual cash inflow from the new equipment. Depreciation is not a cash outlay; thus, it must be added back to adjust net operating income to a cash basis. Second, the payback computation deducts the salvage value of the old machines from the cost of the new equipment so that only the incremental investment is used in computing the payback period.

Since the proposed equipment has a payback period of less than three years, the company's payback requirement has been met.

Payback and Uneven Cash Flows

When the cash flows associated with an investment project change from year to year, the simple payback formula that we outlined earlier cannot be used. Consider the following data:

Year	Investment	Cash Inflow
1	$4,000	$1,000
2		$0
3		$2,000
4	$2,000	$1,000
5		$500
6		$3,000
7		$2,000

EXHIBIT 12–7

Computation of the Payback Period

Step 1: *Compute the net annual cash inflow.* Since the net annual cash inflow is not given, it must be computed before the payback period can be determined:

Net operating income (given above)	$20,000
Add: Noncash deduction for depreciation	10,000
Net annual cash flow	$30,000

Step 2: *Compute the payback period.* Using the net annual cash inflow figure from above, the payback period can be determined as follows:

Cost of the new equipment	$80,000
Less salvage value of old equipment	5,000
Investment required	$75,000

$$\text{Payback period} = \frac{\text{Investment required}}{\text{Net annual cash inflow}}$$

$$= \frac{\$75,000}{\$30,000} = 2.5 \text{ years}$$

EXHIBIT 12–8

Payback and Uneven Cash Flows

Year	Investment	Cash Inflow	Unrecovered Investment*
1	$4,000	$1,000	$3,000
2		$0	$3,000
3		$2,000	$1,000
4	$2,000	$1,000	$2,000
5		$500	$1,500
6		$3,000	$0
7		$2,000	$0

*Year X unrecovered investment = Year X − 1 unrecovered investment + Year X investment − Year X cash inflow

What is the payback period on this investment? The answer is 5.5 years, but to obtain this figure it is necessary to track the unrecovered investment year by year. The steps involved in this process are shown in Exhibit 12–8. By the middle of the sixth year, sufficient cash inflows will be realized to recover the entire investment of $6,000 ($4,000 + $2,000).

The Simple Rate of Return Method

The **simple rate of return** method is another capital budgeting technique that does not involve discounting cash flows. The simple rate of return is also known as the accounting rate of return or the unadjusted rate of return.

Unlike the other capital budgeting methods that we have discussed, the simple rate of return method focuses on accounting net operating income rather than cash flows. To obtain the simple rate of return, the annual incremental net operating income from a project is divided by the initial investment in the project as shown below.

$$\text{Simple rate of return} = \frac{\text{Annual incremental net operating income}}{\text{Initial investment}} \tag{3}$$

Two things should be noted about the simple rate of return. First, net operating income would be net of any depreciation charges that result from making the investment. Second, the initial investment should be reduced by any salvage value realized from the sale of old equipment.

Example G   Brigham Tea, Inc., is a processor of low acid tea. The company is contemplating purchasing equipment for an additional processing line that would increase revenues by $90,000 per year. Incremental cash operating expenses would be $40,000 per year. The equipment would cost $180,000 and have a nine-year life with no salvage value.

Required:
Compute the simple rate of return.

To apply the formula for the simple rate of return, we must first determine the annual incremental net operating income from the project:

Annual incremental revenues		$90,000
Annual incremental cash operating expenses	$40,000	
Annual depreciation ($180,000 − $0)/9	20,000	
Annual incremental expenses		60,000
Annual incremental net operating income		$30,000

Given that the annual incremental net operating income from the project is $30,000 and the initial investment is $180,000, the simple rate of return is 16.7% as shown below:

$$\text{Simple rate of return} = \frac{\text{Annual incremental net operating income}}{\text{Initial investment}}$$

$$= \frac{\$30,000}{\$180,000}$$

$$= 16.7\%$$

Example H   Midwest Farms, Inc., hires people on a part-time basis to sort eggs. The cost of this hand-sorting process is $30,000 per year. The company is investigating an egg-sorting machine that would cost $90,000 and have a 15-year useful life. The machine would have negligible salvage value, and it would cost $10,000 per year to operate and maintain. The egg-sorting equipment currently being used could be sold now for a scrap value of $2,500.

Required:
Compute the simple rate of return on the new egg-sorting machine.

Solution:
This project is slightly different from the preceding project because it involves cost reductions with no additional revenues. Nevertheless, the annual incremental net operating income can be computed by treating the annual cost savings as if it were incremental revenues as follows:

Annual incremental cost savings		$30,000
Annual incremental cash operating expenses	$10,000	
Annual depreciation ($90,000–$0)/15	6,000	
Annual incremental expenses		16,000
Annual incremental net operating income		$14,000

Thus, even though the new equipment would not generate any additional revenues, it would reduce costs by $14,000 a year, which would increase net operating income by $14,000 a year.

Finally, the salvage value of the old equipment offsets the initial cost of the new equipment as follows:

Cost of the new equipment	$90,000
Less: Salvage value of the old equipment	2,500
Initial investment	$87,500

Given the annual incremental net operating income of $14,000 and the initial investment of $87,500, the simple rate of return is 16.0% computed as follows:

$$\text{Simple rate of return} = \frac{\text{Annual incremental net operating income}}{\text{Initial investment}}$$

$$= \frac{\$14,000}{\$87,500}$$

$$= 16.0\%$$

An Amazing Return

Ipswitch, Inc., a software developer and seller, has moved much of its business to the Web. Potential customers can download free trial copies of the company's software at www.ipswitch.com. After the trial period, a customer must return to the Web site to purchase and download a permanent copy of the software. The initial investment in setting up a Web site was modest—roughly $190,000. The cost of keeping the Web site up and running and updated with the latest product information is about $1.3 million a year—mainly in the form of salaries and benefits for eight employees. The company estimates that additional revenues brought in by the Web amount to about $13 million per year and that the company saves about $585,000 per year in direct mail advertising costs by using the Web for much of its advertising instead. Assuming that the cost of sales is almost zero for downloaded software, the accounting rate of return on the initial investment in the Web site is 6,466% ([$13,000,000 − $1,300,000 + $585,000] ÷ $190,000)!

Source: Karen N. Kroll, "Many Happy Returns," *INC,* November 30, 2001, pp. 150–152.

Criticisms of the Simple Rate of Return

The simple rate of return method ignores the time value of money. It considers a dollar received 10 years from now to be as valuable as a dollar received today. Thus, the simple rate of return method can be misleading if the alternatives being considered have different cash flow patterns. Additionally, many projects do not have constant incremental revenues and expenses over their useful lives. As a result, the simple rate of return will fluctuate from year to year, with the possibility that a project may appear to be desirable in some years and undesirable in others. In contrast, the net present value method provides a single number that summarizes all of the cash flows over the entire useful life of the project.

2. If a $300,000 investment has a project profitability index of 0.25, what is the net present value of the project?
   a. $75,000
   b. $225,000
   c. $25,000
   d. $275,000

3. Which of the following statements is false? (You may select more than one answer.)
   a. The payback period increases as the cost of capital decreases.
   b. The simple rate of return will be the same for two alternatives that have identical cash flow patterns even if the pattern of accounting net operating income differs between the alternatives.
   c. The internal rate of return will be higher than the cost of capital for projects that have positive net present values.
   d. If two alternatives have the same present value of cash inflows, the alternative that requires the higher investment will have the higher project profitability index.

Watching the Really Long Term

Forest product companies have some of the longest time horizons of any industry because trees they plant today may not reach their peak for decades. Of the 29 forest product companies that responded to a questionnaire, 9% use the simple rate of return as the primary criterion to evaluate timber investments, 15% use the payback period, 38% use the internal rate of return, and 38% use the net present value. None of the largest forest products companies use either the simple rate of return or the payback method to evaluate timber projects. For other investment decisions—that typically have shorter time horizons—the method used shifted away from net present value and toward the payback period.

Source: Jack Bailes, James Nielsen, and Stephen Lawton, "How Forest Product Companies Analyze Capital Budgets," *Management Accounting,* October 1998, pp. 24–30.

POSTAUDIT OF INVESTMENT PROJECTS

After an investment project has been approved and implemented, a *postaudit* should be conducted. A **postaudit** involves checking whether or not expected results are actually realized. This is a key part of the capital budgeting process because it helps keep managers honest in their investment proposals. Any tendency to inflate the benefits or downplay the costs in a proposal should become evident after a few postaudits have been conducted. The postaudit also provides an opportunity to reinforce and possibly expand successful projects and to cut losses on floundering projects.

The same capital budgeting method should be used in the postaudit as was used in the original approval process. That is, if a project was approved on the basis of a net present value analysis, then the same procedure should be used in performing the postaudit. However, the data used in the postaudit analysis should be *actual observed data* rather than estimated data. This gives management an opportunity to make a side-by-side comparison to see how well the project has succeeded. It also helps ensure that estimated data received on future proposals is carefully prepared, since the persons submitting the data know that their estimates will be compared to actual results in the postaudit process. Actual results that are far out of line with original estimates should be carefully reviewed.

Counting the Environmental Costs

Companies often grossly underestimate how much they are spending on environmental costs. Many of these costs are buried in broad cost categories such as manufacturing overhead. Kestrel Management Services, LLC, a management consulting firm specializing in environmental matters, found that one chemical facility was spending five times as much on environmental expenses as its cost system reported. At another site, a small manufacturer with $840,000 in pretax profits thought that its annual safety and environmental compliance expenses were about $50,000 but, after digging into the accounts, found that the total was closer to $300,000. Alerted to this high cost, management of the company invested about $125,000 in environmental improvements, anticipating a three- to six-month payback period. By taking steps such as more efficient dust collection, the company improved its product quality, reduced scrap rates, decreased its consumption of city water for cooling, and reduced the expense of discharging wastewater into the city's sewer system. Further analysis revealed that spending $50,000 to improve energy efficiency would reduce annual energy costs by about $45,000. Few of these costs were visible in the company's traditional cost accounting system.

Source: Thomas P. Kunes, "A Green and *Lean* Workplace?" *Strategic Finance,* February 2001, pp. 71–73, 83.

Capital Budgeting in Practice

A survey of Fortune 1000 companies—the largest companies in the United States—asked CFOs how often various capital budgeting methods are used in their companies. Some of the results of that survey are displayed below:

Capital Budgeting Tool	Frequency of Use				
	Always	Often	Sometimes	Rarely	Never
Net present value	50%	35%	11%	3%	1%
Internal rate of return	45%	32%	15%	6%	2%
Payback	19%	33%	22%	17%	9%
Accounting rate of return	5%	9%	19%	16%	50%

Many companies use more than one method—for example, they may use both the net present value and the internal rate of return methods to evaluate capital budgeting projects. Note that the two discounted cash flow methods—net present value and internal rate of return—are by far the most commonly used in practice.

A similar survey of companies in the United Kingdom yielded the following results:

Capital Budgeting Tool	Frequency of Use			
	Always	Mostly	Often	Rarely
Net present value	43%	20%	14%	7%
Internal rate of return	48%	20%	10%	5%
Payback	30%	16%	17%	14%
Accounting rate of return	26%	15%	18%	7%

Note that while the results were quite similar for the U.S. and U.K. companies, the U.K. companies were more likely to use the payback and accounting rate of return methods than the U.S. companies.

Sources: Patricia A. Ryan and Glenn P. Ryan, "Capital Budgeting Practices of the Fortune 1000: How Have Things Changed?" *Journal of Business and Management,* Fall 2002, pp. 355–364; and Glen C. Arnold and Panos D. Hatzopoulus, "The Theory-Practice Gap in Capital Budgeting: Evidence from the United Kingdom," *Journal of Business Finance & Accounting* 27(5) & 27(6), June/July 2000, pp. 603–626.

SUMMARY

LOI   Evaluate the acceptability of an investment project using the net present value method.
Investment decisions should take into account the time value of money because a dollar today is more valuable than a dollar received in the future. In the net present value method, future cash flows are discounted to their present value so that they can be compared with current cash outlays. The difference between the present value of the cash inflows and the present value of the cash outflows is called the project's net present value. If the net present value of the project is negative, the project is rejected. The company's cost of capital is often used as the discount rate in the net present value method.

LO2   Rank investment projects in order of preference.
After screening out projects whose net present values are negative, the company may still have more projects than can be supported with available funds. The remaining projects can be ranked using the project profitability index, which is computed by dividing the net present value of the project by the required initial investment.

LO3   Determine the payback period for an investment.
The payback period is the number of periods that are required to recover the investment in a project from the project's cash inflows. The payback period is most useful for projects whose useful lives are short and uncertain. Generally speaking it is not a reliable method for evaluating investment opportunities because it ignores the time value of money and all cash flows that occur after the investment has been recovered.

LO4   Compute the simple rate of return for an investment.
The simple rate of return is determined by dividing a project's accounting net operating income by the initial investment in the project. The simple rate of return is not a reliable guide for evaluating potential projects because it ignores the time value of money.

GUIDANCE ANSWERS TO *DECISION MAKER* AND *YOU DECIDE*

Negotiator for the Red Sox (p. 509)
Apparently, the mayor is suggesting that 100% is the minimum required rate of return. Because the City of Boston does not have shareholders, its cost of capital might be considered the average rate of return that must be paid to its long-term creditors. It is highly unlikely that the city pays interest of 100% on its long-term debt.
      Note that it is very possible that the term *return on investment* is being misused either by the mayor, the media, or both. The mayor's goal might actually be a 100% recovery of the city's investment from the Red Sox. Rather than expecting a 100% return *on* investment, the mayor may simply want a 100% return *of* investment. Taking the time to clarify the mayor's intent might change the course of negotiations.

Financing the Sports Car (p. 515)
The formal analysis, using the least-cost approach, appears below:

Item	Month(s)	Amount of Cash Flows	1% Factor	Present Value of Cash Flows
Pay cash for the car:				
Cash payment	Now	$(21,495)	1.000	$(21,495)
Net present value				$(21,495)
Lease the car:				
Cash payment on lease signing	Now	$(2,078)	1.000	$ (2,078)
Monthly lease payment	1–24	$(300)	21.243	(6,373)
Final payment	24	$(13,776)	0.788	(10,855)
Net present value				$(19,306)
Net present value in favor of leasing				$ 2,189

The leasing alternative is $2,189 less costly, in terms of net present value, than the cash purchase alternative. In addition, the leasing alternative has the advantage that you can choose to not make the final payment of $13,776 at the end of 24 months if for some reason you decide you do not want to keep the car. For example, if the resale value of the car at that point is far less than $13,776, you may choose to return the car to the dealer and save the $13,776. If, however, you had purchased the car outright, you would not have this option—you could only realize the resale value. Because of this "real option," the leasing alternative is even more valuable than the net present value calculations indicate. Therefore, you should lease the car rather than pay cash (and borrow from the credit union).

GUIDANCE ANSWERS TO CONCEPT CHECKS

1. **Choices a and c.** The total-cost and incremental-cost approaches always provide identical results. The present value of a dollar decreases as the time of receipt extends further into the future.
2. **Choice a.** The net present value of the project is $300,000 × 0.25 = $75,000.
3. **Choices a, b, and d.** The payback period does not consider the time value of money; the cost of capital is ignored. The simple rate of return is based on accounting net operating income, not cash flows. If two alternatives have the same present value of cash inflows, the alternative that requires the lower investment, as opposed to the higher investment, will have the higher project profitability index.

REVIEW PROBLEM: COMPARISON OF CAPITAL BUDGETING METHODS

Lamar Company is considering a project that would have an eight-year life and require a $2,400,000 investment in equipment. At the end of eight years, the project would terminate and the equipment would have no salvage value. The project would provide net operating income each year as follows:

Sales		$3,000,000
Less variable expenses		1,800,000
Contribution margin		1,200,000
Less fixed expenses:		
Advertising, salaries, and other		
fixed out-of-pocket costs	$700,000	
Depreciation	300,000	
Total fixed expenses		1,000,000
Net operating income		$ 200,000

The company's discount rate is 12%.

Required:

1. Compute the net annual cash inflow from the project.
2. Compute the project's net present value. Is the project acceptable?
3. Compute the project's payback period.
4. Compute the project's simple rate of return.

Solution to Review Problem

1. The net annual cash inflow can be computed by deducting the cash expenses from sales:

Sales	$3,000,000
Less variable expenses	1,800,000
Contribution margin	1,200,000
Less advertising, salaries, and	
other fixed out-of-pocket costs	700,000
Net annual cash inflow	$ 500,000

Or it can be computed by adding depreciation back to net operating income:

Net operating income	$200,000
Add: Noncash deduction	
for depreciation	300,000
Net annual cash inflow	$500,000

2. The net present value can be computed as follows:

Item	Year(s)	Amount of Cash Flows	12% Factor	Present Value of Cash Flows
Cost of new equipment	Now	$(2,400,000)	1.000	$(2,400,000)
Net annual cash inflow	1–8	$500,000	4.968	2,484,000
Net present value				$ 84,000

Yes, the project is acceptable because it has a positive net present value.

3. The formula for the payback period is:

$$\text{Payback period} = \frac{\text{Investment required}}{\text{Net annual cash inflow}}$$

$$= \frac{\$2,400,000}{\$500,000}$$

$$= 4.8 \text{ years}$$

4. The formula for the simple rate of return is:

$$\text{Simple rate of return} = \frac{\text{Annual incremental net operating income}}{\text{Initial investment}}$$

$$= \frac{\$200,000}{\$2,400,000}$$

$$= 8.3\%$$

GLOSSARY

Capital budgeting   The process of planning significant outlays on projects that have long-term implications such as the purchase of new equipment or the introduction of a new product. (p. 504)

Cost of capital   The average rate of return the company must pay to its long-term creditors and shareholders for the use of their funds. (p. 509)

Internal rate of return   The discount rate at which the net present value of an investment project is zero; the return promised by a project over its useful life. (p. 517)

Net present value   The difference between the present value of the cash inflows and the present value of the cash outflows of an investment project. (p. 506)

Out-of-pocket costs   Actual cash outlays for salaries, advertising, repairs, and similar costs. (p. 511)

Payback period   The length of time that it takes for a project to fully recover its initial cost out of the cash receipts that it generates. (p. 517)

Postaudit   The follow-up after a project has been approved and implemented to determine whether expected results are actually realized. (p. 524)

Preference decision   A decision as to which of several competing acceptable investment proposals is best. (p. 505)

Project profitability index   The ratio of the net present value of a project's cash flows to the investment required. (p. 516)

Screening decision   A decision as to whether a proposed investment passes a preset hurdle. (p. 505)

Simple rate of return   The rate of return computed by dividing a project's annual accounting net operating income by the initial investment required. (p. 521)

Working capital   The excess of current assets over current liabilities. (p. 508)

APPENDIX 12A: THE CONCEPT OF PRESENT VALUE

LEARNING OBJECTIVE 5

Understand present value concepts and the use of present value tables.

A dollar received today is more valuable than a dollar received a year from now for the simple reason that if you have a dollar today, you can put it in the bank and have more than a dollar a year from now. Since dollars today are worth more than dollars in the future, we must weight cash flows that are received at different times so that they can be compared.

The Mathematics of Interest

If a bank pays 5% interest, then a deposit of $100 today will be worth $105 one year from now. This can be expressed as follows:

$$F_1 = P(1 + r) \qquad\qquad (1)$$

where F_1 = the balance at the end of one period, P = the amount invested now, and r = the rate of interest per period.

If the investment made now is $100 deposited in a savings account that earns 5% interest, then P = $100 and r = 0.05. Under these conditions, F_1 = $105, the amount to be received in one year.

The $100 present outlay is called the **present value** of the $105 amount to be received in one year. It is also known as the *discounted value* of the future $105 receipt. The $100 represents the value in present terms of $105 to be received a year from now when the interest rate is 5%.

Compound Interest   What if the $105 is left in the bank for a second year? In that case, by the end of the second year the original $100 deposit will have grown to $110.25:

Original deposit	$100.00
Interest for the first year: $100 × 0.05	5.00
Balance at the end of the first year	105.00
Interest for the second year: $105 × 0.05	5.25
Balance at the end of the second year	$110.25

Notice that the interest for the second year is $5.25, as compared to only $5.00 for the first year. The reason for the greater interest earned during the second year is that during the second year, interest is being paid *on interest*. That is, the $5.00 interest earned during the first year has been left in the account and has been added to the original $100 deposit when computing interest for the second year. This is known as **compound interest.** In this case, the compounding is annual. Interest can be compounded on a semiannual, quarterly, monthly, or even more frequent basis. The more frequently compounding is done, the more rapidly the balance will grow.

We can determine the balance in an account after n periods of compounding using the following equation:

$$F_n = P(1 + r)^n \tag{2}$$

where n = the number of periods of compounding.

If n = 2 years and the interest rate is 5% per year, then the balance in two years will be computed as follows:

$$F_2 = \$100(1 + 0.05)^2$$

$$F_2 = \$110.25$$

Present Value and Future Value   Exhibit 12A–1 shows the relationship between present value and future value. As shown in the exhibit, if $100 is deposited in a bank at 5% interest, it will grow to $127.63 by the end of five years if interest is compounded annually.

Computation of Present Value

An investment can be viewed in two ways. It can be viewed in terms of its future value or in terms of its present value. We have seen from our computations above that if we know the present value of a sum (such as our $100 deposit), the future value in n years can be computed by using equation (1). But what if the tables are reversed and we know the *future* value of some amount but we do not know its present value?

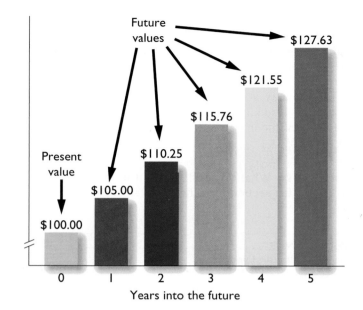

For example, assume that you are to receive $200 two years from now. You know that
the future value of this sum is $200, since this is the amount that you will be receiving in
two years. But what is the sum's present value—what is it worth *right now?* The present
value of any sum to be received in the future can be computed by turning equation (2)
around and solving for *P*:

$$P = \frac{F_n}{(1 + r)^n} \tag{3}$$

In our example, $F_n = \$200$ (the amount to be received in the future), $r = 0.05$ (the
annual rate of interest), and $n = 2$ (the number of years in the future that the amount is to
be received).

$$P = \frac{\$200}{(1 + 0.05)^2}$$

$$P = \frac{\$200}{1.1025}$$

$$P = \$181.40$$

As shown by the computation above, the present value of a $200 amount to be
received two years from now is $181.40 if the interest rate is 5%. In effect, $181.40 received *right now* is equivalent to $200 received two years from now if the rate of return is
5%. The $181.40 and the $200 are just two ways of looking at the same thing.

The process of finding the present value of a future cash flow, which we have just
completed, is called **discounting.** We have *discounted* the $200 to its present value of
$181.40. The 5% interest that we used to find this present value is called the **discount
rate.** Discounting a future sum to its present value is a common practice in business, particularly in capital budgeting decisions.

If you have a power key (y^x) on your calculator, the above calculations are fairly
easy. However, some of the present value formulas we will be using are more complex
and difficult to use. Fortunately, tables are available in which many of the calculations
have already been done for you. For example, Exhibit 12B–3 in Appendix 12B shows
the discounted present value of $1 to be received at various periods in the future at various

interest rates. The table indicates that the present value of $1 to be received two periods from now at 5% is 0.907. In our example, we want to know the present value of $200 rather than just $1; therefore, we need to multiply the factor in the table by $200:

$$\$200 \times 0.907 = \$181.40$$

This answer is the same as we obtained earlier using the formula in equation (3).

Present Value of a Series of Cash Flows

Although some investments involve a single sum to be received (or paid) at a single point in the future, other investments involve a *series* of cash flows. A series (or stream) of identical cash flows is known as an **annuity.** For example, assume that a company has just purchased some government bonds in order to temporarily invest funds that are being held for future plant expansion. The bonds will yield interest of $15,000 at the end of each year and will be held for five years. What is the present value of the stream of interest receipts from the bonds? As shown in Exhibit 12A–2, if the discount rate is 12%, the present value of this stream is $54,075. The discount factors used in this exhibit were taken from Exhibit 12B–3 in Appendix 12B.

Year	Factor at 12% (Table 12B–3)	Interest Received	Present Value
1	0.893	$15,000	$13,395
2	0.797	$15,000	11,955
3	0.712	$15,000	10,680
4	0.636	$15,000	9,540
5	0.567	$15,000	8,505
			$54,075

EXHIBIT 12A–2

Present Value of a Series of Cash Receipts

Two points are important in connection with Exhibit 12A–2. First, the present value of the $15,000 interest declines the further it is received in the future. The present value of $15,000 received a year from now is $13,395, as compared to only $8,505 if received five years from now. This point simply underscores the time value of money.

The second point is that the computations in Exhibit 12A–2 involved unnecessary work. The same present value of $54,075 could have been obtained more easily by referring to Exhibit 12B–4 in Appendix 12B. Exhibit 12B–4 contains the present value of $1 to be received each year over a *series* of years at various interest rates. Exhibit 12B–4 has been derived by simply adding together the factors from Exhibit 12B–3, as follows:

Year	Exhibit 12B–3 Factors at 12%
1	0.893
2	0.797
3	0.712
4	0.636
5	0.567
	3.605

The sum of the five factors above is 3.605. Notice from Exhibit 12B–4 that the factor for $1 to be received at the end of each year for five years at 12% is also 3.605. If we use this factor and multiply it by the $15,000 annual cash inflow, then we get the same $54,075 present value that we obtained earlier in Exhibit 12A–2:

$$\$15,000 \times 3.605 = \$54,075$$

Therefore, when computing the present value of a series (or stream) of equal cash flows that begins at the end of period 1, Exhibit 12B–4 should be used.

To summarize, the present value tables in Appendix 12B should be used as follows:

Exhibit 12B–3: This table should be used to find the present value of a single cash flow (such as a single payment or receipt) occurring at the end of a specified number of periods.

Exhibit 12B–4: This table should be used to find the present value of a series (or stream) of identical cash flows beginning at the end of the current period and continuing at the end of each subsequent period until a specified period.

The use of both of these tables is illustrated in various exhibits in the main body of the chapter. *When a present value factor appears in an exhibit, you should take the time to trace it back into either Exhibit 12B–3 or Exhibit 12B–4 to get acquainted with the tables and how they work.*

SUMMARY OF APPENDIX 12A

LO5   (Appendix 12A) Understand present value concepts and the use of present value tables.
A dollar received today is more valuable than a dollar received a year from now because the dollar received today can be put in the bank to earn interest; therefore, it will be worth more than a dollar a year from now.

The tables shown in Appendix 12B simplify the process of computing the present and future value of cash flows. They summarize the factors used to discount a single sum or annuity received in the future to its present value and the factors used to translate a single sum or annuity to its future value.

GLOSSARY (APPENDIX 12A)

Annuity   A series, or stream, of identical cash flows. (p. 531)
Compound interest   The process of paying interest on interest in an investment. (p. 529)
Discount rate   The rate of return that is used to find the present value of a future cash flow. (p. 530)
Discounting   The process of finding the present value of a future cash flow. (p. 530)
Present value   The value now of an amount that will be received in some future period. (p. 529)

EXHIBIT 12B–1 Future Value of $1. $F_n = (1 + r)^n$

Periods	4%	5%	6%	7%	8%	9%	10%	11%	12%	13%	14%	15%	16%	17%	18%	19%	20%
1	1.040	1.050	1.060	1.070	1.080	1.090	1.100	1.110	1.120	1.130	1.140	1.150	1.160	1.170	1.180	1.190	1.200
2	1.082	1.103	1.124	1.145	1.166	1.188	1.210	1.232	1.254	1.277	1.300	1.323	1.346	1.369	1.392	1.416	1.440
3	1.125	1.158	1.191	1.225	1.260	1.295	1.331	1.368	1.405	1.443	1.482	1.521	1.561	1.602	1.643	1.685	1.728
4	1.170	1.216	1.262	1.311	1.360	1.412	1.464	1.518	1.574	1.630	1.689	1.749	1.811	1.874	1.939	2.005	2.074
5	1.217	1.276	1.338	1.403	1.469	1.539	1.611	1.685	1.762	1.842	1.925	2.011	2.100	2.192	2.288	2.386	2.488
6	1.265	1.340	1.419	1.501	1.587	1.677	1.772	1.870	1.974	2.082	2.195	2.313	2.436	2.565	2.700	2.840	2.986
7	1.316	1.407	1.504	1.606	1.714	1.828	1.949	2.076	2.211	2.353	2.502	2.660	2.826	3.001	3.185	3.379	3.583
8	1.369	1.477	1.594	1.718	1.851	1.993	2.144	2.305	2.476	2.658	2.853	3.059	3.278	3.511	3.759	4.021	4.300
9	1.423	1.551	1.689	1.838	1.999	2.172	2.358	2.558	2.773	3.004	3.252	3.518	3.803	4.108	4.435	4.785	5.160
10	1.480	1.629	1.791	1.967	2.159	2.367	2.594	2.839	3.106	3.395	3.707	4.046	4.411	4.807	5.234	5.695	6.192
11	1.539	1.710	1.898	2.105	2.332	2.580	2.853	3.152	3.479	3.836	4.226	4.652	5.117	5.624	6.176	6.777	7.430
12	1.601	1.796	2.012	2.252	2.518	2.813	3.138	3.498	3.896	4.335	4.818	5.350	5.936	6.580	7.288	8.064	8.916
13	1.665	1.886	2.133	2.410	2.720	3.066	3.452	3.883	4.363	4.898	5.492	6.153	6.886	7.699	8.599	9.596	10.699
14	1.732	1.980	2.261	2.579	2.937	3.342	3.797	4.310	4.887	5.535	6.261	7.076	7.988	9.007	10.147	11.420	12.839
15	1.801	2.079	2.397	2.759	3.172	3.642	4.177	4.785	5.474	6.254	7.138	8.137	9.266	10.539	11.974	13.590	15.407
16	1.873	2.183	2.540	2.952	3.426	3.970	4.595	5.311	6.130	7.067	8.137	9.358	10.748	12.330	14.129	16.172	18.488
17	1.948	2.292	2.693	3.159	3.700	4.328	5.054	5.895	6.866	7.986	9.276	10.761	12.468	14.426	16.672	19.244	22.186
18	2.026	2.407	2.854	3.380	3.996	4.717	5.560	6.544	7.690	9.024	10.575	12.375	14.463	16.879	19.673	22.901	26.623
19	2.107	2.527	3.026	3.617	4.316	5.142	6.116	7.263	8.613	10.197	12.056	14.232	16.777	19.748	23.214	27.252	31.948
20	2.191	2.653	3.207	3.870	4.661	5.604	6.727	8.062	9.646	11.523	13.743	16.367	19.461	23.106	27.393	32.429	38.338
30	3.243	4.322	5.743	7.612	10.063	13.268	17.449	22.892	29.960	39.116	50.950	66.212	85.850	111.065	143.371	184.675	237.376

EXHIBIT 12B–2   Future Value of an Annuity of $1 in Arrears. $F_n = \dfrac{(1+r)^n - 1}{r}$

Periods	4%	5%	6%	7%	8%	9%	10%	11%	12%	13%	14%	15%	16%	17%	18%	19%	20%
1	1.000	1.000	1.000	1.000	1.000	1.000	1.000	1.000	1.000	1.000	1.000	1.000	1.000	1.000	1.000	1.000	1.000
2	2.040	2.050	2.060	2.070	2.080	2.090	2.100	2.110	2.120	2.130	2.140	2.150	2.160	2.170	2.180	2.190	2.200
3	3.122	3.153	3.184	3.215	3.246	3.278	3.310	3.342	3.374	3.407	3.440	3.473	3.506	3.539	3.572	3.606	3.640
4	4.246	4.310	4.375	4.440	4.506	4.573	4.641	4.710	4.779	4.850	4.921	4.993	5.066	5.141	5.215	5.291	5.368
5	5.416	5.526	5.637	5.751	5.867	5.985	6.105	6.228	6.353	6.480	6.610	6.742	6.877	7.014	7.154	7.297	7.442
6	6.633	6.802	6.975	7.153	7.336	7.523	7.716	7.913	8.115	8.323	8.536	8.754	8.977	9.207	9.442	9.683	9.930
7	7.898	8.142	8.394	8.654	8.923	9.200	9.487	9.783	10.089	10.405	10.730	11.067	11.414	11.772	12.142	12.523	12.916
8	9.214	9.549	9.897	10.260	10.637	11.028	11.436	11.859	12.300	12.757	13.233	13.727	14.240	14.773	15.327	15.902	16.499
9	10.583	11.027	11.491	11.978	12.488	13.021	13.579	14.164	14.776	15.416	16.085	16.786	17.519	18.285	19.086	19.923	20.799
10	12.006	12.578	13.181	13.816	14.487	15.193	15.937	16.722	17.549	18.420	19.337	20.304	21.321	22.393	23.521	24.709	25.959
11	13.486	14.207	14.972	15.784	16.645	17.560	18.531	19.561	20.655	21.814	23.045	24.349	25.733	27.200	28.755	30.404	32.150
12	15.026	15.917	16.870	17.888	18.977	20.141	21.384	22.713	24.133	25.650	27.271	29.002	30.850	32.824	34.931	37.180	39.581
13	16.627	17.713	18.882	20.141	21.495	22.953	24.523	26.212	28.029	29.985	32.089	34.352	36.786	39.404	42.219	45.244	48.497
14	18.292	19.599	21.015	22.550	24.215	26.019	27.975	30.095	32.393	34.883	37.581	40.505	43.672	47.103	50.818	54.841	59.196
15	20.024	21.579	23.276	25.129	27.152	29.361	31.772	34.405	37.280	40.417	43.842	47.580	51.660	56.110	60.965	66.261	72.035
16	21.825	23.657	25.673	27.888	30.324	33.003	35.950	39.190	42.753	46.672	50.980	55.717	60.925	66.649	72.939	79.850	87.442
17	23.698	25.840	28.213	30.840	33.750	36.974	40.545	44.501	48.884	53.739	59.118	65.075	71.673	78.979	87.068	96.022	105.931
18	25.645	28.132	30.906	33.999	37.450	41.301	45.599	50.396	55.750	61.725	68.394	75.836	84.141	93.406	103.740	115.266	128.117
19	27.671	30.539	33.760	37.379	41.446	46.018	51.159	56.939	63.440	70.749	78.969	88.212	98.603	110.285	123.414	138.166	154.740
20	29.778	33.066	36.786	40.995	45.762	51.160	57.275	64.203	72.052	80.947	91.025	102.444	115.380	130.033	146.628	165.418	186.688
30	56.085	66.439	79.058	94.461	113.283	136.308	164.494	199.021	241.333	293.199	356.787	434.745	530.312	647.439	790.948	966.712	1181.882

EXHIBIT 12B–3 Present Value of $1. $P_n = \dfrac{1}{(1+r)^n}$

Periods	4%	5%	6%	7%	8%	9%	10%	11%	12%	13%	14%	15%	16%	17%	18%	19%	20%	21%	22%	23%	24%	25%
1	0.962	0.952	0.943	0.935	0.926	0.917	0.909	0.901	0.893	0.885	0.877	0.870	0.862	0.855	0.847	0.840	0.833	0.826	0.820	0.813	0.806	0.800
2	0.925	0.907	0.890	0.873	0.857	0.842	0.826	0.812	0.797	0.783	0.769	0.756	0.743	0.731	0.718	0.706	0.694	0.683	0.672	0.661	0.650	0.640
3	0.889	0.864	0.840	0.816	0.794	0.772	0.751	0.731	0.712	0.693	0.675	0.658	0.641	0.624	0.609	0.593	0.579	0.564	0.551	0.537	0.524	0.512
4	0.855	0.823	0.792	0.763	0.735	0.708	0.683	0.659	0.636	0.613	0.592	0.572	0.552	0.534	0.516	0.499	0.482	0.467	0.451	0.437	0.423	0.410
5	0.822	0.784	0.747	0.713	0.681	0.650	0.621	0.593	0.567	0.543	0.519	0.497	0.476	0.456	0.437	0.419	0.402	0.386	0.370	0.355	0.341	0.328
6	0.790	0.746	0.705	0.666	0.630	0.596	0.564	0.535	0.507	0.480	0.456	0.432	0.410	0.390	0.370	0.352	0.335	0.319	0.303	0.289	0.275	0.262
7	0.760	0.711	0.665	0.623	0.583	0.547	0.513	0.482	0.452	0.425	0.400	0.376	0.354	0.333	0.314	0.296	0.279	0.263	0.249	0.235	0.222	0.210
8	0.731	0.677	0.627	0.582	0.540	0.502	0.467	0.434	0.404	0.376	0.351	0.327	0.305	0.285	0.266	0.249	0.233	0.218	0.204	0.191	0.179	0.168
9	0.703	0.645	0.592	0.544	0.500	0.460	0.424	0.391	0.361	0.333	0.308	0.284	0.263	0.243	0.225	0.209	0.194	0.180	0.167	0.155	0.144	0.134
10	0.676	0.614	0.558	0.508	0.463	0.422	0.386	0.352	0.322	0.295	0.270	0.247	0.227	0.208	0.191	0.176	0.162	0.149	0.137	0.126	0.116	0.107
11	0.650	0.585	0.527	0.475	0.429	0.388	0.350	0.317	0.287	0.261	0.237	0.215	0.195	0.178	0.162	0.148	0.135	0.123	0.112	0.103	0.094	0.086
12	0.625	0.557	0.497	0.444	0.397	0.356	0.319	0.286	0.257	0.231	0.208	0.187	0.168	0.152	0.137	0.124	0.112	0.102	0.092	0.083	0.076	0.069
13	0.601	0.530	0.469	0.415	0.368	0.326	0.290	0.258	0.229	0.204	0.182	0.163	0.145	0.130	0.116	0.104	0.093	0.084	0.075	0.068	0.061	0.055
14	0.577	0.505	0.442	0.388	0.340	0.299	0.263	0.232	0.205	0.181	0.160	0.141	0.125	0.111	0.099	0.088	0.078	0.069	0.062	0.055	0.049	0.044
15	0.555	0.481	0.417	0.362	0.315	0.275	0.239	0.209	0.183	0.160	0.140	0.123	0.108	0.095	0.084	0.074	0.065	0.057	0.051	0.045	0.040	0.035
16	0.534	0.458	0.394	0.339	0.292	0.252	0.218	0.188	0.163	0.141	0.123	0.107	0.093	0.081	0.071	0.062	0.054	0.047	0.042	0.036	0.032	0.028
17	0.513	0.436	0.371	0.317	0.270	0.231	0.198	0.170	0.146	0.125	0.108	0.093	0.080	0.069	0.060	0.052	0.045	0.039	0.034	0.030	0.026	0.023
18	0.494	0.416	0.350	0.296	0.250	0.212	0.180	0.153	0.130	0.111	0.095	0.081	0.069	0.059	0.051	0.044	0.038	0.032	0.028	0.024	0.021	0.018
19	0.475	0.396	0.331	0.277	0.232	0.194	0.164	0.138	0.116	0.098	0.083	0.070	0.060	0.051	0.043	0.037	0.031	0.027	0.023	0.020	0.017	0.014
20	0.456	0.377	0.312	0.258	0.215	0.178	0.149	0.124	0.104	0.087	0.073	0.061	0.051	0.043	0.037	0.031	0.026	0.022	0.019	0.016	0.014	0.012
21	0.439	0.359	0.294	0.242	0.199	0.164	0.135	0.112	0.093	0.077	0.064	0.053	0.044	0.037	0.031	0.026	0.022	0.018	0.015	0.013	0.011	0.009
22	0.422	0.342	0.278	0.226	0.184	0.150	0.123	0.101	0.083	0.068	0.056	0.046	0.038	0.032	0.026	0.022	0.018	0.015	0.013	0.011	0.009	0.007
23	0.406	0.326	0.262	0.211	0.170	0.138	0.112	0.091	0.074	0.060	0.049	0.040	0.033	0.027	0.022	0.018	0.015	0.012	0.010	0.009	0.007	0.006
24	0.390	0.310	0.247	0.197	0.158	0.126	0.102	0.082	0.066	0.053	0.043	0.035	0.028	0.023	0.019	0.015	0.013	0.010	0.008	0.007	0.006	0.005
25	0.375	0.295	0.233	0.184	0.146	0.116	0.092	0.074	0.059	0.047	0.038	0.030	0.024	0.020	0.016	0.013	0.010	0.009	0.007	0.006	0.005	0.004
26	0.361	0.281	0.220	0.172	0.135	0.106	0.084	0.066	0.053	0.042	0.033	0.026	0.021	0.017	0.014	0.011	0.009	0.007	0.006	0.005	0.004	0.003
27	0.347	0.268	0.207	0.161	0.125	0.098	0.076	0.060	0.047	0.037	0.029	0.023	0.018	0.014	0.011	0.009	0.007	0.006	0.005	0.004	0.003	0.002
28	0.333	0.255	0.196	0.150	0.116	0.090	0.069	0.054	0.042	0.033	0.026	0.020	0.016	0.012	0.010	0.008	0.006	0.005	0.004	0.003	0.002	0.002
29	0.321	0.243	0.185	0.141	0.107	0.082	0.063	0.048	0.037	0.029	0.022	0.017	0.014	0.011	0.008	0.006	0.005	0.004	0.003	0.002	0.002	0.002
30	0.308	0.231	0.174	0.131	0.099	0.075	0.057	0.044	0.033	0.026	0.020	0.015	0.012	0.009	0.007	0.005	0.004	0.003	0.003	0.002	0.002	0.001
40	0.208	0.142	0.097	0.067	0.046	0.032	0.022	0.015	0.011	0.008	0.005	0.004	0.003	0.002	0.001	0.001	0.001	0.000	0.000	0.000	0.000	0.000

EXHIBIT 12B–4 Present Value of an Annuity of $1 in Arrears. $P_n = \dfrac{1}{r}\left[1 - \dfrac{1}{(1+r)^n}\right]$

Periods	4%	5%	6%	7%	8%	9%	10%	11%	12%	13%	14%	15%	16%	17%	18%	19%	20%	21%	22%	23%	24%	25%
1	0.962	0.952	0.943	0.935	0.926	0.917	0.909	0.901	0.893	0.885	0.877	0.870	0.862	0.855	0.847	0.840	0.833	0.826	0.820	0.813	0.806	0.800
2	1.886	1.859	1.833	1.808	1.783	1.759	1.736	1.713	1.690	1.668	1.647	1.626	1.605	1.585	1.566	1.547	1.528	1.509	1.492	1.474	1.457	1.440
3	2.775	2.723	2.673	2.624	2.577	2.531	2.487	2.444	2.402	2.361	2.322	2.283	2.246	2.210	2.174	2.140	2.106	2.074	2.042	2.011	1.981	1.952
4	3.630	3.546	3.465	3.387	3.312	3.240	3.170	3.102	3.037	2.974	2.914	2.855	2.798	2.743	2.690	2.639	2.589	2.540	2.494	2.448	2.404	2.362
5	4.452	4.329	4.212	4.100	3.993	3.890	3.791	3.696	3.605	3.517	3.433	3.352	3.274	3.199	3.127	3.058	2.991	2.926	2.864	2.803	2.745	2.689
6	5.242	5.076	4.917	4.767	4.623	4.486	4.355	4.231	4.111	3.998	3.889	3.784	3.685	3.589	3.498	3.410	3.326	3.245	3.167	3.092	3.020	2.951
7	6.002	5.786	5.582	5.389	5.206	5.033	4.868	4.712	4.564	4.423	4.288	4.160	4.039	3.922	3.812	3.706	3.605	3.508	3.416	3.327	3.242	3.161
8	6.733	6.463	6.210	5.971	5.747	5.535	5.335	5.146	4.968	4.799	4.639	4.487	4.344	4.207	4.078	3.954	3.837	3.726	3.619	3.518	3.421	3.329
9	7.435	7.108	6.802	6.515	6.247	5.995	5.759	5.537	5.328	5.132	4.946	4.772	4.607	4.451	4.303	4.163	4.031	3.905	3.786	3.673	3.566	3.463
10	8.111	7.722	7.360	7.024	6.710	6.418	6.145	5.889	5.650	5.426	5.216	5.019	4.833	4.659	4.494	4.339	4.192	4.054	3.923	3.799	3.682	3.571
11	8.760	8.306	7.887	7.499	7.139	6.805	6.495	6.207	5.938	5.687	5.453	5.234	5.029	4.836	4.656	4.486	4.327	4.177	4.035	3.902	3.776	3.656
12	9.385	8.863	8.384	7.943	7.536	7.161	6.814	6.492	6.194	5.918	5.660	5.421	5.197	4.988	4.793	4.611	4.439	4.278	4.127	3.985	3.851	3.725
13	9.986	9.394	8.853	8.358	7.904	7.487	7.103	6.750	6.424	6.122	5.842	5.583	5.342	5.118	4.910	4.715	4.533	4.362	4.203	4.053	3.912	3.780
14	10.563	9.899	9.295	8.745	8.244	7.786	7.367	6.982	6.628	6.302	6.002	5.724	5.468	5.229	5.008	4.802	4.611	4.432	4.265	4.108	3.962	3.824
15	11.118	10.380	9.712	9.108	8.559	8.061	7.606	7.191	6.811	6.462	6.142	5.847	5.575	5.324	5.092	4.876	4.675	4.489	4.315	4.153	4.001	3.859
16	11.652	10.838	10.106	9.447	8.851	8.313	7.824	7.379	6.974	6.604	6.265	5.954	5.668	5.405	5.162	4.938	4.730	4.536	4.357	4.189	4.033	3.887
17	12.166	11.274	10.477	9.763	9.122	8.544	8.022	7.549	7.120	6.729	6.373	6.047	5.749	5.475	5.222	4.990	4.775	4.576	4.391	4.219	4.059	3.910
18	12.659	11.690	10.828	10.059	9.372	8.756	8.201	7.702	7.250	6.840	6.467	6.128	5.818	5.534	5.273	5.033	4.812	4.608	4.419	4.243	4.080	3.928
19	13.134	12.085	11.158	10.336	9.604	8.950	8.365	7.839	7.366	6.938	6.550	6.198	5.877	5.584	5.316	5.070	4.843	4.635	4.442	4.263	4.097	3.942
20	13.590	12.462	11.470	10.594	9.818	9.129	8.514	7.963	7.469	7.025	6.623	6.259	5.929	5.628	5.353	5.101	4.870	4.657	4.460	4.279	4.110	3.954
21	14.029	12.821	11.764	10.836	10.017	9.292	8.649	8.075	7.562	7.102	6.687	6.312	5.973	5.665	5.384	5.127	4.891	4.675	4.476	4.292	4.121	3.963
22	14.451	13.163	12.042	11.061	10.201	9.442	8.772	8.176	7.645	7.170	6.743	6.359	6.011	5.696	5.410	5.149	4.909	4.690	4.488	4.302	4.130	3.970
23	14.857	13.489	12.303	11.272	10.371	9.580	8.883	8.266	7.718	7.230	6.792	6.399	6.044	5.723	5.432	5.167	4.925	4.703	4.499	4.311	4.137	3.976
24	15.247	13.799	12.550	11.469	10.529	9.707	8.985	8.348	7.784	7.283	6.835	6.434	6.073	5.746	5.451	5.182	4.937	4.713	4.507	4.318	4.143	3.981
25	15.622	14.094	12.783	11.654	10.675	9.823	9.077	8.422	7.843	7.330	6.873	6.464	6.097	5.766	5.467	5.195	4.948	4.721	4.514	4.323	4.147	3.985
26	15.983	14.375	13.003	11.826	10.810	9.929	9.161	8.488	7.896	7.372	6.906	6.491	6.118	5.783	5.480	5.206	4.956	4.728	4.520	4.328	4.151	3.988
27	16.330	14.643	13.211	11.987	10.935	10.027	9.237	8.548	7.943	7.409	6.935	6.514	6.136	5.798	5.492	5.215	4.964	4.734	4.524	4.332	4.154	3.990
28	16.663	14.898	13.406	12.137	11.051	10.116	9.307	8.602	7.984	7.441	6.961	6.534	6.152	5.810	5.502	5.223	4.970	4.739	4.528	4.335	4.157	3.992
29	16.984	15.141	13.591	12.278	11.158	10.198	9.370	8.650	8.022	7.470	6.983	6.551	6.166	5.820	5.510	5.229	4.975	4.743	4.531	4.337	4.159	3.994
30	17.292	15.372	13.765	12.409	11.258	10.274	9.427	8.694	8.055	7.496	7.003	6.566	6.177	5.829	5.517	5.235	4.979	4.746	4.534	4.339	4.160	3.995
40	19.793	17.159	15.046	13.332	11.925	10.757	9.779	8.951	8.244	7.634	7.105	6.642	6.233	5.871	5.548	5.258	4.997	4.760	4.544	4.347	4.166	3.999

QUESTIONS

12–1 What is the difference between capital budgeting screening decisions and capital budgeting preference decisions?

12–2 What is meant by the term *time value of money?*

12–3 What is meant by the term *discounting?*

12–4 Why is the net present value method of making capital budgeting decisions superior to other methods such as the payback and simple rate of return methods?

12–5 What is net present value? Can it ever be negative? Explain.

12–6 If a company has to pay interest of 14% on long-term debt, then its cost of capital is 14%. Do you agree? Explain.

12–7 What is meant by an investment project's internal rate of return? How is the internal rate of return computed?

12–8 Explain how the cost of capital serves as a screening tool when dealing with the net present value method.

12–9 As the discount rate increases, the present value of a given future cash flow also increases. Do you agree? Explain.

12–10 Refer to Exhibit 12–2. Is the return on this investment proposal exactly 14%, more than 14%, or less than 14%? Explain.

12–11 Why are preference decisions sometimes called *rationing* decisions?

12–12 How is the project profitability index computed, and what does it measure?

12–13 What is the preference rule for ranking investment projects under the net present value method?

12–14 What is meant by the term *payback period?* How is the payback period determined?

12–15 How can the payback method be useful to managers?

12–16 What is the major criticism of the payback and simple rate of return methods of making capital budgeting decisions?

BRIEF EXERCISES

BRIEF EXERCISE 12–1   Net Present Value Analysis of Competing Projects   [LO2]

Serv U Best, a company that supplies temporary workers for restaurants and other service industries, has $35,000 to invest. Management is trying to decide between two alternative uses for the funds as follows:

	Invest in Project X	Invest in Project Y
Investment required	$35,000	$35,000
Annual cash inflows	$9,000	
Single cash inflow at the end of 10 years		$150,000
Life of the project	10 years	10 years

The company's discount rate is 18%.

Required:

Which alternative would you recommend that the company accept? Show all computations using the net present value approach. Prepare separate computations for each project.

BRIEF EXERCISE 12–2   Net Present Value Method   [LO1]

The management of Kunkel Company is considering the purchase of a $40,000 machine that would reduce operating costs by $7,000 per year. At the end of the machine's eight-year useful life, it will have zero scrap value. The company's required rate of return is 12% on all investment projects.

Required:

1. Determine the net present value of the investment in the machine.
2. What is the difference between the total, undiscounted cash inflows and cash outflows over the entire life of the machine?

BRIEF EXERCISE 12–3   Project Profitability Index   [LO2]
Information on four investment proposals at El Gaucho, a chain of Latin American restaurants, is given
below:

	Investment Proposal			
	A	**B**	**C**	**D**
Investment required..............	$(90,000)	$(100,000)	$(70,000)	$(120,000)
Present value of cash inflows	126,000	90,000	105,000	160,000
Net present value................	$ 36,000	$ (10,000)	$ 35,000	$ 40,000
Life of the project...............	5 years	7 years	6 years	6 years

Required:
1. Compute the project profitability index for each investment proposal.
2. Rank the proposals in terms of preference.

BRIEF EXERCISE 12–4   Payback Method   [LO3]
The management of Unter Corporation, a regional roofing installer, is considering an investment with the
following cash flows:

Year	Investment	Cash Inflow
1	$15,000	$1,000
2	$8,000	$2,000
3		$2,500
4		$4,000
5		$5,000
6		$6,000
7		$5,000
8		$4,000
9		$3,000
10		$2,000

Required:
1. Determine the payback period of the investment.
2. Would the payback period be affected if the cash inflow in the last year were several times as large?
   Explain.

BRIEF EXERCISE 12–5   Simple Rate of Return Method   [LO4]
The management of Ballard MicroBrew is considering the purchase of an automated bottling machine for
$120,000. The machine would replace an old piece of equipment that costs $30,000 per year to operate. The
new machine would cost $12,000 per year to operate. The old machine currently in use could be sold now
for a scrap value of $40,000. The new machine would have a useful life of 10 years with no salvage value.

Required:
Compute the simple rate of return on the new automated bottling machine.

BRIEF EXERCISE 12–6   (Appendix 12A) Basic Present Value Concepts   [LO5]
Solve each of the following parts independently.

1. The Atlantic Medical Clinic can purchase a new computer system that will save $7,000 annually in
   billing costs. The computer system will last for eight years and have no salvage value. Up to how
   much should the Atlantic Medical Clinic be willing to pay for the new computer system if the
   clinic's required rate of return is:
   a.   16%
   b.   20%

2. The Caldwell *Herald* newspaper reported the following story:

   Frank Ormsby of Caldwell is the state's newest millionaire. By choosing the six winning numbers on last week's state lottery, Mr. Ormsby has won the week's grand prize totaling $1.6 million. The State Lottery Commission has indicated that Mr. Ormsby will receive his prize in 20 annual installments of $80,000 each.

   a. If Mr. Ormsby can invest money at a 12% rate of return, what is the present value of his winnings?

   b. Is it correct to say that Mr. Ormsby is the "state's newest millionaire"? Explain your answer.

3. Fraser Company will need a new warehouse in five years. The warehouse will cost $500,000 to build. What lump-sum amount should the company invest now to have the $500,000 available at the end of the five-year period? Assume that the company can invest money at:

   a. 10%

   b. 14%

EXERCISES

EXERCISE 12–7   Basic Net Present Value Analysis   [LO1]

Kathy Myers frequently purchases stocks and bonds, but she is uncertain how to determine the rate of return that she is earning. For example, three years ago she paid $13,000 for 200 shares of Malti Company's common stock. She received a $420 cash dividend on the stock at the end of each year for three years. At the end of three years, she sold the stock for $16,000. Kathy would like to earn a return of at least 14% on all of her investments. She is not sure whether the Malti Company stock provided a 14% return and would like some help with the necessary computations.

Required:

Using the net present value method, determine whether or not the Malti Company stock provided a 14% return. Use the general format illustrated in Exhibit 12–4 and round all computations to the nearest whole dollar.

EXERCISE 12–8   Project Profitability Index   [LO2]

The management of Shilshoe Yacht Brokers is exploring five different investment opportunities. Information on the five projects under study follows:

	Project Number				
	1	**2**	**3**	**4**	**5**
Investment required	$(270,000)	$(450,000)	$(400,000)	$(360,000)	$(480,000)
Present value of cash inflows at a 10% discount rate	336,140	522,970	379,760	433,400	567,270
Net present value	$ 66,140	$ 72,970	$ (20,240)	$ 73,400	$ 87,270
Life of the project	6 years	3 years	5 years	12 years	6 years

The company's required rate of return is 10%; thus, a 10% discount rate has been used in the present value computations above. Limited funds are available for investment, so the company can't accept all of the available projects.

Required:

1. Compute the project profitability index for each investment project.

2. Rank the five projects according to preference, in terms of:

   a. Net present value

   b. Project profitability index

3. Which ranking do you prefer? Why?

EXERCISE 12-9   Net Present Value Analysis of Competing Projects   [LO2]
Perrot & Swan, a jewelry wholesaler, has $100,000 to invest. The company is trying to decide between two alternative uses of the funds. The alternatives are:

	Project A	Project B
Cost of equipment required	$100,000	
Working capital investment required		$100,000
Annual cash inflows	$21,000	$16,000
Salvage value of equipment in six years	$8,000	
Life of the project	6 years	6 years

The working capital needed for project B will be released at the end of six years for investment elsewhere. Perrot & Swan's discount rate is 14%.

Required:
Which investment alternative (if either) would you recommend that the company accept? Show all computations using the net present value format. Prepare separate computations for each project.

EXERCISE 12-10   Payback and Simple Rate of Return Methods   [LO3, LO4]
A piece of laborsaving equipment has just come onto the market that Mitsui Electronics, Ltd., could use to reduce costs in one of its plants in Japan. Relevant data relating to the equipment follow (currency is in thousands of yen, denoted by ¥):

Purchase cost of the equipment	¥432,000
Annual cost savings that will be	
provided by the equipment	¥90,000
Life of the equipment	12 years

Required:
1. Compute the payback period for the equipment. If the company requires a payback period of four years or less, would the equipment be purchased?
2. Compute the simple rate of return on the equipment. Use straight-line depreciation based on the equipment's useful life. Would the equipment be purchased if the company's required rate of return is 14%?

EXERCISE 12-11   Net Present Value Analysis   [LO1]
Windhoek Mines, Ltd., of Namibia, is contemplating the purchase of equipment to exploit a mineral deposit on land to which the company has mineral rights. An engineering and cost analysis has been made, and it is expected that the following cash flows would be associated with opening and operating a mine in the area:

Cost of new equipment and timbers	R275,000
Working capital required	R100,000
Net annual cash receipts	R120,000*
Cost to construct new roads in three years	R40,000
Salvage value of equipment in four years	R65,000
*Receipts from sales of ore, less out-of-pocket costs for salaries, utilities, insurance, and so forth.	

The currency in Namibia is the rand, denoted here by R.
It is estimated that the mineral deposit would be exhausted after four years of mining. At that point, the working capital would be released for reinvestment elsewhere. The company's required rate of return is 20%.

Required:
Determine the net present value of the proposed mining project. Should the project be accepted? Explain.

PROBLEMS

PROBLEM 12–12A   Basic Net Present Value Analysis   [LO1]
The Sweetwater Candy Company would like to buy a new machine that would automatically "dip" choco-lates. The dipping operation is currently done largely by hand. The machine the company is considering costs $120,000. The manufacturer estimates that the machine would be usable for 12 years but would require the replacement of several key parts at the end of the sixth year. These parts would cost $9,000, including installation. After 12 years, the machine could be sold for $7,500.

The company estimates that the cost to operate the machine will be $7,000 per year. The present method of dipping chocolates costs $30,000 per year. In addition to reducing costs, the new machine will increase production by 6,000 boxes of chocolates per year. The company realizes a contribution margin of $1.50 per box. A 20% rate of return is required on all investments.

CHECK FIGURE
(1) $32,000 annual cash flows

Required:
1. What are the net annual cash inflows that will be provided by the new dipping machine?
2. Compute the new machine's net present value. Use the incremental cost approach and round all dollar amounts to the nearest whole dollar.

PROBLEM 12–13A   Ranking of Projects   [LO2]
Oxford Company has limited funds available for investment and must ration the funds among five com-peting projects. Selected information on the five projects follows:

CHECK FIGURE
(1) Project B profitability index: 0.31

Project	Investment Required	Net Present Value	Life of the Project (years)
A	$160,000	$44,323	7
B	$135,000	$42,000	12
C	$100,000	$35,035	7
D	$175,000	$38,136	3
E	$150,000	$(8,696)	6

The net present values above have been computed using a 10% discount rate. The company wants your assistance in determining which project to accept first, second, and so forth.

Required:
1. Compute the project profitability index for each project.
2. In order of preference, rank the five projects in terms of:
   a.   Net present value.
   b.   Project profitability index.
3. Which ranking do you prefer? Why?

PROBLEM 12–14A   Net Present Value Analysis   [LO1]
In eight years, Kent Duncan will retire. He is exploring the possibility of opening a self-service car wash. The car wash could be managed in the free time he has available from his regular occupation, and it could be closed easily when he retires. After careful study, Mr. Duncan has determined the following:

CHECK FIGURE
(1) $49,434 net annual cash flow

a.   A building in which a car wash could be installed is available under an eight-year lease at a cost of $1,700 per month.
b.   Purchase and installation costs of equipment would total $200,000. In eight years the equipment could be sold for about 10% of its original cost.
c.   An investment of an additional $2,000 would be required to cover working capital needs for cleaning supplies, change funds, and so forth. After eight years, this working capital would be released for investment elsewhere.
d.   Both a wash and a vacuum service would be offered with a wash costing $2.00 and the vacuum costing $1.00 per use.

e. The only variable costs associated with the operation would be 20 cents per wash for water and 10 cents per use of the vacuum for electricity.

f. In addition to rent, monthly costs of operation would be: cleaning, $450; insurance, $75; and maintenance, $500.

g. Gross receipts from the wash would be about $1,350 per week. According to the experience of other car washes, 60% of the customers using the wash would also use the vacuum.

Mr. Duncan will not open the car wash unless it provides at least a 10% return.

Required:

1. Assuming that the car wash will be open 52 weeks a year, compute the expected net annual cash receipts (gross cash receipts less cash disbursements) from its operation. (Do not include the cost of the equipment, the working capital, or the salvage value in these computations.)

2. Would you advise Mr. Duncan to open the car wash? Show computations using the net present value method of investment analysis. Round all dollar figures to the nearest whole dollar.

CHECK FIGURE
(2) 15% return

PROBLEM 12–15A   Simple Rate of Return and Payback Methods   [LO3, LO4]
Sharkey's Fun Center contains a number of electronic games as well as a miniature golf course and various rides located outside the building. Paul Sharkey, the owner, would like to construct a water slide on one portion of his property. Mr. Sharkey has gathered the following information about the slide:

a. Water slide equipment could be purchased and installed at a cost of $330,000. According to the manufacturer, the slide would be usable for 12 years after which it would have no salvage value.

b. Mr. Sharkey would use straight-line depreciation on the slide equipment.

c. To make room for the water slide, several rides would be dismantled and sold. These rides are fully depreciated, but they could be sold for $60,000 to an amusement park in a nearby city.

d. Mr. Sharkey has concluded that about 50,000 more people would use the water slide each year than have been using the rides. The admission price would be $3.60 per person (the same price that the Fun Center has been charging for the old rides).

e. Based on experience at other water slides, Mr. Sharkey estimates that annual incremental operating expenses for the slide would be: salaries, $85,000; insurance, $4,200; utilities, $13,000; and maintenance, $9,800.

Required:

1. Prepare an income statement showing the expected net operating income each year from the water slide.

2. Compute the simple rate of return expected from the water slide. Based on this computation, would the water slide be constructed if Mr. Sharkey requires a simple rate of return of at least 14% on all investments?

3. Compute the payback period for the water slide. If Mr. Sharkey accepts any project with a payback period of five years or less, would the water slide be constructed?

PROBLEM 12–16A   Net Present Value; Total and Incremental Approaches   [LO1]
Bilboa Freightlines, S.A., of Panama, has a small truck that it uses for intracity deliveries. The truck is worn out and must be either overhauled or replaced with a new truck. The company has assembled the following information (Panama uses the U.S. dollar as its currency):

CHECK FIGURE
(1) $2,119 NPV in favor of new truck

	Present Truck	New Truck
Purchase cost new	$21,000	$30,000
Remaining book value	$11,500	
Overhaul needed now	$7,000	
Annual cash operating costs	$10,000	$6,500
Salvage value-now	$9,000	
Salvage value-eight years from now	$1,000	$4,000

If the company keeps and overhauls its present delivery truck, then the truck will be usable for eight more years. If a new truck is purchased, it will be used for eight years, after which it will be traded in on another truck. The new truck would be diesel-operated, resulting in a substantial reduction in annual operating costs, as shown above.

The company computes depreciation on a straight-line basis. All investment projects are evaluated using a 16% discount rate.

Required:
1. Should Bilboa Freightlines keep the old truck or purchase the new one? Use the total-cost approach to net present value in making your decision. Round to the nearest whole dollar.
2. Redo (1) above, this time using the incremental-cost approach.

PROBLEM 12–17A Simple Rate of Return and Payback Analyses of Two Machines   [LO3, LO4]
Westwood Furniture Company is considering the purchase of two different items of equipment, as described below:

CHECK FIGURE
(1b) 12.5% return

Machine A

A compacting machine has just come onto the market that would permit Westwood Furniture Company to compress sawdust into various shelving products. At present the sawdust is disposed of as a waste product. The following information is available on the machine:

a. The machine would cost $420,000 and would have a 10% salvage value at the end of its 12–year useful life. The company uses straight-line depreciation and considers salvage value in computing depreciation deductions.
b. The shelving products manufactured from use of the machine would generate revenues of $300,000 per year. Variable manufacturing costs would be 20% of sales.
c. Fixed expenses associated with the new shelving products would be (per year): advertising, $40,000: salaries, $110,000; utilities, $5,200; and insurance, $800.

Machine B

A second machine has come onto the market that would allow Westwood Furniture Company to automate a sanding process that is now done largely by hand. The following information is available:

a. The new sanding machine would cost $234,000 and would have no salvage value at the end of its 13-year useful life. The company would use straight-line depreciation on the new machine.
b. Several old pieces of sanding equipment that are fully depreciated would be disposed of at a scrap value of $9,000.
c. The new sanding machine would provide substantial annual savings in cash operating costs. It would require an operator at an annual salary of $16,350 and $5,400 in annual maintenance costs. The current, hand-operated sanding procedure costs the company $78,000 per year in total.

Westwood Furniture Company requires a simple rate of return of 15% on all equipment purchases. Also, the company will not purchase equipment unless the equipment has a payback period of 4.0 years or less.

Required:
1. For machine A:
   a. Prepare an income statement showing the expected net operating income each year from the new shelving products. Use the contribution format.
   b. Compute the simple rate of return.
   c. Compute the payback period.
2. For machine B:
   a. Compute the simple rate of return.
   b. Compute the payback period.
3. According to the company's criteria, which machine, if either, should the company purchase?

PROBLEM 12–18A Net Present Value Analysis of Securities [LO1]

Linda Clark received $175,000 from her mother's estate. She placed the funds into the hands of a broker, who purchased the following securities on Linda's behalf:

CHECK FIGURE
(1) $7,560 NPV of common stock

a. Common stock was purchased at a cost of $95,000. The stock paid no dividends, but it was sold for $160,000 at the end of three years.
b. Preferred stock was purchased at its par value of $30,000. The stock paid a 6% dividend (based on par value) each year for three years. At the end of three years, the stock was sold for $27,000.
c. Bonds were purchased at a cost of $50,000. The bonds paid $3,000 in interest every six months. After three years, the bonds were sold for $52,700. (Note: In discounting a cash flow that occurs semiannually, the procedure is to halve the discount rate and double the number of periods. Use the same procedure in discounting the proceeds from the sale.)

The securities were all sold at the end of three years so that Linda would have funds available to open a new business venture. The broker stated that the investments had earned more than a 16% return, and he gave Linda the following computation to support his statement:

Common stock:	
Gain on sale ($160,000 − $95,000)	$65,000
Preferred stock:	
Dividends paid (6% × $30.000 × 3 years)	5,400
Loss on sale ($27,000 − $30,000)	(3,000)
Bonds:	
Interest paid ($3,000 × 6 periods)	18,000
Gain on sale ($52,700 − $50,000)	2,700
Net gain on all investments	$88,100

$$\frac{\$88,100 \div 3 \text{ years}}{\$175,000} = 16.8\%$$

Required:

1. Using a 16% discount rate, compute the net present value of *each* of the three investments. On which investment(s) did Linda earn a 16% rate of return? (Round computations to the nearest whole dollar.)
2. Considering all three investments together, did Linda earn a 16% rate of return? Explain.
3. Linda wants to use the $239,700 proceeds ($160,000 + $27,000 + $52,700 = $239,700) from sale of the securities to open a retail store under a 12-year franchise contract. What net annual cash inflow must the store generate for Linda to earn a 14% return over the 12-year period? Round computations to the nearest whole dollar.

PROBLEM 12–19A Keep or Sell Property (LO1)

Raul Martinas, professor of languages at Eastern University, owns a small office building adjacent to the university campus. He acquired the property 10 years ago at a total cost of $530,000—$50,000 for the land and $480,000 for the building. He has just received an offer from a realty company that wants to purchase the property; however, the property has been a good source of income over the years, so Professor Martinas is unsure whether he should keep it or sell it. His alternatives are:

CHECK FIGURE
Keep the property alternative: $309,402 PV of cash flows

Alternative 1: Keep the property. Professor Martinas' accountant has kept careful records of the income realized from the property over the past 10 years. These records indicate the following annual revenues and expenses:

Rental receipts		$140,000
Less building expenses:		
Utilities	$25,000	
Depreciation of building	16,000	
Property taxes and insurance	18,000	
Repairs and maintenance	9,000	
Custodial help and supplies	40,000	108,000
Net operating income		$ 32,000

Professor Martinas makes a $12,000 mortgage payment each year on the property. The mortgage will be paid off in eight more years. He has been depreciating the building by the straight-line method, assuming a salvage value of $80,000 for the building which he still thinks is an appropriate figure. He feels sure that the building can be rented for another 15 years. He also feels sure that 15 years from now the land will be worth three times what he paid for it.

Alternative 2: Sell the property. A realty company has offered to purchase the property by paying $175,000 immediately and $26,500 per year for the next 15 years. Control of the property would go to the realty company immediately. To sell the property, Professor Martinas would need to pay the mortgage off, which could be done by making a lump-sum payment of $90,000.

Required:

Assume that Professor Martinas requires a 12% rate of return. Would you recommend he keep or sell the property? Show computations using the total-cost approach to net present value.

BUILDING YOUR SKILLS

Teamwork in Action   (LO1)

Kingsley Products, Ltd., is using a model 400 shaping machine to make one of its products. The company is expecting to have a large increase in demand for the product and is anxious to expand its productive capacity. Two possibilities are under consideration:

CHECK FIGURE
(1) $30,046 NPV in favor of the model 400 machine

Alternative 1: Purchase another model 400 shaping machine to operate along with the currently owned model 400 machine.

Alternative 2: Purchase a model 800 shaping machine and use the currently owned model 400 machine as standby equipment. The model 800 machine is a high-speed unit with double the capacity of the model 400 machine.

The following additional information is available on the two alternatives:

a. Both the model 400 machine and the model 800 machine have a 10-year life from the time they are first used in production. The scrap value of both machines is negligible and can be ignored. Straight-line depreciation is used.

b. The cost of a new model 800 machine is $300,000.

c. The model 400 machine now in use cost $160,000 three years ago. Its present book value is $112,000, and its present market value is $90,000.

d. A new model 400 machine costs $170,000 now. If the company decides not to buy the model 800 machine, then the old model 400 machine will have to be replaced in seven years at a cost of $200,000. The replacement machine will be sold at the end of the tenth year for $140,000.

e. Production over the next 10 years is expected to be:

Year	Production in Units
1	40,000
2	60,000
3	80,000
4–10	90,000

f. The two models of machines are not equally efficient. Comparative variable costs per unit are:

	Model	
	400	800
Direct materials per unit	$0.25	$0.40
Direct labor per unit	0.49	0.16
Supplies and lubricants per unit	0.06	0.04
Total variable cost per unit	$0.80	$0.60

g.   The model 400 machine is less costly to maintain than the model 800 machine. Annual repairs and maintenance costs on a model 400 machine are $2,500.

h.   Repairs and maintenance costs on a model 800 machine, with a model 400 machine used as standby, would total $3,800 per year.

i.   No other costs will change as a result of the decision between the two machines.

j.   Kingsley Products has a 20% required rate of return on all investments.

Required:

The team should discuss and then respond to the following. All team members should agree with and understand the answers (including the calculations supporting the answers) and be prepared to report the information developed in class. (Each teammate can assume responsibility for a different part of the presentation.)

1.   Which alternative should the company choose? Use the net present value approach.

2.   Suppose that the cost of labor increases by 10%. Would this make the model 800 machine more or less desirable? Explain. No computations are needed.

3.   Suppose that the cost of direct materials doubles. Would this make the model 800 machine more or less desirable? Explain. No computations are needed.

CHECK FIGURE
(1) $78,001 NPV in favor of leasing

Analytical Thinking   (LO1)

Top-Quality Stores, Inc., owns a nationwide chain of supermarkets. The company is going to open another store soon, and a suitable building site has been located in an attractive and rapidly growing area. In discussing how the company can acquire the desired building and other facilities needed to open the new store, Sam Watkins, the company's vice president in charge of sales, stated, "I know most of our competitors are starting to lease facilities rather than buy, but I just can't see the economics of it. Our development people tell me that we can buy the building site, put a building on it, and get all the store fixtures we need for just $850,000. They also say that property taxes, insurance, and repairs would run $20,000 a year. When you figure that we plan to keep a site for 18 years, that's a total cost of $1,210,000. But then when you realize that the property will be worth at least a half million in 18 years, that's a net cost to us of only $710,000. What would it cost to lease the property?"

"I understand that Beneficial Insurance Company is willing to purchase the building site, construct a building and install fixtures to our specifications, and then lease the facility to us for 18 years at an annual lease payment of $120,000," replied Lisa Coleman, the company's executive vice president.

"That's just my point," said Sam. "At $120,000 a year, it would cost us a cool $2,160,000 over the 18 years. That's three times what it would cost to buy, and what would we have left at the end? Nothing! The building would belong to the insurance company!"

"You're overlooking a few things," replied Lisa. "For one thing, the treasurer's office says that we could only afford to put $350,000 down if we buy the property, and then we would have to pay the other $500,000 off over four years at $175,000 a year. So there would be some interest involved on the purchase side that you haven't figured in."

"But that little bit of interest is nothing compared to over 2 million bucks for leasing," said Sam. "Also, if we lease I understand we would have to put up an $8,000 security deposit that we wouldn't get back until the end. And besides that, we would still have to pay all the yearly repairs and maintenance costs just like we owned the property. No wonder those insurance companies are so rich if they can swing deals like this."

"Well, I'll admit that I don't have all the figures sorted out yet," replied Lisa. "But I do have the operating cost breakdown for the building, which includes $7,500 annually for property taxes, $8,000 for insurance, and $4,500 for repairs and maintenance. If we lease, Beneficial will handle its own insurance costs and of course the owner will have to pay the property taxes. I'll put all this together and see if leasing makes any sense with our required rate of return of 16%. The president wants a presentation and recommendation in the executive committee meeting tomorrow. Let's see, development said the first lease payment would be due now and the remaining ones due in years 1–17. Development also said that this store should generate a net cash inflow that's well above the average for our stores."

Required:

1.   Using the net present value approach, determine whether Top-Quality Stores, Inc., should lease or buy the new facility. Assume that you will be making your presentation before the company's executive committee.

2.   How will you reply in the meeting if Sam Watkins brings up the issue of the building's future sales value?

Communicating in Practice (LOI, LO3, LO4)

Use an online yellow pages directory such as www.comfind.com or www.athand.com to find a manufacturer in your area that has a website. Make an appointment with the controller or chief financial officer of the company. Before your meeting, find out as much as you can about the organization's operations from its website.

Required:

After asking the following questions about a capital budgeting decision that was made by the management of the company, write a brief memorandum to your instructor that summarizes the information obtained from the company's website and addresses what you found out during your interview.

1. What was the nature of the capital project?
2. What was the total cost of the capital project?
3. Did the project costs stay within budget (or estimate)?
4. What financial criteria were used to evaluate the project?

Taking It to the Net

As you know, the World Wide Web is a medium that is constantly evolving. Sites come and go and change without notice. To enable periodic updating of site addresses, these problems have been posted to the textbook website (www.mhhe.com/bgn3e). After accessing the site, enter the Student Center and select this chapter to find the Taking It to the Net problems.

13

"How Well Am I Doing?" Statement of Cash Flows

CHAPTER OUTLINE

Chapter Thirteen

DECISION FEATURE

Is the Party Over?

There was a time when many thought that e-tailers (e-retailers) might wipe out traditional retailers. Now investors wonder if any e-tailers will be able to survive. It all boils down to cash flows. Unable to generate the cash needed to support their ongoing operations, the dot.coms are having a hard time raising money. The traditional sources of funds are venture capitalists, Wall Street investors, and banks. Venture capitalists, who often made the initial cash investments required to finance the start-up operations of many e-tailers, are unwilling to invest additional cash. After snatching up the initial public offering of almost any dot.com during the late 1990s, Wall Street investors are now guarded. Banks, quite willing to provide financing to established companies with histories of profitability, are reluctant to loan money to e-tailers because the risk of default is high.

Typically, a potential investor would start with a company's financial statements. The balance sheet provides information about the company's financial condition, and the income statement indicates whether or not a company is profitable, but neither helps to predict whether a company will generate cash. Users of financial statements look to the statement of cash flows for that information.

Market Guide, a Wall Street research firm, analyzes the statements of cash flows of selected e-tailers. Their approach estimates how long it will take for a given company to burn through its available cash. In April 2000, Matt Krantz, a *USA Today* reporter warned that 5 of the 15 companies included in the *USA Today* "Internet 100" could run out of cash by mid-2001. The five companies cited were Drugstore.com, Egghead.com, EMusic, eToys, and Travelocity. Krantz was on target. Shortly thereafter, Egghead.com and eToys went bankrupt and EMusic laid off more than one-third of its staff.

Sources: Matt Krantz, "Dot-Coms Could Run Out of Cash," *USA Today,* August 18, 2000, 1B; Matt Krantz, "E-Retailers Run Low on Fuel," *USA Today,* April 26, 2000, 1B; News.com website; and ecommercetimes website.

LEARNING OBJECTIVES

After studying Chapter 13, you should be able to:

LO1 Classify changes in noncash balance sheet accounts as sources or uses of cash.

LO2 Classify transactions as operating activities, investing activities, or financing activities.

LO3 Prepare a statement of cash flows using the indirect method to determine the net cash provided by operating activities.

LO4 (Appendix 13A) Use the direct method to determine the net cash provided by operating activities.

LO5 (Appendix 13B) Prepare a statement of cash flows using the T-account approach.

Three major financial statements are ordinarily required for external reports—an income statement, a balance sheet, and a statement of cash flows. The **statement of cash flows** highlights the major activities that directly and indirectly impact cash flows and hence affect the overall cash balance. Managers focus on cash for a very good reason—without sufficient cash at the right times, a company may miss golden investment opportunities or may even go bankrupt.

The statement of cash flows answers questions that cannot be easily answered by the income statement and balance sheet alone. For example, the statement of cash flows can be used to answer questions like the following: Where did Delta Airlines get the cash to pay a dividend of nearly $140 million in a year in which, according to its income statement, it lost more than $1 billion? How was The Walt Disney Company able to invest nearly $800 million in expansion of its theme parks, including a major renovation of Epcot Center, despite a loss of more than $500 million on its investment in EuroDisney? Where did Wendy's International, Inc., get $125 million to expand its chain of fast-food restaurants in a year when its net income was only $79 million and it did not raise any new debt? To answer such questions, familiarity with the statement of cash flows is required.

The statement of cash flows is a valuable analytical tool for managers as well as for investors and creditors, although managers tend to be more concerned with forecasted statements of cash flows that are prepared as part of the budgeting process. The statement of cash flows can be used to answer crucial questions such as:

1. Is the company generating sufficient positive cash flows from its ongoing operations to remain viable?
2. Will the company be able to repay its debts?
3. Will the company be able to pay its usual dividend?
4. Why do net income and net cash flow differ?
5. To what extent will the company have to borrow money in order to make needed investments?

This chapter focuses on how to prepare the statement of cash flows and on how to use it to help assess a company's finances.

THE BASIC APPROACH TO A STATEMENT OF CASH FLOWS

LEARNING OBJECTIVE 1

Classify changes in noncash balance sheet accounts as sources or uses of cash.

For the statement of cash flows to be useful to managers and others, it is important that companies use the same definition of cash. It is also important that the statement be constructed using consistent guidelines for identifying activities that are *sources* of cash and *uses* of cash. The proper definition of cash and the guidelines to use in identifying sources and uses of cash are discussed in this section.

Definition of Cash

In a statement of cash flows, *cash* is broadly defined to include both cash and cash equivalents. **Cash equivalents** consist of short-term, highly liquid investments such as Treasury bills, commercial paper, and money market funds that are made solely for the purpose of generating a return on temporarily idle funds. Instead of simply holding cash, most companies invest their excess cash reserves in these types of interest-bearing assets that can be easily converted into cash. Since such assets are equivalent to cash, they are included with cash in a statement of cash flows.

Constructing the Statement of Cash Flows Using Changes in Noncash Balance Sheet Accounts

A type of statement of cash flows could be constructed by simply summarizing all of the debits and credits to the Cash and Cash Equivalents accounts during a period. However, this approach would overlook all of the transactions that involve an implicit exchange of cash. For example, when a company purchases inventory on credit, cash is implicitly exchanged. In essence, the supplier loans the company cash, which the company then uses to acquire inventory from the supplier. Rather than just looking at the transactions that explicitly involve cash, financial statement users are interested in all of the transactions that implicitly or explicitly involve cash. When inventory is purchased on credit, the Inventory account increases, which is an implicit *use* of cash. At the same time, Accounts Payable increases, which is an implicit *source* of cash. In general, increases in the Inventory account are classified as uses of cash and increases in the Accounts Payable account are classified as sources of cash. This suggests that analyzing changes in balance sheet accounts, such as Inventory and Accounts Payable, will uncover both the explicit and implicit sources and uses of cash. And this is indeed the basic approach taken in the statement of cash flows. The logic underlying this approach is demonstrated in Exhibit 13–1.

Exhibit 13–1 shows a seven-step process that can be used to explain net cash flow in terms of net income, dividends, and changes in balance sheet accounts. The first step is to define the balance sheet equation: Assets = Liabilities + Stockholders' Equity. The second step, shown in the second line of the exhibit, is to recognize that assets consist of cash and noncash assets. The third step is to recognize that if the account balances are always equal, then the *changes* in the account balances must be equal too. The fourth step (the fourth line of the exhibit) simply notes that the change in cash for a period is by definition the company's net cash flow. The fifth step is to move the changes in noncash assets from the left-hand side of the equation to the right-hand side. This is done because we are attempting to explain net cash flow, so it should be isolated on the left-hand side of the equation. The sixth step breaks down the "Changes in Stockholders' Equity" into three components—net income, dividends,

EXHIBIT 13–1 Explaining Net Cash Flow by Analysis of the Noncash Balance Sheet Accounts

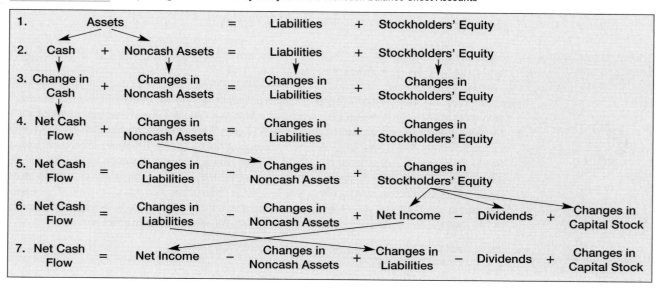

EXHIBIT 13–2

Classifications of Sources and
Uses of Cash

	Sources	Uses
Net income	Always	
Net loss		Always
Changes in noncash assets	Decreases	Increases
Changes in liabilities*	Increases	Decreases
Changes in capital stock accounts	Increases	Decreases
Dividends paid to stockholders		Always
	Total sources −	Total uses = Net cash flow

*Contra asset accounts, such as the Accumulated Depreciation and Amortization account, follow the rules for liabilities.

and changes in capital stock. Net income increases stockholders' equity, while dividends reduce stockholders' equity. The seventh step rearranges two terms in the right-hand side of the equation—changes in liabilities and net income.

According to the equation derived in step 7 in Exhibit 13–1, the net cash flow for a period can be determined by starting with net income, then deducting changes in noncash assets, adding changes in liabilities, deducting dividends paid to stockholders, and finally adding changes in capital stock. It is important to realize that changes in accounts can be either increases (positive) or decreases (negative), and this affects how we should interpret the equation shown in step 7 in Exhibit 13–1. For example, increases in liabilities are added back to net income, whereas decreases in liabilities are deducted from net income to arrive at the net cash flow. On the other hand, increases in noncash assets are deducted from net income while decreases in noncash assets are added back to net income. Exhibit 13–2 summarizes the appropriate classifications—in terms of sources and uses—of net income, dividends, and changes in the noncash balance sheet accounts.

The classifications in Exhibit 13–2 are intuitive. Positive net income generates cash, whereas a net loss consumes cash. Decreases in noncash assets, such as the sale of inventories or property, are a source of cash. Increases in noncash assets, such as the purchase of inventories or property, are a use of cash. Increases in liabilities, such as taking out a loan, are a source of cash. Decreases in liabilities, such as paying off a loan, are a use of cash. Increases in capital stock accounts, such as the sale of common stock, are a source of cash. And payments of dividends to stockholders use cash.

Constructing a simple statement of cash flows is a straightforward process. Begin with net income (or net loss) and then add to it everything listed as sources in Exhibit 13–2 and subtract from it everything listed as uses. This will be illustrated with an example in the next section.

IN BUSINESS

What's Up at Amazon?

Amazon.com, the online retailer of books and other merchandise, may have the best chance of eventually succeeding of any Internet retailer. Even so, "[I]t's no news that Amazon has had troubles, but the numbers are worse than many on Wall Street have admitted." Robert Tracy, a CPA and an analyst on the staff of grantsinvestor.com, took a close look at Amazon's financial statements and found that the company was holding its bills longer than it used to, especially at year-end. The cash flow from this increase in accounts payable exceeded the cash flow from all other operating sources combined. "Bulls [i.e., those who are positive about Amazon.com stock] will commend the company on imaginative cash management. Bears [i.e., those who are skeptical about the stock] will accuse it of financial engineering. What is not debatable is that, by stretching out payments into the new year, Amazon has presented a more liquid face to the world than it could otherwise have done."

Source: James Grant, "Diving into Amazon," *Forbes*, January 22, 2001, p. 153.

AN EXAMPLE OF A SIMPLIFIED STATEMENT OF CASH FLOWS

To illustrate the ideas introduced in the preceding section, we will now construct a *simplified* statement of cash flows for Nordstrom, Inc., one of the leading fashion retailers in the United States. This simplified statement does not follow the format required by the Financial Accounting Standards Board (FASB) for external financial reports, but it is a useful learning aid because it shows where the numbers come from in a statement of cash flows and how they fit together. In later sections, we will show how the same basic data can be used to construct a full-fledged statement of cash flows that would be acceptable for external reports.

Constructing a Simplified Statement of Cash Flows

According to Exhibit 13–2, to construct a statement of cash flows we need the company's net income or loss, the changes in each of its balance sheet accounts, and the dividends paid to stockholders for the year. We can obtain this information from the Nordstrom financial statements that appear in Exhibits 13–3, 13–4, and 13–5. In a few instances, the actual statements have been simplified for ease of computation and discussion.

Note that changes between the beginning and ending balances have been computed for each of the balance sheet accounts in Exhibit 13–4, and each change has been classified as a source or use of cash. For example, the $17 million decrease in accounts receivable has been classified as a source of cash. This is because, as shown in Exhibit 13–2, decreases in noncash accounts, such as accounts receivable, are classified as sources of cash.

A *simplified* statement of cash flows appears in Exhibit 13–6. This statement was constructed by gathering together all of the entries listed as sources in Exhibit 13–4 and all of the entries listed as uses. The sources exceeded the uses by $62 million. This is the net cash flow for the year and is also, by definition, the change in cash and cash equivalents for the year. (Trace this $62 million back to Exhibit 13–4.)

EXHIBIT 13–3

Nordstrom, Inc.*
Income Statement
(dollars in millions)

Net sales..........................	$3,638
Less cost of sales	2,469
Gross margin	1,169
Less operating expenses.........	941
Net operating income	228
Nonoperating items:	
Gain on sale of store	3
Income before taxes	231
Less income taxes...............	91
Net income....................	$ 140

*This statement is loosely based on an actual income statement published by Nordstrom. Among other differences, there was no "Gain on sale of store" in the original statement. This "gain" has been included here to illustrate how to handle gains and losses on a statement of cash flows.

EXHIBIT 13–4

Nordstrom, Inc.*
Comparative Balance Sheet
(dollars in millions)

	Ending Balance	Beginning Balance	Change	Source or Use?
Assets				
Current assets:				
Cash and cash equivalents.........	$ 91	$ 29	+62	
Accounts receivable	637	654	−17	Source
Merchandise inventory	586	537	+49	Use
Total current assets................	1,314	1,220		
Property, buildings, and equipment....	1,517	1,394	+123	Use
Less accumulated depreciation and amortization	654	561	+93	Source
Net property, buildings, and equipment	863	833		
Total assets	$2,177	$2,053		
Liabilities and Stockholders' Equity				
Current liabilities:				
Accounts payable	$ 264	$ 220	+44	Source
Accrued wages and salaries payable.......................	193	190	+3	Source
Accrued income taxes payable	28	22	+6	Source
Notes payable	40	38	+2	Source
Total current liabilities..............	525	470		
Long-term debt....................	439	482	−43	Use
Deferred income taxes	47	49	−2	Use
Total liabilities	1,011	1,001		
Stockholders' equity:				
Common stock	157	155	+2	Source
Retained earnings	1,009	897	+112	†
Total stockholders' equity...........	1,166	1,052		
Total liabilities and stockholders' equity	$2,177	$2,053		

*This statement differs from the actual statement published by Nordstrom.
†The change in retained earnings of $112 million equals the net income of $140 million less the cash dividends paid to stockholders of $28 million. Net income is classified as a source and dividends as a use.

EXHIBIT 13–5

Nordstrom, Inc.*
Statement of Retained Earnings
(dollars in millions)

Retained earnings, beginning balance	$ 897
Add: Net income	140
	1,037
Deduct: Dividends paid	28
Retained earnings, ending balance.......	$1,009

*This statement differs in a few details from the actual statement published by Nordstrom.

EXHIBIT 13–6

Nordstrom, Inc.
Simplified Statement of Cash Flows
(dollars in millions)

Note: This simplified statement is for illustration purposes only. It should *not* be used to complete end-of-chapter homework assignments or for preparing an actual statement of cash flows. See Exhibit 13–11 for the proper format for a statement of cash flows.

Sources		
Net income	$140	
Decreases in noncash assets:		
Decrease in accounts receivable	17	
Increases in liabilities (and contra asset accounts):		
Increase in accumulated depreciation and amortization	93	
Increase in accounts payable	44	
Increase in accrued wages and salaries	3	
Increase in accrued income taxes	6	
Increase in notes payable	2	
Increases in capital stock accounts:		
Increase in common stock	2	
Total sources		$307
Uses		
Increases in noncash assets:		
Increase in merchandise inventory	49	
Increase in property, buildings, and equipment	123	
Decreases in liabilities:		
Decrease in long-term debt	43	
Decrease in deferred income taxes	2	
Dividends	28	
Total uses		245
Net cash flow		$ 62

The Need for a More Detailed Statement

While the simplified statement of cash flows in Exhibit 13–6 is not difficult to construct, it is not acceptable for external financial reports. The FASB requires that the statement of cash flows follow a different format and that a few of the entries be modified. Nevertheless, almost all of the entries on a full-fledged statement of cash flows are the same as the entries on the simplified statement of cash flows—they are just in a different order.

In the following sections, we will discuss the modifications to the simplified statement of cash flows that are necessary to conform to external reporting requirements.

1. Which of the following is considered a source of cash on the statement of cash flows? (You may select more than one answer.)
   a.   A decrease in the accounts payable account.
   b.   An increase in the inventory account.
   c.   A decrease in the accounts receivable account.
   d.   An increase in the property, plant, and equipment account.

CONCEPT
CHECK

IN BUSINESS

Plugging the Cash Flow Leak

Modern synthetic fabrics such as polyester fleece and Gore-Tex have almost completely replaced wool in ski clothing. John Fernsell started Ibex Outdoor Clothing in Woodstock, Vermont, to buck this trend. Fernsell's five-person company designs and sells jackets made of high-grade wool from Europe.

Fernsell quickly discovered an unfortunate fact of life about the wool clothing business—he faces a potentially ruinous cash crunch every year. Ibex orders wool from Europe in February but does not pay the mills until June when they ship fabric to the garment makers in California. The garment factories send finished goods to Ibex in July and August, and Ibex pays for them on receipt. Ibex ships to retailers in September and October, but doesn't get paid until November, December, or even January. That means from June to December the company spends like crazy—and takes in virtually nothing. Fernsell tried to get by with a line of credit, but it was insufficient. To survive, he had to ask his suppliers to let him pay late, which was not a long-term solution. To reduce this cash flow problem, Fernsell is introducing a line of wool *summer* clothing so that some cash will be flowing in from May through July, when he must pay his suppliers for the winter clothing.

Source: Daniel Lyons, "Wool Gatherer," *Forbes,* April 16, 2001, p. 310.

ORGANIZATION OF THE FULL-FLEDGED STATEMENT OF CASH FLOWS

LEARNING OBJECTIVE 2

Classify transactions as operating activities, investing activities, or financing activities.

Concept 13-1

To make it easier to compare statements of cash flows from different companies, the Financial Accounting Standards Board (FASB) requires that companies follow prescribed rules for preparing the statement of cash flows. The FASB requires that the statement be divided into three sections: *operating activities, investing activities,* and *financing activities.* The guidelines for applying these classifications are summarized in Exhibit 13–7 and are discussed below.

Operating Activities

Generally, **operating activities** are those activities that enter into the determination of net income. Technically, however, the FASB defines operating activities as all transactions that are not classified as investing or financing activities. Generally speaking, this includes all transactions affecting current assets and all transactions affecting current liabilities except for issuing and repaying a note payable. Operating activities also include changes in noncurrent balance sheet accounts that directly affect net income such as the Accumulated Depreciation and Amortization account.

EXHIBIT 13–7

Guidelines for Classifying Transactions as Operating, Investing, and Financing Activities

Operating Activities:
- Net income
- Changes in current assets
- Changes in noncurrent assets that affect net income (e.g., depreciation)
- Changes in current liabilities (except for debts to lenders and dividends payable)
- Changes in noncurrent liabilities that affect net income

Investing Activities:
- Changes in noncurrent assets that are not included in net income

Financing Activities:
- Changes in the current liabilities that are debts to lenders rather than obligations to suppliers, employees, or the government
- Changes in noncurrent liabilities that are not included in net income
- Changes in capital stock accounts
- Dividends

Operating, Investing, and Financing Activities

Operating Activities

Investing Activities

Financing Activities

Investing Activities

Generally speaking, transactions that involve acquiring or disposing of noncurrent assets are classified as **investing activities.** These transactions include acquiring or selling property, plant, and equipment; acquiring or selling securities held for long-term investment, such as bonds and stocks of other companies; and lending money to another entity (such as a subsidiary) and the subsequent collection of the loan. However, as previously discussed, changes in noncurrent assets that directly affect net income such as depreciation and amortization charges are classified as operating activities.

Financing Activities

As a general rule, borrowing from creditors or repaying creditors as well as transactions with the company's owners are classified as **financing activities.** For example, when a company borrows money by issuing a bond, the transaction is classified as a financing activity. However, transactions with creditors that affect net income are classified as operating activities. For example, interest on the company's debt is included in operating activities rather than financing activities because interest is deducted as an expense in computing net income. In contrast, a dividend payment to owners does not affect net income and therefore is classified as a financing rather than an operating activity.

Most changes in current liabilities are treated as operating activities unless the transaction involves borrowing money directly from a lender, as with a note payable, or repaying such a debt. Transactions involving accounts payable, wages payable, and taxes payable are included in operating activities rather than financing activities, because these transactions occur on a routine basis and involve the company's suppliers, employees, and the government rather than lenders.

Warning Signs on the Statement of Cash Flows   **IN BUSINESS**

Herb Greenberg, a columnist for *Fortune* magazine, emphasizes the importance of monitoring a company's cash flows:

> [S]tick with two basic indicators: cash flow from operations (how much money the company's core business generates day to day) and total cash flow (which includes the core business, financing, and any investments). Are these two numbers going up or down? Up, it almost goes without saying, is better than down. A slide in both suggested to Bill Fleckenstein of Fleckenstein Capital that Gateway was headed for earnings trouble back in June. Sure enough, in November the company warned of a profit shortfall. "If earnings are growing and the company is consuming cash, that's one of the largest red lights on the balance sheet decoder ring," Fleckenstein says.

Source: Herb Greenberg, "Minding Your K's and Q's," *Fortune*, January 8, 2001, p. 180.

Manipulative Cash Flow Reporting

Professor O. Whitfield Broome from the University of Virginia found a common thread that ties together the fraudulent financial reporting at Tyco International, Dynergy, Qwest Communications International, Adelphia Communications Corporation, and WorldCom. Each company misclassified cash flows among the three sections of the statements cash flows in an effort to inflate their net cash provided by operating activities. For example, Tyco paid more than $800 million to purchase customer contracts from dealers. The cash paid for these contracts was reported in the investing activities section of the statement of cash flows. However, when customers made payments to Tyco under these contracts, all of the cash received was reported in the operating activities section of the statement of cash flows. As another example, WorldCom recorded a substantial amount of its operating expenses as capital investments. Besides inflating net operating income, this manipulation enabled WorldCom to shift cash outflows from the operating activities section of the statement of cash flows to the investing activities section.

Source: O. Whitfield Broome, "Statement of Cash Flows: Time for Change!" *Financial Analysts Journal*, March/April 2004, pp. 16–22.

OTHER ISSUES IN PREPARING THE STATEMENT OF CASH FLOWS

We must consider two other issues before illustrating the preparation of a statement of cash flows that would be acceptable for external financial reports.[1] These issues are (1) whether amounts on the statement should be presented gross or net and (2) whether operating activities should be presented using the direct or indirect method.

Cash Flows: Gross or Net?

For both financing and investing activities, items on the statement of cash flows should be presented in gross amounts rather than in net amounts. To illustrate, suppose that Macy's Department Stores purchases $50 million in property during the year and sells other property for $30 million. Instead of showing the net change of $20 million, the company must show the gross amounts of both the purchases and the sales. The purchases would be recorded as a use of cash, and the sales would be recorded as a source of cash. Similarly, if Alcoa receives $80 million from the issue of long-term bonds and then pays out $30 million to retire other bonds, the two transactions must be reported separately on the statement of cash flows rather than being netted against each other.

The gross method of reporting does *not* extend to operating activities, where debits and credits to an account are ordinarily netted against each other on the statement of cash flows. For example, if Sears adds $600 million to its accounts receivable as a result of sales during the year and $520 million of accounts receivable are collected, only the net increase of $80 million would be reported on the statement of cash flows.

Operating Activities: Direct or Indirect Method?

The net amount of the cash inflows and outflows arising from operating activities, which is known formally as the **net cash provided by operating activities,** can be computed by either the direct or the indirect method.

---

[1] A third issue to consider when creating a statement of cash flows is direct exchange transactions in which noncurrent balance sheet items are swapped. For example, a company might issue common stock in a direct exchange for property. Or creditors might swap their long-term debt for common stock of the company. Direct exchange transactions are not reported on the statement of cash flows; however, they are disclosed in a separate schedule that accompanies the statement. More advanced accounting courses cover this topic in greater detail.

Under the **direct method,** the income statement is reconstructed on a cash basis from top to bottom. For example, in the direct method, cash collected from customers is listed instead of revenue, and payments to suppliers is listed instead of cost of goods sold. In essence, cash receipts are counted as revenues and cash disbursements are counted as expenses. The difference between the cash receipts and cash disbursements is the net cash provided by operating activities for the period.

Under the **indirect method,** the operating activities section of the statement of cash flows is constructed by starting with net income and adjusting it to a cash basis. That is, rather than directly computing cash sales, cash expenses, and so forth, these amounts are arrived at *indirectly* by removing from net income any items that do not affect cash flows. The indirect method has an advantage over the direct method because it shows the reasons for any differences between net income and the net cash provided by operating activities. The indirect method is also known as the **reconciliation method.**

Although both methods will result in exactly the same amount for the net cash provided by operating activities, the FASB *recommends* and *encourages* the use of the direct method for external reports. But there is a catch. If the direct method is used, there must be a supplementary reconciliation of net income with operating cash flows. In essence, if a company chooses to use the direct method, it must also construct a statement that uses a form of the indirect method. However, if a company chooses to use the indirect method for determining the net cash provided by operating activities, there is no requirement that it also report the results of using the direct method.

The Popularity of the Indirect Method

IN BUSINESS

A survey of 600 companies revealed that only 7, or 1.2%, use the direct method to construct the statement of cash flows for external reports. The remaining 98.8% probably use the indirect method because it is simply less work.

Source: American Institute of Certified Public Accountants, *Accounting Trends and Techniques: 2004,* Jersey City, NJ, 2004, p. 549.

While there are some good reasons for using the direct method, we use the indirect method in this chapter because it is by far the most popular method. The direct method is discussed and illustrated in Appendix 13A at the end of the chapter.

2. Which of the following statements is false? (You may select more than one answer.)
   a. Purchasing a new manufacturing plant would be classified as an investing activity.
   b. Paying off accounts payable balances would be classified as a financing activity.
   c. Dividend payments would be classified as a financing activity.
   d. Either the direct or the indirect method can be used to calculate the net cash provided by financing activities.

CONCEPT CHECK ✓

AN EXAMPLE OF A FULL-FLEDGED STATEMENT OF CASH FLOWS

In this section, we apply the FASB rules to construct a statement of cash flows for Nordstrom that would be acceptable for external reporting. The approach we take is based on an analysis of changes in balance sheet accounts, as in our earlier discussion of the simplified statement of cash flows. Indeed, as you will see, the full-fledged statement of cash flows is for the most part just a reorganized form of the simplified statement that appears in Exhibit 13–6.

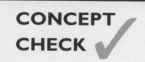

LEARNING OBJECTIVE 3

Prepare a statement of cash flows using the indirect method to determine the net cash provided by operating activities.

	Add (+) or Deduct (−) to Adjust Net Income
Net income	$XXX
Adjustments needed to convert net income to a cash basis:	
Depreciation, depletion, and amortization charges	+
Add (deduct) changes in current asset accounts affecting revenue or expense:*	
Increase in the account	−
Decrease in the account	+
Add (deduct) changes in current liability accounts affecting revenue or expense:†	
Increase in the account	+
Decrease in the account	−
Add (deduct) gains or losses on sales of assets:	
Gain on sales of assets	−
Loss on sales of assets	+
Add (deduct) changes in the Deferred Income Taxes account:	
Increase if a liability; decrease if an asset	+
Decrease if a liability; increase if an asset	−
Net cash provided by operating activities	$XXX

*Examples include accounts receivable, accrued receivables, inventory, and prepaid expenses.
†Examples include accounts payable, accrued liabilities, and taxes payable.

The format for the operating activities section of the statement of cash flows is shown in Exhibit 13–8. Notice that net income is adjusted to net cash provided by operating activities by adding sources of cash and deducting uses of cash. For example, consider the effect of an increase in the Accounts Receivable account on the net cash provided by operating activities. Since the Accounts Receivable account is a noncash asset, we know from Exhibit 13–2 that increases in this account are treated as *uses* of cash. In other words, increases in Accounts Receivable are deducted when determining net cash flows.

Eight Basic Steps to Preparing the Statement of Cash Flows

A number of techniques have been developed to help prepare the statement of cash flows. Preparing a statement of cash flows can be confusing, and important details can be easily overlooked without such aids. We recommend that you use a worksheet, such as the one in Exhibit 13–9, to prepare a statement of cash flows. Another technique relies on the use of T-accounts, which is discussed in Appendix 13B at the end of the chapter.

The worksheet in Exhibit 13–9 can be prepared using the eight steps that follow. This brief summary of the steps will be followed by more detailed explanations later.

1. Copy the title of each account appearing on the comparative balance sheet onto the worksheet except for cash and cash equivalents and retained earnings. Contra asset accounts such as the Accumulated Depreciation and Amortization account should be listed with the liabilities because they are treated the same way as liabilities on the statement of cash flows.
2. Compute the change from the beginning balance to the ending balance in each balance sheet account. Break down the change in retained earnings into net income and dividends paid to stockholders.
3. Using Exhibit 13–2 as a guide, code each entry on the worksheet as a source or a use of cash.

EXHIBIT 13-9

Nordstrom, Inc.
Statement of Cash Flows Worksheet
(dollars in millions)

	(1) Change	(2) Source or Use?	(3) Cash Flow Effect	(4) Adjustments	(5) Adjusted Effect (3) + (4)	(6) Classi-fication*
Assets (except cash and cash equivalents)						
Current assets:						
Accounts receivable	−17	Source	$+17		$+17	Operating
Merchandise inventory	+49	Use	−49		−49	Operating
Noncurrent assets:						
Property, buildings, and equipment	+123	Use	−123	$−15	−138	Investing
Contra Assets, Liabilities, and Stockholders' Equity						
Contra assets:						
Accumulated depreciation and amortization	+93	Source	+93	+10	+103	Operating
Current liabilities:						
Accounts payable	+44	Source	+44		+44	Operating
Accrued wages and salaries payable	+3	Source	+3		+3	Operating
Accrued income taxes payable	+6	Source	+6		+6	Operating
Notes payable	+2	Source	+2		+2	Financing
Noncurrent liabilities:						
Long-term debt	−43	Use	−43		−43	Financing
Deferred income taxes	−2	Use	−2		−2	Operating
Stockholders' equity:						
Common stock	+2	Source	+2		+2	Financing
Retained earnings:						
Net income	+140	Source	+140		+140	Operating
Dividends	−28	Use	−28		−28	Financing
Additional Entries						
Proceeds from sale of store				+8	+8	Investing
Gain on sale of store				−3	−3	Operating
Total (net cash flow)			$+62	$ 0	$+62	

*See Exhibit 13-10 (page 564) for the reasons for these classifications.

4. Under the Cash Flow Effect column, write sources as positive numbers and uses as negative numbers.
5. Make any necessary adjustments to reflect gross, rather than net, amounts involved in transactions—including adjustments for gains and losses. Some of these adjustments may require adding new entries to the bottom of the worksheet. The net effect of all such adjusting entries must be zero.
6. Classify each entry on the worksheet as an operating, investing, or financing activity according to the FASB's criteria, as given in Exhibit 13-7.
7. Copy the data from the worksheet to the statement of cash flows section by section, starting with the operating activities section.
8. At the bottom of the statement of cash flows prepare a reconciliation of the beginning and ending balances of cash and cash equivalents. The net change in cash and cash equivalents shown at the bottom of this statement should equal the change in the Cash and Cash Equivalents accounts during the year.

On the following pages we will apply these eight steps to the data contained in the comparative balance sheet for Nordstrom, Inc., found in Exhibit 13-4. *As we discuss each step, refer to Exhibit 13-4 and trace the data from this exhibit into the worksheet in Exhibit 13-9.*

Setting Up the Worksheet (Steps 1–4)

As indicated above, step 1 in preparing the worksheet is to list all of the relevant account titles from the company's balance sheet. Note that we have done this for Nordstrom, Inc., on the worksheet in Exhibit 13–9. (The titles of Nordstrom's accounts have been taken from the company's comparative balance sheet, which is found in Exhibit 13–4.) The only significant differences between Nordstrom's balance sheet accounts and the worksheet listing are that (1) the Accumulated Depreciation and Amortization account has been moved down with the liabilities on the worksheet, (2) the Cash and Cash Equivalents accounts have been omitted, and (3) the change in retained earnings has been broken down into net income and dividends.

As stated in step 2, the change in each account's balance during the year is listed in the first column of the worksheet. We have entered these changes for Nordstrom's accounts onto the worksheet in Exhibit 13–9. (Refer to Nordstrom's comparative balance sheet in Exhibit 13–4 to see how these changes were computed.)

Then, as indicated in step 3, each change on the worksheet is classified as either a source or a use of cash. Whether a change is a source or a use can be determined by referring back to Exhibit 13–2, where we first discussed these classifications. For example, Nordstrom's Merchandise Inventory account increased by $49 million during the year. According to Exhibit 13–2, increases in noncash asset accounts are classified as uses of cash, so an entry has been made to that effect in the second column of the worksheet for the Merchandise Inventory account.

So far, nothing is new. All of this was done in Exhibit 13–4 when we constructed the simplified statement of cash flows. Step 4 is mechanical, but it helps prevent careless errors. Sources are coded as positive changes and uses as negative changes in the Cash Flow Effect column on the worksheet.

Adjustments to Reflect Gross, Rather than Net, Amounts (Step 5)

As discussed earlier, the FASB requires that gross, rather than net, amounts be disclosed in the investing and financing sections. This rule requires special treatment of gains and losses. To illustrate, suppose that Nordstrom decided to sell an old store and move its retail operations to a new location. Assume that the original cost of the old store was $15 million, its accumulated depreciation was $10 million, and that it was sold for $8 million in cash. The journal entry to record this transaction (in millions) appears below:

Cash Proceeds.............................	8	
Accumulated Depreciation and Amortization.......	10	
Property, Buildings, and Equipment		15
Gain on Sale		3

The $3 million gain is reflected in the income statement in Exhibit 13–3.

We can reconstruct the gross additions to the Property, Buildings, and Equipment account and the gross charges to the Accumulated Depreciation and Amortization account with the help of T-accounts:

Property, Buildings, and Equipment				Accumulated Depreciation and Amortization			
Balance	1,394					561	Balance
Additions (plug*)	138	15	Disposal of store	Disposal of store	10	103	Depreciation charges (plug*)
Balance	1,517					654	Balance

*By *plug* we mean the balancing figure in the account.

According to the FASB rules, the gross additions of $138 million to the Property, Buildings, and Equipment account should be disclosed on the statement of cash flows rather than the net change in the account of $123 million ($1,517 million − $1,394 million = $123 million). Likewise, the gross depreciation charges of $103 million should be disclosed rather than the net change in the Accumulated Depreciation and Amortization account of $93 million ($654 million − $561 million = $93 million). And the cash proceeds of $8 million from sale of the building should also be disclosed on the statement of cash flows. All of this is accomplished, while preserving the correct overall net cash flows on the statement, by using the above journal entry to make adjusting entries on the worksheet. The debits are recorded as positive adjustments, and the credits are recorded as negative adjustments. These adjusting entries are recorded under the Adjustments column in Exhibit 13–9.

It may not be clear why the gain on the sale is *deducted* in the operating activities section of the statement of cash flows. The company's $140 million net income, which is part of the operating activities section, includes the $3 million gain on the sale of the store. But this $3 million gain must be reported in the *investing* activities section of the statement of cash flows as part of the $8 million proceeds from the sale transaction. Therefore, to avoid double counting, the $3 million gain is deducted from net income in the operating activities section of the statement. The adjustments we have made on the worksheet accomplish this. The $3 million gain will be deducted in the operating activities section, and all $8 million of the sale proceeds will be shown as an investing item. As a result, all of the gain will be included in the investing section of the statement of cash flows and none of it will be in the operating activities section. There will be no double counting of the gain.

In the case of a loss on the sale of an asset, we do the opposite. The loss is added back to the net income figure in the operating activities section of the statement of cash flows. Whatever cash proceeds are received from the sale of the asset are reported in the investing activities section.

Before turning to step 6 in the process of building the statement of cash flows, one small step is required. Add the Adjustments in column (4) to the Cash Flow Effect in column (3) to arrive at the Adjusted Effect in column (5).

Classifying Entries as Operating, Investing, or Financing Activities (Step 6)

In step 6, each entry on the worksheet is classified as an operating, investing, or financing activity using the guidelines in Exhibit 13–7. These classifications are entered directly on the worksheet in Exhibit 13–9 and are explained in Exhibit 13–10. Most of these classifications are straightforward, but the classification of the change in the Deferred Income Taxes account may require some additional explanation. Because of the way income tax expense is determined for financial reporting purposes, the expense that appears on the income statement often differs from the taxes that are actually owed to the government. Usually, the income tax expense overstates the company's actual income tax liability for the year. When this happens, the journal entry to record income taxes includes a credit to Deferred Income Taxes:

Income Tax Expense	XXX	
Income Taxes Payable		XXX
Deferred Income Taxes (plug).		XXX

Since deferred income taxes arise directly from the computation of an expense, the change in the Deferred Income Taxes account is included in the operating activities section of the statement of cash flows.

In the case of Nordstrom, the Deferred Income Taxes account decreased during the year. Deferred Income Taxes is a liability account for Nordstrom. Since this liability account decreased during the year, the change is counted as a use of cash and is deducted in determining net cash flow for the year.

EXHIBIT 13–10   Classifications of Entries on Nordstrom's Statement of Cash Flows

Entry	Classification	Reason
• Changes in Accounts Receivable and Merchandise Inventory	Operating activity	Changes in current assets are included in operating activities.
• Change in Property, Buildings, and Equipment	Investing activity	Changes in noncurrent assets that do not directly affect net income are included in investing activities.
• Change in Accumulated Depreciation and Amortization	Operating activity	Depreciation and amortization directly affect net income and are therefore included in operating activities.
• Changes in Accounts Payable, Accrued Wages and Salaries Payable, and Accrued Income Taxes Payable	Operating activity	Changes in current liabilities (except for notes payable) are included in operating activities.
• Change in Notes Payable	Financing activity	Issuing or repaying notes payable is classified as a financing activity.
• Change in Long-Term Debt	Financing activity	Changes in noncurrent liabilities that do not directly affect net income are included in financing activities.
• Change in Deferred Income Taxes	Operating activity	Deferred income taxes result from income tax expense that directly affects net income. Therefore, this entry is included in operating activities.
• Change in Common Stock	Financing activity	Changes in capital stock accounts are always included in financing activities.
• Net Income	Operating activity	Net income is always included in operating activities.
• Dividends	Financing activity	Dividends paid to stockholders are always included in financing activities.
• Proceeds from sale of store	Investing activity	The gross amounts received on disposal of noncurrent assets are included in investing activities.
• Gains from sale of store	Operating activity	Gains and losses directly affect net income and are therefore included in operating activities.

DECISION MAKER   Owner

You are the owner of a small manufacturing company. The company started selling its products internationally this year, which has resulted in a very significant increase in sales revenue and net income during the last two months of the year. The operating activities section of the company's statement of cash flows shows a negative number (that is, cash was *used* rather than *provided* by operations). Would you be concerned?

IN BUSINESS   Evaporating Cash Flow

Investors often assume that it is harder for management to manipulate operating cash flows than reported net earnings. That is often true, but some skepticism is in order. After an investigation by the Securities and Exchange Commission, Dynergy Inc. moved $300 million tied to a complex natural-gas trading arrangement from the operating cash flow section of its already-published statement of cash flows to the financing section. This reduced the company's reported operating cash flow for the year by 37%. And Enron's cash flow from operations was overstated by almost 50% prior to revelations concerning its fraudulent accounting practices.

Sources: Henny Sender, "Cash Flow? It Isn't Always What It Seems," *The Wall Street Journal,* May 8, 2002, pp. C1 & C3; and Tim Reason, "See-Through Finance," *CFO,* October 2002, pp. 45–52.

The Completed Statement of Cash Flows (Steps 7 and 8)

Once the worksheet is completed, the actual statement of cash flows is easy to complete. Nordstrom's statement of cash flows appears in Exhibit 13–11. Trace each item from the worksheet into this statement.

The operating activities section of the statement follows the format laid out in Exhibit 13–8, beginning with net income. The other entries in the operating activities section are adjustments required to convert net income to a cash basis. The sum of all of the entries under the operating activities section is called the "net cash provided by operating activities."

The investing activities section comes next on the statement of cash flows. The worksheet entries that have been classified as investing activities are recorded in this section in any order. The sum of all the entries in this section is called the "net cash used for investing activities."

The financing activities section of the statement follows the investing activities section. The worksheet entries that have been classified as financing activities are recorded in this section in any order. The sum of all of the entries in this section is called the "net cash used in financing activities."

Finally, for step 8, the bottom of the statement of cash flows contains a reconciliation of the beginning and ending balances of cash and cash equivalents.

Concept 13-2

EXHIBIT 13–11

Nordstrom, Inc.*	
Statement of Cash Flows—Indirect Method	
(dollars in millions)	
Operating Activities	
Net income	$140
Adjustments to convert net income to a cash basis:	
Depreciation and amortization charges	103
Decrease in accounts receivable	17
Increase in merchandise inventory	(49)
Increase in accounts payable	44
Increase in accrued wages and salaries payable	3
Increase in accrued income taxes payable	6
Decrease in deferred income taxes	(2)
Gain on sale of store	(3)
Net cash provided by operating activities	259
Investing Activities	
Additions to property, buildings, and equipment	(138)
Proceeds from sale of store	8
Net cash used in investing activities	(130)
Financing Activities	
Increase in notes payable	2
Decrease in long-term debt	(43)
Increase in common stock	2
Cash dividends paid	(28)
Net cash used in financing activities	(67)
Net increase in cash and cash equivalents	62
Cash and cash equivalents at beginning of year	29
Cash and cash equivalents at end of year	$ 91

Reconciliation of the beginning and ending cash balances

*This statement differs from the actual statement published by Nordstrom.

Interpretation of the Statement of Cash Flows

The completed statement of cash flows in Exhibit 13–11 provides a very favorable picture of Nordstrom's cash flows. The net cash flow from operations is a healthy $259 million. This positive cash flow permitted the company to make substantial additions to its property, buildings, and equipment and to pay off a substantial portion of its long-term debt. If similar conditions prevail in the future, the company can continue to finance substantial growth from its own cash flows without the necessity of raising debt or selling stock.

When interpreting a statement of cash flows, it is particularly important to examine the net cash provided by operating activities. This figure indicates how successful the company is in generating cash on a continuing basis. A negative cash flow from operations may be a sign of fundamental difficulties. A positive cash flow from operations is necessary to avoid liquidating assets or borrowing money just to sustain day-to-day operations.

IN BUSINESS

What's Wrong with This Picture?

Getty Images is the world's biggest stock photo company—owning the rights to over 70 million images and 30,000 hours of film. The company gets its revenues from licensing the use of these images. The stock market is impressed with the potential in this market—despite losses of $63 million in the first six months of the year, the company's stock was worth $1.8 billion. "What is there for a growth company to talk about if earnings are so rotten? Anything but earnings . . . Getty Images declared victory in its cash from operations, which it said had swelled to a robust $17.1 million in the second quarter, up from a deficit of $2.6 million in the first. Does that mean Getty collected its bills and whittled down its inventory? Nope. Both receivables and inventory are rising. The cash flow from operations, rather, comes from not paying bills."

Source: Elizabeth MacDonald, "Image Problem," *Forbes*, October 16, 2000, pp. 104–106.

IN BUSINESS

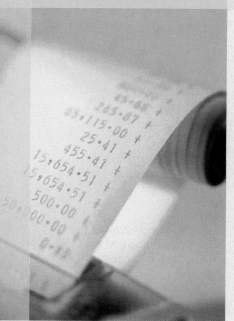

Free Cash Flow: Do the Math

In 1999, Jim Huguet, the manager of IDEX Great Companies mutual fund, was contemplating investing in an energy company with soaring profits. However, something bothered him about this company. Its profits were growing 27% a year, yet its free cash flow was plummeting. How could such a profitable company be bleeding cash? This unsettling contradiction caused Huguet to bypass investing in the highflying energy company Enron. In light of Enron's stunning financial collapse two years later, it turns out that Huguet's decision to focus on cash flow rather than on artificial accounting gimmicks saved his investors a bundle of money.

Free cash flow is a measure of the money that a company has left over after paying its bills. Investors often overlook this number because it is not directly reported in a set of financial statements; nonetheless, it is worth investing the time to do the math. To compute a company's free cash flow, begin with its net operating income, then add back its depreciation and amortization, and deduct its capital expenditures and dividends paid.

Source: Russell Pearlman, "Go With The Cash Flow," *Smart Money*, October 2004, pp. 86–91.

Depreciation, Depletion, and Amortization

A few pitfalls can trap the unwary when reading a statement of cash flows. Perhaps the most common pitfall is to misinterpret the nature of the depreciation charges on the statement of cash flows. Since depreciation is added back to net income, you might think that you can increase net cash flow by increasing depreciation charges. This is false. In a merchandising company like Nordstrom, increasing the depreciation charge by X dollars would decrease net income by X dollars because of the added expense. Adding back the depreciation charge to net income on the statement of cash flows simply cancels out the reduction in net income caused by the depreciation charge. Referring back to Exhibit 13–2, depreciation, depletion, and amortization charges are added back to net income on the statement of cash flows because they are a decrease in an asset (or, an increase in a contra asset)—not because they generate cash.

Portfolio Manager

YOU DECIDE

Assume that you work for a mutual fund and have the responsibility of selecting stocks to include in the fund's investment portfolio. You have been analyzing the financial statements of a chain of retail clothing stores and noticed that the company's cash flow from operations for the quarter ending on December 31 was negative even though the company had a small positive net operating income for the quarter. Further analysis indicated that most of the negative cash flow was due to a large increase in inventories. Should you be concerned?

SUMMARY

LO1 Classify changes in noncash balance sheet accounts as sources or uses of cash.
The statement of cash flows is one of the three major financial statements prepared by organizations. It explains how cash was generated and how it was used during the period. The statement of cash flows is widely used as a tool for assessing the financial health of organizations. In general, sources of cash include net income, decreases in assets, increases in liabilities, and increases in stockholders' capital accounts. Uses of cash include increases in assets, decreases in liabilities, decreases in stockholders' capital accounts, and dividends. A simplified form of the statement of cash flows can be easily constructed using just these definitions and a comparative balance sheet.

LO2 Classify transactions as operating activities, investing activities, or financing activities.
For external reporting purposes, the statement of cash flows must be organized in terms of operating, investing, and financing activities. While there are some exceptions, operating activities include net income and changes in current assets and current liabilities. And, with a few exceptions, changes in noncurrent assets are generally included in investing activities and changes in noncurrent liabilities are generally included in financing activities.

LO3 Prepare a statement of cash flows using the indirect method to determine the net cash provided by operating activities.
The operating activities section of the statement of cash flows can be constructed using the indirect method (discussed in the main body of the chapter) or the direct method (discussed in Appendix 13A). Although the FASB prefers the use of the direct method, most companies use the indirect method. Both methods report the same amount of net cash provided by operating activities.

When the indirect method is used, the operating activities section of the statement of cash flows starts with net income and shows the adjustments required to adjust net income to a cash basis. A worksheet can be used to construct the statement of cash flows. After determining the change in each balance sheet account, adjustments are made to reflect gross, rather than net, amounts involved in selected transactions, and each entry on the worksheet is labeled as an operating, investing, or financing activity. The data from the worksheet are then used to prepare each section of the statement of cash flows, beginning with the operating activities section.

GUIDANCE ANSWERS TO *DECISION MAKER* AND *YOU DECIDE*

Owner (p. 564)

Even though the company reported positive net income, the net effect of the company's operations was to *consume* rather than *generate* cash during the year. Cash disbursements relating to the company's operations exceeded the amount of cash receipts from operations. If the company generated a significant amount of sales just before the end of the year, it is quite possible that cash has not yet been received from the customers. In fact, given that the additional sales were international, a longer collection period would be expected. Nevertheless, as owner, you probably would want to ensure that the company's credit-granting policies and procedures were adhered to when these sales were made, and you should also monitor the length of time it takes to collect accounts receivable.

Portfolio Manager (p. 567)

The low profit (i.e., net operating income) and negative cash flow for the quarter ending December 31 should definitely be of concern for a clothing retailer. Due to the Christmas and Hanukkah holidays, this is traditionally the best quarter of the year for retailers. Furthermore, the increase in inventories is very troubling. This may indicate that sales fell below expectations and that the goods in inventory may have to be deeply discounted in the new year to clear the shelves for new merchandise. At minimum, some very hard questions should be directed to the executives of the clothing chain before buying its stock.

GUIDANCE ANSWERS TO CONCEPT CHECKS

1. **Choice c.** A decrease in a noncash asset, such as accounts receivable, is a source of cash.
2. **Choices b and d.** Paying suppliers is an operating activity. The direct and indirect methods are used to calculate cash from operating activities, not financing activities.

REVIEW PROBLEM

Rockford Company's comparative balance sheet and income statement for the year 2006 follow:

Rockford Company **Comparative Balance Sheet** **December 31, 2006, and 2005** **(dollars in millions)**		
	2006	**2005**
Assets		
Cash	$ 26	$ 10
Accounts receivable	180	270
Inventory	205	160
Prepaid expenses	17	20
Plant and equipment	430	309
Less accumulated depreciation	(218)	(194)
Long-term investments	60	75
Total assets	$700	$650
Liabilities and Stockholders' Equity		
Accounts payable	$230	$310
Accrued liabilities	70	60
Bonds payable	135	40
Deferred income taxes	15	8
Common stock	140	140
Retained earnings	110	92
Total liabilities and stockholders' equity	$700	$650

Rockford Company
Income Statement
For the Year Ended December 31, 2006
(dollars in millions)

Sales	$1,000
Less cost of goods sold	530
Gross margin	470
Less operating expenses	352
Net operating income	118
Nonoperating items:	
Loss on sale of equipment	(4)
Income before taxes	114
Less income taxes	48
Net income	$ 66

Notes: Dividends of $48 million were paid in 2006. The loss on sale of
equipment of $4 million reflects a transaction in which equipment
with an original cost of $12 million and accumulated depreciation of
$5 million was sold for $3 million in cash.

Required:

Using the indirect method, determine the net cash provided by operating activities for 2006 and construct
a statement of cash flows for the year.

Solution to Review Problem

A worksheet for Rockford Company appears below. Using the worksheet, it is easy to construct the statement of cash flows, including the net cash provided by operating activities.

Rockford Company
Statement of Cash Flows Worksheet
For the Year Ended December 31, 2006
(dollars in millions)

	(1) Change	(2) Source or Use?	(3) Cash Flow Effect	(4) Adjust- ments	(5) Adjusted Effect (3) + (4)	(6) Classi- fication
Assets (except cash and cash equivalents)						
Current assets:						
Accounts receivable	−90	Source	$+90		$+90	Operating
Inventory	+45	Use	−45		−45	Operating
Prepaid expenses	−3	Source	+3		+3	Operating
Noncurrent assets:						
Property, buildings, and equipment	+121	Use	−121	$−12	−133	Investing
Long-term investments	−15	Source	+15		+15	Investing
Contra Assets, Liabilities, and **Stockholders' Equity**						
Contra assets:						
Accumulated depreciation	+24	Source	+24	+5	+29	Operating
Current liabilities:						
Accounts payable	−80	Use	−80		−80	Operating
Accrued liabilities	+10	Source	+10		+10	Operating
Noncurrent liabilities:						
Bonds payable	+95	Source	+95		+95	Financing
Deferred income taxes	+7	Source	+7		+7	Operating

(continued)

(concluded)

Rockford Company
Statement of Cash Flows Worksheet
For the Year Ended December 31, 2006
(dollars in millions)

	(1) Change	(2) Source or Use?	(3) Cash Flow Effect	(4) Adjust- ments	(5) Adjusted Effect (3) + (4)	(6) Classi- fication
Stockholders' equity:						
Common stock	+0	—	+0		+0	Financing
Retained earnings:						
Net income	+66	Source	+66		+66	Operating
Dividends	−48	Use	−48		−48	Financing
Additional Entries						
Proceeds from sale of equipment				+3	+3	Investing
Loss on sale of equipment				+4	+4	Operating
Total (net cash flow)			$+16	$ 0	$+16	

Rockford Company
Statement of Cash Flows—Indirect Method
For the Year Ended December 31, 2006
(dollars in millions)

Operating Activities	
Net income	$ 66
Adjustments to convert net income to a cash basis:	
Depreciation and amortization charges	29
Decrease in accounts receivable	90
Increase in inventory	(45)
Decrease in prepaid expenses	3
Decrease in accounts payable	(80)
Increase in accrued liabilities	10
Increase in deferred income taxes	7
Loss on sale of equipment	4
Net cash provided by operating activities	84
Investing Activities:	
Additions to property, buildings, and equipment	(133)
Decrease in long-term investments	15
Proceeds from sale of equipment	3
Net cash used in investing activities	(115)
Financing Activities:	
Increase in bonds payable	95
Cash dividends paid	(48)
Net cash provided by financing activities	47
Net increase in cash and cash equivalents	16
Cash and cash equivalents at beginning of year	10
Cash and cash equivalents at end of year	$ 26

Note that the $16 million increase in cash and cash equivalents agrees with the $16 million increase in the company's Cash account shown in the balance sheet, and it agrees with the total in column (5) in the above worksheet.

GLOSSARY

Cash equivalents   Short-term, highly liquid investments such as Treasury bills, commercial paper, and money market funds that are made solely for the purpose of generating a return on temporarily idle funds. (p. 550)

Direct method   A method of computing the net cash provided by operating activities in which the income statement is reconstructed on a cash basis from top to bottom. (p. 559)

Financing activities   All transactions (other than payment of interest) involving borrowing from creditors or repaying creditors as well as transactions with the company's owners (except stock dividends and stock splits). (p. 557)

Indirect method   A method of computing the net cash provided by operating activities that starts with net income and adjusts it to a cash basis. It is also known as the *reconciliation method.* (p. 559)

Investing activities   Transactions that involve acquiring or disposing of noncurrent assets. (p. 557)

Net cash provided by operating activities   The net result of the cash inflows and outflows arising from day-to-day operations. (p. 558)

Operating activities   Transactions that enter into the determination of net income. (p. 556)

Reconciliation method   See *Indirect method.* (p. 559)

Statement of cash flows   A financial statement that highlights the major activities that directly and indirectly impact cash flows and hence affect the overall cash balance. (p. 550)

APPENDIX 13A: THE DIRECT METHOD OF DETERMINING THE NET CASH PROVIDED BY OPERATING ACTIVITIES

To compute the net cash provided by operating activities under the direct method, we must reconstruct the income statement on a cash basis from top to bottom. Exhibit 13A–1 shows the adjustments that must be made to adjust sales, expenses, and so forth, to a cash basis. To illustrate, we have included in the exhibit the Nordstrom data from the chapter.

Note that the "net cash provided by operating activities" ($259 million) agrees with the amount computed in the chapter by the indirect method. The two amounts agree, since the direct and indirect methods are just different roads to the same destination. The investing and financing activities sections of the statement will be exactly the same as shown for the indirect method in Exhibit 13–11. The only difference between the indirect and direct methods is in the operating activities section.

> **LEARNING OBJECTIVE 4**
>
> Use the direct method to determine the net cash provided by operating activities.

Similarities and Differences in the Handling of Data

Although we arrive at the same destination under either the direct or the indirect method, not all data are handled in the same way in the adjustment process. Stop for a moment, flip back to the general model for the indirect method in Exhibit 13–8, and compare the adjustments made in that exhibit to the adjustments made for the direct method in Exhibit 13A–1. The adjustments for accounts that affect revenue are the same in the two methods. In either case, increases in the accounts are deducted and decreases in the accounts are added. The adjustments for accounts that affect expenses, however, are handled in *opposite* ways in the indirect and direct methods. This is because under the indirect method the adjustments are made to *net income,* whereas under the direct method the adjustments are made to the *expense accounts* themselves.

To illustrate this difference, note the handling of prepaid expenses and depreciation in the indirect and direct methods. Under the indirect method (Exhibit 13–8), an increase in the Prepaid Expenses account is *deducted* from net income in computing the amount of net cash provided by operating activities. Under the direct method (Exhibit 13A–1), an increase in Prepaid Expenses is *added* to operating expenses. The reason for the difference can be explained as follows: An increase in Prepaid Expenses means that more cash has been paid out for items such as insurance than has been included as expense for the period. Therefore, to adjust net income to a cash basis, we must either deduct this increase from net income (indirect method) or we must add this increase to operating expenses (direct method). Either way, we will end up with the same figure for net cash provided by

EXHIBIT 13A–1

General Model: Direct Method of Determining the "Net Cash Provided by Operating Activities"

Revenue or Expense Item	Add (+) or Deduct (−) to Adjust to a Cash Basis	Illustration— Nordstrom (in millions)	
Sales revenue (as reported)		$3,638	
Adjustments to a cash basis:			
Increase in accounts receivable	−		
Decrease in accounts receivable	+	+17	
Total			$3,655
Cost of goods sold (as reported)		2,469	
Adjustments to a cash basis:			
Increase in merchandise inventory	+	+49	
Decrease in merchandise inventory	−		
Increase in accounts payable	−	−44	
Decrease in accounts payable	+		
Total			2,474
Operating expenses (as reported)		941	
Adjustments to a cash basis:			
Increase in prepaid expenses	+		
Decrease in prepaid expenses	−		
Increase in accrued liabilities	−	−3	
Decrease in accrued liabilities	+		
Period's depreciation, depletion, and amortization charges	−	−103	
Total			835
Income tax expense (as reported)		91	
Adjustments to a cash basis:			
Increase in accrued taxes payable	−	−6	
Decrease in accrued taxes payable	+		
Increase in deferred income taxes	−		
Decrease in deferred income taxes	+	+2	
Total			87
Net cash provided by operating activities			$ 259

operating activities. Similarly, depreciation is added to net income under the indirect method to cancel out its effect (Exhibit 13–8), whereas it is deducted from operating expenses under the direct method to cancel out its effect (Exhibit 13A–1). These differences in the handling of data are true for all other expense items in the two methods.

In the matter of gains and losses on sales of assets, no adjustments are needed at all under the direct method. These gains and losses are simply ignored, since they are not part of sales, cost of goods sold, operating expenses, or income taxes. Observe that in Exhibit 13A–1, Nordstrom's $3 million gain on the sale of the store is not listed as an adjustment in the operating activities section.

Special Rules—Direct and Indirect Methods

As stated earlier, when the direct method is used, the FASB requires a reconciliation between net income and the net cash provided by operating activities, as determined by the indirect method. Thus, *when a company elects to use the direct method, it must also present the indirect method* in a separate schedule accompanying the statement of cash flows.

On the other hand, if a company elects to use the indirect method to compute the net cash provided by operating activities, then it must also provide a special breakdown of data. The company must provide a separate disclosure of the amount of interest and the amount of income taxes paid during the year. The FASB requires this separate disclosure so that users can take the data provided by the indirect method and make estimates of what the amounts for sales, income taxes, and so forth, would have been if the direct method had been used instead.

SUMMARY

LO4 (Appendix 13A) Use the direct method to determine the net cash provided by operating activities.

When the direct method is used to determine the net cash provided by operating activities, the income statement is reconstructed on a cash basis. A worksheet, which starts with the major components of the company's income statement (such as sales revenue, cost of goods sold, operating expenses, and income tax expense), can be used to organize the data. Each of the income statement components is adjusted to a cash basis by referring to the changes in the related balance sheet account. (For example, the amount of sales revenue reported on the income statement is converted to the amount of cash received from customers by subtracting the increase, or adding the decrease, in accounts receivable during the period.) Special disclosure rules apply when a company uses the direct method.

APPENDIX 13B: THE T-ACCOUNT APPROACH TO PREPARING THE STATEMENT OF CASH FLOWS

A worksheet approach was used to prepare the statement of cash flows in the chapter. The T-account approach is an alternative technique that is sometimes used to prepare the statement of cash flows. To illustrate the T-account approach, we will again use the data for Nordstrom, Inc. from the chapter.

LEARNING OBJECTIVE 5

Prepare a statement of cash flows using the T-account approach.

The T-Account Approach

Note from Nordstrom's comparative balance sheet in Exhibit 13–4 that cash and cash equivalents increased from $29 million to $91 million, an increase of $62 million during the year. To determine the reasons for this change we will again prepare a statement of cash flows. As before, our basic approach will be to analyze the changes in the various balance sheet accounts. However, in this appendix we will use T-accounts rather than a worksheet.

Exhibit 13B–1 contains a T-account, titled "Cash," which we will use to accumulate the cash "Provided" and the cash "Used." The exhibit also includes T-accounts with the beginning and ending balances for each of the other accounts on Nordstrom's balance sheet. *Before proceeding, refer to Nordstrom's comparative balance sheet in Exhibit 13–4 in the main body of the chapter, and trace the data from this exhibit to the T-accounts in Exhibit 13B–1.*

As we analyze each balance sheet account, we will post the related entry(s) directly to the T-accounts. To the extent that these changes have affected cash, we will also post an appropriate entry to the T-account representing Cash. *As you progress through this appendix, trace each entry to the T-accounts in Exhibit 13B–2. Pay special attention to the placement and description of the entries affecting the T-account representing Cash.*

Observe that in the Cash T-account in Exhibit 13B–2, all operating items are near the top of the Cash T-account, below the net income figure. Also note that the T-account includes a subtotal titled "Net cash provided by operating activities." If the amounts in the "Used" column exceeded the amounts in the "Provided" column, the subtotal would be on the credit side of the T-account and would be labeled "Net cash *used* in operating activities." Also note that all investing and financing items have been placed below the subtotal in the lower portion of the Cash T-account. At the bottom of the T-account is a total titled "Net increase in cash and cash equivalents." If the amounts in the "Used" column exceeded the amounts in the "Provided" column, this total would be on the credit side of the T-account and would be labeled "Net *decrease* in cash and cash equivalents." The entries in the Cash T-account contain all of the entries needed for the statement of cash flows.

EXHIBIT 13B–1   T-Accounts Showing Changes in Account Balances—Nordstrom, Inc. (in millions)

Cash		
	Provided	**Used**
Net cash provided by operating activities		
Net increase in cash and cash equivalents		

Accounts Receivable			Merchandise Inventory			Property, Buildings, and Equipment			Accumulated Depreciation		
Bal.	654		Bal.	537		Bal.	1,394			561	Bal.
Bal.	637		Bal.	586		Bal.	1,517			654	Bal.

Accounts Payable			Accrued Wages and Salaries Payable			Accrued Income Taxes Payable			Notes Payable		
	220	Bal.		190	Bal.		22	Bal.		38	Bal.
	264	Bal.		193	Bal.		28	Bal.		40	Bal.

Long-Term Debt			Deferred Income Taxes			Common Stock			Retained Earnings		
	482	Bal.		49	Bal.		155	Bal.		897	Bal.
	439	Bal.		47	Bal.		157	Bal.		1,009	Bal.

Retained Earnings   The Retained Earnings account is generally the most useful starting point when developing a statement of cash flows. Details of the change in Nordstrom's Retained Earnings account are presented in Exhibit 13–5. Note from the exhibit that net income was $140 million and dividends were $28 million. The entries to record these changes and their effects on Cash are shown below. (The dollar amounts are in millions.)

The entry to record net income and the effect on Cash would be:

(1)

| Cash—Provided .... | 140 | |
| Retained Earnings—Net Income............. | | 140 |

Recall that net income is converted to a cash basis when the indirect method is used to prepare the operating activities section of the statement of cash flows. Since net income is the starting point, the cash effect is included at the top of the Cash T-account.

The entry to record the dividends paid and the effect on Cash would be:

(2)

| Retained Earnings—Dividends.................. | 28 | |
| Cash—Used .... | | 28 |

Since the payment of cash dividends is classified as an investing activity, the cash effect is included in the lower portion of the Cash T-account along with the other investing and financing items.

Once posted to the Retained Earnings T-account in Exhibit 13B–2, these two entries fully explain the change that took place in the Retained Earnings account during the year. We can now proceed through the remainder of the balance sheet accounts in Exhibit 13B–1,

EXHIBIT 13B-2   T-Accounts after Posting of Account Changes—Nordstrom, Inc. (in millions)

Cash						
		Provided	**Used**			
Net income	(1)	140	49	(4)	Increase in merchandise inventory	
Decrease in accounts receivable	(3)	17	3	(5)	Gain on sale of store	
Depreciation and amortization charges	(7)	103	2	(13)	Decrease in deferred income taxes	
Increase in accounts payable	(8)	44				
Increase in accrued wages and salaries payable	(9)	3				
Increase in accrued income taxes payable	(10)	6				
Net cash provided by operating activities		259				
Proceeds from sale of store	(5)	8	28	(2)	Cash dividends paid	
Increase in notes payable	(11)	2	138	(6)	Additions to property, buildings, and equipment	
Increase in common stock	(14)	2	43	(12)	Decrease in long-term debt	
Net increase in cash and cash equivalents		62				

Accounts Receivable				Merchandise Inventory				Property, Buildings, and Equipment				Accumulated Depreciation			
Bal.	654			Bal.	537			Bal.	1,394					561	Bal.
		17	(3)	(4)	49			(6)	138	15	(5)	(5)	10	103	(7)
Bal.	637			Bal.	586			Bal.	1,517					654	Bal.

Accounts Payable				Accrued Wages and Salaries Payable				Accrued Income Taxes Payable				Notes Payable			
		220	Bal.			190	Bal.			22	Bal.			38	Bal.
		44	(8)			3	(9)			6	(10)			2	(11)
		264	Bal.			193	Bal.			28	Bal.			40	Bal.

Long-Term Debt				Deferred Income Taxes				Common Stock				Retained Earnings			
		482	Bal.			49	Bal.			155	Bal.			897	Bal.
(12)	43			(13)	2					2	(14)	(2)	28	140	(1)
		439	Bal.			47	Bal.			157	Bal.			1,009	Bal.

analyzing the change between the beginning and ending balances in each account, and recording the appropriate entries in the T-accounts.

Current Asset Accounts   Each of the current asset accounts is examined to determine the change that occurred during the year. The change is then recorded as a debit if the account balance increased or as a credit if the account balance decreased. The offsetting entry in the case of an increase in the account balance is "Cash—Used"; the offsetting entry in the case of a decrease in the account balance is "Cash—Provided."

To demonstrate, note that Nordstrom's Accounts Receivable decreased by $17 million during the year. The entry to record this change and its effect on Cash would be:

	(3)		
Cash—Provided		17	
Accounts Receivable.			17

The merchandise inventory account increased by \$49 million during the year. The entry to record this change and its effect on Cash would be:

(4)

| Merchandise Inventory . . . . | 49 | |
| Cash—Used . . . . | | 49 |

Note that these two entries result in the correct adjusting entries in the current asset T-accounts so as to reconcile the beginning and ending balances. Also note that the changes in these two current asset accounts are included in the upper portion of the Cash T-account. This is because changes in current assets are considered part of operations and therefore are used to convert net income to a cash basis in the operating activities section of the statement of cash flows.

Property, Buildings, and Equipment and Accumulated Depreciation

The activity in the Property, Buildings, and Equipment account and the Accumulated Depreciation account is analyzed in the chapter beginning on page 562. *Reread the analysis of these accounts before proceeding.* Nordstrom sold a store, purchased property, buildings, and equipment, and recorded depreciation expense during the year. The entries in this case for the T-account analysis are more complex than for current assets. These entries are presented below. You should carefully trace each of these entries to the T-accounts in Exhibit 13B–2.

The entry to record the sale of the store and its effect on Cash would be:

(5)

Cash—Provided	8	
Accumulated Depreciation	10	
Property, Buildings, and Equipment		15
Gain on Sale		3

Since the sale of property, buildings, and equipment is classified as an investing activity, the cash effect is included in the lower portion of the Cash T-account along with the other investing and financing items. The proceeds from the sale, which will be reported in the investing activities section of the statement of cash flows, include the gain that was recognized on the sale of the store. However, this gain was reported on Nordstrom's income statement in Exhibit 13–3 as part of net income, which is the starting point for the operating activities section. As a result, to avoid double counting, the gain must be subtracted (or removed) from net income in the operating activities section of the statement of cash flows. Accordingly, the gain is recorded in the "Used" column in the upper portion of the Cash T-account along with the other operating items.

The entry to record the purchase of property, buildings, and equipment and its effect on Cash would be:

(6)

| Property, Buildings, and Equipment. . . . . | 138 | |
| Cash—Used . . . . | | 138 |

Since the purchase of property, buildings, and equipment is classified as an investing activity, the cash effect is included in the lower portion of the Cash T-account along with the other investing and financing items. Entry (6), along with entry (5) above, explains the change in the Property, Buildings, and Equipment account during the year.

The entry to record depreciation and amortization expense for the year would be:

(7)

| Cash—Provided . . . . | 103 | |
| Accumulated Depreciation . . . . | | 103 |

Note that depreciation and amortization expense does not involve an actual cash outflow. Consequently, depreciation and amortization expense must be added to net income to convert it to a cash basis in the operating activities section of the statement of cash flows. Note that the depreciation and amortization expense is recorded in the "Provided" column in the upper portion of the Cash T-account along with the other operating items. Entry (7), along with entry (5) above, explains the change in the Accumulated Depreciation account during the year.

Current Liabilities The T-accounts in Exhibit 13B–1 show that Nordstrom has four current liability accounts. Three of the four current liability accounts (Accounts Payable, Accrued Wages and Salaries Payable, and Accrued Income Taxes Payable) relate to the company's operating activities. In the entries that follow, increases in current liabilities are recorded as credits, with the offsetting entry being "Cash—Provided." Decreases in current liabilities are recorded as debits, with the offsetting entry being "Cash—Used."

Accounts Payable increased by $44 million during the year. The entry to record this change and its effect on Cash would be:

(8)

| Cash—Provided .... | 44 | |
| Accounts Payable .... | | 44 |

The Accrued Wages and Salaries Payable account increased by $3 million during the year. The entry to record this change and its effect on Cash would be:

(9)

| Cash—Provided .... | 3 | |
| Accrued Wages and Salaries Payable .... | | 3 |

The Accrued Income Taxes Payable account increased by $6 million during the year. The entry to record this change and its effect on Cash would be:

(10)

| Cash—Provided .... | 6 | |
| Accrued Income Taxes Payable .... | | 6 |

Since the changes in these three current liability accounts are considered to be part of operations, their cash effects are included in the upper portion of the Cash T-account along with the other operating items.

The Notes Payable account increased by $2 million during the year. The entry to record this would be:

(11)

| Cash—Provided .... | 2 | |
| Notes Payable .... | | 2 |

Since transactions involving notes payable are classified as financing activities, their cash effects are included in the lower portion of the Cash T-account along with the other investing and financing items.

Long-Term Debt Nordstrom's Long-Term Debt account decreased by $43 million during the year. The entry to record this would be:

(12)

| Long-Term Debt .... | 43 | |
| Cash—Used................................ | | 43 |

Since transactions involving long-term debt are classified as financing activities, their cash effects are included in the lower portion of the Cash T-account along with the other investing and financing items.

Deferred Income Taxes The activity in Deferred Income Taxes is analyzed in the chapter beginning on page 563. *Reread the analysis of this account before proceeding.* The entry to record the activity in this account and its effect on Cash would be:

(13)

Deferred Income Taxes.........................	2	
Cash—Used..............................		2

Since changes in the Deferred Income Taxes account are classified as part of operations, its cash effects are included in the upper portion of the Cash T-account along with the other operating items.

Common Stock The Common Stock account increased by $2 million. The entry to record this would be:

(14)

Cash—Provided	2	
Common Stock		2

With this entry, our analysis of changes in Nordstrom's balance sheet accounts is complete. At this point, the subtotal titled "Net cash provided by operating activities" can be computed. To ensure that all activity has been properly recorded in the Cash T-account, the total titled "Net increase in cash and cash equivalents" should also be computed (by adding the investing and financing items in the lower portion of the Cash T-account to the subtotal of the upper portion). The $62 million net increase in cash and cash equivalents that is detailed in the Cash T-account in Exhibit 13A–2 equals the increase in cash and cash equivalents shown on Nordstrom's comparative balance sheet in Exhibit 13–4.

Preparing the Statement of Cash Flows from the Completed T-Accounts

The Cash T-account in Exhibit 13B–2 now contains the entries for those transactions that have affected Nordstrom's cash balance during the year. Our only remaining task is to organize these data into a formal statement of cash flows. The statement is easy to prepare since the data relating to the operating activities are grouped in the upper portion of the Cash T-account and the data relating to investing and financing activities are grouped in the lower portion of the account.

The technique used to gather and organize data for the preparation of a statement of cash flows does not affect the preparation of the statement itself. The end result is the same. The statement of cash flows for Nordstrom, Inc., is presented in the chapter in Exhibit 13–11. *Refer to the Cash T-account in Exhibit 13B–2, and trace the entries in this T-account to Nordstrom's statement of cash flows in Exhibit 13–11.* Note that the subtotal, "Net cash provided by operating activities," and the total, "Net increase in cash and cash equivalents," in the Cash T-account match the amounts reported on Nordstrom's statement of cash flows.

SUMMARY

LO5 (Appendix 13B) Prepare a statement of cash flows using the T-account approach.
The T-account approach is an alternative technique that can be used to gather and organize the data required to prepare a statement of cash flows. T-accounts are created for each balance sheet account. Each of these accounts is analyzed, and the related entries are posted directly to the T-accounts. The offsetting entry in most cases is Cash. Debits to Cash are labeled "Cash—Provided" and credits are labeled "Cash—Used." Operating items are listed near the top of the Cash T-account and investing and financing items are listed in the lower portion of the Cash T-account. The completed Cash T-account is used to prepare each section of the statement of cash flows, beginning with the operating activities section.

QUESTIONS

13–1 What is the purpose of a statement of cash flows?

13–2 What are *cash equivalents,* and why are they included with cash on a statement of cash flows?

13–3 What are the three major sections on a statement of cash flows, and what are the general rules that determine the transactions that should be included in each section?

13–4 Why is interest paid on amounts borrowed from banks and other lenders considered to be an operating activity when the amounts borrowed are financing activities?

13–5 If an asset is sold at a gain, why is the gain deducted from net income when computing the net cash provided by operating activities under the indirect method?

13–6 Why aren't transactions involving accounts payable considered to be financing activities?

13–7 Assume that a company repays a $300,000 loan from its bank and then later in the same year borrows $500,000. What amount(s) would appear on the statement of cash flows?

13–8 How do the direct and the indirect methods differ in their approach to computing the net cash provided by operating activities?

13–9 A business executive once stated, "Depreciation is one of our biggest sources of cash." Do you agree that depreciation is a source of cash? Explain.

13–10 If the balance in Accounts Receivable increases during a period, how will this increase be handled under the indirect method when computing the net cash provided by operating activities?

13–11 (Appendix 13A) If the balance in Accounts Payable decreases during a period, how will this decrease be handled under the direct method in computing the net cash provided by operating activities?

13–12 During the current year, a company declared and paid a $60,000 cash dividend and a 10% stock dividend. How will these two items be treated on the current year's statement of cash flows?

13–13 Would a sale of equipment for cash be considered a financing activity or an investing activity? Why?

13–14 (Appendix 13A) A merchandising company showed $250,000 in cost of goods sold on its income statement. The company's beginning inventory was $75,000, and its ending inventory was $60,000. The accounts payable balance was $50,000 at the beginning of the year and $40,000 at the end of the year. Using the direct method, adjust the company's cost of goods sold to a cash basis.

BRIEF EXERCISES

BRIEF EXERCISE 13–1 Classifying Transactions as Sources or Uses (LO1)
Below are transactions that took place in Placid Company during the past year:

a. Equipment was purchased.
b. A cash dividend was declared and paid.
c. Accounts receivable decreased.
d. Short-term investments were purchased.
e. Equipment was sold.
f. Preferred stock was sold to investors.
g. Interest was paid to long-term creditors.
h. Salaries and wages payable decreased.
i. Stock of another company was purchased.
j. Bonds were issued that will be due in 10 years.
k. Rent was received from subleasing space, reducing rents receivable.
l. Common stock was repurchased and retired.

Required:
For each of the above transactions, indicate whether it would be classified as a source or a use (or neither) on a simplified statement of cash flows.

BRIEF EXERCISE 13–2   Classifying Transactions as Operating, Investing, or Financing   (LO2)
Refer to the transactions for Placid Company listed in Brief Exercise 13–1.

Required:
For each of the transactions in Brief Exercise 13–1, indicate whether it would be classified as an operating, investing, or financing activity (or would not be reported) on the statement of cash flows.

BRIEF EXERCISE 13–3   Net Cash Provided by Operating Activities (Indirect Method)   (LO3)
For the just completed year, Hanna Corporation, an air conditioning equipment supplier and installer, had net income of $35,000. Balances in the company's current asset and current liability accounts at the beginning and end of the year were:

	End of Year	Beginning of Year
Current assets:		
Cash	$30,000	$40,000
Accounts receivable ..	$125,000	$106,000
Inventory	$213,000	$180,000
Prepaid expenses	$6,000	$7,000
Current liabilities:		
Accounts payable	$210,000	$195,000
Accrued liabilities	$4,000	$6,000

The Deferred Income Taxes liability account on the balance sheet increased by $4,000 during the year, and depreciation charges were $20,000.

Required:
Using the indirect method, determine the net cash provided by operating activities for the year.

BRIEF EXERCISE 13–4   (Appendix 13A) Net Cash Provided by Operating Activities (Direct Method)   (LO4)
Refer to the data for Hanna Corporation in Brief Exercise 13–3. The company's income statement for the year appears below:

Sales	$350,000
Less cost of goods sold	140,000
Gross margin	210,000
Less operating expenses	160,000
Income before taxes	50,000
Less income taxes	15,000
Net income	$ 35,000

Required:
Using the direct method (and the data from Brief Exercise 13–3), convert the company's income statement to a cash basis.

BRIEF EXERCISE 13–5   (Appendix 13B) Posting Account Changes to Cash T-Account   (LO5)
Refer to the data for Hanna Corporation in Brief Exercise 13–3.

Required:
Using the indirect method (and the data from Brief Exercise 13–3), post the account changes to a Cash T-account to determine the net cash provided by operating activities for the year.

EXERCISE 13–6   Net Cash Provided by Operating Activities (Indirect Method)   [LO3]

Changes in various accounts and gains and losses on the sale of assets during the year for Argon Company, a caterer, are given below:

Item	Amount
Accounts Receivable	$90,000 decrease
Accrued Interest Receivable	$4,000 increase
Inventory	$120,000 increase
Prepaid Expenses	$3,000 decrease
Accounts Payable	$65,000 decrease
Accrued Liabilities	$8,000 increase
Deferred Income Taxes Payable	$12,000 increase
Sale of equipment	$7,000 gain
Sale of long-term investments	$10,000 loss

Required:

Prepare an answer sheet using the following column headings:

Item	Amount	Add	Deduct

For each item, place an X in the Add or Deduct column to indicate whether the dollar amount should be added to or deducted from net income under the indirect method when computing the net cash provided by operating activities for the year.

EXERCISE 13–7   Prepare a Statement of Cash Flows (Indirect Method)   [LO2, LO3]

Comparative financial statement data for Carmono Company follow:

	2005	2004
Cash	$ 3	$ 6
Accounts receivable	22	24
Inventory	50	40
Plant and equipment	240	200
Less accumulated depreciation	(65)	(50)
Total assets	$250	$220
Accounts payable	$ 40	$ 36
Common stock	150	145
Retained earnings	60	39
Total liabilities and stockholders' equity	$250	$220

For 2005, the company reported net income as follows:

Sales	$275
Less cost of goods sold	150
Gross margin	125
Less operating expenses	90
Net income	$ 35

Dividends of $14 were declared and paid during 2005.

Required:

Using the indirect method, prepare a statement of cash flows for 2005.

EXERCISE 13–8   (Appendix 13A) Net Cash Provided by Operating Activities (Direct Method)   [LO4]
Refer to the data for Carmono Company in Exercise 13–7.

Required:
Using the direct method, convert the company's income statement to a cash basis.

EXERCISE 13–9   Prepare a Statement of Cash Flows (Indirect Method)   [LO2, LO3]
The following changes took place during the year in Pavolik Company's balance sheet accounts:

Cash	$5 D	Accounts Payable	$35 I
Accounts Receivable	$110 I	Accrued Liabilities	$4 D
Inventory	$70 D	Bonds Payable	$150 I
Prepaid Expenses	$9 I	Deferred Income Taxes	$8 I
Long-Term Investments	$6 D	Common Stock	$80 D
Plant and Equipment	$200 I	Retained Earnings	$54 I
Accumulated Depreciation	$(60) I		
Land	$15 D		

D = Decrease; I = Increase.

Long-term investments that had cost the company $6 were sold during the year for $16, and land that had cost $15 was sold for $9. In addition, the company declared and paid $30 in cash dividends during the year. No sales or retirements of plant and equipment took place during the year.
The company's income statement for the year follows:

Sales		$700
Less cost of goods sold		400
Gross margin		300
Less operating expenses		184
Net operating income		116
Nonoperating items:		
Gain on sale of investments	$10	
Loss on sale of land	6	4
Income before taxes		120
Less income taxes		36
Net income		$ 84

The company's beginning cash balance was $90, and its ending balance was $85.

Required:
1. Use the indirect method to determine the net cash provided by operating activities for the year.
2. Prepare a statement of cash flows for the year.

EXERCISE 13–10   (Appendix 13A) Adjust Net Income to a Cash Basis (Direct Method)   [LO4]
Refer to the data for Pavolik Company in Exercise 13–9.

Required:
Use the direct method to convert the company's income statement to a cash basis.

PROBLEMS

  PROBLEM 13–11A   Prepare a Statement of Cash Flows (Indirect Method)   [LO2, LO3]
Comparative financial statements for Weaver Company follow:

CHECK FIGURE
(1) Net cash provided by operating activities: $104

Weaver Company
Comparative Balance Sheet
December 31, 2005 and 2004

	2005	2004
Assets		
Cash	$ 9	$ 15
Accounts receivable	340	240
Inventory	125	175
Prepaid expenses	10	6
Plant and equipment	610	470
Less accumulated depreciation	(93)	(85)
Long-term investments	16	19
Total assets	$1,017	$840
Liabilities and Stockholders' Equity		
Accounts payable	$ 310	$230
Accrued liabilities	60	72
Bonds payable	290	180
Deferred income taxes	40	34
Common stock	210	250
Retained earnings	107	74
Total liabilities and stockholders' equity	$1,017	$840

Weaver Company
Income Statement
For the Year Ended December 31, 2005

Sales		$800
Less cost of goods sold		500
Gross margin		300
Less operating expenses		213
Net operating income		87
Nonoperating items:		
Gain on sale of investments	$7	
Loss on sale of equipment	4	3
Income before taxes		90
Less income taxes		27
Net income		$ 63

During 2005, the company sold some equipment for $20 that had cost $40 and on which there was accumulated depreciation of $16. In addition, the company sold long-term investments for $10 that had cost $3 when purchased several years ago. Cash dividends totaling $30 were paid during 2005.

Required:
1. Using the indirect method, determine the net cash provided by operating activities for 2005.
2. Using the information in (1) above, along with an analysis of the remaining balance sheet accounts, prepare a statement of cash flows for 2005.

PROBLEM 13–12A **(Appendix 13A) Prepare a Statement of Cash Flows (Direct Method) [LO2, LO4]**
Refer to the financial statement data for Weaver Company in Problem 13–11A.

CHECK FIGURE
(2) Net decrease in cash: $6

Required:
1. Using the direct method, adjust the company's income statement for 2005 to a cash basis.
2. Using the information obtained in (1) above, along with an analysis of the remaining balance sheet accounts, prepare a statement of cash flows for 2005.

PROBLEM 13–13A   Classifying Transactions on a Statement of Cash Flows   [LO1, LO2]
Below are a number of transactions that took place in Seneca Stores, Inc., during the past year:

a.   Common stock was sold for cash.
b.   Interest was paid on a note, decreasing Interest Payable.
c.   Bonds were retired.
d.   A long-term loan was made to a subsidiary.
e.   Interest was received on the loan in (d) above, reducing Interest Receivable.
f.   A stock dividend was declared and issued on common stock.
g.   A building was acquired by issuing shares of common stock.
h.   Equipment was sold for cash.
i.   Short-term investments were sold.
j.   Cash dividends were declared and paid.
k.   Preferred stock was converted into common stock.
l.   Deferred Income Taxes, a long-term liability, was reduced.
m.   Dividends were received on stock of another company held as an investment.
n.   Equipment was purchased by giving a long-term note to the seller.

Required:
Prepare an answer sheet with the following column headings:

Transaction	Source, Use, or Neither	Activity			Reported in a Separate Schedule	Not on the Statement
		Operating	Investing	Financing		

Enter the letter of the transaction in the left column and indicate whether the transaction would be a source, use, or neither. Then place an X in the appropriate column to show the proper classification of the transaction on the statement of cash flows, or to show if it would not appear on the statement at all.

PROBLEM 13–14A   Prepare a Statement of Cash Flows (Indirect Method)   [LO2, LO3]
Balance sheet accounts for Joyner Company contained the following amounts at the end of Years 1 and 2:

File Edit View Insert Format Tools Data Window Help

	A	B	C	D
1		Year 2	Year 1	
2	*Debit Balance Accounts*			
3	Cash	$ 4,000	$ 21,000	
4	Accounts Receivable	250,000	170,000	
5	Inventory	310,000	260,000	
6	Prepaid Expenses	7,000	14,000	
7	Loan to Hymas Company	40,000	-	
8	Plant and Equipment	510,000	400,000	
9	Total debits	$1,121,000	$ 865,000	
10				
11	*Credit Balance Accounts*			
12	Accumulated Depreciation	$ 132,000	$ 120,000	
13	Accounts Payable	310,000	250,000	
14	Accrued Liabilities	20,000	30,000	
15	Bonds Payable	190,000	70,000	
16	Deferred Income Taxes	45,000	42,000	
17	Common Stock	300,000	270,000	
18	Retained Earnings	124,000	83,000	
19	Total credits	$1,121,000	$ 865,000	
20				

The company's income statement for Year 2 follows:

Sales	$900,000
Less cost of goods sold	500,000
Gross margin	400,000
Less operating expenses	328,000
Net operating income	72,000
Gain on sale of equipment	8,000
Income before taxes	80,000
Less income taxes	24,000
Net income	$ 56,000

Equipment that had cost $40,000 and on which there was accumulated depreciation of $30,000 was sold during Year 2 for $18,000. Cash dividends totaling $15,000 were declared and paid during Year 2.

Required:

1. Using the indirect method, compute the net cash provided by operating activities for Year 2.
2. Prepare a statement of cash flows for Year 2.
3. Briefly explain why cash declined so sharply during the year.

PROBLEM 13–15A   (Appendix 13A) Prepare and Interpret a Statement of Cash Flows (Direct Method)   [LO2, LO4]

Refer to the financial statement data for Joyner Company in Problem 13–14A. Sam Conway, president of the company, considers $15,000 to be the minimum cash balance for operating purposes. As can be seen from the balance sheet data, only $4,000 in cash was available at the end of the current year. The sharp decline is puzzling to Mr. Conway, particularly since sales and profits are at a record high.

CHECK FIGURE
(1) Net cash provided by operating activities: $20,000

Required:

1. Using the direct method, adjust the company's income statement to a cash basis for Year 2.
2. Using the data from (1) above and other data from the problem as needed, prepare a statement of cash flows for Year 2.
3. Explain why cash declined so sharply during the year.

PROBLEM 13–16A   Prepare and Interpret a Statement of Cash Flows (Indirect Method) [LO2, LO3]

Mary Walker, president of Rusco Products, considers $14,000 to be the minimum cash balance for operating purposes. As can be seen from the statements below, only $8,000 in cash was available at the end of 2005. Since the company reported a large net income for the year, and also issued both bonds and common stock, the sharp decline in cash is puzzling to Ms. Walker.

CHECK FIGURE
(1) Net cash provided by operating activities: $18,000

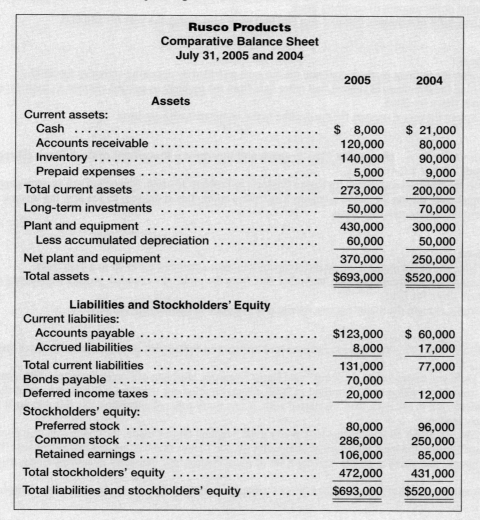

Rusco Products
Comparative Balance Sheet
July 31, 2005 and 2004

	2005	2004
Assets		
Current assets:		
Cash	$ 8,000	$ 21,000
Accounts receivable	120,000	80,000
Inventory	140,000	90,000
Prepaid expenses	5,000	9,000
Total current assets	273,000	200,000
Long-term investments	50,000	70,000
Plant and equipment	430,000	300,000
Less accumulated depreciation	60,000	50,000
Net plant and equipment	370,000	250,000
Total assets	$693,000	$520,000
Liabilities and Stockholders' Equity		
Current liabilities:		
Accounts payable	$123,000	$ 60,000
Accrued liabilities	8,000	17,000
Total current liabilities	131,000	77,000
Bonds payable	70,000	
Deferred income taxes	20,000	12,000
Stockholders' equity:		
Preferred stock	80,000	96,000
Common stock	286,000	250,000
Retained earnings	106,000	85,000
Total stockholders' equity	472,000	431,000
Total liabilities and stockholders' equity	$693,000	$520,000

Rusco Products
Income Statement
For the Year Ended July 31, 2005

Sales		$500,000
Less cost of goods sold		300,000
Gross margin		200,000
Less operating expenses		158,000
Net operating income		42,000
Nonoperating items:		
Gain on sale of investments	$10,000	
Loss on sale of equipment	2,000	8,000
Income before taxes		50,000
Less income taxes		20,000
Net income		$ 30,000

The following additional information is available for the year 2005.

a. Dividends totaling $9,000 were declared and paid in cash.
b. Equipment was sold during the year for $8,000. The equipment had originally cost $20,000 and had accumulated depreciation of $10,000.
c. The decrease in the Preferred Stock account is the result of a conversion of preferred stock into an equal dollar amount of common stock.
d. Long-term investments that had cost $20,000 were sold during the year for $30,000.

Required:
1. Using the indirect method, compute the net cash provided by operating activities for 2005.
2. Using the data from (1) above, and other data from the problem as needed, prepare a statement of cash flows for 2005.
3. Explain the major reasons for the decline in the company's cash position.

CHECK FIGURE
(2) Net cash used for investing activities: $112,000

PROBLEM 13–17A   (Appendix 13A) Prepare and Interpret a Statement of Cash Flows (Direct Method)   [LO2, LO4]
Refer to the financial statements for Rusco Products in Problem 13–16A. Since the Cash account decreased so dramatically during 2005, the company's executive committee is anxious to see how the income statement would appear on a cash basis.

Required:
1. Using the direct method, adjust the company's income statement for 2005 to a cash basis.
2. Using the data from (1) above, and other data from the problem as needed, prepare a statement of cash flows for 2005.
3. Briefly explain the major reasons for the sharp decline in cash during the year.

CHECK FIGURE
(2) Net cash used for investing activities: $570,000

PROBLEM 13–18A   Worksheet; Prepare and Interpret a Statement of Cash Flows (Indirect Method)   [LO2, LO3]
"See, I told you things would work out," said Barry Kresmier, president of Lomax Company. "We expanded sales from $1.6 million to $2.0 million in 2005, nearly doubled our warehouse space, and ended the year with more cash in the bank than we started with. A few more years of expansion like this and we'll be the industry leaders."

"Yes, I'll admit our statements look pretty good," replied Sheri Colson, the company's vice president. "But we're doing business with a lot of companies we don't know much about and that worries me. I'll admit, though, that we're certainly moving a lot of merchandise; our inventory is actually down from last year."

A comparative balance sheet for Lomax Company containing data for the last two years follows:

Lomax Company
Comparative Balance Sheet
December 31, 2005 and 2004

	2005	2004
Assets		
Current assets:		
Cash	$ 61,000	$ 40,000
Accounts receivable	710,000	530,000
Inventory	848,000	860,000
Prepaid expenses	10,000	5,000
Total current assets	1,629,000	1,435,000
Long-term investments	60,000	110,000
Loans to subsidiaries	130,000	80,000
Plant and equipment	3,170,000	2,600,000
Less accumulated depreciation	810,000	755,000
Net plant and equipment	2,360,000	1,845,000
Patents	84,000	90,000
Total assets	$4,263,000	$3,560,000
Liabilities and Stockholders' Equity		
Current liabilities:		
Accounts payable	$ 970,000	$ 670,000
Accrued liabilities	65,000	82,000
Total current liabilities	1,035,000	752,000
Long-term notes	820,000	600,000
Deferred income taxes	95,000	80,000
Total liabilities	1,950,000	1,432,000
Stockholders' equity:		
Common stock	1,740,000	1,650,000
Retained earnings	573,000	478,000
Total stockholders' equity	2,313,000	2,128,000
Total liabilities and stockholders' equity	$4,263,000	$3,560,000

The following additional information is available about the company's activities during 2005:

a.   Cash dividends declared and paid to the common stockholders totaled $75,000.
b.   Long-term notes with a value of $380,000 were repaid during the year.
c.   Equipment was sold during the year for $70,000. The equipment had cost $130,000 and had $40,000 in accumulated depreciation on the date of sale.
d.   Long-term investments were sold during the year for $110,000. These investments had cost $50,000 when purchased several years ago.
e.   The company's income statement for 2005 follows:

Sales		$2,000,000
Less cost of goods sold		1,300,000
Gross margin		700,000
Less operating expenses		490,000
Net operating income		210,000
Nonoperating items:		
Gain on sale of investments	$60,000	
Loss on sale of equipment	20,000	40,000
Income before taxes		250,000
Less income taxes		80,000
Net income		$ 170,000

Required:

1. Prepare a worksheet like Exhibit 13–9 for Lomax Company.
2. Using the indirect method, prepare a statement of cash flows for the year 2005.
3. What problems relating to the company's activities are revealed by the statement of cash flows that you have prepared?

CHECK FIGURE
Net cash provided by operating activities: $356,000

PROBLEM 13–19A   **(Appendix 13A) Adjusting Net Income to a Cash Basis (Direct Method)**   **[LO4]**

Refer to the data for the Lomax Company in Problem 13–18A. All of the long-term notes issued during 2005 are being held by Lomax's bank. The bank's management wants the income statement adjusted to a cash basis so that it can compare the cash basis statement to the accrual basis statement.

Required:

Use the direct method to convert Lomax Company's 2005 income statement to a cash basis.

BUILDING YOUR SKILLS

Communicating In Practice   **(LO3, LO4)**

Use an online yellow pages directory such as www.athand.com to find a company in your area that has a website on which it has an annual report, including a statement of cash flows. Make an appointment with the controller or chief financial officer of the company. Before your meeting, find out as much as you can about the organization's operations from its website.

Required:

After asking the following questions, write a brief memorandum to your instructor that summarizes the information obtained from the company's website and addresses what you found out during your interview.

1. Does the company use the direct method or the indirect method to determine the net cash provided by operating activities when preparing its statement of cash flows? Why?
2. How is the information reported on the statement of cash flows used for decision-making purposes?

Analytical Thinking   **[LO2, LO3]**

Oxident Products manufactures a vitamin supplement. The following *changes* have taken place in the company's balance sheet accounts as a result of the past year's activities:

CHECK FIGURE
Net cash used for investing activities: $580,000

Debit Balance Accounts	Net increase (Decrease)
Cash	$ (10,000)
Accounts Receivable	(81,000)
Inventory	230,000
Prepaid Expenses	(6,000)
Long-Term Loans to Subsidiaries	100,000
Long-Term Investments	(120,000)
Plant and Equipment	500,000
Net increase	$ 613,000

Credit Balance Accounts	Net increase (Decrease)
Accumulated Depreciation	$ 90,000
Accounts Payable	(70,000)
Accrued Liabilities	35,000
Bonds Payable	400,000
Deferred Income Taxes	8,000
Preferred Stock	(180,000)
Common Stock	270,000
Retained Earnings	60,000
Net increase	$ 613,000

The following additional information is available about last year's activities:

a. The company sold equipment during the year for $40,000. The equipment originally cost $100,000 and it had $70,000 in accumulated depreciation at the time of sale.

b. Net income for the year was $ ____?____.

c. The balance in the Cash account at the beginning of the year was $52,000; the balance at the end of the year was $ ____?____.

d. The company declared and paid $30,000 in cash dividends during the year.

e. Long-term investments that had cost $120,000 were sold during the year for $80,000.

f. The balances in the Plant and Equipment and Accumulated Depreciation accounts for the past year are given below:

	Ending	Beginning
Plant and Equipment	$3,200,000	$2,700,000
Accumulated Depreciation	$1,500,000	$1,410,000

g. If data are not given explaining the change in an account, make the most reasonable assumption as to the cause of the change.

Required:

Using the indirect method, prepare a statement of cash flows for the past year. Show all computations for items that appear on your statement.

Taking It to the Net

As you know, the World Wide Web is a medium that is constantly evolving. Sites come and go and change without notice. To enable periodic updating of site addresses, these problems have been posted to the textbook website (www.mhhe.com/bgn3e). After accessing the site, enter the Student Center and select this chapter to find the Taking It to the Net problems.

14

"How Well Am I Doing?" Financial Statement Analysis

CHAPTER OUTLINE

A LOOK BACK

In Chapter 13 we showed how to construct the statement of cash flows and discussed the interpretation of the data found on that statement.

A LOOK AT THIS CHAPTER

In Chapter 14 we focus on the analysis of financial statements to help forecast the financial health of a company. We discuss the use of trend data, comparisons with other organizations, and fundamental financial ratios.

Limitations of Financial Statement Analysis

- Comparison of Financial Data
- The Need to Look beyond Ratios

Statements in Comparative and Common-Size Form

- Dollar and Percentage Changes on Statements
- Common-Size Statements

Ratio Analysis—The Common Stockholder

- Earnings per Share
- Price-Earnings Ratio
- Dividend Payout and Yield Ratios
- Return on Total Assets
- Return on Common Stockholders' Equity
- Financial Leverage
- Book Value per Share

Ratio Analysis—The Short-Term Creditor

- Working Capital
- Current Ratio
- Acid-Test (Quick) Ratio
- Accounts Receivable Turnover
- Inventory Turnover

Ratio Analysis—The Long-Term Creditor

- Times Interest Earned Ratio
- Debt-to-Equity Ratio

Summary of Ratios and Sources of Comparative Ratio Data

Chapter Fourteen

DECISION FEATURE

Biotech Companies Go Out of Favor

A venture capitalist invests in a start-up company with the hope of recognizing a significant profit when the start-up company goes public by selling shares of its stock on the open market. During the 1980s and early 1990s, investments by venture capitalists in biotechnology companies helped fund the development of drugs used to treat a variety of diseases that were previously considered untreatable (e.g., cancer, kidney failure, heart attacks, arthritis, and the AIDS virus, among others). However, in 1997, a reallocation of funds took place in the venture capital market. Software vendors, health care service providers, and Internet-based businesses came into favor, and biotech companies went out of fashion. Instead of waiting for returns on biotech investments that took years to realize because of the length of time required to get drugs to market, venture capitalists opted for the quicker payoffs in other industries. Payoffs were especially rapid on investments in dot.com companies, which were managing to go public long before they reached profitability. By 1999, even biotech companies with experienced management teams and well-conceived development plans for a multitude of drugs were finding it difficult, if not impossible, to raise money.

Cynthia Robbins-Roth, the founding partner of Bio Venture Consultants, believes that the venture capitalists' decision-making model was flawed. Part of the problem is the tendency for investors to jump on board when a hot new fad (such as the dot.com one) surfaces. She emphasizes the need to separately analyze each company, rather than analyzing just one and then investing in similar companies. Robbins-Roth is also critical of the technical expertise of the analysts that were working for venture capital firms. She highlights the mounting need for new drugs as the population ages and the opportunities provided by recent leaps in biotechnology that will make possible the development of those drugs.

Source: Cynthia Robbins-Roth, "Seduced & Abandoned," *Forbes ASAP,* May 29, 2000, pp. 153–154.

All financial statements are historical documents. They tell what *has happened* during a particular period. However, most users of financial statements are concerned with what *will happen* in the future. For example, stockholders are concerned with future earnings and dividends and creditors are concerned with the company's future ability to repay its debts. While financial statements are historical in nature, they can still provide valuable insights to users regarding financial matters. These users rely on *financial statement analysis,* which involves examining trends in key financial data, comparing financial data across companies, and analyzing financial ratios to assess the financial health and future prospects of a company. In this chapter, we focus our attention on the most important ratios and other analytical tools that financial analysts use.

In addition to stockholders and creditors, managers are also vitally concerned with the financial ratios discussed in this chapter. First, the ratios provide indicators of how well the company and its business units are performing. Some of these ratios might be used in a balanced scorecard approach as discussed in Chapter 8. The specific ratios selected depend on the company's strategy. For example, a company that wants to emphasize responsiveness to customers may closely monitor the inventory turnover ratio discussed later in this chapter. Second, since managers must report to stockholders and may wish to raise funds from external sources, managers must pay attention to the financial ratios used by external investors to evaluate the company's investment potential and creditworthiness.

LIMITATIONS OF FINANCIAL STATEMENT ANALYSIS

Although financial statement analysis is a useful tool, it has two limitations that should be mentioned before proceeding any further. These two limitations involve the comparability of financial data between companies and the need to look beyond ratios.

Comparison of Financial Data

Comparisons of one company with another can provide valuable clues about the financial health of an organization. Unfortunately, differences in accounting methods between companies sometimes make it difficult to compare their financial data. For example, if one company values its inventories by the LIFO method and another company by the average cost method, then direct comparisons of their financial data such as inventory valuations and cost of goods sold may be misleading. Sometimes enough data is presented in footnotes to the financial statements to restate data to a comparable basis. Otherwise, the analyst should keep in mind any lack of comparability before drawing definite conclusions. Even with this limitation in mind, comparisons of key ratios with other companies and with industry averages often suggest avenues for further investigation.

The Need to Look beyond Ratios

Ratios should not be viewed as an end, but rather as a *starting point*. They raise many questions and point to opportunities for further analysis, but they rarely answer any questions by themselves. In addition to ratios, the analyst should evaluate industry trends, technological changes, changes in consumer tastes, changes in broad economic factors, and changes within the company itself.

STATEMENTS IN COMPARATIVE AND COMMON-SIZE FORM

An item on a balance sheet or income statement has little meaning by itself. Suppose a company's sales for a year were $250 million. In isolation, that is not particularly useful information. How does that stack up against last year's sales? How do the sales relate to the cost of goods sold? In making these kinds of comparisons, three analytical techniques are widely used:

LEARNING OBJECTIVE 1

Prepare and interpret financial statements in comparative and common-size form.

1. Dollar and percentage changes on statements (*horizontal analysis*).
2. Common-size statements (*vertical analysis*).
3. Ratios.

Concept 14-1

The first and second techniques are discussed in this section; the third technique is discussed in the remainder of the chapter. Throughout the chapter, we will illustrate these analytical techniques using the financial statements of Brickey Electronics, a producer of specialized electronic components.

Dollar and Percentage Changes on Statements

Horizontal analysis (also known as **trend analysis**) involves analyzing financial data over time. This can involve nothing more complicated than showing year-to-year changes in each financial statement item in both dollar and percentage terms. Exhibits 14–1 and 14–2 show Brickey Electronics' financial statements in this *comparative form*. The dollar changes serve to highlight the changes that are the most important economically; the percentage changes serve to highlight the changes that are the most unusual.

Horizontal analysis can be even more useful when data from a number of years are used to compute *trend percentages*. To compute **trend percentages,** a base year is selected and the data for all years are stated in terms of a percentage of that base year. To illustrate, consider the sales and net income of McDonald's Corporation, the world's largest food service retailer, with more than 31,000 restaurants worldwide:

	2002	2001	2000	1999	1998	1997	1996	1995	1994	1993
Sales (millions)	$15,406	$14,870	$14,243	$13,259	$12,421	$11,409	$10,687	$9,795	$8,321	$7,408
Net income (millions)	$894	$1,637	$1,977	$1,948	$1,550	$1,642	$1,573	$1,427	$1,224	$1,083

Be careful to note that the above data have been arranged with the most recent year on the left. This may be the opposite of what you are used to, but it is the way financial data are commonly displayed in annual reports and other sources. By simply looking at

EXHIBIT 14–1

Brickey Electronics
Comparative Balance Sheet
December 31, 2005 and 2004
(dollars in thousands)

	2005	2004	Increase (Decrease) Amount	Increase (Decrease) Percent
Assets				
Current assets:				
Cash	$ 1,200	$ 2,350	$(1,150)	(48.9)%*
Accounts receivable, net	6,000	4,000	2,000	50.0%
Inventory	8,000	10,000	(2,000)	(20.0)%
Prepaid expenses	300	120	180	150.0%
Total current assets	15,500	16,470	(970)	(5.9)%
Property and equipment:				
Land	4,000	4,000	0	0%
Buildings and equipment, net	12,000	8,500	3,500	41.2%
Total property and equipment	16,000	12,500	3,500	28.0%
Total assets	$31,500	$28,970	$ 2,530	8.7%
Liabilities and Stockholders' Equity				
Current liabilities:				
Accounts payable	$ 5,800	$ 4,000	$ 1,800	45.0%
Accrued payables	900	400	500	125.0%
Notes payable, short term	300	600	(300)	(50.0)%
Total current liabilities	7,000	5,000	2,000	40.0%
Long-term liabilities:				
Bonds payable, 8%	7,500	8,000	(500)	(6.3)%
Total liabilities	14,500	13,000	1,500	11.5%
Stockholders' equity:				
Preferred stock, $100 par, 6%	2,000	2,000	0	0%
Common stock, $12 par	6,000	6,000	0	0%
Additional paid-in capital	1,000	1,000	0	0%
Total paid-in capital	9,000	9,000	0	0%
Retained earnings	8,000	6,970	1,030	14.8%
Total stockholders' equity	17,000	15,970	1,030	6.4%
Total liabilities and stockholders' equity	$31,500	$28,970	$ 2,530	8.7%

*The change between 2004 and 2005 is expressed as a percentage of the dollar amounts for 2004. For example, Cash decreased by $1,150 between 2004 and 2005. This decrease expressed in percentage form is computed as follows: $1,150 ÷ $2,350 = 48.9%. Other percentage figures in this exhibit and Exhibit 14–2 are computed in the same way.

these data, one can see that sales increased every year, but the net income has not. However, recasting these data into trend percentages aids interpretation:

	2002	2001	2000	1999	1998	1997	1996	1995	1994	1993
Sales (millions)	208%	201%	192%	179%	168%	154%	144%	132%	112%	100%
Net income (millions) ...	83%	151%	183%	180%	143%	152%	145%	132%	113%	100%

In the above table, both sales and net income have been put into percentage terms, using 1993 as the base year. For example, the 2002 sales of $15,406 are 208% of the 1993

EXHIBIT 14-2

Brickey Electronics
Comparative Income Statement and Reconciliation of Retained Earnings
For the Years Ended December 31, 2005 and 2004
(dollars in thousands)

	2005	2004	Increase (Decrease) Amount	Percent
Sales............................	$52,000	$48,000	$4,000	8.3%
Cost of goods sold	36,000	31,500	4,500	14.3%
Gross margin	16,000	16,500	(500)	(3.0)%
Operating expenses:				
Selling expenses	7,000	6,500	500	7.7%
Administrative expenses	5,860	6,100	(240)	(3.9)%
Total operating expenses	12,860	12,600	260	2.1%
Net operating income	3,140	3,900	(760)	(19.5)%
Interest expense	640	700	(60)	(8.6)%
Net income before taxes	2,500	3,200	(700)	(21.9)%
Less income taxes (30%)	750	960	(210)	(21.9)%
Net income........................	1,750	2,240	$ (490)	(21.9)%
Dividends to preferred stockholders,				
$6 per share (see Exhibit 17-1)	120	120		
Net income remaining for common				
stockholders......................	1,630	2,120		
Dividends to common stockholders,				
$1.20 per share....................	600	600		
Net income added to retained				
earnings	1,030	1,520		
Retained earnings, beginning				
of year..........................	6,970	5,450		
Retained earnings, end of year	$ 8,000	$ 6,970		

sales of $7,408. This trend analysis is particularly striking when the data are plotted as in Exhibit 14–3. McDonald's sales growth was impressive throughout the entire 10-year period and was closely tracked by net income for the first part of this period, but net income faltered in 1998 and then plummeted in 2001 and 2002.

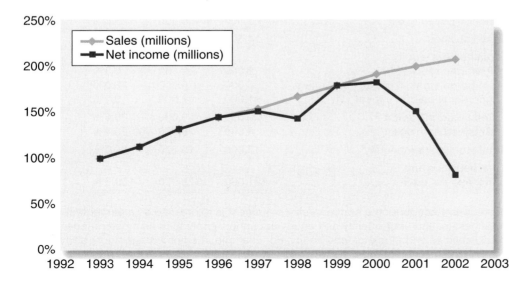

EXHIBIT 14-3

McDonald's Corporation: Trend Analysis of Sales and Net Income

Common-Size Statements

Horizontal analysis, which was discussed in the previous section, examines changes in a financial statement item over time. **Vertical analysis** focuses on the relations among financial statement items at a given point in time. A **common-size financial statement** is a vertical analysis in which each financial statement item is expressed as a percentage. In income statements, all items are usually expressed as a percentage of sales. In balance sheets, all items are usually expressed as a percentage of total assets. Exhibit 14–4 contains a common-size balance sheet for Brickey Electronics and Exhibit 14–5 contains a common-size income statement for the company.

EXHIBIT 14–4

Brickey Electronics
Common-Size Comparative Balance Sheet
December 31, 2005 and 2004
(dollars in thousands)

| | | | Common-Size Percentages | |
	2005	2004	2005	2004
Assets				
Current assets:				
Cash	$ 1,200	$ 2,350	3.8%*	8.1%
Accounts receivable, net	6,000	4,000	19.0%	13.8%
Inventory	8,000	10,000	25.4%	34.5%
Prepaid expenses	300	120	1.0%	0.4%
Total current assets	15,500	16,470	49.2%	56.9%
Property and equipment:				
Land	4,000	4,000	12.7%	13.8%
Buildings and equipment, net	12,000	8,500	38.1%	29.3%
Total property and equipment	16,000	12,500	50.8%	43.1%
Total assets	$31,500	$28,970	100.0%	100.0%
Liabilities and Stockholders' Equity				
Current liabilities:				
Accounts payable	$ 5,800	$ 4,000	18.4%	13.8%
Accrued payables	900	400	2.9%	1.4%
Notes payable, short term	300	600	1.0%	2.1%
Total current liabilities	7,000	5,000	22.2%	17.3%
Long-term liabilities:				
Bonds payable, 8%	7,500	8,000	23.8%	27.6%
Total liabilities	14,500	13,000	46.0%	44.9%
Stockholders' equity:				
Preferred stock, $100, 6%	2,000	2,000	6.3%	6.9%
Common stock, $12 par	6,000	6,000	19.0%	20.7%
Additional paid-in capital	1,000	1,000	3.2%	3.5%
Total paid-in capital	9,000	9,000	28.6%	31.1%
Retained earnings	8,000	6,970	25.4%	24.1%
Total stockholders' equity	17,000	15,970	54.0%	55.1%
Total liabilities and stockholders' equity	$31,500	$28,970	100.0%	100.0%

*Each asset account on a common-size statement is expressed as a percentage of total assets, and each liability and equity account is expressed as a percentage of total liabilities and stockholders' equity. For example, the percentage figure above for Cash in 2005 is computed as follows: $1,200 ÷ $31,500 = 3.8%.

EXHIBIT 14–5

Brickey Electronics
Common-Size Comparative Income Statement
For the Years Ended December 31, 2005 and 2004
(dollars in thousands)

	2005	2004	Common-Size Percentages 2005	Common-Size Percentages 2004
Sales	$52,000	$48,000	100.0%	100.0%
Cost of goods sold	36,000	31,500	69.2%	65.6%
Gross margin	16,000	16,500	30.8%	34.4%
Operating expenses:				
Selling expenses	7,000	6,500	13.5%	13.5%
Administrative expenses	5,860	6,100	11.3%	12.7%
Total operating expenses	12,860	12,600	24.7%	26.3%
Net operating income	3,140	3,900	6.0%	8.1%
Interest expense	640	700	1.2%	1.5%
Net income before taxes	2,500	3,200	4.8%	6.7%
Income taxes (30%)	750	960	1.4%	2.0%
Net income	$ 1,750	$ 2,240	3.4%	4.7%

*Note that the percentage figures for each year are expressed as a percentage of total sales for the year. For example, the percentage figure for cost of goods sold in 2005 is computed as follows: $36,000 ÷ $52,000 = 69.2%

Notice from Exhibit 14–4 that placing all assets in common-size form clearly shows the relative importance of the current assets as compared to the noncurrent assets. It also shows that significant changes have taken place in the composition of the current assets over the last year. For example, accounts receivable have increased in relative importance and both cash and inventory have declined in relative importance. Judging from the sharp increase in accounts receivable, the deterioration in the cash balance may be a result of an inability to collect from customers.

Shifting now to the income statement, in Exhibit 14–5 the cost of goods sold as a percentage of sales increased from 65.6% in 2004 to 69.2% in 2005. Or looking at this from a different viewpoint, the *gross margin percentage* declined from 34.4% in 2004 to 30.8% in 2005. Managers and investment analysts often pay close attention to this measure of profitability. The **gross margin percentage** is computed as follows:

$$\text{Gross margin percentage} = \frac{\text{Gross margin}}{\text{Sales}}$$

The gross margin percentage should be more stable for retailing companies than for other companies since the cost of goods sold in retailing excludes fixed costs. When fixed costs are included in the cost of goods sold, the gross margin percentage should increase and decrease with sales volume. With increases in sales volume, the fixed costs are spread across more units and the gross margin percentage improves.

Common-size statements are particularly useful when comparing data from different companies. For example, in 2002, Wendy's net income was $219 million, whereas McDonald's was $894 million. This comparison is somewhat misleading because of the dramatically different sizes of the two companies. To put this in better perspective, net income can be expressed as a percentage of the sales revenues of each company. Since Wendy's sales revenues were $2,730 million and McDonald's were $15,406 million,

Wendy's net income as a percentage of sales was about 8.0% and McDonald's was about 5.8%. In this light, McDonald's performance does not compare favorably with Wendy's performance.

Gross Margins Can Make the Difference

After announcing a 42% increase in quarterly profits, Dell Inc.'s shares fell over 6%. Why? According to *The Wall Street Journal*, investors focused on the company's eroding profit margins. "Analysts . . . said that a decline in gross margins was larger than they had expected and indicated a difficult pricing environment. Gross margins fell nearly a full percentage point to 21.5% of sales, from 22.4%." Dell had cut its prices to increase its market share, which worked, but at the cost of lowered profitability.

Source: Gary McWilliams, "Dell Net Rises, but Margins Spur Worries," *The Wall Street Journal*, May 19, 1999, p. A3.

RATIO ANALYSIS—THE COMMON STOCKHOLDER

LEARNING OBJECTIVE 2

Compute and interpret financial ratios that would be useful to a common stockholder.

Concept 14-2

A number of financial ratios are used to assess how well a company is doing from the standpoint of its stockholders. These ratios focus on net income, dividends, and stockholders' equity.

Earnings per Share

An investor buys a share of stock in the hope of realizing a return in the form of either dividends or future increases in the value of the stock. Since earnings form the basis for dividend payments, as well as the basis for future increases in the value of shares, investors are always interested in a company's *earnings per share*. Probably no single statistic is more widely quoted or relied on by investors than earnings per share, although it has some inherent limitations, as discussed below.

Earnings per share is computed by dividing net income available for common stockholders by the average number of common shares outstanding during the year. "Net income available for common stockholders" is net income less dividends paid to the owners of the company's preferred stock.[1]

$$\text{Earnings per share} = \frac{\text{Net income} - \text{Preferred dividends}}{\text{Average number of common shares outstanding}}$$

Using the data in Exhibits 14–1 and 14–2, we see that the earnings per share for Brickey Electronics for 2005 would be computed as follows:

$$\frac{\$1,750,000 - \$120,000}{(500,000 \text{ shares*} + 500,000 \text{ shares})/2} = \$3.26$$

*$6,000,000 ÷ 12 = 500,000 shares.

---

[1]Another complication can arise when a company has issued securities such as executive stock options or warrants that can be converted into shares of common stock. If these conversions were to take place, the same earnings would have to be distributed among a greater number of common shares. Therefore, a supplemental earnings per share figure, called diluted earnings per share, may have to be computed. Refer to a current intermediate financial accounting text for details.

Pennies Matter!

In January 2005, online auctioneer eBay announced that its fourth-quarter earnings for 2004 rose 44% compared with the same quarter of the prior year. While eBay's fourth quarter earnings of 30 cents per share matched the company's own forecast, it came up short of Wall Street analysts' forecasts by an average of four cents per share. Consequently, eBay's stock price tumbled $15.36 in less than 24 hours. Given that eBay had about 662 million shares of common stock outstanding at the time, the company's stockholders saw more than $10 billion of wealth evaporate in one day.

eBay's experience clearly illustrates how Wall Street investors exert pressure on publicly traded companies to deliver quarterly earnings that meet expectations. While it may be easy from a theoretical standpoint to advocate the value of taking a long-run point of view when making decisions, managers face the cold, hard reality that if their companies fail to meet Wall Street investors' quarterly earnings forecasts, their stock prices will probably take a beating.

Source: Mylene Mangalindan, "EBay Posts 44% Jump in Profit; Forecast Is Tepid," *The Wall Street Journal,* January 20, 2005, p. A3.

Price-Earnings Ratio

The relationship between the market price of a share of stock and the stock's current earnings per share is often stated in terms of a **price-earnings ratio.** If we assume that the current market price for Brickey Electronics' stock is $40 per share, the company's price-earnings ratio is computed as follows:

$$\text{Price-earnings ratio} = \frac{\text{Market price per share}}{\text{Earnings per share}}$$

$$\frac{\$40 \text{ per share}}{\$3.26 \text{ per share}} = 12.3$$

The price-earnings ratio is 12.3; that is, the stock is selling for about 12.3 times its current earnings per share.

The price-earnings ratio is widely used by investors. A high price-earnings ratio means that investors are willing to pay a premium for the company's stock—presumably because the company is expected to have higher than average future earnings growth. Conversely, if investors believe a company's future earnings growth prospects are limited, the company's price-earnings ratio will be relatively low. For example, not long ago, the stock prices of some dot.com companies—particularly those with little or no earnings—were selling at levels that gave rise to unprecedented price-earnings ratios. However, these price-earnings ratios were unsustainable in the long run and the companies' stock prices eventually fell.

Dividend Payout and Yield Ratios

Investors in a company's stock make money in two ways—increases in the market value of the stock and dividends. In general, earnings should be retained in a company and not paid out in dividends as long as the rate of return on funds invested inside the company exceeds the rate of return that stockholders could earn on alternative investments outside the company. Therefore, companies with excellent prospects of profitable growth often pay little or no dividend. Companies with little opportunity for profitable growth, but with steady, dependable earnings, tend to pay out a higher percentage of their earnings as dividends.

The Dividend Payout Ratio   The **dividend payout ratio** gauges the portion of current earnings being paid out in dividends. Investors who seek stock price growth would like this ratio to be small, whereas investors who seek dividends prefer it to be large. This ratio is computed by dividing the dividends per share by the earnings per share for common stock:

$$\text{Dividend payout ratio} = \frac{\text{Dividends per share}}{\text{Earnings per share}}$$

For Brickey Electronics, the dividend payout ratio for 2005 is computed as follows:

$$\frac{\$1.20 \text{ per share (see Exhibit 14-2)}}{\$3.26 \text{ per share}} = 36.8\%$$

There is no such thing as a "right" dividend payout ratio, although the ratio tends to be similar for companies within the same industry. As noted above, companies with ample growth opportunities at high rates of return tend to have low payout ratios, whereas companies with limited reinvestment opportunities tend to have higher payout ratios.

The Dividend Yield Ratio   The **dividend yield ratio** is computed by dividing the current dividends per share by the current market price per share:

$$\text{Dividend yield ratio} = \frac{\text{Dividends per share}}{\text{Market price per share}}$$

The market price for Brickey Electronics' stock is $40 per share so the dividend yield is computed as follows:

$$\frac{\$1.20 \text{ per share}}{\$40 \text{ per share}} = 3.0\%$$

The dividend yield ratio measures the rate of return (in the form of cash dividends only) that would be earned by an investor who buys common stock at the current market price. A low dividend yield ratio is neither bad nor good by itself.

Return on Total Assets

The **return on total assets** is a measure of operating performance. It is defined as follows:

$$\text{Return on total assets} = \frac{\text{Net income} + [\text{Interest expense} \times (1 - \text{Tax rate})]}{\text{Average total assets}}$$

Adding interest expense back to net income results in an adjusted earnings figure that shows what earnings would have been if the company had no debt. With this adjustment, the return on total assets can be compared for companies with differing amounts of debt or for a single company that has changed its mix of debt and equity over time. Notice that the interest expense is placed on an after-tax basis by multiplying it by the factor $(1 - \text{Tax rate})$.

The return on total assets for Brickey Electronics for 2005 is computed as follows (from Exhibits 14–1 and 14–2):

Net income	$ 1,750,000
Add back interest expense: $640,000 × (1 − 0.30)	448,000
Total (a)	$ 2,198,000
Assets, beginning of year	$28,970,000
Assets, end of year	31,500,000
Total	$60,470,000
Average total assets: $60,470,000 ÷ 2 (b)	$30,235,000
Return on total assets, (a) ÷ (b)	7.3%

Brickey Electronics has earned a return of 7.3% on average total assets employed over the last year.

Return on Common Stockholders' Equity

The **return on common stockholders' equity** is based on the book value of common stockholders' equity. It is computed as follows:

$$\frac{\text{Return on common}}{\text{stockholders' equity}} = \frac{\text{Net income} \;-\; \text{Preferred dividends}}{\text{Average common stockholders' equity}}$$

where

$$\frac{\text{Average common}}{\text{stockholders' equity}} = \frac{\text{Average total stockholders' equity}}{\;-\; \text{Average preferred stock}}$$

For Brickey Electronics, the return on common stockholders' equity is computed as follows:

Net income	$ 1,750,000
Deduct preferred dividends	120,000
Net income remaining for common stockholders (a)	$ 1,630,000
Average stockholders' equity	$16,485,000*
Deduct average preferred stock	2,000,000†
Average common stockholders' equity (b)	$14,485,000
Return on common stockholders' equity, (a) ÷ (b)	11.3%

*$15,970,000 + $17,000,000 = $32,970,000; $32,970,000 ÷ 2 = $16,485,000.
†$2,000,000 + $2,000,000 = $4,000,000; $4,000,000 ÷ 2 = $2,000,000.

Compare the return on common stockholders' equity above (11.3%) with the return on total assets computed in the preceding section (7.3%). Why is the return on common stockholders' equity so much higher? The answer lies in *financial leverage.*

Financial Leverage

Financial leverage results from the difference between the rate of return the company earns on investments in its own assets and the rate of return that the company must pay its creditors. If the rate of return on the company's assets exceeds the rate of return the company pays its creditors, *financial leverage is positive.* If the rate of return on the company's assets is less than the rate of return the company pays its creditors, *financial leverage is negative.*

Comparing Banks

IN BUSINESS

Deutsche Bank, the German banking giant, fares poorly in comparisons with its global rivals. Its net-income-to-assets ratio (i.e., return on assets) is only 0.26%, while its peers such as Citigroup and Credit Suisse have ratios of up to 0.92%. Its return on equity is only 10%, whereas the return on equity of almost all its peers is in the 14% to 16% range. One reason for Deutsche Bank's anemic performance is the bank's bloated and expensive payroll. Deutsche Bank's earnings average about $23,000 per employee. At HSBC (Hong Kong and Shanghai Banking Corporation) the figure is $32,000 per employee and at Credit Suisse it is $34,000.

Source: Justin Doebele, "Best Bank Bargain?" *Forbes,* August 9, 1999, pp. 89–90.

Financial Leverage

| Creditors/Preferred Stockholders | Common Stockholders | Creditors/Preferred Stockholders | Common Stockholders |

Positive Financial Leverage   **Negative Financial Leverage**

For example, suppose that CBS's after-tax return on total assets is 12%. If the company can borrow from creditors at an after-tax cost of 7%, then financial leverage is positive. The difference of 5% (12% − 7%) will go to the common stockholders.

We can see financial leverage in operation in the case of Brickey Electronics. Notice from Exhibit 14–1 that the company pays 8% interest on its bonds payable. The after-tax interest cost of these bonds is only 5.6% [8% interest rate × (1 − 0.30) = 5.6%]. As shown earlier, the company's after-tax return on total assets is 7.3%. Since the return on total assets of 7.3% is greater than the 5.6% after-tax interest cost of the bonds, leverage is positive, and the difference goes to the common stockholders. This explains in part why the return on common stockholders' equity of 11.3% is greater than the return on total assets of 7.3%. If financial leverage is positive, having some debt in the capital structure can substantially benefit the common stockholder. For this reason, companies often try to maintain a level of debt that is considered to be normal within their industry.

Unfortunately, leverage is a two-edged sword. If assets do not earn a high enough return to cover the interest costs of debt and preferred stock dividends, then the common stockholder suffers. In that case, financial leverage is negative.

Book Value per Share

Book value per share measures the amount that would be distributed to holders of each share of common stock if all assets were sold at their balance sheet carrying amounts (i.e., book values) and if all creditors were paid off. Book value per share is based entirely on historical costs. The formula for computing it is:

$$\text{Book value per share} = \frac{\text{Common stockholders' equity}}{\text{Number of common shares outstanding}}$$

where

$$\text{Common stockholders' equity} = \frac{\text{Total stockholders' equity}}{- \text{ Preferred stock}}$$

Total stockholders' equity (see Exhibit 14–1)	$17,000,000
Deduct preferred stock (see Exhibit 14–1)	2,000,000
Common stockholders' equity	$15,000,000

The book value per share of Brickey Electronics' common stock is computed as follows:

$$\frac{\$15,000,000}{500,000 \text{ shares}} = \$30 \text{ per share}$$

If this book value is compared with the $40 market value of Brickey Electronics' stock, the stock may appear to be overpriced. However, as we discussed earlier, market prices reflect expectations about future earnings and dividends, whereas book value largely reflects the results of events that have occurred in the past. Ordinarily, the market value of a stock exceeds its book value. For example, in one year, Microsoft's common stock traded at over 4 times its book value, and Coca-Cola's market value was over 17 times its book value.

RATIO ANALYSIS—THE SHORT-TERM CREDITOR

Short-term creditors, such as suppliers, want to be repaid on time. Therefore, they focus on the company's cash flows and on its working capital because these are the company's primary sources of cash in the short run.

LEARNING OBJECTIVE 3

Compute and interpret financial ratios that would be useful to a short-term creditor.

Working Capital

The excess of current assets over current liabilities is known as **working capital.**

$$\text{Working capital} = \text{Current assets} - \text{Current liabilities}$$

The working capital for Brickey Electronics is computed below:

	2005	2004
Current assets	$15,500,000	$16,470,000
Current liabilities	7,000,000	5,000,000
Working capital	$ 8,500,000	$11,470,000

Ample working capital provides some assurance to short-term creditors that they will be paid by the company. However, maintaining large amounts of working capital isn't free. Working capital must be financed with long-term debt and equity—both of which are expensive. Therefore, managers often want to minimize working capital.

A large and growing working capital balance may not be a good sign. For example, it could be the result of unwarranted growth in inventories. To put the working capital figure into proper perspective, it should be supplemented with the following four ratios—the current ratio, the acid-test (quick) ratio, the accounts receivable turnover, and the inventory turnover.

Current Ratio

The elements involved in the computation of working capital are frequently expressed in ratio form. A company's current assets divided by its current liabilities is known as the **current ratio:**

$$\text{Current ratio} = \frac{\text{Current assets}}{\text{Current liabilities}}$$

For Brickey Electronics, the current ratios for 2004 and 2005 would be computed as follows:

2005	2004
$\dfrac{\$15,500,000}{\$7,000,000} = 2.21$	$\dfrac{\$16,470,000}{\$5,000,000} = 3.29$

Although widely regarded as a measure of short-term debt-paying ability, the current ratio must be interpreted with great care. A *declining* ratio, as above, might be a sign of a deteriorating financial condition. On the other hand, it might be the result of eliminating obsolete inventories or other stagnant current assets. An *improving* ratio might be the result of stockpiling inventory, or it might indicate an improving financial situation.

In short, the current ratio is useful, but tricky to interpret. To avoid a blunder, the analyst must take a hard look at the individual assets and liabilities involved.

The general rule of thumb calls for a current ratio of at least 2. However, many companies successfully operate with a current ratio below 2. The adequacy of a current ratio depends heavily on the *composition* of the assets. For example, as we see in the table below, both Worthington Corporation and Greystone, Inc., have current ratios of 2. However, they are not in comparable financial condition. Greystone is likely to have difficulty meeting its current financial obligations, since almost all of its current assets consist of inventory rather than more liquid assets such as cash and accounts receivable.

	Worthington Corporation	Greystone, Inc.
Current assets:		
Cash	$ 25,000	$ 2,000
Accounts receivable, net	60,000	8,000
Inventory	85,000	160,000
Prepaid expenses	5,000	5,000
Total current assets (a)	$175,000	$175,000
Current liabilities (b)	$ 87,500	$ 87,500
Current ratio, (a) ÷ (b)	2	2

Acid-Test (Quick) Ratio

The **acid-test (quick) ratio** is a more rigorous test of a company's ability to meet its short-term debts than the current ratio. Inventories and prepaid expenses are excluded from total current assets, leaving only the more liquid (or "quick") assets to be divided by current liabilities.

$$\text{Acid-test ratio} = \frac{\text{Cash} + \text{Marketable securities} + \text{Current receivables}}{\text{Current liabilities}}$$

where

$$\text{Current receivables} = \frac{\text{Accounts receivable}}{+ \text{Short-term notes receivable}}$$

The acid-test ratio is designed to measure how well a company can meet its obligations without having to liquidate or depend too heavily on its inventory. Ideally, each dollar of liabilities should be backed by at least $1 of quick assets. However, acid-test ratios as low as 0.3 are common.

The acid-test ratios for Brickey Electronics for 2004 and 2005 are computed below:

	2005	2004
Cash (see Exhibit 14–1)	$1,200,000	$2,350,000
Accounts receivable (see Exhibit 14–1)	6,000,000	4,000,000
Total quick assets (a)	$7,200,000	$6,350,000
Current liabilities (see Exhibit 14–1) (b)	$7,000,000	$5,000,000
Acid-test ratio, (a) ÷ (b)	1.03	1.27

Although Brickey Electronics has an acid-test ratio for 2005 that is within the acceptable range, an analyst might be concerned about several trends revealed in the company's balance sheet. Notice in Exhibit 14–1 that short-term debts are rising, while the cash position seems to be deteriorating. Perhaps the lower cash balance is a result of the substantial increase in accounts receivable. In short, as with the current ratio, the acid-test ratio should be interpreted with one eye on its basic components.

IN BUSINESS

Too Much Cash?

Microsoft has accumulated an unprecedented hoard of cash and cash equivalents—over $49 billion at the end of fiscal year 2003 and this cash hoard is growing at the rate of about $1 billion per month. This cash hoard is large enough to give every household in the U.S. a check for $471. What does Microsoft need all this money for? Why doesn't it pay more dividends? Microsoft executives say the cash is needed for antitrust lawsuits. Critics of the company's power, including some of its competitors, claim that the cash gives the company a huge competitive advantage. Because of this huge reserve of cash, the company can afford to lose money to enter risky new markets like the Xbox game console.

Sources: Jay Greene, "Microsoft's $49 Billion 'Problem,'" *BusinessWeek,* August 11, 2003, p. 36 and the Microsoft Annual Report for the year 2003.

Accounts Receivable Turnover

The *accounts receivable turnover* and *average collection period* ratios are used to measure how quickly credit sales are converted into cash. The **accounts receivable turnover** is computed by dividing sales on account (i.e., credit sales) by the average accounts receivable balance for the year:

$$\text{Accounts receivable turnover} = \frac{\text{Sales on account}}{\text{Average accounts receivable balance}}$$

Assuming that all of Brickey Electronics' sales for the year were on account, its accounts receivable turnover for 2005 would be computed as follows:

$$\frac{\text{Sales on account}}{\text{Average accounts receivable balance}} = \frac{\$52,000,000}{(\$4,000,000 + \$6,000,000)/2} = 10.4$$

The turnover can then be divided into 365 days to determine the average number of days required to collect an account (known as the **average collection period**).

$$\text{Average collection period} = \frac{365 \text{ days}}{\text{Accounts receivable trunover}}$$

The average collection period for Brickey Electronics for 2005 is computed as follows:

$$\frac{365 \text{ days}}{10.4} = 35 \text{ days}$$

This means that on average it takes 35 days to collect a credit sale. Whether this is good or bad depends on the credit terms Brickey Electronics is offering its customers. Most customers will tend to withhold payment for as long as the credit terms allow. If the credit terms are 30 days, then a 35-day average collection period would usually be viewed as very good. On the other hand, if the company's credit terms are 10 days, then a 35-day average collection period is worrisome. A long collection period may result from having too many old uncollectible accounts, failing to bill promptly or follow up on late accounts, lax credit checks, and so on. In practice, average collection periods ranging from 10 days all the way to 180 days are common, depending on the industry.

Inventory Turnover

The **inventory turnover ratio** measures how many times a company's inventory has been sold and replaced during the year. It is computed by dividing the cost of goods sold by the average level of inventory on hand:

$$\text{Inventory turnover} = \frac{\text{Cost of goods sold}}{\text{Average inventory balance}}$$

The average inventory is the average of the beginning and ending inventory balances. Since Brickey Electronics has a beginning inventory of $10,000,000 and an ending inventory of $8,000,000, its average inventory for the year would be $9,000,000. The company's inventory turnover for 2005 is computed as follows:

$$\frac{\text{Cost of goods sold}}{\text{Average inventory balance}} = \frac{\$36,000,000}{\$9,000,000} = 4$$

The number of days being taken on average to sell the entire inventory (called the **average sale period**) can be computed by dividing 365 by the inventory turnover:

$$\text{Average sale period} = \frac{365 \text{ days}}{\text{Inventory turnover}}$$

$$= \frac{365 \text{ days}}{4 \text{ times}} = 91\tfrac{1}{4} \text{ days}$$

The average sale period varies from industry to industry. Grocery stores, with significant perishable stocks, tend to turn their inventory over very quickly. On the other hand, jewelry stores tend to turn their inventory over very slowly. In practice, average sales periods of 10 days to 90 days are common, depending on the industry.

A company whose inventory turnover ratio is much slower than the average for its industry may have too much inventory or the wrong sorts of inventory. Some managers argue that they must buy in large quantities to take advantage of quantity discounts. But these discounts must be compared with the added costs of insurance, taxes, financing, and risks of obsolescence and deterioration that result from carrying added inventories.

Inventory turnover should increase in companies that adopt lean production. If properly implemented, lean production should result in both a decrease in inventories and an increase in sales due to better customer service.

CONCEPT CHECK

1. Total sales at a store are $1,000,000 and 80% of those sales are on credit. The beginning and ending accounts receivable balances are $100,000 and $140,000, respectively. What is the accounts receivable turnover?
   a.   3.33 times
   b.   6.67 times
   c.   8.33 times
   d.   10.67 times
2. A retailer's total sales are $1,000,000 and the gross margin percentage is 60%. The beginning and ending inventory balances are 240,000 and 260,000, respectively. What is the inventory turnover?
   a.   1.60 times
   b.   2.40 times
   c.   3.40 times
   d.   3.60 times

YOU DECIDE   **Portfolio Manager**

Assume that you work for a mutual fund and have the responsibility of selecting stocks to include in its investment portfolio. You have been analyzing the financial statements of a chain of retail clothing stores and noticed that the company's current ratio has increased, but its acid-test (quick) ratio has decreased. In addition, the company's accounts receivable turnover has decreased and its inventory turnover ratio has decreased. Finally, the company's price-earnings ratio is at an all-time high. Would you recommend buying stock in this company?

Vice President of Sales

Although its credit terms require payment within 30 days, your company's average collection period is 33 days. A major competitor has an average collection period of 27 days. You have been asked to explain why your company is not doing as well as the competitor. You have investigated your company's credit policies and procedures and have concluded that they are reasonable and adequate under the circumstances. What rationale would you consider to explain why (1) the average collection period of your company exceeds the credit terms, and (2) the average collection period of your company is higher than that of its competitor?

Watch Those Receivables and Inventories!

Herb Greenberg, an investment columnist for *Fortune* magazine, warns investors to look out for two "sure warning signs: receivables and inventory that rise faster than sales . . . A fast rise in receivables could mean that the company is pulling out all the stops to get customers to take its products. That's good, *unless* it means stealing sales from future quarters. As for a rise in inventory: If finished goods are piling up in warehouses—absent some reasonable explanation, like a looming product launch—they must not be selling." To monitor these possibilities, watch the accounts receivable turnover or average collection period for the receivables and the inventory turnover or average sale period for the inventories.

Source: Herb Greenberg, "Minding Your K's and Q's," *Fortune*, January 8, 2001, p. 180.

Warning Signs at Amazon.com

Ravi Suria, a debt analyst at Lehman Brothers, sounded an early warning about Amazon.com's finances. Amazon's inventory turnover plummeted from 8.5 times to 2.9 times within two years. And in a year in which its sales grew 170%, its inventories skyrocketed by 650%. Suria points out that "When a company manages inventory properly, it should grow along with its sales growth rate." When inventory grows faster than sales, "it means simply that they're not selling as much as they are buying."

Source: Robert Hof, Debra Sparks, Ellen Neuborne, and Wendy Zellner, "Can Amazon Make It?" *BusinessWeek*, July 10, 2000, pp. 38–43.

RATIO ANALYSIS—THE LONG-TERM CREDITOR

Long-term creditors are concerned with a company's ability to repay its loans over the long run. For example, if a company were to pay out all of its retained earnings in the form of dividends, then nothing would be left to pay back creditors. Consequently, creditors often seek protection by requiring that borrowers agree to various restrictive covenants, or rules. These restrictive covenants typically include restrictions on payment of dividends as well as rules stating that the company must maintain certain financial ratios at specified levels. Although restrictive covenants are widely used, they do not ensure that creditors will be paid when loans come due. The company still must generate sufficient earnings to cover payments.

> **LEARNING OBJECTIVE 4**
> Compute and interpret financial ratios that would be useful to a long-term creditor.

Times Interest Earned Ratio

The most common measure of the ability of a company's operations to provide protection to long-term creditors is the **times interest earned ratio.** It is computed by dividing earnings *before* interest expense and income taxes (i.e., net operating income) by interest expense:

$$\text{Times interest earned ratio} = \frac{\text{Earnings before interest expense and income taxes}}{\text{Interest expense}}$$

For Brickey Electronics, the times interest earned ratio for 2005 is computed as follows:

$$\frac{\$3,140,000}{\$640,000} = 4.9$$

The times interest earned ratio is based on earnings before interest expense and income taxes because that is the amount of earnings that is available for making interest payments. Interest expenses are deducted *before* income taxes are determined; creditors have first claim on the earnings before taxes are paid.

Clearly, a times interest earned ratio of less than 1 is inadequate because the interest expense exceeds the earnings that are available for paying interest. In contrast, a times interest earned ratio of 2 or more may be considered sufficient to protect long-term creditors.

Debt-to-Equity Ratio

Long-term creditors are also concerned with a company's ability to keep a reasonable balance between its debt and equity. This balance is measured by the **debt-to-equity ratio:**

$$\text{Debt-to-equity ratio} = \frac{\text{Total liabilities}}{\text{Stockholder's equity}}$$

The debt-to-equity ratios for Brickey Electronics in 2004 and 2005 are computed below:

	2005	2004
Total liabilities (a)	$14,500,000	$13,000,000
Stockholders' equity (b)	$17,000,000	$15,970,000
Debt-to-equity ratio, (a) ÷ (b)	0.85	0.81

The debt-to-equity ratio indicates the relative proportions of debt and equity on the company's balance sheet. In 2005, creditors of Brickey Electronics were providing 85 cents for each $1 being provided by stockholders.

Creditors and stockholders have different views about the optimal level of the debt-to-equity ratio. Ordinarily, stockholders would like a lot of debt to take advantage of positive financial leverage. On the other hand, because equity represents the excess of total assets over total liabilities and hence a buffer of protection for the creditors, creditors would like to see less debt and more equity.

In practice, debt-to-equity ratios from 0.0 (no debt) to 3.0 are common. Generally speaking, in industries with little financial risk, creditors tolerate high debt-to-equity ratios. In industries with more financial risk, creditors demand lower debt-to-equity ratios.

CONCEPT CHECK ✓

3. Total assets are $1,500,000 and stockholder's equity is $900,000. What is the debt-to-equity ratio?
   a.   0.33 to 1
   b.   0.50 to 1
   c.   0.60 to 1
   d.   0.67 to 1

SUMMARY OF RATIOS AND SOURCES OF COMPARATIVE RATIO DATA

Exhibit 14–6 contains a summary of the ratios discussed in this chapter. The formula for each ratio and a summary comment on each ratio's significance are included in the exhibit.

EXHIBIT 14–6   Summary of Ratios

Ratio	Formula	Significance
Gross margin percentage	Gross margin ÷ Sales	A broad measure of profitability
Earnings per share (of common stock)	(Net income − Preferred dividends) ÷ Average number of common shares outstanding	Tends to have an effect on the market price per share, as reflected in the price-earnings ratio
Price-earnings ratio	Market price per share ÷ Earnings per share	An index of whether a stock is relatively cheap or relatively expensive in relation to current earnings
Dividend payout ratio	Dividends per share ÷ Earnings per share	An index showing whether a company pays out most of its earnings in dividends or reinvests the earnings internally
Dividend yield ratio	Dividends per share ÷ Market price per share	Shows the return in terms of cash dividends being provided by a stock
Return on total assets	{Net income + [Interest expense × (1 − Tax rate)]} ÷ Average total assets	Measures how well assets have been employed by management
Return on common stockholders' equity	(Net income − Preferred dividends) ÷ Average common stockholders' equity (Average total stockholder' equity − Average preferred stock)	When compared to the return on total assets, measures the extent to which financial leverage is working for or against common stockholders
Book value per share	Common stockholders' equity (Total stockholders' equity − Preferred stock) ÷ Number of common shares outstanding	Measures the amount that would be distributed to common stockholders if all assets were sold at their balance sheet carrying amounts and if all creditors were paid off
Working capital	Current assets − Current liabilities	Measures the company's ability to repay current liabilities using only current assets
Current ratio	Current assets ÷ Current liabilities	Test of short-term debt-paying ability
Acid-test (quick) ratio	(Cash + Marketable securities + Current receivables) ÷ Current liabilities	Test of short-term debt-paying ability without having to rely on inventory
Accounts receivable turnover	Sales on account ÷ Average accounts receivable balance	A rough measure of how many times a company's accounts receivable have been turned into cash during the year
Average collection period (age of receivables)	365 days ÷ Accounts receivable turnover	Measures the average number of days taken to collect an account receivable
Inventory turnover ratio	Cost of goods sold ÷ Average inventory balance	Measures how many times a company's inventory has been sold during the year
Average sale period (turnover in days)	365 days ÷ Inventory turnover	Measures the average number of days taken to sell the inventory one time
Times interest earned ratio	Earnings before interest expense and income taxes ÷ Interest expense	Measures the company's ability to make interest payments
Debt-to-equity ratio	Total liabilities ÷ Stockholders' equity	Measures the amount of assets being provided by creditors for each dollar of assets being provided by the stockholders

EXHIBIT 14–7   Sources of Financial Ratios

Source	Content
Almanac of Business and Industrial Financial Ratios, Aspen Publishers; published annually	An exhaustive source that contains common-size income statements and financial ratios by industry and by the size of companies within each industry.
AMA Annual Statement Studies, Risk Management Association; published annually.	A widely used publication that contains common-size statements and financial ratios on individual companies; the companies are arranged by industry.
EDGAR, Securities and Exchange Commission; website that is continually updated www.sec.gov	An exhaustive database accessible on the Internet that contains reports filed by companies with the SEC; these reports can be downloaded.
FreeEdgar, EDGAR Online, Inc.; website that is continually updated; www.freeedgar.com	A site that allows you to search SEC filings; financial information can be downloaded directly into Excel worksheets.
Hoover's Online, Hoovers, Inc.; website that is continually updated; www.hoovers.com	A site that provides capsule profiles for 10,000 U.S. companies with links to company websites, annual reports, stock charts, news articles, and industry information.
Industry Norms & Key Business Ratios, Dun & Bradstreet; published annually	Fourteen commonly used financial ratios are computed for over 800 major industry groupings.
Mergent Industrial Manual and Mergent Bank and Finance Manual; published annually	An exhaustive source that contains financial ratios on all companies listed on the New York Stock Exchange, the American Stock Exchange, and regional American exchanges.
Standard & Poor's Industry Survey, Standard & Poor's; published annually	Various statistics, including some financial ratios, are given by industry and for leading companies within each industry grouping.

Exhibit 14–7 contains a listing of public sources that provide comparative ratio data organized by industry. These sources are used extensively by managers, investors, and analysts in doing comparative analyses and in attempting to assess the well-being of companies. The Internet contains a wealth of financial and other data. A search engine such as Google can be used to track down information on individual companies. Many companies post their latest financial reports and news of interest to potential investors on their own websites. The *EDGAR* database listed in Exhibit 14–7 is a particularly rich source of data. It contains copies of all reports filed by companies with the SEC since about 1995—including annual reports filed as form 10-K.

IN BUSINESS

XBRL: The Next Generation of Financial Reporting

In 2005, the Securities and Exchange Commission (SEC) announced that it would allow companies to submit financial reports using a computer code known as Extensible Business Reporting Language, or XBRL for short. XBRL is a "financial reporting derivation of Extensible Markup Language, or XML—a framework that establishes individual 'tags' for elements in structured documents, allowing specific elements to be immediately accessed and aggregated."

XBRL dramatically improves the financial reporting process in two ways. First, data are tagged in accordance with a generally accepted framework. This simplifies the process of making apples-to-apples comparisons of financial results across companies. For example, "many of the components of a 'property, plant and equipment' listing on a balance sheet . . . may be described differently by different companies, but when tagged in XBRL, a straight comparison becomes much simpler."

Second, XBRL simplifies the exchange of financial data. Without XBRL, a company's financial data are typically stored in a format that is unique to that company's specific financial software application and that cannot be easily read by other financial software. This problem is overcome with XBRL because the tagged data become "independent of the originating application and can readily be shared with any application that recognizes XBRL. This feature of XBRL makes the markup language very attractive for government regulators and financial analysts."

Sources: Glenn Cheney, "U.S. gets its XBRL in gear: SEC, FDIC OK tagged data," *Accounting Today*, March 14–April 3, 2005, pp. 26–27; Neal Hannon, "XBRL Fundamentals," *Strategic Finance*, April 2005, pp. 57–58; and Ghostwriter, "From Tags to Riches," *CFO-IT*, Spring 2005, pp. 13–14.

SUMMARY

LO1   Prepare and interpret financial statements in comparative and common-size form.
It is difficult to interpret raw data from financial statements without standardizing the data in some way so that it can be compared over time and across companies. For example, all of the financial data for a company can be expressed as a percentage of the data in some base year. This makes it easier to spot trends over time. To make it easier to compare companies, common-size financial statements are often used in which income statement data are expressed as a percentage of sales and balance sheet data are expressed as a percentage of total assets.

LO2   Compute and interpret financial ratios that would be useful to a common stockholder.
Common stockholders are concerned with the company's earnings per share, price-earnings ratio, dividend payout and yield ratios, return on total assets, book value per share, and return on common stockholders' equity. Generally speaking, the higher these ratios, the better it is for common stockholders.

LO3   Compute and interpret financial ratios that would be useful to a short-term creditor.
Short-term creditors are concerned with the company's ability to repay its debt in the near future. Consequently, these investors focus on the relation between current assets and current liabilities and the company's ability to generate cash. Specifically, short-term creditors monitor working capital, the current ratio, the acid-test (quick) ratio, accounts receivable turnover, and inventory turnover.

LO4   Compute and interpret financial ratios that would be useful to a long-term creditor.
Long-term creditors have many of the same concerns as short-term creditors, but also monitor the times interest earned ratio and the debt-to-equity ratio. These ratios indicate the company's ability to pay interest out of operations and how heavily the company is financially leveraged.

GUIDANCE ANSWERS TO *DECISION MAKER* AND *YOU DECIDE*

Portfolio Manager (p. 606)
All of the ratios—current ratio, acid-test (quick) ratio, accounts receivable turnover, and inventory turnover ratio—indicate deteriorating operations. And yet the company's price-earnings ratio is at an all-time high, suggesting that the stock market is optimistic about the company's future and its stock price. It would be risky to invest in this company without digging deeper and finding out what has caused the deteriorating operating ratios.

Vice President of Sales (p. 607)
An average collection period of 33 days means that on average it takes 33 days to collect a credit sale. Whether the average of 33 days is acceptable or not depends on the credit terms that your company offers to its customers. In this case, an average collection period of 33 days is good because the credit terms offered by your company are net 30 days. Why might the average collection period exceed the credit terms? Some customers may misjudge the amount of time that it takes mail to reach the company's offices. Certain customers may experience temporary cash shortages and delay payment for short periods of time. Others might be in the process of returning goods and have not paid for the goods that will be returned because they realize that a credit will be posted to their account. Still others may be in the process of resolving disputes regarding the goods that were shipped.

Turning to the competitor's average collection period of 27 days, it is possible that the competitor's credit terms are 25 days rather than 30 days. Or, the competitor might be offering sales discounts to its customers (e.g., 2/10, n/30) for paying early. Sales discounts are offered as an incentive to customers to motivate them to pay invoices well in advance of the due date. If enough customers take advantage of the sales discounts, the average collection period will drop below 30 days.

GUIDANCE ANSWERS TO CONCEPT CHECKS

1. **Choice b.** The accounts receivable turnover is $800,000 of credit sales ÷ $120,000 average accounts receivable balance = 6.67 times.
2. **Choice a.** First, calculate the cost of goods sold as follows: $1,000,000 × (1 − 0.60) = $400,000. Next, the inventory turnover is calculated as follows: $400,000 of cost of goods sold ÷ $250,000 average inventory = 1.60 times.
3. **Choice d.** Total assets of $1,500,000 − $900,000 of stockholders' equity = $600,000 of total liabilities. The debt-to-equity ratio is $600,000 ÷ $900,000 = 0.67 to 1.

REVIEW PROBLEM: SELECTED RATIOS AND FINANCIAL LEVERAGE

Starbucks Coffee Company is the leading retailer and roaster of specialty coffee in North America with over 1,000 stores offering freshly brewed coffee, pastries, and coffee beans. Data (slightly modified) from its financial statements are given below:

Starbucks Coffee Company
Comparative Balance Sheet
(dollars in millions)

	End of Year	Beginning of Year
Assets		
Current assets:		
Cash	$ 113	$ 71
Marketable securities	107	61
Accounts receivable	90	76
Inventories	221	202
Other current assets	63	48
Total current assets	594	458
Property and equipment, net	1,136	931
Other assets	121	103
Total assets	$1,851	$1,492
Liabilities and Stockholders' Equity		
Current liabilities:		
Accounts payable	$ 128	$74
Short-term bank loans	62	56
Accrued payables	245	174
Other current liabilities	10	8
Total current liabilities	445	312
Long-term liabilities	30	32
Total liabilities	475	344
Stockholders' equity:		
Preferred stock	0	0
Common stock and additional paid-in capital	792	751
Retained earnings	584	397
Total stockholders' equity	1,376	1,148
Total liabilities and stockholders' equity	$1,851	$1,492

Starbucks Coffee Company
Income Statement
(dollars in millions)

	Current Year
Revenue	$2,678
Cost of goods sold	1,113
Gross margin	1,565
Operating expenses:	
Store operating expenses	875
Other operating expenses	93
Depreciation and amortization	164
General and administrative expenses	151
Total operating expenses	1,283

(continued)

(concluded)

Starbucks Coffee Company
Income Statement
(dollars in millions)

	Current Year
Net operating income	282
Less internet investment losses	3
Plus interest income	11
Less interest expense	0
Net income before taxes	290
Income taxes (about 37%)	108
Net income	$ 182

Required:
For the current year:

1. Compute the return on total assets.
2. Compute the return on common stockholders' equity.
3. Is Starbucks' financial leverage positive or negative? Explain.
4. Compute the current ratio.
5. Compute the acid-test (quick) ratio.
6. Compute the inventory turnover.
7. Compute the average sale period.
8. Compute the debt-to-equity ratio.

Solution to Review Problem

1. Return on total assets:

$$\text{Return on total assets} = \frac{\text{Net income} + [\text{Interest expense} \times (1 - \text{Tax rate})]}{\text{Average total assets}}$$

$$= \frac{\$182 + [\$0 \times (1 - 0.37)]}{(\$1,851 + \$1,492)/2} = 10.9\% \text{ (rounded)}$$

2. Return on common stockholders' equity:

$$\text{Return on common stockholders' equity} = \frac{\text{Net income} - \text{Preferred dividends}}{\text{Average common stockholders' equity}}$$

$$= \frac{\$182 - \$0}{(\$1,376 + \$1,148)/2} = 14.4\% \text{ (rounded)}$$

3. The company has positive financial leverage because the return on common stockholders' equity of 14.4% is greater than the return on total assets of 10.9%. The positive financial leverage was obtained from current and long-term liabilities.

4. Current ratio:

$$\text{Current ratio} = \frac{\text{Current assets}}{\text{Current liabilities}}$$

$$= \frac{\$594}{\$445} = 1.33 \text{ (rounded)}$$

5. Acid-test (quick) ratio:

$$\text{Acid-test ratio} = \frac{\text{Cash} + \text{Marketable securities} + \text{Current receivables}}{\text{Current liabilities}}$$

$$= \frac{\$113 + \$107 + \$90}{\$445} = 0.70 \text{ (rounded)}$$

6. Inventory turnover:

$$\text{Inventory turnover} = \frac{\text{Cost of goods sold}}{\text{Average inventory balance}}$$

$$= \frac{\$1,113}{(\$221 + \$202)/2} = 5.26 \text{ (rounded)}$$

7. Average sale period:

$$\text{Average sale period} = \frac{365 \text{ days}}{\text{Inventory turnover}}$$

$$= \frac{365 \text{ days}}{5.26} = 69 \text{ days (rounded)}$$

8. Debt-to-equity ratio:

$$\text{Debt-to-equity ratio} = \frac{\text{Total liabilities}}{\text{Stockholders' equity}}$$

$$= \frac{\$445 + \$30}{\$1,376} = 0.35 \text{ (rounded)}$$

GLOSSARY

(Note: Definitions and formulas for all financial ratios are shown in Exhibit 14–6. These definitions and formulas are not repeated here.)

Common-size financial statements   A statement that shows the items appearing on it in percentage form as well as in dollar form. On the income statement, the percentages are based on total sales revenue; on the balance sheet, the percentages are based on total assets. (p. 596)

Financial leverage   A difference between the rate of return on assets and the rate paid to creditors. (p. 601)

Horizontal analysis   A side-by-side comparison of two or more years' financial statements. (p. 593)

Trend analysis   See *Horizontal analysis.* (p. 593)

Trend percentages   Several years of financial data expressed as a percentage of performance in a base year. (p. 593)

Vertical analysis   The presentation of a company's financial statements in common-size form. (p. 596)

QUESTIONS

14–1   Distinguish between horizontal and vertical analysis of financial statement data.

14–2   What is the basic purpose for examining trends in a company's financial ratios and other data? What other kinds of comparisons might an analyst make?

14–3   Assume that two companies in the same industry have equal earnings. Why might these companies have different price-earnings ratios?

14–4   Would you expect a company in a rapidly growing technological industry to have a high or low dividend payout ratio?

14–5   Distinguish between a manager's *financing* and *operating* responsibilities. Which of these responsibilities is the return on total assets ratio designed to measure?

14–6   What is meant by the dividend yield on a common stock investment?

14–7   What is meant by the term *financial leverage?*

14–8   If a stock's market value exceeds its book value, then the stock is overpriced. Do you agree? Explain.

14–9   Weaver Company experiences a great deal of seasonal variation in its business activities. The company's high point in business activity is in June; its low point is in January. During which month would you expect the current ratio to be highest?

14–10 A company seeking a line of credit at a bank was turned down. Among other things, the bank stated that the company's 2 to 1 current ratio was not adequate. Give reasons why a 2 to 1 current ratio might not be adequate.

BRIEF EXERCISES

BRIEF EXERCISE 14–1   Trend Percentages   [LO1]
Rotorua Products, Ltd., of New Zealand markets agricultural products for the burgeoning Asian consumer market. The company's current assets, current liabilities, and sales have been reported as follows over the last five years (Year 5 is the most recent year):

	Year 5	Year 4	Year 3	Year 2	Year 1
Sales	$NZ2,250,000	$NZ2,160,000	$NZ2,070,000	$NZ1,980,000	$NZ1,800,000
Cash	$NZ 30,000	$NZ 40,000	$NZ 48,000	$NZ 65,000	$NZ 50,000
Accounts receivable, net	570,000	510,000	405,000	345,000	300,000
Inventory	750,000	720,000	690,000	660,000	600,000
Total current assets	$NZ1,350,000	$NZ1,270,000	$NZ1,143,000	$NZ1,070,000	$NZ 950,000
Current liabilities	$NZ 640,000	$NZ 580,000	$NZ 520,000	$NZ 440,000	$NZ 400,000

$NZ stands for New Zealand dollars.

Required:
1. Express all of the asset, liability, and sales data in trend percentages. (Show percentages for each item.) Use Year 1 as the base year and carry computations to one decimal place.
2. Comment on the results of your analysis.

BRIEF EXERCISE 14–2   Common-Size Income Statement   [LO1]
A comparative income statement is given below for McKenzie Sales, Ltd., of Toronto:

McKenzie Sales, Ltd. Comparative Income Statement		
	This Year	**Last Year**
Sales	$8,000,000	$6,000,000
Less cost of goods sold	4,984,000	3,516,000
Gross margin	3,016,000	2,484,000
Less operating expenses:		
Selling expenses	1,480,000	1,092,000
Administrative expenses	712,000	618,000
Total expenses	2,192,000	1,710,000
Net operating income	824,000	774,000
Less interest expense	96,000	84,000
Net income before taxes	$ 728,000	$ 690,000

Members of the company's board of directors are surprised to see that net income before taxes increased by only $38,000 when sales increased by two million dollars.

Required:
1. Express each year's income statement in common-size percentages. Carry computations to one decimal place.
2. Comment briefly on the changes between the two years.

BRIEF EXERCISE 14–3   Financial Ratios for Common Stockholders   [LO2]
Comparative financial statements for Weller Corporation, a wholesale distributor, for the fiscal year ending December 31 appear below. The company did not issue any new common or preferred stock during the year. A total of 800,000 shares of common stock were outstanding. The interest rate on the bonds payable

was 12%, the income tax rate was 40%, and the dividend per share of common stock was $0.25. The market value of the company's common stock at the end of the year was $18. All of the company's sales are on account.

Weller Corporation
Comparative Balance Sheet
(dollars in thousands)

	This Year	Last Year
Assets		
Current assets:		
Cash	$ 1,280	$ 1,560
Accounts receivable, net	12,300	9,100
Inventory	9,700	8,200
Prepaid expenses	1,800	2,100
Total current assets	25,080	20,960
Property and equipment:		
Land	6,000	6,000
Buildings and equipment, net	19,200	19,000
Total property and equipment	25,200	25,000
Total assets	$50,280	$45,960
Liabilities and Stockholders' Equity		
Current liabilities:		
Accounts payable	$9,500	$8,300
Accrued payables	600	700
Notes payable, short term	300	300
Total current liabilities	10,400	9,300
Long-term liabilities:		
Bonds payable	5,000	5,000
Total liabilities	15,400	14,300
Stockholders' equity:		
Preferred stock	2,000	2,000
Common stock	800	800
Additional paid-in capital	2,200	2,200
Total paid-in capital	5,000	5,000
Retained earnings	29,880	26,660
Total stockholders' equity	34,880	31,660
Total liabilities and stockholders' equity	$50,280	$45,960

Weller Corporation
Comparative Income Statement and Reconciliation
(dollars in thousands)

	This Year	Last Year
Sales	$79,000	$74,000
Cost of goods sold	52,000	48,000
Gross margin	27,000	26,000
Operating expenses:		
Selling expenses	8,500	8,000
Administrative expenses	12,000	11,000
Total operating expenses	20,500	19,000

(continued)

(concluded)		
Weller Corporation		
Comparative Income Statement and Reconciliation		
(dollars in thousands)		
	This Year	Last Year
Net operating income	6,500	7,000
Interest expense	600	600
Net income before taxes	5,900	6,400
Less income taxes	2,360	2,560
Net income	3,540	3,840
Dividends to preferred stockholders	120	400
Net income remaining for		
common stockholders	3,420	3,440
Dividends to common stockholders	200	200
Net income added to retained earnings	3,220	3,240
Retained earnings, beginning of year	26,660	23,420
Retained earnings, end of year	$29,880	$26,660

Required:
Compute the following financial ratios for common stockholders for this year:

1. Gross margin percentage.
2. Earnings per share of common stock.
3. Price-earnings ratio.
4. Dividend payout ratio.
5. Dividend yield ratio.
6. Return on total assets.
7. Return on common stockholders' equity.
8. Book value per share.

BRIEF EXERCISE 14–4   Financial Ratios for Short-Term Creditors   [LO3]
Refer to the data in Brief Exercise 14–3 for Weller Corporation.

Required:
Compute the following financial data for short-term creditors for this year:

1. Working capital.
2. Current ratio.
3. Acid-test (quick) ratio.
4. Accounts receivable turnover. (Assume that all sales are on account.)
5. Average collection period.
6. Inventory turnover.
7. Average sale period.

BRIEF EXERCISE 14–5   Financial Ratios for Long-Term Creditors   [LO4]
Refer to the data in Brief Exercise 14–3 for Weller Corporation.

Required:
Compute the following financial ratios for long-term creditors for this year:

1. Times interest earned ratio.
2. Debt-to-equity ratio.

EXERCISES

EXERCISE 14–6   Selected Financial Measures for Short-Term Creditors   [LO3]
Norsk Optronics, ALS, of Bergen, Norway, had a current ratio of 2.5 on June 30 of the current year. On that date, the company's assets were:

Cash	Kr	90,000
Accounts receivable, net		260,000
Inventory		490,000
Prepaid expenses		10,000
Plant and equipment, net		800,000
Total assets	Kr	1,650,000

The Norwegian currency is the krone, denoted here by the symbol Kr.

Required:
1. What was the company's working capital on June 30?
2. What was the company's acid-test (quick) ratio on June 30?
3. The company paid an account payable of Kr40,000 immediately after June 30.
   a. What effect did this transaction have on working capital? Show computations.
   b. What effect did this transaction have on the current ratio? Show computations.

EXERCISE 14–7   Selected Financial Ratios for Common Stockholders   [LO2]
Selected financial data from the June 30 year-end statements of Safford Agricultural Services Corporation are given below:

Total assets	$3,600,000
Long-term debt (12% interest rate) ...	$500,000
Preferred stock, $100 par, 8%	$900,000
Total stockholders' equity	$2,400,000
Interest paid on long-term debt	$60,000
Net income	$280,000

Total assets at the beginning of the year were $3,000,000; total stockholders' equity was $2,200,000. There has been no change in preferred stock during the year. The company's tax rate is 30%.

Required:
1. Compute the return on total assets.
2. Compute the return on common stockholders' equity.
3. Is financial leverage positive or negative? Explain.

EXERCISE 14–8   Selected Financial Ratios   [LO3, LO4]
The financial statements for Castile Products, Inc., an importer of consumer products, are given below:

Castile Products, Inc.
Balance Sheet
December 31

Assets	
Current assets:	
Cash	$ 6,500
Accounts receivable, net	35,000
Merchandise inventory	70,000
Prepaid expenses	3,500
Total current assets	115,000
Property and equipment, net	185,000
Total assets	$300,000
	(continued)

(concluded)

Castile Products, Inc.
Balance Sheet
December 31

Liabilities and Stockholders' Equity
Liabilities:

Current liabilities		$ 50,000
Bonds payable, 10%		80,000
Total liabilities		130,000

Stockholders' equity:

Common stock, $5 per value	$ 30,000	
Retained earnings	140,000	
Total stockholders' equity		170,000
Total liabilities and stockholders' equity		$300,000

Castile Products, Inc.
Income Statement
For the Year Ended December 31

Sales	$420,000
Cost of goods sold	292,500
Gross margin	127,500
Operating expenses	89,500
Net operating income	38,000
Interest expense	8,000
Net income before taxes	30,000
Income taxes (30%)	9,000
Net income	$ 21,000

Account balances at the beginning of the year were: accounts receivable, $25,000; and inventory, $60,000. All sales were on account.

Required:
Compute financial ratios as follows:

1. Gross margin percentage.
2. Current ratio.
3. Acid-test (quick) ratio.
4. Debt-to-equity ratio.
5. Average collection period.
6. Average sale period.
7. Times interest earned.
8. Book value per share.

EXERCISE 14–9   Selected Financial Ratios for Common Stockholders   [LO2]
Refer to the financial statements for Castile Products in Exercise 14–8. In addition to the data in these statements, assume that Castile Products, paid dividends of $2.10 per share during the year. Also assume that the company's common stock had a market price of $42 at the end of the year and there was no change in the number of outstanding shares of common stock during the year.

Required:
Compute financial ratios as follows:

1. Earnings per share.
2. Dividend payout ratio.
3. Dividend yield ratio.
4. Price-earnings ratio.

Refer to the financial statements for Castile Products in Exercise 14–8. Assets at the beginning of the year totaled $280,000, and the stockholders' equity totaled $161,600.

Required:
Compute the following:

1. Return on total assets.
2. Return on common stockholders' equity.
3. Was financial leverage positive or negative for the year? Explain.

PROBLEMS

eXcel

PROBLEM 14–11A Common-Size Statements and Financial Ratios for Creditors [LO1, LO3, LO4]
Paul Sabin organized Sabin Electronics 10 years ago to produce and sell several electronic devices on which he had secured patents. Although the company has been fairly profitable, it is now experiencing a severe cash shortage. For this reason, it is requesting a $500,000 long-term loan from Gulfport State Bank, $100,000 of which will be used to bolster the Cash account and $400,000 of which will be used to modernize equipment. The company's financial statements for the two most recent years follow:

CHECK FIGURE
(1e) Inventory turnover this year: 5.0
(1g) Times interest earned last year: 4.9

Sabin Electronics
Comparative Balance Sheet

	This Year	Last Year
Assets		
Current assets:		
Cash	$ 70,000	$ 150,000
Marketable securities	0	18,000
Accounts receivable, net	480,000	300,000
Inventory	950,000	600,000
Prepaid expenses	20,000	22,000
Total current assets	1,520,000	1,090,000
Plant and equipment, net	1,480,000	1,370,000
Total assets	$3,000,000	$2,460,000
Liabilities and Stockholders' Equity		
Liabilities:		
Current liabilities	$ 800,000	$ 430,000
Bonds payable, 12%	600,000	600,000
Total liabilities	1,400,000	1,030,000
Stockholders' equity:		
Preferred stock, $25 par, 8%	250,000	250,000
Common stock, $10 par	500,000	500,000
Retained earnings	850,000	680,000
Total stockholders' equity	1,600,000	1,430,000
Total liabilities and equity	$3,000,000	$2,460,000

Sabin Electronics
Comparative Income Statement and Reconciliation

Sales	$5,000,000	$4,350,000
Cost of goods sold	3,875,000	3,450,000
Gross margin	1,125,000	900,000
Operating expenses	653,000	548,000
Net operating income	472,000	352,000
Interest expense	72,000	72,000
Net income before taxes	400,000	280,000

(continued)

(concluded)

Sabin Electronics
Comparative Income Statement and Reconciliation

	This Year	Last Year
Income taxes (30%)	120,000	84,000
Net income	280,000	196,000
Dividends paid:		
Preferred dividends	20,000	20,000
Common dividends	90,000	75,000
Total dividends paid	110,000	95,000
Net income retained	170,000	101,000
Retained earnings, beginning of year	680,000	579,000
Retained earnings, end of year	$ 850,000	$ 680,000

During the past year, the company introduced several new product lines and raised the selling prices on a number of old product lines in order to improve its profit margin. The company also hired a new sales manager, who has expanded sales into several new territories. Sales terms are 2/10, n/30. All sales are on account. Assume that the following ratios are typical of companies in the electronics industry:

Current ratio	2.5
Acid-test (quick) ratio	1.3
Average collection period	18 days
Average sale period	60 days
Debt-to-equity ratio	0.90
Times interest earned	6.0
Return on total assets	13%
Price-earnings ratio	12

Required:
1. To assist the Gulfport State Bank in making a decision about the loan, compute the following ratios for both this year and last year:
   a. The amount of working capital.
   b. The current ratio.
   c. The acid-test (quick) ratio.
   d. The average collection period. (The accounts receivable at the beginning of last year totaled $250,000.)
   e. The average sale period. (The inventory at the beginning of last year totaled $500,000.)
   f. The debt-to-equity ratio.
   g. The times interest earned ratio.
2. For both this year and last year:
   a. Present the balance sheet in common-size format.
   b. Present the income statement in common-size format down through net income.
3. Comment on the results of your analysis in (1) and (2) above and make a recommendation as to whether or not the loan should be approved.

PROBLEM 14–12A   Financial Ratios for Common Stockholders   [LO2]
Refer to the financial statements and other data in Problem 14–11A. Assume that you are an account executive for a large brokerage house and that one of your clients has asked for a recommendation about the possible purchase of Sabin Electronics' stock. You are not acquainted with the stock and for this reason wish to do some analytical work before making a recommendation.

Required:
1. You decide first to assess the well-being of the common stockholders. For both this year and last year, compute:
   a. The earnings per share. There has been no change in preferred or common stock over the last two years.
   b. The dividend yield ratio for common stock. The company's stock is currently selling for $40 per share; last year it sold for $36 per share.

CHECK FIGURE
(1a) EPS this year: $5.20
(1c) Dividend payout ratio last year: 42.6%

    c.   The dividend payout ratio for common stock.

    d.   The price-earnings ratio. How do investors regard Sabin Electronics as compared to other companies in the industry? Explain.

    e.   The book value per share of common stock. Does the difference between market value and book value suggest that the stock is overpriced? Explain.

2. You decide next to assess the company's rate of return. Compute the following for both this year and last year:

    a.   The return on total assets. (Total assets at the beginning of last year were $2,300,000.)

    b.   The return on common stockholders' equity. (Stockholders' equity at the beginning of last year was $1,329,000.)

    c.   Is the company's financial leverage positive or negative? Explain.

3. Would you recommend that your client purchase shares of Sabin Electronics' stock? Explain.

PROBLEM 14–13A   Comprehensive Ratio Analysis   [LO2, LO3, LO4]
You have just been hired as a loan officer at Slippery Rock State Bank. Your supervisor has given you a file containing a request from Lydex Company, a manufacturer of safety helmets, for a $3,000,000, five-year loan. Financial statement data on the company for the last two years follow:

CHECK FIGURE
(2a) EPS this year: $9.28
(2b) Dividend yield ratio
last year: 3.6%

Lydex Company Comparative Balance Sheet	This Year	Last Year
Assets		
Current assets:		
Cash	$ 960,000	$ 1,260,000
Marketable securities	0	300,000
Accounts receivable, net	2,700,000	1,800,000
Inventory	3,900,000	2,400,000
Prepaid expenses	240,000	180,000
Total current assets	7,800,000	5,940,000
Plant and equipment, net	9,300,000	8,940,000
Total assets	$17,100,000	$14,880,000
Liabilities and Stockholders' Equity		
Liabilities:		
Current liabilities	$ 3,900,000	$ 2,760,000
Note payable, 10%	3,600,000	3,000,000
Total liabilities	7,500,000	5,760,000
Stockholders' equity:		
Preferred stock, 8%, $30 par value	1,800,000	1,800,000
Common stock, $80 par value	6,000,000	6,000,000
Retained earnings	1,800,000	1,320,000
Total stockholders' equity	9,600,000	9,120,000
Total liabilities and stockholders' equity	$17,100,000	$14,880,000

Lydex Company Comparative Income Statement and Reconciliation	This Year	Last Year
Sales (all on account)	$15,750,000	$12,480,000
Cost of goods sold	12,600,000	9,900,000
Gross margin	3,150,000	2,580,000
Operating expenses	1,590,000	1,560,000
Net operating income	1,560,000	1,020,000
Interest expense	360,000	300,000

(continued)

(concluded)

Lydex Company
Comparative Income Statement and Reconciliation

	This Year	Last Year
Net income before taxes	1,200,000	720,000
Income taxes (30%)	360,000	216,000
Net income	840,000	504,000
Dividends paid:		
Preferred dividends	144,000	144,000
Common dividends	216,000	108,000
Total dividends paid	360,000	252,000
Net income retained	480,000	252,000
Retained earnings, beginning of year	1,320,000	1,068,000
Retained earnings, end of year	$ 1,800,000	$ 1,320,000

Helen McGuire, who just a year ago was appointed president of Lydex Company, argues that although the company has had a "spotty" record in the past, it has "turned the corner," as evidenced by a 25% jump in sales and by a greatly improved earnings picture between last year and this year. McGuire also points out that investors generally have recognized the improving situation at Lydex, as shown by the increase in market value of the company's common stock, which is currently selling for $72 per share (up from $40 per share last year). McGuire feels that with her leadership and with the modernized equipment that the $3,000,000 loan will permit the company to buy, profits will be even stronger in the future. McGuire has a reputation in the industry for being a good manager who runs a "tight" ship.

Not wanting to botch your first assignment, you decide to generate all the information that you can about the company. You determine that the following ratios are typical of companies in Lydex Company's industry:

Current ratio	2.3
Acid-test (quick) ratio	1.2
Average collection period	30 days
Average sale period	60 days
Return on assets	9.5%
Debt-to-equity ratio	0.65
Times interest earned	5.7
Price-earnings ratio	10

Required:
1. You decide first to assess the rate of return that the company is generating. Compute the following for both this year and last year:
   a. The return on total assets. (Total assets at the beginning of last year were $12,960,000.)
   b. The return on common stockholders' equity. (Stockholders' equity at the beginning of last year totaled $9,048,000. There has been no change in preferred or common stock over the last two years.)
   c. Is the company's financial leverage positive or negative? Explain.
2. You decide next to assess the well-being of the common stockholders. For both this year and last year, compute:
   a. The earnings per share.
   b. The dividend yield ratio for common stock.
   c. The dividend payout ratio for common stock.
   d. The price-earnings ratio. How do investors regard Lydex Company as compared to other companies in the industry? Explain.
   e. The book value per share of common stock. Does the difference between market value per share and book value per share suggest that the stock at its current price is a bargain? Explain.
   f. The gross margin percentage.
3. You decide, finally, to assess creditor ratios to determine both short-term and long-term debt-paying ability. For both this year and last year, compute:
   a. Working capital.
   b. The current ratio.

   c.   The acid-test (quick) ratio.
   d.   The average collection period. (The accounts receivable at the beginning of last year totaled $1,560,000.)
   e.   The inventory turnover. (The inventory at the beginning of last year totaled $1,920,000.) Also compute the average sale period.
   f.   The debt-to-equity ratio.
   g.   The times interest earned ratio.
4. Make a recommendation to your supervisor as to whether the loan should be approved.

PROBLEM 14–14A   Common-Size Financial Statements   [LO1]
Refer to the financial statement data for Lydex Company given in Problem 14–13A.

Required:
For this year and last year:

   1. Present the balance sheet in common-size format.
   2. Present the income statement in common-size format down through net income.
   3. Comment on the results of your analysis.

PROBLEM 14–15A   Financial Ratios for Common Stockholders   [LO2]
(Problems 14–16A and 14–17A delve more deeply into the data presented below. Each problem is independent.) Empire Labs, Inc., was organized several years ago to produce and market several new "miracle drugs." The company is small but growing, and you are considering the purchase of some of its common stock as an investment. The following data on the company are available for the past two years:

CHECK FIGURE
(1a) EPS this year: $4.65
(2a) Return on total assets last year: 14.0%

Empire Labs, Inc.
Comparative Income Statement
For the Years Ended December 31

	This Year	Last Year
Sales	$20,000,000	$15,000,000
Cost of goods sold	13,000,000	9,000,000
Gross margin	7,000,000	6,000,000
Operating expenses	5,260,000	4,560,000
Net operating income	1,740,000	1,440,000
Interest expense	240,000	240,000
Net income before taxes	1,500,000	1,200,000
Income taxes (30%)	450,000	360,000
Net income	$ 1,050,000	$ 840,000

Empire Labs, Inc.
Comparative Retained Earnings Statement
For the Years Ended December 31

	This Year	Last Year
Retained earnings, January 1	$2,400,000	$1,960,000
Add net income (above)	1,050,000	840,000
Total	3,450,000	2,800,000
Deduct cash dividends paid:		
Preferred dividends	120,000	120,000
Common dividends	360,000	280,000
Total dividends paid	480,000	400,000
Retained earnings, December 31 ...	$2,970,000	$2,400,000

Empire Labs, Inc.
Comparative Balance Sheet
December 31

	This Year	Last Year
Assets		
Current assets:		
Cash	$ 200,000	$ 400,000
Accounts receivable, net	1,500,000	800,000
Inventory	3,000,000	1,200,000
Prepaid expenses	100,000	100,000
Total current assets	4,800,000	2,500,000
Plant and equipment, net	5,170,000	5,400,000
Total assets	$9,970,000	$7,900,000
Liabilities and Stockholders' Equity		
Liabilities:		
Current liabilities	$2,500,000	$1,000,000
Bonds payable, 12%	2,000,000	2,000,000
Total liabilities	4,500,000	3,000,000
Stockholders' equity:		
Preferred stock, 8%, $10 par	1,500,000	1,500,000
Common stock, $5 par	1,000,000	1,000,000
Retained earnings	2,970,000	2,400,000
Total stockholders' equity	5,470,000	4,900,000
Total liabilities and stockholders' equity	$9,970,000	$7,900,000

After some research, you have determined that the following ratios are typical of companies in the pharmaceutical industry:

Dividend yield ratio	3%
Dividend payout ratio	40%
Price-earnings ratio	16
Return on total assets	13.5%
Return on common stockholders' equity	20%

The company's common stock is currently selling for $60 per share. Last year the stock sold for $45 per share.

There has been no change in the preferred or common stock outstanding over the last three years.

Required:

1. In analyzing the company, you decide first to compute the following ratios for last year and this year:
   a. The earnings per share.
   b. The dividend yield ratio.
   c. The dividend payout ratio.
   d. The price-earnings ratio.
   e. The book value per share of common stock.
   f. The gross margin percentage.
2. Next, you decide to determine the rate of return that the company is generating by computing the following ratios for last year and this year:
   a. The return on total assets. (Total assets were $6,500,000 at the beginning of last year.)
   b. The return on common stockholders' equity. (Common stockholders' equity was $2,900,000 at the beginning of last year.)
   c. Is financial leverage positive or negative? Explain.
3. Based on your work in (1) and (2) above, does the company's common stock seem to be an attractive investment? Explain.

PROBLEM 14–16A   Creditor Ratios   [LO3, LO4]

Refer to the data in Problem 14–15A. Although Empire Labs, Inc., has been very profitable since it was organized several years ago, the company is beginning to experience some difficulty in paying its bills as they come due. Management has approached Security National Bank requesting a two-year, $500,000 loan to bolster the cash account.

Security National Bank has assigned you to evaluate the loan request. You have gathered the following data relating to companies in the pharmaceutical industry:

Current ratio	2.4
Acid-test (quick) ratio	1.2
Average collection period	16 days
Average sale period	40 days
Times interest earned	7
Debt-to-equity ratio	0.70

The following additional information is available on Empire Labs, Inc.:

a.   All sales are on account.
b.   At the beginning of last year, the accounts receivable balance was $600,000 and the inventory balance was $1,000,000.

Required:

1.   Compute the following amounts and ratios for both last year and this year:
   a.   The working capital.
   b.   The current ratio.
   c.   The acid-test (quick) ratio.
   d.   The average collection period.
   e.   The average sale period.
   f.   The times interest earned ratio.
   g.   The debt-to-equity ratio.
2.   Comment on the results of your analysis in (1) above.
3.   Would you recommend that the loan be approved? Explain.

PROBLEM 14–17A   Common-Size Statements   [LO1]

Refer to the data in Problem 14–15A. The president of Empire Labs, Inc., is deeply concerned. Sales increased by $5 million from last year to this year, yet the company's net income increased by only a small amount. Also, the company's operating expenses went up this year, even though a major effort was launched during the year to cut costs.

Required:

1.   For both last year and this year, prepare an income statement and a balance sheet in common-size format. Round computations to one decimal place.
2.   From your work in (1) above, explain to the president why the increase in profits was so small this year. Were any benefits realized from the company's cost-cutting efforts? Explain.

PROBLEM 14–18A   Interpretation of Financial Ratios   [LO1, LO2, LO3]

Paul Ward is interested in the stock of Pecunious Products, a company that sells drilling equipment to the oil industry. Before purchasing the stock, Mr. Ward would like your help in analyzing the data that are available to him as shown below:

	Year 3	Year 2	Year 1
Sales trend	128.0	115.0	100.0
Current ratio	2.5	2.3	2.2
Acid-test (quick) ratio	0.8	0.9	1.1
Accounts receivable turnover	9.4	10.6	12.5
Inventory turnover	6.5	7.2	8.0
Dividend yield	7.1%	6.5%	5.8%
Dividend payout ratio	40%	50%	60%
			(continued)

(concluded)

	Year 3	Year 2	Year 1
Return on total assets	12.5%	11.0%	9.5%
Return on common stockholders' equity	14.0%	10.0%	7.8%
Dividends paid per share*	$1.50	$1.50	$1.50

*There have been no changes in common stock outstanding over the three-year period.

Mr. Ward would like answers to a number of questions about the trend of events in Pecunious Products over the last three years. His questions are:

a. Is it becoming easier for the company to pay its bills as they come due?
b. Are customers paying their accounts at least as fast now as they were in Year 1?
c. Is the total of accounts receivable increasing, decreasing, or remaining constant?
d. Is the level of inventory increasing, decreasing, or remaining constant?
e. Is the market price of the company's stock going up or down?
f. Is the earnings per share increasing or decreasing?
g. Is the price-earning ratio going up or down?
h. Is the company employing financial leverage to the advantage of its common stockholders?

Required:
Answer each of Mr. Ward's questions and explain how you arrived at your answers.

PROBLEM 14–19A   Effects of Transactions on Various Ratios   [LO3]
Denna Corporation provides services to high-end restaurants. The company's working capital accounts at the beginning of the year are given below:

CHECK FIGURE
(1c) Acid-test ratio: 1.4

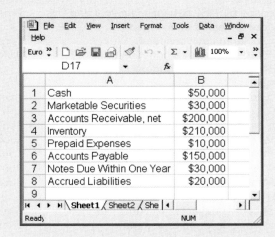

	A	B
1	Cash	$50,000
2	Marketable Securities	$30,000
3	Accounts Receivable, net	$200,000
4	Inventory	$210,000
5	Prepaid Expenses	$10,000
6	Accounts Payable	$150,000
7	Notes Due Within One Year	$30,000
8	Accrued Liabilities	$20,000

During the year, Denna Corporation completed the following transactions:

x. Paid a cash dividend previously declared, $12,000.
a. Issued additional shares of common stock for cash, $100,000.
b. Sold inventory costing $50,000 for $80,000, on account.
c. Wrote off uncollectible accounts in the amount of $10,000, reducing the accounts receivable balance accordingly.
d. Declared a cash dividend, $15,000.
e. Paid accounts payable, $50,000.
f. Borrowed cash on a short-term note with the bank, $35,000.
g. Sold inventory costing $15,000 for $10,000 cash.
h. Purchased inventory on account, $60,000.
i. Paid off all short-term notes due, $30,000.
j. Purchased equipment for cash, $15,000.
k. Sold marketable securities costing $18,000 for cash, $15,000.
l. Collected cash on accounts receivable, $80,000.

Required:

1. Compute the following amounts and ratios as of the beginning of the year:
   a.   Working capital.
   b.   Current ratio.
   c.   Acid-test (quick) ratio.
2. Indicate the effect of each of the transactions given above on working capital, the current ratio, and the acid-test (quick) ratio. Give the effect in terms of increase, decrease, or none. Item (x) is given below as an example of the format to use:

	The Effect on		
Transaction	**Working Capital**	**Current Ratio**	**Acid-Test Ratio**
(x) Paid a cash dividend previously declared	None	Increase	Increase

PROBLEM 14–20A   Effects of Transactions on Various Financial Ratios   [LO2, LO3, LO4]
In the right-hand column below, certain financial ratios are listed. To the left of each ratio is a business transaction or event relating to the operating activities of Delta Company.

Business Transaction or Event	**Ratio**
1. Declared a cash dividend.	Current ratio
2. Sold inventory on account at cost.	Acid-test (quick) ratio
3. Issued bonds with an interest rate of 8%. The company's return on assets is 10%.	Return on common stockholders' equity
4. Net income decreased by 10% between last year and this year. Long-term debt remained unchanged	Times interest earned
5. Paid a previously declared cash dividend.	Current ratio
6. The market price of the company's common stock dropped from 24½ to 20. The dividend paid per share remained unchanged.	Dividend payout ratio
7. Obsolete inventory totaling $100,000 was written off as a loss.	Inventory turnover ratio
8. Sold inventory for cash at a profit.	Debt-to-equity ratio
9. Changed customer credit terms from 2/10, n/30 to 2/15, n/30 to comply with a change in industry practice.	Accounts receivable turnover ratio
10. Issued a dividend to common stockholders.	Book value per share
11. The market price of the company's common stock increased from 24½ to 30.	Book value per share
12. Paid $40,000 on accounts payable.	Working capital
13. Issued a common stock dividend to common stockholders.	Earnings per share
14. Paid accounts payable	Debt-to-equity ratio
15. Purchased inventory on account.	Acid-test (quick) ratio
16. Wrote off an uncollectible account against the Allowance for Bad Debts.	Current ratio
17. The market price of the company's common stock increased from 24½ to 30. Earnings per share remained unchanged.	Price-earnings ratio
18. The market price of the company's common stock increased from 24½ to 30. The dividend paid per share remained unchanged.	Dividend yield ratio

Required:
Indicate the effect that each business transaction or event would have on the ratio listed opposite to it. State the effect in terms of increase, decrease, or no effect on the ratio involved, and give the reason for your

answer. In all cases, assume that the current assets exceed the current liabilities both before and after the event or transaction. Use the following format for your answers:

Effect on Ratio	Reason for Increase, Decrease, or No Effect
1.	
Etc.	

BUILDING YOUR SKILLS

Ethics Challenge   [LO3, LO4]

Venice InLine, Inc., was founded by Russ Perez to produce a specialized in-line skate he had designed for doing aerial tricks. Up to this point, Russ has financed the company with his own savings and with cash generated by his business. However, Russ now faces a cash crisis. In the year just ended, an acute shortage of high-impact roller bearings developed just as the company was beginning production for the Christmas season. Russ had been assured by his suppliers that the roller bearings would be delivered in time to make Christmas shipments, but the suppliers had been unable to fully deliver on this promise. As a consequence, Venice InLine had large stocks of unfinished skates at the end of the year and had been unable to fill all of the orders that had come in from retailers for the Christmas season. Consequently, sales were below expectations for the year, and Russ does not have enough cash to pay his creditors.

Well before the accounts payable were due, Russ visited a local bank and inquired about obtaining a loan. The loan officer at the bank assured Russ that there should not be any problem getting a loan to pay off his accounts payable—providing that on his most recent financial statements the current ratio was above 2.0, the acid-test ratio was above 1.0, and net operating income was at least four times the interest on the proposed loan. Russ promised to return later with a copy of his financial statements.

Russ would like to apply for an $80,000 six-month loan bearing an interest rate of 10% per year. The unaudited financial reports of the company appear below:

Venice InLine, Inc.
Comparative Balance Sheet
As of December 31
(dollars in thousands)

	This Year	Last Year
Assets		
Current assets:		
Cash	$ 70	$150
Accounts receivable, net	50	40
Inventory	160	100
Prepaid expenses	10	12
Total current assets	290	302
Property and equipment	270	180
Total assets	$560	$482
Liabilities and Stockholders' Equity		
Current liabilities:		
Accounts payable	$154	$ 90
Accrued payables	10	10
Total current liabilities	164	100
Long-term liabilities	—	—
Total liabilities	164	100
Stockholders' equity:		
Common stock and additional paid-in capital	100	100
Retained earnings	296	282
Total stockholders' equity	396	382
Total liabilities and stockholders' equity	$560	$482

Venice InLine, Inc.
Income Statement
For the Year Ended December 31
(dollars in thousands)

	This Year
Sales (all on account)	$420
Cost of goods sold	290
Gross margin	130
Operating expenses:	
Selling expenses	42
Administrative expenses	68
Total operating expenses	110
Net operating income	20
Interest expense	—
Net income before taxes	20
Income taxes (30%)	6
Net income	$ 14

Required:

1. Based on the above unaudited financial statements and the statement made by the loan officer, would the company qualify for the loan?
2. Last year Russ purchased and installed new, more efficient equipment to replace an older plastic injection molding machine. Russ had originally planned to sell the old machine but found that it is still needed whenever the plastic injection molding process is a bottleneck. When Russ discussed his cash flow problems with his brother-in-law, he suggested to Russ that the old machine be sold or at least reclassified as inventory on the balance sheet because it could be readily sold. At present, the machine is carried in the Property and Equipment account and could be sold for its net book value of $45,000. The bank does not require audited financial statements. What advice would you give to Russ concerning the machine?

Communicating In Practice   (LO1, LO2, LO3, LO4)

Typically, the market price of shares of a company's stock takes a beating when the company announces that it has not met analysts' expectations. As a result, many companies are under a lot of pressure to meet analysts' revenue and earnings projections. To manage (that is, to inflate or smooth) earnings, managers sometimes record revenue that has not yet been earned by the company, delay the recognition of expenses that have been incurred or employ other accounting tricks.

A wave of accounting scandals related to earnings management swept over the capital markets in the wake of the collapse of Enron in 2002. Some earlier examples illustrate how companies have attempted to manage their earnings. On March 20, 2000, MicroStrategy announced that it was forced to restate its 1999 earnings; revenue from multiyear contracts had been recorded in the first year instead of being spread over the lives of the related contracts as required by GAAP. On April 3, 2000, Legato Systems Inc. announced that it had restated its earnings; $7 million of revenue had been improperly recorded because customers had been promised that they could return the products purchased. As further discussed in this chapter, America Online overstated its net income during 1994, 1995, and 1996. In May 2000, upon completing its review of the company's accounting practices, the SEC levied a fine of $3.5 million against AOL. Just prior to the announcement of the fine levied on AOL, Helane Morrison, head of the SEC's San Francisco office, reemphasized that the investigation of misleading financial statements is a top priority for the agency. [Sources: Jeff Shuttleworth, "Investors Beware: Dot.Coms Often Use Accounting Tricks," *Business Journal Serving San Jose & Silicon Valley,* April 14, 2000, p. 16; David Henry, "AOL Pays $3.5M to Settle SEC Case," *USA Today,* May 16, 2000, p. 3B.]

Required:

Write a memorandum to your instructor that answers the following questions. Use headings to organize the information presented in the memorandum. Include computations to support your answers, when appropriate.

1. Why would companies be tempted to manage earnings?
2. If the earnings that are reported by a company are misstated, how might this impact business decisions made about that company (such as the acquisition of the company by another business)?
3. What ethical issues, if any, arise when a company manages its earnings?
4. How would investors and financial analysts tend to view the financial statements of a company that has been known to manage its earnings in the past?

Teamwork In Action   (LO1, LO2, LO4)

Gauging the success of a company usually involves some assessment of the company's earnings. When evaluating earnings, investors should consider the quality and sources of the company's earnings as well as their amount. In other words, the source of earnings is as important a consideration as the size of earnings.

Your team should discuss and then respond to the following questions. All team members should agree with and understand the answers (including the calculations supporting the answers) and be prepared to report in class. Each teammate can assume responsibility for a different part of the presentation.

Required:

1. Discuss the differences between operating profits and the bottom line—profits after all revenues and expenses.
2. Do you think a dollar of earnings coming from operations is any more or less valuable than a dollar of earnings generated from some other source below operating profits (e.g., one-time gains from selling assets or one-time write-offs for charges related to closing a plant)? Explain.
3. What is the concept of operating leverage? What is the relation between operating leverage and operating profits?
4. What is the concept of financial leverage? What is the relation between financial leverage and return on common stockholders' equity?

Analytical Thinking   [LO2, LO3, LO4]

Incomplete financial statements for Pepper Industries follow:

Pepper Industries
Balance Sheet
March 31

Current assets:	
Cash	$?
Accounts receivable, net	?
Inventory	?
Total current assets	?
Plant and equipment, net	?
Total assets	$?
Liabilities:	
Current liabilities	$ 320,000
Bonds payable, 10%	?
Total liabilities	?
Stockholders' equity:	
Common stock, $5 par value	?
Retained earnings	?
Total stockholders' equity	?
Total liabilities and stockholders' equity	$?

Pepper Industries
Income Statement
For the Year Ended March 31

Sales	$4,200,000
Cost of goods sold	?
Gross margin	?
Operating expenses	?
Net operating income	?
Interest expense	80,000
Net income before taxes	?
Income taxes (30%)	?
Net income	$?

The following additional information is available about the company:

a. All sales during the year were on account.
b. There was no change in the number of shares of common stock outstanding during the year.
c. The interest expense on the income statement relates to the bonds payable; the amount of bonds out-
    standing did not change during the year.
d. Selected balances at the *beginning* of the current year were:

Accounts receivable	$270,000
Inventory	$360,000
Total assets	$1,800,000

e. Selected financial ratios computed from the statements above for the current year are:

Earnings per share	$2.30
Debt-to-equity ratio	0.875
Accounts receivable turnover	14.0
Current ratio	2.75
Return on total assets	18.0%
Times interest earned	6.75
Acid-test (quick) ratio	1.25
Inventory turnover ratio	6.5

Required:
Compute the missing amounts on the company's financial statements. (Hint: What's the difference between
the acid-test ratio and the current ratio?)

Taking It to the Net
As you know, the World Wide Web is a medium that is constantly evolving. Sites come and go and change
without notice. To enable periodic updating of site addresses, these problems have been posted to the textbook website (www.mhhe.com/bgn3e). After accessing the site, enter the Student Center and select this
chapter to find the Taking It to the Net problems.

PHOTO CREDITS

INDEX